Ancient Greece from Homer to Ale:

Blackwell Sourcebooks in Ancient History

This series presents readers with new translations of the raw material of ancient history. It provides direct access to the ancient world, from wars and power politics to daily life and entertainment, allowing readers to discover the extraordinary diversity of ancient societies.

Published

The Ancient Near East
Edited Mark W. Chavalas

The Roman Games
Alison Futrell

Alexander the Great
Waldemar Heckel and J. C. Yardley

The Hellenistic Period
Roger Bagnall and Peter Derow

Ancient Greek Religion
Emily Kearns

Ancient Greece from Homer to Alexander
Joseph Roisman; translations by J. C. Yardley

In Preparation

Sexuality in the Classical World
Holt Parker

Ancient Greece from Homer to Alexander

The Evidence

Joseph Roisman

Translations by J. C. Yardley

WILEY-BLACKWELL

A John Wiley & Sons, Ltd., Publication

Blackwell Publishing was acquired by John Wiley & Sons in February 2007. Blackwell's publishing program has been merged with Wiley's global Scientific, Technical, and Medical business to form Wiley-Blackwell.

Registered Office
John Wiley & Sons Ltd, The Atrium, Southern Gate, Chichester, West Sussex, PO19 8SQ, United Kingdom

Editorial Offices
350 Main Street, Malden, MA 02148-5020, USA
9600 Garsington Road, Oxford, OX4 2DQ, UK
The Atrium, Southern Gate, Chichester, West Sussex, PO19 8SQ, UK

For details of our global editorial offices, for customer services, and for information about how to apply for permission to reuse the copyright material in this book please see our website at www.wiley.com/wiley-blackwell.

The right of Joseph Roisman to be identified as the author of this work has been asserted in accordance with the UK Copyright, Designs and Patents Act 1988.

Library of Congress Cataloging-in-Publication Data

Roisman, Joseph, 1946–
Ancient Greece from Homer to Alexander: the evidence / Joseph Roisman.
    p. cm. — (Blackwell sourcebooks in ancient history)
  Includes bibliographical references and index.
  ISBN 978-1-4051-2775-2 (hardcover: alk. paper)—ISBN 978-1-4051-2776-9 (pbk.: alk. paper) 1. Greece—Civilization—To 146 B.C.—Sources. 2. Greece—History—To 146 B.C.—Sources. I. Title.
  DF12.R65 2011
  938—dc22

                                                                                2010025066

A catalogue record for this book is available from the British Library.

This book is published in the following electronic formats: ePDFs 9781444390773; ePub 9781444390780

Set in 10/13pt Stone Serif by SPi Publisher Services, Pondicherry, India

1 2011

Contents

Illustrations

Maps

Preface and Acknowledgments

The aim of this book is to acquaint the reader with the main evidence for Greek history from Homer and the end of the Dark Age to Alexander the Great (ca. 800–323 BCE). Although the editor hopes to have covered diverse political, social, and cultural aspects of Archaic and Classical Greece, he does not strive to be exhaustive or to provide a substitute for a textbook on the subject. Indeed, much of the volume deals with the Greek mainland and is less concerned with Greeks in the western Mediterranean. Similarly, the bibliography of modern scholarship at the end of each chapter does not aim to be comprehensive but is limited to works in English, with a clear preference for more recent publications. (Only the author and the year of publication are given in these bibliographical notes. Fuller details can be found in the References at the end of the book.) Finally, the selection of the evidence may at times reflect the personal interests of the editor. Yet an attempt was made to create a continuity of themes and processes by placing the evidence in a broader historical context and by linking various documents together. A companion website provides further evidence and explanations in addition to those offered here as well as links to relevant online sites.

The volume is the collaborative work of Joseph Roisman, who has selected, introduced, and annotated the evidence, and John Yardley, who translated nearly all of the texts from their Greek and Latin originals. All dates in this book are BCE unless otherwise noted. Dates of key events are given in the timeline at the front of the book and in parentheses in the text. Frequently dates show an overlap of two consecutive years (e.g., 455/4); this is due to the difficulty of matching the modern calendar year with the Athenian one, which began around July. Square brackets indicate editorial comments and modern restorations of words and lines in inscriptions. They also enclose authors whose identity is in doubt. Greek names are Latinized to promote accessibility, although some inconsistency is not always avoidable. The transliteration of Greek terms includes an accent only where necessary to distinguish the term's pronunciation from English usage.

Acknowledgment is due to previous publications that have been helpful in the preparation of this book, especially to E. David, *The Classical Democracy* (Jerusalem, 2003; Hebrew); M. Dillon and L. Garland, *Ancient Greece: Social and Historical Documents from Archaic Times to the Death of Socrates (c.800–399 BC)*, 2nd ed. (London and New York, 2000); and P.J. Rhodes, *A History of the Classical Greek World: 478–323 BC* (Malden, MA, 2006). The editor and translator are equally grateful to the anonymous readers of the manuscript for their most helpful comments. We also wish to thank Al Bertrand, Haze Humbert, Brigitte Lee Messenger, and Louise Butler of Wiley-Blackwell for their assistance.

This book is dedicated to Hanna, Elad, and Shalev Roisman, to my mentor Professor Zeev W. Rubinsohn and his wife Nadia, and to the memory of Iolo Davies.

How to Use This Book

The following book is divided into chapters, which in turn are divided into sections. Chapters and sections are labeled and titled individually. For example, Chapter 1 is titled "The World of Homer," and section 7 within it, labeled 1.7, is titled "Household and Community." For the sake of clarity, cross-references to documents outside the chapter include the section title where appropriate, for example, "see 1.7 ('Household and Community')."

The book is accompanied by a website available at www.wiley.com/go/AncientGreece that includes supplementary written and electronic material. The labeling of the documents on the web corresponds to as well as complements that of the book. To facilitate the identification of web documents and links, every web section or chapter is accompanied by the icon 🖥. In the contents list, this icon distinguishes items on the web from items in the book. For example, the web section "🖥 1.10 A Trial Scene" follows "1.9 Kings, Council, and Assembly," which appears in the book. Cross-references in the book to items on the web identify them using the term "WEB" followed, where appropriate, by the section title, for example, "see WEB 9.2 ('Draco's Harsh Laws')." Cross-references on the web to sections in the book are prefixed by the label "BOOK."

Abbreviations

AJA	*American Journal of Archaeology*
AJP	*American Journal of Philology*
Ath. Pol.	Aristotle (?), *Athenaion Politeia* ("The Constitution of the Athenians")
CAH	*Cambridge Ancient History*, 2nd and 3rd eds.
Campbell	Campbell, D.A., ed. 1989–1993. *Greek Lyric* (Loeb Classical Library). 5 vols. Cambridge, MA
CJ	*Classical Journal*
ClAnt	*Classical Antiquity*
CPh	*Classical Philology*
CQ	*Classical Quarterly*
DK	Diels, H. and W. Kranz. 1960–1961. *Die Fragmente der Vorsokratiker*[10] (Diels-Kranz). Berlin
F, FF, fr., frs.	fragment(s)
FGrHist	Jacoby, F., ed. 1957–1969. *Die Fragmente der griechischen Historiker.* 18 vols. Leiden
Fornara	Fornara, C.W., ed. 1983. *Archaic Times to the End of the Peloponnesian War.* 2nd ed. Cambridge
G&R	*Greece & Rome*
Gerber	Gerber, D.E., trans. 1999. *Greek Elegiac Poetry: From the Seventh to the Fifth Centuries BC* (Loeb Classical Library). Cambridge, MA
GRBS	*Greek, Roman, and Byzantine Studies*
Harding	Harding, P., ed. 1985. *From the End of the Peloponnesian War to the Battle of Ipsus.* Cambridge
HSCP	*Harvard Studies in Classical Philology*
IG	*Inscriptiones Graecae*
Jensen	Jensen, Chr. 1963. *Hyperides: Orationes.* Stuttgart
JHS	*Journal of Hellenic Studies*

LP	Lobel, E. and D.L. Page, eds. 1955. *Poetarum Lesbiorum Fragmenta.* Oxford
ML	Meiggs, R. and D. Lewis, eds. 1988. *A Selection of Greek Historical Inscriptions to the End of the Fifth Century.* Rev. ed. Oxford
Page	Page, D., ed. 1962. *Poetae Melici Graeci.* Oxford
R&O	Rhodes, P.J. and R. Osborne, eds. 2003. *Greek Historical Inscriptions: 404–323 BC.* Oxford
Radt	Radt, S., ed., 1977. *Tragicorum Graecorum Fragmenta,* vol. 4: *Sophocles.* Gottingen
SEG	*Supplementum Epigraphicum Graecum*
TAPhA	*Transactions of the American Philological Association*
Tod	Tod, M.N., ed. 1985. *Greek Historical Inscriptions: From the Sixth Century BC to the Death of Alexander the Great in 323 BC.* 2 vols. Reprint. Chicago
West	West, M.L. 1989–1992. *Iambi et Elegi Graeci ante Alexandrum Cantati.* 2 vols. Oxford
YCS	*Yale Classical Studies*
ZPE	*Zeitschrift für Papyrologie und Epigraphik*

Glossary

Agon	Contest
Amphictyonic League	Group of states that supervised Apollo's sanctuary at Delphi
Antidosis	"Giving in exchange": a legal procedure aiming to transfer a costly public duty (liturgy) to an allegedly richer man
Apoikia	Independent settlement abroad
Archon	Chief Athenian official
Areopagus	Athenian council of former archons that served as a homicide court and, up to the 460s, supervised public officials
Aretê	Excellence; valor
Basileus	King; chieftain; Athenian archon who managed religious affairs
Boeotarch	Senior magistrate in the Boeotian League
Boulê	Council
Choregy	Public service by rich citizens that involved producing and financing performances in Athenian festivals
Cleruchy	Athenian colony
Common Peace	Peace agreement among Greeks imposed by hegemonic power(s)
Decarchy	Government of ten men supported by the Spartans
Demagogue	Popular leader; leader of the people
Demos	The people; commoners; democracy; township (deme)
Dikasterion	Jury court
Dikê	Justice; private legal action
Dionysia	Athenian festival in honor of Dionysus that included dramatic performances

Dokimasia	Examination of an individual's eligibility for office or citizenship
Eisangelia	Legal procedure of impeachment against officials or leaders
Eisphora	Property tax designed to finance military projects
Ekklesia	Popular citizens' assembly
Eleutheria	Freedom
Ephebes	Young adults trained by the state in the military and good citizenship
Ephors	Annual magistrates in Sparta
Erastês	"Lover," the elder partner in a homosexual relationship
Eromenos	"Beloved," the younger partner in a homosexual relationship
Ethnos	People, tribal state
Eunomia	Good order
Euthynai (pl.)	Giving of accounts by officials at the end of their term in office
Gerousia	Spartan council of elders
Graphê	Public legal action
Graphê paranomon	Legal action against decrees that allegedly contradicted existing laws
Harmost	Spartan governor and commander of a garrison
Heliaea	"People's Court," the largest court in Athens under the presidency of the Thesmothetae ("Lawgivers")
Hellenotamiai (pl.)	Treasurers of the Greeks: Athenian officials who collected the allies' tributes
Helots	People of servile status in Sparta
Hetaira	"Female companion," courtesan
Hetaireia	Companionship
Hetairoi (pl.)	Companions of Homeric and Macedonian kings
Hippeis	Cavalry; the second richest class in Solon's system
Homoioi (pl.)	"Similar ones," Spartan full citizens
Hoplites	Heavy infantrymen
Isegoria	The equal right to speak in public
Isonomia	Equality before the law
Kaloi k'agathoi (pl.)	"The beautiful and good," description of the elite
Kleros	Plot of land
Koinon	League, federation
Krypteia	Killing of helots by stealth
Kyrios	Head of household; husband; male guardian
Liturgy	Rich man's tax designed to finance festivals (choregy) or the upkeep of a battleship (trierarchy)
Medism	Supporting or collaborating with the Persian enemy
Metic	Resident alien

Nomos (pl. *nomoi*)	Law(s), convention(s)
Oikistês	Leader of a new settlement; founder
Oikos	Household; family
Oliganthropia	Shortage of men (especially in Sparta)
Ostracism	Voting a citizen to ten-year exile
Panathenaea	Athenian festival in honor of Athena
Parrhesia	The right to speak one's mind in a public forum
Perioeci (*perioikoi*)	"Dwellers around": Sparta's free subjects who provided the state with military and economic services
Phoros	"Tribute," the allies' payment to the Delian League
Phratry	"Brotherhood," a social and religious association
Phylê	Tribe
Polemarch	Military leader/magistrate
Polis	City-state
Politeia	Government, constitution
Proskynesis	Obeisance performed in sanctuaries or for Persian superiors
Prytany	One-tenth of the Athenian year. During this term, fifty prytanies (presidents) per tribe presided over the Council and the assembly. The Prytaneum was the town hall
Psephisma	Decree
Pythia	Apollo's priestess at the oracle at Delphi
Rhetores (pl.)	Orators, public speakers, and leaders
Rhetra	"Utterance," Spartan law
Sacred Band	Theban elite military unit
Sarissa	Pike used in particular by the Macedonian phalanx
Sophists	Teachers of wisdom, experts
Sophrosynê	Self-control, moderation
Stasis	Civil conflict within a city-state
Strategos	General (an elected official in Athens)
Symposion	"Drinking together," a banquet
Synedrion	A league's council
Syssition	"Sitting together," a common mess
Theoric Fund	Athenian fund for civilian projects such as festivals
Thirty, the	Oligarchic government in Athens (404–403)
Trierarchy	Public service by rich citizens that involved financing a warship (trireme) for one year
Trireme	Galley whose oarsmen sat in three rows
Tyrant (*tyrannos*)	Non-elected ruler or a man who ruled contrary to tradition
Xenia, proxenia	Guest-friendship

Greek Weights, Measures, Coins, and the Athenian Calendar

Weights

Cotylê: cup, ca. ¼ liter
Choinix (pl. *choinikes*): Four cups, ca. 1 liter
Medimnos: "measure," ca. 1.5 bushels or 52 liters of grain. 1 liquid *medimnos* = 48 *choinikes*
Chous: ca. 3.25 liters
Mina: ca. 0.4 kilogram or 1 pound

Measures

Pechys: (Latin cubit) = ca. 45 cm (18 inches)
Stadion: stade, ca. 180 m or ca. 590 ft

Coins

1 drachma = 6 obols
1 stater = 2 drachmas
1 (Athenian) mina = 100 drachmas
1 talent = 60 minas = 6,000 drachmas

The Athenian Calendar

The Athenian calendar was lunar and the Attic year began in the summer.

Hecatombaeon – July/August
Metageitnion – August/September

Boedromion – September/October
Pyanepsion – October/November
Maemacterion – November/December
Poseideon – December/January
Gamelion – January/February
Anthesterion – February/March
Elaphebolion – March/April
Mounychion – April/May
Thargelion – May/June
Scirophorion – June/July

Timeline

ca. 3000–1200 BCE	Bronze Age Greece
ca. 1260	Trojan War
ca. 1200–800/700	Dark Age
800/700–500	Archaic Age
776	First Olympic Games
ca. 750	Foundation of Pithecoussae
ca. 735–650	Sparta's Messenian Wars
ca. 651/0	Foundation of Selinus
ca. 650–625	Cypselus' tyranny in Corinth
632	Cylon's attempt at tyranny in Athens
631	Foundation of Cyrene
625–585	Periander's tyranny in Corinth
621/0	Draco's legislation
594/3	Solon's archonship
ca. 580/575–530	Cyrus the Great of Persia
561/0	Peisistratus' first tyranny at Athens
560–546	Croesus of Lydia
ca. 557–530	Reign of Cyrus the Great of Persia
556	Peisistratus' second tyranny at Athens
ca. 550	Sparta's war against Tegea
ca. 547	Cyrus' defeat of Croesus of Lydia
546/5–528/7	Peisistratus' third tyranny at Athens
528/7–511/0	Hippias' and Hipparchus' tyranny at Athens
522–486	Darius (I) the Great of Persia
ca. 520–490/89	Cleomenes I
513	Darius' Scythian expedition
500–338/323	Classical Age
519	Plataea's alliance with Athens
514/3	Tyrannicides Harmodius and Aristogeiton

511/0	Expulsion of Hippias from Athens
508/7	Cleisthenes' reforms at Athens
499–494	Ionian Revolt
490	Battle of Marathon
486–465	Xerxes I of Persia
483	Themistocles' shipbuilding program
480–479	Xerxes' invasion of Greece: battles of Artemisium, Thermopylae, and Salamis
479	Battles of Plataea and Mycale
478	Formation of the Delian League
477/6	Cimon's capture of Eion
476/5	Cimon's capture of Scyros
474–470	Pausanias' recall to Sparta
ca. 472	Carystus joins the Delian League
471/0	Themistocles' ostracism
469–466	Battle of Eurymedon
465–424	Artaxerxes I of Persia
465/4–463/2	Thasos' revolt
ca. 465	Naxos joins the Delian League
464–460	Helots' revolt and Mt. Ithome
462/1	Ephialtes' reforms
461/0	Athens' clash with Corinth over Megara
460	Athenian expedition to Egypt
458	Building of Athens' Long Walls; battle of Tanagra
454/3	First tribute quota list; transfer of league's treasury to Athens
453/2	Erythraean decree
451	Five years' peace
451/0	Pericles' citizenship law
450?	Peace of Callias
448/7–426/5	Cleinias decree
447–445	Foundation of Brea
447–432	Building of the Parthenon
446/5	Peloponnesian invasion of Attica; the Thirty-Year Peace
444/3	Foundation of Thurii
441/0	Samian Revolt
437/6	Foundation of Amphipolis
436–433	Epidamnus affair
433–432	Potidaea affair
432?	Megarian decree
432/1–424/3	Methone decree
431–404	Peloponnesian War
431–421	Archidamian War
430–426	Plague at Athens
428–427	Mytilenean Revolt

425/4	Pylos campaign; Thudippus decree; coinage decree
424	Brasidas' capture of Amphipolis; Thucydides' exile
424–404	Darius II (Ochus) of Persia
422	Death of Brasidas and Cleon in Amphipolis
421	Peace of Nicias
418	Battle of Mantinea (I)
416	Melos' revolt; Egesta's request for Athenian aid
415–413	Sicilian expedition; Alcibiades' exile
415	Herms and Mysteries affairs
413–404	The Decelean War
411	Oligarchy at Athens
407	Selymbrian decree
407/6	Lysander's victory at Notium; Alcibiades' second exile
406/5	Arginusae affair
405	Battle of Aegospotami
405–359	Artaxerxes II of Persia
404	Athens' surrender and the end of the Peloponnesian War
404–403	The rule of the Thirty at Athens
403	Amnesty at Athens and restoration of democracy
400–360/59	Agesilaus II of Sparta
400–399	Expedition of Cyrus the Younger; Cinadon's conspiracy
399	Socrates' trial
396–394	Agesilaus in Asia Minor
395–387/6	Corinthian War
394	Battle of Cnidus
390	Battle of Lechaeum
388/7	Peace of Antalcidas
382	Spartan occupation of the Cadmea
379/8	Sphodrias' attempt to capture Piraeus
378/7	Formation of the second Athenian League
375/7	Coinage certification decree
374/3	Agyrrhius' decree
371	Battle of Leuctra
370/69	Foundation of Messene
367	Theban common peace
365	Dissolution of the Peloponnesian League; Athens' colonization of Samos
364	Thebes' destruction of Orchomenus
362	Battle of Mantinea II
359–336	Philip II of Macedonia
359–338	Artaxerxes III of Persia
357–355	Social War
356–346	Third Sacred War
352	Battle of the Crocus Field
348	Philip's capture of Olynthus

346	Peace of Philocrates
340	Athens and Philip at war
338	Battle of Chaeronea
ca. 338–330	Darius III of Persia
336	Philip II's death
336–323	Alexander (III) the Great
335	Destruction of Thebes
334	Alexander's invasion of Asia Minor and the battle of the Granicus
333	Battle of Issus
332/1	Alexander visits the Oracle of Ammon at Siwa
331	Battle of Gaugamela
330	Alexander at Persepolis
326	Alexander's invasion of India
324	Opis mutiny
323	Alexander's death

Map 0.1 Map of Greece and the Aegean.

Introduction

The Evidence for Greek History and Culture

Ancient Greece from Homer to Alexander: The Evidence, First Edition. Joseph Roisman.
© 2011 Blackwell Publishing Ltd. Translations © 2011 John Yardley. Published 2011 by Blackwell Publishing Ltd.

The purpose of this book is to present readers with the main evidence for Greek history from Homer to Alexander the Great (roughly 800–323). It follows the course of this history both chronologically and thematically, with each chapter introducing a period or topic. The chapters consist of sections that provide literary or material evidence related to the topic, place the evidence in its context, clarify it, and cite modern interpretations of issues raised by the chapter. Most sections and all chapters in the book are followed by questions whose aim is to help readers review the material, provide a focus, and, hopefully, trigger discussion of the documents or the topic. Some questions require a greater interpretative effort than others, and it is up to the individual's discretion whether or not to take up the challenge. The book is accompanied by a website that includes additional chapters as well as supplementary evidence and explanations. Best results would be achieved by reading the chapters in conjunction with the website material so as to enrich and deepen familiarity with the subject. The questions and suggested readings at the close of each chapter relate to material both in the book and on the website. The book and online documents are numbered consecutively. While documents in the book are labeled without any distinguishing icon, online documents are prefixed by the term "WEB" (for example, WEB **1.3**) and accompanied by a computer icon. References to external web links should not be construed as full endorsement of their contents. Unless otherwise noted, all dates in this book are BCE.

The purpose of this Introduction is to acquaint readers with the nature of the extant ancient evidence for Greek history. It discusses problems of interpreting the evidence and methods of dealing with it. The task of comprehending a civilization that existed so many centuries ago can be daunting. The evidence is often incomplete, marred by problems of transmission, and even our understanding of it may be tainted by our own experiences and perspectives. This is true for the two main categories of evidence that historians use to reconstruct Greek history: physical – including archaeological – evidence, and ancient literary accounts. In this chapter we illustrate the chief features of both types and suggest ways of using them. We shall discuss the nature of material evidence as illustrated by an archaeological survey of the Argolid and an excavation of a monumental structure on the island of Euboea. In both cases there is no literary evidence that can significantly illuminate the findings. The chapter also includes brief, illustrated discussions of pottery and coinage. The section on written evidence deals with the problems of identifying lost sources of extant ancient histories and the works of authors who are used frequently in this book, such as the historians Herodotus, Thucydides, Xenophon, and Diodorus of Sicily, the biographer Plutarch, and the Attic orators.

I The Archaeological Evidence

The physical evidence for ancient Greece comprises the geographical and climatic environments of various Greek sites and their material remains. It allows us to reconstruct historical events, and especially the technological level, material culture, and social history of the ancient Greeks. Archaeology is responsible for much of our material evidence in the form of artifacts and structures. Until recently these artifacts tended to come mostly from urban centers, and much of the evidence used in this book illustrates their value. An increasing number of archaeologists, however, are now interested in non-urban life and so add to our meager knowledge of this topic. Moreover, for a number of reasons, not the least budgetary, many archaeologists are engaged not in digs but in survey or surface archaeology.

For example, an archaeological survey of the southern Argolid in the north-eastern Peloponnese has located farms, country shrines, and storehouses in addition to villages and towns. Among the finds are stone tools whose use, surprisingly, did not stop at the end of the Stone Age (ca. 3000 BCE). Archaeologists found that the residents of the region from prehistoric to historic times used flake-stone tools such as flints, sickles, scrappers as well as containers. Some were made of obsidian (volcanic glass), which is locally unavailable, and this suggests a probable trade with the closest source of this raw material, the island of Melos. Stone was also used for grinding grain and pressing oil. The finds show that in Classical times (ca. 500–323) grinders were imported ready-made from distant quarries. They also show that oil was introduced into the local economy only at the end of the Archaic period (800/700–500), but continued to thrive until the end of the Roman period (fourth to fifth centuries CE). Rotary mills that used water or wind as sources of power rather than animals were introduced into the region only around the second century BCE. Such information is helpful for the reconstruction of daily and communal life, economy, trade, and communication in a region that is otherwise poorly recorded in other sources.

Archaeological finds, however, can be puzzling, especially in the absence of other evidence. A case in point is a spectacular find in Lefkandi on Euboea, an island that stretched along the Athenian and Boeotian coasts in central Greece. An examination of the site and its modern interpretations may illustrate how to approach material evidence, as well as the limits of this evidence.

Between ca. 1125 and 950 and even later, the slopes near the settlement of Lefkandi were used for cemeteries. We do not know what made the inhabitants choose this ground for their graveyards. In fact, even the name Lefkandi is modern, although some would identify it with ancient Lelanton, which gave its name to the nearby Lelantine plain. On one of the slopes, a hill called Toumba (a modern name), a monumental structure was found (Figure I.1). Potsherds in and around it date the building to ca. 950. It measured 45 meters long by 10 meters wide, was covered by a peaked roof, and had a number of rooms, colonnades, verandas, and an eastern doorway almost 5 meters wide. The evidence shows that the structure was partly dismantled not long after it had been erected and a mound, or tumulus, was raised on its top.

The building included several rooms, the central and largest of which was over 22 meters long. It housed two box-like containers that were filled respectively with stones and ashes and burnt animal bones. The room also had two large burial shafts. One contained a Bronze Age bronze vase (amphora) of Cypriot origin which held the ashes and cremated remains of a man and a

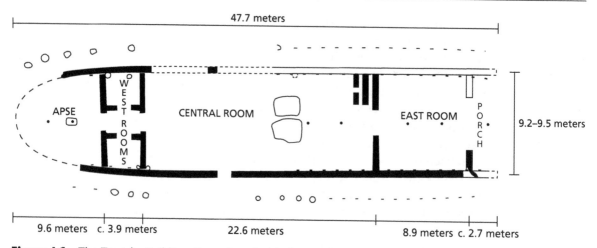

Figure I.1   The Toumba Building. Reproduced with the permission of the British School at Athens.

rich shroud. Next to the vase were a sword, the remains of a wooden scabbard, an iron spearhead and razor, and a whetstone. Around the vase was found the skeleton of a woman wearing a rich dress and golden jewelry. For some scholars the fact that her hands and feet were close together and that an iron knife was found next to her head suggested that she had been bound and sacrificed. Human sacrifice, however, is very rarely attested in ancient Greece. The man's age was estimated at between 30–45 years and the woman's teeth indicated that she was in her late twenties. Next to the grave were found a huge vase (*kratêr*) and an ash box. The second grave contained four horses with iron bits.

How to interpret these findings? The cemeteries in Toumba and the ones close to it, and even the Lefkandi settlement, show no comparable monumentality or riches. In fact, it is hard to find a parallel with the building elsewhere in Greece, which makes identifying its function such a challenge. The building has no central hearth and shows very little evidence of food utensils that would suggest residential use. It was therefore speculated that the structure was designed to glorify the dead man, and that the horses were supposed to accompany him in the afterlife. The practice of horse sacrifice is attested in other graves on the hill. Yet it is unclear why the structure was destroyed shortly after its construction. Equally unknown is the man's role entitling him to such honor. Unlike later periods, Greeks of the Dark Age did not inscribe grave steles to commemorate their dead. The arms suggested that he was a warrior, but we do not really know if this was the reason for the honor accorded him. There are other warrior graves in nearby Athens, but even if they inspired the Lefkandians, no Athenian grave resembles the scale of that in Lefkandi. It was also suggested that the building was a shrine for a hero, a *heroön* or cult center where the community strengthened its cohesion through rituals and sacrifices. Some scholars identify the site as the house of a founder of a settlement, an *oikistês* (see **4.4**: "The Foundation of Cyrene"). All suggestions, while attractive, are hardly more than speculative. It is unclear why the community decided to stop gathering in the building, and there are no signs of cultic activity around the mound, not to mention the fact that shrines for heroes are known only from later times. Undoubtedly, the man enjoyed posthumous prestige because later and poorer graves were dug next to the mound. Anthropological studies of societies dominated by chieftains or "big men" could be useful in identifying the status of the grave occupant as a big chief, but they still do not take us beyond the realm of supposition. In sum, archaeological evidence is informative about material context, but to attain full cultural meaning it needs to be supplemented by theories and, if one is lucky, literary evidence.

Questions

1. What are the advantages and disadvantages of material evidence in reconstructing ancient history?
2. What are the strengths and weaknesses of the different interpretations of the Toumba building?

I.1   Pottery

Pottery occupies a place of honor among ancient remains. It had practical uses in the form of containers, utensils, lamps, pipes, tiles, and other articles. Distribution of pottery is a valuable indication of production and trade and can be used for dating remains and their provenance. Especially informative are illustrated vases. They tell us about daily life and the systems of beliefs and values of their users as well as about artistic accomplishments and trends. One example (shown in Figure I.2) may illustrate the kind of information that can be elucidated from this evidence.

This famous Athenian vase of ca. 540–530 is an amphora, used as a container for liquid, mostly wine or oil, and in this case also primarily for display. It is decorated in the so-called "black-figure" technique, which portrayed figures in black against the background of the natural reddish color of the local clay, with red and white colors added. The artists scraped the paint with a graver to delineate the figures' details and lines. Black-figure vases were popular in Athenian workshops from at least the seventh century up to around 525 when "red-figure" vases replaced them.

The vase displays two scenes. One side depicts the family of the mythological twins Castor and Polydeuces (or Pollux). The other side, shown here, depicts the Homeric heroes Ajax, on the right, and Achilles, on the left, playing dice or a board game. Their names, in the possessive genitive, are written next to their respective heads, and out of Ajax's lips comes the word *tria*, "three," while Achilles "says" *tesara*, "four." Over Achilles' back is written *Exekias*

Figure I.2
Exekias Vase with
Ajax and Achilles.
© TopFoto.

epoiesen, "Exekias made [me? it?]," while over Ajax's back is written *Onetorides kalos,* Onetorides is beautiful." The decorative patterns above the panel, at the base, and on the handles are generic.

The scene shows two Homeric heroes, but their weapons are contemporary of the painter's time. The helmets, spears, body armor, greaves, and the leaning shields all belong to heavy infantrymen called hoplites (see Chapter 8). No poetic tradition has survived about the episode painted here, but many other artistic depictions of it existed. It is likely, then, that artists invented the episode and contributed to its popularity. The warriors are playing a game, but the fact that they did not take off their armor shows that it is just a short respite. Scholars disagree on the suggested meaning of the scene. Their interpretations range from allusions to contemporary Athenian events (i.e., to some Athenians who were absent from a battlefield) to references to later events in the Trojan myth such as the heroes' tragic deaths. The writing on the vase demonstrates the increased literacy of late Archaic Athens. The "signature" by Exekias indicates pride in the product by a craftsman in a society that disparaged manual workers. The inscription "Onetorides is beautiful," which praises the beauty of this man, appears on other vases by Exekias. The term *kalos,* "beautiful," was often associated in Archaic times with aristocratic lineage and homoerotic love. Lastly, the vase, now in the Vatican museum, was found in the Etruscan town of Vulci and confirms the popularity of Athenian vases and Greek mythology in Etruria.

Questions

1. What can a Greek historian learn from illustrative evidence?
2. How does the Exekias Vase appeal to its contemporary viewers?

II Coins

Like illustrated vases, ancient coins combine literary with artistic evidence. They are also useful tools for dating. Early Greek coins appeared first in Asia Minor ca. 600 and showed the influence of neighboring Lydian coinage. The date of their appearance is significant because it renders later literary traditions about pre-600 coinage unreliable. Alternatively, it could be that the sources refer to proto-coins in the form of metal bullions or spits. Many early coins were made of electrum, a natural alloy of gold and silver. Since coins could be minted by both individuals and states, each with its own weight and value system, the worth of a coin was judged by its weight, the value of its metal components, and its stamp of authority. Early coins resembled other forms of portable wealth. Many came in large denominations, which suggests that they were used for large-scale payments such as state taxes or wages for mercenaries. Yet the coexistence of smaller denominations indicates that coins could also be used for retail. Starting from ca. 580, coinage spread into Greece and the west. Greek coins were made mostly of silver. Coins of small denominations used for retail appeared as early as the late sixth century but became very common in the fourth century.

Coins were made of cast blanks that were then struck with engraved dies. They could also be struck over by new dies. The faces of coins often displayed a local divinity and/or symbols associated with it, say, a grape cluster and Dionysus. When Alexander the Great conquered Asia and Egypt, he used local mints for his coinage.

The (10.09 g) silver tetradrachm (four drachmas) shown in Figure I.3 is dated to around 332–323. It was minted in Memphis, Egypt, and like other coins of Alexander was based on the Attic standard, which made it more interchangeable than the coins of Alexander's Macedonian predecessors. The obverse shows the head of Heracles wearing a lion skin in reference to the myth of his killing the Nemean lion. It is uncertain to what extent, if at all, the portrait bears a resemblance to Alexander. The reverse shows a crowned Zeus seated on a throne holding an eagle in his right hand and a scepter in his left. The word *Alexandrou* (of Alexander) is written on the right, and the monogram DI O under the throne identifies the moneyers and/or magistrates who minted the coin. The symbol on the left is of a rose, which appears on many other coins of Alexander and Ptolemy I, his successor in Egypt. Possibly the coin carried a political message. The images of Zeus and Heracles go back to earlier Macedonian coins, but also had universal Greek appeal. Zeus and Heracles were also Alexander's ancestors.

Figure I.3
A silver tetradrachm from Memphis, Egypt, 332–323. Reproduced with the permission of MoneyMuseum Zurich.

Questions

1. How were coins struck and for what purposes?
2. What messages does the Alexander coin convey?

III   The Written Evidence

The most informative evidence on ancient Greece comes from ancient texts. The texts can be very short, such as those written on pots or coins, but the most detailed are found in inscriptions and manuscripts.

Many extant Greek inscriptions record texts that were of an official nature and intended for public display, be they laws, treaties, or commemorations of individuals and communities. However, epigraphic evidence may be of limited value because inscriptions often record information whose larger context is unknown or unclear, or which is pertinent only to specific historical moments. When inscriptions have no date, scholars have to rely on dating methods such as letterforms which are not always accurate or universally accepted. Many inscriptions are fragmentary, and their restoration by epigraphists is speculative to varying degrees. Yet inscriptions can also provide specific information that is otherwise unknown. This book includes many inscriptions that show their evidentiary value.

The most common and informative evidence consists of literary texts. Modern historians of ancient Greece use ancient histories and supplement them with Greek fiction, drama, and poetry as well as philosophical and scientific texts. Some of these texts were found on Egyptian papyri that copied literary works or recorded public and private documents. The degree of preservation of papyri varies greatly, but the surviving texts can be invaluable. Much information on Athenian history and administration comes from a lengthy papyrus that was discovered in the nineteenth century, commonly known by the abbreviation *Ath. Pol.* for *Athenaion Politeia*, or "The Constitution of the Athenians." The present book quotes generously from this work. It also reproduces passages from another papyrus, found in the Egyptian town of Oxyrhynchus, which has partially preserved the work of an anonymous fourth-century BCE historian commonly known as the Oxyrhynchus Historian. Other papyri used here are copies, sometimes fragmented, of Greek lyric poetry.

Greek poetry and drama are highly useful for reconstructing the cultural, social, and political environment of ancient Greece. Indeed, among the most important sources for Dark Age and early Archaic Greece are the poems of Homer and Hesiod (see Chapters 1 and 2). Shorter poetic compositions by Archaic poets are no less useful. Inspired by communal or individual experiences, or even when they are works of pure fiction, poems tell much about the city-state's politics and society. They describe gender relationships, religious beliefs, practices, conventions, and ideals. Tragedy and comedy are equally important sources in spite of the constraints of their respective genres. Tragedy normally situates its characters in mythical times, but the plays are never far removed from the historical context in which they were written. The present collection, then, uses dramatic passages to illustrate political, social, and intellectual issues that interested ancient spectators. It includes the tragic playwrights Aeschylus (425–456), who fought the Persian invaders in Greece, the highly successful and respected Sophocles (496–406), who held important Athenian offices, and Euripides (490–406), whose plays both responded to and shaped the culture of Athens. Finally, the comic poet Aristophanes (?460–386) wrote plays that were firmly embedded in the reality and changing atmosphere of Athens. He is an excellent informant about his times, even though his comic depiction of individuals and society can distort them beyond repair.

Of the written evidence, however, the most important and informative are ancient histories. Conventionally, these accounts are divided into primary and secondary sources. A primary source is a first account of an event, actors, or topic that ideally was written by an eyewitness or a contemporary. Not that immediacy guarantees credibility, but it is potentially preferable to authors who gathered their information second hand and hence are classified as secondary sources. Such authors often wrote long after the events they described and were forced to rely on older primary sources or on oral traditions that were susceptible to changes and manipulations. Much of the information we have on the Archaic and Classical ages of Greece comes from secondary and even tertiary sources. A well-established field within the study of ancient historiography (the writing of history) deals with identifying the sources of our extant ancient accounts and assesses their value. Often these primary sources are no longer extant or have survived only in fragments.

III.1   Investigation of Sources and Fragments of Lost Historians

A major criterion in judging the value of ancient historical work is the quality of its sources. Scholars wish to know about the careers of the author and of his informants, how they obtained their information, the scope and aim of their work, their methods and historiographic guidelines, their literary tendencies, and such like. Answers to these questions will, it is hoped, help us to assess the accuracy of our extant ancient sources.

The German classicist and philologist Felix Jacoby arguably contributed more than any other modern scholar to identifying and evaluating lost historical works that survived only in fragmentary form. In his monumental seventeen-volume collection of fragments of Greek historians, *Die Fragmente der griechischen Historiker* (Berlin and Leiden, 1923–1957), commonly abbreviated as *FGrHist*, Jacoby identified and commented on historical works that were used and cited by extant ancient sources. The impact of Jacoby is attested by a new version of his project, *Brill's New Jacoby*, Volume 1. An online edition (editor-in-chief Ian Worthington) offers new translations of and commentary on the historical fragments.

Jacoby called the remains of ancient texts fragments, but the term can be misleading. When an ancient historian used a previous work, he did not always cite it verbatim but more often paraphrased or summarized it. Hence Jacoby's frequent insistence that we have the authentic remains of a lost work may be open to question. The secondary source had its own interest and perspective, not to mention a mixed loyalty to the text it used, which influenced the nature of the "fragment." In addition, it is hard to judge where a fragment begins and ends because authors rarely bothered to mark the boundaries of their use of the original work. The following example illustrates both the advantages and pitfalls of what is known as *Quellenforschung*, or investigation of sources, that purports to recover lost portions of ancient histories.

In 331, Alexander the Great took his campaign to Egypt where he decided to visit an ancient oracle in the oasis of Siwa on the Libyan–Egyptian border. It was an important event because Alexander heard there that he was the son of the Egyptian god Ammon, whom the Greeks and Macedonians identified with Zeus. We shall discuss Alexander's divine sonship and aspirations as well as their impact on him and his contemporaries in **39.6** ("Alexander Visits the Oracle of Ammon at Siwa") and **39.11** ("Alexander Turns 'Asian'"). Here we focus on the geographer Strabo's depiction of Alexander's visit to the oracle that used as its source the now lost history of Callisthenes.

Strabo *Geography* 17.1.43 = Callisthenes *FGrHist* 124 F 14

I have already spoken a great deal about Ammon, but I want to make this one point, that for the ancients prophecy as a whole and oracles were more respected, whereas these days they are much despised. The Romans content themselves with the oracles of the Sibyl and with the Tyrrhenian prophecies that derive from entrails, observing birds, and signs in the sky. This is why the oracle of Ammon has been all but abandoned, though it was formerly held in honor. This is best demonstrated by the historians of Alexander, who impose all kinds of abject flattery on their accounts, but also produce some worthwhile information.

Callisthenes, at least, states that Alexander greatly sought fame for making his way up-country to the oracle, since he had been told that both Perseus and Heracles had earlier made the journey. He set off from Paraetonium, says Callisthenes, and, despite the onset of the south winds, struggled on. He was thrown off course by a dust storm, and owed his rescue to rainstorms and two crows that led the way, though these are brought in to flatter the king, as are the details that follow. For Callisthenes claims that it was only the king that the priest allowed to enter the temple in his usual attire, and that the others changed their clothes; that they all heard from outside the oracles that were given, apart from Alexander who heard them within. The oracular responses were not delivered through words, he says, as at Delphi and among the Branchidae, but by signs and symbols, as in Homer (*Iliad* 1.528):

"And Cronus' son gave the sign of assent with his dark eyebrows"

with the prophet playing the part of Zeus. And the man expressly told the king that he was the son of Zeus.

Callisthenes also adds some dramatic elaboration. Apollo had abandoned the oracle amongst the Branchidae, he says, after the temple was plundered by the Branchidae when they supported the Persians in the time of Xerxes, and the spring had also failed.[1] But on that occasion the spring welled up again, and Milesian ambassadors transported many oracles to Memphis concerning Alexander's descent from Zeus, his forthcoming victory at Arbela, the death of Darius, and the revolutionary movements in Lacedaemon.[2] Callisthenes further says that the Erythraean Athenais also made an announcement about Alexander's high birth, and notes that this woman was similar to the ancient Sibyl of Erythrae...

Notes

1. *The Branchidae were priests of Apollo at Didyma, Asia Minor. The Persian king Xerxes invaded Greece in 480–479.*
2. *Alexander defeated Darius III at Arbela, or Gaugamela, in 331, when a Spartan insurrection against Macedonia had also failed.*

We have other accounts of Alexander's visit to Siwa according to which Alexander learned that he would be the ruler of the inhabited world and that he had punished all of his father's murderers (see **39.6**: "Alexander Visits the Oracle of Ammon at Siwa"). Strabo's silence about these revelations makes it likely that Callisthenes did not report them. Investigation of sources may help in deciding which account is preferable.

To assess the value of Strabo's account, we first need to investigate who he was and the nature of his work, the *Geography*. Briefly, Strabo lived ca. 64 BCE–19 CE, that is, about three centuries after the event described here. His work was multidisciplinary in nature and includes myths, ethnography, history, and geographical knowledge. In order to describe Alexander's visit of the oracle, Strabo used Callisthenes, a Greek historian who joined Alexander's campaign and was probably the first to record it (until probably 327 when he was arrested or executed). The fact that some of the details in Strabo's story, such as the guidance rendered by the two crows, recur in other accounts makes it likely that they too relied directly or indirectly on Callisthenes as their source. But before placing trust in Strabo's version due to its reliance on a companion of Alexander, it should be noted that Strabo records the story of Alexander's visit not out of an interest in Alexander, but out of an interest in the oracle of Siwa and the stories associated with it. Did his focus on the oracle impact his use of Callisthenes who focused on the king? It is also uncertain how faithful Strabo was otherwise in reproducing his source, and judging his accuracy on the basis of his reproduction of sources elsewhere gives us no more than an indication. Clearly, however, Strabo's judgment that Callisthenes flattered Alexander colored his reading and paraphrasing of this historian. Apart from Strabo's fidelity to his sources, there is also the question of how reliable Callisthenes was as a historian. Thus we do not really know whether Callisthenes took part in the trip to Siwa or whether he learned about it from others. In addition, The Hellenistic historian Polybius criticized Callisthenes' description of one of Alexander's battles as inept (Polybius 12.17–22), and Strabo in the cited passage thought that he wished to flatter Alexander. Against these discouraging views of Callisthenes are many fragments attributed to him that do not always justify Strabo's characterization of the historian as Alexander's flatterer. Indeed, later in the campaign Callisthenes forcefully opposed Alexander's attempt to appropriate divine honors, an opposition that does not easily tally with his reported account of the king's visit to Siwa. As the above problems demonstrate, any investigation of a lost historian is bound to run into difficulties of assessing how reliable his account is, how authentic his fragments are, and whether his version should be preferred to others that differ from it. At least in the case of Alexander's visit to Siwa, archaeological evidence seems to support Callisthenes' account of the consultation of the oracle in comparison to others that describe an exchange of questions and answers between the king and the local priest. The remains of the shrine in Siwa strongly suggest that no one outside could have heard what was going on in the inner sanctum.

In sum, investigation of sources is marred by problems of restoring faithfully the remains of lost works. Nevertheless, these remains are important for reconstructing the development and range of Greek historiography and, in the absence of better evidence, suggest the reliability of the information provided by their ancient users.

Questions

1. What are the challenges of identifying a lost work from its use by later extant authors?
2. Is it possible to separate Callisthenes' original from Strabo's narrative? How does such an exercise impact our knowledge of the event described in the document?

Every modern historian of Archaic and Classical Greece has to rely extensively on the three great ancient historians of these periods, namely, Herodotus, who is often called "the father of history," Thucydides, and Xenophon.

Our knowledge of Herodotus' life comes from very late sources whose information is difficult to ascertain. He was born in Halicarnassus in Asia Minor around 480 and died around 420, either in Thurii in southern Italy or in Pella, Macedonia. His native town, Halicarnassus, was a Dorian Greek city with close ties to the local Carian population. The city came under Persian control around the mid-sixth century. This cultural mix, as well as the historian's travels in Greece and the Near East, probably after he had gone into exile, accounted for much of his respectful attitude toward cultures other than Greek.

The declared aim of Herodotus' *historiai*, "inquiries" or "investigations," was to fight oblivion by recording the fame and accomplishments of Greeks and barbarians (non-Greeks). In describing the latter, he paid special attention to peoples he considered least resembling the Greeks, particularly the Egyptians and the Scythians. Herodotus' other goal was to report on the conflict between the Greeks and the Persians, and especially the great Persian War (480–479). By recording the fame, or *kleos*, of the participants in the conflict, Herodotus followed Homer, who also immortalized the Trojan War and its heroes.

Herodotus' Aims

Herodotus 1. *Preface*

Here the results of Herodotus of Halicarnassus' research are laid out. My aim is to prevent the deeds of men from fading out with the passage of time, and to see that the great and amazing achievements brought off by both Greeks and barbarians not lose their fame. Amongst the material under discussion the reason for their going to war is of particular significance.

To accomplish his goal, Herodotus gathered information from what he saw, heard, and read. He was not the first Greek to write history. Others had written before him, in prose or in verse, about Greek local histories and wars, and on the Persians, Lydians, Egyptians, and other non-Greek peoples. However, there is no certainty about how much, if at all, Herodotus consulted them, with the exception of Hecataeus of Miletus who had tried to put in order and make sense of mythic genealogies. Wherever possible, Herodotus used his own observations to describe the geographical and cultural setting of peoples. At the end of his description of the Egyptian land and civilization, he states that he would write its history based on local, mostly priestly, accounts. Yet he interspersed these accounts with his own observations.

Herodotus and His Sources

Herodotus 2.99.1–4

(**2.99.1**) All the material that I have thus far presented derives from my own observation, judgment, and research. From this point, however, I shall be giving Egyptian accounts, which I have supplemented with what I saw myself.

(**99.2**) The priests said that Min was the first king of Egypt and that it was he who built the dykes to safeguard Memphis. They explained that the whole river used to flow past the sandy mountains toward Libya, but that upstream, about a hundred stades [ca. 18 km] from Memphis, Min built dams to create the bend that lies to the south. He thus dried up the old riverbed, diverting the river so that it flowed between the mountains. (**99.3**) Even today this bend of the Nile is still kept under strict surveillance by the Persians to insure that it keeps to its banks, the dams being strengthened every year. For should the river choose to break the dams and overflow just here, Memphis faces a threat of total inundation. (**99.4**) Thanks, then, to this Min, who was the first king of Egypt, what had been cut off became dry land, and on it he founded a city, which today is called Memphis – for Memphis, too, lies in the narrow part of Egypt. Outside the city, to the north and west (the Nile itself bounds the city to the east), he made a lake using the river water, and he also built within it the shrine of Hephaestus, a great and truly remarkable edifice.

Herodotus also used informants who recalled the more remote past based on oral traditions, and eyewitnesses for more recent history. He then had to decide what to include in his work and how reliable his information was. His approach to both questions can be described as inclusive. At times Herodotus incorporated in his narrative accounts of fantastic phenomena and marvelous deeds because they were good stories. They were also suitable to the parts of his history that he read in public; indeed, the performative aspect of his work is recognizable in some of its episodes. Herodotus' inclusiveness was also based on the old Greek wisdom that one's circumstances were transitory and that it was possible to judge only at the endpoint (*telos*) whether an individual or a city were great, prosperous, happy, and so on. Because this endpoint might still be in the future, Herodotus refused to limit his narrative to reports on great men or large cities. He makes this principle explicit after recounting what Greeks and Persians said on the ancient origins of their conflict.

Herodotus on the Ancient Origins of the Persian War

Herodotus 1.5.3–4

(**1.5.3**) Such are the accounts of the Persians and the Phoenicians. Personally, I am not going to declare things happened in one way or another, but I will put my finger on the man who I myself know first launched unjustifiable aggression against the Greeks, and then I shall go on with my narrative, devoting equal discussion to large and small communities of people. (**5.4**) For many of those that were great in the past have now become insignificant, and those that were great during my time were insignificant earlier. So, well aware as I am that the wealth of peoples never remains in the same place, I shall make mention of both of these alike.

Herodotus' assessment of the information he found was similarly broad-minded. When he came across contradictory reports or traditions, he often recorded both versions, leaving the reader to decide which was preferable. Although he was not gullible, he knowingly included in his work stories of dubious credibility, either because he felt that he was not qualified to disregard them, or because he thought that what people told him and how had both literary and cultural value. Besides, the information was important to the informants or to the story and so was worth recording. Herodotus clarifies his manner of handling sources in the context of his report on Argos' neutrality during the war between the Greeks and the Persians in 480–479. There were different versions of the reasons for Argos' controversial position, some friendlier to the city than others. Herodotus recounts them and then states the rules he followed in writing down what he had found out.

Herodotus' Methods

Herodotus 7.152.1–3

(**7.152.1**) I cannot say for sure whether [the Persian king] Xerxes sent a herald to Argos with this message [affirming Argos' friendship with him] or whether messengers from Argos went inland to Susa and asked Artaxerxes about a pact of friendship. And I am not putting forward any opinion on these events contrary to the one the Argives voice themselves. (**152.2**) But this much I do know. If all men brought their own troubles with them to market, wanting to make an exchange with their neighbors, every one of them would, after a close look at the troubles of those next door, be quite happy to carry back home what he had brought. (**152.3**) So what was done by the Argives was not the worst that could be done. I am obliged to record what I have been told, but I am certainly not obliged to believe it – and let that statement apply to all my writing. For this story is also told, that it was the Argives who invited the Persian into Greece, and that they did so because the war with the Spartans had gone badly for them, and they wanted for themselves anything other than their current misery.

Modern readers are bound to be baffled by the way Herodotus arranged the enormous amount of information he gathered. He tells stories in a linear manner, but often digresses to tell other stories in order to report on people or places his narrative has taken him to. He also travels easily in time from the present to the past. Nevertheless, there are recurrent motifs that often serve as organizing principles. These include the growth of Persian power, which eventually led to the conflict with the Greeks, and the concept of reciprocity, both negative and positive, that explains people's actions and the course of events. For example, the mythic origins of the conflict between Greece and Persia, or Europe and Asia, went back to mutual abductions of women by both sides (1.1–5). Related to this concept were *tisis*, divine retribution, and *hubris*, human insolence, which triggered divine envy and punishment. Finally, Herodotus often discusses reversals of fortune and the operation of fate in human affairs.

Questions

1. What were Herodotus' aims in writing his history and how did he set out to accomplish them?
2. What were Herodotus' sources and how did they impact his work?
3. What are the advantages and disadvantages of Herodotus' historiographical approach?

III.3   Thucydides

Thucydides was a contemporary of Herodotus. Although scholars have portrayed him as Herodotus' polar opposite, the two shared many historiographic attributes, including an interest in military history and the psychology of actions.

Thucydides, son of Olorus, was born ca. 460 to an elite Athenian family. During the Peloponnesian War between Athens and Sparta, he served as general in 424/3 in the northern Aegean. But when the Spartan general Brasidas captured the important city of Amphipolis on Thucydides' watch, the historian went into exile. Thucydides spent the rest of the war outside Athens until his return there at the end of the war in 404/3. He died ca. 400, or perhaps a few years later.

His work, *The Peloponnesian War*, is divided, probably not originally, into eight books, the bulk of which records the origins and course of the war between Athens and Sparta (431–404). The narrative was supposed to end at the conclusion of the war in 404, but it breaks off abruptly in 411, presumably due to the author's death. In the following passage Thucydides describes how he arranged his work. He argues that the Peace of Nicias that intervened in the course of the war was not a real peace. He also recounts how his exile was conducive to his history.

Thucydides' Inclusive View of the Peloponnesian War and His Exile

Thucydides 5.26.1–5

(**5.26.1**) The same Thucydides of Athens also wrote a history of these events, presenting them in chronological order, by summers and winters, down to the time when the Spartans and their allies brought the Athenian empire to an end, and captured both the Long Walls and Piraeus [404]. The years of war down to that point totaled twenty-seven; (**26.2**) and one would be making an error of judgment in not considering the interval of the treaty [i.e., the Peace of Nicias in 421] to be part of the war. For let someone simply consider how the peace was punctuated by military action and he will find that it is unreasonable to judge that to be peace. In that period neither side gave back or got back all that was agreed upon, and apart from that there were infractions of the treaty in the Mantinean and Epidaurian Wars and other cases, too, while the allies in Thrace did not relax their hostility to Athens, and the Boeotians had a truce that was renewed every ten days. **(26.3)** Thus, with the first war lasting ten years, followed by the questionable peace and then the war that came after it, one will find the aforementioned total (calculating by seasons), plus a few extra days, and that this is the only case where those who have faith in oracles turned out to be correct. **(26.4)** For I myself remember that, at the beginning of the war and right to its end, it was declared by many that it had to last "thrice nine years." **(26.5)** I lived through it all; and I was mature enough to have understanding and also focused my attention on it so that I would acquire accurate intelligence. It also transpired that I was exiled from my country for twenty years after my time as general at Amphipolis. Thus I had contact with both sides' affairs, especially those of the Spartans because of my exile and, having time on my hands, could acquire some better understanding of them...

Unlike Herodotus, Thucydides had little respect for accounts that could not be corroborated. This was one of the reasons he chose to focus on events of his own time rather than on the distant past. In addition, while Herodotus presented the reader with more than one version of events, Thucydides preselected and recorded only the version he deemed the correct one. His sources included his own observations, eyewitness accounts, official documents, and, at times, oral traditions. Like many other ancient historians, he was highly competitive; hence, he characterized the war he described as the greatest and most significant in Greek history, and others' view of history and historical evidence as faulty. He describes his approach to the evidence early in his work.

Thucydides Contrasts Historical Fallacies with His Accuracy

Thucydides 1.20.1, 20.3–22.4

(1.20.1) Such are my findings on the Archaic period, although it is difficult to give credence to every single piece of evidence. For people accept from each other hearsay accounts of events of the past without questioning them, even if they concern their own country.

Thucydides goes on to criticize the Athenian collective memory of a conspiracy against the tyrants of the city in 514/3 (see WEB **10.11**: "Thucydides on the Athenian Tyrannicides").

(1.20.3) The other Greek peoples also entertain wrong-headed ideas about many other matters that actually belong in the present and have not been forgotten with the passage of time. Examples of this are the belief that the kings of the Spartans have two votes to express their opinion, not one, and that the Spartans have a "Pitane" army unit, which in fact has never existed.[1] So undiscriminating are the masses in their search for the truth, preferring rather to resort to notions that are readily available.

(**1.21.1**) Nevertheless, on the basis of the evidence presented, one would not be mistaken in accepting my account to be quite accurate. One should not rely more on the accounts that the poets have chanted with their embellishment and exaggeration, or on those of the chroniclers whose compositions were aimed at pleasing the ear rather than reaching the truth. Such works cannot be verified, and the majority of them have, with the passage of time, won their way into the realms of mythology and become unbelievable. My findings, based as they are on the clearest evidence, should be regarded as being sufficiently reliable, given the antiquity of the period. (**21.2**) Men inevitably judge the war in which they are currently engaged to be the greatest war of all, but when they have finished it they regard the feats of antiquity with increased admiration. However, for he whose view of it is based on the facts, this war will be clearly seen to have been greater than all the others in the past.

(**22.1**) With regard to the speeches made by various people when they were about to go to war or were already in it, it was difficult for me to report from memory the exact words that were spoken, both those I heard myself and those communicated to me from different places. The speeches therefore represent the sort of things that seemed to me the most appropriate for the various speakers to say about the particular situation prevailing at the time, while I have also kept as close as possible to the general sense of what was actually delivered. (**22.2**) As for the actions taken [*erga*] in the war, I did not think it appropriate to write down what I was told by just anybody, or what to me seemed the likely scenario. Rather, after an inquiry as minute as possible into every detail, I have described events that I witnessed myself and those that I heard about from others. (**22.3**) The research was arduous because those present at the various events in question did not give similar accounts of the same incident, the differences arising from the witnesses' partiality to one or other side or from their memories. (**22.4**) And the absence of the mythological element from my narrative will possibly make it seem less enjoyable to listen to. But there will be those wanting a clear insight into the events of the past and also of those that will happen again in more or less the same way (human nature being what it is), and it will suffice for me if these judge my work to be of use. My history has been composed as a possession for eternity, not as a prize piece that is only for immediate hearing.

Note

1. *The two "mistakes" concerning Sparta are found in Herodotus (6.57.5; 9.53.2).*

The most troublesome of the above statements are those regarding the speeches. It is not easy to reconcile Thucydides' striving for an accurate, factual account with his use of speeches delivered by others but written by the historian himself. Scholarly opinion has ranged between regarding the speeches as pure inventions to viewing them as sincere efforts to reproduce the essence of what the speakers said. It may be advisable to follow Thucydides in regarding the narrative as having a better claim to accuracy than the speeches.

In many respects Thucydides' history reflects his own times. His work shows the impact of intellectuals of the period, called sophists, whose range of teaching included philosophy, politics, rhetoric, and science (see Chapter 23). Like the sophists, Thucydides was fond of contrasting what people said (*logos*) with what they actually did (*ergon*), or showing that social conventions (sg. *nomos*) were weaker than, and often disguised, one's true nature (*physis*). Unlike Herodotus, he refused to see divine intervention behind individual and collective conduct. Instead, he often detected in people's behavior the motivating power of self-interest and the ambition to attain or augment power. He also observed the working of "human nature," which revealed itself under different circumstances across time. The following example illustrates the operation of fear, honor, and self-interest in Athenian history. It comes from a speech that Thucydides ascribes to an Athenian delegation to Sparta which tried to dissuade the Spartans from going to war against Athens. The Athenians justified the way they came to hold and maintain imperial power following the Persian War.

Thucydides on Human Nature

Thucydides 1.75.1–3

(**1.75.1**) Men of Sparta: In view of our readiness to act at that time and the wisdom of our judgment, surely we do not deserve this excessive resentment felt for us, or at least for our empire, by the Greeks? (**75.2**) And, in fact, we did not acquire that empire by force. We did so after you refused to continue the fight against what remained of the barbarian forces, when the allies came to us and of their own free will asked us to assume command. (**75.3**) It was as a result of accepting it that we were initially constrained to enlarge our empire to its present extent, mostly from fear, then from honor, and finally from self-interest...

In the course of describing a vicious civil war (*stasis*) on the island of Corcyra in 427, Thucydides uses human nature to explain why it spread like a disease to the rest of Greece.

Thucydides 3.82.1–2

(**3.82.1**) With such cruelty did the strife [*stasis*] progress, and because this was one of the first instances of it, that cruelty appeared all the greater. Later, virtually the whole of the Greek world was convulsed, as conflict broke out everywhere, with the leaders of the popular parties wanting to call in the Athenians, and the oligarchs wanting to call in the Spartans. In peacetime they would have had neither the excuse nor the inclination to invite them in. Now, however, the two states were at war, and for both factions, if they were eager for revolutionary change, opportunities were readily available for bringing in allies to inflict damage on their opponents and at the same time to further their own agenda. (**82.2**) And many were the sufferings that befell the city-states in times of civil strife; these things happen and always will while human nature remains the same, but they can be more or less intense and different in character as circumstances vary from one case to another. For in time of peace and prosperity city-states and individuals observe a higher code of behavior through not being faced with grim necessity. But war, in taking away easy access to one's daily needs, is a violent teacher who adapts most people's attitudes to the prevailing circumstances...

Scholars have lauded Thucydides as the first "scientific historian." He is still, arguably, the best extant historian to come from the Greco-Roman world, but in recent decades greater attention has been paid to his literary devices, judgmental presentation (often implicit) of individuals and events, selective points of view, biases, and even carelessness. Yet the work that continues his narrative, Xenophon's *Hellenikê* (or *Hellenica*), causes many readers to miss him.

Questions

1. What impact did Thucydides' career have on his history?
2. What were Thucydides' guidelines in assessing and using historical evidence?
3. What, according to Thucydides, are the driving forces of history? Is he right?

III.4   Xenophon

Xenophon, son of Gryllus, was born ca. 430–425 to a wealthy Athenian family and studied under Socrates. In 401 he joined other Greek mercenaries in the army of Cyrus the Younger in a failed attempt to take over the Persian throne. Xenophon later wrote the story of this campaign and the return of the Greeks to Europe in *Anabasis* (lit. "marching up"). During the 390s Xenophon enjoyed the patronage of the Spartan king Agesilaus II, whom he praised in a number of works. He was exiled from Athens for his pro-Spartan activities and lived in Elis on an estate he obtained from the Spartans. While in exile he wrote his historical, philosophical, and educational works. After 371 he was allowed to return to Athens, but apparently preferred to move to Corinth where he died ca. 355.

Xenophon's history of the Greek world, *Hellenica*, begins where Thucydides' narrative breaks off. It describes affairs in Greece and Asia Minor from 411 to the Battle of Mantinea (II) in 362. Scholars are divided among the "unitarians," who argue that he wrote the entire work late in life, and the "analysts," who divide it into two parts: Books 1–2.3.10, which continues the story of the Peloponnesian War to its end and which was written early in Xenophon's exile (ca. 380?), and the rest of the work (2.3.11–7.5.27), which Xenophon wrote in old age. The problem of the time of composition is closely linked to Xenophon's sources. It appears that he relied on his memory, but mostly on other informants' recollections. Such sources may explain the omission of important details and events from his narrative, although some gaps were deliberate, as when he fashioned a story to compliment his hero, Agesilaus.

Xenophon thought that his history could teach readers both practical and moral lessons. His historiographic approach resembled that of Herodotus more than that of Thucydides. (In antiquity, Xenophon was more popular than Thucydides largely because of his more accessible and engaging style.) Like Herodotus, Xenophon accorded the divine a role in shaping events. The following remarks are also reminiscent of Herodotus' justification for writing about things big and small and about fame and human accomplishments. Xenophon makes these comments in the context of the replacement of the Spartan admiral Teleutias in 389.

Xenophon *Hellenica* 5.1.3–4

(**5.1.3**) After this the admiral Hierax arrived from Sparta. He assumed command of the fleet, and Teleutias set sail for home amidst great euphoria. As he went down to the sea to start the homeward voyage, there was not a single one of his soldiers who did not greet him, one putting a garland on him, another a headband, and the late-comers, even though he had already cast off, nevertheless threw garlands into the sea and called down many blessings upon him. (**5.1.4**) I realize that, in describing this incident, my subject is not expenditure of funds, a dangerous situation, or some note-worthy stratagem; but *for heaven's sake* it seems to me worthwhile for a person to reflect on what Teleutias did to have such an influence on his subordinates. Indeed, for a man this is an achievement more remarkable than spending a lot of money or facing many dangers.

III.5   Diodorus of Sicily

Diodorus of Sicily (Diodorus Siculus) was a first-century historian who wrote the "Library" (*Bibliotekê*), a universal history that covers Greek and Sicilian history from their mythical origins to ca. 60. Only fifteen of the original forty books have survived intact; the rest are in fragments. For the period covered in this book, Diodorus is especially valuable for the Classical Age (500–323).

Like many other ancient historians, Diodorus promulgated the moral and didactic value of his history.

Diodorus of Sicily 37.4

The historian Diodorus says this: I shall mention certain men for the sake of example, because they deserve praise and also because this benefits the lives of us all. Its aim [i.e., of history] is to have the wicked amongst mankind turn away from their evil impulses through the censure of history, and the good aspire to noble behavior because of the praise that accrues to everlasting glory.

Diodorus hoped that one benefit of reading his history would be to teach people how to contend with fortune (*tychê*), which according to him played a significant role in human affairs.

Diodorus relies for his history on earlier written accounts. Scholars are divided about whether Diodorus preferred to use one main source or more, including his own investigations. When he supplemented his source with others, he did not always reconcile them and at times even recorded conflicting accounts. Yet the old scholarly view that regarded him as an unintelligent copier of earlier sources has been challenged by recent readers, who have pointed to his critical ability and original contributions, and who have recommended treating his history as an independent text.

For his account of the Classical Age, Diodorus chiefly used the fourth-century historian Ephorus of Cyme, who wrote a universal history from mythical times to 340. Ephorus was a highly respected historian in antiquity, and the surviving fragments of his work indicate a strong Herodotean influence and a moralistic tone. Diodorus also used Timaeus (ca. 350–260), who was arguably the most important ancient historian of Sicily and the western Mediterranean. The second-century Greek historian Polybius, however, criticized Timaeus' methodology and describes Ephorus as a historian who sets great store by autopsy, or personal observations.

Polybius 12.27.1–7

(**12.27.1**) … We have from nature two devices for gaining knowledge and conducting research, hearing and sight, and of these, according to [the philosopher] Heracleitus, the more reliable by far is sight – the eyes are more accurate witnesses than the ears. (**27.2**) Timaeus, however, embarked on his researches by taking the more pleasant but also the inferior of the two paths. (**27.3**) For he totally avoided material gathered using his eyes and worked instead with hearsay. Hearsay is also of two kinds, that based on written materials … but Timaeus was careless in gathering information from witnesses, as has been demonstrated above. (**27.4**) The reason for his making this choice is easy to see. Research into materials in books can be done without danger or discomfort if one takes care simply to live in a town with a rich store of documents or else have a library in one's neighborhood. (**27.5**) For the rest all one has to do is research the question, lying at one's ease, and compare the mistakes of earlier historians with no discomfort whatsoever. (**27.6**) Personal investigation, however, calls for considerable hardship and expense, but it is very useful and is the major part of historiography. (**27.7**) This is clear from those who are actually engaged in the composition of historical documents. Ephorus says that if the writers could themselves be present at all the events they cover, this would be by far the best experience for them.

Questions

1. What are the purposes of writing history according to Xenophon and Diodorus of Sicily?
2. What faults does Polybius find in the sources that Diodorus would eventually use?

III.6   Plutarch

Plutarch of Chaeronea was not a historian but a biographer of historical figures. He lived in the second century CE and, in addition to biographies, wrote essays on a wide range of literary, philosophical, moral, and other issues.

He published his biographies in pairs of Greek and Roman individuals and added a comparison between the two. In his biography of Alexander the Great, Plutarch insists on distinguishing between biography and history. He was well read and used a great number of sources, now lost, for his biographies.

Plutarch *Alexander* 1.1–3

(**1.1**) I shall in this book write of the life of Alexander the king and of the Caesar by whom Pompey was brought low. Because of the large number of their exploits, all I shall do by way of preface is ask my readers not to complain if I do not narrate all their famous exploits, or treat any particular one of them exhaustively, but instead deal only briefly with the majority of them. (**1.2**) For it is not history that I am writing, but biography. And as far as famous exploits are concerned, a man's virtues or shortcomings are not always revealed by them; often, indeed, it is a trivial thing, a remark or a joke, that reflects character more than battles in which thousands are killed, or huge arrays of soldiers, or blockades of cities. (**1.3**) Painters take the likenesses of their subjects from the face and the look of the eyes, which is where character manifests itself, giving very little heed to the other parts of the body. So, too, I must be allowed to go more into the items that mirror a person's soul, and to use these to build a picture of the life of each of my subjects, leaving to others the great exploits and the battles.

III.7   The Attic Orators

Among the most important sources for Athenian history in the fourth century are speeches that various Athenians delivered in courts and in the Athenian popular assembly. The ancients already singled out for prominence ten Attic orators, whose speeches have been preserved to varying degrees. The speeches are conventionally divided into three categories: (1) deliberative speeches that were given in the popular assembly or in the city council and which focused on public policy; (2) forensic speeches that were delivered in different Athenian courts; and (3) epideictic (display) speeches that celebrated the city or individual Athenians. The authenticity of the speeches and the value of the information they provide are not without problems. There are speeches that are wrongly attributed to a certain speaker or for which the speaker is unknown. Moreover, many speeches, and in particular forensic speeches, were written by speechwriters (logographers) for litigants, who delivered them as if they were their own creations, and their depiction of a case was highly partisan. Finally, scholars disagree on the extent to which the extant written speeches were revised for publication after their delivery. The position taken here is that most speeches were more faithful to their actual delivery than not. In spite of these and other constraints, orations are an invaluable source for the political, social, legal, and cultural history of fourth-century Athens.

The following passage is taken from a speech that the Athenian orator and politician Demosthenes delivered in 352 in the Athenian assembly. It illustrates how a speaker addresses an assembly as well as his use of information and persuasive devices to move his hearers to approve his policy. Demosthenes calls upon the Athenians to take action against the Macedonian king Philip II, whom the orator presents as a great danger to the city. He speaks as a counselor and makes efforts to present himself as better than other speakers who compete with him for political influence. He then rebukes the Athenians for their inaction over Philip, but also argues that the situation is not beyond repair. The impact of his speech on the Athenians was fairly minimal.

Demosthenes 4 *First Philippic* 1–3

(**1**) Men of Athens, were it a new subject that had been put to us for discussion, then I would have held back until most of our customary speakers had expressed their opinions. I would have held my tongue if any of their suggestions pleased me, and tried to give my own thoughts only if they did not. However, since it transpires that we are now actually considering matters on which they have often spoken in the past, I think I can reasonably expect to be pardoned for being the first to take the floor. For if in the past these men had given you the advice that was needed, it would not have been necessary for you to deliberate the issue today.

(**2**) First of all, Men of Athens, you should not be discouraged by the current situation, even if it seems totally desperate. For the worst of what has happened in the past is actually what gives us our best hope for the future. How is that so? It is because this dire situation is the result of your failure to do any of the things you ought to have done. For if this situation obtained even though you had taken all the appropriate action, then there would be no hope of its improving. (**3**) Next, you must bear in mind that you have been told by others how great Spartan power was not so long ago (and some of you actually know it from personal recollection) and how you nonetheless, with appropriate nobility, faced it with action completely worthy of your city, taking on a war against them for a just cause. Why do I make mention of this? So that you may realize and understand, Men of Athens, that you have nothing to fear as long as you are on your guard, and that you can also, if you are dilatory, expect to have none of the things you might want. As witness to this, consider the strength of Sparta, which you conquered by paying attention to your affairs, and the overconfidence of this man [Philip II] which discomforts us because we are not focusing on what we should.[1]

Note

1. See **38.8** (*"Demosthenes' War Plan Against Philip"*) for other passages of this speech.

Question

1. What problems may impede historical investigation that is based solely on Plutarch's biographies or on the Attic orators?

Review Questions

1. What aspects of a historical investigation are best served by material evidence?
2. The Greeks preserved stories of their migrations into or within Greece in prehistoric times. We know of them from much later written accounts, but in a number

of cases archaeological evidence fails to show signs of the arrival of newcomers. In case of such a conflict between types of evidence, which should prevail and why?

3. Use the criteria of source investigation (**III.1**: "Investigation of Sources and Fragments of Lost Historians") to assess the validity of Polybius' criticism of Timaeus and Ephorus (**III.5**: "Diodorus of Sicily").

4. Compare and contrast the aims and methods of Herodotus, Thucydides, Xenophon, and Plutarch.

Suggested Readings

Archaeological evidence: Snodgrass 1987; Morris 1994; Renfrew and Bahn 1996. *Southern Argolid and stone tools*: Runnels et al. 1995, esp. 74–139. *Greek pottery*: Boardman 2006. *Athenian Greek vases*: Boardman 1974, 1975, 1989; M. Robertson 1992. *The Exekias amphora*: Boardman 1978; Hedreen 2001, Ch. 3; Woodford 2003, 116–118. *Greek coins and money*: Kraay 1976; Carradice 1995; Meadows and Shipton 2001; Schaps 2004. *Selected images of Greek coins*: http://tjbuggey.ancients.info/Greek.html. *Alexander's coinage*: Bellinger 1963; Price 1991 (the Memphis coin: no. 3971, p. 498); Troxell 1997; Dahmen 2007. *Epigraphy*: Bodel 2001; R&O, i–xxvii; Hedrick 2006. *Herodotus*: Lateiner 1989; Bakker et al. 2002; Dewald and Marincola 2006. *Commentaries on Thucydides*: Gomme et al. 1945–1981; Hornblower 1991–2008. *Thucydides' history*: Connor 1984; Rood 1998; Stahl 2003; Rengakos and Tsakmakis 2006. *Xenophon*: Gray 1989; Tuplin 1993, 2004; Dillery 1995. *Commentary on the Hellenica Bks. 1–4.2*: Krentz 1989–1995. *Diodorus*: Rubicam 1987; Sacks 1990; Green 2006, 1–47. *Ephorus*: Pearson 1984; Barber 1993; Pownall 2004, 113–142. *Plutarch*: Stadter 1992; Mossman 1997; Russell 2001. *Greek rhetoric and the oratorical evidence*: Kennedy 1963; Ober 1989; Usher 1999; Worthington 2007.

1

The World of Homer

CHAPTER CONTENTS

Ancient Greece from Homer to Alexander: The Evidence, First Edition. Joseph Roisman.
© 2011 Blackwell Publishing Ltd. Translations © 2011 John Yardley. Published 2011 by Blackwell Publishing Ltd.

This chapter briefly surveys the so-called Homeric Question, including the relations between the Homeric epics and material evidence. Its major focus, however, is on the society and institutions depicted in the epics, which are assumed here to be largely historic. On that assumption, Homer is a valuable source for two main reasons. Firstly, the poet describes institutions and practices that were likely to have existed no later than the early Archaic period. Secondly, his heroes often served as models for generations of ancient Greeks, especially members of the elite. The Homeric value system, then, was relevant to many Greeks far beyond his age. In general, the *Odyssey* is more informative on Homeric society, and the *Iliad* on political institutions and war. The following sections discuss the Homeric family and household, their relationship to the community, political institutions and leadership, values, and social networks.

Scholarly interest in the Homeric epics goes back to ancient times. It has often focused on the so-called Homeric Question, which may be more aptly termed the Homeric Controversy. Readers have failed to agree on the identity of Homer; the time and the manner by which the *Iliad* and the *Odyssey* were composed or edited; the origins of the epics and their unique language; and the historicity of the poems.

Briefly, already in ancient times readers doubted whether Homer was a historical figure or if he wrote both the *Iliad* and the *Odyssey*. Many modern scholars would answer both questions in the positive. They assume that he wrote, or orally composed, first the *Iliad*, and then the *Odyssey*, based on oral traditions. Indeed, the epics reveal their oral origins in their language, which used a special rhythmic form, the hexameter, and many repetitive descriptive words or phrases (epithets) that were well suited to recitations.

Students of history are particularly interested in how historical the events and the society described in the epics are and to what period they should be dated. The *Iliad* in particular describes a long war between a large Greek expedition and a well-fortified Troy. The nineteenth-century excavator Heinrich Schliemann identified the site of Troy in the mound of Hissarlik in Asia Minor near the Dardanelles. Yet the site has revealed the existence of nine cities as well as sub-settlements dating from the Bronze Age to Roman times. Identifying which of these is the Troy of the Trojan War has been a bone of scholarly contention since Schliemann. The Greeks could not have mounted a large expedition following the destructions and consequent decline of many Bronze Age sites around 1200. This means that only Troy VIh, ca. 1300, or Troy VIi (formerly known as VIIa), ca. 1210–1180, would be good candidates. Yet both were relatively small settlements that appear to have suffered no human destruction, although recent excavators of the site interpret some findings as signs of a much larger site and even of human destruction for Troy VIi.

Many scholars agree that the Homeric epics may retain ancient memories, but that they also project on mythical times realities that better fit the poet's own era, perhaps between the second half of the eighth century and the first half of the seventh. This does not mean that the world depicted by the poet is consistent or securely fixed in this period. The epics mix elements from different times and locales in a way that has caused some readers to regard attempts to historicize the Homeric world as futile.

The following example illustrates the complexity of attempts to compare the Homeric evidence with archaeological findings.

1.1   A Funeral Scene on a Dipylon Vase

Figure 1.1 shows a grave marker in the form of a very large crater or mixing bowl from the Dipylon cemetery in Athens. It was made ca. 750 by a potter known as the "Dipylon Master." It depicts a dead man surrounded by more than forty male and female mourners, who are making the same gesture of (probably) tearing their hair. Chariots are driving by, and a ship is depicted under the handle. The painter is possibly describing the dead man's military exploits. Homer describes a chariot parade around the corpse of Patrocles, Achilles' friend (*Iliad* 23.12–16). It could be that Homer's description is based on a practice current in his own day, or that he inspired the painter. No less likely, however, is that both poet and artist, in their different ways, mix fiction and reality.

Questions

1.   What is the Homeric Question?
2.   Can the Homeric epics be used as historical documents?

Figure 1.1
A funeral scene on a Dipylon Vase. © Photo 12 – Oronoz.

1.2 The Homeric Household (*Oikos*)

The historian M.I. Finley provides a definition of the Homeric household that conveys its critical importance:

> The authoritarian household, the *oikos*, was the center around which life was organized, from which flowed not only the satisfaction of material needs, including security, but ethical norms and values, duties, obligations and responsibilities, and relations with the gods. The *oikos* was not merely the family, it was all the people of the household together with its lands and goods. (Finley 1978, 57–58)

When wandering Odysseus reached the blessed land of the Phaeacians, he came upon an idealized palatial home and household that belonged to their king, Alcinous. The great house is a center of political, social, and economic activity, bedecked with gold, silver, and bronze.

Homer *Odyssey* 7.95–132

(**95**) Inside, seats were installed along the walls on both sides, from the palace threshold to its center, and on them were drapes of fine embroidery, the work of the women of the house. On these seats sat the leaders of the Phaeacians, eating and drinking, and lacking nothing. (**100**) Golden statues of youths stood on firm pedestals, and in their hands they held blazing torches, brightening the night for the diners throughout the hall. Alcinous has in the house fifty female slaves, some of them grinding yellow grain with hand-mills, (**105**) and others sitting and plying the loom and spinning wool, which flutters like leaves on a lofty poplar. From the tightly woven fabric seep beads of oil. And as the Phaeacians surpass all men in the skill of sailing a ship swiftly on the sea, so their women excel in the work of the loom; (**110**) for to them especially has Athena granted the knowledge and wit to produce fine works of art.

Outside the palace courtyard, close to its doors, stands a large four-acre garden encircled by a hedge. Here grow tall trees in full bloom – (**115**) pear and pomegranate, apple trees with glistening fruit, sweet fig and rich olive trees. Their fruit grows constantly, never dying and never failing winter or summer; and the west wind is constantly breathing on it, bringing some to birth and some to ripeness. (**120**) And one pear follows another pear in ripening, one apple another apple, one bunch of grapes another bunch, and one fig another fig. There, too, Alcinous has a bountiful vineyard planted, part of which is a warm area on level ground where grapes are being dried in the sun, (**125**) while others his people are gathering or treading. In front of this are unripe grapes that are dropping their blossom, and others that are starting to turn dark. And there, too, parallel to the last row of vines, are planted well-ordered gardens of all sorts of herbs that are constantly fresh and lush, and two springs, one diffusing water to the whole garden (**130**) and the other flowing toward the lofty palace, under the entranceway to the courtyard (and from this the town's inhabitants have their water-supply). Such were the splendid gifts of the gods in the palace of Alcinous.

For women and slaves in the Homeric household, see WEB **1.3–4**.

Questions

1. Describe the economic and social activities that take place in Alcinous' household.
2. What does Homer's description of the household suggest about the status of its head?

1.5 The Measure of Happiness

A man's happiness was often measured by the well-being of his family and household. Thus Menelaus, king of Sparta, describes the good fortune of Nestor, the old ruler of Pylos.

Homer *Odyssey* 4.207–211

It is easy to recognize the son of a man whom Cronus' son [Zeus] destined for happiness both when he married and when he produced children! Just as now to Nestor he has granted happy days everlasting, allowing him to grow old in his palace, and have sons who are wise and excellent wielders of the spear.

1.6 A Household in Trouble

While Alcinous' and Nestor's households were prosperous and secure, Odysseus' house in Ithaca was in turmoil. In his absence, local nobles pressured his wife, Penelope, to marry one of them. They also invaded Odysseus' house and squandered its resources.

In the following exchange between Odysseus' young son, Telemachus, and the most evil of the suitors, Antinous, Telemachus articulates the notion that the male head of the *oikos* should have sole control over its assets. The prince tries to assert his authority, but also alludes to the unstable nature of dynastic power. In spite of Telemachus' protests, the suitors continued to behave insolently until Odysseus exacted revenge on them.

Homer *Odyssey* 1.365–398

(**1.365**) There was a noisy response from the suitors throughout the shady hall, and they all prayed to lie in bed alongside Penelope. But quick-witted Telemachus began to address them:

"Suitors of my mother, with your brash arrogance, let us now enjoy our feast, (**370**) and let there be no shouting; for it is good to listen to a singer such as this with a god-like voice. In the morning let us go and sit in the assembly so that I can tell you something straight – to leave these halls! Prepare other banquets for yourselves, (**375**) eating your own provisions and going from one house to another. But if you think it nicer and better to waste the possessions of a single individual without compensation, then eat up! I shall call upon the ever-living gods for Zeus to grant me my revenge, (**380**) with you dying in these halls – and without compensation!"

So spoke Telemachus, and with teeth fastened in their lips they were all amazed at his confident address. Then Antinous, son of Eupeithes, spoke:

"Telemachus, those very gods certainly teach you to play the bold orator (**385**) and speak with confidence. May the son of Cronus not make you the king in sea-washed Ithaca, your birthright though that be!"

And quick-witted Telemachus gave him this reply:

"Antinous, I may annoy you with what I say, (**390**) but if Zeus granted me the throne, I would happily take it. Are you saying that this is the worst thing on earth? To be a king is not a bad thing, for the king's house quickly gains wealth and he himself gains greater honor. However, there are many other kings of the Achaeans, both young and old, (**395**) on sea-washed Ithaca, and one of these may gain this prize, since noble Odysseus is dead.[1] But I shall be master of my own house and of the slaves that noble Odysseus took as plunder."

Note

1. *See* **1.8–9** *on Homeric kingship. Telemachus presents kingship as accessible to local leaders, also called kings.*

1.7 Households and Community

Telemachus' words show how a man's responsibility and loyalty centered on his family and household. Attitudes toward the community derived largely from these sentiments. When the Trojan hero Hector exhorts the troops to fight the enemy, this is what he proclaims.

Homer *Iliad* 15.494–499

And any of you meeting his death and his fate from a missile or blow, well, let him die. It is no shame for him to die defending his fatherland. Indeed, his wife and children, who live on after him, and his home and property [*kleros*][1] will remain inviolate if the Achaeans should reach their native country with their ships.

Note

1. Kleros, *lit. "lot," refers to an inherited land or property that was distributed among the heirs by lot.*

Questions

1. Contrast the description of Nestor's household (**1.5**) with that of Odysseus (**1.6**). What might account for the difference?
2. What distinctions does Telemachus make between domestic and public authority (**1.6**)?
3. How does Hector link household to country (**1.7**)?

1.8 Homeric Leaders

Any investigation of Homeric leadership and political institutions and their relation to history is bound to run into difficulties. In addition to the epics' mixture of reality and fiction, the poems describe unusual circumstances, such as men at war in the *Iliad* and a leaderless household and community in the *Odyssey*, but seldom examine the operation of political institutions under more ordinary circumstances. Moreover, the epics might have artificially combined political realities from different times and locales. Nevertheless, they show that at the head of the hierarchy of power stood the king (*basileus*). His power was based on his large household, companions (*hetairoi*), and followers (and their followers), whom he had attracted. The king's ability to exert power, however, varied. A king like Agamemnon, the leader of the Greek expedition to Troy, inherited a scepter that came from Zeus, thus indicating divine confirmation of his rule. But the competitive principle of "ever to be the best and excel among others" (*Iliad* 6.208) affected leadership as well. It created an expectation of kings to legitimize their power, preferred status, greater honor, and large economic assets through their personal performance. Thus, when Sarpedon, the king of the Lycians and a Trojan ally, encourages his companion Glaucus to fight the Greeks, he highlights displays of strength and courage as justifications of their leadership position.

Homer *Iliad* 12.310–321

(**12.310**) Glaucus, why is it that we two are held in the greatest honor in Lycia, with thrones, meat, and cups full of wine, while all look upon us as gods? And why do we have a large plot of land to live on by the banks of the Xanthus, well blessed with vineyards and wheat-bearing soil? (**315**) It is for this that we must now take our position in the front lines of the Lycians and face the raging fight, so that any man of the well-armed Lycians may say: "Our kings who rule over us in Lycia are not without fame, these men who eat fat sheep (**320**) and drink our sweet vintage wines. No, indeed! They have outstanding strength, for they fight in the front lines of the Lycians."

1.9 Kings, Council, and Assembly

A leader's authority was largely based on his wealth, his excellence in fighting, and on attracting fellowship through feasting and gift-giving. He thus resembled a type of ruler that anthropologists, and following them historians, have labeled the "big chief" (or "big man"). A king, however, was also exposed to challenges and criticism from others who saw themselves as his equals or even superior in merit and resources. Indeed, the title "king" appears to denote a level of authority rather than an office, because in Homer there are kings who are more "kingly" than others. Telemachus' concession to others of the right to be king (**1.6**) shows the weakness of an inherited claim to the throne. Conversely, an inherited claim combined with a measure of divine favor legitimized Agamemnon's leadership to some degree. It could be that the epics retained memories of leadership by "divine right," as well as a different conception, later or coeval, based on personal performance.

Homer also described councils consisting of other "kings" or "elders" (*gerontês*), who were convened by the leading king to advise him and discuss mutual concerns. Ideally, all participants were supposed to agree on a common course.

The assembly was made up of adult males from both the elite and the masses. Leaders used this arena to garner public support, inform the people, and prevail upon rivals. Some scholars regard these functions as an indication of significant popular power, which Homer, who wrote for an elite audience, tried to minimize or even to denigrate. Those who put more credence in Homer note that, in the poems, members of the elite call the assembly, do most of the talking, and take no popular vote.

The following description shows the working of Homeric kingship, council, and assembly. It also describes an unusual and failed attempt by someone outside the leading elite, the Greek Thersites, to upset the political and social hierarchy of the camp. The poet is clearly hostile toward attempts to challenge those in power.

The episode commences with a dream, sent by Zeus, that urged Agamemnon to do battle with the Trojans.

Homer *Iliad* 2.16–59, 71–154, 182–277

(**2.16**) With these words, and on hearing the order, the dream went on its way. It came quickly to the swift ships of the Achaeans and went to Agamemnon, son of Atreus, whom it found sleeping in his hut wrapped in a sleep divine. (**20**) Standing over him in the form of Neleus' son, Nestor – whom Agamemnon respected most among the elders – the god-sent dream addressed him:

"You are asleep, son of wise Atreus, tamer of horses. A man responsible for giving guidance should not sleep all night, (**25**) not when an army is under his command and so much is his concern. Now quick, listen to me! I come to you as a messenger from Zeus, who, far off though he is, has great concern and pity for you. He tells you to put the longhaired Achaeans under arms post-haste, for this is when you might take the broad-wayed city of the Trojans – (30) the immortals who have their homes on Olympus are no longer in disagreement on this. Hera has changed the minds of all with her entreaties and over the Trojans hang troubles sent by Zeus. But see that you keep this in mind and do not let forgetfulness take hold of you when honey-sweet sleep lets you go."

(35) So saying, the dream departed, leaving Agamemnon there to ponder in his thoughts things that were not to come about. He thought he was going to the city of Priam on that day – silly man, ignorant as he was of the designs that Zeus had in mind. (40) For the god was going to bring distress and groaning on Trojans and Danaans alike in dire conflict.

Agamemnon awoke from his sleep and the divine voice still rang about him. He sat up straight, put on his soft tunic, a handsome, newly made garment, and threw around him his great cloak. Beneath his shining feet he bound his fine sandals, (45) and over his shoulders he slung his silver-studded sword. He took up the ever-imperishable scepter of his forefathers, and with it proceeded to the ships of the bronze-mailed Achaeans.

And so the goddess Dawn arrived on high Olympus, announcing day's arrival to Zeus and the other gods. (50) And Agamemnon instructed the clear-voiced heralds to summon the longhaired Achaeans to an assembly, and when they summoned them the Achaeans quickly gathered.

The king first held a council of the greathearted elders beside the ship of Nestor, the king born in Pylos. (55) Calling together the elders he devised a cunning strategy.

"Listen, friends," he said. "A heavenly dream came to me in my sleep during the divine night, and in form, size, and stature it most resembled illustrious Nestor. It stood over me and addressed me as follows:

Agamemnon repeats the dream's words.

(71) With these words the dream went flying away, and sweet sleep let go of me. But come now, let us try to put the sons of the Achaeans under arms. But I shall test their spirit with an address, as is appropriate, and will order them to take to flight with their many-benched ships. (75) But your task is to try to restrain them with your words from your various positions.

With that Agamemnon sat down, and Nestor arose amongst them, the lord of sandy Pylos. He addressed them warm-heartedly. "Friends," he said, "leaders and rulers of the Argives: (80) had it been any other of the Achaeans telling of this dream, we might call it a lie and be inclined to disregard it. But the man who saw it is he who professes to be the best of the Achaeans. So come now, let us try to put the sons of the Achaeans under arms."

So saying, he led the exodus from the meeting, (85) and the other scepter-bearing kings stood up and followed the lead of the shepherd of the people. The rank and file came swiftly to meet them. It was as when the thronging swarms of bees come forth from a hollowed rock in a continual stream, hovering in groups over the flowers of spring, and congregating in clusters on this side and that. (90) Just so did the numerous tribes of men come forward in companies from ships and huts to the assembly ground, before the low-lying shore. And amongst them blazed Rumor, messenger of Zeus, urging them on; and so they came together. (95) Confusion now reigned in the assembly. As the men took their seats the earth groaned beneath them, and there was general uproar. Nine heralds cried out in an attempt to restrain them, hoping to make them quell their clamor and listen to the kings who are blessed by Zeus. Only with difficulty could the common soldiers be brought to sit and keep to their seats, (**100**) and end their shouting. Their ruler Agamemnon then stood up, holding the scepter that was the handiwork of Hephaestus. Hephaestus had given it to lord Zeus, Cronus' son, and then Zeus had in turn given it to the guiding god, the killer of Argos. Lord Hermes had then given it to the charioteer Pelops, (**105**) and Pelops had given it to Atreus, the shepherd of his people. When Atreus died he left it to Thyestes, the owner of large flocks, and Thyestes then left it to the hands of Agamemnon, for him to become ruler of many islands and all of Argos.

Agamemnon now leaned on the scepter as he addressed the Argives.

(**110**) "Friends," he said, "Danaan warriors, squires of Ares! Zeus the son of Cronus had me tightly enmeshed in terrible folly – a merciless god who earlier made me the solemn undertaking that I should return home after sacking strongly fortified Troy. Now it transpires that he has played a foul trick on me, and he bids me go back to Argos in disgrace (**115**) after sustaining so many losses. That is probably going to be the decision of all-powerful Zeus who has brought low the battlements of many cities, and will do so again in future, his power being the greatest. This is a disgraceful thing for future generations to hear, (**120**) that an Achaean force of such quality and size should be fruitlessly engaged in a hopeless fight and struggle against an inferior enemy, with no end yet in sight. For suppose we Achaeans and Trojans were prepared to establish a binding truce and be counted, (**125**) and the Trojans were to agree to a count of all with homes in the city and we Achaeans to be divided up into units of ten. Suppose then that each of our units should choose a Trojan to serve its wine – many such groups of ten would be without a wine-steward! Such is the numerical superiority of the sons of the Achaeans over the Trojans who live in the city. (**130**) However, they have allies present, spearmen from many cities, and these are a great hindrance, and do not allow me to fulfill my wish of sacking the populous city of Ilium. Nine of great Zeus' years have already gone by, (**135**) and our ships' timbers have rotted and their rigging has disintegrated. And I expect our wives and little children are sitting in our halls waiting for us, while for us the task for which we came is nowhere near to being accomplished. So come now, let us all follow my instructions. (**140**) Let us retreat with our ships to our own country, since we shall not now take Troy with its broad streets."

Such were Agamemnon's words, and amongst the assembled multitude he stirred the hearts in the breasts of those who were not party to the plan. The meeting was moved like the towering waves of the deep – of the Icarian Sea – (**145**) which the east and south winds whip up, swooping down from the clouds of Father Zeus. It was as when the west wind comes and sets a deep cornfield in motion with its swift onrush, so that its corn-ears nod in the breeze. Just so was the movement of the whole assembly. They rushed to the ships with a cheer, (**150**) the dust rising high from beneath their feet. They urged each other to seize the ships and drag them to the divine sea, and they proceeded to clear the launching paths. Their shouts went up to heaven as they eagerly set off for home, and they began to remove the props from beneath the vessels.

The enthusiastic response to the idea of sailing home alarms the goddesses Hera and Athena. Athena urges Odysseus to put a stop to it.

(**182**) Such were Athena's words, and Odysseus heard the goddess speaking to him. He began to run, throwing aside his cloak, which the herald Eurybates of Ithaca, his squire, gathered up, (**185**) and he came to Agamemnon, son of Atreus, from whom he received the everlasting scepter of the royal house. With that in hand he proceeded to the ships of the mail-clad Achaeans.

On coming upon a king or a man of distinction, Odysseus would stand beside him and hold him back with gentle words. (**190**) "My friend," he would say, "it would be improper for me to try to intimidate you like a coward; just sit yourself down and tell the others to be seated. For you do not know yet what the son of Atreus has in mind. This is a test he is conducting, (**195**) and soon he will deliver a blow to the sons of the Achaeans. Did we not all hear what he had to say in the council? I am afraid that in his anger he may inflict injury on the sons of the Achaeans. Kings, cherished by Zeus, possess violent tempers; their honor comes from Zeus, and all-wise Zeus loves them."

When, however, he spied a member of the common people and found him shouting, he would strike him with the scepter and threaten him, saying: (**200**) "My friend, sit down quietly and listen to what others have to say, men better than you – you who are a cowardly weakling and never of any use in battle or debate. We Achaeans shall not all play the king here – the rule of many is not a good thing! (**205**) There should be one ruler, one king, the man to whom the son of cunning Cronus has granted that power."

Thus, with authority, he set the army back in order, and the men came swiftly streaming back to the assembly from the ships and the huts, creating a noise like that (**210**) when a wave of the deafening deep thunders on an open shore and a roaring comes from the sea.

The others sat down and remained in order in their seats, with the sole exception of the loudmouthed Thersites, who kept up his noisy tirade. In his mind he had a large store of indecent language with which to squabble with the kings in a reckless and unseemly manner, (**215**) saying whatever he thought would make the Argives laugh. He was the ugliest man who came to Troy. He was bow-legged, and lame in one foot; and his shoulders were rounded and bent down over his chest. Above that he had a pointed head with thin, straggly hair sprouting on it. (**220**) He more than anyone was detested by Achilles and Odysseus, whom he made a habit of reproaching, but on that occasion it was against noble Agamemnon that he directed his reproaches with piercing screams. In fact, the Achaeans were furious with him, and had indignation in their hearts. But he kept up his noisy shouts of abuse against Agamemnon.

(**225**) "Son of Atreus," he said, "what are you grumbling about now and what do you want? Your huts are full of bronze and you have lots of women in them, a choice bevy which we the Achaeans grant to you first whenever we take a town. Can it be that you still need gold – (**230**) gold that one of the horse-taming Trojans will bring from Ilium as ransom for his son, a man that I, or another of the Achaeans, brought in irons? Or is it a young woman you need, one to make love with and keep on the side for yourself? But one who is their leader should not be bringing the sons of the Achaeans into trouble. (**235**) You softies, you miserable cowards, you who are Achaean women rather than Achaean men, let us go back home with our ships. Let us leave this fellow here in Troy to bask in his honors and see whether or not we are a help to him. He has even shown disrespect for Achilles, a much better man than he is – (**240**) he has seized Achilles' prize for himself, and still holds on to it. And it's not that Achilles does not feel resentment in his heart – he's just apathetic! Otherwise, son of Atreus, this would now be the last insult of which you would be guilty!"

Such were Thersites' reproaches against Agamemnon, the shepherd of his people. But noble Odysseus swiftly came up to him and, (**245**) with a withering look, gave him a severe dressing down.

"You loudmouth, Thersites," he said, "you have a shrill tongue but you can stop now and put an end to your one-man rant against your leaders. In my opinion there is no more worthless being than you amongst the men who came to Ilium with the sons of Atreus. (**250**) So none of this chatter and talk about your kings now, and no hurling abuse at them as you seek an opportunity to get home! We do not yet have a clear picture of how these things will turn out, of whether we sons of Achaea will go home with success or failure to our credit. So there you are hurling reproaches at

Agamemnon son of Atreus, the shepherd of his people, (**255**) because the Danaan warriors give him many presents, and your words are completely insulting. But I tell you something, and it is going to happen. If I find you once more ranting like this, (**260**) I shall take hold of you and strip you of your clothing, your cloak and your tunic that cover your private parts, and I shall send you weeping and wailing to the swift ships, driving you from the assembly with a shameful beating. If I do not, then let my head not remain on my shoulders and let me no longer be called the father of Telemachus!"

(**265**) Such were Odysseus' words, and with the scepter he beat the man on his back and shoulders. Thersites cowered, and a large tear fell from his eye, while a bloody weal arose on his back from the golden scepter. He sat down aghast; and in pain and with a look of bewilderment he wiped away his tears. (**270**) Vexed though they were the soldiers laughed heartily at him and, looking at a comrade close by, one of them would say: "Good heavens! Odysseus has countless great deeds to his credit as the author of fine plans and as a leader in battle; but this is now the best thing of all that he has done amongst the Argives, (**275**) namely, putting a stop to this foul cheap-talker's ranting. For sure his headstrong spirit will never again drive him to assail his rulers with insulting language."

See WEB **1.10** for a description of a trial scene in Homer.

Questions

1. What legitimized the power of the Homeric leaders according to sections **1.8** and **1.9**?
2. What does the story of Agamemnon's dream and its consequences tell about the respective powers of the king, council, and assembly?
3. Were Thersites' complaints justified? How were they addressed? Why did his fellow warriors not support him?

1.11 Homeric Values: Honor and Excellence

To a large extent, what separated the good man (*agathos*) from the bad (*kakos*) in the Homeric world were his social status and personal performance. Hence the importance of the concept of *aretê*, which equated virtue with competitive excellence and being better than another man. It also identified defeat with shame. However, this individualistic, competitive ethos did not exclude adherence to cooperative values such as aid, magnanimity, and helping the community. Honor (*timê*) and shame (*aidos*) were often functions of keeping up with society's expectations and showing acute awareness of what others might think or say about one's conduct. A man of honor was anxious to increase or maintain it and defend it from challenges and insults. He also looked to gain fame or glory (*kleos*) that could immortalize him.

All these perceptions are recognizable in the response of the Trojan hero Hector to the pleading of his wife, Andromache. She asks him to have mercy on his family and defend Troy from behind the walls instead of on the battlefield. Hector's words evince sensitivity to public opinion as well as to his own self-image, and distinguish between the good and courageous man and the bad and cowardly one.

Homer *Iliad* 6.441–446

Yes, my wife, all that is on my mind, too, but I would feel deep shame [*aideomai*] in front of the Trojan men and the long-robed Trojan women if, like a coward [*kakos*], I keep out of the battle. Nor does my heart tell me to do that; for I have learned ever to be courageous and fight in the front lines of the Trojans, gaining great renown [*kleos*] for my father and for myself.

1.12   Reciprocity and Guest-Friendship (*Xenia*)

One of the governing principles of social and political interaction in Homer is reciprocity. It existed between a leader and the community when the people gave their chief material gifts, and he reciprocated in the form of common feasts, sacrifices, military and political service, and individual rewards. Reciprocity also guided the conduct of members of the elite who exchanged gifts, services, and favors with one another. The men involved in the exchange were not blind to its material value, but it was primarily designed to establish and regulate social and political relationships. Reciprocal gift-giving and hospitality were also the mark of *xenia* (Homeric Greek: *xeinia*), or guest-friendship, between prominent individuals from different places. *Xenia* was hereditary and, as shown in the following case, could even supersede one's allegiance to fellow combatants. Thus, the Greek Diomedes and the Trojan ally Glaucus decide to avoid fighting each other after discovering that they are guest-friends (*xenoi*) through their grandfathers. They affirm their relationship with a gift exchange, in which Glaucus' greater gift suggests perhaps his inferior status to Diomedes.

The scene commences with Diomedes, son of Tydeus, and Glaucus, son of Hippolochus, meeting in the space between the two armies. Diomedes acknowledges Glaucus' courage and military prowess and asks for his identity. Glaucus assures Diomedes that he is not a god in disguise and identifies himself through his lineage. He focuses especially on the tale of his grandfather, Bellerophon, who was forced to leave his native land near Argos and go to Lycia. There, after performing some heroic feats, the local king "recognized him [Bellerophon] as the noble son of a god, he kept him there, giving him his daughter in marriage and half his royal honors" (6.194–196). Bellerophon fathered three children, including Hippolochus.

Homer *Iliad* 6. 206–236

(6.206) Hippolochus fathered me, and of him, I declare, am I born. He sent me to Troy and time and again impressed upon me ever to be the best and excel among others, and not to bring dishonor on the line of my forefathers, **(210)** who were by far the bravest men in Ephyra and broad Lycia. This is the family and bloodline that I declare myself to belong to."

Such were Glaucus' words, and Diomedes of the great war cry was delighted. He thrust his spear into the fertile earth, and addressed the shepherd of the people with gentle words:

(215) "So then," he said "you must have long-standing ties of guest-friendship with my father's house. For noble Oeneus [Diomedes' grandfather] entertained the peerless Bellerophon in his home, keeping him there for twenty days, and they exchanged fine presents to mark their friendship. Oeneus gave a belt of gleaming purple, **(220)** and Bellerophon gave a golden cup with two handles, which I left behind in my house when coming here. I do not remember Tydeus since I was small when he left, at the time when the Achaean army perished at Thebes. And so I am now your host in the midst of Argos, **(225)** and you are mine in Lycia whenever I might come to the country of those people. Let us avoid each other's spears, even in the thick of the fray; for there are large numbers of Trojans and of their famous allies to make my victims, any that a god puts before me or I catch by the speed of my feet, **(230)** and for you there are many Achaeans to kill if you can. But let us exchange armor, so that men here may also know that we proudly declare that we are friends [*xeinoi*] through our fathers."

With these words they leapt from their chariots, clasped each other's hands, and swore an oath of friendship. **(235)** But then Zeus the son of Cronus deprived Glaucus of his wits, for he exchanged with Tydeus' son Diomedes armor of gold for armor of bronze, a hundred oxen's worth in return for nine.

For a link to a Roman copy of a bust of Homer, see WEB **1.13**.

Review Questions

1. What constituted a desirable, i.e., "good," Homeric man?
2. Describe the structure and role of the Homeric household on the basis of the documents in **1.2** and **1.5**, and WEB **1.3** and **1.4**.
3. How was power distributed in the Greek camp and in Ithaca? Also consult the trial scene in WEB **1.10**.
4. Identify Homeric ideals and explain how they were anchored in their social and economic environment.

Suggested Readings

Homer, history, and archaeology: Project Troia, http://www.uni-tuebingen.de/troia/eng/index.html; Kolb 2004 (against identifying Troy VI as Homeric Troy); Jablonka and Rose 2004 (*contra* Kolb); see also Strauss 2006. *Homer, artistic evidence, and the Dipylon*

Vase: Hurwit 1985, 93–124; Snodgrass 1997. *Homeric society and its historicity*: Finley 1978 (highly influential and still quite valuable); see also Raaflaub 1998a. *Homeric household and family*: Lacy 1968, 33–50. *Homeric social and political institutions*: Donlan 1997; Raaflaub 1997; Hammer 2002. *Homeric values*: Adkins 1960, 30–60 (*contra*: Cairns 1993, 48–146); Donlan 1980. *Homeric chiefs, friendship, and xenia*: Donlan 1989, 1993; van Wees 1992; Herman 1987; Zanker 1994; Konstan 1997, 24–42. *Greek concepts of reciprocity*: C. Gill et al. 1998.

2

The World of Hesiod

CHAPTER CONTENTS

This chapter examines the society depicted by the poet Hesiod in his *Works and Days*. It includes passages dealing with attitudes toward men of the elite and their treatment of people weaker than them, as well as perceptions of women and work. The chapter also illustrates through a vase aspects of Asian influence on Greek culture in this early period.

As with Homer, it is not certain whether Hesiod wrote the poems ascribed to him. According to one scholarly view, the ancients attributed different poetic traditions of various times to Hesiod. We shall follow the orthodox view, which largely assumes the authenticity of his authorship.

Hesiod was a contemporary or near contemporary of Homer (ca. 700). According to his own account in *Works and Days*, his father had emigrated from Cyme in Asia Minor to Ascra in Boeotia, where he became a farmer. When Hesiod's father died, his inheritance was divided between Hesiod and his brother Perses, although Hesiod complained that Perses took more than his rightful share following a crooked judgment.

In his *Theogony*, Hesiod systematized Greek myths of heroes and gods. In his later poem, *Works and Days*, written around 700, he remonstrates with his brother for his misconduct over the inheritance. Yet mostly he imparts folk wisdom and advice on issues of justice, morality, religion, seafaring, and especially farming. While the *Iliad* and the *Odyssey* focus on the elite, *Works and Days* deals with the ways of life, beliefs, and mores of those who, while not downtrodden, are still less privileged – in other words, small to middling landholders.

Accordingly, *Works and Days* describes no big chiefs on the Homeric scale. Instead there are "gift-eating kings," powerful individuals who dispense injustice. They reside in the neighboring polis Thespia, which probably controlled Ascra at that time. In his appeal to the Thespian elite and to his brother, Hesiod deifies justice (*dikê*) and retribution (*atê*), and suggests that injustice will result in suffering for the family and community. Leaders are expected to show public responsibility.

2.1 Individual, Communal, and Divine Justice

Hesiod *Works and Days* 213–273

(**213**) You, Perses, should listen to Right [*Dikê*]; do not promote Violence [*Hubris*]. Violence is bad for a poor man; (**215**) even a man of substance cannot bear it easily, and is oppressed by it when he meets Retribution [*Atê*]. Better to take the road on the other side, the one leading to righteousness, for in the end Justice prevails over Violence. The fool learns this only through suffering the consequences; for Oath straightway keeps pace with perverse judgments. (**220**) There is uproar when Right is forcibly dragged wherever bribe-devouring men take her, adjudicating claims with perverse verdicts. She follows in tears to those men's abodes in their community [*polis*], wrapped in mist and bringing misfortune to the men who drove her out and did not dispense straightforward justice.

(225) But those who give straight judgments to foreigners and local people, and do not stray from the path of justice, these men see their community flourish, and their populations prospering in it. There is throughout their land a peace that fosters children, and never does far-seeing Zeus apportion grievous war to them. (230) Never do famine or retribution afflict men who give fair judgments, and they enjoy much feasting as they till the fields they care for. For them the earth provides a rich livelihood, and on the hills the oak tree bears acorns on the exterior and bees within. They have fleecy sheep laden with wool, (235) and their wives bear children who resemble their fathers. They always have an abundance of good things; they do not make sea journeys, and their farmland is productive and bears them fruit.

To those who are given to iniquitous violence and evil deeds, however, far-seeing Zeus apportions punishment. (240) Often an entire community has suffered because of one man who does wrong and has iniquitous designs. On such folk the son of Cronus brings suffering from heaven in the form of famine and plague, and the people die out. The women fail to produce children, and their households fade away through the design of Olympian Zeus. (245) Sometimes, too, the son of Cronus destroys their broad army or their city wall, or wrecks their ships upon the sea.

Oh kings, you too should take note of this punishment. For there are immortals rubbing shoulders with humans and (250) observing those who exhaust their fellow men with perverse judgments with no thought for punishment from the gods. Zeus has thirty thousand immortal spirits on the fertile earth watching mortal men, and these keep an eye on judgments and wicked deeds, (255) clothed in mist and roaming everywhere in the world.

And there is the maiden, Justice, who is the daughter of Zeus, an illustrious maiden respected by the gods who live on Olympus. And whensoever someone does her harm with unjust censure she straightway takes a seat beside Cronus' son Zeus (260) and apprises him of the wicked thoughts of men so that the people may pay for the iniquities of their leaders who, with evil thoughts in their hearts, make fraudulent statements and pervert the course of Justice. Be on your guard against this, you kings, and make your judgments straight, you who swallow bribes – forget all about perverse judgments.

(265) The man who inflicts wickedness on another inflicts wickedness on himself, and an evil plan turns out most evil for the planner.

The eye of Zeus sees all things, and takes account of all things; and it looks down on these things, too, if it wishes, not failing to see the quality of the justice that a community employs within it. (270) In the present circumstances I would not myself be "righteous" amongst men, or have my son be so, for it is bad for a man to be "righteous" if the less righteous man will have the greater right.

Questions

1. What were the relationships between divine and human justice according to Hesiod?
2. What, according to Hesiod, are the incentives and deterrents that should guide the conduct of leaders? Are they effective in your opinion?

2.2 Women and Pandora's Jar

The desirable Hesiodic *oikos* is relatively modest in size. It consists of a husband, wife, preferably one son, a small number of male and female slaves, and farm animals and equipment. Hesiod believes that young women who are modest, docile, and concerned about the family's good name may turn into good wives (cf. *Works and Days* 519–522). However, his version of the myth of Pandora reveals masculine concerns, fears, and stereotypes of women. The speaker in lines 57–58 is Zeus, who has decided to punish Prometheus' theft of fire from the gods by unleashing suffering on humans. Pandora (lit., "gift for all") was given a jar, which she opened and so let loose evils on humankind.

Hesiod *Works and Days* 59–82; cf. 373–375

(59) So saying, the father of gods and men laughed aloud. And he ordered the renowned god Hephaestus to mix earth and water immediately, to set in the mixture the voice and strength of a human being, and to mold the delightful form of a lovely maiden with the features of the immortal goddesses. Athena he ordered to teach her handiwork, how to weave the intricate web; (65) while Aphrodite was to shower upon her head both painful desire and enfeebling cares. And he bade Hermes, the messenger god and killer of Argos, to set in her the mind of a bitch and a perfidious nature.

Such were his orders, and the deities obeyed their master, Zeus son of Cronus. (70) The famous lame god [Hephaestus] immediately molded from clay, in accordance with the plans of the son of Cronus, the figure of a modest girl. The gray-eyed goddess Athena clothed her and decked her out; the divine Graces and Queen Seduction [Aphrodite] placed golden necklaces upon her; (75) and the lovely-tressed Seasons made a garland of spring flowers for her head. The messenger, the killer of Argos [Hermes], created in her breast lies, wheedling words, and a cunning nature, after the plans of loud-thundering Zeus. (80) And the herald of the gods also put a voice within her, and named this woman Pandora, because all those having their homes on Olympus contributed to her – a disaster for men who live on bread.

 See WEB **2.3** for Hesiod on desirable household and marriage.

Questions

1. What feminine attributes are highlighted in the creation of Pandora?
2. Based on the myth of Pandora and the descriptions of household and marriage in WEB **2.3**, how were men to contend with the harmful potential of women?

2.4   The Value of Labor

It may be expected that a farming community would endorse the value of hard work. Hesiod accordingly extols labor as a key to material prosperity and as a moral virtue that separates the honorable from the shameful. Homer associates excellence (*aretê*), fame, and competitiveness with combat, courage, and leadership qualities. *Works and Days* links these values to wealth that comes from labor, and contextualizes them in farming and other working environments. In spite of Hesiod's praise of work, leisure continued to distinguish the elite from the masses and to signal the former's social and moral superiority.

Hesiod *Works and Days* 299–318

(**299**) But you, divine-born Perses, set yourself to work so that hunger may hate you and venerable well-garlanded Demeter may love you, filling your barn with sustenance. For hunger is always the companion of the idle man. Gods and men feel rancor against the man who lives in idleness, (**305**) being in his nature similar to the stingless drones who, eating without working, consume the fruits of the bees' labor. Your efforts should be directed toward putting your work in proper order, so that your barns may be full of the food of each season. It is from work that men have abundant flocks and wealth, (**310**) and those who work are more loved by the immortals. Work is no disgrace; disgrace lies in not working. And if you work the idle man will soon be jealous of your growing wealth; and rank [*aretê*] and honor [*kudos*] go along with wealth. But whatever your fortune, work is the better course, (**315**) if you direct your foolish heart away from other people's possessions and focus on work as I tell you. A discreditable shame accompanies the man in need – shame which can harm men greatly, but also greatly benefit them.

See WEB **2.5.I–II** for Hesiod on slaves and competitiveness, and WEB **2.5.III** for a link to a bust of Hesiod.

Question

1. What makes working preferable to idleness according to Hesiod?

2.6   The Orientalizing Period

Occurring close to, or contemporary with, the world of Hesiod was what modern scholars have termed the "orientalizing period" (ca. 725–650). It is characterized by a strong eastern influence on Greeks in many areas, but especially in the realms of religion, myth, writing, and art. Indeed, some critics have attributed the direct or indirect origins of Hesiod's *Works and Days* to the so-called wisdom literature that flourished in Mesopotamia and Egypt. Oriental influences were imported either by Greeks from the east or by

Figure 2.1 A griffin jug from Aegina. © The Granger Collection/TopFoto.

Egyptians or Phoenicians who settled in and traded with the west. Cults like that of Adonis or the later Orphic religion, Greek cosmology, and the systematization of gods and heroes demonstrated similarities with more ancient Mesopotamian and Egyptian beliefs and practices. The Greeks adopted and modified the Phoenician alphabet, though it is unclear where this script was first introduced and how it was diffused. The orientalizing style in vase-painting began around 725 with what is known as the proto-Corinthian style and continued for about a century. Naturalist motifs, many of them imported from the east, replaced or supplemented earlier Geometric patterns. They included, among others, rosettes, lotus flowers, and even animals like panthers that the artists knew only from oriental art and myths.

The jug shown in Figure 2.1 exemplifies the mixture of Geometric and orientalizing elements. Produced around 675 in one of the Cycladic islands, it was found on the island of Aegina near Attica. The top is shaped like a griffin, a motif adopted from Syria and modified by Greek artists. The central panel depicts the eastern motif of a lion and its prey next to a grazing horse, which is a scene that appears already in the Geometric style. The bottom combines Geometric triangles with oriental flower patterns. It might be significant that the jug was found in Aegina, a thriving trade center, and not in an inland settlement like Hesiod's Ascra. In an agriculture-based community, wealth and worth were probably measured differently than in towns where overseas trade constituted a major economic activity.

Review Questions

1. What were the dominant moral values in the society described by Hesiod?
2. Describe the structure and activities of the Hesiodic household based on the documents in **2.4**, WEB **2.3**, and WEB **2.5.I–II**.
3. Describe the relations between leader and community as characterized by Hesiod. How did they resemble and differ from similar relations in Homer?

Suggested Readings

Society and politics in Hesiodic Ascra: Millett 1984; Tandy 1997; Thomas and Conant 1999, 144–161; A. Edwards 2004. *Hesiod's conflict with Perses*: in addition to the above see Gagarin 1974, but also Clay 2003, 34–38. *Women in Hesiod (and in other Greek authors)*: Arthur 1973; Zeitlin 1996, 53–86. *Pandora*: Ogden 1998. *Hesiodic household*: Hanson 1999, 90–106. *Hesiod and the value of hard work*: G. Nussbaum 1960. *On the Hesiodic value system as the opposite of Homer's*: Zanker 1986, but also Pearson 1962, 72–73, 82–83. *Orientalizing period*: Burkert 1992, 2004; Murray 1993, 81–101.

3

The Early Greek Polis (City-State) and the *Ethnos*

CHAPTER CONTENTS

Ancient Greece from Homer to Alexander: The Evidence, First Edition. Joseph Roisman.
© 2011 Blackwell Publishing Ltd. Translations © 2011 John Yardley. Published 2011 by Blackwell Publishing Ltd.

The term *polis* (pl. *poleis*) is usually translated as city-state, although the degree of urbanization of a polis may have varied over time or from one place to another. Recent exhaustive studies of the subject have produced a definition of the Greek polis in its ideal, largely Classical Greek form as "a highly institutionalized and highly centralized micro-state consisting of one town (often walled) with its immediate hinterland and settled with a stratified population, of whom some are citizens, some foreigners and, sometimes, slaves." The territory and the politically privileged segment of the population are small. The town is "the economic, the religious, the military, and the political center of the city-state," and the city-state "is a self-governing polity, but not necessarily an independent and autonomous state" (Hansen 2000, 18). The definition does not fit every stage in the development of the polis, and especially not its earlier phases. Yet it shows that the Greek city-state is recognizable by its territory, community, public buildings, and urban center (*asty*).

This chapter examines the Greek polis from different perspectives. It presents perceptions of the polis and its origins in the writings of Homer and Aristotle. It shows the spatial dimensions of an early Greek settlement on the island of Andros, and concludes with a discussion of the Greek concept of *ethnos* ("tribal state"), which identified Greeks and created ties among them in ways that were unrelated to the polis.

3.1 The Homeric Polis

An early type of polis appears already in Homer. When Odysseus meets the Phaeacian princess Nausica on the island of Scheria, she describes her city through its physical attributes, which are typical of a (coastal) town: walls, harbor, assembly, and a precinct (*temenos*) for a god. See WEB **3.2** for the description of this walled Homeric polis and for a link discussing it.

When Odysseus wanders into the land of the Cyclopes, he describes them as lacking in all that a Greek would identify with a polis, namely, public institutions and space, common laws and customs, communal habitation and spirit, technology, and civilized existence.

Homer *Odyssey* 9.105–115

(**9.105**) From there we sailed on with heavy heart and reached the land of the insolent and lawless Cyclopes, who neither plant nor plow with their hands but leave everything to the gods. Even so everything grows for them without planting and plowing – (**110**) wheat, barley, and vines that produce wine from large-clustered grapes fattened by the rain of Zeus. They have no assemblies for discussion and no legal usage; rather, they live on the peaks of lofty mountains, in hollow caverns, and they all individually lay down the laws for their own wives and children and have no interest in each other's welfare.

Question

1. What constituted a city according to Homer's description of the Cyclopes (**3.1**) and of a walled city (WEB **3.2**)?

3.3   An Early Settlement on Andros (Zagora; ca. 700)

The origins of the polis are unclear and the subject of a lively debate. Recent opinion suggests that the concept was imported from long-existing city-states in Phoenicia or Mesopotamia and that it was implemented in Greek colonies. Public space and common cult contributed as well to the notion of citizenship in the polis.

Archaeological finds reveal regional differences in the emergence of the polis as a focus of habitation. A polis is larger than a village, and in Attica, for example, the significant increase in the number of graves around 750 suggests a population growth (whose rate is still debated). Elsewhere in Greece, large temples were set up at the center of Greek settlements, on their frontiers, but also in territory accessible to more than one community. They were the recipients of a massive amount of votives, including some that were expensive, which formerly had been placed in individual graves. The movement toward communal space and activity was balanced in some settlements by the demarcation of the private sphere: courtyard houses gradually replaced oval huts and open space, which were typical of Dark Age villages.

Figure 3.1 shows the plan of a settlement in Zagora (a modern name) on the Aegean island of Andros. The settlement was abandoned around 700 when its inhabitants apparently moved to the nearby newer city of Palaeopolis. As with many other Dark Age settlements, Zagora was located on a high headland, probably for security reasons, with two bays in its vicinity. A massive wall guarded the main access to town, which was protected by natural barriers on its other sides. The similar alignment of the houses' walls suggests a single planner, and streets may have existed around where houses D3 or H18 are situated. D6 and D7 have open courtyards. The temple at the center of the settlement, H30/31, is separated from the house clusters and was used even after the settlement had been abandoned. Cluster J seems to be later than clusters D and H and may be the result of population growth.

See WEB **3.4** for links to the archaeology of the island of Andros and excavations of an early settlement in Azoria, Crete.

Question

1. What public needs did the settlement in Zagora try to meet and how?

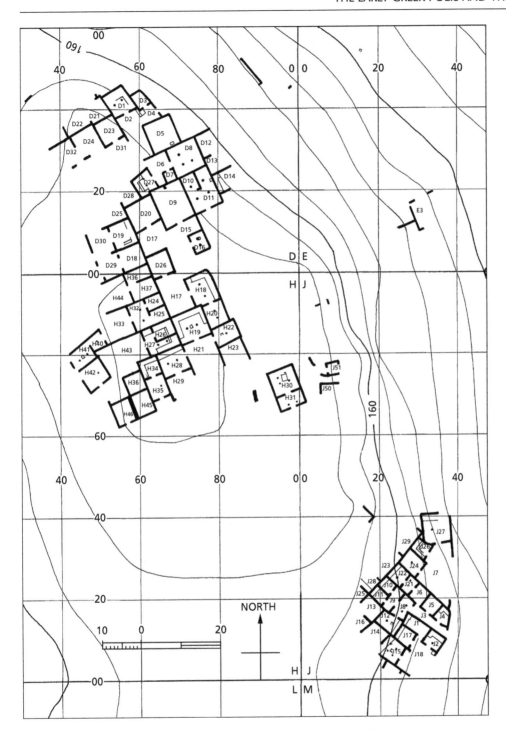

Figure 3.1 The settlement in Zagora, Andros. Based on J.M. Coldstream, *Geometric Greece 900–700 BC*, 2nd ed. (London and New York: Routledge, 2003), p. 307. Plan J. Coulton *apud* Cambitoglou, *Praktika tês Archaiologikês Hetaireias* (1972), p. 260. Reprinted with kind permission of Professor Cambitoglou.

3.5   Ancient Views of the Origins of the Polis

Unlike modern scholars, ancient Greeks rarely paid attention to material evidence when they reconstructed the emergence of their respective poleis. Instead, they relied on traditions that dated the foundations of cities to mythical times. For example, the cities of Argos and Sparta in the Peloponnese attributed their foundations to Dorian Greeks. The latter were led by the Heraclidae, Heracles' descendants, who came to reclaim the inheritance of their divine ancestor. Some ancient accounts record a process of "settling together" (*synoikismos*) of neighboring villages and towns that formed a polis. Thus, local traditions in Athens told of a mythical ruler, Theseus, who unified politically different poleis into a single Athenian polis. The historicity of these traditions has often been contested, but it shows how Classical Athenians imagined the origins of their state.

3.5.A   Theseus' Unification of Attica

Thucydides 2.15.1–2

(**2.15.1**) This had been the case with the Athenians more than with the other Greeks, and from a very early period. For in the time of Cecrops and the earliest kings, right down to Theseus, Attica had always been a collection of separate poleis with their own town halls [*prytaneia*] and magistrates. Whenever they were not under threat, they would not meet with the king to formulate policy; rather, they had their own government and established their own policy, some of them, on occasion, even making war on the king, as the people of Eleusis and Eumolpus did on Erechtheus.[1] (**15.2**) But then Theseus came to the throne, and through a combination of ability and intelligence he effected a basic reorganization of the land. In particular, he made a unified body of all the poleis. He abolished all local councils [sg. *boulêuterion*] and magistracies and united all the various poleis into what is today's polis, establishing a single council and a single town hall. The people all lived on their own lands as before, but Theseus obliged them to recognize only the one acropolis (that which we have today). With all the citizens now contributing to it, the city had become very great by the time it was passed on to his successors by Theseus, and because of that the Athenians even now celebrate the Unification [*Synoikia*] as a publicly funded festival.

Note

1. *Cecrops and Erechtheus were the legendary first and sixth kings of Athens, respectively. Eumolpus was one of the mythical founders of the Mysteries at Eleusis (see **14.4**: "Greek Temples and the Mysteries of Demeter in Eleusis"). Prytaneia were public buildings that in historical times were used for religious functions, as state archives, and to entertain individuals who were publicly honored.*

The fourth-century philosopher Aristotle provides the most detailed ancient analysis of the formation of the polis. He envisions an evolutionary process that begins with the union of a male and female and culminates in the creation of the polis. His description is likely based on his and others' theories of social interactions, local traditions, and perhaps contemporary or near-contemporary experiences of foundations of cities. Aristotle's view that living in a polis was "natural," that is, culturally desirable and correct, was typical of many Greeks.

3.5.B   Aristotle on the Evolution of the Polis

Aristotle *Politics* 1.1.3–9 1252a24–53a7

(**1.1.3**) As in other matters, it is by observing the evolution of phenomena from their earliest phase that we would gain the best insight into them. (**1.4**) The first unions must perforce be those of people who cannot exist apart, like the male and the female who unite for the sake of reproduction. This is not a matter of choice but a natural law, which also applies to all other living beings and plants, that is the desire to leave behind another being like oneself. The same applies to the union of the natural ruler and the naturally ruled, which is for the sake of security; for the one capable of foresight – thanks to his intelligence – is a natural ruler and natural master, while the one physically able to do his bidding is the subject, and a slave by nature. (Thus the relationship is mutually beneficial to master and slave alike.) (**1.5**) Accordingly there is a distinction made by nature between the female and the slave (for nature never produces anything with a view to economy, like the metalworkers with their Delphic knife [i.e., having multiple uses], but creates one thing for one purpose. In this way each instrument could be best perfected, serving not a number of purposes but only one). Amongst the barbarians the female and the slave have the same status. The reason for this is that barbarians do not have a natural ruler – their unions are those of female slave and male slave, which is why the poets say that "it is right for Greeks to rule over barbarians" [Euripides *Iphigenia in Aulis* 1400], the barbarian and the slave being by nature the same thing.

(**1.6**) It is from such unions of two people that the household [*oikia*] is first formed, and Hesiod was right to say in his poem: "First of all <acquire> a house [*oikos*], a woman, and an ox for plowing" [*Works and Days* 405], the ox representing a slave laborer for the poor. So the union established by nature for everyday life is the household, whose members Charondas calls "table-fellows" and Epimenides the Cretan "mess-mates."[1]

(**1.7**) The union formed from a plurality of households for needs beyond the daily is the village [*komê*]. More than anything the village would seem to be a colony [*apoikia*] of the household, and its members some call "fellow-nurselings," namely, children and grandchildren. That is why the cities [*poleis*] were originally ruled by monarchs and why tribal communities [*ethnê*] still are, for they are an amalgam formed from peoples ruled by kings. For every household is ruled by its eldest member, and thus the "colonies" are as well, because they are all related. This is what Homer means by saying:

"they all individually lay down the laws for their own wives and children" [*Odyssey* 9.114–115; see **3.1**].

For they were scattered families, and that is how they were originally constituted.

In the case of the gods, too, all men claim that these have a king. The reason is that some people are still ruled by kings today, and others were in the distant past – they attribute to the gods their own way of life, just as they attribute to them their own appearance.

(**1.8**) The end product of the union of a number of villages is the city [*polis*], which now has reached the perfect state of virtually total self-sufficiency. Established merely for living, it actually serves the purpose of living well. Thus every city is a natural formation, inasmuch as the original unions are natural, too. For the city is the end result of those unions, and the end result is something's nature. For what each thing is when its development is complete is what we call its nature, as with a man, a horse, or a household. In addition, the completed end for which something exists is also its best condition, and self-sufficiency is a completed end and the best condition. (**1.9**) From this it is clear that the city is a natural formation, that it is natural for a man to live in a polis,[2] and that a man who is without a city thanks to his nature, not chance, is either worthless or greater than a man. He is like the man reproached by Homer – "without clan, without law, without hearth" [*Iliad* 9.63].

Notes

1. *Charondas: the lawgiver of Sicilian Catana. Epimenides: a seer who was called to purify the city of Athens ca. 630.*
2. *It is common to mistranslate the phrase* politikon zô(i)on *as "man is a political animal."*

 See WEB **3.7** for links to the Greek polis and to the rise of the polis.

Questions

1. How would Theseus' unification of Attica (**3.5.A**) fit with Aristotle's description of the evolution of the polis (**3.5.B**)? Can it add to Aristotle's analysis?
2. What needs do the different kinds of partnership mentioned by Aristotle meet?
3. What are the relationships between gender and polis according to Aristotle?

3.6   *Ethnos*: The Ionians

The commonest way to identify a person in Greece was by his or her patronymic and polis of origin, for example, Pericles son of Xanthippus of Athens. Yet alongside the poleis, and at times preceding or incorporating them, were communities whose residents perceived themselves as members of the same *ethnos*, often translated as people or tribe. Ethnic identity consists chiefly of a belief in common kinship and often in past collective migration. It also comprises an affiliation with a particular region, cult, or religious sanctuary. This identity was not static but was susceptible to local and chronological variations, illustrating both its flexible nature and the fact that it was subjectively constructed and perceived. Until the Classical period, ethnic identity made only few attempts at self-definition in terms of "us" versus other ethnic groups.

The manipulability of ethnic identities and the late literary evidence for them make it difficult to trace their origins. The following example illustrates how they might be constructed. The Ionians were a prominent ethnic group of Greeks who shared a common dialect, names of months and tribes, religious cults and customs, and alleged common ancestry and history. They were located mostly in Attica and central Asia Minor. The fifth-century historian Herodotus recorded traditions that established mythological links among these communities. The first document describes how Ion, who gave his name to the Ionians, made Athens Ionian. According to some traditions, Ion was the mythical son of Apollo and Creusa, the daughter of the Athenian king Erechtheus, while according to others, he was the son of her husband Xuthus.

3.6.A   Ion's Ancestors

Herodotus 8.44.2

When the Pelasgians occupied what is now called Hellas, the Athenians were Pelasgians who went by the name of Cranae.[1] In the time of king Cecrops they were called Cecropidae, and on Erechtheus' accession to the throne they changed their name to Athenians. When Ion son of Xuthus became the leader of the army of the Athenians they were called Ionians after him.

Note

1. *The Pelasgians were the pre-Hellenic inhabitants of Greece. The Athenians regarded themselves as* autochtonoi, *those who had occupied their land since time immemorial. It is likely, however, that this belief did not precede the fifth century.*

Another tradition links Athens to Ionian settlements in Asia Minor, especially Miletus (see Herodotus 1.146.2–3: **4.7**: "Settlers and Locals"). Although archaeologists have found links between Attica and Miletus that go back to the Dark Age, these links do not make the tradition recorded here more credible. There was also a tradition that the Ionians were driven out from the Peloponnese by the Achaeans.

3.6.B   Ionians in the Peloponnese

Herodotus 7.94

The Ionians supplied a hundred ships and wore Greek clothes and armor. Greek tradition has it that, as long as the Ionians lived in the Peloponnese, in what is now called Achaea, before the arrival in the Peloponnese of Danaus[1] and Xuthus, they were called Aegialian Pelasgians, but later they were called Ionians after Xuthus' son Ion.

Note

1. *Danaus was a mythical hero and king of Argos.*

The second-century CE traveler Pausanias preserves an attempt to systematize all these tales. It is hard to assess their historicity because the archaeological evidence for an Ionian migration to Asia Minor is meager. In addition, some traditions link Ionian settlements to non-Ionian founders. It is possible, then, that the myths sought to establish a common ethnic identity between Athens and Ionian settlements in Asia Minor at times when either side deemed such links useful, politically or culturally. The author first describes Ion's tribulations, which landed him in Elis in the Peloponnese. He became its local ruler and called those under his rule Ionians.

3.6.C   The History of the Ionians

Pausanias *Description of Greece* 7.1.5–2.1

(**7.1.5**) At that time, during the reign of Ion, the Eleusinians had opened hostilities against Athens and the Athenians brought in Ion to assume leadership in the war. Ion's fate overtook him in Attica, and his monument stands in a Potamian deme.[1] Ion's descendants held sway over the Ionians until they and the common people were driven out by the Achaeans. It transpired that, at that time, the Achaeans themselves had been driven from Lacedaemon and Argos by the Dorians.

(**1.7**) When the sons of Achaeus gained power in Argos and Lacedaemon, Archandrus forced the name Achaeans on the people of those regions. That was the general name for these peoples, while the Argives had their own particular name of "Danaeans." At the time referred to above, when the Achaeans were driven out of Argos and Lacedaemon by the Dorians, they and their king, Orestes' son Tisamenus, sent the Ionians a message in which they proposed settling amongst them without warfare.

Note

1. *There were two Athenian demes (townships) called Potamion, but it is uncertain in which one the monument stood.*

The Ionians refused, went to war against the Achaeans, and lost.

(**1.9**) The Ionians then came to Attica where the Athenians and their king Melanthus son of Andropompus welcomed them as settlers, no doubt because of Ion and what he achieved for the Athenians as their leader in war [*polemarchos*]. It is also said that the Athenians regarded the Dorians with suspicion, fearing that they would not be willing to leave them in peace, and they welcomed the Ionians as settlers among them more to bolster their own strength than from any kindly feelings toward them.

(**2.1**) Not many years later Codrus' eldest sons, Medon and Neileus, were in dispute over the throne, and Neileus declared that he would not put up with being ruled over by Medon because the latter was lame in one foot. The two decided to refer the issue to the oracle at Delphi, where the Pythia [Apollo's priestess at the oracle] assigned rule over the Athenians to Medon. Neileus and the rest of Codrus' sons therefore set off to found a colony [in Asia Minor]. They took along with them any of the Athenians who wished to go, but Ionians formed the largest part of the expedition.

Questions

1. Construct the career of Ion based on the documents in **3.6A–C.**
2. What established the identity of ethnic groups according to the traditions on the Ionian migrations?

Review Questions

1. How did the Greeks account for the rise of the city-states?
2. What made a polis for the Greeks?
3. What role did leadership have in the formation of city and *ethnos*?
4. Discuss the relationship between myth and identity based on the descriptions of polis and *ethnos* in this chapter.

See WEB **3.7** for links on *ethnos* and on the Ionians.

Suggested Readings

The Homeric polis: Scully 1981; Raaflaub 1997, 645–647, 629–630. The Copenhagen Polis Center under the directorship of M. H. Hansen has published several works on the Greek polis. Especially relevant are Hansen 1993, 2006a. *The early polis*: Mitchell and Rhodes 1997 (esp. chapters by Davies and Donlan). *Archaeological evidence on the early polis*: Snodgrass 1980, modified by Morris 1987; Coldstream 2003, esp. 303–312; Osborne 1996, esp. 70–104. *Zagora*: Coldstream 2003, 210–213, 304–312, 424, 430, but also Demand 1990, 21–22. *Greek houses (including in this period)*: Nevett 1999; Ault and Nevett 2005. *Thucydides and early Attica*: Hornblower 1991–2008, 1: 259–269; Gouschin 1999. For opposite views of the historical validity of Aristotle's analysis, see Coldstream 2003, 406–407 and Davies 1997, 26–27. *The construction of an Ionian identity (as well as other ethnic identities)*: Sakellariou 1990; Hall 1997, 51–56; 2002, 67–71; cf. K. Morgan 2003, 187–188. Gorman 2001, 31–40 supports the tradition that Athens was Miletus' mother-city.

4

Settlements Across the Sea

Greek "Colonization"

Ancient Greece from Homer to Alexander: The Evidence, First Edition. Joseph Roisman.
© 2011 Blackwell Publishing Ltd. Translations © 2011 John Yardley. Published 2011 by Blackwell Publishing Ltd.

The movement of Greek settlers across the sea and the foundation of poleis there are commonly known as "Greek colonization." Yet the terms "colonization" and "colonies" are anachronistic because they connote the annexation of overseas territory to the settlers' place of origin. In fact, most Greek settlements abroad (sg. *apoikia*) were politically independent from their mother-cities or their original *ethnos*, possibly from the beginning of their existence. Recent scholarship is also disinclined to identify the origins of many colonies with organized state enterprises. We use the terms "colonies" and "colonization" as a concession to their common use rather than in support of their validity.

Early Greek overseas settlement spanned from the Dark to the Archaic ages, and those who participated in it came from many corners of the Greek world. In due course, colonies spawned their own colonies, resulting in Greek settlements all over the Mediterranean from Massilia (Marseille) in the west to Naucratis in Egypt in the east. Their presence was most heavily felt in Sicily, southern Italy, the Aegean, which became a Greek sea, and the Black Sea. Colonization continued, although on a smaller scale, during the Classical Age and later. In addition to colonies, many Greeks established trading posts (sg. *emporion*).

The causes of colonization varied. It is commonly assumed that population growth led to a shortage of farmland in the communities of origin and consequently to migration. Yet scholars have recently contested the role of land shortage in encouraging emigration (Foxhall 2004), offering as a no less likely cause the depletion of local resources by the existing population. Trade opportunities and the exploitation of desirable resources (e.g., metals) were concomitant inducements. See p. 62 for additional motives.

This chapter shows the extent of Greek settlements in the western Mediterranean, and provides information on the foundation of the earliest of these settlements on the island of Pithecoussae (Ischia). Traditions concerning the foundation of Cyrene in Libya tell us about the process of sending settlers abroad. Thucydides' report of a conflict between Corinth, Corcyra, and Epidamnus illustrates the mutual expectations of mother-cities and colonies, while a tradition on Miletus describes Greek settlers' treatment of the local inhabitants. Finally, a plan of the city of Selinus in Sicily reveals how the Greeks shaped their settlement.

4.1 Greek Settlements in the Western Mediterranean

See Map 4.1, opposite, for Greek settlements in southern Italy and Sicily.

4.2 The Settlement at Pithecoussae (ca. 750)

The earliest Greek colony in the western Mediterranean was Pithecoussae, situated on the island of Ischia across from Cumae and Neapolis in Italy. It was founded around 750 by settlers from the cities of Chalcis and Eretria on the island of Euboea. Archaeological excavations have confirmed its agricultural character. Two structures in the colony were identified as blacksmiths' workshops where iron from the island of Elba was smelted. The cemetery

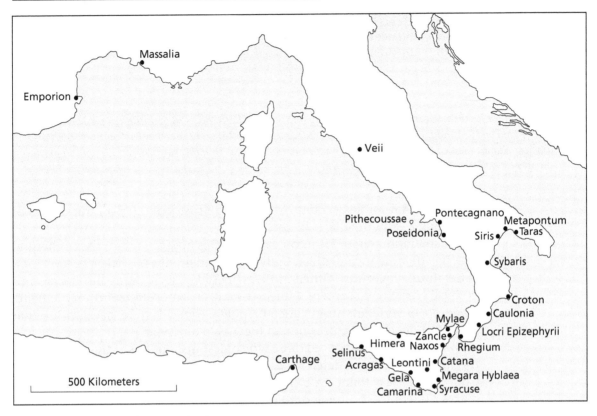

Map 4.1   Greek settlements in the west.

reveals the use of local, Italian, Euboean, Corinthian, Rhodian, Anatolian, Levantine, and Egyptian pottery and artifacts. The finds suggest not so much the commercial character of the colony as a market for a wide-range of Mediterranean trade. Some graves indicate the presence of the local population and Phoenicians in the colony.

The late first-century Greek geographer and historian Strabo reports on the foundation and history of the settlement.

4.2.A   The Settling of Pithecoussae

Strabo *Geography* 5.4.9

The island of Prochute lies in front of Misenum and is a piece of land broken off from Pithecoussae. It was the Eretrians and the Chalcidians who colonized Pithecoussae. Thanks to the fertility of the soil and to their gold mines, the colonists prospered, but they left the island in a time of civil discord [*stasis*], and later on they were also driven away by earthquakes, and by eruptions involving fire, the sea, and hot waters. For the island produces this sort of volcanic activity, and this was also why the people who had been sent out later by Hiero tyrant of Syracuse [in 474] left the fortified town they had built and, indeed, the entire island, after which the people of Neapolis came to take it over...[1]

Note

1. *The fact that Ischia's volcanic soil is good mostly for vines, and that no great quantities of gold ornaments were found on the island, raises questions about Strabo's interpretation of the colonists' motives. He is also unclear about the fate of the colony. One possible interpretation is that one segment of the population (the Eretrians?) left for Cumae following civil strife, and the rest followed in the wake of later eruptions.*

 See WEB **4.3** for an account by the Roman historian Livy on the settlers of Pithecoussae and their later history.

The abandonment of Pithecoussae illustrates how domestic crises or natural disasters (famine included) led individuals and groups of settlers to look for a better future overseas. Other motives included local wars and social and political unrest or discontent. Pithecoussae also demonstrates how settlements made up of residents from different poleis were likely to develop internal *stasis*, although conflict was not an inevitable outcome.

Pithecoussae has produced one of the oldest inscriptions of the Archaic Age. It is inscribed on a cup dated to ca. 735–720, commonly known as the "Nestor Cup," which was found in a child's tomb. It is possible that the inscription makes a reference to Homer or to rival epic traditions, and perhaps it contains a magical incantation. It is written from right to left in a script that was used in Chalcis, Euboea.

4.2.B   The "Nestor Cup"

ML no. 1

Translation: B. Powell 1989, p. 338

> I am Nestor's cup, delightful to drink from
> Whoever drinks this cup, straight away
> The desire of beautifully crowned Aphrodite will seize.

 See WEB **4.9** for a link to an image of the "Nestor Cup" and additional information about it.

Questions

1. What moved settlers to found and then desert Pithecoussae according to Strabo (**4.2.A**) and Livy (WEB **4.3**)?
2. What can be learned from the "Nestor Cup" about Pithecoussan society?

4.4   The Foundation of Cyrene (631)

A well-attested foundation story concerns the settlement of Cyrene in Libya in 631 by men from the island of Thera. See WEB **4.5** for Herodotus' narrative of Cyrene's foundation, and WEB **4.5.I** for a brief description of, and links about, the Delphic oracle and how it played an important role in this and other foundations.

Sometime in the fourth century, the Cyreneans decided, perhaps following a Theran request, to grant citizen rights to Theran residents in Cyrene and to Therans who wished to join their city. In justification of the motion, its proposer recalled customs that regulated the relationship between the mother-city and her colony that went back, he said, to the time of its foundation. A decree recording the grant of citizenship was set up in the local temple of Apollo Pythius. The second part of the inscription purports also to record the original decision to found the settlement. It describes the conditions imposed on the settlers and the role of the leader and founder of the colony, the *oikistês*. He was a Greek aristocrat whom the colony often honored post-humously with a cult or festival. The scholarly view that the settlers' oath is authentic has found more favor than that regarding it as a late fabrication.

The Cyrenean decree ML no. 5 = Fornara no. 18

God. Good Fortune. Damis, son of Bathycles, proposed as follows. With regard to the declaration of the people of Thera [and] Cleudamas,[1] son of Euthycles, and in order that the polis may flourish and the Cyrenean people prosper, we grant the Therans (**5**) citizenship. We do this in accord with our ancestral custom which our ancestors formulated, both those who settled Cyrene from Thera and those who remained in Thera, just as Apollo gave good fortune to Battus and the people of Thera if they kept to the sworn agreement that our ancestors themselves made with them (**10**) when they sent out the colony at the command of Apollo Archagetas. With good fortune it was resolved by the people [*demos*] that the Therans should retain equal citizenship in Cyrene, too, on the same terms as before. All the Therans living in Cyrene are to take the same oath as the others once (**15**) swore; and they are to be assigned to a tribe [*phylê*], a phratry, and nine companionships [*hetairiai*].[2] This decree is to be engraved on a marble stone, and the stone is to be placed in the ancestral temple of Pythian Apollo. And the sworn agreement that the colonists made after sailing to Libya – from Thera to Cyrene – (**20**) with Battus, shall also be engraved on the stone. With regard to the necessary expenditures for the stone or its engraving, the officials for accounts draw them from the incoming funds of Apollo...

Sworn Agreement of the Colonists. The following was decided by the Assembly [*ekklesia*]. Since Apollo in a spontaneous prophecy instructed B[at]tus (**25**) and the Therans to colonize Cyrene, the people of Thera resolve to send to Libya Battus as founder [*archagetas*][3] and king, with the Therans accompanying him on the voyage. They are to sail according to family, on fair and equal terms, with one son conscripted from each [...] and (**30**) adults and free persons of the other Therans [...] are to sail. If the colonists settle the colony, anyone of their relatives later sailing to Libya is to have citizenship and political offices, along with them, and to be allotted land that is not under ownership. And if they do not settle the colony, and if the Therans cannot help them (**35**) and if they suffer hardship for five years, then they may return to their own property in Thera from the country without fear, and be citizens. Anyone refusing to sail when the city sends him is to be liable to the death penalty and his property to confiscation. Any man taking him in or protecting him, be it a father [helping] a son or a brother a brother (**40**), shall suffer the same as the man refusing to sail.

On these conditions those who stayed here and those sailing to found the colony made a sworn agreement, putting curses on those who violated them and refused to stand by them, whether it be those settling in Libya or those remaining here. They made wax images and burned them, and uttered this curse (**45**) while they all joined together – men and women, boys and girls: "Whosoever fails to abide by this sworn agreement but instead violates it, let him melt and liquefy like the images, the man himself, his offspring, and his property. But for those who abide by this sworn agreement, both those (**50**) sailing to Libya and [those] remaining in Thera, may there be many good things both for them [and] their offspring.

Notes

1. *Cleudamas was perhaps the leader of the Therans.*
2. *Tribe, phratry, and companionships were subgroups of the citizenry.*
3. *Archagetas means most likely a ruler and leader.*

 A link to reports of recent excavations in Cyrene can be found in WEB **4.9**.

Questions

1. What moved Thera to send settlers abroad, and what difficulties did they encounter according to Herodotus' narrative of the foundation of Cyrene (WEB **4.5**)?
2. Discuss the relationships between Thera and the settlers of Cyrene in light of Herodotus' foundation stories (WEB **4.5**) and the Cyrenean decree (**4.4**).

3. What role did Delphi play in Cyrene's foundation (cf. WEB **4.5.I**)?

4.6 Mother-City and Colony: Corinth, Corcyra, and Epidamnus (435)

The relations between colonies and their mother-cities (sg. *metropolis*) varied considerably. The Therans, for example, insisted that Cyrene would break away from them. In other cases colonies remained dependent to varying degrees on their mother-cities. Often colonies may be described as having a "special relationship" with their mother-cities, in which the two states acknowledged their historic, cultural, and religious ties. Festivals served as occasions to show respect toward the mother-city, and Corinth even provided her colony Potidaea in Chalcidice with annual magistrates (Thucydides 1.56.2).

Thucydides' account of a conflict in 435 between Corcyra and its colony Epidamnus (today Durazzo), and Corinth's involvement in it, belongs to the Classical Age. Yet it illustrates well the ties between a mother-city and her colonies, the parties' mutual expectations, and the manipulation of these expectations. The dispute between Epidamnus and Corcyra escalated into a military conflict between Corinth and Corcyra, which precipitated the outbreak of the Peloponnesian War between Athens and Sparta (see WEB **24.2.I**: "The Epidamnus Affair"). Generally, it was considered unseemly for a colony to wage war on its mother-city.

Thucydides 1.24.1–26.1

(**1.24.1**) On the right-hand side as one sails into the Ionian Gulf is the city of Epidamnus, bordering on which is a barbarian tribe, the Taulantians, who are of Illyrian stock. (**24.2**) Epidamnus was a colony of the Corcyrans, but its founder [*oikistês*] was Phalius son of Eratocleides. He was a Corinthian by nationality, and a descendant of Heracles,[1] and in accordance with long-established practice he had been summoned from the mother-state to lead the colonization. A number of Corinthians and members of the other Dorian groupings also took part in the settlement [627]. (**24.3**) As time went on the Epidamnians became a powerful and populous nation. (**24.4**) However, they experienced many years of civil discord, it is said, and suffered disastrous losses from a war with their barbarian neighbors which stripped them of most of their power. (**24.5**) Eventually, before the outbreak of this war [the Peloponnesian War], the common people [*demos*] drove out the most prominent citizens, and these, banding together with barbarians, attacked and conducted predatory raids by land and sea on those left in the city. (**24.6**) Under severe pressure, the Epidamnians remaining in the city sent a delegation to Corcyra, since it was their mother-state. They begged the Corcyrans not to stand by and watch them being destroyed, but to effect a reconciliation with the exiles on their behalf and bring their war with the barbarians to an end. (**24.7**) And they made this entreaty seated as suppliants in the temple of Hera. The Corcyrans, however, turned a deaf ear to their suppliant plea and sent them away empty handed.

(**25.1**) Aware now that no assistance was forthcoming from Corcyra, the Epidamnians were at a loss how to solve the problem facing them. They therefore sent representatives to Delphi and asked the god whether they should put their city in the Corinthians' hands, since these were their original founders, and try to elicit some assistance from them. The god's reply was that they should put the city in the hands of the Corinthians and appoint them their leaders.

(**25.2**) In accordance with the oracle the Epidamnians went to Corinth and handed over the colony. They pointed out to the Corinthians that their founder came from Corinth, and acquainted them with the content of the oracle, after which they begged them to come to their assistance and not stand by and watch them being destroyed. (**25.3**) The Corinthians undertook to help them. There was justification for it, they thought, because the colony was as much theirs as it was Corcyra's, but they were also motivated by hatred for the Corcyrans for the disdain that they felt, their colonists though they were, for the Corinthians. (**25.4**) In fact, at the festivals that they held in common, they did not accord them the usual privileges and would not give a Corinthian the first portion from the sacrifices as other colonies did. Rather, they felt only contempt for Corinth, being, as they then were, on a par with the richest of the Greek peoples economically and even stronger in military capability. Indeed, they actually boasted sometimes that they far surpassed the Corinthians at sea, relating this to Corcyra being formerly occupied by the Phaeacians, who were famous for their ships. This actually made the Corcyrans continue to build up their navy, in which they were certainly not weak, possessing as they did 130 triremes [galleys] at the commencement of hostilities. (**26.1**) Feeling aggrieved over all these issues, the Corinthians were happy to send to Epidamnus the assistance it needed, and they bade anyone who so wished to go there to settle, sending as well a garrison made up of Ambracians, Leucadians, and their own citizens.[2]

Notes

1. See **3.5** (*"Ancient Views of the Origins of the Polis"*) *for Heracles' descendants (the Heraclidae).*
2. *Both Ambracia and Leucas were Corinthian colonies.*

Question

1. Judging by Thucydides' account, what grievances might colonies and mother-cities have against one another? What do such complaints tell us about their mutual expectations?

4.7   Settlers and Locals

There was no single pattern of relationship between Greek settlers and local populations. Ideally, colonists would have liked to settle in uninhabited land, like the island next to the Cyclopes' land that Odysseus noticed (**3.1**: "The Homeric Polis"). The tradition concerning Cyrene records cautious cooperation with the local Libyans. The story of the foundation of the Greek city of Miletus in Asia Minor, however, suggests that settlers arrived without their families, eliminated the local male population, and married the local women.

Herodotus 1.146.2–3

(**1.146.2**) Those who set off from the Prytaneum [town hall] of Athens and who considered themselves the most aristocratic of the Ionians did not take wives with them on their colonizing expedition. Instead, they had with them some Carian women whose fathers they had killed. (**146.3**) Because of this murder the women made themselves take an oath, which they also passed on to their daughters, making it a practice for them not to take their meals with their husbands or call out a husband's name. This was in recognition of the fact that the men had killed their fathers, their husbands, and their children, and then married them after doing so. This happened in Miletus.

Figure 4.1   Selinus site plan. © Dieter Mertens. Printed in *Stadte und Bauten der Westgriechen*, ed. Hirmer (Munich, 2006), ed. L'Erma di Bretschneider (Rome, 2006), p. 174, ill. 303. Reprinted with kind permission of Dieter Mertens.

4.8   Selinus (651/0?)

The history and the site of the city of Selinus in Sicily exemplify many of the aspects discussed so far. Thucydides (6.4.2) reports that Selinus was founded by neighboring Megara Hyblaea and that her *oikistês* was Pamillus, who came from the Greek city of Megara, the mother-city of the founding city. He dates the foundation to 628/7, though the later Greek historian Diodorus of Sicily (13.59.4) dates it to 651/0, and pottery finds seem to support the earlier date. There is also archaeological evidence of an indigenous stratum from the eighth to seventh centuries, topped by a mixed indigenous–Greek level, which is covered in turn by a late seventh-century purely Greek level. Future excavations may reveal whether these finds suggest initial peaceful coexistence between Greeks and locals, followed by the latter's expulsion.

The site plan of Selinus (Figure 4.1) shows a town flanked by two rivers and the sea. The blocks of residential houses on Manuzza Hill and next to the acropolis reveal a division between public and private spaces and a grid design, which is dated to 580–570. Manuzza Hill also had a necropolis. Structures A, D, C, and O on the acropolis, G, F, and E on the East Hill, and M on Gaggera Hill are temples, some of which were built later. The unlettered structure on Gaggera Hill is Demeter sanctuary, and M is probably a temple of Heracles. The city wall dates to the mid-sixth century, as does the monumental Temple C, perhaps of Apollo. Selinus' monumental temples (A–G, O) suggest great wealth, which came from exporting wheat, manufacturing, trade, and other sources. Its urban population is estimated at between 6,500 and 10,000 residents, and the polis' territory at ca. 1,500 sq. km. The size of the rural population is unknown. Selinus was destroyed by Carthage in 409/8.

Question

1. Compare Selinus' town plan with that of Zagora (**3.3**: "An Early Settlement on Andros"). What does each plan tell us about the division between public and private spaces and the city's communal needs and resources?

Review Questions

1. What expectations did settlers have of their new polis?
2. Describe the role of the *oikistês* (settlement leader) based on the traditions of the foundation of Cyrene (**4.4** and WEB **4.5**).

3. Describe the relationship between Greek settlers and locals in Cyrene (WEB **4.5**), Miletus (**4.7**), and Selinus (**4.8**).
4. What might strengthen or disrupt relationships between mother-cities and their colonies?

Suggested Readings

Colonization: Jeffrey 1976, 50–62; Graham 1983; Boardman 1999. *Colonization and religion*: Polignac 1995, 89–127; *and Delphi*: Malkin 1987: 17–91; *and the indigenous population*: Descoeudres 1990; *motives*: Purcell 1990, 44–49. *Pithecoussae (including the Nestor Cup)*: Ridgeway 1992, 31–120; Faraone 1996; Tandy 1997, 66–72; Coldstream 2003, 225–228, 395. *The foundation of Cyrene and the settlement decree*: Boardman 1966; Graham 1983, 27, 29, 64; Malkin 1994, 89–111; Osborne 2002, 505–508. *A narratological analysis of the story of the foundation as a myth*: Calame 2003. *Corinth, her colonies, and their conflict*: Graham 1983, 118–153; Salmon 1984, 62–74, 93–96, 211–219; Crane 1998: 97–124. *Selinus*: De Angelis 2003, 101–199; Marconi 2007 (temples and sculpture).

5

Aristocratic Power and Attitudes

Ancient Greece from Homer to Alexander: The Evidence, First Edition. Joseph Roisman.
© 2011 Blackwell Publishing Ltd. Translations © 2011 John Yardley. Published 2011 by Blackwell Publishing Ltd.

Many colonial enterprises were led by aristocrats who were either unhappy with the situation in their native home or ambitious for greater power, prestige, and wealth. Indeed, aristocrats dominated the Archaic Age both politically and culturally. What distinguished them from non-aristocrats was their birth, wealth (which came from agriculture, trade, or both), and lifestyle. Our sources are too late to provide a reliable account of how aristocrats replaced the kings in power. Yet if, as Aristotle surmised (WEB **5.2**), legitimate royal power depended on personal and family *aretê* (excellence) and on an ability to serve one's city or *ethnos*, then men other than kings could claim these qualifications. Aristocracy seemed to have replaced monarchy without much of an upheaval.

This chapter deals with the political power of Athenian aristocracy in the early Archaic Age. It also examines aristocratic attitudes toward non-aristocrats and the elite's concern with their status, as articulated by the Megarian poet Theognis.

5.1   Aristocratic Power and Offices in Athens

Aristotle or one of his contemporaries wrote a work commonly known as "The Constitution of the Athenians" (*Athenaion Politeia*, henceforth *Ath. Pol.*), which described in its early chapters the process by which Archaic Athens became an aristocratic republic. There is no telling how typical of other cities Athens was in its political development, but many historians regard it as an example of the gradual transfer of power in Greece from monarchy to aristocracy.

According to Athenian traditions of uncertain date and reliability, the last Athenian king, Codrus, was succeeded by thirteen archons (chief magistrates), who each served for life in succession. They were followed by seven archons, each serving a ten-year term. Starting from 683/2, the archonship was limited to one year.

Ath. Pol. 3.1–6

(**3.1**) The structure of the ancient constitution before Draco[1] was as follows:

The Athenians established magistracies on the basis of noble birth and wealth, with magistrates at first holding power for life, and subsequently for a ten-year period. (**3.2**) The supreme, and the earliest, magistracies were those of the king [*basileus*], the polemarch [*polemarchos*], and the archon.[2] The most ancient of these three was that of king – which dated from earliest times – and the second to be established was the polemarchy, whose origin derived from the fact that some kings had no aptitude for warfare (that, in fact, was why the Athenians, under pressure, sent for Ion). (**3.3**) The last-established magistracy was that of archon, with most authorities ascribing its introduction to the time of Medon, but some to the time of Acastus.[3] As evidence for the latter view its proponents adduce the fact that the nine archons swear to fulfill their oaths "as under Acastus," which suggests that it was in his reign that the descendants of Codrus ceded the throne in return for the privileges accorded to the archon. Whichever of these positions is correct, the chronology is little affected, but that the archonship was the last of the offices established is indicated by the fact that the archon, unlike the king and the polemarch, has none of the early governmental functions, only functions later added to the office. And this explains why it was only recently – enhanced as it was by these added functions – that the office became important.

(**3.4**) The election of Thesmothetae[4] took place many years later when the Athenians were already holding annual elections for the magistracies, and their *raison d'être* was the transcription and safeguarding of the laws for the arbitration of disputes. Thus this was the only office whose tenure was never for more than one year…

(**3.5**) This was how the magistracies functioned. (**3.6**) The council of the Areopagus[5] had responsibility for maintaining the laws, and had the greatest and most important functions in the community as the supreme arbiters of punishment and fines for all malefactors. In fact, the selection of archons depended on noble birth and wealth, and members of the Areopagus were ex-archons. And that is why, of the Athenian offices, this is the only one that has remained to this time with life-long tenure.

Notes

1. *Draco was a lawgiver active in 621. See **9.1** ("Draco's Law of Homicide").*
2. *In later times the king archon (archon basileus) oversaw the city's religious cults and festivals and judged cases concerning religion. The polemarchos was the military leader. After the creation of the office of strategos (general), he supervised cases involving family matters and resident aliens. The archon was probably the chief magistrate, who in later times gave his name to the year (archon eponymous). Together with the Thesmothetae (see note 4), these office-holders were called the "nine archons." On Ion, see **3.6** ("Ethnos: The Ionians").*
3. *Medon and Acastus were the first archons for life.*
4. *The author ascribes to the Thesmothetae powers that he probably deduced from the etymology of their names (lit. "lawgivers"). In later periods they had judicial duties.*
5. *The Areopagus was a council that met on the hill of the god of war, Ares (hence the name). It oversaw the laws, supervised office-holders, and had extensive judicial powers. According to Ath. Pol. 8.2, the Areopagus appointed archons to office.*

Questions

1. What gave rise to monarchy, according to Aristotle (WEB **5.2**)?
2. Which powers did Athenian magistrates hold (**5.1**)?
3. What made the council of the Areopagus the most powerful institution in Athens (**5.1**)?

5.3 Aristocratic Exclusiveness

The passage in **5.1** shows how aristocrats limited access to power to their exclusive group. At the same time, they tried to regulate and distribute power evenly among themselves. However, the aristocrats' political and social dominance was challenged from within and without. In his *Works and Days* (see **2.1**: "Individual,

Communal, and Divine Justice"), Hesiod complained about rulers' insolent abuse of power, the distress of the poor, and the absence of justice in the polis. The seventh-century poet Theognis of Megara provides an aristocratic perspective on this and other protests. Scholars disagree on the exact date of Theognis' career and the authorship of the poems in his corpus. His authorship of the next poem, however, is less in doubt. Addressing his youthful beloved, Cyrnus, son of Polypais, Theognis defends aristocratic claims to moral excellence and sees those outside its circle as threatening the rule of justice in the polis.

5.3.A   The Unworthy

Theognis 53–68 (Gerber)

Cyrnus, this city remains a city but its people are different. Those who formerly knew neither justice nor the laws but who wore out goat hides on their flanks and grazed the areas outside the city like deer – even these are now our worthies, son of Polypais. Those who were men of repute before are now worth nothing. Who could bear to see this happen? They laugh at each other and cheat each other, knowing the thoughts of neither the good nor the bad.

   Make a close friend of none of these fellow-citizens of ours, son of Polypais, no matter what benefit you have in prospect. Rather, seem from your language to be a friend to all, but join none of them in any serious business at all. For you will find them to have the hearts of wretched beings, with no trust to be accorded to their actions. Rather, they love deceit, treachery, and cunning, like men who are beyond redemption.

Much to Theognis' chagrin, the blue-blooded aristocracy actually courted the former goatskin-wearers if they happened to be rich. Half ironically and half in earnest, he laments this breach of social solidarity and exclusivity, using a metaphor that for modern readers reads as chillingly eugenic.

5.3.B   Do Not Marry a Commoner

Theognis 183–192 (Gerber)

Cyrnus, we look for good bloodlines in rams, asses, and horses, and a person wants them to mate with noble stock. But a man of standing does not worry about marrying the common daughter of a common man if that man gives him a lot of money. Nor does a woman object to being the wife of a common man if he is rich – no, she prefers a wealthy man to a good one. For it is riches they honor. So the man of standing marries someone of bad stock, and the commoner someone of good stock, and wealth has sullied the race. So do not be surprised, son of Polypais, at the lapse into obscurity of the line of our fellow-citizens – for the bad is mixed with the good.

Questions

1. What criteria does Theognis use to distinguish the socially superior from their inferiors?
2. Discuss attitudes toward wealth in Theognis (**5.3.B**), Hesiod (**2.1**, **2.4**, WEB **2.5.II**), and Homer (**1.6**, **1.8**).

5.4 Aristocratic Anxiety

For Theognis of Megara, the social and moral crises faced by the aristocracy affect the entire polis. A city that is unjust and where the base mixed with nobility is bound to experience political crisis. The poet is concerned that setting the city to rights will give rise to a single ruler, probably a tyrant. It is unclear whether he has in mind Theagenes, the tyrant of Megara in the second half of the seventh century, or a different man.

Theognis 39–52 (Gerber)

Cyrnus, this city is pregnant, and I fear she may bring forth a man who will put our foul, outrageous conduct to rights. For though these fellow-citizens of ours still have good sense, the leaders have turned and are heading for the depths of wickedness. No city, Cyrnus, has yet been ruined by good men. But when bad men take pleasure in outrageous conduct, corrupting the common people and making judgments in favor of the wicked in order to promote their own profits and power – do not then expect that city to remain peaceful for long, even if now it enjoys deep tranquility. Do not expect that to happen when these dishonest profits please the wicked, coming as they do to the public detriment. For from them arise sedition [*stasis*], slaughter amongst the people and autocrats.[1] May such things never please this city!

Note

1. *Theognis uses the term* mounarchoi *(Ionic for* monarchoi*), which means single rulers, either kings or tyrants.*

Review Questions

1. How did the Athenian elite secure its political power according to *Ath. Pol.* (**5.1**)?
2. Discuss the relationship between power, class, and morality in Athens (**5.1**) and Megara (**5.3**, **5.4**).
3. Could the governmental structure of Athens (**5.1**) lead to anxieties such as those articulated by Theognis in the final document (**5.4**)?

Suggested Readings

Early Greek political development: Starr 1986; Murray 1993, 35–54; J. Hall 2007, 119–144. *Early Athenian constitution*: Hignett 1952, 33–195; Stanton 1990, 6–33; Rhodes 1993, 84–118. *Theognis and Megara of his times*: Legon 1981, 88–119; Figueira and Nagy 1985, esp. 9–21, 22–81, 112–158; Lane Fox 2000; van Wees 2000b.

6

Archaic Tyranny

CHAPTER CONTENTS

Ancient Greece from Homer to Alexander: The Evidence, First Edition. Joseph Roisman.
© 2011 Blackwell Publishing Ltd. Translations © 2011 John Yardley. Published 2011 by Blackwell Publishing Ltd.

During the seventh and sixth centuries many Greek city-states experienced tyranny. The word *tyrannos*, "tyrant," perhaps of Lydian origin, came to denote a single ruler who usurped power. The evidence for the tyrants' rise to power and the nature of their regime is highly problematic. Many of the extant accounts were written considerably later than the events they describe. They also reflected their authors' own experiences with later tyranny as well as hostile oligarchic and democratic attitudes toward tyranny. Yet the sources seem to agree that tyrants tended to come from within the elite and at times of social and political turmoil. Once in power, they enacted measures to address these problems. Many accounts stress the tyrant's isolation, his personal (as opposed to communal) concerns, and his harsh treatment of real or suspected opposition. Yet no ruler could rule by himself, and many tyrants enjoyed support from members of both the masses and the elite. Hostility toward tyrants had much to do with their later biased depiction, partly inspired by the second generation of tyrants, who were often the sons of the first tyrants and who resorted to violence and oppression in response to pressure from the people and aristocrats to share power. Many tyrants were consequently banished or eliminated. Tyranny, however, did not become extinct. During the Classical Age tyrants, often acting as military leaders, ruled important cities and communities in Sicily as well as in Greece.

This chapter reproduces Aristotle's survey of the different ways Greek tyrants attained power in different poleis. It illustrates tyrannical rule through the Corinthian tyranny of Cypselus and his son Periander. The chapter concludes with the Olympic victor Cylon's failed attempt to become a tyrant in Athens. Relevant to this discussion is the tyranny in Athens less than a century later, which is examined in Chapter 10.

6.1   How Tyrants Attained Power

Aristotle, like Plato, characterizes tyranny as the worst possible government. In his *Politics*, he discusses how tyrants seized power.

Aristotle *Politics* 5.8.2–4 1310b13–31

(**5.8.2**) The tyrant, on the other hand, is appointed by the people and the masses to champion them against the notables, so that the commons suffer no injury at their hands. (**8.3**) This is made clear by past examples; for, generally speaking, most tyrants have come from amongst what one might call "demagogues" [popular leaders], who won support by criticizing the notables. It was in this way that tyrannies became established at the time when the cities had already grown in power.[1] Those established before that time arose from monarchs overriding the established norms of their position and aiming at more despotic power. Others likewise arose from men selected for the highest offices (for in the early days the people gave long tenure of office to magistracies [*demiourgiai*][2] and ambassadorial posts with religious functions), and yet others from the process of oligarchies selecting a single individual to have authority over their highest offices. (**8.4**) In all of these ways men could easily achieve their end, if they simply had the ambition, because the power was already in their hands, in some cases regal power and in others that of high office. Take, for example, Pheidon of Argos[3] and the other men, too, who established themselves as tyrants when they already had regal power, while the tyrants of Ionia and Phalaris[4] acquired their positions after holding high office. On the other hand, Panaetius in Leontini,[5] Cypselus in Corinth, Peisistratus in Athens, Dionysius in Syracuse,[6] and others achieved their position in one and the same manner, that is from being demagogues.

Notes

1. *The historian Thucydides (1.13.1) also links tyranny to the growth in Greece's power and to the increased revenues of states and individuals.*
2. *The demiourgia was a high magistracy whose function changed from one polis to another.*
3. *Pheidon ruled Argos probably in the first half of the seventh century. He is said to have defeated Sparta and Elis, only to be defeated later by a coalition of the two.*
4. *Phalaris ruled Acragas in Sicily in the second quarter of the sixth century. He allegedly roasted people in a hollow bronze bull that amplified their screams to sound like bellowing. The story served Greek and Roman authors as an illustration of the cruelty of tyrants.*
5. *Little is known of Panaetius, who ruled Sicilian Leontini in the early sixth century.*
6. *See **6.3** below for Cypselus, tyrant of Corinth, and Chapter 10 for Peisistratus, an Athenian tyrant. Dionysius I of Syracuse, ca. 430–367, was one of the most powerful rulers of his age. His successor and son, Dionysius II, went into exile in Corinth in 344.*

Aristotle suggests that tyrants used political office and popular discontent to attain power. Scholars identified this discontent with the rise of newly rich and middle-income groups who were blocked by the nobility from political power. Others point to the emergence of a hoplite (heavy infantry) class and mentality that emphasized collective military effort and contribution, thus undermining the legitimacy of the aristocratic monopoly over leadership (but see Chapter 8: "Hoplites and Their Values"). Scholars also regarded tyranny as a trendy political phenomenon that encouraged would-be tyrants to imitate the success of others. Indeed, tyrants tended to help each other. It should be noted, however, that the evidence to support each of these theories is tenuous.

Tyrants legitimized their rule through various means. Like Homeric leaders, they claimed personal distinction in war and sport. They built monumental public buildings, especially temples, and initiated public works to glorify themselves and to gain public gratitude and support. They also relied on non-aristocratic segments of the population by trying to help and patronize them.

Question

1. What, according to Aristotle, were the origins of tyrants and their means of attaining power?

6.3   Cypselus' Tyranny in Corinth (ca. 650–625)

Corinth, famous for its wealth, was ruled by hereditary kings, and from 747 by the aristocratic clan of the Bacchiadae. In the 650s, Cypselus usurped power from the Bacchiads, to whom he was related through his mother. The two chief sources on his career are Herodotus and the first-century historian Nicolaus of Damascus.

Herodotus framed the story of the Corinthian tyranny in a speech delivered by a Corinthian who dissuaded Sparta from restoring tyranny in Athens sometime after 509. For Herodotus' history, see **Introduction III.2**. Herodotus depicts most Greek tyrants as bad despotic rulers whose autocracy led to their downfall. His narrative on Cypselus focuses on the latter's family and birth. It was foretold that Cypselus would fall like a rock on Corinth's rulers, and after he was born the Bacchiads sent assassins to kill him. The baby's smile, however, melted the emissaries' hearts and his mother saved his life by hiding him in a chest (*kypselos*, hence his name). (See WEB **6.2** for Herodotus on Cypselus' birth and rescue.) When it comes to describing Cypselus' tyranny, Herodotus is brief.

6.3.A   Cypselus' Harsh Tyranny

> ## Herodotus 5.92e.2–f1
>
> (**5.92e.2**) …and Cypselus' tyranny was characterized by his expelling a large number of men, and depriving a large number of their wealth – but also by his depriving by far the largest number of their lives.
>
> (**92f.1**) Cypselus ruled for thirty years and ended his life well, and his son Periander succeeded to the tyranny.

Nicolaus of Damascus provides more details on Cypselus' regime. His account is based on the fourth-century historian Ephorus, who wrote a universal history and other works. According to Nicolaus, following Cypselus' miraculous survival his father took him to Olympia, and then to neighboring Cleonae. When Cypselus reached manhood, he decided to return to Corinth.

Nicolaus of Damascus *FGrHist* 90 F 57.4–8

(**57.4**) In the course of time Cypselus, wishing to return to Corinth, consulted the oracle at Delphi. When he received a favorable response he lost no time in coming to Corinth, where he quickly became one of the most admired people in town because he seemed to be courageous, intelligent, and a good man of the people – in contrast to the rest of the Bacchiads, who were violent and haughty. (**57.5**) After serving as polemarch[1] he was held in even greater affection, being by far the best of all who had held the office up to that time. For he was righteous in all his actions, and particularly in the following. There was a law in Corinth that those convicted in court were to be hauled before the polemarch and imprisoned for the payment of their fines, part of which actually went to the polemarch. Cypselus, however, neither imprisoned nor put in irons any citizen. Instead, he released some after recognizing people as guarantors for them, and in the case of others he himself became the guarantor; and in all cases he renounced his own share of the fine. As a result he was very much loved among the common people.

(**57.6**) When Cypselus saw that the Corinthians were ill disposed toward the Bacchiads, but that they did not have a champion whose lead they could follow to put them down, he offered his services and became the leader of the common people.[2] He told them of the oracle by which the elimination of the Bacchiads at his hands had been foretold, and how, because of this, they were in the past eager to destroy him when he was born and now, too, wished to ensnare him. But they had not been able to alter the course of destiny. The Corinthians accepted his words with relish, being hostile to the Bacchiads and well disposed toward Cypselus, and taking his courage as the surest guarantee of success in his project. Eventually, he put together a band of supporters [*hetairikon*][3] and killed the current ruler, Patrocleides,[4] who was an oppressive despot. The people swiftly made Cypselus king in his place.[5]

(**57.7**) Cypselus recalled the exiles and restored their rights to those who had been deprived of them by the Bacchiads; and thanks to that he could rely on them for whatever he wanted to do. Those not supporting him he deported to settlements abroad to facilitate his rule over the others. He sent them to Leucas and Anactorium, appointing his illegitimate sons Pylades and Echiades as their colony-founders.[6] The Bacchiads he drove into exile, confiscating their property for the state (they went to Corcyra). (**57.8**) Cypselus' rule over Corinth was easygoing; he had no bodyguard and was not disliked by the Corinthians. He died after a rule of thirty years [625], leaving four sons, of whom one, Periander, was legitimate, and the others bastards.

Notes

1. *The title polemarch implies a military function in addition to the duties mentioned in the passage.*
2. *Aristotle (Politics 5.7.4 1310b29–31, 9.22 1315b25–29) says that Cypselus was a leader of the people (demagogos) who needed no bodyguard, and that he came into power through demagoguery.*
3. *The word* hetairikon *implies an aristocratic association.*
4. *A different reading of the manuscript tradition suggests that his name was Hippocleides.*
5. *It is not unlikely that Cypselus gave himself the title of a king; cf. Salmon (1984, 190).*
6. *The names of Cypselus' illegitimate sons are different in other sources.*

Questions

1. What role does the supernatural play in Cypselus' story according to Herodotus (WEB **6.2**)?
2. According to Nicolaus' account (**6.3.B**), how did Cypselus attain power, and who benefited from his rule?
3. How would you explain the contrasting depictions of Cypselus' tyranny in Herodotus and Nicolaus?

6.4 Periander's Tyranny in Corinth (625–585)

Periander, Cypselus' son, ruled Corinth from 625 to ca. 585. Herodotus' account of his regime includes some famous advice to tyrants to secure their rule by eliminating aristocratic opposition. Tyrants who followed this advice gave rise to hostile aristocratic traditions about them and tyranny in general. (However, Aristotle *Politics* 3.7.2–4 1284a 17–37, 5.7.7 1311a8–23 notes that democracy and oligarchy used similar methods.) Periander's allegedly stripping Corinthian wives of their clothes and his necrophilia probably owed their origins to such traditions as well as to the image of tyrants as men whose power enabled them to cross moral and social boundaries.

Herodotus 5.92.f1–g4

(**5.92.f1**) …At the beginning of his reign Periander was more lenient than his father Cypselus, but when he struck up a relationship with Thrasybulus, tyrant of Miletus, through correspondence, he became far more murderous than Cypselus had been.[1] (**92f.2**) He sent a messenger to Thrasybulus, and from the tyrant learned the best manner of ruling his city-state while maintaining his security. When the man came to him from Periander, Thrasybulus took him out of the city to a cultivated piece of land. He went through the crop in the field, all the time questioning and cross-examining the messenger about why he had come from Corinth. And as he did so, he would break off any ear of wheat that he saw standing above the others, and after breaking it off he would throw it away, until in this manner he had destroyed the finest and richest stalks of the crop. (**92f.3**) After traversing the field and offering not a single word of advice he sent the messenger home.

When the messenger returned to Corinth Periander was eager to learn what advice Thrasybulus had for him. The messenger, however, said that Thrasybulus gave no advice, and added that he was amazed at Periander sending him to such a person. He was a madman who destroyed his own property, said the messenger, who gave an account of what he had seen of Thrasybulus' behavior. (**92g.1**) Periander, however, understood what Thrasybulus had been doing and worked out that he had been advising him to put to death citizens who stood out, and from that point on he brought upon his fellow-citizens all manner of misery. Anything that Cypselus had left undone in his period of butchery and oppression Periander finished off.

One day Periander stripped naked all the women of Corinth, and this was because of his own wife, Melissa.[2] (**92g.2**) Periander had sent a delegation to the oracle of the dead on the Acheron River in Thesprotia to inquire about some money that had been given in trust to a friend of his.[3] The specter of Melissa appeared there, declaring that she would not identify or describe the location of the money since she was cold and naked. She could not make use of the clothes Periander had buried with her, she explained, since they had not been burned. As evidence for him that she was telling the truth in this matter, she declared that Periander had put his bread in a cold oven. (**92g.3**) Now this testimonial was convincing to Periander, who had had sexual relations with Melissa when she was dead, and when it was reported back to him he immediately issued an edict for all the women of Corinth to go from their homes to the temple of Hera. Assuming they were going to a festival, the women went dressed in their finest apparel. Periander, however, had surreptitiously stationed his bodyguards at the temple, and he made all the women disrobe, free persons and handmaids alike. He then gathered all the clothing together in a ditch and burned it, offering a prayer to Melissa. (**92g.4**) After doing this he sent a second embassy to the oracle where Melissa's ghost now revealed the spot where she had put the money of the friend.

Notes

1. *Thrasybulus was the tyrant of Miletus at the beginning of the sixth century. In Aristotle's version of this story (Politics 3.8.3 1284a26–33), it is Periander who advises Thrasybulus. Some tyrants, including Periander, were famous for their sagacity.*
2. *Melissa was the daughter of Procles, the tyrant of Epidaurus, whom Periander is said to have murdered (Herodotus 3.52).*
3. *The oracle of the dead at Ephyra was linked to Odysseus' journey to Hades.*

See WEB **6.5** for additional information on tyranny in Corinth, including a link to a bust of Periander.

Tyranny ended in Corinth three years after Periander's death, when his heir and nephew, Psammetichus, was killed following either a domestic plot (Nicolaus *FGrHist* 90 F 60.1) or Spartan intervention (Plutarch *Moralia* 859c–d).

Questions

1. What mores has Periander violated?
2. Describe the relationship between the Corinthian tyrants and the city's elite (**6.3**, **6.4**, and WEB **6.2**).

6.6 A Failed Attempt at Tyranny in Athens: Cylon (632)

At the time that Corinth was ruled by tyrants, the Athenian Cylon tried unsuccessfully to establish a tyranny in his homeland. Cylon had won the footrace in the 640 Olympics, and some time later – many scholars favor

632 – he seized the Athenian acropolis. He was aided by local friends and troops procured from his father-in-law, Theagenes, the tyrant of Megara. Because our sources are chiefly interested in the subsequent curse on those responsible for killing Cylon's supporters, they fail to discuss his motives. He likely hoped that his Olympic glory would earn him support and legitimacy as a man of excellence. He failed on account of the impious act of occupying a religious site, or because his foreign troops may have alienated the Athenians. Indeed, there is no solid evidence that Athens at that time experienced a social or political crisis that Cylon could have exploited.

Thucydides relates Cylon's attempt in the context of a Spartan demand on the eve of the Peloponnesian War (431) to banish the "cursed," i.e., Pericles, from Athens. Among those involved in the killing of the Cylonians was Pericles' maternal ancestor, Megacles, of the prominent Alcmeonid family (Plutarch *Solon* 12.1). The curse made those who were responsible for killing the Cylonians, including their descendants, both polluted and polluting. Judging by the history of the Alcmeonid family, however, it did not have a devastating effect on their political fortunes.

Herodotus' brief account of the Cylon affair (WEB **6.7**) was written before Thucydides. It differs from him in calling the officials responsible for the Cylonians' murder not archons but "*prytaneis* of the naucraries." The identity of these officials is uncertain. Possibly naucraries were groups of people taxed to finance a warship, and their presidents (*prytaneis*) were officials in charge of collecting the tax as well as having other financial and military duties. Herodotus also indicates that Cylon and his brother did not escape but were killed. Despite scholarly attempts, the two accounts cannot be comfortably reconciled. Plutarch (*Solon* 12.1–2) also reports on the plot.

Thucydides 1.126.3–12

(**1.126.3**) Now the history of this curse was as follows:

In the distant past there lived an Athenian Olympic victor, Cylon. He was of noble birth and very powerful, and he had married a daughter of a Megarian, Theagenes, who was at the time tyrant of Megara. (**126.4**) Consulting the Delphic oracle, Cylon was instructed by the god to seize the acropolis of Athens during the greatest festival of Zeus. (**126.5**) Cylon then acquired an armed troop from Theagenes and also persuaded his friends to join him; and when the Olympic festival in the Peloponnese came round he seized the acropolis, with the intention of establishing a tyranny. He thought that this was the greatest festival of Zeus, and that it had special relevance for him as an Olympic victor. (**126.6**) But whether it was the "greatest festival" in Attica or in another location that was meant Cylon did not stop to consider, nor did the oracle make it clear. Now, in fact, the Athenians do have the so-called Diasia, a festival of Zeus Meilichius [Gracious], their greatest festival of Zeus. It is held outside the city and the whole population participates, offering not many animal sacrifices, but rather offerings specific to the locality. Cylon, then, believed his assessment to be correct and proceeded with the coup. (**126.7**) When the Athenians heard about it, they came from the fields in large numbers to resist the conspirators, and took up a position to blockade them. (**126.8**) As time went on, however, most of the Athenians tired of the siege and went home, leaving it to the nine archons to supervise the operation and giving them full powers to settle the whole affair as they thought best – in that period the nine archons handled most affairs of state. (**126.9**) Cylon and his men were hard pressed by the siege as food and water ran out. (**126.10**) Cylon and his brother therefore slipped away. The rest were under severe pressure and a number were starving to death, and so they proceeded to sit as suppliants before the altar on the acropolis.

(**126.11**) When those of the Athenians charged with supervising the situation saw the men expiring in the precinct, they raised them to their feet on the understanding that they would do them no harm. Then they led them off and executed them. Some of the conspirators even sat at the altars of the Solemn Goddesses[1] as they were passing by, but the Athenians killed them, too. As a result, the perpetrators, and their descendants after them, were termed accursed and offenders against the goddess. (**126.12**) The Athenians therefore drove out these accursed individuals, and so too, later on, did the Spartan Cleomenes[2] along with some disaffected Athenians. They expelled the living and dug up and threw out of the land the bones of the dead. At a later date, however, the exiles returned, and their descendants still remain in the city.

Notes

1. *The Solemn Goddesses are the Erinyes or Eumenidae (Kindly Ones).*
2. *Cleomenes was a Spartan king who banished the tyrant Hippias from Athens ca. 509 (see **10.12**: "The Expulsion of the Tyrants").*

See Chapter 10 for tyranny in Athens in the second half of the sixth century.

Review Questions

1. Why did Cypselus succeed in becoming a tyrant while Cylon failed? (See **6.3**, **6.6** and WEB **6.5**, **6.7**.)
2. Discuss the links between religion and power in the stories of the Corinthian tyrants and Cylon.
3. What role did the people play in the rise of tyranny?
4. Discuss the relationship between tyrants and aristocracy.

Suggested Readings

Greek tyranny: Andrewes 1956; McGlew 1993; Cawkwell 1995; G. Anderson 2005. *Tyrants and new wealth*: Ure 1922. *Tyrants and hoplites*: Salmon 1977. *Tyrants as a political trend*: Murray 1993, 144–145. *Tyranny in Corinth*: Salmon 1984, 186–230; Murray 1993, 145–153. *Herodotus on Corinthian and other tyrants*: Vernant 1982; Lateiner 1989, 169–175; Gray 1996; Dewald 2003. *The oracles about Cypselus*: Parke and Wormell 1956, 1: 116–117;

McGlew 1993, 61–74. *The Delphic oracle*: Parke and Wormell 1956; Fontenrose 1978; Bowden 2005. *Nicolaus on Cypselus*: Salmon 1984, 188–192. *Tyrants and freedom from restraints*: McGlew 1993, 26–30. *Corinthian pottery and trade*: Salmon 1984, 101–158. *Cylon's coup*: Lang 1967; Lambert 1986 (but also Wallinga 2000, esp. 140 for the naucraries); Hornblower 1991–2008, 1: 202–210. *The curse*: R. Parker 1983, 16–17.

7

Archaic and Classical Sparta

CHAPTER CONTENTS

Ancient Greece from Homer to Alexander: The Evidence, First Edition. Joseph Roisman.
© 2011 Blackwell Publishing Ltd. Translations © 2011 John Yardley. Published 2011 by Blackwell Publishing Ltd.

The history of early and even Classical Sparta is handicapped by our problematic evidence. Except for very few Spartan sources, most of the accounts on Sparta were written by outsiders, some without the benefit of having visited the state. Significant information comes from late authors who anachronistically attributed to early Sparta later laws and practices based on the Spartan belief in the intact preservation of their institutions and way of life. In the Hellenistic period, the Spartan kings Agis IV and Cleomenes III legitimized their reforms by presenting them as based on alleged precedents from an earlier and better Sparta. Their actions and propaganda had an impact on depictions of Archaic Sparta in some sources.

Authors were also impressed by the prolonged political and military dominance of Sparta in Greece, which stretched from the Archaic period to Sparta's defeat by Thebes in the battle of Leuctra in 371. Sparta's success led many Greeks to view it as a desirable model and to idealize its community and institutions. The Spartans themselves contributed to the bias of their history by imagining themselves and their ancestors as living in the best-governed Greek polis. The result was what modern scholars have termed a "Spartan mirage," a distorted or fictional image of Sparta that held sway over the Spartans themselves and colored ancient and modern perceptions. This was a construct of a politically stable state with an egalitarian and well-ordered society. It characterized the Spartans as excelling other Greeks in character, communal spirit, and especially in military achievement. It depicted Spartan men as strong, highly disciplined, fearing shame more than death, and eager to sacrifice their lives for the common good. Spartan men were supported by equally dedicated women. This construct was not entirely imaginary, but it represented an idealized state more than the real Sparta.

This chapter discusses Spartan images, ideology, and practices, including those that violated Spartan ideals. Although recent studies claim that many Spartan practices and concepts should be dated to no earlier than the Classical Age, it is assumed that the phenomena described here belonged to Archaic times, and even if archaized, the desire to make them ancient is worthy of consideration. Accordingly, the chapter discusses Sparta's early wars with its neighbors and its treatment of the occupied population, especially the helots. It deals with the Spartan lawgiver Lycurgus, the regulations attributed to him, and the city's political leaders and institutions. The examination of Spartan society includes the relationship between family and state, the schooling of boys and girls, the nature of Spartan marriage, and the common messes. Spartan values and the relations between ideology and reality are illustrated as well. The chapter concludes by discussing Sparta's relationships with states in and outside the Peloponnese.

See WEB **7.1** for Sparta's origins and Thucydides' description of fifth-century Sparta as an undistinguished settlement.

7.2 The Messenian Wars (735–650) and the Conquered Population

The Spartan expansion in Laconia and westward into Messenia in the eighth century had a pivotal impact on the state and Spartan way of life.

Sparta completed its occupation of Messenia following two wars, which many historians date to ca. 735–715 and ca. 660–650, respectively. The dates are not secure, but it is safe to say that Messenia was finally subjugated by the end of the seventh century. To some extent Messenia substituted for the Spartans the search for resources overseas, which in part motivated Greek colonization (see Chapter 4). Sparta's only colony was Taras (Tarentum) in southern Italy, which, according to unreliable traditions, was founded by a group of undesirable Spartans around 706.

The most informative sources on the Messenian wars are unfortunately too late or heavily influenced by tendentious and unreliable earlier sources. Yet a fragmentary poem by the Archaic poet Tyrtaeus is instructive about the First Messenian War. Tyrtaeus was a Spartan by birth or by naturalization, and, according to a late source, was a contemporary of the Second Messenian War. The rich land of Messenia mentioned in his poem probably constituted a major incentive for its occupation.

Tyrtaeus fr. 5 (West)

To our king Theopompus, loved by the gods, thanks to whom we captured broad Messene – Messene that is good for plowing and good for planting. Over this land the warrior fathers of our fathers fought without pause for nineteen years, with hearts ever courageous. In the twentieth year the Messenians fled from great mountains of Ithome, leaving behind their rich farms.[1]

Note

1. *The fragment is collated from three different sources. King Theopompus is also reputed to have helped shape the Spartan government and introduced the office of the ephorate.*

The occupied land of Messenia was divided among the conquerors. In Sparta, land ownership was of crucial importance because owning a plot of land (*kleros*) and contributing produce to the common messes (see **7.22**) were among the conditions for Spartan citizenship.

7.3   The Helots

The Spartans divided the pre-Dorian population in both Laconia and Messenia into two main categories. The more privileged group comprised perioeci (*perioikoi*, lit. "dwellers around"). They enjoyed personal freedom and local autonomy, but had no political rights in Sparta. Many of them were farmers. After Spartan male citizens made themselves an elite whose sole legitimate occupation was fighting, the perioeci filled the vacuum by becoming craftsmen and traders. They were obliged to obey Spartan calls to military duty, and in the late fifth century they served as hoplites with Spartans in the same units. The perioeci cooperated only rarely with the other category of the subjugated population – helots – against the Spartans.

Helots ("captives") comprised the second category of the occupied population. In some respects they resembled chattel slaves, and in others they stood between slaves and medieval serfs. The Spartans helotized local inhabitants already in Laconia, but the bulk were Messenian Greeks. The state assigned Spartan masters to helots, who lived on lands that used to be their own.

Tyrtaeus describes the treatment of helots in verses which the second-century CE geographer and traveler Pausanias paraphrases. The reference to helots' wives suggests that, unlike chattel slaves, they were allowed to have families. Indeed, in the 460s the Spartans permitted rebel helots to leave Messenia with their wives and children (Thucydides 1.103).

7.3.A   Tyrtaeus on the Helots

Tyrtaeus frs. 6–7 (West) = Pausanias *Description of Greece* 4.14.4–5

(**Fr. 6**) Like asses in distress under heavy loads, bearing to their masters from wretched necessity half of all the fruits the land produces.

(**Fr. 7**) The Messenians, they and their wives alike, mourned for their masters whenever death's tragic lot overtook one of them.

It appears that the helots were sharecroppers, who gave up half of their crop. This form of payment constituted an easier and more flexible burden than fixed taxes. The state also set limits on the power of the Spartan masters over their helots. The first-century geographer Strabo describes the origins of helotage, based on the fourth-century historian Ephorus.

Strabo *Geography* 8.5.4

... But Agis,[1] son of Eurysthenes, took from them [i.e., those who lived around Sparta] their constitutional equality and commanded that they pay taxes to Sparta. All obeyed apart from the Heleians, who live in Helos. They revolted, and after being defeated in battle they were condemned to serfdom on certain fixed conditions, namely that no owner was to liberate them or sell them beyond the country's borders.[2] This conflict was called "The War with the Helots." In fact, the helot system, which lasted right down to the time of the Roman hegemony, was pretty well the invention of Agis and his courtiers.[3] For the Lacedaemonians kept the helots virtually as slaves of the state, assigning to them places to live and specific jobs to do.

Notes

1. *Agis I was the founder of the Agiad royal dynasty in Sparta, presumably in the tenth century.*
2. *The meaning of this restriction is unclear and refers perhaps to a ban on selling helots outside Sparta.*
3. *Since the historian Ephorus died prior to the Roman hegemony, it is unlikely that the second half of this passage is taken from him.*

It is a matter of debate how public or private the helots' servitude was, although it is safe to say that the Spartan state had a paramount interest in keeping them subjugated. For helots provided the infrastructure necessary for the Spartans to concentrate on training for war and maintaining their way of life. Additionally, without helots working his land, a Spartan would be unable to meet one of the conditions for citizenship, which was to contribute food to his common mess (*syssition*; see **7.22**). Yet the helots also threatened the very existence of the state.

Spartan demography is a knotty problem if only because the Spartans kept the number of their citizens secret. The number of helots is even more difficult to estimate, although it is a fair assumption that there were many more helots than Spartans. The threat of revolt, especially by Messenian helots, must have weighed heavily on Spartan minds. The fourth-century philosophers Plato and Aristotle mention frequent helot revolts (Plato *Laws* 6.777b–c: WEB **36.5.I** Aristotle *Politics* 2.5.2 1269a37–39).

Spartans resorted to different measures to deal with the threat, some of which were drastic and inhuman. In 424, the Spartan government permitted its general Brasidas to recruit helots for a campaign in northeastern Greece. Thucydides says that, fearing sedition, it gladly allowed Brasidas to take the helots away, then describes a mass killing of helots at an uncertain date.

7.4 Eliminating Helots

Thucydides 4.80.3–4

(**4.80.3**) At all times Lacedaemonian policy was mostly focused on protective measures against the helots, and through fear of their propensity for mischief and of their numbers the Spartans once took the following course of action. They issued a public order for a selection to be made of all helots who felt they had provided the Spartans with particularly distinguished service against the enemy, apparently to grant them their freedom. They were, in fact, putting them to a test, thinking that it was precisely those individuals who thought they should be freed first who would be the ones most likely to have the spirit to attack them. (**80.4**) They selected about 2,000, and these men put on garlands and went around the temples as though they had already been freed. Not long afterwards, however, the Spartans did away with them, with no one knowing how each of them met his end.

7.5 The *Krypteia*

It is likely that the Spartans' treatment of the helots was closely linked to their evolution into a community of warriors. Fear of helots encouraged the Spartans to promote ideals of military excellence, exclusivity, and communal equality that fostered solidarity among citizens. Concerns about the helots also had an impact on Sparta's foreign policy, which was cautious and sought to prevent runaway helots from finding shelter.

Plutarch reports on the institution of the *krypteia*, an elite group of young men that was sent to kill helots in the fields. The license to kill, as well as frequent declarations of war on the helots, freed the killers from punishment and pollution. Some scholars have interpreted the *krypteia* as an initiation rite to adulthood, which the Spartans incorporated into the socialization of their youth. In Plato's *Laws* 1.633b, it is described only as a test of enduring cold in the winter, which appeared to have been required of any Spartan male youth. The sending of selected young men to kill helots suggests that the state, rather than the individual landowner, controlled the helots' fate. The mockery and humiliation of helots as reported by Plutarch illustrates their otherness in comparison with the Spartans.

Plutarch *Lycurgus* 28.1–13

(**28.1**) In these measures there is not a trace of injustice or high-handedness, the criticism that some people level against the laws of Lycurgus, saying that they are effective in fostering courage but wanting in terms of justice. (**28.2**) Now the so-called *krypteia* (if indeed it is one of Lycurgus' institutions, as Aristotle recorded) might have given Plato, as well as Aristotle, such an opinion about the constitution and the man.[1]

(**28.3**) The *krypteia* functioned as follows. Those in charge of the youth would occasionally send those young men who seemed the most intelligent into different parts of the countryside, taking nothing with them other than their daggers and such food as they needed. (**28.4**) In the daytime the youths would scatter into coverts, concealing themselves and resting, but at night they would come down to the roads and cut the throats of any helots they caught. (**28.5**) Often, too, they would make their way into the fields, where they would kill the strongest and most enterprising of them. (**28.6**) In the same vein, Thucydides, in his *Peloponnesian War*, tells [4.80.3–4: see **7.4**] of some helots who had been singled out for their courage by being crowned with garlands by the Spartiates, as though they had been freed, and then going around the temples of the gods. Shortly afterwards, however, they all disappeared, more than two thousand of them, without anyone being able to account for their loss, either at the time or later. (**28.7**) And there is especially the statement of Aristotle that, at the beginning of their term of office, the ephors formally declared war on the helots so that killing them would involve no pollution.

(**28.8**) In general, the Spartiates were ruthless and cruel in their treatment of the helots. They would force them to drink large amounts of unmixed wine and bring them into their communal messes to show their children what drunkenness was. (**28.9**) And they would order them to sing vile and ludicrous songs and dance vile and ludicrous dances, and to avoid those that were suitable for free men. (**28.10**) And so it is said that, later on, during the expedition of the Thebans into Laconia [370/69], the helots taken by the Thebans refused an order to sing the works of Terpander, Alcman, and Spendon the Laconian, saying it was against their masters' wishes.[2] (**28.11**) Thus those who say that in Lacedaemon the free man is truly free while a slave is truly a slave have well understood the difference between the two.

(**28.12**) In my opinion, such instances of cruelty began later amongst the Spartiates, and did so especially after the great earthquake when, historians tell us, the helots joined the Messenians to attack them, inflicting serious damage on the countryside and putting the city in the greatest danger [ca. 460].[3] (**28.13**) For I personally could not ascribe to Lycurgus such a brutal institution as the *krypteia*, not if I judge his character from his general kindness and uprightness – a character to which the god also bore witness.

Notes

1. *Aristotle discussed these practices in his* Constitution of the Lacedaemonians, *now lost. For Plato see the introduction to this passage.*
2. *Terpander was a poet from Lesbos, who won the musical contest in the Spartan festival of the Carnea in 676. Alcman was a seventh-century Spartan poet who wrote hymns to the gods and choral songs sung by maidens in Spartan festivals (see **7.17**). Spendon is unknown.*
3. *See **18.12** ("Sparta's Wars in the Peloponnese") for these events.*

Questions

1. What motivated the Spartans to wage war on the Messenians?
2. In what ways were the helots similar to but also different from slaves?
3. How did the Spartans control the perioeci and the helots (**7.3–5**)?

7.6 Lycurgus' Regulations

The Spartans would not acknowledge that their relationship with the helots contributed to the way their society and state were shaped. By their account, they owed their government and way of life to their lawgiver, Lycurgus.

The Spartans believed that Lycurgus saved them from a prolonged crisis. Literary and archaeological evidence indeed points to a state of inequality and restlessness in seventh- and sixth-century Sparta. See WEB **7.7.I–II** on the crisis and economic disparity in early Sparta.

The many contradictory traditions about Lycurgus make it impossible to ascertain when or if he ever existed. Whether Lycurgus was a historical or invented figure, it is fair to assume that he was used by the Spartans to legitimize existing and even new practices and institutions by attributing them to him. Scholars tend to place the reforms ascribed to Lycurgus at the end of the seventh century or even later. See WEB **7.7.III** for the second-century CE biographer Plutarch's summary of ancient views about Lycurgus' identity, which reveal the lack of consensus about him. For Plutarch, see **Introduction III.6**.

According to the Spartans, Lycurgus established *eunomia*, a political and social system that guaranteed law, order, and enduring stability. The system allowed for personal fulfillment through service to the polis and supposedly made the Spartans superior to other Greeks. The Spartans proudly believed that Lycurgus' measures remained unchanged since he introduced them.

Herodotus 1.65.2–66.1

(**1.65.2**) How the Spartans changed to a good, lawful government [*eunomia*] was as follows. Lycurgus was a prominent Spartiate who went to consult the oracle at Delphi. As soon as he entered the great hall of the temple, the Pythian priestess said to him: (**65.3**) "So you have arrived at my rich temple, Lycurgus, you who are dear to Zeus and to all who have their homes on Olympus! I ask myself whether I shall call you a god or a man in my prophecy, but I think rather that you are a god, Lycurgus." (**65.4**) Some people say that, in addition to this, the Pythia revealed to him the system of government that the Spartiates have today. In the account of the Spartans themselves, however, Lycurgus brought these institutions back from Crete[1] when he had become the guardian of Leobotas, his nephew who was a king of Sparta.[2] (**65.5**) For as soon as he took up his position as guardian he changed all the rules of the society and saw to it that no one broke them. It was also Lycurgus who later on established all the military institutions, the sworn companies [*enomotiai*], the Thirties [*triakades*], and the messes [*syssitia*] as well as the ephors and the council of elders.[3] (**66.1**) With these changes the Spartans achieved good government. When Lycurgus died they built him a shrine and they hold him in high esteem.

Notes

1. *A common ancient tradition held that the Spartans were influenced by Cretan practices, but the similarities could be due to their common Dorian heritage.*

2. *Leobotas is said to have reigned in the ninth century. Aristotle (*Politics *2.7.1 1271b25–26) and Plutarch (*Lycurgus *3.4) name Lycurgus' ward, Charilaus.*
3. *The sworn company was a military unit comprising thirty-five to forty men during the Classical era. The Thirty is an unknown military unit. See this chapter for the other terms.*

Questions

1. What difficulties beset Sparta prior to Lycurgus' legislation according to the testimonies in WEB **7.7.I–II**?
2. Discuss the problems of authenticating Lycurgus' legislation in light of the traditions about him in Herodotus (**7.6**) and Plutarch (WEB **7.7.III**).

7.8   The Spartan Government and the *Great Rhetra*

The Spartans were very proud of their government and noted that, unlike other poleis, they experienced no tyranny. Needless to say, the Spartan political structure evolved and changed over time.

The most ancient sources on the early government of Sparta are a poem by Tyrtaeus and an archaic document cited by the biographer Plutarch, who might have found it in Aristotle's *Constitution of the Lacedaemonians* (now lost).

Tyrtaeus' poem, entitled *Eunomia* ("good government"), survived only in fragments. The first fragment (fr. 2) calls upon the Spartans to obey their kings – Sparta was unique in having two royal houses of the Agiad and Europontid dynasties. The second fragment (fr. 4) mentions an oracle, which according to the historian Diodorus of Sicily (7.12.5–6) was given to Lycurgus. The poem is not entirely clear about the division of power in the state. Tyrtaeus tells the Spartans that Apollo confirmed the power of the kings and elders to counsel the city. The people should respond with straight *rhetrai* (lit. "utterances"), which probably means laws or agreements. This gives the people power to approve or reject the kings' and elders' counsel. Yet the Greek can also be understood as if the people "respond to *rhetrai*" of the kings and elders, which suggests a significantly lesser power. The fragmentary lines that precede the first fragment have been restored as a call to obey the kings.

7.8.A   Tyrtaeus on the Spartan Government

Tyrtaeus frs. 2, 4 (West)

(**Fr. 2**) For the son of Cronus and husband of beautifully garlanded Hera, Zeus himself, has given this city to the Heraclidae, with whom, leaving windy Erineus, we reached the broad island of Pelops.[1]

(**Fr. 4**) After hearing Phoebus [Apollo], they brought home from Pytho the oracles and sure predictions of the god. He told the kings – who are honored by the gods and who care for the lovely city of Sparta – and the hoary elders to commence their consultation. And the common people he told to answer with straightforward utterances [*rhetrai*], making good comments, taking just action in everything, and not delivering crooked advice to the city.[2] Victory and strength would attend the mass of the people, he said. Such was Phoebus' declaration to the city on such matters.

Notes

1.   *Erineus, in Doris in central Greece, was regarded as the mother-city of the Dorians. The island of Pelops was the Peloponnesian peninsula.*
2.   *The line is corrupt, and the word "crooked" is a modern emendation.*

Plutarch cites the so-called *Great Rhetra*, which provides additional information on the government of Sparta. This highly controversial document mentions the *gerousia*, a council of elders that included the kings. The kings in the following document seem to have less authority than they do in Tyrtaeus' poem. The *rhetra* also gives the people power to approve or reject the elders' proposals. Many scholars, however, agree that what Plutarch describes as a later rider setting limits on popular power was, in fact, part of the original *rhetra*.

7.8.B   Plutarch on Lycurgus' *Rhetra*

Plutarch *Lycurgus* 6.1–9

(**6.1**) So enthused was Lycurgus about this form of government [of the elders] that he brought back from Delphi an oracle on the subject which they call a "*rhetra*." (**6.2**) It runs as follows: "Having founded a sanctuary of Zeus Syllanius and Athena Syllania;[1] having formed tribes and made '*obai*';[2] and having set up a *gerousia* of thirty members, including the *archagetai* [leaders] – after this hold an Apella [*appelazein*] from time to time between Babyca and Cnacion, and thus make proposals and lodge objections. But the people are to have the authority [*kyria*] and the power."[3]

(**6.3**) In the above "form tribes" and "make *obai*" refer to dividing and arranging the citizen body in groups, some of which Lycurgus called "tribes" and others "*obai*." "*Archagetai*" means "kings," and "hold an Apella" means "hold an assembly," because it refers to Apollo as the origin and source of the constitution.[4] (**6.4**) Babyca they now call [...] and Cnacion they call Oenus (Aristotle claims Cnacion is a river and Babyca a bridge). The Spartans held their assemblies between the two, as there were no halls or any other permanent structure. (**6.5**) Lycurgus did not think that such things were helpful for sound deliberation, that they were, in fact, detrimental to it. For he believed they stupefied and befuddled the intellects of those assembled with fatuous thoughts, one's attention during the meetings being turned to statues and pictures, or to the stage ornamentation in theaters, or to the excessively detailed work on the roofs of meeting halls.

(**6.6**) When the populace had gathered, Lycurgus permitted no one other than the elders and kings to make a proposal, but the people were sovereign in judging the measures that they put forward. (**6.7**) Later, however, the common people began distorting and perverting the proposals by subtracting from them and making additions, and so the kings Polydorus and Theopompus [ca. 760–700] added the following article to the *rhetra*: (**6.8**) "If the people vote for a crooked motion, the elders and leaders are authorized to set it aside," which is to say not confirm the decision, but instead completely break up and dismiss the assembly of the people on the grounds that they are making changes and amendments to a proposal contrary to the state's best interests. (**6.9**) The kings also persuaded the citizens that the addition was authorized by the god, as Tyrtaeus possibly suggests in the following: [continues as Tyrtaeus fr. 4 above].

Notes

1. *Syllanian Zeus and Athena are unknown cults. Yet Zeus was the father of Heracles, the ancestor of the Spartan kings, and Athena was the city's patron goddess.*
2. *The Spartans were divided into three tribes. The* obai *were local and kinship units, probably the villages that comprised Sparta.*
3. *The text of this sentence is corrupt.*
4. *The assembly's association with Apollo's festivals suggests that these were monthly meetings.*

Questions

1. Compare and contrast the powers of the kings, council, and assembly as described by Tyrtaeus and Plutarch (**7.8.A–B**).
2. What might aristocrats as well as commoners find appealing in the Spartan political system?

7.9 Spartan Kingship

The Spartans explained the origins of their dual kingship by attributing it to twin descendants of Heracles. The privileges and powers of the early Spartan kings are shrouded in mystery. In Archaic and Classical times, however, they held supreme command over the military and so could influence foreign policy as well. They fulfilled certain religious and judicial duties and enjoyed special honors in life and death. Their death rites indicated their heroization – they were, after all, Heracles' descendants – as well as their identification with the state. Herodotus describes their powers and honors. See WEB **7.10** for Xenophon's account of additional royal honors and powers in Sparta.

Herodotus 6.56–59

(**6.56**) The Spartiates have conferred the following privileges on their kings. They both hold two priest-hoods, that of Lacedaemonian Zeus and that of Heavenly Zeus, and can commence a war on any country they choose, and no Spartiate may stand in their way, on pain of bringing a curse upon himself. On campaign the kings take the lead in the advance, and are last in retreat; and they have a bodyguard of a hundred handpicked men in the field. On their expeditions they have at their disposal as much live-stock as they wish, and they may take for themselves the hides and backs of all sacrificed animals.

(**57.1**) Such are their privileges in war; in peacetime they have been granted others, which are as fol-lows. At a public sacrifice, the kings are the first seated for the feast, and the servants must start with them, giving each of them twice as much of everything as the other diners. They have the right to make the first libation, and to take the hides of the sacrificed animals. (**57.2**) At every new moon, and on the seventh of the month, they are each given a full-grown sacrificial animal, at public expense, for sacrifice in the temple of Apollo, and along with it a bushel of barley-meal and a Laconian quart of wine. They also have select seating at all the games. In addition, it is the prerogative of the kings to appoint citizens of their choice as *proxenoi* [guest-friends], and of each of them to select two Pythians, officials who deal with Delphi, and who take their meals with the kings at public expense. (**57.3**) If the kings decline to attend the public dinner, two *choinikes* [3.10 liters] of barley-meal and a *cotylê* [0.38 liter] of wine are sent to each of them at his home; and if they do attend they must be given double helpings of everything.[1] The same honor must be accorded them if they are invited to dinner by private individuals. (**57.4**) It is they who guard the oracles that are received (and the Pythians also have knowledge of these). The kings' jurisdictional functions are limited to the follow-ing, but in them they have sole authority. If a girl has been left as an heiress without her father having betrothed her, it is they who decide to whom she should be married, and they also have jurisdiction over public roads.[2] (**57.5**) Furthermore, if a person wants to adopt a child, that has to be done before the kings. They also have the right to sit with the elders, who are twenty-eight in number. If they do not wish to attend, those of the elders who are most closely related to them are entitled to assume the kings' privileges, casting two proxy votes for them, and a third for themselves.[3]

(**58.1**) Such are the rights accorded the kings during their lifetime by the community of Spartiates, and in death they receive the following. Horsemen carry news of the event throughout Laconia, and women beat cauldrons as they wend their way through the city. When this has taken place, two free persons from each house, a man and a woman, are obliged to befoul themselves in mourning, and failure to do so incurs heavy fines. (**58.2**) Lacedaemonian custom on the deaths of their kings is the same as that of barbarians in Asia, for most barbarians observe that very custom on their kings' deaths. When a king of the Lacedaemonians dies, not only the Spartiates but a fixed number of the perioeci are obliged to attend the funeral from all over Lacedaemon. (**58.3**) When these, the helots, and the Spartiates themselves are gathered together in one place, many thousands strong, they, in company with the women, fervently beat their foreheads and break into interminable lamentation, declaring on each occasion that the last of their kings to die was the very best of their kings. If any of the kings dies in battle, they make a statue of him, set it on a richly covered bier, and carry it out for burial. When they have buried it, there is no commercial business or electoral meeting for a period of ten days, days which they devote entirely to mourning.

(**59**) There is another practice in which the Spartans resemble the Persians. When another king takes the throne after the previous king's death, the new king releases from his obligations any of the Spartiates indebted to the crown or the state. Amongst the Persians, too, the king releases all the cities from any outstanding tribute when he ascends the throne.

Notes

1. *Apparently the kings were not obliged to participate in the common messes, or lost this privilege in the late fifth century (Plutarch* Lycurgus *12.3). The kings did not have to go through the Spartan education system either.*
2. *It is unclear if the royal jurisdiction over heiresses and adoption was real or a mere formality. In the fourth century this power was largely transferred to private individuals.*
3. *Thucydides, who understood Herodotus to mean that each king had two votes, sharply disagreed (1.20.3).*

Questions

1. What were the powers of the Spartan kings according to Herodotus (**7.9**) and Xenophon (WEB **7.10**)?
2. Which communal values were confirmed in the honors paid to the Spartan kings?

7.11   The Spartan *Gerousia* (Council)

The political power of the Spartan kings was constrained by the powers of the *gerousia* (council of elders) and the popular assembly. The *gerousia* was made up of the two kings and twenty-eight men, aged sixty and over, who were probably of elite background and who served for life. The manner of their election by acclamation, which was also used in other voting in the assembly (Thucydides 1.87.2), reflected the Spartan devaluation of individualism. In the *gerousia*, however, voting was not done by shouting. The *gerousia* sat in judgment of criminal cases, including those of the kings, and as suggested by the great *rhetra*, had the power to initiate policy, make proposals, and even reject popular decisions. Its members enjoyed the prestige of the office and the respect accorded old age in Sparta.

Plutarch *Lycurgus* 26.1–5

(**26.1**) As noted above, Lycurgus initially saw to the appointment of elders himself, choosing from amongst those who had taken part in his project, but later he established a system whereby a man judged to be of the highest quality [*aretê*] amongst those who were over sixty replaced an elder who died. (**26.2**) And this was regarded as the most important contest in the world, and the most keenly fought. For the judgment bore not on who was the swiftest among the swift, or the strongest among the strong, but on who amongst the good and the sound-minded [*sophron*] was the best and most sound-minded. And the reward he received for his excellence was a lifelong power within the government that was virtually absolute, it being for him to decide whether citizens were to live or die, or be dishonored – to decide, generally, on the most important things in life.

(**26.3**) The electoral process was as follows. The assembly would be convened, and a number of chosen individuals would be secluded in a room close by, unable to see the assembly or be seen by it, and only hearing the shouts of its members. (**26.4**) For, as in other matters, it was by acclamation that they judged the candidates. These did not all appear together but were brought in individually, in an order decided by lot, and they would walk in silence through the assembly. (**26.5**) The sequestered men had writing-tablets and on them they recorded for each person the volume of the applause. They were unaware of the man's identity, knowing only that he was first, second, third, or whatever he was, of those brought in. Whoever received the longest and loudest applause they declared elected.

Question

1. What was Spartan in the qualifications of candidates to the *gerousia*?

7.12   The Ephors

The popular assembly, composed of male Spartan citizens, elected men to office and voted on legislation and matters of policy, including war and peace. But its lack of initiative, and the fact that speakers in it tended to be the kings, elders, and magistrates called ephors, demonstrate the limited extent of popular power in Sparta.

The ephors (*ephoroi*, "overseers") were five annually elected officials. They are not mentioned in Tyrtaeus' poem and the *Great Rhetra*, which implies that they became powerful relatively late in Spartan history. The Spartans, however, ascribed the ephorate either to Lycurgus (Herodotus 1.65.5: see **7.6**), or to the eighth-century king Theopompus (see WEB **7.13.I** for the ephors and king Theopompus). The third-century CE author Diogenes Laertius (1.68–73) attributes the ephorate to the sixth-century Spartan sage Chilon. See WEB **7.13.II** for Aristotle on the mixed constitution in which the ephorate serves as a constraint upon kingship.

The ephors accompanied the kings on campaigns and sat with the *gerousia* in judgment of them. The ephors also fulfilled some religious and judicial functions and oversaw the draft. They were active in foreign policy, supervised Spartan education, and proclaimed war on the helots as well as the notorious *xenalasia*, or periodic expulsion of foreigners. The last-mentioned practice, which was motivated either by security considerations or by xenophobia, and which was attested for the Classical Age, offended the norms of Greek hospitality and gave ammunition to Sparta's critics. Plutarch, however, finds merit in this custom as well as in the restriction of Spartans traveling abroad.

Plutarch *Lycurgus* 27.7–9

(**27.7**) This was also why he [Lycurgus] would not grant his permission to those who wanted to leave the country and travel abroad, where they would pick up foreign customs and start imitating unenlightened lifestyles and different political systems. Indeed, he even drove out of Sparta people who came streaming into the city in large numbers for no useful purpose. This was not because he feared, as Thucydides claims [2.39.1], that they would copy his political structure or learn some valuable moral lesson; rather, it was to prevent these people from teaching anything bad. (27.8) For along with foreign personages foreign ideas necessarily enter a society, and new ideas bring new value judgments. From these inevitably come many sentiments and choices that are out of tune with the harmony, as it were, of the established political system. (27.9) Lycurgus accordingly thought it was his duty to keep the city free from infection by bad habits – more so than physical illnesses – that might enter it from outside.

7.14 State and Family: The Scrutiny of Spartan Babies

In Sparta the community controlled the right of babies to live. Elsewhere, whether infants survived or were exposed was normally at the discretion of parents. The scrutiny of infants in Sparta also illustrates the honorary place old men held there and the tensions that existed between state and family.

Plutarch *Lycurgus* 16.1–2

(16.1) After the child was born the father did not have the authority to bring it up. Instead, he would take it in his arms to a place called "Leschê," where the eldest members of his tribe would sit in council. The elders would examine the baby, and if it was robust and sturdy they would give the order for it to be brought up, assigning to it one of the 9,000 plots of land.[1] (16.2) If, however, it was in poor condition and deformed, they would send it to the so-called "Apothetae," a precipice near Mt. Taugetus. Their reasoning was that it was better, both for the child itself and for the city, that a child born poorly formed at the start in terms of health and strength not continue its life.

Note

1. *Plutarch follows the tradition that Lycurgus fixed the number of Spartan citizens at 9,000, each with a plot of land.*

7.15 The Schooling of Boys

In addition to shaping the Spartan government, Lycurgus was credited with introducing the Spartan education system, called *agoge* (lit. "raising") in Hellenistic times. Spartan education was not static but was reformed and changed throughout its history. It is likely, however, that the following passages give a credible account of its character during the Classical Age, if not earlier.

The Spartans trained and indoctrinated young boys into becoming men, citizens, and warriors. While in most Greek states education was private and voluntary, Spartan education was public and obligatory. It constituted a precondition for Spartan citizenship, and was supervised by the state and the community.

Boys started their education at the age of seven. They were taken away from their families and grouped together by age in bands, whose names were borrowed from cattle herding. In addition to reading, writing, music, and dancing, the boys were trained in physical endurance. Plutarch *Lycurgus* 18.1 tells an unlikely story of a hungry boy who hid a fox cub under his garment, and died because he let the cub gnaw his guts rather than reveal the theft. The story illustrates the value the Spartans placed on endurance and fear. The fourth-century historian Xenophon gives our earliest account of Spartan education. (For Xenophon, see **Introduction III.4**.) He highlights the teaching of self-denial and fortitude, which were attained mostly by punitive means. Generally, Xenophon tries to rationalize and defend Spartan education, which led to his functionalist interpretation of customs such as stealing cheese and punishing those who failed by whipping. Yet the original purpose of these customs could have been ritualistic. Noteworthy also is the use of competition in training young Spartans.

Xenophon *The Constitution of the Lacedaemonians* 2.1–13

(**2.1**) Amongst the rest of the Greeks, those who claim to give their sons the best education appoint tutors [*paidagogoi*] to look after them just as soon as the boys can understand what they are being told.[1] They also immediately send them to school to learn letters, music, and the sports of the wrestling-ground [*palaestra*]. In addition, they make the children's feet tender by supplying them with sandals, and soften their bodies with changes of clothing. They also think their bellies should tell the children how much food they should eat.

(**2.2**) Lycurgus, however, instead of leaving each individual to appoint slaves as tutors, put one man in charge of directing the boys, a man selected from the class from which the chief magistracies were filled. He was given the title supervisor [*paidonomos*], and to him Lycurgus granted the authority to assemble the boys, and, in the process of inspecting them, to punish severely any misbehavior. He also assigned to him a group of young men who carried whips, and who were to take disciplinary action whenever necessary. The result is a combination in Sparta of great modesty and strict obedience.

(**2.3**) Instead of making tender the boys' feet with sandals, Lycurgus ordered that they harden them by dispensing with footwear. He thought that if they practiced doing this, they would find it much easier to climb hills, and much safer to go down slopes; and also that they would have more speed in leaping, jumping, and running. (**2.4**) And rather than have them pampered with clothing, he established the custom that they wear a single garment throughout the year, for he thought that in this way they would be better prepared to face cold and heat. (**2.5**) He also ordered the team-leader [*eirên*][2] to have with him for distribution only a limited amount of food, to insure that the boys would not be weighed down from gorging, and would not lack the experience of going without. He thought that those brought up in this way would be better able to labor on, if necessary, without food, and better able to last a longer time on the same food rations if so ordered. They would also have less need of delicacies, and would the more easily accept all sorts of food; and they would, in addition, be in a healthier state. Lycurgus was also of the opinion that a regime that made for leanness in the physique would also contribute to height, more than one that broadened a person with its food.

(**2.6**) But to prevent the boys being oppressed too much by hunger, while he would not grant them the freedom to take all that they needed, he did permit them to steal some things to stave off the hunger pangs. (**2.7**) It was not because he was short of the sustenance to give them that he let them acquire food by their own devices, as I think everyone is aware. Obviously, the person who is going to steal must stay awake at night and also use his wits and lie in ambush by day, and the one who is likely to catch something must prepare his lookouts. By all of this Lycurgus clearly wanted to make the boys more resourceful in acquiring supplies, and make them more proficient fighters, and that was the point of this type of training. (**2.8**) Someone may pose the question, "Well, if Lycurgus thought stealing was good, why would he have the boy who was caught severely flogged?" My reply is this: because, as with all other subjects they teach, people punish the student who does not perform well. The Spartans therefore punish those who get caught as being bad thieves.[3] (**2.9**) What is demonstrated here is that where speed is needed the idler gains the least and has the most trouble.

(**2.10**) So the boys would not be without a master even if the supervisor went away, Lycurgus arranged that one of the citizens present at the time should take charge; he could command the boys to do whatever he thought good, and punish them for any misbehavior. By doing this he achieved the further end of making the boys more respectful; for in Sparta there is nothing that either boys or men respect as much as those in power. (**2.11**) And so that the boys would not be without a master even if no adult male happened to be present, Lycurgus arranged that the most capable of the team-leaders [*eirenes*] should have authority over each team [*ilê*]. The result is that boys there are never without a master.

(**2.12**) I think I must say something about love affairs with boys, for that, too, bears on education. In the case of the other Greeks, man and boy live together as a couple (as in the case of the Boeotians) or else the men enjoy the beauty of the boys through services that they have performed for them (as with the Elians). Some again have a total ban on lovers conversing with the boys. (**2.13**) Lycurgus' opinion ran contrary to all this. He approved if someone who, being himself a moral person and according the due respect to the soul of the boy, tried to make him moral, too, and to spend time with him for that, and he considered this an excellent form of education. But if a man was clearly only attracted to a boy's body, he regarded that as absolutely disgraceful, and he saw to it that, in Lacedaemon, such lovers refrained from sexual relationships with boys no less than parents see to that in the case of their children, and brothers in the case of their sisters.[4]

Notes

1. *Xenophon mentions three age groups:* paides *(boys),* meirakioi *(youngsters), and* hebontes *(youth). Plutarch (Lycurgus 16) has finer age distinctions, but his information may reflect later times.*
2. *The word for the team-leaders,* eirenes, *is a later emendation (also in 2.11). The* eirenes *were the youngest of the adult group and often the boys' lovers.*
3. *The point of the test was to steal as many pieces of cheese as possible from the altar of Artemis Orthia, a goddess associated with rites of passage for both boys and girls. In Roman times the ritual evolved into a flagellation show for tourists.*
4. *See* **12.2** *("Homoerotic Couples"),* **12.3** *("Courting Men and Women"), and* **12.4** *("Cretan Lovers") on Archaic Greek homosexuality. In the case of Spartan pederasty, the pairing of elite boys seemed to have been arranged. The Athenians associated the Spartans with homosexual practices.*

See Xenophon in WEB **7.16** for additional information on the schooling of boys in Sparta.

Questions

1. What were the Spartans' educational principles and how did they implement them?
2. To what extent was the community involved in Spartan education?
3. Xenophon both reports on and interprets the Spartan educational system (**7.15** and WEB **7.16**). Try to separate his interpretation from the practices he describes. Can you find alternative interpretations to his?

7.17   Girls' Education and Rituals

Spartan education was unique in its inclusion of girls. Xenophon notes that in other Greek states girls were taught moderation, woolwork, and how to remain sedentary, that is, to stay indoors. In Sparta, girls exercised outdoors in the aim of making them healthy mothers. Unlike boys, however, Spartan girls lived at home until they married.

7.17.A   Girls' Education

> ### Xenophon *The Constitution of the Lacedaemonians* 1.3–4
>
> (**1.3**) First, then, childbearing, so that I may start at the beginning. In the case of girls who are to bear children, and are thought fit to be given an appropriate education, other peoples give them as moderate a diet as possible, with the smallest amount of delicacies. As for wine, they either keep them away from it altogether, or have them drink it very well watered. In addition, the other Greeks think girls should be quiet and work in wool, seated like the majority of their tradesmen. If girls are brought up like that, then, how can one expect them to produce fine offspring? (**1.4**) Lycurgus, however, considered slaves sufficiently capable of providing clothing; for free women the most important thing, he thought, was childbearing. Accordingly, he first gave orders that the female sex should take physical training to no less an extent than the male, and then he instituted competitions in running and physical strength for women, as well as men, in the belief that more robust children would be born from parents who were both strong.

Plutarch (WEB **7.18**) provides additional information on girls' education, their participation in religious festivals, and their role in instilling desirable manly values in Spartan youth.

The socialization of Spartan girls included participation in religious rituals. The Archaic poet Alcman (ca. 600) composed poems that were performed by choruses of girls in front of a mixed audience, (as attested by Plutarch). The following fragmentary poem mentions two chorus leaders, Agido and Hagesichora (lit. "chorus leader"), and illustrates the role that competitiveness and homoeroticism played in their rituals and social life. The poem also suggests girls' knowledge and perhaps practice of horsemanship.

7.17.B   Spartan Maidens and Rituals

Alcman *Partheneion* 1.40–91 (Page)

(**1.40**) I sing of Agido's radiance. I see her shining as the sun, which Agido calls to witness for us. But the famed leader of our choir allows me neither to praise her nor find fault with her in any way. (**45**) For she appears to be preeminent, just as if a person were to place among grazing animals a strong prize-winning horse with ringing feet, a horse such as is found in winged dreams.

(**50**) Do you not see? The racehorse is Venetic;[1] but the hair of Hagesichora my cousin has the sheen of pure gold. (**55**) And her silver face – but why do I tell you openly? Such is Hagesichora. But she who is second to Agido in beauty will run as a Colaxaean horse against an Ibenian.[2] (**60**) For the Pleiads[3] at dawn rise like the star of Sirius through the ambrosial night, fighting against us as we carry the plow.

(**65**) For we have not enough purple [raiment] to protect ourselves, nor a many-hued snake all made of gold, nor Lydian headband, the ornament of dark-eyed girls, (**70**) nor Nanno's hair, nor again god-like Areta nor Sylacis nor Cleisesera; nor will you go to Aenesimbrota's home and say: (**75**) "Let Astaphis be mine and let Philylla look at me, and Damareta and lovely Ianthemis. But Hagesichora torments me.[4] For is not Hagesichora of the beautiful ankles right here? (**80**) Is she not staying close to Agido and praising our festival?" Accept their prayers, you gods. For accomplishment and fulfillment are in the gods' hands. Chorus-leader, I would speak, (**85**) I who am myself just a girl; I have vainly screeched as an owl from a roof-beam. But I desire to please Aotis most of all, since she has been the healer of our sufferings.[5] (**90**) But it was because of Hagesichora that the girls embarked upon lovely peace.

Notes

1. *Venetic horses probably came from the Adriatic (cf. Strabo 1.3.21; 5.1.4) and were used mostly for chariot riding.*
2. *A Colaxaean horse was probably a Scythian pony, and an Ibenian was perhaps a Celtic or Ionian horse.*
3. *Pleiads refer either to stars or to a rival girls' chorus.*
4. *The text can be read also to mean that Hagesichora "guides me" or "exhausts me with love."*
5. *An attached commentary to the poem identifies Aotis with Orthia, a goddess associated with Artemis. See also note 3 on Xenophon* The Constitution of the Lacedaemonians *2.8 (**7.15**).*

7.17.C   A Female Spartan Runner

The Archaic bronze figurine shown in Figure 7.1 was found in the sanctuary of Zeus in Dodona, Epirus. The second-century CE scholar Pollux (7.54–55)

Figure 7.1   An Archaic bronze figurine of a young Spartan female, dressed as a runner.
© The Trustees of the British Museum.

describes Spartan girls as wearing a chiton (tunic) with a high slit, while a scholiast on Euripides *Hecube* argues, based on the Archaic poet Anacreon, that Dorian women showed themselves naked (schol. *Eurip. Hec.* 934 = Anacreon 399).

Questions

1. What were the Spartans' expectations of women according to Xenophon (**7.17.A**) and Plutarch (WEB **7.18**)? What do they tell us about the status of Spartan women?
2. What might non-Spartans find offensive in the education of Spartan girls, and why?
3. What can we learn from Alcman's poem (**7.17.B**) about the interests and concerns of Spartan girls, and about the world of their imagination?
4. In what ways do Alcman's poem (**7.17.B**) and the figurine in Figure 7.1 add to, confirm, or contradict the descriptions of girls' education by Xenophon (**7.17.A**) and Plutarch (WEB **7.18**)?

7.19   Spartan Marriage

As in other Greek societies, marriage was considered the most important and formative event in a woman's life. Spartan women likely married later than their Athenian counterparts, maybe around the age of eighteen to twenty. Plutarch describes Spartan marriage customs whose antiquity is hard to ascertain. They include the abduction of the bride, dressing her in men's clothes, and cutting off her hair. Spartan men, on the other hand, grew their hair long. The bride's being made to simulate a man has been variously interpreted. Some regard it as a rite of passage to womanhood, others see an attempt to make her resemble a man's homosexual partners during his education, and still others consider it as intended to conceal the woman's identity from evil forces. Plutarch's explanation of the married couple's conduct appears to be influenced by Xenophon's commentary on the topic (*The Constitution of the Lacedaemonians* 1.5).

Plutarch *Lycurgus* 15.4–10

(**15.4**) Marriage was conducted with the abduction of the bride, who was not now a small girl unripe for marriage but in her prime and completely mature. (**15.5**) The woman who was called the bridesmaid took the abducted bride, cut her hair close to the skin, dressed her in a man's cloak and sandals, and set her on a pallet of straw, where she was left alone and without light. (**15.6**) The bridegroom, who was not drunk or drowsy, but sober, as he always was after dining in the *phidition* [common mess], would come in and undo her girdle and, lifting her up, would carry her to the bed. (**15.7**) He would not spend much time there, and would take his leave in a respectable manner to sleep amongst the other young men, where he had normally slept before his marriage. (**15.8**) And that is what he did later, too, spending the day amongst his comrades and sleeping amongst them, as well. He would come to his wife in secret and with caution, embarrassed and fearful that someone in the house might see him, while the wife would use her resourcefulness to arrange ways that the two could meet at appropriate moments without being observed. (**15.9**) The couple would do this for quite some time, with the result that some husbands had children born to them before they set eyes on their own wives in daylight. (**15.10**) Meeting in this manner was not only a training in self-control and moderation. It also brought the two together for sexual union when their bodies were fertile, and when they were fresh and eager for lovemaking, not sated and jaded from unlimited sexual relations, since they always left in each other some remnant of passion and affection to keep them excited.

7.20   Wife-Sharing

The primary expectation of a married couple in Greece was to produce children. In Sparta this expectation had special meaning given that helots outnumbered citizens. Spartans even allowed wife-sharing for the purpose of procreation. Xenophon thinks that the reason was to produce strong warriors, but the practice might have less to do with patriotism than with pragmatism.

He and the later historian Polybius suggest that wife-sharing bonded two families together without having to split the inheritance among many heirs. The husband's agreement to wife-share excluded such an arrangement from the category of adultery, which was regarded by other Greeks as a punishable offense: see, for example, the Cretan and Athenian dealings with adultery (WEB **13.2**: "The Gortyn Law on Sexual Misconduct" and WEB **13.4**: "Solon's Laws Concerning Inheritance, Dowry, Women Outdoors, Parental Support, and Sexual Misconduct").

7.20.A   Xenophon on Wife-Sharing

Xenophon *The Constitution of the Lacedaemonians* 1.6–9

(**1.6**) In addition, Lycurgus also put a stop to men taking a wife whenever they wanted, and ordered them to marry in the prime of their physical strength, for he thought that this, too, promoted eugenics. (**1.7**) In the case of an old man having a young spouse, however, he observed that older men kept a particularly close watch over their wives, and his ideas in this case were very different. He instituted the practice that an old man should bring home, for the purposes of procreation, a male whose physical and inner qualities he admired. (**1.8**) And if anyone did not wish to cohabit with a wife, but did want exemplary children, Lycurgus also established that the man could – if he persuaded the lady's husband – have children by any woman he saw who had fine children and was of noble birth.

(**1.9**) Lycurgus agreed to many such relationships. For the women want to be mistresses of two households, and the men want to gain as brothers for their sons boys who share with them heredity and influence within the family, but lay no claim to its property.

7.20.B   Polybius on Wife-Sharing

Polybius 12.6b8

In fact it was amongst the Lacedaemonians a traditional custom, one widely practiced, for three or four men – even more if they were brothers – to have one wife, and for their children to be regarded as common to all of them. When a man had sired enough children it was quite proper, and a commonplace occurrence, for him to pass his wife on to one of his friends.

Both the marriage ritual and wife-sharing made Spartan women somewhat passive and instrumental in male transactions. Yet as wives and mothers of warriors, Spartan women enjoyed more liberties than, say, Athenian women. As co-heirs or sole heirs they could also own real property. In the late fourth century, Aristotle complained that women owned almost two-fifths of Spartan land (*Politics* 2.6.10 1270a23–27). In addition, women, especially in their roles as mothers, were expected to support the Spartan martial and patriotic value system. See WEB **7.21** for sayings attributed to Spartan mothers.

Questions

1. What do the marriage ritual and polyandry (multiple husbands) tell us about the standing of Spartan women?
2. Describe the integration of women into Spartan society based on the wedding ritual (**7.19**), sharing of wives (**7.20.A–B**), and sayings attributed to Spartan mothers (WEB **7.21**).

7.22 The Common Messes

The preconditions for Spartan citizenship were Spartan parentage, completion of the education process, a plot of land (*kleros*), and a contribution to the common messes. Absence of one of these criteria disqualified a man from obtaining, or keeping, his citizenship.

The common messes, called *syssitia* (sitting together), *syskenia* (tent-companies), or *pheiditia* (frugal meal), were associations of Spartans who got together both in the city and over a campaign. Xenophon idealized this institution as promoting sharing, sobriety, and proper conduct. Aristotle, however, criticized the obligation to contribute to the common mess as discriminatory against the poor, who lost their citizenship for lack of means (see WEB **7.23**). A rejected member was deprived of his civic rights and socially demoted.

7.22.A Xenophon on the Common Messes

Xenophon *The Constitution of the Lacedaemonians* 5.2–7

(**5.2**) Finding the Spartiates settled in at home like the rest of the Greeks, Lycurgus realized that this was the cause of considerable mischief. He therefore instituted public messes in the open, believing that in this way men would be least likely to disobey commands. (**5.3**) He also rationed their food so that they would not gorge themselves, but not go short, either. In fact, many unexpected additions to the meals also come from the spoils of the hunt, and sometimes, instead of these, the rich make contributions of bread. Accordingly the table is never bare of food until everyone leaves, nor is it extravagantly supplied. (**5.4**) Lycurgus also put a stop to obligatory drinking at a party, which is mentally and physically debilitating, but he allowed everyone to drink whenever he was thirsty, thinking that this was the least harmful and most pleasurable form of drinking.

How could anyone sharing a mess in this way ruin himself or his household by gluttony or drunkenness? (**5.5**) For in the other city-states, generally speaking, men keep company with their contemporaries, amongst whom they feel very little embarrassment. Lycurgus, however, [introduced] the system in Sparta that such company be of various ages [so that] the younger men would learn most from the experience of their elders.[1] (**5.6**) And, in fact, the custom of the land at the common meals was for discussion to center on whatever good one could do in the city-state, so that there was very little outrageous behavior, very little drunken violence, and very little indecency in conduct and conversation. (**5.7**) There are also the following beneficial consequences from taking meals outdoors. The men are obliged to walk about when they leave for home, and have to make sure that they do not keel over from drunkenness, for they know that they will not be staying in the place where they had dinner. Also, they must negotiate their way in darkness as well as they can in daylight, for anyone liable for guard duty is not even allowed to walk with the aid of a torch.

Note

1. *The restorations are due to lacunae in the text.*

7.22.B   Plutarch on the Common Messes

Plutarch adds information about the admission process to the *syssition* (at the age of twenty), and the institution's rules of conduct.

Plutarch *Lycurgus* 12.3–7

(**12.3**) They would come together in groups of fifteen, or slightly fewer or slightly more than that. Each of the diners brought, every month, a *medimnos* [ca. 1.5 bushels] of barley-meal, eight *choes* [ca. 26 liters] of wine, five *minae* [ca. 2.2 kilos] of cheese, two and a half *minae* [ca. 1.1 kilos] of figs, and in addition just a little money for the purchase of fish. (**12.4**) Besides this, anyone who had sacrificed would send the first fruits of the offering to the mess, and anyone who had hunted would send part of the catch. For a man could dine at home whenever he was late through offering sacrifice or hunting, but all others had to attend the mess. (**12.5**) The practice of communal eating they religiously preserved for a long time. At any rate, when king Agis[1] returned from campaign after defeating the Athenians and, wishing to dine with his wife, sent for his parts of the meal, the polemarchs [senior officers] refused his request. And when, in anger, Agis did not the following day make a sacrifice that he should have made, they fined him.

(**12.6**) Even male children used to frequent the common messes, and were taken to them as if they were schools of temperance. There they would listen to political talk, and observe games suitable for free persons; and they became habituated to playing these games, and also to making jokes without coarseness, and being the butt of jokes without becoming annoyed.[2] (**12.7**) For it was thought a particularly Laconian quality to be able to take a joke; but anyone unable to do so could ask the joker to stop and he did so at once.

Questions

1. What rules governed admittance to and participation in the Spartan common mess according to Xenophon and Plutarch (**7.22.A–B**)?
2. How did the common mess contribute to, but also violate, the ideology of Spartan equality?

7.24 Spartan Equality: Ideology and Reality

The sources associate the sharing of food and company and the universal obligation to attend the *syssition* with the Spartan ideology of an egalitarian and austere society. The Spartans paid respect to this ideology when they called themselves *homoioi*, "the similar ones." Plutarch reproduces this ideology in the following traditions about Lycurgus' distribution of land among the Spartans. The Spartans were reputed to hold the possession of money in low regard. For money they used iron ingots as well as standard foreign currency.

7.24.A   Lycurgus' Egalitarian Measures

Plutarch *Lycurgus* 8.1–9

(**8.1**) The second, and the most enterprising, of Lycurgus' reforms is the redistribution of land. (**8.2**) The inequality of holdings had become extreme, and there were many poor and indigent people threatening the well-being of the state, while the wealth had fallen completely into the hands of a few. (**8.3**) Lycurgus now wanted to drive out arrogance, jealousy, criminality, luxury, and those ills of the state even more inveterate and serious than these, namely wealth and poverty. He therefore persuaded the Spartans to put all their land at the disposal of the community, to agree to a new division, and to live all together on an equal footing with the same amount of property for their livelihood, seeking distinction only by virtue. (**8.4**) There would be no difference or inequality between one person and another except that created by the censure of wicked acts and praise of noble ones.

(**8.5**) Following words with action, Lycurgus divided the rest of Laconia into thirty thousand lots [*kleroi*] for the perioeci, but the city land belonging to the city of Sparta he divided into nine thousand, which became the lots of the Spartiates. (**8.6**) Some say that Lycurgus' division created only six thousand city parcels, and that three thousand were subsequently added by [king] Polydorus. Others claim that half of the nine thousand were created by Polydorus, and the other half by Lycurgus. (**8.7**) Each man's lot was big enough to bear seventy *medimnoi*[1] of barley for a man and twelve for his wife, with a proportionate amount of fruit. (**8.8**) For Lycurgus believed that this was sufficient nourishment for them for their health and strength, and that they would need nothing more. (**8.9**) It is said that, later, on his return from a voyage, he was going through the countryside when it had just been harvested. Seeing the stacks of grain standing next to each other, all alike, he smiled and said to those present that all of Laconia seemed to belong to a large band of brothers who had just divided it amongst themselves.

Note

1.   A medimnos *equals about 52 liters or 1.5 bushels of grain.*

7.24.B   The Similar Ones (*Homoioi*)?

Archaeological and literary evidence, however, suggests that the image of austere and equal Spartans requires modification. The fact that the Spartans could bequeath their plots of lands (*kleroi*) to male or female heirs or give them to others as a gift (but not apparently to sell them) testifies against egalitarian land ownership. These practices challenge the common ancient (and modern) assumption that land in Sparta was owned by the state. It appears that the Spartans, like other Greeks, maintained a fairly common pattern of land ownership. However, Spartans and other Greeks of later years cultivated the ideology of egalitarian Spartan society. Thus, Plutarch's figures for plots of land are based on testimonies that are no earlier than the Hellenistic period.

In addition, until sometime in the sixth century, the city of Sparta showed few signs of leading an austere lifestyle, and even later Spartans continued to collect and keep valuables, although they avoided ostentation. Both Archaic and Classical sources tell us about wealthy Spartans and inequality after Lycurgus (e.g., Herodotus 6.61.3 [WEB **7.29.IV**]; 7.134.2).

The Laconian cup shown in Figure 7.2, attributed to the "Naucratis Painter," is dated to around 565. It depicts a lifestyle typical of the elite in other contemporary Greek states, but contradicts the asceticism ascribed to Sparta by the sources. The cup shows five men reclining in a *symposion* (banquet). The *symposion* was very much an aristocratic institution, and included drinking wine, entertainment (including by female pipe players depicted on other Laconian vases), male bonding, and erotic pursuit (see **12.8**: "The Banquet"). The scene on the cup portrays five bearded (i.e., adult) banqueters, and a naked young cupbearer who stands next to the wine jar (*kratêr*). Two sirens and two winged creatures are carrying wreaths. The meaning of the winged figures is unclear. Perhaps they represent benevolent supernatural beings, perhaps divine approval of the participants. They were possibly borrowed from Near Eastern iconography.

Figure 7.2
The *Symposion* of Five Cup, ca. 565.
© RMN/Hervé Lewandowski.

Questions

1. What constituted Spartan equality or similarity?
2. Is it possible to reconcile the scene depicted on the Laconian cup (Figure 7.2) with Xenophon's description of the common mess (**7.22.A**)? Explain why or why not.

7.25 Courage and Cowardice in Sparta

The ideal of homogeneity helped to promote communal solidarity and conformity, which were espoused also in the Spartan army. The Spartan man spent his days exercising, training, and hunting in readiness for the next campaign. On the battlefield he fought alongside his comrades and was expected to return, according to a proverbial Spartan saying, "with the shield, or on the shield." We shall revisit Spartan warriors in the chapter on the hoplite army (**8.6**: "The Spartan or Hoplite Ideology"). The following passage describes how the Spartan community ritualized the shaming of individuals who failed to meet its standards of manly courage and comradeship. Cowards in Sparta were labeled *tresantes*, lit. "tremblers" (see also Plutarch *Agesilaus* 30.3–4).

Xenophon *The Constitution of the Lacedaemonians* 9.1–6

(**9.1**) This, too, was a praiseworthy accomplishment of Lycurgus: he managed to make a noble death preferable to a dishonorable life in the city-state of Sparta. And, in fact, anyone looking into the matter would find that fewer of these Spartans actually lose their lives than do those who choose to retreat from a fearful situation. (**9.2**) To tell the truth, salvation more often goes along with courage than it does with cowardice, for courage is easier, sweeter, more inventive, and stronger. And it is obvious that glory also follows closely on valor, for all people want to be allied with the brave in some way.

(**9.3**) One should also not pass over the means that Lycurgus employed to bring this about. Quite clearly he provided happiness for the brave and unhappiness for the cowardly. (**9.4**) In other city-states, when a man turns coward all he receives is the name "coward," and he still frequents the same marketplace as the brave man, and he sits beside him and exercises with him, if he wishes.[1] In Lacedaemon, however, everybody would be ashamed to have a coward as his messmate, or as an opponent in a wrestling match. When people pick sides for a ball game, such a person is often left unchosen, and in choral dancing he is sent off to the shameful positions. In the streets he has to step out of others' way, and when it comes to seating he must cede his even to younger men. At home he must support his unmarried female relatives, and he must put up with being blamed by them for their unmarried state. He must endure a hearth without a wife (**9.5**) and yet he must pay the penalty for it. He must not walk about looking comfortable, or have the appearance of men beyond reproach; otherwise he must endure a beating from his betters. (**9.6**) I am not at all surprised that in Sparta – since such disgrace hangs over cowards – death is preferred to a life of disgrace and shame like this.

Note

1. *In fact, Athenian law from the Classical Age punished desertion with partial disenfranchisement* (atimia).

Question

1. How did the Spartans shame those deemed cowards? Where else in Sparta was shame used to promote conformity to ideals?

7.26 The Peloponnesian League and Spartan Alliances

Spartan foreign policy relied greatly on alliances with other states. Often alliances were based on ties of individual *xenia* between prominent Spartans, especially the kings, and other Greek and non-Greek notables. Yet more reliable or stable alliances were those between states. Sparta formed a system of alliances called the Peloponnesian League, which included many states both inside and outside the Peloponnese. Among the first communities to become a Spartan ally was the Arcadian city of Tegea. Herodotus reports that around the mid-sixth century the Spartans tried to subjugate neighboring Tegea and probably to helotize it. They overcame the Tegeans only after acquiring the (alleged) bones of the mythical Orestes, the son of Agamemnon and his Spartan wife Clytemnestra. The establishment of a cult for Orestes in Sparta, and the recovery from Achaea of the (alleged) bones of Orestes' son, Tisamenus, have been interpreted as part of a Spartan propaganda campaign that aimed to establish Spartan hegemony over other Peloponnesian states on the basis of their Achaean, i.e., pre-Dorian, heritage. See Herodotus' description of how the Spartans obtained Orestes' bones in WEB **7.27.I**.

The Spartans did not annex Tegea to their state but signed a treaty with it, which Plutarch found in Aristotle's *Constitution of the Lacedaemonians* and partially preserves. The treaty forbade giving shelter to runaway helots.

--- **7.26.A   The Spartans' Agreement with Tegea**

Plutarch *Greek Questions* 5 (*Moralia* 292B) = Arist. F 592

"Who are the 'good men' amongst the Arcadians and Lacedaemonians?"

When the Lacedaemonians became reconciled with the people of Tegea, they signed a treaty and erected a stele together on the banks of the Alpheus.[1] Among other things, the following was inscribed on it: "They must expel the Messenians from the country, and making them 'good' is forbidden."[2] Now Aristotle, in his explanation of this, says that its meaning is that the death penalty is not to be applied for assistance given to those Tegeans sympathizing with Sparta.

Notes

1. *The Alpheus River was either in Olympia or somewhere between Sparta and Tegea.*
2. *The phrase "making them good/useful" was often applied to the dead. The Spartans requested that their Tegean friends not be executed.*

Most likely the treaty included additional provisions. Sparta's relations with its allies in the Archaic period suggest that some of its alliance terms might have resembled the conditions accepted by the city of Olynthus when it surrendered to Sparta in 379. The agreement with Olynthus demonstrates the unequal relationship between Sparta and its allies. The allies were linked to Sparta but not to each other, and the Spartans were not obliged to reciprocate their services.

--- **7.26.B   The Spartans' Treaty with Olynthus**

Xenophon *Hellenica* 5.3.26

The Olynthians were in an absolutely terrible state from famine because they were deriving no food from their land, and none was being brought in to them by sea. [The Spartan commander] Polybiades then forced them to send a deputation to Lacedaemon to sue for peace. The spokesmen came with plenipotentiary authority, and they concluded a treaty by which they were to recognize the same enemies and friends, follow the Spartans wherever they would lead them, and join their alliance. After swearing to abide by these terms, they returned home.

During the Archaic Age Sparta gained many allies in and outside the Peloponnese, and thus attained hegemonic status in Greece. However, in 506 and 504, Sparta's most powerful ally Corinth successfully opposed two attempts by the Spartan king Cleomenes I to forcibly install his friends in power in Athens. Corinth's opposition might have led to the establishment of an assembly of allies' representatives whose approval was required before taking action. Each member had one vote, and decisions were made by majority vote. Nevertheless, the Spartans still retained the exclusive right to call the allies together, and certainly to decline pursuing the course of action advocated by them. See WEB **7.27.II–III** for Herodotus' report on the Corinthian opposition to Cleomenes' policy.

Questions

1. What were the obligations of the members of the Peloponnesian League?
2. Describe the evolution of the Peloponnesian League from the wars against Tegea (**7.26.A** and WEB **7.27.I**) to Cleomenes' failed mobilization of the Peloponnesians against Athens following Corinth's opposition (WEB **7.27.II–III**).

7.28   King Cleomenes, Plataea, and Athens (519)

As a hegemonic and powerful state, Sparta was often courted by other Greeks to become their ally. Plataea's request and rejection reveal some of the considerations that influenced Spartan foreign policy. The episode involves one of the more formidable Spartan kings, Cleomenes I.

In 519 Cleomenes led a Spartan force to Boeotia. He was approached by the city of Plataea, which was threatened by its neighbor Thebes, with a request to become Sparta's ally. The Spartans declined on account of their geographical distance from Plataea, which rings true in view of their apprehension of helots and far-flung campaigns. Instead, they recommended an alliance with Athens, which was closer by and ruled at the time by their friend, the tyrant Hippias. It was the beginning of a wonderful friendship between Athens and Plataea. It also displayed Cleomenes' astuteness, since his policy won Athenian gratitude and curbed Thebes' power. (Herodotus, however, attributes more sinister motives to the Spartans.)

Herodotus recounts the Plataean episode in the context of the preliminaries of the battle of Marathon between the Persians and Athenians and their Plataean allies (490; see Chapter 15: "The Ionian Revolt: Persians and Greeks").

Herodotus 6.108.1–6

(**6.108.1**) The Plataeans had earlier put themselves under the protection of the Athenians, and the Athenians had already shouldered many burdens on their behalf. How the Plataeans came to put themselves under their protection is as follows:

(**108.2**) The Plataeans, under pressure from the Thebans, first of all offered to put themselves under the protection of Cleomenes son of Anaxandrides and the Lacedaemonians, who happened to be in the area. The Lacedaemonians, however, refused, saying to them: "We live too far away, and such help as might come to you would be in vain – you might be enslaved many times over before any of us learned of it! (**108.3**) Our advice to you is to offer yourselves to the Athenians; they live next door and are competent to help you." It was not out of regard for the Plataeans that the Lacedaemonians gave this advice, but because they wanted to see the Athenians have problems in their relations with the Boeotians.

(**108.4**) The Plataeans did not disregard the advice that the Lacedaemonians gave them. When the Athenians were holding a sacrifice for the twelve [Olympian] gods, they sat as suppliants at the altar [in the agora], and put themselves under Athenian protection. On learning of this, the Thebans launched a campaign against the Plataeans, and the Athenians came to their defense. (**108.5**) But as they were about to join battle the Corinthians would not allow them to proceed. They happened to be in the area, and they effected a reconciliation between the two parties, who both turned to them for arbitration. The Corinthians marked out a boundary line in the land, on condition that the Thebans leave in peace any Boeotians not wishing to belong to the Boeotian League. After rendering this judgment, the Corinthians left. As the Athenians were pulling back, however, the Boeotians attacked them, but were defeated in the battle. (**108.6**) The Athenians then passed over the boundaries that the Corinthians established for the Plataeans, and made the Asopus River itself the border between Theban territory and that of Plataea and Hysiae.

That was how the Plataeans put themselves under Athenian protection, and on that occasion they came to Marathon to help them.

See WEB **7.29.I–V** for the remarkable story of king Cleomenes I, which tells much about Spartan customs, domestic affairs, and foreign policy.

WEB **7.30** has useful links to the website of the Sparta Museum, including images of ancient Spartan remains and artifacts, to two resources for Spartan history, and to some Spartan poetry.

Questions

1. Who was involved in the Plataean affair and what role did they play?
2. What can the Plataean episode tell us about the workings of Greek diplomacy?

Review Questions

1. Describe the categories of inhabitants in the Spartan state and how this stratification was reflected in Spartan culture (**7.2–5**, WEB **7.7.I–II**, WEB **7.23**).

2. How was power distributed in Sparta? Was the Spartan political structure a mixed constitution with adequate checks and balances (**7.8–9**, **7.11–12**, WEB **7.10**, WEB **7.13.I–II**)?

3. What values did Spartans highlight in their education of boys and girls, and how did they teach these values (**7.15**, **7.17**, WEB **7.16**, WEB **7.18**)?

4. Describe how the socialization of Spartan men and women continued after they became adults (**7.19**, **7.22**, **7.25**, WEB **7.21**, WEB **7.23**).

5. What tensions between family and state in Sparta existed on or beneath the surface? How did the Spartans deal with these tensions (**7.14**, **7.15**, **7.17**, **7.19**, **7.20**, **7.22**)?

6. What contributed to the Spartan egalitarian ideology and how (**7.22, 24**)?

7. How did Sparta become a dominant power in Greece (**7.26**, WEB **7.27.I–III**)?

8. What does the story of Demaratus' birth and dethroning (WEB **7.29.IV**) tell us about Spartan queens?

9. Herodotus' account of Cleomenes I appears to be based on hostile sources (WEB **7.29.I–V**). Without forcing the issue, try to give a more sympathetic account of the king's career.

Suggested Readings

Ancient sources on Sparta and the Spartan "mirage": Tigerstedt 1965–1978; Hodkinson 1997, 83–88; Flower 2002. *Spartan archaeology*: Cartledge 1992, esp. 53. *Messenian Wars*: Hodkinson 2000, 2, 76. *Land ownership in Sparta*: Hodkinson 2000, 19–112; Figueira 2004. *Spartan currency*: Christien 2002; Figueira 2002. *Krypteia*: Cartledge 1987, 30–32; *as an initiation rite*: Vidal-Naquet 1986, 106–128. *Perioeci*: Cartledge 1979, 160–196; Shipley 1997b; Eremin 2002; Mertens 2002. *Helots*: Hodkinson 2000, 113–150; Luraghi and Alcock 2003 (includes studies questioning the great demographic disparity between helots and Spartans). *Thucydides and massacre of helots*: Paradiso 2004 (doubts the report); Harvey 2004 (defends it). *Laconian art in its social context*: Lane 1933–1934; Pipili 1987; A. Powell 1998. *The Symposion cup*: Pipili 1987, 71–72; A. Powell 1998, 123–126. *Lycurgus and his reforms*: Andrewes 1956, 66–77; Finley 1986, 161–178; V. Parker 1993; Cartledge 2002, 27–29, 57–68. *Spartan education*: Kennel 1995; Cartledge 2001; Ducat 2006. *Spartan pederasty*: Cartledge 2001, 91–105. *Spartan girls and women*: Dewald 1981; Scanlon 1998; Cartledge 2001, 106–126; Pomeroy 2002. *Spartan maiden songs*: Robbins 1994; Calame 1997. *Spartan rhetra and government*: Cartledge 1987, 116–132; van Wees 1999. *Common messes*: Singor 1999; Hodkinson 2000, 216–218. *The Peloponnesian League*: Ste Croix 1972, 101–124; Cartledge 1987, 9–13, 242–273. *Sparta's Achaean policy*: Leahy 1955, but see Boedeker 1993 and Welwei 2004. *Cleomenes and his reign*: Jeffrey 1976, 123–127; Cawkwell 1993; Ste Croix 2004, 421–440.

8

Hoplites and Their Values

CHAPTER CONTENTS

Ancient Greece from Homer to Alexander: The Evidence, First Edition. Joseph Roisman.
© 2011 Blackwell Publishing Ltd. Translations © 2011 John Yardley. Published 2011 by Blackwell Publishing Ltd.

The hoplites (heavy infantrymen) long dominated Greek land warfare as well as perceptions of desirable martial and manly conduct. Some characteristics of hoplite warfare, such as fighting en masse, can be found already in Homer (e.g., *Iliad* 13.129–133). Archaeological evidence shows hoplite weapons in use in the late eighth century. There is a lively debate among scholars about when the Greeks fully adopted the hoplite style of warfare and even about the nature of hoplite warfare itself, with some dating it to as late as the fifth century. The current chapter follows the more "orthodox" view, which suggests that by the sixth century hoplite warfare dominated the battlefield and continued with variations down to the Hellenistic Age.

This chapter discusses hoplite weapons and formations as well as expectations of hoplites on the battlefield. It also examines the supposed impact of hoplite warfare on the politics of Archaic Greece.

8.1 Hoplites and Their Weapons

The term hoplite (*hoplitês*) probably means "armed," although the historian Diodorus of Sicily (15.44.3) argues, possibly wrongly, that it comes from *hoplon*, a later term for shield. The circular hoplite shield was concave, about 1 meter in diameter, made of wooden planks covered with polished bronze, and weighed around 6 kilos (ca. 12–16 pounds). It was held by a supportive arm-strap and handgrip. The Archaic hoplite wore a bronze helmet that often covered his head, ears, nose, and neck. A crest made the soldier look taller. The protection provided by the helmet came at the expense of good hearing and peripheral vision, and by the late fifth century the helmet had been modified so that it protected only the crown of the head. A bronze corselet protected the upper body. Due to its weight (ca. 16 kilos/35 pounds), unwieldiness, and lack of ventilation, the corselet was later replaced by lighter protective gear or was completely discarded. Bronze greaves protected the legs, and, during the early Archaic Age wealthy hoplites even wore bronze foot-guards. The hoplite's major offensive weapon was the spear, used chiefly for stabbing. It was 2–2.5 meters long, made of wood, with a spearhead and a spike butt. The sword, measuring up to 0.6 meter, was a secondary weapon which the soldier used for hand-to-hand combat and to strike fallen or wounded enemies. In the fifth century a single-edge slashing sword replaced the cut-and-thrust type. All together, the panoply (outfit) could weigh up to ca. 23–30 kilos, and its cost put it out of reach of the poor, although it was affordable to the middle-income and higher class. The equipment was rarely uniform, and starting from the sixth century it became lighter, more selective, and hence within the means of many Greeks.

The soldier shown in Figure 8.1 is part of a frieze that decorated a bronze jar, ca. 530–520, known as the Vix Krater, which was found in the tomb of a Celtic princess in southern France. Most scholars identify the krater as a Laconian product, but Corinthian or Southern Italian origins have also been suggested. The hoplite is shown wearing most of the weapons described above, except

Figure 8.1   A soldier on the frieze of the Vix Krater, ca. 530–520. The Art Archive/
Archaeological Museum, Châtillon-sur-Seine/Gianni Dagli Orti.

for the sword. The spear in his right hand has been lost. Note the warrior's
long hair, which was sported especially by the Spartans. Normally a leather
apron riveted to the base of the cuirass (breastplate) protected the groin.

8.2   Standing in a Phalanx Formation

The hoplite's weapons were designed to be used for both fighting in formation
and individual combat. The scene of hoplite battle in both the Archaic and
Classical periods was a combination of conventions, attempts at disciplined
conduct, and chaos. Before battle the opposing armies chose a level terrain as
their battleground. Following a sacrifice and divination ceremonies, the generals exhorted their armies to battle. The soldiers stood and advanced in a
phalanx (rank-and-file) formation, often eight rows deep. Ideally they were
supposed to retain their cohesive formation. Indeed, reliance on fellow-soldiers
and the desire to attain full protection explain both the strengths and disadvantages of hoplite warfare. The shield held on the left arm offered better

protection to the warrior's left side than to his right. This resulted in hoplites seeking additional protection under the shields of the soldier to their right, and in a movement described by Thucydides in his account of the battle of Mantinea (I) in 418 between Spartan and Mantinean coalitions.

Thucydides 5.71.1

The following is something that occurs to all armies. They become over-extended on the right wing when they clash, and both sides thus outflank the left wing of their opponents with their right. This is because, from fear, each man tries to bring his unprotected side under the cover of the shield of the man posted to his right, and believes that the greatest protection lies in the closeness of the interlocking of the shields. And the man most to blame for this is the man standing in the first position on the right wing, for he is always eager to remove his own uncovered side from the enemy, and the rest follow his lead from a similar fear.

Question

1. Compare Thucydides' description of the hoplites' line with Demaratus' description of the Spartan warriors in Herodotus (**8.6**). How do the two passages inform each other?

8.3 Hoplite Battles

It is possible that early hoplite battles consisted chiefly of duels between individuals or small groups. In contrast to the Classical period, Archaic hoplites fought alongside light-armed troops such as archers and slingers. The initial onslaught was carried out by the first three ranks. Raising war cries, the soldiers ran toward the enemy, trying to break its formation by stabbing and shoving. The rear ranks watched the battle, and helped when needed by pushing the front ranks or by filling gaps where soldiers had fallen. Close-rank fighting is attested no earlier than ca. 500. When the ranks disintegrated, the fighting changed to hand-to-hand combat. Often, however, the enemy fled, discarding its heavy weapons. Casualties in hoplite battles could be relatively low, though they greatly increased as time progressed. It has been estimated that the victors could lose on average 5 percent and the vanquished about 14 percent of their total strength (Krentz 1985). The victorious side, heavily clad, tended to give up pursuit and claimed victory by stripping the enemy dead of their weapons. The request by the vanquished side to reclaim its dead and wounded confirmed the battle's outcome, and the victor in most cases granted it. In the Classical Age, the winning side asserted its victory by erecting a trophy on the battlefield, made of weapons affixed to a stand.

Figure 8.2 The Chigi Vase, ca. 640. © The British Library Board. X.423/1337.

The battle frieze shown in Figure 8.2 comes from a Corinthian pitcher ca. 640 that was found in Veii in Etruria. It depicts an early form of hoplite battle. At the center are two rows of warriors holding their spears upright ready to engage in battle. The second spear each holds may indicate that they are in the stage of hurling spears at one another from a distance. Note that the left group has ten legs as opposed to four shields and spears, indicating a longer row of men. The group on the right is about to be joined by running hoplites still far off. The group on the left is also about to be reinforced by warriors who are partly marching, partly running, and who are still not close enough to join the fray. The boy piper in the middle has been interpreted as playing a marching rhythm for the troops, but it is possible that he is sounding the alarm to the men on the left.

Question

1. Try to reconstruct the contribution to battle made by individual hoplites based on the Vix Krater (Figure 8.1), the Chigi Vase (Figure 8.2), and Thucydides' account (**8.2**).

8.4 Hoplite Ideals

The model hoplite was physically strong, disciplined, and courageous. He maintained the group's male solidarity and contributed to the interdependence of its members. In many Greek states, hoplite values were identical to, or incorporated into, the civic and masculine ethos, which promoted cooperation, solidarity, bodily strength, patriotism, valor, order, and self-control. The seventh-century poet Tyrtaeus wrote poems that instilled these values in young Spartan warriors primarily through fear of shame. Death on the battlefield was noble as opposed to disgraceful flight, and courage and excellence were equated with standing one's ground in close formation. Tyrtaeus also refers to the mingling of light-armed and hoplites in the fighting. Later they would be separated into different units, with the light-armed suffering lower prestige in comparison with the hoplites.

8.4.A   Do Not Flee But Stand Your Ground

Tyrtaeus fr. 11 (West)

You are descendants of unconquerable Heracles – so take heart! Not yet does Zeus have his neck turned aside.[1] Do not fear the large numbers of men and do not be dismayed. Let each man hold his shield straight toward the enemy front line, **(5)** regarding life as being hateful and the black shades of death as being as lovely as the rays of the sun.

For you know how destructive are the works of Ares who brings many tears, and you have great experience of the character of painful warfare. **(10)** Young men, you have been with those in flight as well as those in pursuit, and you have had a surfeit of both. Now, those who stand at each other's side and dare to advance to fight at close quarters in the front ranks – these die in fewer numbers, and they keep safe the host behind them. But when men flee in fear, all valor [*aretê*] is lost; **(15)** for no one could put into words all the ills that befall a man if he suffers dishonor. For it is a terrible thing to stab a fleeing man in the back in lethal combat; and shameful is a man's corpse that lies in the dust, **(20)** his back run through by the point of a spear.

Instead, with both feet set solidly on the ground and biting his lip with his teeth, let each man take a firm stand, covering with the belly of his broad shield his thighs, **(25)** his shins below, his breast, and his shoulders. Let him brandish his strong spear in his right hand, and shake the fearful crest above his head. Let him learn soldiering from doing mighty deeds, and not stand holding his shield out of range of spears. No, rather let each man come to close quarters and take on the enemy, **(30)** wounding him with his long lance or sword; and with foot set against foot, and pressing shield on shield, crest against crest, and helmet against helmet, let him fight a man, with sword-hilt or long spear in hand. **(35)** And you, skirmishers, take cover beneath the shield at your various stations, and strike them with your great stones, hurling at them your smooth spears as you stand next to the heavy-armed.

Note

1. *The line is unclear, and possibly means that Zeus has not turned away from the Spartans.*

Tyrtaeus gives *aretê* (excellence) the exclusive meaning of military courage. Contesting the Homeric forms of excellence in sport, physical strength and beauty, kingly status, and speaking skills, Tyrtaeus dwells on discipline and the courage of standing one's ground. The reward for the dead soldier is communal honor and (Homeric) fame for him and his family. The surviving soldiers enjoyed the respect of all. About three centuries later, both Plato and Aristotle would criticize Sparta for restricting excellence to military courage at the expense of other virtues, especially wisdom.

8.4.B The Worthy Man in War

Tyrtaeus fr. 12 (West)

I would not mention a man, or have any regard for him, for achievement in the foot-race or wrestling, not even if he possessed the stature and strength of the Cyclopes and outran Thracian Boreas, (**5**) or if he were better-looking than Tithonus and richer than Midas or Cinyras.[1] Not even if he were a better king than Pelops son of Tantalus, and had the sweet-talking tongue of Adrastus – not, in fact, if he had reputation for anything at all, apart from furious strength in battle.[2] (**10**) For the only worthy man [*aner agathos*] in war is he who can stand the sight of bloody slaughter and who, at close quarters, lunges at the foe. This is excellence [*aretê*]; this is the best prize amongst mankind, the finest a young man can win. (**15**) This is a benefit alike for the state and all its people – a soldier standing ever firm in the front ranks, completely oblivious to shameful flight, keeping resolute his heart and spirit, and encouraging with his words the man at his side.

(**20**) This is the man who has worth in war. Quickly he turns the enemy's rugged battle-line, and by his efforts halts the tide of battle. When this man falls in the front ranks and loses the life dear to him, he brings glory to his city, his people, and his father, (**25**) with many wounds to the front, through his chest, his bossed shield, and breastplate. Young and old alike grieve for him, and the whole city mourns, sorely missing him. His grave and his children are celebrated amongst men, (**30**) and so are his children's children and his lineage thereafter. Never does his great fame and his name perish and, beneath the earth though he be, he remains immortal – any man, that is, who was doing battle with valor, standing his ground and fighting for his land and children when raging Ares finished him. (**35**) And if he avoids the doom of death that lays a man out, and with victory has his prayer for glory in the battle fulfilled, all men, young and old alike, honor him, and he goes to Hades having experienced much joy. As he ages, he enjoys distinction amongst the people of his town, (**40**) and no one wishes to do him harm in respect of his reputation or rights. All yield their seats to him, the young, those of his age, and his elders alike. It is the peak of this *aretê* that each man should now steel his heart to reach, with no cessation of hostilities.[3]

Notes

1. *Boreas was the north wind. Tithonus was a handsome Trojan youth, whom the goddess Eos (Dawn) took for a lover. Cinyras was the first king of Cyprus.*
2. *Pelops was Agamemnon's grandfather, who (among other individuals) was said to have founded the Olympics. Adrastus was the king of Argos and the leader of the Seven against Thebes.*
3. *Reading* hos d'aut' en.

See WEB **8.5** for the "Battle of Champions" between Sparta and Argos ca. 545, which was inspired by the hoplite and Homeric ethos.

Questions

1. How does Tyrtaeus relate actions in battle to martial values?
2. What means does Tyrtaeus use to indoctrinate his audience into becoming ideal warriors?
3. What constituted victory and merit according to Tyrtaeus (**8.4**) and the story of the Battle of Champions (WEB **8.5**)?

8.6 The Spartan or Hoplite Ideology

The Spartan army was considered the best in the Greek world, largely because it excelled in meeting the standards of hoplite warfare. Herodotus describes the Spartan hoplite ethos in a speech he attributes to the exiled Spartan king Demaratus, who joined the Persian king Xerxes in the invasion of Greece in 480. Demaratus informs Xerxes of the character of Spartan warriors in a way that foretells their fighting to the death in the battle of Thermopylae (for which see **17.11**: "The Battle of Thermopylae"). Other Greeks shared the Spartans' martial values described here.

Herodotus 7.104.3–5

(**7.104.3**) Personally, I do not claim to be able to fight ten men, or two men, and I would not willingly fight one-on-one. If it were necessary, however, or if there were some great struggle that stirred my spirit, then I would be the most pleased fighting one of these men who claim to be able to take on three Greeks each. (**104.4**) That is how it is with the Lacedaemonians. Fighting as individuals they are inferior to no men, but in a body they are the finest warriors alive. For though they are free, they are not entirely free. They have a master, the law, and they stand in far greater awe of it than your subjects do of you. (**104.5**) At all events, they carry out its bidding to the letter, and its bidding is always the same – it does not allow them to run from battle before any multitude of men, but they must remain in their posts, and conquer or fall. If you think I'm talking nonsense when I say this, then I will remain silent in future – I only spoke on this occasion because I was made to. However, may matters turn out as you wish, Your Majesty.

Question

1. What was expected of the Spartan hoplite?

8.7 Hoplites and Politics

According to Aristotle, the hoplites' contribution on the battlefield was translated into political gains and made the politics of the polis more participatory. Scholars are divided on the merits of his thesis. Some agree with the philosopher, arguing that the dependence of the polis on non-elite hoplites for its security encouraged hoplites to seek and attain political power. Others maintain that hoplites supported tyrants against the established aristocracy, or shaped the dominant ideology and practices of Sparta. Yet there are historians who dispute any link between military tactics and political power. They argue that the commoners had always made a significant contribution to the military, but still remained politically weak. They note that there is no evidence that the army of the polis changed its composition from cavalry, manned by nobles, to hoplites, and that not all hoplites were equal or gained political power. The correlation between political and military dominance, then, simplifies a more complex evolutionary process. The debate is unlikely to be resolved soon.

Aristotle *Politics* 4.10.10–11 1297b16–28

... The first political organization amongst the Greeks in the period following the monarchies was made up of warriors, and initially of cavalrymen. This is because it was with cavalry that strength and superiority in battle lay. Heavy infantry is useless without tactical configuration, and knowledge of such matters, and fighting in ranks, did not exist amongst the ancients, so that their strength lay in the cavalry. As the city-states grew, however, and armed infantry became more important, more people began to be involved in the political process. This is why what we now call "constitutions" the men of former times called "democracies." Now the ancient constitutions were, naturally, oligarchic and regal in nature; for, given the smallness of their population, the city-states did not possess much of a middle class, with the result that these people, being few in number as well as in terms of political organization, were more ready to accept being ruled.

See WEB **8.8** for a link to depictions of hoplites on Greek vases.

Review Questions

1. What did the hoplites' equipment consist of and how did it relate to the hoplite formation (**8.1–3**)?
2. What were the cardinal values that guided hoplites in battle (**8.4–6**)?
3. To what extent were hoplite warfare and ideals community bound?
4. In what way did the Spartan education of boys and girls (**7.15**, **7.17**) contribute to the Spartans' excellence as hoplites?
5. Try to reconstruct a battle scene using the visual evidence produced here (Figures 8.1, 8.2), Thucydides' description of battle (**8.2**), and Tyrtaeus' poems (**8.4**).

Suggested Readings

Hoplite weapons and warfare: Snodgrass 1967, 48–76; Krentz 1985; Hanson 1991, 1998, 219–286; Schwartz 2009; but also van Wees 2004, 47–60. *The Chigi Vase*: Snodgrass 1964, 138; *contra*: van Wees 2000a, 134–139, but see also Schwartz 2009, 62–63, 122–133. *Hoplites' impact on politics*: Andrewes 1956, 34–38; Hanson 1998; Cartledge 2001, 153–166; *contra*: Raaflaub 1999; van Wees 1995, 2004, 77–86.

9

Archaic Athens from Draco to Solon

CHAPTER CONTENTS

Ancient Greece from Homer to Alexander: The Evidence, First Edition. Joseph Roisman.
© 2011 Blackwell Publishing Ltd. Translations © 2011 John Yardley. Published 2011 by Blackwell Publishing Ltd.

The government of Archaic Athens was in the hands of the *eupatridai* (well-born), who dominated Athenian politics, justice, and economy. Nobles held office as archons (chief magistrates), and at the end of their term they joined the Areopagus, a council with extensive political and judicial powers. We do not know what role the popular assembly (*ekklesia*) played at this time.

Athenian free men were members first of all of their respective households, then of their *genos* (clan), which was a group of households linked by a common ancestor, and finally of a phratry (*phratria*, brotherhood), which consisted of several clans. The phratry was an association that conferred legitimacy on the household's members. Membership in these institutions was also one of the criteria for Athenian citizenship. As with other Ionians, the Athenians were divided into four tribes (*phylai*), each providing a contingent for the army.

In the late seventh century, the aristocrat Cylon tried unsuccessfully to establish a tyranny in Athens (see **6.6**: "A Failed Attempt at Tyranny in Athens: Cylon"). It is possible that his failure and the Alcmeonid execution of his followers provided the background for the legislative work of Draco around 621/0. Later Athenians legitimized policies and measures by attributing them anachronistically to Draco, while other Athenians, who opposed these "Draconian" regulations, criticized "his" laws. See WEB **9.2** for Draco's harsh laws.

This chapter discusses Athenian politics and society from Draco to Solon (621/0–594). It includes epigraphic evidence of Draco's homicide law, and descriptions of the conditions that led to Solon's reforms. It documents economic, political, and judicial regulations attributed to Solon as well as his poetic depictions of his policy and vision of the state.

 For Archaic Greek laws as well as Solon's laws, see WEB Chapter 13: "Archaic Law."

9.1 Draco's Law of Homicide (621/0)

We know very little about Draco's background, authority base, and the nature of most of his laws, if only because Solon is said to have abolished them, except for those concerning homicide. The scholarly view that Draco codified Athenian laws or substituted unwritten with written laws is unwarranted. Draco appears only to have collected and inscribed existing laws, which now coexisted with unwritten laws. By writing and publicly displaying the laws, he aimed to inform the public about them and to establish judicial procedures. It has been claimed that he intended to check the power of judicial magistrates, but it is no less likely that by confirming the existing laws, he sought in fact to preserve the status quo. The laws were inscribed on wooden blocks (*axones*).

In 409/8, the Athenians decided to revise or republish their earlier laws, including Draco's homicide law. A highly fragmented inscription records a popular decree to inscribe this law on a stone stele and to place it next to the Stoa of the Archon Basileus. The preserved part of the inscription deals with unintentional homicide, which was punished by exile, as opposed to murder, which was punishable by death. It was up to the victim's relatives to bring the killer to justice and to prosecute him. The law regulated disputes within the kinship group over pardoning involuntary killers and limited the scope of revenge.

ML no. 86

(**10**) And if a person [kills someone] without premeditation, [he is to be exiled.] The kings[1] are to judge him guilty of homicide ... [either the perpetrator or] the man who plotted the death. The Ephetae[2] are to give the verdict. [But he can be pardoned if the father] is alive, or brother or sons are all in agreement, or the one [opposing it prevails. If, however, (**15**) none] such are alive, then if all to the degree of cousin's son and [cousin, if all] wish to give a pardon, the opposition will [prevail. But if none such are alive] and the killing was involuntary, and the Fifty [One, the Ephetae, judge that the killing was] involuntary, the [his ten phratry members] may admit him, [if they wish.] And the Fifty One may [choose according to merit]. (**20**) And let those who committed homicide earlier [be subject to this law. And a proclamation] is to be made against the killer in the agora, [by those to the degree of male cousin and first cousin]. [Prosecution is to be made jointly by] cousins, [sons of cousins, sons-in-law, fathers-in-law] and phratry members ... guilty of homicide ... [the Fifty] One ... guilty of homicide ...

(**26**) And if anyone [kills the killer or is responsible for his death, though he has kept away from the market] on the border, [from the games and the Amphictyonic rites, then he is to be regarded as being just like anyone] who has killed an Athenian, and the Ephetae [are to judge the case].[3]

Notes

1. *The kings are either the king archons of different years, or tribal officials. In Classical times, the king archon presided over homicide trials in the open air, since homicide involved pollution.*
2. *The Ephetae were a group of fifty-one (?) judges who in later periods dealt with justified and unintentional homicide and with killers already in exile.*
3. *The purpose of these restrictions is to prevent the killer from polluting Athenians, including those attending Panhellenic events.*

Questions

1. How did the Athenians decide the fate of persons charged with unintentional homicide?
2. What does Draco's law tell us about the relationship between state and family authority in Athens?

9.3   The Background to Solon's Legislation

Athenians of the Classical Age considered Athens' next lawgiver, Solon, as the originator of many of their political and judicial practices and institutions. Moreover, both democrats and their critics saw him as their ideological forerunner and sought to legitimize their measures and political ideas by attributing them to Solon. This anachronism makes it difficult to ascertain Solon's original work or his authorship of poems attributed to him. Nevertheless, poems whose authenticity is less controversial do tell us about the background to his legislation. Additional information comes from the Aristotelian work on the Athenian government, *Ath. Pol.*, and Plutarch's biography of Solon, both of which make extensive use of Solon's poems.

9.3.A   The Situation Before Solon's Archonship

Ath. Pol. 2.1–3

(**2.1**) After this [Cylon's attempt at tyranny], it so happened that there was a long factional dispute between the leading citizens and the commons. (**2.2**) Their constitution, in fact, was in all respects oligarchic, and in particular the poor, along with their children and wives, were subject to the rich. They were called "dependants" and "sixth-part men" [*hektemoroi*],[1] for that was the amount they paid for working the fields of the rich, all the land being in the hands of a few men. If they failed to make their payments, they, and their children along with them, were liable to seizure. And in all cases the security for their debt was, until the time of Solon, their own persons. It was Solon who became the first champion of the people. (**2.3**) For most of them the most difficult and bitter hardship of all aspects of the constitution was their servitude, which does not mean that they were not aggrieved with all its other aspects as well, for they had practically no part in any of it.

Note

1. *Leading scholarly opinion identifies "sixth-part men" as people who mortgaged their land and paid a "sixth part" interest on their loan. They may have reached this status after going into debt.*

The origins of this social distress are unclear, although scholars favor the idea that the elite increased pressure on dwellers on the land to intensify their cultivation. The crisis called for extraordinary measures, and in 594 Solon was empowered to put an end to the *stasis* through legislation. He owed his authority to his position as archon and mediator as well as to his aristocratic background (although he was not a wealthy man). Helpful too was the public recognition he had gained after vocally supporting Athens' war with Megara over control of the nearby island of Salamis. Solon mastered the art of conveying messages to a largely illiterate audience through poetry. He had an aura of inspired wisdom, which people associated with poets who were called to help the state (Tyrtaeus in Sparta is another example).

9.3.B   Solon's Election

Ath. Pol. 5.1–2

(**5.1**) Such being the order established in the constitution, with the majority in subjection to the few, the people rebelled against the leading citizens. (**5.2**) The factional struggle [*stasis*] was violent, and the opposing parties faced each other over a long period. Then both sides together chose Solon as a mediator [*diallaktês*] and as archon, and they put the constitution in his hands after he composed the elegy whose beginning is as follows:

"I know, and there is pain in my breast at the sight of Ionia's oldest land declining." [Fr. 4a West]

In the poem he fights each side on the other's behalf, and disagrees with each, after which he encourages them to end the strife that exists between them.

Questions

1. What was the nature of the Athenian crisis prior to Solon's archonship?
2. What might the alternatives have been to Solon's election as a mediator (cf. WEB **9.5**)?

9.4   Solon's Middle-of-the-Road Policy (594)

Solon depicted his actions as fair and non-partisan in the face of opposing expectations: the poor wished him to radically change the status quo, while the rich expected him to preserve it. He avoided taking measures that might alienate either side. He also stressed (perhaps with a hint of threat) that he could easily have become a tyrant but refused to follow this tack (Plutarch *Solon* 14.4–6: WEB **9.5**).

Ath. Pol. 12.1–2, 5

(**12.1**) Everybody agrees that these events took place in this way, and in particular Solon himself recalls the events in his poetry, with these words:

"To the people I gave an appropriate measure of honor, not depriving them of, or adding to, their worth. And as to those who held power and were admirably blessed with wealth – I took measures to insure that they, too, were not badly treated. I stood holding a strong shield over both sides,[1] not allowing either to be unjustly victorious over the other." (Fr. 5 West)

(**12.2**) And again, when he was stating how the common people should be treated:

"The people would do best to follow their leaders, being neither too independent nor subjected to undue force. For excess brings forth insolence [*hubris*] when great wealth comes to men whose mind is not ready for it." (Fr. 6 West)

(**12.5**) And he also reproaches both parties for the complaints they made later:

"If I must make a public reproach against the people, I say they would never have seen in their dreams what they now have ... But the greater men who have more might would praise me and call me their friend." (Fr. 37 West)

For, he says, if another had gained this magistracy:

"He would not have held back the people and would not have stopped before he had churned up the milk and taken away the cream. I, on the other hand, stood like a boundary marker between their two armies."

Note

1. *The metaphor is inspired by hoplite imagery.*

Questions

1. Judging by the fragments of Solon's poems alone, what did people and the elite demand, and what fault did Solon find in them? (See also **9.6**.)
2. Why did Solon refuse to become a tyrant? (See also WEB **9.5**.)

9.6 Solon's Economic Regulations: Land and Debts

Solon's regulations may be conveniently divided into economic, political, and judicial reforms. For the latter, see also WEB **13.4**: "Solon's Laws Concerning Inheritance, Dowry, Women Outdoors, Parental Support, and Sexual Misconduct."

While the poor wished Solon to introduce a more egalitarian system of land distribution, Solon declared that he would not resort to such tyrannical measures. Instead, he abolished debt-enslavement and canceled debts. The author of *Ath. Pol.* (6.1; 12.4) identifies these reforms with what was known as the "shaking off of burdens" (*seisachtheia*), but his interpretation is open to dispute (see Plutarch *Solon* 15.2–4). If the "burden" removed was the marker posts mentioned in Solon's poem (**9.6.B**), which signaled that the land and those who tilled it were under the claim of another Athenian, he might (in a way) have redistributed land after all.

_____   9.6.A   Solon's Regulations Concerning Debts

Ath. Pol. 6.1

When Solon came to power he set the commons free both at the time and for the long term by forbidding loans to be made on the security of one's person. He also enacted laws, and effected a cancelation of debts, both private and public. These measures they call "the shaking off of burdens" [*seisachtheia*], since people had shaken a load off themselves.

_____   9.6.B   Solon on His Regulations

Ath. Pol. 12.4 (Solon fr. 36 Gerber)

"Which of the goals for which I united the people did I not achieve before I stopped? In the court of time I shall have the finest witness to this – the great mother of the Olympian gods, black Earth, (**5**) whose boundary stones [*horoi*] I once removed, fixed as they were in many places. She was enslaved earlier, and now she is free. And I brought back to Athens, their divinely founded homeland, many who had been sold, some illegally, (**10**) some legally, and also those who had fled the country from dire necessity – men who, as a result of their wandering far and wide, no longer spoke the Attic tongue. And I liberated those in shameful slavery here at home, trembling before their masters' whims. (**15**) These measures I forced into practice, yoking might and right, and I followed through on my commitment. I drafted laws for the lower and upper classes alike, preparing fair legislation for every individual. (**20**) If someone other than I, some unscrupulous and greedy man, had taken the stick in hand, he would not have kept the common people in check. For had I been willing to do what was pleasing to the opposition, and then do what the others wanted, (**20**) the city would have lost many men. That was why I took defensive measures for all parties, turning around like a wolf amid a large pack of dogs."

See WEB **9.7** for Solon's regulations of export and trade and on the Athenian economy.

Questions

1. Divide into categories Solon's regulations as reported here and those in WEB **9.7**. Who benefited from his laws?
2. Try to reconstruct from Solon's legislation the issues and problems that preceded it.

9.8 Solon's Political Regulations

Politically, Solon changed the criterion for attaining political power from birth to wealth measured in agricultural produce. Aristocrats now had to share high office such as archonships and positions as treasurer with other men of relatively high income.

9.8.A   Solon's Classes and Their Respective Offices

Ath. Pol. 7.3–4

(**7.3**) He organized the constitution in the following manner. He divided the population into four classes,[1] on the basis of property ratings, in the same manner as they had been earlier divided: the *Pentakosiomedimnos* ["five-hundred measure man"], the *Hippeus* ["horseman"], the *Zeugites* ["yoke man"],[2] and the *Thês* ["laborer"].[3] He distributed all the offices amongst the *Pentakosiomedimnoi*, the *Hippeis*, and the *Zeugitai* (that is, the positions of the nine archons, the *Tamiai* [Treasurers], the *Poletai* [Sellers],[4] the Eleven,[5] and the *Kolakretai* [Financial Officers]), giving the various offices to the various classes according to the level of their property ratings. To those rated as *Thetes* he granted only membership of the assembly and law courts. (**7.4**) A man who produced from his estate five hundred measures [*medimnoi*], liquid and dry[6] combined, had to be rated as a *Pentakosiomedimnos*; those producing three hundred had to be rated a *Hippeis*, though according to some this class depended on the ability to maintain a horse ... Those producing two hundred liquid and dry measures were to be rated as *Zeugitai*; and all the others were rated as *Thetes*, and held no public office. Thus, even today, when a person asks someone who is about to draw lots for any magistracy the class to which he belongs, no one would say he was a *Thês*.

Notes

1.   *Unlike scholars who regard the four classes as a later invention, it is assumed here that, except for the* Pentakosiomedimnoi, *all other appellations preceded Solon, who gave them a new meaning.*
2.   *The term* Zeugitai *refers either to soldiers (i.e., hoplites) of the same rank, or to men who owned a pair of yoked oxen, that is, middle-income farmers.*
3.   *The* Thetes *were often identified with the poor.*
4.   *In the Classical period, the Sellers (Poletai) dealt with state contracts and confiscated property.*
5.   *The Eleven were in charge of prison and execution. They were aided by a force of public slaves, the "Scythian Archers," in the performance of some policing duties.*
6.   *The liquid and dry measures refer to products such as oil or wine (liquid) and grain (dry).*

Solon made election to the archonship more accessible. He increased the number of candidates for the office to forty and subjected the choice of archon to the lot. The tyrants would later change it to an open election (*Ath. Pol.* 22.5). Solon is also said to have instituted the *Boulê*, or Council. Scholars are divided on the historicity of this tradition, which is assumed here to be credible. According to Plutarch *Solon* 19.1, the council played a probouleutic (preparatory) role when it debated and approved in advance issues for the assembly's agenda. The Areopagus retained its power to oversee the administration and the political system.

9.8.B   Solon and Election to Offices

Ath. Pol. 8.1–2, 4–5

(**8.1**) He had appointments to magistracies made by lot, the slate of candidates being selected by vote by each of the tribes.[1] Each tribe chose ten candidates for the nine archonships, and they picked the nine from these by lot. An indication that Solon based the election to the offices on the property classes is the law relating to the Treasurers that the Athenians still have in force today; for this ordains that the Treasurers must be selected by lot from the *Pentakosiomedimnoi*. (**8.2**) Such then was Solon's legislation with regard to the nine archons; for in early times the Council of the Areopagus called in people it considered suitable for each of the magistracies and put them in office for a year...

(**8.4**) Solon also created a Council of four hundred, a hundred from each tribe, but he authorized the Council of the Areopagus to oversee the laws, as it had earlier been the overseer of the constitution. This body supervised the largest number of the state's functions, and its most important ones; it disciplined offenders, and had the authority to inflict fines and punishments. It could also bring to the acropolis the money gathered in fines without registering the reason for them, and try people conspiring to overthrow the state. Solon had established a legal process [*eisangelia*: denouncement] for prosecuting them.[2] (**8.5**) He could see that the city was frequently subject to civil strife, and that a number of citizens, through apathy, would merely accept whatever came along. He therefore passed a law with specific reference to such people: anyone failing to take up arms in support of either party in a time of civil strife was to be deprived of citizen rights [*atimos*] and no longer be a member of the city-state.[3]

Notes

1. *This version is preferable to the tradition that Solon did not change the mode of election of magistrates (Aristotle Politics 2.9.1–4 1273b35–1274a17).*
2. *The judicial procedure of denouncement and the role of defending democracy belonged to later times.*
3. *If authentic, the law against neutrality was probably designed to encourage civic engagement.*

Questions

1. How was political power distributed in Solon's Athens?
2. Who was most affected by Solon's political reforms and how?

9.9   Solon's Judicial Regulations

Many of Solon's judicial reforms had political ramifications. Speaking in hindsight, the fourth-century author of the *Ath. Pol.* could even call them democratic. Indeed, Solon's proclamation in his poem above that he gave similar laws to the high and low (*Ath. Pol.* 12.5: **9.4**) is akin to the democratic principle of *isonomia*, or equality before the law.

Ath. Pol. 9.1; cf. Plutarch *Solon* 18.2–3

(**9.1**) Such, then, was the character of the reforms of the magistracies. These three features of Solon's constitution appear to be the most democratic: first and foremost, the ban on loans made on the security of one's person; secondly, the feasibility granted to anyone who wanted it to claim redress on behalf of wronged parties; and, third, the right of appeal to the courts.[1] It was in this last, they say, that the power of the common people lay; for when the commons are master of the vote they are master of the constitution.

Note

1. *The author calls the popular court* dikasterion *(jury court), which is a later democratic term. The Solonian term for the court was* heliaia, *which referred to the popular assembly in its judicial capacity.*

The permission Solon gave to third parties to sue on behalf of those who had been wronged expanded the legal sphere to any interested citizen. Following Solon, legal actions were divided into two types. One was the private suit (*dikê*), which allowed only those parties personally involved in the dispute, or their relatives, to prosecute, as in the case of theft or certain kinds of homicide. The other type was the public action (*graphê*), which any citizen could initiate, as in the case of impiety or insolent behavior (*hubris*). Public actions undertaken by a third party exposed the wrongdoer to suits even when the victim was reluctant to prosecute, perhaps out of fear of repercussions or ignorance of the law. They also made officials accountable to the state, although the initiative to bring charges against office-holders was left to volunteer citizens. Public actions, then, were more egalitarian and civic-minded than private suits because they gave protection to the weaker party and encouraged citizens toward greater civic engagement in public affairs. In addition, the right to appeal magistrates' verdicts (*ephesis*) in the popular court empowered the people.

For regulations concerning public and private conduct and family property attributed to Solon, see WEB **13.4**: "Solon's Laws Concerning Inheritance, Dowry, Women Outdoors, Parental Support, and Sexual Misconduct."

All in all, Solon sought to unify the Athenians around the idea that membership in the polis meant taking responsibility for its welfare. He construed the city-state as a political community, in which every citizen, regardless of his status, had a share. The shares were unequal, but they entailed an obligation to participate in public life and the responsibility to insure communal peace. He hoped to gain maximum support for his policy and vision by decrying what was universally condemned, namely, selfishness, greed, injustice, and hubristic behavior, and advocating what was universally condoned, namely, justice and self-control. Political and social justice would prevent *stasis* from destroying what all Athenians were supposed to aspire to: a city governed by good order (*eunomia*).

Solon fr. 4 (Gerber)

Our city-state will never perish through the decree of Zeus and the will of the blessed undying gods; for a great-hearted goddess, Pallas Athena, our protectress and daughter of a mighty father, holds her hands over it. (**5**) But the citizens themselves, putting their trust in money, are willing to destroy a great city by their folly, and the thinking of the leaders of the people is unjust – sure to suffer many woes are they because of their great arrogance. For they do not know how to hold back their excesses or (**10**) to hold now the good cheer of the banquet in peace … they become rich, trusting in unjust deeds … sparing neither religious nor secular property, they steal right and left, having no respect for the holy foundations of Justice (**15**), who knows well, silent though she be, the present and the past, and who in the fullness of time advances inexorably to exact her punishment. This comes now as an unavoidable wound upon the whole city, and the state has swiftly reached the point of foul slavery that rouses internecine strife and sleeping war, (**20**) which destroys the lovely youth of many. For, at the hands of the enemy, our much-loved town is being ruined in meetings dear to the unjust. Such evils are rampant amidst the people, and many of the poor are going to foreign lands, (**25**) sold as slaves and shackled in shameful chains …. Thus the common evil comes to each man's house, and the courtyard gate can no longer lock it out. It leaps over the high wall, and inevitably finds a man even if he seeks refuge in a corner of his bedroom.

(**30**) This is what my heart tells me to teach the Athenians, that Bad Government [*dysnomia*] provides much ill for the city, and Good Government [*eunomia*] makes everything orderly and correct, often putting chains on the unjust. Good Government makes the rough smooth, arrests excess, impairs insolence, (**35**) withers the flourishing weeds of ruin, corrects crooked judgments, softens arrogant deeds, puts a stop to seditious actions, and ends the anger that produces deadly strife. Under her guidance mankind's affairs are correct and prudent.

Questions

1. According to Solon, what dangers did "our city-state" face and how was it supposed to deal with them?

2. Where would Solon's judicial legislation (**9.9**) fit in his vision of Athens (**9.10**)?

3. Compare Solon's concerns about the situation in Athens with Hesiod's grievances (**2.1**: "Individual, Communal, and Divine Justice"). Has there been an improvement since Hesiod's day?

 See WEB **9.11** for a link to a bust of Solon.

Review Questions

1. What challenges did Solon face and how did he deal with them (**9.3–4**, **9.6**, **9.8–9**, WEB **9.7**)?
2. Describe the links between economic and political status in Solon's Athens (**9.3**, **9.8**).
3. Solon portrayed himself as a man who occupied the middle ground (**9.4**); did he?
4. Who was bound to be satisfied or dissatisfied with Solon's regulations and why (**9.4**, **9.6**, **9.8–9**; cf. **10.2**: "Athens after Solon")?
5. Which of Solon's regulations later support the claim that he is the father of Athenian democracy, and which do not (**9.8–9**)?

Suggested Readings

Early Greek law, including Draco: Stroud 1968; Gagarin 1986; Hölkeskamp 1992; Carawan 1998, 33–43, 70–77. *Solon's poems, reforms, and their background*: Andrewes 1982a, 375–391; Manville 1990; Wallace 1998 (democratically oriented reforms); Foxhall 1997 (traditional and elitist measures); Block and Lardinois 2006. *Solon's Council as a later invention*: Hignett 1952, 92–96; G. Anderson 2003, 57–76; *for its historical existence*: Rhodes 1985, 208–209; Stanton 1990, 72. *Solon and Athenian vases*: Morris 1991, 34–35; *and the polis of Athens*: Almeida 2003. *Later images of Solon*: Hansen 1990a; Mossé 2004.

10

Tyranny in Athens

CHAPTER CONTENTS

Ancient Greece from Homer to Alexander: The Evidence, First Edition. Joseph Roisman.
© 2011 Blackwell Publishing Ltd. Translations © 2011 John Yardley. Published 2011 by Blackwell Publishing Ltd.

The sources report that at the end of Solon's term in office, he left Athens to travel in the east. Herodotus (1.30.1) reports that he visited the Lydian king Croesus and the Egyptian king Amasis. Since both kings significantly postdated Solon's archonship of 594/3 – Croesus ruled in 560–546, and Amasis in 570–526 – some scholars have dated Solon's laws to as late as the 570s. The traditional date, however, is much better attested. Solon undoubtedly traveled abroad (before or after taking office), but the traditions about his visiting potentates and teaching them wisdom belong more to the realm of folktale and fiction than to history. See WEB **10.1** for a popular story about Solon's visit with Croesus the Lydian that is informed by Archaic moral concepts.

This chapter focuses on the tyranny that followed Solon's reforms in Athens. It describes popular disappointment with Solon's regulations and the resultant competition for political power among elite leaders. The ultimate victor was Peisistratus, whose failed and successful attempts at tyranny are documented in this chapter. Also examined here are the nature of Peisistratus' rule and that of his sons, as well as their relationship with the Athenian elite and demos. Finally, the chapter describes how tyranny was eliminated, investigating Athenian memories of the tyrants and of those who contributed to their fall.

Judging by their immediate outcomes, Solon's reforms failed to solve the political crisis. Even his abolition of debt-servitude, one of Solon's major accomplishments, might have deterred potential lenders from giving loans to people in need. In fact, rather than reconciling opposing sides in Athens, Solon managed to disappoint or antagonize both.

10.2 Athens after Solon

Ath. Pol. 11.2, 13.3

(**11.2**) At the same time Solon found that he had many of the aristocrats against him because of the debt-cancelations, and that both sides had changed their minds because the settlement had not been what they had expected. The people thought he would bring about total redistribution of property, the nobles that he would reestablish the same order, or make only insignificant changes. Solon, however, opposed both parties; and though he could have become tyrant by siding with whichever party he wished, he chose to incur the animosity of both by saving his country and establishing the legislation that was best for it.

(**13.3**) In short, the Athenians continued in their state of factional strife. Some saw their motivation and justification in the cancelation of debts, which had in their case resulted in their becoming poorer; others were dismayed with the constitution because of the great change that had occurred; and some were driven by personal rivalry that existed among them.

10.3 Rivalry for Power

The crisis resulted in irregular archonships. There were two years without an archon (*anarchia*) in 590/89 and 586/5, and one archon, Damasias, held the office for two years and two months (582–580). There was also a board of ten archons of mixed income and social background that followed Damasias for an unspeci-fied time (*Ath. Pol.* 13.1–2). It appears that Solon's reforms destabilized the politi-cal system. They also fostered divisions within the elite, with some ambitious Athenians looking for support outside its circle. Eventually, the contest over power revolved around three rival aristocrats, each with his regional power base.

Herodotus 1.59.3

Later on, a factional dispute arose amongst the Athenians, between the men of the coast and those of the plain, the former under the leadership of Megacles son of Alcmaeon, and the latter under Lycurgus son of Aristolaedes. Peisistratus, aiming at tyranny, formed a third party: gathering together his partisans, he championed the cause of "the men of the hills"...[1]

Note

1. *Herodotus calls Peisistratus' followers* hyperakrioi, *i.e., those who live across the hills. Other sources (Ath. Pol. 13.4; Plutarch Solon 29.1) call them* diakrioi, *the hill-men. Diakria was a region in northeast Attica.*

The author of the *Ath. Pol.* (13.4) anachronistically attributes to the three leaders political orientations that appear only later in Athenian history. He claims that Megacles stood for a moderate government, Lycurgus for an oligar-chy, and Peisistratus for a "most democratic" agenda (cf. Plutarch *Solon* 13.1, who wrongly dates the conflict to before Solon, but also ibid. 29.1).

All three contestants for power were likely noblemen. The "coast" led by the Alcmeonid Megacles centered on the west coast of Attica. The "plain" led by Lycurgus was the central plain close to the city, while Peisistratus' "men of the hills" came from northeast Attica. It appears that Megacles stood at the head of mid-income farmers and the non-aristocratic rich. Lycurgus might have represented the established elite of large landowners, and Peisistratus led the poor and other elements who were unhappy with the status quo. But since none of these social groups resided exclusively in one region, their geographi-cal appellations represented only the core support of each leader.

Question

1. Why were people dissatisfied with Solon's reforms? How did this dissatis-faction relate to the rival factions that followed his archonship?

10.4 Peisistratus' First Attempt at Tyranny (561/0)

Peisistratus had captured the Megarian port of Nisaea during Athens' protracted war with the city, which gave him political capital. He tried to cash it into tyranny, but without success. The stories of Peisistratus' attempts at tyranny, his eventual success, and the later expulsion of his sons from Athens are all tainted by partisan traditions, some favorable, some hostile, which complicate any reconstruction of his career. Hostility toward tyrants, first from aristocrats, and later from democrats, led to their depiction as arch-enemies of legitimate government. Prominent families also had an interest in dissociating themselves from tyrants, Peisistratus' included. While the following traditions on Peisistratus and his tyranny are only partially reliable, even these doubtful accounts are valuable in revealing how Classical Athenians viewed this chapter of their history.

Peisistratus first tried to become a tyrant in 560/1 using trickery, which would become one of his hallmarks.

Herodotus 1.59.4–60.1

(**1.59.4**) Peisistratus inflicted wounds on his own person and on his mules and drove his cart to the agora, pretending to have escaped from his enemies who, he claimed, had tried to kill him as he was driving into the country. He then requested of the people that he be supplied with a bodyguard; and he had, in fact, won a good reputation as a commander in the campaign against Megara, when he took Nisaea and had other great exploits to his credit. (**59.5**) The Athenian people were duped by his story, and they selected and assigned to him a number of citizens, who became Peisistratus' "club-bearers" (rather than spearmen, inasmuch as they followed him around carrying wooden clubs). (**59.6**) These joined Peisistratus in a revolt and took possession of the acropolis.[1] Peisistratus then began to rule Athens without disturbing the existing offices or making any changes to the laws. Instead, he administered the city according to the constitution, with good and orderly governance.

(**60.1**) Not much later, however, the supporters of Megacles and those of Lycurgus came to an understanding and expelled him. So it was that Peisistratus first came to rule in Athens, but since the tyranny he held was not firmly rooted he lost it again.

Note

1. Ath. Pol. *(14.1–3) and Plutarch* (Solon 30) *give a similar account, adding that the Athenian Aristion made the motion to give Peisistratus the "club-bearers," and that Solon unsuccessfully opposed it. I follow here Rhodes' (1993, 198) chronology of Peisistratus' career. The meaning of the "club-bearers" is unclear, especially as many tyrants used spear-bearers as bodyguards. They have been interpreted as instruments of punishment, revenge, and the meting out of justice (McGlew 1993, 74–78).*

Question

1. What does the story of Peisistratus' first tyranny tell us about the nature of political leadership in Athens? What role did the people play in it?

10.5   Peisistratus' Second Attempt at Tyranny, His Exile and Return (556–546)

Around 556 Peisistratus got a second chance. After falling out with Lycurgus, Megacles arranged for Peisistratus to come back and marry his daughter. Peisistratus returned, triumphantly accompanied by a woman disguised as Athena. Judging by his later tyranny, he may have intended to elevate the cult of Athena Paeania in central Attica into a state cult at the expense of cults dominated by local aristocrats. Not long after, however, the coalition between Megacles and Peisistratus fell apart because Peisistratus refused to impregnate his new wife.

10.5.A   Peisistratus Marries Megacles' Daughter

Herodotus 1.61.1–4

(**1.61.1**) On recovering the tyranny in the manner explained above, Peisistratus married Megacles' daughter in accordance with the agreement he had made with him. He had sons of his own, however, and the Alcmeonids were purportedly under a curse,[1] and so he did not want to have children by his new bride. He therefore did not have sexual intercourse with her in the normal way. (**61.2**) At first the wife kept the matter secret, but later she told her mother (whether or not the mother inquired about it is unclear), who then told her husband. Megacles was angry and made up with the opposing party. When Peisistratus learned of the action being taken against him, he left the country completely and, coming to Eretria, he discussed the situation with his sons. (**61.3**) Hippias' opinion, that they should recover the tyranny, prevailed, and they next began to solicit contributions from those cities that were under any kind of obligation to them. Many of the cities provided large sums of money, but the Thebans outstripped all with their contribution. (**61.4**) Not to drag out the story, all preparations for their return were eventually made. Argive mercenaries arrived from the Peloponnese, and a Naxian called Lygdamis, coming to them of his own volition, provided a great boost in morale by bringing both money and fighting men.[2]

Notes

1. See **6.6** (*"A Failed Attempt at Tyranny in Athens: Cylon"*) for the Alcmeonid curse.
2. *Peisistratus would reciprocate the favor by helping Lygdamis become the tyrant of Naxos. He also sent Athenian hostages to Naxos. The Spartans expelled Lygdamis from the island in 525.*

As suggested by Herodotus, Peisistratus succeeded during his exile in creating an independent power base by accumulating wealth and making powerful foreign friends. His capture of Sigeum on the northwestern coast of Asia Minor from the Mytileneans shows how members of the elite used private military campaigns overseas in their competitions for power in their native city. See WEB **10.6** on Peisistratus' acquisition of resources and friends in exile. Helped by these resources, Peisistratus was able to effect his third return to Athens in 546. He landed in Marathon, where he enjoyed local support, although his popular appeal crossed over to other districts. Even Herodotus, who is critical of Peisistratus' followers, admits that many Athenians joined his camp.

10.5.B   Peisistratus' Exile

Herodotus 1.62.1–2

(**1.62.1**) Leaving Eretria, they returned home after a ten-year absence, and the first place they took in Attica was Marathon. While they were encamped at Marathon, their partisans from the city joined them, and others – men to whom tyranny was more welcome than freedom – came streaming to them from the demes. And so Peisistratus' forces began to assemble. (**62.2**) The Athenians in the city had not been at all concerned while Peisistratus was soliciting funds, nor later when he took Marathon; only now, when they learned that he was marching on the city from Marathon, did they come out against him.

Questions

1. List Peisistratus' foreign friends and resources (**10.5.A–B**, WEB **10.6**). How could aristocratic networks and wealth both benefit and endanger the polis?
2. Aristotle (**6.1**: "How Tyrants Attained Power") names Peisistratus as one of the Greek tyrants who attained power as leaders of the people (demagogues). Do Peisistratus' three attempts at tyranny confirm his observation?

10.7   Peisistratus' Tyranny (546–528/7)

Accompanied by local and foreign supporters and mercenaries, and aided by a favorable oracle, Peisistratus defeated the opposition in a battle at Pallene. As befitted his trickster image, he cunningly caught the opposing army unprepared, even deceiving the battle refugees into submission (Herodotus 1.62–63). He ruled Athens until his death in 528/7.

The historical traditions on Peisistratus' tyranny are largely positive. They may go back to the popular rather than aristocratic view of the ruler, who had helped the common people. Perhaps they acknowledge his largely tolerant policies, in contrast to the despotic rule of his son, as well as his contribution to the polis. While Peisistratus reportedly adopted the typical tyrannical measures of disarming the people, relying on mercenaries, and taking his rivals' children hostage upon assuming power, there is also a tradition that compares his regime to the "age of Cronus," or the golden age, and both *Ath. Pol.* (below) and Thucydides (WEB **10.8.I**) describe his rule as mild in nature. Peisistratus helped the agrarian poor with loans and instituted local judges for the people, which reduced farmers' dependence on local aristocrats in legal matters and saved them a trip to the city. He might have used the tithe he collected (Thucydides in WEB **10.8.I** reports on a tax of 5 percent) not just to line his own pockets, but also to finance loans to the poor. These loans and the exemption of some people from paying taxes demonstrate Peisistratus ruling through personal patronage (cf. Athenaeus 12.532f–533a).

Ath. Pol. 16.1–10

(**16.1**) This was how Peisistratus' tyranny was originally established, and such were his vicissitudes. (**16.2**) As noted already, Peisistratus' administration of affairs of state was measured and more consistent with constitutional than tyrannical rule. He was in all respects humane and mild, and was forgiving with those who did wrong. Furthermore, he advanced loans of money to the needy for their work so that they could make a living from agriculture. (**16.3**) He had two aims in doing this. The first was that these people should not remain in the city but be scattered throughout the territory; and the second was that, having moderate means and being occupied with their own business, they would have neither the inclination nor the time to become involved in public affairs.[1] (**16.4**) A side benefit was that Peisistratus' revenues increased as a result of the cultivation of the land, since he levied a tax of one tenth on all produce. (**16.5**) For the same reasons he instituted deme judges, and frequently went himself into the countryside to make inspections and settle disputes. This was to prevent people from coming into the city and neglecting their farm work.

(**16.6**) It was when Peisistratus was on one such journey, they say, that the incident occurred involving the man who was working the land on Hymettus later called the "tax-free district." Peisistratus saw a man digging up and working terrain that was nothing but rock. Surprised, he ordered his slave to ask him what the produce of that land was. "Aches and pains," said the man, "and Peisistratus should get his tenth of these aches and pains." The man made his reply because he was unaware of his questioner's identity. Peisistratus, however, pleased with his outspokenness and industry, exempted him from all taxation. (**16.7**) In other matters, too, he caused the people no annoyance in his rule, but was always trying to provide them with peace and to assure their tranquility – and so it could often be heard said that the tyranny of Peisistratus meant living in the age of Cronus. For the rule turned out to be much more severe when his sons later succeeded him.

(**16.8**) But the greatest of Peisistratus' reported attributes were his common touch and gentle nature. In all matters, he wanted his administration to follow the laws, giving him no personal advantage.[2] In fact, on one occasion he was summoned to the Areopagus on a charge of homicide, and he actually made an appearance to defend himself, but his prosecutor became frightened and dropped the case.

(**16.9**) The result of all this was that Peisistratus long remained in power, and every time he was expelled he easily regained his position. For that was the wish of most of the aristocrats as well as the common people. The former he won over by socializing with them, the latter by helping them in their private affairs; and he was by nature well disposed to both. (**16.10**) Furthermore, the laws of the Athenians relating to tyrants were generally mild in those days, particularly the law concerning the establishment of tyranny.[3] This law of theirs ran as follows: "These are the laws and ancestral statutes of the Athenians: any attempting to establish a tyranny, or anyone abetting the tyranny, shall be deprived, both he and his family, of the rights of a citizen [*atimos*]."

Notes

1. *The argument that tyrants tried to keep the people busy away from the city in order to curtail their political involvement is also found in Aristotle* Politics *5.8.7 1311a13–15, 5.9.4 1313b21–25.*

2. *Thucydides (WEB* **10.8.I***) similarly asserts that the existing laws were preserved; cf. Herodotus 1.59.6. Ath. Pol. 22.1, however, argues that the tyrants did away with Solon's laws through neglect. The last statement may refer to Peisistratus' successors, and perhaps the tyrants followed Solon's laws selectively.*
3. *The author regards the anti-tyranny law as mild because in his day atimia meant the loss of civic rights. In Archaic Athens, however, outlawry involved execution or exile and confiscation of property.*

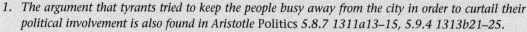 See WEB **10.8.II** for early Athenian coins and the city of Athens under the tyrants, including links to images of Athenian fountain houses.

Questions

1. Describe Peisistratus' style of leadership. In what ways did it conflict with or complement the working of state institutions?

2. On the assumption that the tyrants initiated public projects in Athens, how did the community and the tyrants benefit from them (WEB **10.8.I–II**)?

10.9   Tyranny and the Athenian Elite: The Archon List

The relationship of the Athenian elite with Peisistratus and his successors was complex. On the one hand, Herodotus states that some of Peisistratus' opponents "had died in battle, and others, along with the Alcmeonids, fled their homeland" (1.64.3). On the other hand, *Ath. Pol.* 16.9 (**10.7**: "Peisistraus' Tyranny, 546–528/7") argues that both the aristocrats (*gnorimoi*, notables) and the people (*demos*) supported him. Peisistratus also allowed prominent noblemen to return from exile. Even the Alcmeonids seemed to have enjoyed a period of good relationships with the tyrants. They and another prominent family, the Philaids, later claimed hatred of tyranny. The Alcmeonids also said that they went into exile on this account. A fifth-century fragmentary inscription, however, lists archons who served during the tyranny of Peisistratus' sons; it includes the Alcmeonid Cleisthenes, son of Megacles, and the Philaid Miltiades. It is not easy to reconcile Cleisthenes' magistracy with Herodotus' statement, derived perhaps from a family source, that the Alcmeonids "were in exile during all the time of the tyrants" (6.123.1; cf. *Ath. Pol.* 20.4). The family may have left Athens following Peisistratus' victory in 546 and returned after obtaining his or his son's permission to go into exile again only after Cleisthenes' archonship.

ML no. 6, A List of Athenian Archons

[On]eto[rides] (or, [On]eto[r])	(527/6)
[H]ippia[s]	(526/5)
[C]leisthen[es]	(525/4)
[M]iltiades	(524/3)
[Ca]lliades	(523/2)
[Peisi]strat[us]	(522/1)[1]

Note

1. *Onetorides is unknown. Hippias was Peisistratus' son and heir. Miltiades' archonship and his dispatch to the Chersonese with the tyrant's blessing undermine the credibility of the story that his father was later murdered by Peisistratus' sons (Herodotus 1.103). Calliades is unknown, but the name sounds aristocratic. Peisistratus (the Younger) was Hippias' son (see also Thucydides 6.54.6–7).*

Question

1. How did Peisistratus treat the Athenian elite according to *Ath. Pol.* (**10.7**), Thucydides (WEB **10.8.I**), and the archon list (**10.9**)?

10.10   The Athenian Tyrannicides (514/3)

When Peisistratus died in 528/7, the tyranny devolved without apparent difficulties to his sons Hippias and Hipparchus. Thucydides (1.20.1–2; 6.54.2, 55.1–3) insists that Hippias was the elder brother and the man in charge of public affairs; *Ath. Pol.* (18.1), perhaps influenced by this historian, characterized Hipparchus as interested in love affairs and the arts. But another, more popular, tradition, identified Hipparchus as a tyrant and the older of the brothers, and even Thucydides and *Ath. Pol.* treat them at times as partners. Because tyranny was not an official institution, the division of power between the brothers was likely informal.

A pivotal event was the assassination of Hipparchus in 514/3 by the Athenian notables and lovers Harmodius and Aristogeiton. Thucydides gives the most informative account of the assassination, which he uses to demonstrate the unreliability of collective memory as opposed to his own relentless historical investigation. See WEB **10.11** for Thucydides' version of the Athenian tyrannicides.

Unlike Thucydides, who tried to discredit the plotters' political motivation, there was a popular tradition that made civic heroes of the tyrannicides. Indeed, following the tyrants' expulsion, and especially after Hippias' failed attempt to return to Athens in 490 backed by a Persian force, the tyrannicides Harmodius and Aristogeiton came to symbolize freedom and equality for both democrats and aristocrats. Drinking songs (*skolia*), which were popular in Athenian banquets, celebrated their deed (cf. *Ath. Pol.* 19.3: **10.12**).

10.10.A   Drinking Songs Honoring the Tyrannicides

Athenaeus *Learned Conversationalists at Table* (*Deipnosophistae*) 15.695a–b

In a branch of myrtle I shall carry my sword, like Harmodius and Aristogeiton when they killed the tyrant and gave equality of rights [*isonomia*] to Athens.[1]

Dearest Harmodius, you are not dead, I think. No, they say that you are in the Isles of the Blest where fleet-footed Achilles is to be found along with, they say, valiant Diomedes son of Tydeus.

In a branch of myrtle I shall carry my sword, like Harmodius and Aristogeiton when, during Athena's sacred rites, they killed the tyrant Hipparchus.

Dearest Harmodius and Aristogeiton, your glory will always live on the earth because you killed the tyrant and gave us equality.

Note

1. *Aristocratic* isonomia *meant equality of the privileged as opposed to tyranny and democracy.*

The tyrannicides were the first historical Athenians to be heroized. They were given a state's cult and their descendants were honored with the right to dine at public expense in the Prytaneum (town hall). The sculptor Antenor cast bronze statues of them that were put in the agora. It was probably because of their symbolic value that Xerxes transferred their statues to the Persian capital of Susa in 480, and Alexander the Great sent them back to Athens in 330. The Athenians, however, did not wait for the statues' return, and in 477/6 they commissioned the sculptors Critus and Nestius to recast them. A Roman copy of the later group was found in Hadrian's villa in Tivoli. Both men are holding swords, with Aristogeiton, the older of the two, trying to shield Harmodius with his hand extended. The copies of the statues stand about 6 feet tall, and Aristogeiton's head is restored. A probable base of this group was found in Athens, bearing an inscription that commenced: "A great light came upon the Athenians when Aristogeiton and Harmodius killed Hipparchus"

(*IG* I³ 502). The scene of the couple about to strike Hipparchus was highly popular in Classical Athenian art.

_____ 10.10.B   The Statues of Harmodius and Aristogeiton

Figure 10.1   The statues of Harmodius and Aristogeiton. © Mimmo Jodice/CORBIS.

Questions

1. Was the assassination of Hipparchus a political murder? What does Thucydides' account of it (WEB **10.11**) tell us about the relationship between public and private spaces in Athens?
2. How did the Athenians commemorate the killing of Hipparchus? What messages did the different memorializations convey?

10.12   The Expulsion of the Tyrants (511/0)

Hipparchus' murder did not lead to liberation but to a harsher tyrannical regime, executions, and exiles. In Herodotus' opinion (6.123), the Alcmeonids did more to liberate Athens than Harmodius and Aristogeiton. This is, indeed, Herodotus' own view, and there is no need to regard it as an Alcmeonid claim for the credit of setting Athens free to rival the story of the tyrannicides Harmodius and Aristogeiton. There was also no public amnesia about the Spartans' role in the affair. The Athenian memory of these events included several traditions, and highlighting one or other element depended on its relevance to historical circumstances, the informants, and a score of other factors.

Ath. Pol. gives a concise account of resistance to Hippias' rule and of the Alcmeonids' influence in Delphi that was instrumental in his expulsion by the Spartans.

Ath. Pol. 19.1–6, 20.4; cf. Herodotus 5.62–65

(**19.1**) After this the tyranny became much harsher. Because of the vengeance taken for his brother, and because of his execution and expulsion of many people, Hippias became suspicious and bitter toward everyone. (**19.2**) Some three years after the death of Hipparchus, the situation in the city was very unsettled, and Hippias began to fortify Munychia, with the intention of moving there.[1] In the meantime, however, he was expelled by king Cleomenes of Sparta, who was acting in response to oracles constantly instructing the Spartans to crush the tyranny.[2] This all came about as follows.

(**19.3**) The Athenian exiles, with the Alcmeonids at their head, were unable to bring about their return by their own efforts alone. They were constantly experiencing setbacks, and all their plans turned out to be complete failures, one especially. They built the stronghold of Leipsydrium in the country below Mt. Parnes,[3] and some of their supporters in the city came to join them. But they were blockaded by the tyrants and forced to capitulate, and so they later used to refer to the disaster in their drinking-songs:

> "Alas, Leipsydrium,[4] betrayer of your companions,
> What men have you destroyed!
> Men good at fighting and noble [*eupatridai*]
> Who showed from what fathers they came!"

(**19.4**) Failing in all their enterprises, the exiles accepted a contract to build the temple in Delphi,[5] and from this they made sufficient profit to acquire the help of the Lacedaemonians. The Pythian priestess, too, kept suggesting to the Lacedaemonians, whenever they consulted the oracle, that they free Athens, until she finally persuaded the Spartiates, despite the fact that the Peisistratids were their guest-friends [*xenoi*]. What contributed no less to the Spartans' enthusiasm for the task was the friendship that existed between the Peisistratids and the Argives. (**19.5**) Their first move, then, was to send Anchimolus[6] with troops by sea, but he was defeated and killed because the Thessalians came to the aid of the tyrants with a thousand cavalrymen. Furious over what had happened, the Spartans sent their king, Cleomenes, overland with a larger force, and he defeated the cavalry of the Thessalians when they tried to stop him marching into Attica. Cleomenes then pinned Hippias down at the Pelargic Wall,[7] and with the help of the Athenians proceeded with a blockade. (**19.6**) While the king was prosecuting the siege, it happened that the sons of the Peisistratids were captured as they attempted to slip away. After these were captured, the tyrants came to terms on condition that their children would remain safe, and they would remove their possessions within five days. They surrendered the acropolis to the Athenians in the archonship of Harpactides [511/0]. They had held the tyranny for about seventeen years after their father's death, and the total reign, including that of the father, was forty-nine years.

(**20.4**) The people then assumed control of the state, and Cleisthenes became their leader and champion.[8] For those primarily responsible for driving out the tyrants were the Alcmeonids, who achieved it in large part by forming an opposition party. But even before the Alcmeonids, Cedon[9] made an attack on the tyrants, and so people would sing of him, too, in their drinking songs:

> "Pour a cup for Cedon, too, serving-lad, and do not forget him,
> If we must pour a toast for brave men."

Notes

1. *Thucydides (6.59.4) seems to agree on the date, but [Plato] Hipparchus 229b gives Hippias three more years. Munychia was a fortified hill east of the Piraeus.*
2. *For Cleomenes, see WEB **7.29.I–V**.*
3. *The text is emended from "above" to "below" Mt. Parnes.*
4. *Leipsydrium was located in a hilly region north of Athens.*
5. *The temple was destroyed by fire in 548.*
6. *Herodotus (5.63) calls the Spartan general Anchimolius.*
7. *The Pelargic Wall was probably a late Bronze Age wall, which the Athenians believed to have been built by the prehistoric Pelasgians. Parts of it survived.*
8. *The "champion of the people" (prostates tou demou, lit. "he who stands before the people") was a term for later popular leaders such as orators.*
9. *Cedon is unknown.*

Questions

1. Who were responsible for the expulsion of the tyrants and why?
2. Describe the links between religion and politics in the stories of the tyrannicides (WEB **10.11**) and the expulsion of the tyrants.

Review Questions

1. Why did Peisistratus succeed in his third attempt at tyranny when his previous attempts had failed (**10.2–5**, WEB **10.6**)?

2. Describe Peisistratus' economic measures. What can we learn from them about rural Athenians (**10.7**, WEB **10.8.I–II**)?

3. How did Peisistratus succeed where Solon failed and why (**10.2**, **10.7**, **10.9**, WEB **10.8.I**)?

4. Who was responsible for driving out tyranny from Athens (**10.10**, **10.12**, WEB **10.11**)?

5. Why did the people, who seemed to benefit from tyranny, not stand by the tyrants against their enemies?

Suggested Readings

Between Solon and Peisistratus: Rhodes 1993, 179–188; Lavelle 2005, 66–97. *Traditions on the tyrants*: Sancisi-Weerdenburg, 2000. *Peisistratus' failed attempts at tyranny*: Connor 1987; Lavelle 2005. *Peisistratus in exile*: Lavelle 2005, 116–133. *Early Athenian coinage*: Hopper 1968; Kroll and Waggoner 1984; van der Vin 2000. *Tyranny and art*: H. Shapiro 1989. *The tyrants, religious cults, and civic and religious projects*: Boersma 1970, 11–27; Shear 1978; H. Shapiro 1989; R. Parker 1996, 67–121. *Tyranny and poets*: Slings 2000 (questioning Peisistratid patronage). *Peisistratid building*: G. Anderson 2003, 87–119. *The tyrannicides' sculptures*: Taylor 1991, 13–21; Stewart 1997, 70–75; Ober 2005, 212–248. *The traditions on the end of tyranny*: Fornara 1970; R. Thomas 1989, 238–282; Lavelle 1993, esp. 59–86 (arguing for an attempt to suppress collaboration with the tyrants).

11

Cleisthenes and Athenian Democracy (508/7)

Ancient Greece from Homer to Alexander: The Evidence, First Edition. Joseph Roisman.
© 2011 Blackwell Publishing Ltd. Translations © 2011 John Yardley. Published 2011 by Blackwell Publishing Ltd.

This chapter discusses the establishment of democracy in Athens following tyranny. It documents the struggles of the Alcmeonid Cleisthenes with his domestic and foreign foes, and describes his reforms that gave power to the people. The chapter then examines the nature of the Athenian township (demos), which was a building block in Cleisthenes' reconstruction of the city administration. Finally, it reports on two measures that were associated, rightly or wrongly, with Cleisthenes: ostracism and the creation of the office of general (*strategos*).

Athenian democracy, and Cleisthenes' reforms that contributed to it, was born out of a domestic conflict that spilled over into clashes with other states. The two chief sources for Cleisthenes' reforms are Herodotus and *Ath. Pol.*, which differ over their date. While Herodotus (5.66.1–2) dates Cleisthenes' reforms to the period of his struggle with Isagoras, *Ath. Pol.* (21.1) dates them to its aftermath in 508/7, and the majority of scholars agree with the latter version. Both sources depict the rivalry between the leaders as a typical aristocratic contest, in which each man was helped by his respective *hetaireia* (companionship). In later times, and especially in the late fifth century, *hetaireiai* were groups of men of similar age and elite background who aided their members in politics and litigation. The nature of these associations in the late Archaic period is poorly attested, but they might have resembled the fellowships that supported Peisistratus and his rivals prior to his tyranny. Combining the testimonies of both Herodotus and *Ath. Pol.* suggests that Cleisthenes initially lost ground to Isagoras. In response, he imitated the tyrants by reaching out for popular support and expanded his group of friends to include the people (demos). Isagoras called in his Spartan friends, and it was ultimately the Council's and people's resistance to Isagoras and his Spartan allies that decided the struggle in Cleisthenes' favor. The evidence is insufficient, however, to settle the scholarly debate between those who see the workings of a spontaneous popular revolution and others who doubt the extent of the people's power or ability to act without guidance from the elite and Cleisthenes. In any case Cleisthenes' democratic reforms institutionalized the rising power of non-elite Athenians.

11.1 Cleisthenes and His Opposition

Herodotus 5.66.1–67.1, 69.2–70.2, 72.1–73.1

(**5.66.1**) Athens, great before, became greater when delivered from her tyrants, and the two men who had power in the city were Cleisthenes, an Alcmeonid, who is reputed to have bribed the Pythian priestess, and Isagoras son of Tisandrus. Although Isagoras came from a respected family, what his precise origins were I am unable to say, but his kinsmen sacrifice to Carian Zeus.[1] (**66.2**) These men were locked in a struggle for power, and when Cleisthenes began to lose he proceeded to associate himself [*prosetairizetai*] with the common people. Later he divided the Athenians, who initially had four tribes, into ten, and changed their names. Formerly they were called after the sons of Ion – Geleon, Aegicores, Argades, and Hoples – but Cleisthenes created for them names taken from other heros native to the land. Ajax was an exception, and he added him because, though a foreigner, he had been a neighbor and ally.[2]

(**67.1**) In this, I think, Cleisthenes was following his own grandfather on his mother's side, Cleisthenes, tyrant of Sicyon.

Notes

1. *Elite families were often recognized by the cult they worshipped and controlled.*
2. *Ajax came from the island of Salamis. For the selection of tribal names, see Ath. Pol. 21.5: **11.2**.*

Herodotus goes on to discuss the tribal reforms of Cleisthenes' grandfather in Sicyon in support of his own thesis that Cleisthenes changed the Ionian tribal system from four to ten in order to distinguish the Athenians from the Ionians.

(**5.69.2**) After winning the support of the Athenian common people, which had formerly been given slight regard, Cleisthenes renamed the tribes and increased their number. He appointed ten tribe-leaders [*phylarchoi*] in place of the earlier four, and assigned demes to each tribe; and having thus brought the common people to his side he was far stronger than his opponents.

(**70.1**) Isagoras, now being worsted in his turn, devised the following countermeasure. He called for assistance from Cleomenes of Sparta, who had been a guest-friend [*xenos*] of his since the siege of the Peisistratids; and Cleomenes was actually accused of having sexual relations with Isagoras' wife. (**70.2**) Cleomenes' first move was to send a herald to Athens to order the expulsion of Cleisthenes and many other Athenians (whom he called "accursed," an addition to his message made on the instructions of Isagoras). For the Alcmeonids and their partisans stood accused of the killing here referred to, whereas neither Isagoras himself nor his friends had had any part in it…

Herodotus proceeds to recount the Cylon affair and the Alcmeonid curse (see WEB **6.7**: "Herodotus on Cylon").

(**5.72.1**) When Cleomenes sent orders for the expulsion of Cleisthenes and the "accursed" Athenians, Cleisthenes himself left town. Cleomenes nevertheless appeared in Athens after that with a small detachment, and on his arrival he expelled seven hundred families, which Isagoras identified for him, to remove the curse. He next tried to disband the Council,[1] and proceeded to transfer its powers to three hundred of Isagoras' partisans. (**72.2**) The Council, however, resisted and would not accept this; and so Cleomenes, along with Isagoras and his supporters, seized the acropolis. The rest of the Athenians then united and blockaded them for two days. On the third, all the Spartans amongst them left the country under the terms of a truce.

(**72.3**) So it was that the prophetic utterance came true for Cleomenes. For when he mounted the acropolis intending to take possession of it, he approached the temple of the goddess in order to address a prayer to her, but before he passed the doors the priestess arose from her seat and said: "Spartan stranger, go back and do not enter the shrine – Dorians are not allowed in here." "I am not a Dorian, lady," Cleomenes replied, "but an Achaean."[2] (**72.4**) And so, paying no attention to her warning, he carried on with his enterprise, and thus was once more expelled with his Lacedaemonians. As for the others, the Athenians imprisoned them under sentence of death, and they included Timesitheus the Delphian, whose feats of strength and bravery were, as I could tell, very great.[3]

(**73.1**) After the execution of the prisoners, the Athenians recalled Cleisthenes and the seven hundred families expelled by Cleomenes. They also sent a delegation to Sardis, since they wanted to form an alliance with the Persians, knowing as they did that they had provoked the Lacedaemonians and Cleomenes into war against them.

Notes

1. *The exact identity of the Council is uncertain. It could have been Solon's Council of 400, Cleisthenes' new Council of 500, or the Areopagus. The first possibility is more attractive.*
2. *Cleomenes' answer is enigmatic. Perhaps he claimed pre-Dorian descent as an Achaean.*
3. *Regrettably, Herodotus failed to record this man's story.*

In return for a Persian alliance the local satrap in Sardis demanded that the Athenians give the Persian king earth and water as tokens of subjugation. The Athenian envoys agreed but were blamed for it upon their return.

Cleomenes then tried and failed to lead an army of the Peloponnesian League against Athens, which was attacked also by Boeotian and Chalcidian forces (506/5). The Peloponnesians retreated and the Athenians defeated the other invaders. Cleomenes tried once more to make Spartan allies of Athens and her rulers when he planned to restore Hippias to power ca. 505, only to be rebuffed by the Corinthians again (Herodotus 5.90–93: WEB **7.27.III** "The Second Corinthian Opposition to King Cleomenes I"). By this time, however, Cleisthenes' reforms were very much at work.

Questions

1. What led to Cleisthenes' defeats and later success in his struggle with Isagoras?
2. How did Isagoras resemble Peisistratus?
3. What were the Spartans' reported motives for intervening in the conflict? What do the motives suggest about the sources, or Spartan foreign policy?

11.2 Cleisthenes' Reforms (508/7)

The most informative source on Cleisthenes' reforms is *Ath. Pol.* 21. To better understand the account, it is helpful to look at Cleisthenes' reorganization of the city's political structure from its basic unit, the demos (deme).

Generally, Cleisthenes divided the citizens into demes (townships) that made up larger districts called *trittyes* (thirds), which in turn comprised larger groups called tribes.

The word *demos* could mean the entire people, the masses, the rule of the people (democracy), and a local settlement or township. It is the last unit, which scholars have termed "deme," that formed the basis of Cleisthenes' reforms. Cleisthenes expanded the basis of citizenship from kinship to include free aliens and other disenfranchised residents who lived in the demes (see Aristotle in WEB **11.3**). The new citizens probably supported him in his struggle against Isagoras. Many demes existed prior to Cleisthenes' reforms, and together with the new demes he created, they now numbered 140. Cleisthenes created thirty districts called *trittyes*. A *trittys* might consist of a number of demes, which were not always in close proximity, or of a single deme if it was large enough. Cleisthenes also divided Attica into three regions: city (*asty*), coast (*paralia*), and inland (*mesogeios*). The names resembled those of the regions that supported Peisistratus and his rivals, with the significant exception of the "aristocratic" plain, which now disappeared into the "city" and "inland." Each region included ten *trittyes*. Using lots, Cleisthenes joined three *trittyes*, one from each region, into an artificial body called a tribe (*phylê*). In other words, a tribe consisted of one *trittys* from the city, one from the coast, and one from the inland. "Deme," "tribe," and "*trittys*" were old, familiar terms, and Cleisthenes further mitigated his departure from the past by giving each of his ten new tribes an eponymous hero who had a well-established cult and known myths. Yet he changed the substance of tribal affiliation when he transformed the old four-tribes system based on (fictitious) kinship to ten tribes made up of disjointed territories. The four old tribes continued to fulfill religious duties but lost their political powers to the ten new tribes. By making the new tribes the basis for recruiting Council members, troops, and tribal choruses who competed with one another in the city festivals, Cleisthenes fostered solidarity within the new tribes as well as mixing elite and non-elite Athenians in the city's institutions.

11.2.A   Cleisthenes' Measures

Ath. Pol. 21.1–5

(21.1) It was for these reasons, then, that the demos put their trust in Cleisthenes. At that time he became the leader of the people, and now, three years after the overthrow of the tyrants, and in the archonship of Isagoras [508/7] **(21.2)** he first of all divided the whole citizen body into ten tribes to replace the four then in existence. His object was to mix them up, so that more people would participate in the government; hence the saying "Do not investigate by tribes," directed at those wanting to look into people's families.[1]

(21.3) Next Cleisthenes established a Council of 500, to replace the existing Council of 400, fifty members coming from each tribe, whereas at the time it was a hundred from each [of the four]. His reason for not organizing the people into twelve tribes was to obviate the use of the already-existing *trittys* (there being twelve *trittyes* in the four tribes). That would have meant failing to achieve the mixture of the population that he wanted. (21.4) He also divided up the land amongst the demes, forming thirty units, ten in the area of the city [*asty*], ten on the coast [*paralia*], and ten in the inland area [*mesogeios*]. These units he now termed *trittyes*, and he assigned three by lot to each tribe so that each would have one part in all three areas.[2] And all living in each of the demes he made fellow-demesmen to each other. This was to stop people from using the father's name in forms of address, thereby exposing the newly enfranchised citizens; instead, they would refer to them by their demes, which is why Athenians use the demes in their nomenclature.[3]

(21.5) Cleisthenes also appointed demarchs [heads of demes], and these had the same functions as the earlier *naukraroi*, for he replaced the *naukrariai*[4] with the demes. He gave names to the demes, some of them deriving from their localities but some, too, from the people who founded them, since the demes did not all now have the same geographical location as the place-name. But as far as clans, phratries [brotherhoods], and priesthoods were concerned, he allowed ancestral custom to prevail throughout. As eponymous heroes of the tribes he instituted ten that the Pythian priestess chose from a shortlist of a hundred.

Notes

1. *Since the new tribe was a discontinuous territorial unit, inquiring after the family background by tribe would have been unproductive. Yet citizens continued to be identified by their father's name.*
2. *Because the number of citizens in each* trittys *was roughly similar but not equal, there was a chance that the lot would join together three small or large* trittyes, *thus undermining the principle of similar size among the ten tribes. Perhaps the lot was "assisted," or was fortuitously fair; in any case, it was considered divinely guided.*
3. *Cleisthenes' attempt to allow new citizens to hide their parentage failed. In Athens citizens were identified by their patronymic and deme, for example, Pericles son of Xanthippus of Cholargus.*
4. *See* **6.6** *("A Failed Attempt at Tyranny in Athens: Cylon") for the naucraries' possible function.*

11.2.B   Athenian Demes

Cleisthenes' reforms had far-reaching outcomes. The link between deme membership and citizenship undercut the advantage of kinship and birth and created greater equality among citizens. Cleisthenes also removed political power from kinship groups and religious organizations such as the clans, phratries, and cults. The influence of regionally based politicians was curbed. The tribes, which functioned as political and military units, required politicians and citizens to take into account "national" rather than local interests. For example, Cleisthenes' Council (*boulê*) consisted of 500 members, fifty per tribe, who presided over the Council for one-tenth of the year (*prytaneia*) as its presidents (*prytaneis*). The members' diverse political base and the rotating presidency guaranteed that power in the polis would not be regionally based. (The view

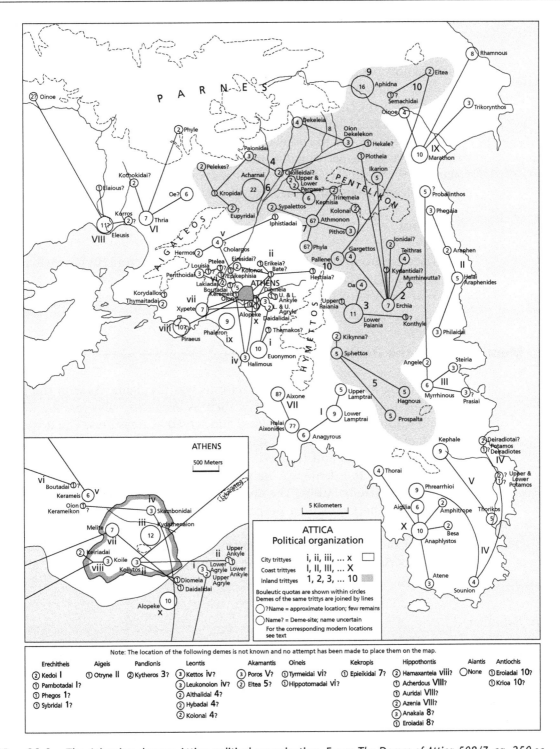

Map 11.1   The Athenian demes: Attica political organization. From *The Demes of Attica 508/7–ca. 250 BC* by David Whitehead (Princeton: Princeton University Press, 1986). © Princeton University Press. Reprinted by permission of Princeton University Press.

that Cleisthenes' tribal system was geared to insure Alcmeonid influence in three tribes [e.g., Stanton 1990, 148–159] has not gained much support.) Moreover, the new system strengthened the links between the city and the more remote parts of Attica. Finally, the mobilization of hoplites by demes and tribes, as opposed to the old system, significantly increased their numbers and consequently the city's military power. Indeed, Athens soundly defeated armies from Boeotia and Chalcis that threatened the new regime (Herodotus 5.77).

The Areopagus was the body that legislated measures. However, Cleisthenes did not change property qualifications for public office or diminish the Areopagus' power to supervise the political system. This was accomplished by later popular leaders who continued the democratization of the city.

Questions

1. Trace the group affiliations of an Athenian citizen from his family to larger groups. What civic engagement was entailed in each group?
2. Why did Athens become more democratic following Cleisthenes' reforms?

11.4 Membership in the Deme

The building block of Cleisthenes' reforms was the deme. As with the polis, the deme had local elected officials such as *demarchs*, who ran the deme's assembly, implemented its decisions, and served as treasurers. The deme was in charge of local temples and religious activity, including contributions to the polis's sacrifices and festivals. Many demes had an agora and a theater. Membership in the deme was hereditary and stayed with a man even if he moved elsewhere in Attica. The deme also served as a military unit and sent members to the Council in proportion to its size within the fifty-member quota allotted to a tribe.

Ath. Pol. describes a late fourth-century procedure for registering and reviewing membership in the deme, whose core may go back to Cleisthenes' time.

Ath. Pol. 42.1–2

(**42.1**) The constitution is currently structured as follows. Citizenship is limited to those whose parents are both citizens, and these are registered amongst the deme-members at the age of eighteen.[1] At the time of their registration, the deme-members make the decision on their membership by a vote taken under oath. They decide first whether candidates seem to have reached the age prescribed by the law, and if they do not, they rejoin the ranks of the boys, and secondly whether the candidate is free and of legitimate birth. If by their vote they judge him not to be free, he then appeals to the law courts, and the deme-members choose five men from amongst their number to present the case against him. If the court decides that the person has no right to be registered, then the state sells him off; but if he prevails, the deme-members are obliged to register him. (**42.2**) After this the Council conducts a review of all who have been registered and, in the event of its deciding that someone is younger than eighteen, it fines the deme-members who enrolled him ...

Note

1. *Prior to Pericles' law of 451/0, only paternal citizenship was required for granting a man Athenian citizenship.*

Questions

1. What were the criteria for Athenian citizenship, and how did the state try to prevent false claims to it?
2. What prevented members of the deme from abusing their power to admit or refuse admittance of new members to their group?

11.5 Ostracism (*Ostrakismos*)

Ostracism was a procedure that allowed Athenians to exile a citizen for a ten-year period. The term *ostrakismos* comes from *ostrakon* (pl. *ostraka*), a potsherd on which the name of the candidate for ostracism was scratched or, less often, painted. Voting with potsherds was called *ostrakophoria*. Philochorus (ca. 340–260), the historian and chronograph of Attica (Attidograph), provides useful information about the way ostracism was conducted. Plutarch (*Aristides* 7.5) has a similar account, though his version that it required a minimum of 6,000 citizens to make the vote valid, and that the man ostracized received the majority of these votes, is preferable to Philochorus' report. Philochorus' claim that the term of exile was changed from ten to five years is questionable.

11.5.A   Trial by Potsherds

Philochorus *FGrHist* 328 F 30 (Lexicon Rhet. Cantab.)

Procedure for ostracism: Philochorus describes ostracism in his third book in the following manner:

The people would, before the eighth prytany, hold a preliminary vote on whether they wanted to hold the ostracism.[1] When they decided to go ahead, the agora was fenced in with planks, with ten entrances left open through which the people would enter according to their tribes, and put in their *ostraka*, turning the written face downwards. The nine archons and the Council would preside. When the count of who received most votes was made – the quorum being 6,000 – that individual was obliged, within ten days, to settle any private litigation in which he was involved either as accuser or defendant, and leave the city for ten years (later it became five). He continued to enjoy the income from his own property, but was not allowed to come closer to Athens than Geraestus and the tip of Euboea. Hyperbolus was the only dishonorable man to be ostracized for moral turpitude and not for being suspected of tyrannical aspirations.[2] After him the practice was terminated. It originated with

Cleisthenes' legislation, which was designed to enable him, when he brought down the tyrants, to drive out their friends along with them.

Notes

1. Ath. Pol. *(43.5) states that the preliminary vote was taken in the sixth prytany. The ostracism took place in the eighth prytany, around February/March.*
2. *Hyperbolus was ostracized between 416 and 415, when two of his political rivals colluded with their supporters against him:* **27.1.D** *("Alcibiades and the Ostracism of Hyperbolus").*

Archaeologists have found thousands of discarded *ostraka* in the agora, the Kerameikos quarter, and the northern slope of the acropolis. The published *ostraka* show that voters often identified candidates for exile by their names and patronymics, and, at times, by their demes as well. Some motivated Athenians supplemented their vote with unkind words about the candidates for exile.

11.5.B   *Ostraka*

Lang 1990, 134, no. 1065

"This *ostrakon* says that Xanthippus, son of Ariphron, does the most wrong of the accursed leaders [*prytaneis*]."

Xanthippus, who was ostracized in 485/4, was Pericles' father and married to the Alcmeonid Agariste (II). The curse refers to leaders generally or to his Alcmeonid connection. The *ostrakon*, in the form of an elegiac couplet, was incised around the foot of a black-glazed vase.

Themistocles played a key role in the Persian War of 480–479. There are more than 2,600 *ostraka* bearing his name. One hundred and ninety of them were found in a well on the acropolis' north slope and were written by only fourteen scribes. Although never used, these *ostraka* show how resourceful Athenians sought to assist illiterate voters, or no less likely influence the vote against this famous politician. The thirteen *ostraka* in Figure 11.1, all wine cup (*kylix*) bases, were written by the same hand ("Hand C").

 See WEB **11.6** for *Ath. Pol.* on ostracized Athenians, as well as for the problems of dating the introduction of ostracism and its role in Athenian democracy.

Questions

1. Who made a good candidate for ostracism according to documents in **11.5.A–B** and WEB **11.6**?
2. What might have facilitated the abuse of the "trial by potsherds"?

Figure 11.1
Ostraka with inscription: "Themistocles, son of Neocles." From M. L. Lang, *Ostraka* (*Agora XXV*) (Princeton: Princeton University Press, 1990), pl. 6, nos. 1211 C–1223 C. Courtesy of the Trustees of the American School of Classical Studies at Athens.

3. Was ostracism fair? Was it democratic?
4. Regardless of whether Cleisthenes instituted ostracism, was it in line with his reforms? How?

11.7 Generalship

Another democratic change, which *Ath. Pol.* 22.2 dates to no earlier than 501/0, involved the election of ten generals (sg. *strategos*), one per tribe. Some time later, the procedure for electing generals was changed to allow the election of two generals from the same tribe, and in the late fourth century the Athenians elected the generals regardless of their tribal affiliation (*Ath. Pol.* 61.1).

Starting from 487/6, the Athenians selected nine archons, including the *polemarchos* (military chief), by lot from a panel of 100 pre-elected candidates. If prior to the election of archons by lot the archon polemarch had higher authority over the generals, it soon became too risky to allow luck to decide who would command the army. Selection by lot also reduced the prestige of the archonship (and consequently that of the Areopagus, which consisted of former archons). The result was a rise in the authority and status of the generals. The office differed from most other magistracies in that there was no limit on reelection to it. This, and the strong link between military and political leadership, made the office of *strategos* highly attractive for the elite. The people too tended for a long time to elect elite members as generals because of the belief that they had leadership qualifications, experience, and a traditional claim to power.

Ath. Pol. 22.2

First of all, in the fifth year after these [Cleisthenes' laws] were enacted, in the archonship of Hermocreon [501/0], they instituted the oath for the Council of 500, which they take even today. Then they began electing the generals by tribes, one from each tribe, and the polemarch was in command of the whole army.

 See WEB **11.8** for public works at Athens that possibly date from this period and an agora boundary stone.

Review Questions

1. Describe the democratization of Athens following Cleisthenes' reforms (**11.2**, **11.5**, **11.7**, WEB. **11.3**, WEB **11.6**). In what aspects was Athens not fully democratic even within the group of male adult citizens?
2. Rank in power Athenian political institutions and offices after Cleisthenes (**11.2**, **11.7**).
3. Was *stasis* (strife) good or bad for Athenian democracy?
4. Compare and contrast Solon's political and judicial regulations (**9.8–9**) with the reforms of Cleisthenes (**11.2**).

5. WEB **11.8** has a link to an image of a stone that marked the boundary between public and private spaces in the Athenian agora. Show how Cleisthenes integrated both spaces in his reforms.

Suggested Readings

Cleisthenes' rise to power and reforms: Ober 1996, 35–52; 1998b (a people's revolution); *contra*: Raaflaub 1998b, 1998c; Samons 1998; G. Anderson 2003, esp. 76–83; see also Develin and Kilmer 1997; Ste Croix 2004, 129–179. *Reforming the army*: Signor 2000; G. Anderson 2003, 147–157. *Demes*: Traill 1975, 1986; Osborne 1985a; Whitehead 1986. *Ostracism and its ideology*: Stanton 1990, 173–186; Forsdyke 2005. *Ostraka*: Lang 1990. *Boundaries of the ostracized*: Figueira 1993. *Generals and archons*: Badian 1971; Fornara 1971; Hamel 1998, 79–87; Mitchell 2000. *Athenian public space and new democracy*: Camp 2001, 39–47.

12

Archaic Society and Culture

Gender, Sexuality, Banquets, and Competition

CHAPTER CONTENTS

Ancient Greece from Homer to Alexander: The Evidence, First Edition. Joseph Roisman.
© 2011 Blackwell Publishing Ltd. Translations © 2011 John Yardley. Published 2011 by Blackwell Publishing Ltd.

This chapter discusses three related topics that figured prominently in Archaic culture and society: gender, sexuality, and competition. It examines societal expectations of young men and the protocols of homosexual and heterosexual courtship as depicted in literary and artistic evidence. It deals with male-dominated institutions such as banquets and sport, as well as poetic depictions of homosexual and heterosexual love and sex. It concludes with a poem by the Archaic poet Semonides that reveals expectations of as well as concerns about wives.

Much of the evidence about Archaic gender and sexuality comes from lyric poetry and illustrated pottery and sculpture. Generally, erotic scenes on vases were popular between ca. 574 and 450, and findings in Etruscan tombs indicate local demand for the more explicit of them. Both artistic and literary depictions of men and women chiefly revolved around members of the elite.

12.1   Manly Youth: A *Kouros*

The socialization of Archaic males into manhood began in childhood, but we are best informed on male youths and adults. Between the seventh and early fifth centuries, families in different parts of Greece put up life-size marble statues of male and female youth known respectively as *kouroi* (sg. *kouros*) and *kourai* (sg. *kourê*). Their function is unclear: perhaps they served as dedications to gods, perhaps as grave markers. One famous example of a male *kouros* ca. 530 is of Croesus of Attica (Figure 12.1). The name suggests a possible *xenia* (guest-friendship) with the famous Lydian king, Croesus.

The statue appears to depict an ideal male youth. The perfect masculine body, the restrained demeanor, and the inscription that commemorates Croesus' death in battle, embody elite males' self-perception as courageous men who are *kaloi k'agathoi*, "the beautiful and good."

The inscription is written in epic hexameter and reads:

"Stand and take pity besides the memorial of the dead Croesus, whom violent Ares once destroyed in the front rank." (Trans. Hall 2007, 170)

12.2   Homoerotic Couples

Croesus' youthful beauty makes him also an ideal beloved (*eromenos*). Homoerotic relationships between adolescents and more adult men played a major role in the introduction of elite youth into manhood.

The literary evidence for Greek homosexuality becomes abundant later than Homer and Hesiod. In the Archaic Age, homoerotic relationships between coevals or adults are less frequently attested and certainly less approved of than pederastic relationships.

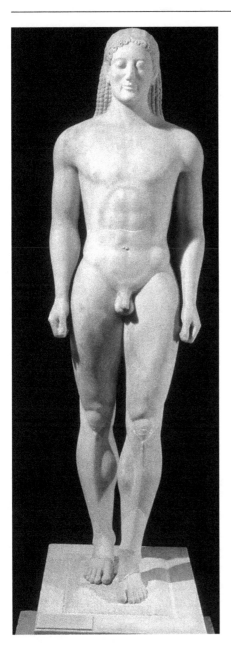

Figure 12.1   A *kouros*. © Gianni Dagli Orti/CORBIS.

At least until the end of the sixth century, a typical homoerotic couple consisted of an adult man in his twenties or older, called "lover" (*erastês*), and a
youth of about sixteen to eighteen years old who had yet to grow a beard,
called "beloved" (*eromenos*). The active and passive modes of the terms "lover"
and "beloved" reflected social expectations of both. The lover was supposed to
initiate the relationship, be active in courting the beloved, and more desirous
of the two. This is how a lover in a collection of poems by Theognis of Megara
appeals to a prospective beloved.

Theognis 1327–1334 (Gerber)

As long as you have a smooth chin, boy, I shall never cease from your praises, not even if I am fated to die. It is a decent thing for you the giver, and for me the lover it is not shameful to ask. But I beg you in the name of our parents, boy, have respect for me, granting me your favor; and if ever you, too, shall possess the gift of the violet-crowned goddess, born on Cyprus [Aphrodite], and you approach another, may the god grant that you meet with the same words as I shall now.

12.3   Courting Men and Women

The social protocols that governed the beloved's behavior encouraged him to play the reluctant object of the lover's affections, decline his sexual advances, and when he yielded, not to shame himself or his lover. Ideally, *eros* helped the lover and other adults to mentor the beloved in excellence (*aretê*), and in becoming a good man and citizen. The desirable adult man and citizen was a free male, in control of his desires and conduct, active, better than other men, and sensitive of his honor.

These expectations influenced the courtship and even sexual conduct of homoerotic couples. The lover might be burning with desire, but he was also supposed to be careful not to feminize the beloved, a future man and citizen. He would give him gifts but never money, which was the mode of exchange with prostitutes. An Attic red-figure wine cup (*kylix*), signed by Peithinus ca. 500, illustrates homosexual and heterosexual encounters (Figure 12.2). The side that depicts male couples has scenes of varied intimacy. Next to the lonely young lover on the left stands a couple, the younger *eromenos* holding in his left hand an apple, which was a popular gift among lovers. He gazes modestly down. The other *eromenoi* too indicate their modesty by covering their heads with their cloaks. The next couple is kissing, with the lover fondling the beloved's genitalia – a common courtship gesture – and the beloved restraining him. The lover of the next pair tries to insert his penis between the beloved's legs but the latter holds him back. Although lovers practiced anal intercourse, artists largely preferred to depict them engaged in intercrural sex, which did not feminize the beloved as anal sex did. Indeed, scenes of heterosexual copulation tend to favor rear entry or anal sex (which also functioned as a contraceptive measure). The lover of the last couple tries to embrace the boy who grasps his hand. The strigils (cleaning blades) and oil flasks hanging on the wall indicate that the courtships are taking place in the *gymnasion* (exercise ground) or the *palaestra* (wrestling school), both favorite hangouts for boys and their suitors.

The other side of the cup shows interactions between male and female youths (Figure 12.3). The men hold walking sticks, which Greek men used to take outdoors, and both they and the women gaze modestly down. The woman at the center offers the man a flower. The scene is very proper. It also

Figure 12.2
The Peithinus
Cup: male
couples. bpk/
Antiken-
sammlung, SMB/
Johannes
Laurentius.

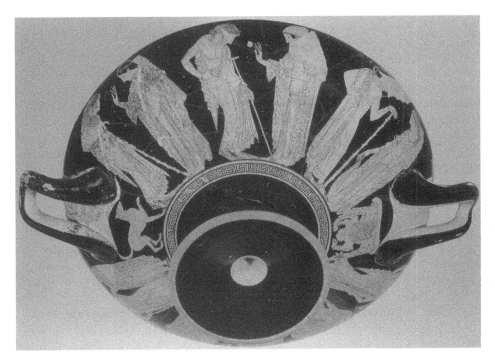

Figure 12.3
The Peithinus
Cup: young men
and women. bpk/
Antiken-
sammlung, SMB/
Johannes
Laurentius.

differs from the homoerotic courtship scenes on the same vase in that it shows no physical contact.

Questions

1. Judging by the *kouros* statue (Figure 12.1), the vase (Figures 12.2 and 12.3), and Theognis' poem (**12.2**), what made a male youth a desirable partner? What gave him power over his suitor?
2. What is proper and improper in the conduct of the persons depicted in Figures 12.2 and 12.3 and Theognis' poem (**12.2**)?

12.4   Cretan Lovers

A Cretan custom that dates probably to Archaic times involved the ritualistic kidnapping of a boy by his lover, and their bonding in nature through the masculine pursuits of hunting, feasting, and presumably sex. Abusive conduct by the lover was supposed to terminate the relationship. The custom has been widely interpreted as a rite of passage that prepared the boy for manhood, and perhaps it did. Yet the author of the following passage associates the practice with the youth's attaining high status rather than with his transition to adulthood. Strabo's source is the fourth-century historian Ephorus.

Strabo *Geography* 10.4.21

The Cretans have a peculiar custom *vis-à-vis* erotic relationships: they win their loved ones not by persuasion but by kidnapping. The lover gives the beloved's friends three or more days' notice of his intention to effect the kidnapping, but for these to hide the boy, or not allow him to take the road envisaged, is most disgraceful inasmuch as it is an admission that the boy does not deserve to encounter such a lover. If, when they meet, the kidnapper turns out to be someone who is the boy's equal or superior in distinction and other qualities, the friends chase him and seize him, but only gently, thereby observing the custom. Then they gladly put the boy in his hands to take away. If the kidnapper is an unworthy person, however, they take the boy from him. The end of the pursuit comes only when the boy is taken to the kidnapper's *andreion* [common mess].

Desirability is considered to lie not in superior looks but in manliness and decent behavior. After bestowing gifts on him, the lover takes the boy to wherever he likes in the country, and those who attended the kidnapping go along with them. They dine with them and hunt with them for two months – detaining the boy for a longer period is not allowed – and then return to the city. The boy is let go after being presented with gifts of a soldier's uniform, an ox, a drinking cup – these are the customary ones – and others which are more numerous and expensive, so that the friends make a contribution toward them because of the high cost involved. Next, the boy sacrifices the ox to Zeus and hosts a dinner for those who returned with him. He then makes revelations about his time spent with the lover, indicating whether or not he was satisfied with it; and the law gives him this right so that if any violence befell him during the kidnapping he can then and there take his revenge and rid himself of the man.

   For good-looking boys with distinguished ancestry it is a disgrace not to find a lover, as though they experienced this failure because of their character. But the *parastathentes* (such is the name given to those who have been kidnapped)[1] receive honors: they have the foremost places at the dances and races, and are allowed to wear clothing superior to everybody else's – the clothing given them by their lovers. And this applies not just to that time; even when they are adults they wear distinctive garb from which each of them will be recognized as having become *kleinos* (for they call the beloved *kleinos* and the lover *philetor*). Such, then, are Cretan customs in erotic relationships.

Note

1. Parastathentes *literally means those who stand by or support.*

See WEB **12.5** for an Athenian law that sought to prevent slaves from courting free boys.

Questions

1. How did Cretan society supervise the conduct of the adult lover?
2. What roles did the friends of the kidnapper play?
3. Discuss the relationship between courtship and status in Crete and in Athens (WEB **12.5**).

12.6   Sex, Power, and the Eurymedon Vase

Since the late 1970s scholars of Greek sexuality have emphasized the power and dominance of the lover in homo- or hetero-erotic relationships. They have defined even sexual acts in terms of power relationships in which adult males dominated women, minors, and the unfree. This view has been recently modified in favor of a more egalitarian relationship between sexual partners and against the centrality of dominance in them. Anacreon's poem (WEB **12.7.I**), for example, indicates the beloved's power over the lover. A mid-fifth-century sympotic vase (Figure 12.4) has attracted much attention in the controversy over sex and power. It depicts on one side a young man marching forward holding his penis in his hand. The other side shows a man in barbarian attire, bending forward with a quiver dangling from his arm, and with his hands raised in a gesture of fear or surrender. An inscription between the two scenes reads: "I am Eurymedon I stand bent over." If "Eurymedon" refers to an Athenian victory over the Persians around 467 next to the mouth of the Eurymedon River in Asia Minor (**18.9**: "Operations in Asia Minor and the Battle of Eurymedon"), then victory, power, and

Figure 12.4
The Eurymedon
Vase. Museum für
Kunst und
Gewerbe,
Hamburg,
Germany.
Photograph
courtesy of the
museum.

superiority were clearly associated with buggery. But the attribution of the vase to this historical event is uncertain. In any case the vase polarizes a manly young Greek with an inferior barbarian, whom the scene derides. The more feminine partner in homosexual relationships was often mocked too for his questionable masculinity.

Questions

1. How could love and wine drinking threaten masculinity (WEB **12.7.I–II**)?
2. What made banqueting and homosexuality popular with the elite?

12.8   The Banquet (*Symposion*)

The banquet or *symposion* (lit. "drinking together") functioned as an institution of socialization and male bonding. Members of the upper class got together in the *andron* (men's room), which was the largest room in the house and accommodated normally no more than thirty people. The host and his male guests dined together, and after the meal reclined on couches, shared drinks, ideas, and songs, and played games. Female members of the household of free status were excluded from this company. In contrast, young male cupbearers, singing and dancing flute girls, courtesans, and prostitutes attended the *symposion*, and provided entertainment as well as sexual services.

Figure 12.5 A banquet scene, Paestum, Italy. akg-images/Erich Lessing.

In an attempt to control behavior and prevent shameful drunkenness (as opposed to merry drinking), the wine's potency was moderated by mixing it with water in a mixing bowl (*kratêr*). However, a *symposion* might develop under the influence of wine into outdoor revelry (*komos*) and unruly behavior.

The scene shown in Figure 12.5 is from the inside walls of a stone sarcophagus ca. 480, found in a tomb in the Greek city of Paestum in Italy. The dead hoped to reexperience the pleasures of the banquets they had enjoyed when alive. The symposiasts are reclining in couples, wearing wreaths, playing music, and one of them is playing the popular game of *kottabos*, which involved throwing dregs of wine at a target.

See WEB **12.7.I–II** for poems declaring desire for a boy and about wine drinking and self-control.

12.9 Competition and the Rewards of Victory

Archaic Greek men of the elite showed as great an interest in sport as in going to a banquet. They wholeheartedly embraced the competitive spirit that inspired the Homeric heroes, their role models. The institution of contest (*agon*) provided a framework for displays of individual worth and claims of excellence (*aretê*) in arenas that ranged from politics and war to sport.

Competitive sport allowed elite members to establish and celebrate difference in an age that opened up the field of politics to non-aristocratic groups, and which promoted collective rather than individual goals and spirit. Indeed, for a period of time, participation in sport competitions was largely limited to the wealthy elite who had the leisure to train for them. Wealth was especially recognizable in the costly chariot race. In short, sport enabled members of the elite to demonstrate their individual superiority over peers and commoners. There was no team sport. See WEB **12.10** for additional information on Greek games, links to websites on ancient Greek sport, and for a dissenting voice that questioned the value Greeks set on athletic victories and victors.

The most famous Greek games were international. In addition, there were many local games. Among the most renowned were the Panathenaic games, which were held every four years in the Great Panathenaea festival in Athens that honored the goddess Athena. They were open to non-Athenians as well.

12.9.A   A Prize in the Panathenaic Games

The oil jar dating from ca. 520 shown in Figure 12.6 was a prize in the Panathenaic games. It shows, from left to right, a long jumper with weights that were held while jumping, a javelin thrower, a discus thrower, and another javelin thrower. Both training and competition were performed in the nude.

Soon institutions like the *gymnasion* and the *palaestra* appeared, which served also as centers of social life for the male residents of the polis. In later periods they came to connote urban existence and Greekness.

The reward of winning the games could be monetary, but it was especially fame and prestige. Hence the prizes for the victors were symbolic and comprised wreaths or vases. Victory brought legitimate pride to the individual and his family, who made considerable efforts to spread their new claim to fame. The Theban poet Pindar (518–438) hired his poetic genius to members of the elite who wished to advertise their own or their relative's success in athletic competitions. In a victory ode written for the winner of the boy wrestling competition in the Pythian games of 446, Pindar articulated well the rewards and joy of victory that included the pleasure of witnessing the humiliation of the losers.

12.9.B   A Victory Ode

Pindar *Pythian Victory Odes* 8.81–97

(**81**) You, with fierce intent, flung yourself upon the bodies of four others. For these there was not ordained at the Pythian festival such a cheerful homecoming as yours, nor when they went back to their mothers did sweet laughter bring delight. Instead, keeping their distance from their foes, they went slinking along alleyways, stung by their misfortune.

Figure 12.6
A Panathenaic oil jar. © The Trustees of the British Museum.

(**88**) But he who has won recent glory in his tender years is raised up by his great hopes on the wings of his manly achievements, having thoughts that rise above wealth. In a brief moment does the happiness of mortals grow; and likewise does it fall to the ground when shaken by adverse doom.

(**95**) Beings of a day! What is anyone? What is he not? Man is a dream of a shadow. But when a god-given sunbeam comes upon them, a brilliant splendor and a gentle life rests upon men.

In addition to attaining personal fame, the victor in a Panhellenic festival brought pride to his city, which rewarded him with public honors. The would-be Athenian tyrant Cylon probably relied on his Olympic victory to garner local support for his unsuccessful attempt at tyranny (see **6.6**: "A Failed Attempt at Tyranny in Athens: Cylon").

12.11   Archaic Women: Sappho on Love

In Chapter 7 we discussed women's roles, status, and images in Archaic Sparta. In this section we look at Athenian and other Archaic Greek women, mostly from the elite.

One such woman was the poetess Sappho from the island of Lesbos, whose fame and popularity earned her the title "the female Homer" (*Palatine Anthology*

9.26.3). It is very unfortunate, therefore, that her surviving love poems are mostly fragmentary. Sappho lived in the late seventh century, and much later traditions describe her as a head of a school for girls or as their chief priestess, although these could be speculations. The frequent marriage motif in her poems suggests that she mentored maidens toward marriage. As was the case with other lyric poets, many of Sappho's compositions were performed. Hence, the poems cited here were not necessarily autobiographical.

In a farewell poem to a girl, Sappho intimates the homoerotic relationship between the girl and the speaker. Female homoeroticism is rarely attested in Greek sources due to the dominance of male Greek poets and their male audience. But as in the case of male homosexuality, Greek men did not disapprove of lesbian relationships, certainly not before marriage, or regard them as a threat to heterosexuality.

12.11.A   "She Left Me"

Sappho fr. 94 (Campbell)

I really want to be dead! With gushing tears she left me with these words: "Ah, how terribly have we suffered! (5) Sappho, it truly is against my will that I leave you."

And thus did I answer her: "Go now – fare you well and remember me, for you know how we cherished you. If you do not, I want to remind you ... (11) and the happy times we had. (14) You put on many chaplets of violets and roses, standing at my side, and many garlands woven of flowers did you put round your tender neck ... and you anointed yourself with rich perfume fit for royalty (20) ... and on soft beds you satisfied your desire ..."

The following poem ranks the beauty of love for a woman above the masculine aesthetic of war and the military.

12.11.B   What is Beauty?

Sappho fr. 16 (Campbell)

Some say the most beautiful thing on the black earth is a host of cavalry, others that it is one of infantry, and others one of ships – but personally I say it is whatever a person loves. (4) It is very easy to make everyone realize this. For Helen, who far surpassed all human beings in beauty, left her husband, for all his nobility, and went sailing off to Troy with no thought whatsoever for her child or dear parents. No, <the Cyprian> led her astray (12)

... and has reminded me now of Anectoria, (16) who is not here. Her lovely walk and the bright sparkle of her face I would rather see than chariots of Lydia and (20) infantry fully armed.

See WEB **12.12.I** for an additional poem by Sappho about Aphrodite and female sexuality, and WEB **12.12.II** for a statue and inscription commemorating a dead female youth.

Questions

1. How might Sappho's poems appeal to both men and women?
2. What themes do Sappho's images allude to? What do they tell us about female experience?
3. Can Sappho's description of passionate women (**12.11**) be reconciled with their depiction in art (WEB **12.12.II**)?

12.13   Seducing Maidens

According to one tradition, the seventh-century poet Archilochus of Paros wished to marry Neobule, but her father, Lycambes, would not allow it. To avenge the insult, Archilochus reportedly wrote poems maligning Lycambes' daughters, and they committed suicide because of the shame. The following fragmentary poem describes Archilochus' seduction of a young girl, perhaps Neobule's sister. It also depicts Neobule as promiscuous and faithless, characterizing her as "over-ripe" in an allusion to her sexual indulgence. Women were often viewed as too weak to control their desires.

The fragment commences with the girl trying to reject the narrator's advances. According to one interpretation, he promised to avoid penetration, but the unclear last line makes it uncertain if he kept his word.

Archilochus fr. 196A (West)

... keeping away entirely. And likewise dare ... But if you insist and your desire drives you on, there is a beautiful young virgin in our house who now greatly desires ... My opinion is that she has an appearance without blemish; make her your lover.

So she spoke, and I answered her: "Daughter of Amphimedo (who was a good and ... woman, one whom now the dark earth holds), the joys of the goddess are many for young men, even apart from the divine deed,[1] and one of these will do. You and I shall, with the help of god, consider these matters at our leisure when it grows dark. I shall do as you say. Much ... me. But, dear girl, do not refuse me ... much ... under the eaves and the gates. For I shall head for the grassy garden, and you can now be sure of this. Neobule – let another man have her. Ah, she's over-ripe and twice your age; and the flower of her virginity has gone along with the charm she formerly possessed. For there is no satisfying [her?], and the frenzied woman has shown the measure ... To hell with her! Let not ... this, so that I become a figure of fun for my neighbors having a wife like that. I want you dearly... For you are not deceitful or perfidious. She, however, is hot-headed and makes many men her lovers. I fear that I if I rush impetuously ahead I may, like the bitch, produce blind children born at the wrong time."

Such were my words, and taking the girl I laid her down on a bed of lush flowers. Covering her with a soft cloak and holding her neck with my arm … she stopped like a young deer. I gently took her breasts in my hands … she showed the fresh color, the onset of youth … and feeling her beautiful body all over I released my white strength as I touched her blond hair.

Note

1. *The "divine deed" refers to either marriage or lovemaking. Other sexual metaphors in the poem involve eaves, gates, garden grass, flowers, and the like.*

 See WEB **12.14** for Anacreon's poem comparing a girl to a Thracian filly that requires taming.

Questions

 1. Compare the poems of Archilochus (**12.13**) and Anacreon (WEB **12.14**) describing the courtship of young women with the description of the courtship of young men (**12.1–4**, **12.6**, WEB **12.5**). In what ways are the courtship rituals different and why?
2. What masculine concerns about women can be gleaned from Archilochus' poem?

12.15 Portraits of Wives

The seduction of girls such as described above might have ended in marriage. Hesiod (*Works and Days* 695–705) advises a farmer to choose for his wife a maiden, who is more docile than an adult woman, from among his neighbors in order to reduce the risk of undiscovered bad qualities or an evil reputation. Members of the elite were equally interested in having a "good wife" of sound repute, but their marriages were primarily designed to foster political alliances or to consolidate property within the family. They attained these goals through arranged marriages that were negotiated between the bride's adult male guardian (*kyrios*), often the father or the brother, and the bridegroom or his father. The bride came with a dowry, and the wedding sealed her transfer from her guardian's authority and natal home to the household and the guardianship of her husband. (See WEB **13.4** for Solon's regulations concerning dowry.) Athenian vases show wedding rituals that included a bridal bath and the couple riding a chariot or a cart to the bridegroom's house accompa-nied by a procession of family members and guests. See WEB **12.16.I** for Sappho's poem describing the arrival of the bride Andromache in Troy, the city of Priam and her husband Hector.

The wife was expected to produce children, weave, run the *oikos*, and thus contribute to the household's welfare and economy. The Archaic poet Semonides of Amorgus uses the tradition of fables, which appealed to a non-elite audience, to satirize women in their roles as wives. His verses reflect his contemporaries' expectations of a wife to serve her husband and the household, keep things in order, and not to shame her family. The view of women as consumers rather than producers, as unstable, and as "mad for love" reappears in one form or another in other sources. But Semonides also praises the busy "bee woman," and his depiction of other wives, comic and unkind as it is, shows that women were not merely passive and submissive toward their male partners.

Semonides fr. 7.1–20, 43–70, 83–118 (West)

(**1**) God at the start made the mind of a woman different from a man's. He made one from a bristly sow. In her house everything lies in disorder, soiled with filth, and rolling about on the floor. She herself, unwashed and wearing unwashed clothes, grows fat sitting in a shit-pile.

(**7**) Another God made from the villainous fox to be a woman who knows everything – nothing escapes her notice, whether it is good or bad. In fact, the good she often calls bad, and the bad she often calls good. She has a temper that changes from one moment to the other.

(**12**) Another he made from the bitch, a wicked woman and just like her mother. She wants to hear everything and know everything; and peering about and sauntering around everywhere, she barks even if she sees no one. Her husband could not stop her, not by threatening her and not even if he knocked her teeth out with a stone in a fit of anger; nor by talking to her sweetly, and not even if she happens to be sitting with guests. She has to have her useless yapping…

(**43**) Another he made from the dusty gray and obstinate ass. She barely does her work, and only under duress and with threats – after all, she puts up with everything. Meanwhile, all day and all night, she is eating in her own quarters and eating at the hearth. And she's just the same with sex, taking on as her partner anyone who comes along.

(**50**) Another wretched and miserable class he made from the weasel. Nothing in her is attractive or agreeable, nothing delightful or pleasant. She's crazy for lovemaking, but nauseates the man she's with. She does her neighbors great harm by her stealing and is often eating up sacrificial offerings not yet consecrated.

(**57**) Another is born of the dainty mare with the long mane. She shuns menial work and hardship. She would never touch a mill, take up a sieve, or sweep the shit out of the house, nor would she sit by the oven – she's avoiding the soot! She makes love to her husband only when compelled to. She cleanses the dirt from herself twice every day, sometimes three times, and smears herself with perfumes. She always has her hair well combed and garlanded with flowers. And such a woman is therefore a beautiful sight for other men, but for the husband she becomes a problem, unless one is a tyrant or a king, a person whose heart is delighted by this sort of thing…

(**83**) Another he made from the bee, and anyone who gets her is lucky. To her alone there clings no blame, and thanks to her a man's life flourishes and prospers. She grows old with her loving husband – by whom she herself is loved – after bearing handsome and illustrious children. She becomes noted amongst all women, and a divine grace surrounds her. She takes no pleasure in sitting amongst the women where they tell tales of sex. Such are the finest and wisest wives that Zeus grants to men. But through the design of Zeus all these other groups of women are, and will remain, a misery for men.

(**94**) For it was Zeus who made this greatest abomination, women. Even if they appear to be doing some good they are more than anything else harmful to the husband. Anyone living with a woman never passes a whole day in good spirits; nor will he quickly drive hunger from his house – hunger, the hated lodger and inimical god. When a man seems to be happy in his home, thanks to heaven's blessing or the favor of man – that is just when she finds cause to blame him and girds herself for battle. For wherever there's a woman people cannot give a warm welcome to a guest. And it is that woman who seems the most reasonable who is actually the worst offender: while her husband gapes at her, the neighbors are happy at seeing how he, like them, is deceived. And each man will praise his own wife when he thinks about her, and find fault with his neighbor's – we do not recognize that we share the same misfortune. For this is the greatest curse that Zeus has created, throwing about us an unbreakable shackle to keep us fettered.

For courtesans (sg. *hetaira*), who were not attached to the traditional household, see WEB **37.14**: "The Courtesan Neaera."

See also WEB **12.16.II** for an aristocratic tradition about the marriage of Agariste, the daughter of Cleisthenes, the tyrant of Sicyon, which reflects many of the social institutions and values described here.

Questions

1. Make a composite of "the bad wife" from the portraits in Semonides' poem. What would be her worst features and why?
2. What powers did women have over their male partners according to Semonides?
3. Discuss the fear of other men in Semonides' poem.

Review Questions

1. What were the social protocols governing the courtship of males and females (**12.2–4**, WEB **12.5**, WEB **12.7.I**)?

2. What roles did men's friends or age-mates play in homosexual relationships (**12.2**, **12.4**, **12.8**, WEB **12.7.II**)?

3. Were there differences between male and female perceptions of female sexuality (**12.1–4**, **12.6**, **12.11**, **12.13**, WEB **12.7.I**, WEB **12.12**, WEB **12.14**)?
4. What complicated Greek attitudes toward sexual desire?

5. What complicated displays of masculinity in banquets and sport (**12.8–9**, WEB **12.7.II**, WEB **12.10**)?

6. What could mar relationships between Greek husbands and wives (especially **12.15**)?

7. What gender expectations and social values are reflected in the story of Agariste's marriage (WEB **12.16.II**)?

Suggested Readings

Kouroi and kourai: Richter 1970. *Croesus' statue*: Stewart 1997, 63–70. *The Eurymedon Vase: victory and buggery*: Dover 1989, 105; A. Smith 1999; *contra*: Davidson 1997, 170–171, 180–182. *Archaic Greek sexuality*: Skinner 2005, 45–111. *Greek sexuality and power*: Foucault 1986; Halperin 1990. *Greek homosexuality*: Dover 1989, with the qualifications and criticism of Davidson 1997, 166–169, 78–79, and 2007; Hubbard 1988, 70–72; cf. Hubbard 2003. *Initiatory pederasty*: Bremmer 1980; Sergent 1986; Percy 1996; but see Dover 1988, 115–134. *Symposion*: Murray 1990; Davidson 1997, 3–72. *Symposion, pederasty, and sex*: Bremmer 1990; Keuls 1993, 160–169. *Greek competitiveness and athletics*: Murray 1993, 204–207; Golden 1998, esp. 1–103; S. Miller 2004 (relying extensively on archaeological evidence). *Ancient Olympics*: see the above authors as well as those in Phillips and Pritchard 2003, 1–74. *Panathenaea*: Phillips 2003. *Sappho*: Winkler 1990, 162–187; H. Parker 1993; L. Wilson 1996; Skinner 2005, 58–61, 71–78. *Female homoeroticism*: Sorkin Rabinowitz 2002. *Phrasiclea*: Svenbro 1993, esp. 8–25. *Archilochus' poem*: Lefkowitz 1976; Skinner 2005, 52–54. *Semonides*: Lloyd-Jones 1975. *Archaic women and wives*: Arthur 1973; Pomeroy 1975, 32–56; Fantham et al. 1994, 44–53.

13

Archaic Law

CHAPTER CONTENTS

Ancient Greece from Homer to Alexander: The Evidence, First Edition. Joseph Roisman.
© 2011 Blackwell Publishing Ltd. Translations © 2011 John Yardley. Published 2011 by Blackwell Publishing Ltd.

14

Archaic Greek Religion

CHAPTER CONTENTS

Ancient Greece from Homer to Alexander: The Evidence, First Edition. Joseph Roisman.
© 2011 Blackwell Publishing Ltd. Translations © 2011 John Yardley. Published 2011 by Blackwell Publishing Ltd.

Greek religion was an amalgam of elements from different times and origins. Some practices and beliefs went back to the Bronze Age, others developed locally during the Dark Age, and still others were acquired from the east. This chapter discusses just a few aspects of this large topic. It reproduces the historian Herodotus' view of the impact of the Homeric and Hesiodic popular poems on Greek religion. It documents the Greek concept of worship and illustrates a place of worship and its administration through the Mysteries of Demeter in Eleusis. Epigraphic evidence for Athens' regulation of the offering of first-fruits to the goddess shows the relationship between cult and polis.

Generally, the Greeks divided their divinities into immortal gods and heroes. The latter were children of gods and mortals who had performed great deeds during their lifetime and became the focus of local cults after their death. The hero's tomb and the area surrounding it, called *heroôn*, were sacred. Like several other chthonic deities, heroes lived in or beneath the earth and received liquid offerings, fruits, and holocausts (burnt sacrificial offerings). This book does not discuss heroes' cults, and only mentions by way of illustration the Spartan cults of Orestes (see WEB **7.27.I**: "Sparta Obtains the Bones of Orestes") and that of the Dioscuri, Helen's brothers Castor and Pollux who were the sons of Zeus and mortal Leda. The Dioscuri were housed with their sister and her husband Menelaus in the sanctuary of the Menelaion. Their images accompanied the Spartan kings to battle, perhaps to draw attention to the kings' divine ancestry that went back to Zeus.

More important than heroes were gods, who were identified by their name, an epithet that defined their function, and their locale. For example, Athena Polias (of the polis) of Athens was the patroness of the city of Athens, while Apollo Pythius watched over the oracle at Delphi. The traditions and practices associated with the Olympic gods, worshipped by all Greeks, were taken from various local cults. Many scholars agree with Herodotus that poets like Homer and Hesiod (in his *Theogony*) contributed to the sorting out of these Panhellenic deities according to family relations, roles, powers, fundamental traits, and appearance.

14.1 Herodotus on Homer and Hesiod's Contribution to Greek Religion

Herodotus 2.53.1–3

(**2.53.1**) How individual gods arose, however, whether all of them had always been in existence, and what forms they had – this the Greeks did not know until, as one might say, yesterday or the day before. (**53.2**) For I think that Homer and Hesiod are to be dated four hundred years – no more than that – before my time, and it was they who created for the Greeks the divine genealogy, and who gave the gods their various names, assigned to them their honors and special functions, and described their appearance. (**53.3**) The poets who are said to have preceded these two men were, to my mind, later than them. The first part of what I have said here is what the priestesses in Dodona claim; but the later material relating to Hesiod and Homer is what I claim myself.

Question

1. What did Greeks need to know about their gods, according to Herodotus?

Religion was practiced most intensively on the local level, that is, at home, and less frequently in the village, the city, and Panhellenic sanctuaries.

Early Greek sanctuaries were established in places regarded as sacred, at the boundaries of the polis, or according to the function of the god, say, Zeus of the agora. At the center of the cult stood an altar, which was oriented to the east in the case of a sky-god. An enclosed area formed the sacred precinct (*temenos*), which was protected by the god and included asylum granted to people seeking shelter. A polluted person was barred from entering the sanctuary area so as not to deter the god from attending it. Pollution was perceived as contagious dirt that could be acquired through sexual intercourse, childbirth, attending funerals, and murder. Purification rituals and the passage of time could cleanse a person from pollution.

See WEB **14.2** for the Athenian purification of the island of Delos in 426/5.

14.3 Worship

The Greeks worshipped their gods in the hope that they would look upon them with favor, assist and reward them, or not cause them harm. People used gifts to honor and gain favor with the gods or heroes, just as they would do with highborn or powerful mortals. Gifts came in the form of dedications, votives, and especially sacrifices. Sacrifices were often a communal affair during festivals organized by the city or its component groups. Hesiod advises worshippers to be pure and honor the gods with sacrifices.

> ### Hesiod *Works and Days* 336–341
>
> Sacrifice to the immortal gods as well as you can, in a pure and clean manner, and burn splendid thighbones for them. At other times appease them with libations and offerings, both when you go to bed and when the holy light returns, so that they may have kindly feelings and thoughts toward you – in order that you may buy up another man's estate, and not another man yours!

Question

1. What were the rewards of purity according to Hesiod (**14.3**) and Thucydides (WEB **14.2**)?

14.4   Greek Temples and the Mysteries of Demeter in Eleusis

Prior to the polis' supervision of religious activity, many cults were controlled by noble families, whose members served as priests, priestesses, and religious experts. In many cases priestly duties, which were not exacting or time-consuming, included performing religious acts and rituals. Generally, statues and temples were built either by tyrants or by the polis, which also regulated religious duties and officials.

During the Archaic Age, and especially the sixth century, many monumental temples were constructed for the gods. In Asia Minor, for example, enormous temples were built such as those at Ephesus for the cult of Artemis, at Samos for the cult of Hera, and at Didyma near Miletus for the cult of Zeus. Besides piety and local patriotism, building activity was designed to attract adherents from the region and beyond. Scholars have hypothesized that the building of monumental temples indicated the existence of self-assertive poleis and a new communal effort. Indeed, during the eighth century, people who in the past had placed metal dedications in graves now placed them in temples. Other scholars explained the building of temples at a distance from the polis as a boundary marker of its territory. Still others surmise that these sanctuaries were the work of powerful individuals and that they were designed to serve more than one community.

The multifaceted character of Greek religion can be illustrated through the working of the cult of Demeter and Persephone at Eleusis in Attica. The cult incorporated local, state, and Panhellenic characteristics, some of them unique to Attica and others common to other cults.

The Greeks used myths to explain the origins of cults and their own relationship with their deities. The most detailed account of the myth of Demeter and Persephone is the seventh-century Homeric *Hymn to Demeter*, which tells of the abduction of Persephone by Hades and her subsequent reunion with her mother Demeter. See WEB **14.5** for the *Hymn to Demeter*.

The Athenian cult of Demeter was famous for its initiation rites, the Mysteries, which were supposed to promote agricultural fertility and provide initiates with an afterlife free from suffering and troubles. Persephone was queen of the underworld for a third of the year, namely, the winter, when seeds planted in the fall were dormant.

14.4.A   The Mysteries and Hades

Sophocles fr. 837 (Radt)

Three times happy are those mortals who go to Hades having seen these rites. For to these alone is it granted to have life there – the others are allowed to have only all manner of ills.

The rites were open to any Greek-speaking adult, slaves included, but not murderers. Although the *Hymn* proclaims the rituals secret, and divulging them was punishable by death, some of the proceedings are known. The Great Mysteries at Eleusis were preceded by the Lesser Mysteries, which were celebrated seven months before the Great Mysteries in the sanctuary of the Mother (whose identity is debated). The purpose of the Lesser Mysteries was probably to purify initiates in preparations for the Great Mysteries. The latter took place in early autumn in Eleusis, 23 kilometers west of Athens. First, initiates went to the Attic port of Phaleron where they washed piglets in the sea and sacrificed them at the altar of the Eleusinion in Athens. Then, on a designated day, a great procession marched on the Sacred Way that led from the Altar of the Twelve Gods in Athens to Eleusis. At Eleusis, participants sacrificed to Demeter, Persephone, and Hades and commemorated the reunion between mother and daughter. Like Demeter in the *Hymn*, they fasted, drank a mixed drink called *kykeon*, and joked in imitation of Iambe (or Baube). The Mysteries were performed inside the temple of Demeter, which is mentioned in the *Hymn*, and which is otherwise known as the Telesterion (Hall of Initiation). They took place at night, with torches providing light. The initiates heard about the birth of a child, possibly called Brimus, who may have represented Plutus (Wealth) or agricultural abundance.

Two prominent priestly families supervised the initiations. One was the Ceryces, who served in the Mysteries as the "torch bearers": Demeter used torches in her search for her daughter. The other was the Eumolpidae, who claimed as their ancestor the Eleusinian ruler Eumolpus (mentioned in the *Hymn*). The Eumolpidae displayed sacred objects, which might have included an ear of grain. The priests also proclaimed a sacred truce of fifty-five days to protect persons going to the Mysteries at Eleusis and served as experts in this cult's traditions and practices.

14.4.B   The Macron Cup with Triptolemus

An Attic red-figure cup by Macron ca. 480 is shown in Figure 14.1 (p. 188). At the center sits the Eleusinian prince Triptolemus on a winged chariot, holding ears of grain and ready to spread agriculture in the world. According to some versions, his chariot was pulled by serpents. He is flanked by Demeter in front and Persephone at the back, each carrying a torch.

A link to additional information on the Mysteries and images of related artifacts can be found in WEB **14.7**.

Questions

1. What religious lessons might a Greek draw from the *Hymn to Demeter* (WEB **14.5**)?

**Figure
14.1** The
Macron Cup with
Triptolemus. ©
The Trustees of
the British
Museum.

2. Which agricultural motifs appeared in the myth of Demeter and the Mysteries ritual (**14.4**, WEB **14.5**)?

3. Discuss local Eleusinian elements in the myth of Demeter and the rituals (**14.4**, WEB **14.5**).

14.6   The Decree of Offering First-Fruits in Eleusis (420s)

The Athenians were very proud of their affiliation with the Mysteries cult. The fourth-century author Isocrates even praised Athens for generously sharing it with others (Isocrates 4 *Panegyricus* 28–29). The Athenians also strove to enhance the status of the Eleusinian Mysteries in the Greek world. A highly detailed inscription, perhaps from the 420s, obliged the Athenians and their then allies/subjects to give as "first-fruits" to the goddesses Demeter and Persephone at Eleusis 1/1600 of all the barley and 1/1200 of all the wheat they produced. The decree strongly encouraged other Greeks to make this contribution too, perhaps because Athens failed to get an oracle ordering them to do so. The wheat was stored and sold in the market, and Athenian officials supervised these activities. The income, and the fee that the initiates paid for attending the rites, made the cult quite prosperous.

ML 73 = Fornara no. 140

Translation: Fornara, pp. 161–162

Decree regulating the offering of first-fruits at Eleusis

[Timo]tel[e]s of Acharnae was Secretary. Resolved by the Boulê [Council] and the People, Cecropis held the prytany, Timote[les] was Secretary, Cycneas presided. The following the Commissioners [*syngrapheis*] drafted: First-fruits shall be offered to the two goddesses, in accordance with ancestral custom and the (**5**) oracular response from Delphi, by the Athenians (as follows): from each one hundred *medimnoi*[1] of barley not less than one-sixth (of one *medimnos*); of wheat, from each hundred *medimnoi*, not less than one-twelfth. If anyone produces more grain than [this amount] or less, he shall offer first-fruits in the same proportion. Collection shall be made by [the] Demarchs[2] deme by deme and they shall deliver it to the Hieropoioi[3] (**10**) from Eleusis at Eleusis. (The Athenians) shall construct three (storage) pits at Eleusis in accordance with the ancestral custom, at whatever place seems to the Hieropoioi and the architect to be suitable, out of the funds of the two goddesses. The grain shall be put in there which they receive from the Demarchs. The allies as well shall offer first-fruits according to the same procedure. The cities shall have collectors (**15**) chosen for the grain by whatever means seems best to them for grain collection. When it has been collected, they shall send it to Athens, and those who have brought it shall deliver it to the Hieropoioi from Eleusis at Eleusis. If (the latter) do not take delivery of it within five days after it has been reported to them, although it was offered by (the envoys) of whatever city [was the source] (**20**) of the grain, the Hieropoioi at their *euthynae*[4] shall be fined one thousand drachmas [each]. They shall also receive it from the Demarchs in accordance with the same procedure. [Heralds] shall be chosen by the Boulê, which shall send them to the cities announcing [the present] decree of the People, in the present instance as quickly as possible and in the future, whenever it (the Boulê) thinks best. Let an exhortation be pronounced both by the Hierophant[5] and by [the] (**25**) Daidouchos[6] for the Hellenes to make offerings of the first-fruits at the Mysteries in accordance with the ancestral custom and the oracular response from Delphi. After writing on a notice board the weight of the grain (received) from the Demarchs according to deme and of that [received] from the cities according to city, (the Hieropoioi) shall set up (copies of) it in the Eleusinion in Eleusis and in the Bouleuterion [Council house]. (**30**) The Boulê shall also send a proclamation to the other cities, [the] Hellenic cities in their entirety, wherever it seems to the Boulê to be feasible, telling them the principles on which the Athenians and their allies are offering first-fruits, and not ordering them but urging them to offer first-fruits, if they so desire, in accordance with the ancestral custom and the oracular response from Delphi. The acceptance (**35**) of any (grain) that anyone may bring from these cities as well shall be the duty of the Hieropoioi according to the same procedure. They shall perform sacrifice with the pelanos[7] in accordance with what the Eumolpidae and (they shall sacrifice) the triple sacrifice, first, a bull with gilt horns to each of the two goddesses separately, out of (proceeds from) the barley and the wheat; and to Triptolemus and to the [god] and the goddess and Euboulus[8] a full-grown victim each; and (**40**) to Athena a bull with gilt horns. The rest of the barley and wheat shall be sold by the Hieropoioi together with the Boulê and they shall have votive offerings dedicated to the two goddesses, having made whatever seems best to the People of the Athenians, and they shall inscribe on the votive offerings that it was out of the first-fruits of the grain that they were dedicated, and (the name) of every Hellene [Greek] who made the offense of first-fruits. [For those] who do this (**45**) there shall be many benefits in abundance of good harvests if they are men who do not injure the Athenians or the city of the Athenians or the two goddesses. Lampon[9] made the motion: Let all the rest be as (advised) in the draft-decree (of the Commissioners) for the first-fruits of the grain for the goddesses. But their draft-decree and this decree shall be inscribed by the Secretary of the Boulê on two steles of marble (**50**) and set up, the one in the sanctuary in Eleusis, the other on the Acropolis. The Poletai[10] are to let out the contract for the two steles. The Kolakretai[11] are to supply the money. These things concerning the first-fruits of the grain to the two goddesses shall be inscribed on the two steles. There shall be intercalation of the month Hecatombaeon [July/August] by the new Archon.[12] The King (Archon) shall delimit the sanctuaries in the (**55**) Pelargicon,[13] and in the future altars shall not be erected in the Pelargicon without the consent of the Boulê and the People, nor shall (anyone) cut stones out of the Pelargicon, or remove soil or stones. If anyone transgresses any of these regulations, he shall be fined five hundred drachmas and impeached by the King (Archon) before the Boulê. As to the first-fruits of olive oil, a draft-decree (**60**) shall be produced by Lampon before the Boulê in the ninth prytany and the Boulê shall be obliged to bring it before the People.

Notes

1. *See the list of weights and measures on p. xl.*
2. *A demarch was the leading official of the deme.*
3. *The Hieropoioi were state officials in Eleusis in charge of the cult's property.*
4. *The* euthynae *was giving accounts at the end of an official's term in office.*
5. *Hierophants were priests who initiated worshippers. They came exclusively from the Eumolpid family.*
6. *The* daidouchos, *or "torch-bearer," was a priestly office at the Eleusinian Mysteries.*
7. *The* pelanos *was a wheat and barley cake. For the Eumolpidae see note 5.*
8. *The identity of Euboulus, an underworld deity, is uncertain: it may be Pluto, Persephone, or another god.*
9. *Lampon was probably one of the founders of Thurii in Italy in 444/3.*
10. *The Poletai were elected state auctioneers or sellers.*
11. *The Kolakretai were financial office-holders.*
12. *Normally the month Gamelion (January/February) was duplicated in an intercalary year. On this occasion the first Attic month, Hecatombaeon (July/August), was duplicated, perhaps to give the worshippers extra time.*
13. *The Pelargicon was a site below the acropolis. For an oracle forbidding other uses of the place, see Thucydides 2.17.1–2.*

Questions

1. List the various office-holders mentioned in the inscription and their functions.
2. How did Athens benefit from the Mysteries cult?

 For Athenian religion, see also WEB Chapter 22: "The City of Athens," which has sections on the Parthenon, the acropolis, and the City Dionysia.

Review Questions

 1. Describe the relationship between the polis and religion based on the documents reproduced in this chapter as well as in WEB **14.2** and WEB **14.5**.
 2. What elements of the myth of Demeter and Persephone were replicated in the Mysteries (**14.4** and WEB **14.5**)?

3. What can we learn from the *Hymn to Demeter* about Greek perceptions of their gods (WEB **14.5**)? How were these perceptions reflected in Greek religious practices?

Suggested Readings

Greek religion: Burkert 1985; Bremmer 1994; R. Parker 1996; S. Price 1999; Mikalson 2005. *Pollution, purification, and cults' regulations*: R. Parker 1983; Dillon 1997, 149–182, 204–227. *The Hymn to Demeter*: Richardson 1974; Foley 1994; Suton 2002. *The Eleusinian Mysteries*: Mylonas 1962; Burkert 1987; Clinton 1974, 1993; Mikalson 2005, 82–90. *Taxes for Eleusis*: Lewis 1994. *The first-fruits decree*: Cavanaugh 1996; Clinton 2009 (both date it to 435); Lawton 2009 (dates to 421–413).

15

The Ionian Revolt

Persians and Greeks

CHAPTER CONTENTS

In the second half of the sixth century the Greeks of Asia Minor were annexed by the Persian king into his empire. The results of this encounter were to affect Greek history all the way to the Hellenistic Age.

Our information about the ancient Persians comes from archaeology, Persian inscriptions, and Greek, Mesopotamian, Egyptian, and Hebrew accounts. The main sources on Persian–Greek relations were written by Greeks, chief among them Herodotus. The Greeks regarded the Persians as "barbarians," which in a neutral sense signified non-Greeks. Yet the meaning of this cultural construct was not static or uniform, ranging from ethnic affiliation and association with an alien civilization to being the polar opposite of what constituted Greek culture and way of life.

The Persian Empire was created by Cyrus II (the Great). He first led the Persians to victory over the Medians, their neighbors and rulers (the Greeks identified these different ethnic groups with one another), and then expanded his rule from India to the Aegean. Cyrus' expansion westward was in response to a Lydian attack on his realm. Croesus, who was king of Lydia in Asia Minor, subjugated the Asian Greeks before going against Persia ca. 547. See WEB **15.1.I** on Croesus' kingdom.

Herodotus (1.46–52) recounts that Croesus found the oracle of Delphi most reliable and showered it with very expensive gifts. When Croesus asked the oracle if he should fight the Persians, he received a response that became proverbial for its ambiguity, namely, that he would destroy a great kingdom. See WEB **15.1.II** on Croesus and the Delphic oracle.

Croesus' army and Cyrus' larger force clashed in the battle of Pteria in Cappadocia, which ended with Croesus retreating to his capital of Sardis. Cyrus followed him there and captured the king and the city. He did not kill Croesus, but included him in his retinue (see WEB **10.1**: "Solon and King Croesus"). It was an example of the Persians' tolerant policy toward the vanquished, which helped them to present themselves as heirs to, rather than usurpers of, local rulers and regimes.

It took the Persians four years to complete the conquest of Ionia. This chapter discusses the Persians' relations with the Ionians and the tyrants who ruled Greek cities in Asia Minor with the endorsement of the Persian administration. The chapter then examines the causes of the Ionian revolt and the efforts of its leader, Aristagoras, to obtain military aid from Sparta and Athens. It documents the fall of Miletus at the end of the revolt and the reaction to it in Athens. The chapter concludes with a description of a change in Persian policy in Ionia following the revolt.

Our primary informant for the Ionian revolt and the later Persian War is Herodotus' history, for which see **Introduction III.2**.

15.2 Persia and the Ionians

As subjects of the Persian Empire, the Ionians had to pay tribute to the king and provide troops and rowers to the Persian armed forces. Only the inhabitants of Phocaea and Teos chose to leave and settle elsewhere. Herodotus

(1.169) thinks highly of their action, which he describes as motivated by the Greek ideal of freedom (*eleutheria*) as opposed to servitude under foreign rule.

Cyrus incorporated members of the local elite into his administration. He and his successors installed or tolerated tyrants in many Greek cities. He also made efforts in Asia Minor and elsewhere to gain the favor of local sanctuaries. As the benefactor and protector of deities in his empire, he expected to gain the local population's good will and prevent revolts. An inscription from the time of Darius I (r. 522–486), which was reinscribed in the second century CE, tells of the royal benefactions given to the sanctuary of Apollo near Magnesia on the Meander that went back to Darius' predecessors.

Darius' letter (ML no. 12)

The King of kings, Darius son of Hystaspes, says the following to his slave Gadatas:[1]

I am told that you are not complying entirely with my instructions. Inasmuch as you are working my land, planting in the area of Western Asia fruit trees from beyond the Euphrates, I commend your design and there will therefore be much gratitude in store for you in the palace of the King. But inasmuch as you are obliterating my religious policy, I shall let you have the proof of my injured spirit, unless you effect changes. For you have been exacting tribute from the gardeners sacred to Apollo, and you ordered the digging up of land as being unhallowed. You are unaware of how my ancestors felt about the god, who told the Persians ... exact truth ...

Note

1. *Gadatas was a Persian official apparently in charge of the local royal park, the so-called Persian paradise. The Greek text describes Gadatas as* doulos, *a servant or slave, which is much harsher than the probable Persian original* bandaka, *"faithful."*

 See WEB **15.3.I** for Herodotus on the Ionian reaction to the Persian occupation and his low opinion of them; WEB **15.3.II** on Cyrus the Great's disdainful response to a Spartan claim to protect the Greeks; and WEB **15.3.III** for evidence of Greco-Persian cultural exchange.

Questions

 1. Discuss the Persian kings' dealings with local rulers in light of Darius' letter (**15.2**) and Cyrus' treatment of Croesus (WEB **10.1**: "Solon and King Croesus").

 2. Compare and contrast Herodotus' descriptions of the Ionians' response to the Persian occupation with that of the Spartans (WEB **15.3.I–II**). What might account for the differences?

15.4   The Greek Tyrants at the Bridge (ca. 513)

Cyrus died in 530, and in 522 Darius I, following a coup, ascended the throne and ruled the empire until his death in 486. Darius married Cyrus' daughter and, by co-opting her father into his family, established the Achaemenid royal dynasty. Darius instituted governmental and administrative changes that shaped the Persian Empire for years to come. Like his predecessors, he divided the empire into provinces and appointed Persian nobles as their governors, or satraps. The satrap was the king's personal representative in the region, and his tasks included the collection of tribute and troops and securing Persian rule in his satrapy. Local cities kept their autonomy, but answered to the satrap. See WEB **15.5** for King Darius I and his administrative reforms.

Darius' expedition against the Scythians around 513 brought the Persians into the Greek mainland. Herodotus' account of this campaign does not clarify its aims (3.134; 4.1–40). Perhaps the king sought to annex southern Russia to the empire, or he may have tried to prevent the Scythians from raiding Thrace, his new acquisition. The campaign, however, was unsuccessful, and Darius retreated back to Asia. Yet he made the Danube the limit of his empire and might even have placed the Macedonian kingdom under a Persian protectorate (Herodotus 5.18–20; 7.22).

Among those who contributed forces to the Scythian expedition were Greek cities from Asia Minor, the islands, the Hellespont, and the Propontis. According to Herodotus, when Darius went inland to conquer the Scythians he instructed the Greek tyrants of these cities to guard a bridge over the Danube. Among the tyrants was the Athenian Miltiades the Younger, son of Cimon, who in 490 would lead the Athenians against the Persians in Marathon. In about 516, he succeeded his uncle and namesake as the ruler of a Greek settlement in the Thracian Chersonese. It is reported that Miltiades supported cooperation with the Scythians against Darius, although the story may have been intended to exonerate him from the charge of assisting Darius. In any case, Histiaeus, the tyrant of Miletus, opposed the idea and carried the day. According to Herodotus (4.142), the Scythians reproached the Ionians for being worthless slaves.

Herodotus 4.137–138

(**4.137.1**) The Ionians proceeded to deliberate on the matter. The Athenian Miltiades, who was a general and tyrant of the Hellespontine Chersonese, held the view that they should listen to the Scythians and liberate Ionia. (**137.2**) Histiaeus of Miletus, however, opposed this, saying that it was thanks to Darius that they were now all tyrants in their own cities. If Darius' power were crushed, he argued, he himself would not be able to rule over the Milesians nor any other of them over anyone, since each of the cities would prefer a democratic government to tyranny. (**137.3**) When Histiaeus made known his opinion all immediately changed their minds, though they had earlier accepted Miltiades' view.

(**138.1**) The following were those who participated in the voting and were highly regarded by the king. There were the Hellespontine tyrants Daphnis of Abydus, Hippoclus of Lampsacus, Herophantus of Parion, Metrodorus of Proconnesus, Aristagoras of Cyzicus, and Ariston of Byzantium. (**138.2**) Such were the tyrants of the Hellespont. From Ionia there was Strattis of Chios, Aiaces of Samos, Laodamas of Phocaea, and Histiaeus of Miletus, the man who put forward the proposal that countered Miltiades'. Of the Aeolians the only man of note was Aristagoras of Cyme.

Question

1. Describe the Persian rule of Ionia in light of the debate on the bridge and Herodotus' description of Darius' reforms (WEB **15.5**).

15.6   The Causes of the Ionian Revolt (499–494)

Herodotus thinks that the Ionian revolt against Persia, and the Athenians' aid in support of it, were among the main causes of the Persian expeditions to Greece in 490 and 480–479 (Herodotus 5.97.3, 105; 7.5.2, 8b). It is largely because of Herodotus, however, that modern historians find it hard to ascertain the causes of the Ionian revolt, and even its course. He treats the revolt as an enterprise that was doomed to fail, and criticizes it as "the beginning of evils for Greeks and barbarians" (5.97.3). As he does elsewhere, he explains events in terms of the personal motivation of the chief actors: Histiaeus, the tyrant of Miletus, and his successor Aristagoras.

According to Herodotus, Darius became concerned about Histiaeus' ambitions and resources. He invited him to his court in Susa, and honored him with the titles of "counselor" and "tablemate." Both honors established Histiaeus' proximity to the king, but they also meant that he could not return home. Histiaeus planned to return by encouraging Aristagoras, his brother-in-law and successor as ruler of Miletus, to start a revolt in the hope that the king would send Histiaeus back to Ionia to help put it down (Herodotus 5.23–25, 35).

Aristagoras, however, had his own reasons to rebel. Around 500/499, he wanted to restore exiles from Naxos to the island, but because he lacked adequate resources he invited the local Persian satrap, Artaphrenes, to join him in the expedition.

15.6.A   Aristagoras' Naxian Campaign

Herodotus 5.31.1–4

(**5.31.1**) When Aristagoras reached Sardis, he explained to Artaphrenes that while Naxos was an island of no great size, it was beautiful, fertile, close to Ionia, and endowed with great wealth and many slaves. "Lead an army against this land," he said, "and restore those exiled from it. (**31.2**) If you do that, I have ready money in large quantities for you, enough for everything but the war-expenses (for as far as these are concerned, it is fair that we who are leading the expedition should supply them). Moreover, you will annex some islands to the king's realm – Naxos itself, and those islands dependent on it, Paros, Andros, and others that are called the Cyclades. (**31.3**) Setting off from these you will easily be able to attack Euboea, a great and prosperous island, no smaller than Cyprus and very easy to take. A hundred ships are enough to overpower all these islands."

Artaphrenes gave him the following reply: (**31.4**) "You are the bringer of good things for the house of the king, and this advice of yours is fine in all details except the number of ships. Instead of a hundred you will find two hundred vessels ready for you in the spring. But the king's personal approval of these projects is also needed."

Bickering between Aristagoras and Megabates, the Persian commander of the expedition, as well as the Naxians' successful resistance led the Persians to abandon the project. Fearing for his rule, Aristagoras contemplated defection. At that moment a message arrived from Histiaeus encouraging him to revolt. Herodotus (5.35.1–4) says that Histiaeus tattooed the message on the messenger's head and then allowed his hair to grow back. For Herodotus' account and a summary of scholarly views on the causes of the Ionian revolt, see WEB **15.7**.

Because Aristagoras' best prospects of matching Persian power was on the sea, he took command of the fleet that sailed to Naxos. He then substituted tyranny with *isonomia* (equality before the law), thus creating a link between the war, freedom, and democratic ideology.

15.6.B   Aristagoras Banishes Tyrants

Herodotus 5.37.2

Aristagoras' first move was to renounce his tyranny and establish equal rights [*isonomia*] in Miletus, in order to make the Milesians willing to join the rebellion. He then did the same thing throughout Ionia. Some of the tyrants he expelled, but the others, whom he had taken from the ships that had sailed with him to Naxos, he surrendered and restored to the various cities from which they had come, a measure designed to please the city-states.

Questions

1. From the attempt to capture Naxos, what can be deduced about the relationship between the Persian satrap and the Greek rulers?
2. Were Histiaeus and Aristagoras freedom fighters?

15.8   Aristagoras' Quest for Help in Greece (500)

 Aristagoras sailed to Sparta in search of allies. Herodotus describes in vivid detail his unsuccessful attempt to persuade king Cleomenes I to join the conflict (WEB **15.9**).

Aristagoras had more success in Athens and in Eretria on the island of Euboea. Traditional views that Athens was the mother-city of Miletus and that Eretria owed a debt of gratitude to Miletus should not be discounted as motives in their support of the rebels. In addition, by intervening in Ionia, Athens staked a claim as an international player. The prospect of raiding the wealthy Persians may have played a part too, although Herodotus, who implied this motive, was critical of it. He also says that the Persians wanted the Athenians to take Hippias back, but they would not hear of it. It was at this moment that Aristagoras showed up in Athens.

Herodotus 5.97.1–3, 99.1–2

(**5.97.1**) Such was the temper of the Athenians, and slanderous comments were also being made about them to the Persians. It was at this point that Aristagoras of Miletus, having now been driven out of Sparta by Cleomenes the Lacedaemonian, arrived in Athens – for this city was much more powerful than the others. Aristagoras came before the people and said just what he had said in Sparta about the wealth to be found in Asia, and about the Persian manner of warfare, how they used neither shield nor spear, and would be easy to defeat.[1] (**97.2**) To these comments he added a number of others. The Milesians were settlers from Athens, he said, and it was reasonable for the Athenians, being a very powerful people, to come to their rescue. So desperate was his need, in fact, that there was nothing he did not promise, and he did eventually win them over. Evidently it is easier to dupe a large number than it is one person, if Aristagoras could not dupe Cleomenes the Lacedaemonian, one man, but could dupe 30,000 Athenians.[2] (**97.3**) Won over, the Athenians voted to send twenty ships to assist the Ionians, appointing as their commander Melanthius, an Athenian citizen with a good all-round reputation. It was these ships that were to start the troubles for the Greeks and the barbarians…

(**99.1**) The Athenians arrived with their twenty ships,[3] and at the same time brought with them five triremes of the Eretrians. The Eretrians were on the campaign as a favor not to the Athenians but to the Milesians themselves. They were repaying a debt to them, for the Milesians had earlier assisted the Eretrians in their war against the Chalcidians, in which the Samians helped the Chalcidians against the Eretrians and the Milesians.[4] When the ships arrived, and the rest of the Ionian allies appeared on the scene, Aristagoras proceeded with the campaign against Sardis. (**99.2**) He did not take part in it personally, but remained behind in Miletus, appointing two others to command the Milesian forces, his own brother Charopinus and another citizen, Hermophantus.

Notes

   1. *See WEB* **15.7***.*
   2. *The number of citizens probably reflects Herodotus' time of composition rather than Athens in 499.*

3. *It is uncertain whether the Athenian fleet comprised a large or small part of the entire Athenian navy; probably the former.*
4. *Eretria's war with Chalcis in the late eighth century is known as the Lelantine War. The cities fought over the Lelantine plain in Euboea.*

Questions

1. Why did Aristagoras' mission fail in Sparta (WEB **15.9**) but succeed in Athens (**15.8**)?
2. To what extent does the story of Aristagoras' visit to Sparta (WEB **15.9**) confirm, add to, or modify the depiction of the Spartan political structure (**7.8–9**, **7.11–12**)?
3. Were Cleomenes, the Athenians, and the Eretrians right or wrong to respond to Aristagoras' request as they did?

15.10 The Fall of Miletus and Phrynichus' *Capture of Miletus* (494)

The first significant Ionian action was to raid Sardis, the seat of Persian power. But the attackers failed to capture the well-fortified citadel or to plunder the city because of a raging fire, which also destroyed a local temple of Cybele. Persian reinforcements from the surrounding regions pursued the retreating Ionians and defeated them in a battle near Ephesus. The Athenians, having had enough, sailed back home and kept out of the conflict (Herodotus 5.100–103). The Persians, however, noted the Athenian involvement and would use it to justify a campaign against them in 490.

Nevertheless, Greek cities all the way from the Hellespont to Caria and Cyprus joined the Ionians' cause. The Persian army recaptured many coastal towns, thus depriving the Ionian navy of its bases. Aristagoras met his death in battle in Thrace, while Histiaeus, who had returned to the region, failed to gain the trust of many Ionians and was eventually captured and executed by the Persians. In a last-ditch effort, the Ionians assembled a large fleet in 494, but it did not match the size of the Persian navy, moored near the island of Lade across from Miletus. Disunity among the Ionians and the Persians' skillful use of former tyrants to encourage Greek defections led a large part of the Samian fleet to change sides in mid-battle. The Ionians were defeated, and the city of Miletus was left to fend for itself.

Herodotus' report (below) on Phrynichus' play *The Capture of Miletus* has been variously interpreted. Some see the play as an attempt by Athenian political leaders, especially Themistocles, to use Miletus' fate as a warning to encourage Athens to take steps against a future Persian offensive. Others highlight the play's cultural significance, pointing to its unusual dramatization of a contemporary event while other classical dramas used mythical stories. The Athenian prohibition on reproducing the play shows an early attempt to control artistic expression in a public space out of concern for the community.

Herodotus 6.18–21.2

(**6.18**) After defeating the Ionians at sea, the Persians laid siege to Miletus by land and sea, undermining its walls and bringing up to them all kinds of siege engines. In the sixth year after Aristagoras' revolt [494] they took it completely, and reduced the whole city to slavery. Thus its fate was consistent with the oracle that had been given about Miletus.

(**6.19.1**) The Argives had been consulting the shrine in Delphi about the security of their city, and they were given a joint response: some of it referred to the Argives themselves, but there was an additional part that concerned the Milesians. (**19.2**) The section pertaining to the Argives I shall recount when I reach the appropriate point in my narrative,[1] but the prediction concerning the Milesians, who were not present, runs as follows:

> "At that time, Miletus, contriver of evil deeds, you will become a banquet and a splendid gift for many. Your wives will wash the feet of many long-haired men, and others will have responsibility for my temple at Didyma."

(**19.3**) This was what befell the Milesians at that time. Most of their men were killed by the Persians, who are long-haired; their women and children were reduced to slavery; and the temple at Didyma, both the sanctuary and the oracle, were pillaged and burned. Of the riches in that temple I have frequently made mention elsewhere in my account.[2]

(**20**) The Milesians who had been taken captive were then brought to Susa. King Darius did them no further harm and settled them on what is called the Red Sea in the city of Ampe, which the Tigris flows past before it empties into the sea. As for the territory of the Milesians, the Persians themselves took possession of the area around the city and of the plain, but they put the uplands in the hands of the Carians of Pedasa.

(**21.1**) When these punishments were inflicted on the Milesians by the Persians, the people of Sybaris, who were living in Laos and Scidrus after having their city taken from them, failed to pay a debt they owed them. For when Sybaris was captured by the people of Croton [510], all the Milesians, from boys up, shaved their heads and went into deep mourning. Of all the cities I know these two enjoyed the closest ties of friendship. The Athenians' reaction was not at all like that of the Milesians. (**21.2**) The Athenians made clear their great distress at the capture of Miletus in many ways, and in particular, when Phrynichus wrote and staged his drama "The Capture of Miletus," the audience broke into tears and the people fined him a thousand drachmas for reminding them of their own troubles. They also forbade anyone to stage the play in future.

Notes

1. *Herodotus 6.77.*
2. *Herodotus 1.92; 5.36.*

Questions

1. What punishments did the Persians mete out to the people of Miletus?
2. What principle should govern relationships between poleis according to Herodotus' description of the fall of Miletus?
3. How can the Athenian reaction to the fall of Miletus be reconciled with Athens' early withdrawal from the Ionian revolt?

15.11   The Change of Persian Policy in Ionia

The Persians also treated Chios, Lesbos, and Tenedos harshly. Their policy toward other Ionians was more conciliatory though no less firm. In 493 the satrap Artaphrenes established Persian peace and order in the region. In 492, Mardonius, Darius' nephew and son-in-law, led an expedition to northern Greece, and on his way there replaced Ionian tyrants with democracies. Scholars have been hesitant to accept Herodotus' report of the Persians' endorsement of democracies in Ionia, especially because the Persians used and reinstated tyrants during the Ionian revolt and its aftermath. Yet Darius probably realized that tyranny had led many Ionians to rebel. It appears that the Persians left some tyrants in place but also did not change the democracies that Aristagoras had established. As long as the Ionians remained loyal, it made little difference what government they had.

Herodotus 6.42.1–43.4; cf. Diodorus of Sicily 10.25.4

(**6.42.1**) That year [493] there were no further hostilities mounted against the Ionians by the Persians; in fact, a number of events that occurred in the course of the year were very favorable for them. Artaphrenes, governor of Sardis, sent for deputations from the various city-states and forced the Ionians to negotiate settlements amongst themselves so their relations would be based on law instead of mutual harassment and plundering. (**42.2**) After obliging them to do this, Artaphrenes also measured their lands in parasangs, the Persian word for an area of thirty stades [ca. 5.5 km], and then assessed the tribute for each of the cities on the basis of those measures. Since that time the tribute has remained in place, as prescribed by Artaphrenes, right down to my own day. The rate, though, was much the same as it had been before. Such were the peaceful measures that were taken by the Persians.

(**43.1**) In the spring [492], after the other generals had been relieved of their commands, Mardonius son of Gabrias – a young man who had recently married Artozostre, a daughter of Darius – came down to the coast with a sizable army and fleet. (**43.2**) When Mardonius arrived in Cilicia at the head of these troops, he himself boarded ship and sailed off with the rest of the fleet, while other officers led the land army to the Hellespont. (**43.3**) Mardonius reached Ionia after skirting the coast of Asia, and my account of what happened there will truly amaze those Greeks who refuse to believe that Otanes expressed to the Seven Persians the opinion that Persia should become a democracy![1]

Mardonius actually dismissed all the Ionian tyrants and established democracies in their cities. (**43.4**) That done, he sped to the Hellespont, and after a large number of ships and a large army had been assembled there, the Persians crossed on the ships. They then proceeded with their march through Europe, and their march on Eretria and Athens.

Note

 1. *Herodotus refers to his account of a debate in the Persian court over the best government that Persia should adopt prior to Darius' ascension of the throne (see WEB 23.6.I: "A Debate over the Merits of Democracy, Oligarchy, and Monarchy"). Clearly, his audience had doubts about the historicity of the debate.*

Question

1. What expectations informed Persian policy in Asia Minor following the Ionian revolt?

Review Questions

 1. How did the Persians treat their subject populations (**15.2**, **15.4**, **15.6**, **15.10–11**, WEB **15.3.I–III**, WEB **15.5**)?
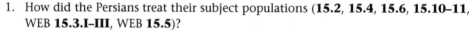 2. What were the causes of the Ionian revolt according to Herodotus (**15.6**, **15.8**, WEB **15.7**)?
 3. Explain the reactions in Greece to the Ionian revolt (**15.8**, **15.10**, WEB **15.9**).
 4. How did Greeks and barbarians perceive one another (**15.8**, WEB **15.3.II–III**, WEB **15.9**)?
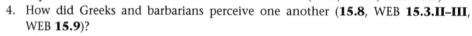 5. What moralistic and political perceptions inform Herodotus' account of the fall of Croesus (WEB **15.1**, WEB **15.1.II**) and of the Ionian revolt (**15.10–11**)?

Suggested Readings

The Persian Empire and civilization: Gershevitz 1985; Khurt 2001; Briant 2002a; Brosius 2006. *Darius and the Greek sanctuary*: Briant 2002a, esp. 491–493. *Cyrus, Darius I, and the Ionians*: Balcer 1995; Briant 2002a, 62–146. *Cultural contacts between Greeks and Persians*: M. Miller 1997, 89–108. *The Ionian revolt*: Lateiner 1982; Balcer 1995, 169–191; Gorman 2001, 129–145; Briant 2002a, 141–156. *Isonomia, freedom, and democracy*: Ostwald 1969, 161–167; Raaflaub 2004, 58–117. *Phrynichus*: Roisman 1988; Rosenbloom 1993.

16

The Battle of Marathon (490)

CHAPTER CONTENTS

Ancient Greece from Homer to Alexander: The Evidence, First Edition. Joseph Roisman.
© 2011 Blackwell Publishing Ltd. Translations © 2011 John Yardley. Published 2011 by Blackwell Publishing Ltd.

According to Herodotus, Darius was incensed with Athens and Eretria for their participation in the raid on Sardis in 499 that resulted in the burning of the temple of Cybele there. He sought to exact revenge by enslaving these cities and burning their sanctuaries (Herodotus 5.102.1, 105). If this is true, Darius must have savored his revenge served cold, because it was not until 491 that he began preparing the expedition against both cities. Before then his general Mardonius captured Aegean islands and in 492 reoccupied Thrace. Mardonius also added the island of Thasos and the kingdom of Macedonia to the empire. It appears that Darius was less interested in Athens than in securing and expanding Persian rule over the Aegean and northern Greece.

In 491 (or 492), however, the king directed his attention to the Greek mainland. This chapter discusses the famous battle of Marathon between the Athenians and a Persian expeditionary force. It deals with Darius' initial demand of surrender from mainland Greeks, the Persian expedition to Eretria and Athens, and Athens' request for help from Sparta. It then describes the battle of Marathon, the failed Persian attempt to capture the city, possibly with local help, and Athenian pride in and commemoration of the battle.

16.1   Darius Demands Surrender

Around 492 Darius sent envoys to Greek cities requesting earth and water, a demand that, depending on the circumstances, could mean surrender, alliance, or hospitality.

Herodotus 6.48.1–49.1

(**6.48.1**) Darius next tried to ascertain whether the Greeks intended to fight him or to surrender. (**48.2**) He sent heralds to various parts of Greece with instructions to ask for earth and water for the king, and while he was dispatching these to Greece he sent other messengers to the tribute-paying coastal cities, ordering them to build warships and vessels for transporting horses. (**49.1**) These people did indeed start on the work. In the meantime, many of the mainlanders gave the heralds who came to Greece the items the Persian asked for, and so did all the islanders to whom they came with the request. And notable amongst the islanders who gave Darius his earth and water were the people of Aegina.[1]

Note

 1. *Athens was upset by Aegina's action and asked Sparta to intervene. See WEB **7.29.III** for Cleomenes campaign against Aegina and his sending of Aeginetan hostages to Athens.*

Unlike Aegina, Athens and Sparta rejected the demand and even killed the Persian envoys in violation of both religious and diplomatic conventions. The rationale for this action is unclear; perhaps it aimed to send a strong message of resistance to Persia both at home and abroad. See WEB **16.2** for Herodotus' description of the Spartans' later attempt to atone for their crime by sending two messengers to the Persian king so *he* could kill them (he refused).

Questions

1. How did the Greeks react to Darius' demand for earth and water?
2. What does the story of the Spartan heralds' trip to Persia (WEB **16.2**) to pay for the killing of the Persian envoys with their lives suggest about the Spartans, the Persians, and their images?

16.3   The Persian Expedition and Athens' Request for Help (490)

Herodotus (6.95) tells us that a Persian expeditionary force made up of infantry, cavalry, and 600 ships (a likely exaggeration) assembled in Cilicia under its commanders, Datis and Artaphrenes (the Younger). In 490 they sailed into the Aegean and captured island after island from Naxos to Euboea. The Aegean Sea was now under almost complete Persian control. Cities that surrendered were spared, but Eretria in Euboea resisted and was enslaved, plundered, and its temples set on fire.

16.3.A   The Persians Arrive at Marathon

Herodotus 6.102

After overpowering Eretria the Persians waited a few days and then sailed on to Attica, putting severe pressure on the Athenians and fancying that they would do to them what they had done to the Eretrians. Marathon was the most suitable place in Attica for cavalry action, and also the closest spot to Eretria, and so it was toward this spot that Hippias son of Peisistratus guided them.

Hippias, the exiled tyrant of Athens, joined the Persian invaders as military advisor and prospective ruler of Athens under Persian control. He probably hoped to repeat his father's landing in Marathon that had preceded his tyranny (**10.5**: "Peisistratus' Second Attempt at Tyranny").

The Athenians for their part mobilized their army and asked Sparta for help. Their messenger, Philippides, reported on his return home that on his way to

Sparta he had met the Arcadian god Pan, who complained that the Athenians did not care for him. After the battle, the Athenians built a temple for Pan at the bottom of the acropolis. According to Herodotus, the Spartans refused to come to help right away for religious reasons. Plato, however, explains the Spartans' reticence by their need to fight the Messenians (*Laws* 692b; 698e). In either case, it is unlikely that they looked for a pretext because they did come with an army as soon as they could (Herodotus 6.120).

16.3.B   Athens Requests Help from Sparta

Herodotus 6.105.1, 106.1–3

(**6.105.1**) And at first, while they were still in the city, the generals sent Philippides[1] to Sparta with a message. He was an Athenian, a "day-runner," who made that his profession …

(**106.1**) Sent by the generals on the mission – during which he claimed Pan appeared to him – Philippides reached Sparta the day after leaving the town of Athens. He came to the Spartan archons[2] and said: (**106.2**) "Lacedaemonians: The Athenians earnestly request that you help them and not allow the most ancient city in Greece to fall into slavery at the hands of barbarians. Eretria has now been enslaved and Greece is weaker through the loss of a renowned city." (**106.3**) After Philippides delivered this message to them as ordered, the Lacedaemonians decided to help the Athenians, but it was not possible for them to do so immediately as they were unwilling to break a law of theirs. It was the ninth day of the month, and they claimed that they would not conduct an expedition on the ninth, nor would they until there was a full moon.[3]

Notes

1. *Another tradition names the runner Pheidippides.*
2. *It took Philippides one day to cover the ca. 250 km distance between Athens and Sparta. The "archons" he addressed were presumably the ephors.*
3. *To judge from other Dorian calendars, the Spartans must have referred to the law against fighting not during the first half of every month but during the second lunar month, when the Carnean festival was celebrated.*

Questions

1. How might the presence of the former tyrant Hippias among the invading Persians have affected the Athenians (**16.3.A**)?
2. Add to Philippides' address to the Spartans (**16.3.B**) two or more persuasive arguments.

16.4 The Battle of Marathon (490)

At the time of the battle of Marathon the only allies to come to Athens' help were their Plataean neighbors. The Plataeans had been Athens' ally since Cleomenes recommended they become so in 519 (**7.28**: "King Cleomenes, Plataea, and Athens").

The most informative source for the battle of Marathon is Herodotus, who includes no figures for the rival armies. Sources from the Roman imperial period give the Athenians 9,000 hoplites, including old warriors and freed slaves (Pausanias *Description of Greece* 7.15.7; 10.20.2), and 1,000 troops to Plataea (Cornelius Nepos *Miltiades* 5; Justin 2.9). Recorded numbers for the Persians are impossible and range from 80,000 (Apuleius 5.9) to 600,000 (Justin 2.9). Modern estimates put the numbers at between 15,000 and 25,000 men. The desire to extol the victory of the few against the many inspired the ancient accounts.

While the bulk of the Greek army was made up of hoplites, the Persians came with heavy infantrymen, archers, and cavalry. The Persian infantry wore to battle a felt hat or turban, a decorated long-sleeved tunic and trousers, and jewelry. They had iron breastplates, wicker shields, and spears and swords that were slightly shorter than those used by the Greeks.

The Greek army camped next to Heracles' temple in Marathon. Herodotus reports that the Athenian generals debated whether they should offer battle, and that one general, the archon polemarch, was selected by lot. Yet the selection of archons by lot was introduced only later in 487/6 (*Ath. Pol.* 22.5). Moreover, in later times command over the army belonged to a board of generals, not to this one archon. It is possible, however, that around 490 the archon polemarch held supreme authority over the other generals (cf. *Ath. Pol.* 22.2).

Herodotus highlights the leading role that general Miltiades played in urging the Athenians to offer battle. Miltiades, who escaped the Persians from his settlement on the Chersonese and went to Athens in 493, had a strong incentive to fight the invaders (cf. **15.4**: "The Greek Tyrants at the Bridge"). See WEB **16.7.III** for other claimants to Marathon fame. The battle was fought on September 11, 490.

16.4.A The War Council Before Battle and the Fighting in Marathon

Herodotus 6.109.1–114, 117.1

(**6.109.1**) The Athenian generals were divided in their opinions, some calling for no confrontation (on the grounds that they were too few to confront the Medic army), and others, including Miltiades, urging it … (**109.2**) When they were thus divided, the more cowardly of the opinions began to prevail. Now there was an eleventh person with a vote, the man who had gained the post of polemarch by lot – for the Athenians had long ago given the polemarch equal voting rights with the generals – and the polemarch at the time was Callimachus of Aphidnae. Miltiades approached this man, and said: (**109.3**) "It now rests with you, Callimachus. Either you enslave Athens or, by keeping her free, you leave a memorial to yourself that will last as long as men will live, a memorial unmatched even by Harmodius and Aristogeiton.[1] For the Athenians have now come into the greatest danger they have known since their beginnings, and if they buckle before the Medes it is clear what they will suffer when they are put into Hippias' hands. If this city survives, however, it can become the foremost of the cities of Greece.

(**109.4**) How this can be accomplished, and how it is that a decision in this matter lies with you, I shall now explain. We, the ten generals, are split in our opinion, with some urging confrontation, and others not. (**109.5**) If we do not engage now, I expect some civil discord will descend upon us, shaking the will of the Athenians to the point of making them Medize [i.e., collaborate with the Persians]. If, however, we *do* engage before some crazy idea comes into the heads of certain Athenians, then, supposing that the gods deal fairly, we can win the engagement. (**109.6**) This all rests with you and depends on you. Support my view and your country is free, your city the foremost in Greece. Accept the view of those actively discouraging engagement and you will set in motion events that will give the opposite of the blessings I have mentioned."

(**110**) By these words Miltiades brought Callimachus on side, and with the addition of the polemarch's vote the decision to engage was reached.[2] After that, the generals who voted for engaging surrendered their prerogative to Miltiades when their day of command came round to each of them, and though Miltiades accepted, he did not actually engage until his own day of command arrived.

(**111.1**) When Miltiades' turn came round, the Athenians were deployed for the engagement in the following manner. Commanding the right wing was the polemarch Callimachus, for it was at that time the practice amongst the Athenians for the polemarch to have charge of the right. After that came the tribes, following each other in their fixed order, and finally there were the Plataeans, taking up their position on the left wing. (**111.2**) (In fact, a custom has prevailed ever since that battle. When the Athenians offer sacrifices at their national quadrennial festivals, the Athenian herald makes a prayer that all the blessings prayed for be granted both to the Athenians and to the Plataeans.) (**111.3**) The Athenian deployment at Marathon resulted in the following configuration. The Athenian line matched the Persian in length, but the center was only a few ranks deep, and this was where the line was weakest, each wing being numerically strong.

(**112.1**) When the force was deployed and the sacrificial omens were good, the Athenians were unleashed and they charged the barbarians at running pace. There was a space of no less than eight stades [ca. 1,500 meters] between them. (**112.2**) Seeing them coming at a run, the Persians prepared to take them on, and they attributed the Athenians' behavior to a derangement that was going to destroy them completely; for they could see that they were few in number but were nevertheless charging at running pace, with no cavalry or archers in support. (**112.3**) Such was the Persians' thinking, but when the Athenians came to grips with them at close quarters they put up a remarkable fight. As far as I know, they were the first of the Greeks to make a running charge at an enemy, and the first to withstand the sight of Medic dress and the men wearing it. Up to that point even the sound of the name "Mede" inspired fear in the Greeks.

(**113.1**) The fighting at Marathon went on for a long time. The barbarians were victorious in the center of the line where the Persians themselves and the Sacae were positioned, and after getting the upper hand here, they broke through and chased the Greeks inland. On the two wings, however, the Athenians and the Plataeans carried the day. (**113.2**) Victorious at those points, they allowed those of the barbarians that they had routed to run off, while they brought the two wings together and began to fight those who had broken the center; and here, too, they prevailed. They kept following the fleeing Persians, cutting them down, until they reached the sea, where they proceeded to call for fire and to attack the ships.[3]

(**114**) In the struggle here the polemarch was killed while putting up a brave fight, and one of the generals, Stesilaus son of Thrasylus, also died. Here, too, fell Cynegeirus son of Euphorion – his hand lopped off by a battle-axe as he grasped the stern of a ship[4] – and many other notable Athenians...

(**117.1**) In this battle at Marathon some 6,400 of the barbarians lost their lives, and 192 Athenians...[5]

Notes

1. *For these tyrannicides, see* **10.10** *("The Athenian Tyrannicides"),* **10.12** *("The Expulsion of the Tyrants"), WEB* **10.11** *("Thucydides on the Athenian Tyrannicides"), and Figure 10.1.*
2. *The first-century* CE *Roman biographer Cornelius Nepos (Miltiades 4.4–5.2) reports that, before marching to Marathon, the Athenian generals debated in Athens whether to fight the Persians or find shelter behind the walls, and that Miltiades convinced them to fight. Aristotle mentions a decree of Miltiades, which instructed the Athenians to take provisions and the field (Rhetoric 1411a10; cf. Demosthenes 19.303). If there was only one debate, Herodotus' testimony is preferable.*
3. *The description of the battle by the ships has a Homeric ring: see Homer Iliad 15.178.*
4. *Cynegeirus was the brother of the playwright Aeschylus, who also fought at Marathon.*
5. *The late Roman historian Justin puts the number of the Persian dead at 2,000.*

See WEB **16.7.I** for a link to an image of a vase depicting a Greek soldier fight- ing a Persian.

One of the main questions about the battle concerns the absence of the Persian cavalry, which was a highly skilled attacking force. The Persians had picked the Marathon plain as the battleground largely to accommodate their cavalry (Herodotus 6.102). An enigmatic entry in the Byzantine lexicon *Suda* adds the following information.

16.4.B   The Persian Cavalry

Suda, s.v. *Choris hippeis* ("the cavalry are apart")

During the time of Datis' landing in Attica, they say that the Ionians climbed some trees after he moved off, and signaled to the Athenians that the cavalry were separated from the force. Miltiades, understanding that they were separated, engaged and won the victory. This is why, they claim, the saying is applied to those who break ranks.

Perhaps the cavalry were instructed to guard the road to Athens, and perhaps they were put aboard the ships in order to capture Athens while her army was away. Another puzzle concerns Herodotus' description of the charging Greek troops, which has them running in heavy hoplite armor for almost 1.5 km. It is possible they started running only when they reached the ca. 160-meter range of the Persian archers so as to minimize their impact. (Herodotus is wrong in crediting the Athenians as the first force to charge at a run.)

16.4.C   Monuments of the Battle of Marathon

The traveler-writer Pausanias visited Marathon around the mid-second century CE. His description of monuments in Marathon and wondrous tales associated with the site add information about the battle.

Pausanias *Description of Greece* 1.32.3–5

(**1.32.3**) Before I turn to my island narrative, I shall again go back to the matter of the demes. There is a deme, Marathon, which is equidistant from the city of Athens and from Carystus in Euboea. It was at this point in Attica that the barbarians landed and were defeated in battle, losing a number of their ships when they put out to sea again. There is a tomb of the Athenians on the plain, and on it are grave steles providing the names of the fallen who are listed by their various tribes; and there is a second tomb for the Plataeans of Boeotia and for the slaves – for slaves were in battle on that occasion, for the first time.

(**32.4**) There is also a separate monument dedicated to Miltiades son of Cimon, though his death fell at a later date, after he failed in Paros and was brought to trial for it by the Athenians. At Marathon, throughout the night, the sound of horses neighing and men fighting can be heard. No good has come to any person deliberately placing himself there to witness the phenomenon, but the gods show no anger toward anyone there unawares or by chance. The people of Marathon worship the men who died in battle there (they call them heroes), as well as the Marathon from whom the deme gets its name and Heracles whom they say they were first among the Greeks to recognize as a god.

(**32.5**) There also happened to be a man present at the battle, they say, who looked and dressed like a peasant. He killed large numbers of the enemy with a plow, but disappeared after the action. When the Athenians consulted the oracle about it the god made no response apart from ordering them to honor Echetlaius as a hero. A trophy of white marble is also erected there. The Athenians claim to have buried the Persians since religious law emphatically demands that a man's body be hidden beneath the earth, but I could find no grave. There was no mound or other sign of burial to be seen there; the Athenians merely bore them to a ditch and threw them in indiscriminately.

Questions

1. How did the preliminaries to the battle of Marathon and the Athenian lines reflect Athenian democracy?

2. What were the Athenians' political and military concerns on the eve of the battle?
3. Try to reconstruct the course of the battle from the documents reproduced in this section.

—————————— **16.5 An Attempt to Capture the City with Alcmeonid Aid?**

While the forces were engaged in fighting, the Persian fleet failed to capture the city by surprise. Herodotus reports a story that the Alcmeonids helped them with a signal, only to reject it in very strong terms. In spite of the historian's protests, there is no need to label the story as hostile fabrication. The Persians often relied on the help of local sympathizers, to which Miltiades alludes in his appeal to the polemarch Callimachus (Herodotus 6.109.5: see **16.4.A**). *Ath. Pol.* 22.5–6 says that the Athenians ostracized the friends of the tyrants in the years following the battle (487/6–484/3), and in the decade following Marathon, two Alcmeonids faced ostracism. The meaning of the signal could have been that the city was free for the taking, or conversely, that the Athenians were aware of the plot.

The Athenian army prevented the capture of the city by hastily marching there, and the Persians sailed back to Asia. Late traditions tell about a runner, Eucles or Philippides, who ran ahead of the army, announced the victory, and dropped dead. The modern Marathon run is slightly longer than the original one because the course was extended in the second modern Olympics so that runners would pass by Buckingham Palace.

Herodotus 6.115

The Athenians overwhelmed seven ships in this way. The barbarians backed water with the others and, after picking up the Eretrian captives from the island on which they had left them, they rounded Sunium – they wanted to reach the city before the Athenians. In Athens the accusation was made that they intended doing this because of a piece of trickery on the part of the Alcmeonids. These, it was said, had made a deal with Persians, and held up a shield to signal to them when they were aboard the ships.

Later in his narrative Herodotus rebuffs the charge of Alcmeonid collaboration with the Persians.

Herodotus 6.123.1–124.2

(**6.123.1**) The Alcmeonids were actually no less haters of the tyrants than was Callias. I am therefore amazed at, and do not believe, the charge that it was they who put up the shield as a signal – they were in exile throughout the entire period of the tyrants, and it was thanks to their machinations that the Peisistratids lost their tyranny. (**123.2**) In my estimation, the Alcmeonids were liberators of Athens to a much greater extent than were Harmodius and Aristogeiton. For the latter, by their assassination of Hipparchus, only infuriated the rest of the Peisistratids, and did nothing more to end the tyranny. The Alcmeonids, however, clearly did free the land, if it really was they who, as I indicated above [5.90], convinced the Pythia to give the oracle instructing the Lacedaemonians to liberate Athens.

(**124.1**) The objection will perhaps be made that the Alcmeonids betrayed their native land over some grudge that they had against the common people of Athens. But amongst the Athenians none were more esteemed or more respected than they, and (**124.2**) so, logically, the shield could not have been put up by them for reasons of that sort. Now a shield was held up, and there is no denying it. It happened. As to the identity of the culprit, I can say no more than I have.

Questions

1. Construct a counter-argument to Herodotus' defense of Alcmeonid innocence.
2. Regardless of whether the Alcmeonids helped the Persians or not, what do the allegation and its denial tell us about the Athenians during and after the Persian invasion?

16.6   The Fame of Marathon and Its Commemoration

The battle of Marathon is important as much for its symbolic value as for its military significance. For the defeated Persians it meant the frustration of their limited goal of punishing Athens. Indeed, the relatively small force they sent and the king's absence from the campaign indicate that they did not aim seriously to conquer Greece at this stage. The battle also had no impact on Persian control of the Aegean islands and Asia Minor. However, Marathon motivated Darius to plan a larger expedition that aimed to occupy the whole of Greece. But an Egyptian revolt intervened and Darius died before he could follow up on his plan. See WEB **16.7.IV** for Darius' war plans after Marathon.

For the Athenians, Marathon was one of the most illustrious battles in their history. It was a victory for the Athenian polis over the mighty Persian king and his empire, of democracy over tyranny, and of freedom over barbarian servitude. The Greek agonistic culture turned Marathon into a claim for military and moral superiority over other Greeks as well. Some of these perceptions informed an epigram by Simonides of Cos that commemorated the dead of Marathon and was probably inscribed on their tomb. The source for the epigram is an ancient commentator on Aristophanes' play *Peace*.

16.6.A   An Elegy on Marathon

Simonides *Elegies* 9 (Campbell III, p. 512)

"Daughter of Zeus: If honoring a person who is the best comic poet in the world, and the most famous, is reasonable, then our poet says that he is worthy of high praise" [Aristophanes *Peace* 736–738].

Scholiast:

This is after Simonides, from his elegies:

But, Daughter of Zeus, if honoring excellence is reasonable, then the Athenian demos accomplished it unaided.

Marathonomachai, "those who fought in Marathon," became Athenian models of valiant warriors. When the great tragic poet Aeschylus died in Sicily in 456/5, his epitaph mentioned none of his literary accomplishments, only his participation in the battle.

16.6.B   Aeschylus' Epitaph

Athenaeus *Learned Conversationalists at Table* (*Deipnosophistae*) 627c; cf. Pausanias 1.14.5

At any rate the first boast of Archilochus, who was a fine poet, was that he was able to take part in the competitive activities of the city, and only after that did he mention his poetic gifts. He says:

"I am a servant of Lord Enyalius [Ares], and I am familiar, too, with the lovely gift of the Muses."

Likewise Aeschylus, despite having such a great reputation for his poetry, nevertheless thought his bravery more important for the inscription on his tomb. He wrote:

"The grove at Marathon could tell of his famed courage, and so could the long-haired, who experienced it."

Figure 16.1 The mound at Marathon. George Tsafos/Lonely Planet Images.

In his comedy *Acharnians*, produced in 425, Aristophanes calls old men who represent traditional masculine values and courage "those who fought at Marathon." See WEB **16.7.II** for Aristophanes on the warriors of Marathon.

Marathon even led Athenian oligarchs to rank hoplite warfare above maritime victories attained by the lowlier oarsmen.

The glorification of Marathon and its warriors assumed many forms. Public monuments linked the battle to the city as well as to local and national cults. There were also commemorations of individual contributions to the battle that aimed to shape public memory or claim individual and family prestige. See again **16.4.C** for Pausanias' description of monuments in Marathon, and WEB **16.7.III** for questions concerning the memory of Miltiades and his inglorious career following the battle. For additional commemorations of Marathon, see WEB **18.8.II** ("Cimon and Theseus").

16.6.C   The Mound at Marathon

The most conspicuous of the battle's commemorations is arguably the mound (*soros*) for the Athenian dead that still stands on the Marathon plain (but at a distance from the battlefield; Figure 16.1). It is 9 (originally perhaps 12) meters high and 50 meters in diameter. A significantly smaller mound, 2.5 kilometers away, has been identified by its excavator as the tomb of the Plataeans and slaves, though the identification has been disputed. The Persian tombs were unmarked, and a mass grave, perhaps belonging the them, was found next to marshes near the site of the battle.

Notwithstanding individual claims to fame, all Athenians saw themselves as entitled to share in the battle's glory. They celebrated the victory in the annual festival of Artemis Agrotera, to whom they had sacrificed before the battle. They also built a temple to Eucleia (Glory) in grateful memory of Marathon (Pausanias 1.14.5). The southern frieze of the later temple of Nike on the acropolis and the Parthenon frieze have been interpreted as commemorations of the battle. In Greece, Athens advertised its valor by dedicating spoils of the battle to Apollo at Delphi (Pausanias 10.10.1–2, 11.5; Fornara no. 50).

Questions

1. What was the battle's significance for both victor and vanquished (**16.6**, WEB **16.7.II**)?
2. Discuss the forms of memorializing Marathon and their goals (**16.6**; see also **16.4.C**, WEB **16.7.III–IV**).

Review Questions

1. What did the Persians seek to achieve through Darius' campaign (**16.1**)?
2. Describe the Greeks' reaction to Darius' demands for earth and water and the Marathon campaign (**16.1**, **16.3–4**).
3. Was Athens united in its opposition to the Persian invasion (**16.4–5**)?
4. What were the key stages in the battle of Marathon and what is puzzling about it (**16.4–5**)?
5. How did the Athenians shape the memory of Marathon (**16.6**, WEB **16.7.II–III**)?

Suggested Readings

The battle of Marathon: Whatley 1964; Lazenby 1993, 48–80; Briant 2002a, 157–161; Sekunda 2002. *The legacy of Marathon, including in art*: Harrison 1972; Loraux 1986, esp. 57–62, 155–171; Castoria 1992, 28–32, 134–183. *Miltiades and Paros*: Develin 1977; Hamel 1998, 168–171.

17

The Persian War (480–479)

CHAPTER CONTENTS

Ancient Greece from Homer to Alexander: The Evidence, First Edition. Joseph Roisman.
© 2011 Blackwell Publishing Ltd. Translations © 2011 John Yardley. Published 2011 by Blackwell Publishing Ltd.

This chapter focuses on the Persian invasion of Greece, which the Greeks regarded as a defining event in their history. It reproduces Greek perspectives on the Persian War and documents the Athenian naval program that preceded it. The chapter then describes the galleys (triremes), that Athens and other Greeks used in their naval battles. It reports Greek responses to the invasion and their establishment of an anti-Persian alliance. The course of the war is examined through the Greek retreat from Thessaly, the famous battle of Thermopylae, the evacuation of Athens, the Greek naval victory at Salamis, and the land victory at Plataea and its commemorations. The battle of Mycale on the Ionian coast concludes the chapter.

17.1   Greek Perspectives of the Persian War

In the eyes of the Greeks, and especially the Spartans and the Athenians, the war against Persia in 480–479 confirmed their claim to both military and moral excellence and to hegemony over other Greeks. It was a new Trojan War, of Europe versus Asia, only this time the invaders were foreigners who wished to enslave the free Greeks. The Persians resembled the Trojans in wealth, but they were also imperialistic and sacrilegious. The Greek victory created and reaffirmed stereotypes of the Persians as inferior and of their king as a despotic ruler who was lacking in self-control and blinded by *hubris*. Such images color our sources and test the historical reconstruction of both events and policies. Two sources that reflected and contributed to these images were Herodotus and the poet Aeschylus, whose tragedy *Persians*, produced in 472, focused on the Greek naval victory over the Persian fleet in Salamis. Both authors describe as hubristic King Xerxes' construction of a floating bridge over the Hellespont so that his army could cross over to Europe, and especially his scourging of the sea after a storm had broken the bridge. In Aeschylus *Persians*, Darius' ghost gives a Greek perspective of the bridge over the water.

17.1.A   The Bridging of the Hellespont

Aeschylus *Persians* 745–752

Xerxes expected to stay the flow of the holy Hellespont with shackles, like a slave – the Bosporus, a stream of the god! He tried to make a new road, and by throwing on it fetters made by the hammer he changed the nature of the passage and produced a wide pathway for his mighty army. Mortal though he was, he thought – not with good sense – that he would get the better of all the gods, Poseidon included. A sickness of the mind must have overtaken my son for him to do this. I am afraid that my treasure, won by great effort on my part, may be overthrown and become the prey of the opportunist.

Herodotus adds the story of Xerxes' punishing the sea for destroying his bridge.

17.1.B   Punishing the Hellespont

Herodotus 7.34.3–35.2

(7.34.3) The men given the task therefore bridged the span over to this headland, starting from Abydos, the Phoenicians making their bridge from white flax, and the Egyptians making the other from papyrus. From Abydos to the coast opposite is a distance of seven stades [ca. 1,260 meters]. The strait was barely bridged when a violent storm descended, which shattered and destroyed the entire structure.

(35.1) When he learned of this, Xerxes was livid, and he gave orders for the Hellespont to be given three hundred lashes and for a pair of fetters to be thrown into the sea. I also heard at one time that he sent professional branders to put his brand on the Hellespont. **(35.2)** He certainly did order his men to make barbarous and insolent utterances, saying as they thrashed the water: "Bitter water, your master is inflicting this punishment on you for wronging him although you had suffered no wrong at his hands. King Xerxes will cross you, whether you like it or not. Quite just it is that nobody sacrifices to you, since you are a muddy and salty stream." So it was that Xerxes ordered these men to punish the sea, and he also ordered those who had been in charge of bridging the Hellespont to be beheaded.[1]

Note

1. *According to Herodotus (7.54), Xerxes later regretted his action and tried to placate the local gods.*

In Aeschylus' *Persians* (929–930), Xerxes and a chorus of Persians lament their defeat and conclude that "the land of Asia, oh monarch of the country, has been terribly, terribly brought to her knees."

   See WEB **17.2.I** for a fuller version of Aeschylus' depiction of the Persian defeat and humiliation, and WEB **17.2.II** for Plato's linking, more than a century later, of Persian royal decadence to unmanly educators and schooling.

Question

   1. What was barbarian in the Persian conduct and foretold their defeat according to Greek authors (**17.1.A–B** and WEB **17.2.I–II**)?

17.3   Themistocles and His Naval Program

Xerxes, who succeeded Darius in 486, began his preparations for the invasion of Greece two years later. Meanwhile, post-Marathon Athens ostracized men charged with tyrannical ambition or connections. The charges, whether warranted or not, reflected the link between tyranny and foreign invasion that was forged at Marathon. The city also witnessed the rise to prominence of one of its most famous politicians, Themistocles, son of Neocles. Themistocles lacked the social status of other members of the Athenian elite, but he compensated for it with a fierce political ambition and competitiveness. The historian Thucydides depicts him as a man of exceptional strategic foresight (1.138.3). In his account of the Athenians' rebuilding of the city walls in 478 following the Persian sack of Athens, he ascribes to Themistocles a plan to turn Athens into a maritime empire.

17.3.A   Themistocles' Plan

Thucydides 1.93.3–4

(**1.93.3**) Themistocles convinced the Athenians to finish the work still to be done in the Piraeus, a start having been made on it earlier (during the year that he was archon in Athens [493]). He thought the area had great potential, having as it did three natural harbors, and that for the Athenians to become a seafaring people would greatly help their acquisition of power. (**93.4**) It was, in fact, Themistocles who first ventured to say that they should focus on the sea, and he now at once began to help them establish their empire.

In 483/2 Themistocles succeeded in persuading the people to set the city on a shipbuilding program. Scholars have disagreed on his purpose, but there is no need to attribute to him a scheme for using Athens' war against Aegina in 483/2 as a pretext for preparing the city for a future conflict with Persia (thus Herodotus in WEB **17.4**). Driven by commercial rivalry, Athens had been involved in a war with Aegina since the end of the sixth century, and now, apparently, she sought to defeat her on the sea. *Ath. Pol.* as well as Plutarch *Themistocles* 4.1–3 set the projected number of triremes at one hundred, in contrast to Herodotus' probably erroneous two hundred.

17.3.B   Themistocles' Naval Project

Ath. Pol. 22.7

Two years later, in the archonship of Nicomedes [483/2], a hundred talents came to the city from operations at the silver mines that had been discovered at Maroneia[1], and some recommended that the money be distributed amongst the people. Themistocles, however, blocked the proposal, but did not say how he would spend the money.[2] Instead, he urged that they lend it out to the hundred richest Athenians, giving them one talent each. If what it was spent on met with approval, then the city would benefit, and if it did not they should take the money back from the borrowers. He was allowed to dispose of the money on these terms, and he had a hundred triremes built, each of the borrowers being responsible for building one ship; and it was with these that the Athenians fought the barbarians in the naval battle of Salamis. At this time, too, Aristides son of Lysimachus was ostracized.[3]

Notes

1. *Maroneia was a mining area in Laurium.*
2. *Themistocles' silence about spending the money is both unexplained and unlikely. More probable was his appointing rich men to build the ships.*
3. *According to ancient sources, Aristides was Themistocles' major rival. He was a better-connected politician with a reputation for honesty in contrast to Themistocles' trickery. For Aristides' ostracism, see also Plutarch Aristides 7.*

Questions

1. What led to Themistocles' naval program and how was it implemented according to *Ath. Pol.* (**17.3.B**) and Herodotus (WEB **17.4**)?
2. What were the consequences of the naval project?
3. What kind of opposition might the naval project have faced?

17.5   The Athenian Trireme

The trireme was the Athenians' maritime weapon of choice. The word "trireme" comes from the Greek *trieres*, "three-rower," which refers to the three levels of oarsmen who rowed the ship. The ship was introduced in the Levant no later than the sixth century and became the Greeks' standard warship during the Classical Age. The trireme was about 40 meters long, 5.4 meters wide, and 2.4 meters above the water. It had limited space, which forced the crew to disembark in order to eat or rest. The trireme used two masts as well as sails that were removed before battle. The standard crew of an Athenian trireme included 200 men: 170 oarsmen, 20 marines (*epibatai*) armed like hoplites, 4 archers, various seamen, the captain (trierarch), and the pilot who navigated the ship with two steering oars in the stern. The marines and the rest of the crew sat on the deck. The oarsmen were crowded on three levels under the deck, sitting on benches one on top of the other.

17.5.A   The Lenormant Relief of a Trireme

The Lenormant Relief, named after the French scholar who found it on the Athenian acropolis in the mid-nineteenth century, is one of the most informative

Figure 17.1   The Lenormant Relief of a trireme in the Acropolis Museum. © Luisa Ricciarini/TopFoto.

artistic renditions of a trireme (Figure 17.1). It was made ca. 410–400 and depicts a section of a trireme's side. A small fragment of this relief discovered later shows part of the side of the boat with an upper-level oarsman and two men on deck.

17.5.B   *Olympia* at Sea

Thanks to the efforts of British and Greek scholars, engineers, shipbuilders, and workmen, a classical trireme named *Olympia* has been reconstructed and was first tested at sea in 1987 (Figure 17.2, p. 222).

See WEB **17.6** for explanatory comments on the trireme's structure, tactics, its personnel, and the image of oarsmen.

17.7   Greek Responses to Xerxes' Invasion

While Athens was building its navy, which was the largest in the Greek world, Xerxes was already preparing his Greek campaign. Herodotus reports on a debate in the Persian court between Xerxes' cousin, the aggressive and impetuous

Figure 17.2 *Olympia*, a reconstruction of a classical trireme. M. Andrews/Ancient Art & Architecture Collection Ltd.

Mardonius, who advocated going to war, and Xerxes' uncle, the wise and cautious Artabanus, who opposed it. Greek advisors and heaven-sent dreams induced Xerxes to opt for war (Herodotus 8.6–19). In the end, Xerxes followed his father Darius' plan. Like his royal predecessors, he sought to support his status as the Great King through territorial expansion and military glory.

The king made advanced preparations for the invasion, and when he and his army reached Sardis, he resorted to the traditional Persian strategy of dividing the enemy. He sent heralds to request earth and water from the Greeks, except for the Spartans and the Athenians. He was quite successful: Argos refused to join the Greeks, and Xerxes heard from his heralds that there were other Medized (collaborating) Greeks in central Greece. The Ionians of Asia had already joined forces with him.

Herodotus 7.131–132.2

(**7.131**) … The heralds that had been sent to Greece to ask for earth returned, some with nothing, others with earth and water.

(**132.1**) Amongst those who actually gave these items were the following: the Thessalians, the Dolopians, the Enienians, the Perrhaebians, the Locrians, the Magnesians, the Melians, the Achaeans of Phthiotis, and the Thebans, along with all the other Boeotians apart from the Thespians and the Plataeans. (**132.2**) The Greeks who undertook to fight the barbarian took a solemn oath directed against these peoples. The oath stipulated that, if things went well for them in the war, they would dedicate to the god in Delphi a tenth of the property of all those who had surrendered to the Persians although they were Greeks and had not been forced into submission.

The leaders of the anti-Persian front were Sparta and Athens. Sparta had opposed Persia and Persian friends in Greece since the reign of Cleomenes. The presence of the exiled Spartan king Demaratus in the Persian court and the Spartans' fear of losing their hegemonic position in Greece motivated them to support fighting the invaders. Athens had been on Persia's enemy list since the Ionian raid of Sardis in 499, and the Persian defeat at Marathon made punishing Athens even more imperative.

In 481/0 Athens recalled ostracized citizens, including the politician Aristides. According to Plutarch, the man responsible for the measure was Themistocles, who had also been the most active in ostracizing Aristides in the first place: see WEB **17.8**, which also has links to Themistocles' bust and an *ostrakon* inscribed with Aristides' name.

Question

1. How did the Greek coalition try to deter other Greeks from surrendering to the Persians?

17.9   The Hellenic Alliance Against Persia

In 481, Athens, Sparta, and twenty-nine other Greek states met together in Corinth to form what modern historians call the "Hellenic League." They resolved to fight the invaders and made several operative and strategic decisions. The Hellenic oath (Herodotus 7.132.2 = **17.7**), which aimed to dissuade states from supporting the Persians, was probably a product of this meeting too.

17.9.A   The Greeks' Decisions About the War

Herodotus 7.145.1–2

(**7.145.1**) ...All the Greeks who were loyal to the Greek cause now came together to hold discussions and make solemn commitments. In their deliberations, they first of all decided to terminate their feuding and their wars with each other (and there were a number of these at the time, the greatest of them being that between Athens and Aegina). (**145.2**) Then, when they learned that Xerxes was at Sardis with his army, they decided to send spies to Asia to gather intelligence on the king's movements. They further agreed to dispatch deputations to Argos to form a defensive alliance with the city against Persia, and to send requests for assistance for Greece to Gelon son of Deinomenes in Sicily, to Corcyra, and to Crete. Their intention, since the pressing danger threatened all Greeks alike, was to have a unified Greek force with all its peoples coming together and acting in unison. Gelon's power was said to be great, far surpassing that of any of the Greeks.

None of those who were asked to support the league did so. The allies, many of them Peloponnesians, gave Sparta command over both the Greek army and navy. When Herodotus discusses the preparations for a later naval engagement at Artemisium (480), he praises the Athenians for giving up on the joint naval command and for ranking Greek unity above considerations of prestige and power. He thus endorses the Athenians' self-congratulatory view of their contribution to the war. It does not mean, however, that Athens did not deserve praise or that Herodotus sought to propagate it.

17.9.B   The Greek Command

Herodotus 8.2.1–3.2

(**8.2.1**) These were the men who fought at Artemisium, and I have also noted the numbers of ships the various states supplied. The total number of ships that assembled at Artemisium was (pentecontgers excepted) 271.[1] (**2.2**) But the admiral with supreme command, Eurybiades son of Eurycleides, was provided by the Spartans, because the allies declared that they would not follow Athenian leaders and would abort the projected expedition if a Laconian were not overall commander.

(**3.1**) In fact, at the start of the campaign, before the Greeks sent to Sicily for an alliance, there had been talk of entrusting the naval campaign to the Athenians. When the allies objected, however, the Athenians acquiesced, thinking that what was most important was the survival of Greece, and realizing that Greece would be destroyed if they bickered over leadership. And they were right; for internal quarreling is worse than a united military front to the same degree that war is worse than peace. (**3.2**) So, aware of this, they did not press their claim but gave way – but only for as long as they had a serious need of the Spartans, as they later showed. For when they had driven the Persian back, and they were now in a struggle for *his* territory, they wrested the command from the Lacedaemonians on the pretext of Pausanias' arrogant behavior. But this came later.[2]

Notes

1. *The penteconter had only fifty oarsmen, hence the name.*
2. *See WEB **18.4** ("Pausanias Seeks Support from Xerxes") and WEB **18.13.II** ("Pausanias' Second Recall and Death") for Pausanias' conduct after the war and its consequences.*

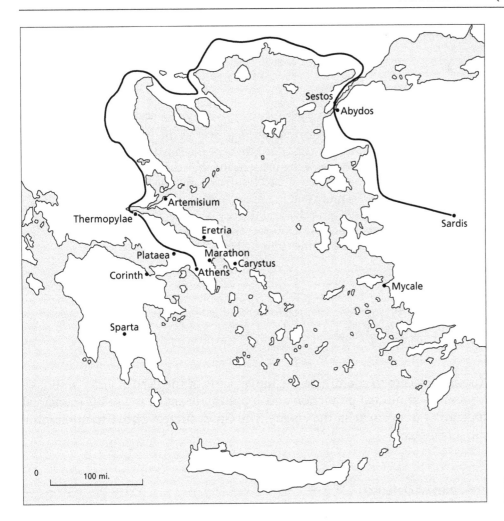

Map 17.1
Xerxes' expedition.

Questions

1. What measures did the Greeks take in preparation for the Persian invasion?
2. What issues might have divided the Greek front and how were they resolved?

17.10   The Greek Retreat from Thessaly and its Aftermath (480)

The first joint action of the Greeks was to try to keep Thessaly and its cavalry on the Greek side by defending the Tempe pass between Lower Macedonia and Thessaly. They sent 10,000 hoplites there (with Themistocles leading the Athenian contingent), and their army was joined by the Thessalian cavalry. But the Greek force retreated from the pass shortly after, and Thessaly went over to the Persian side.

17.10.A   Retreat from Thessaly

Herodotus 7.173.3–4

(**7.173.3**) The Greeks remained there only a few days. For messengers arrived from the Macedonian, Alexander, son of Amyntas,[1] advising them to leave rather than stay in the pass and be trampled under by the advancing Persian army – and they informed them of the Persian troop numbers and naval strength. The Greeks followed the advice of the messengers; they thought it was sound, and that the Macedonian was well disposed toward them. (**173.4**) In my opinion, however, it was fear that persuaded them, for they were now learning that there was another pass into Thessaly, one running through inland Macedonia, by way of Perrhaebia and the city of Gonnus (and this was actually the one by which Xerxes' army did come into the country). The Greeks accordingly went down to their ships and started on their return journey to the Isthmus.

Note

1. *The Macedonian king, Alexander I (498–454). His appellation "Philhellenê," lover of the Greeks, appears to be a much later addition.*

Xerxes took care to coordinate the movements of the Persian army and navy for reasons of mutual protection and supplies. He aimed to use his numerical superiority to overwhelm the enemy. The Greek strategy strove to undermine this advantage.

17.10.B   The Greeks' Lines of Defense

Herodotus 7.175.1–2

(**7.175.1**) When they reached the Isthmus, the Greeks began to discuss, in light of the information from Alexander, how and where to make their stand. The opinion that prevailed was that they should defend the pass at Thermopylae: it was clearly narrower than the pass into Thessaly and was at the same time closer to home. (**175.2**) Before they came to Thermopylae and were given the information by the Trachinians, they had no knowledge of the existence of the path that brought about the downfall of the Greeks at Thermopylae. They therefore decided on defending this pass to block the barbarians' advance into Greece, while the fleet would sail to Artemisium in the territory of Histiaea. The two places are close to each other, and thus both armies could gain information on each other's movements.

Question

1. Why did the Greeks retreat from Tempe and what did it mean for their strategy?

17.11   The Battle of Thermopylae (480)

Following the retreat from Thessaly, the Greeks' goal was to stop the Persians before they advanced into central Greece and Attica. Both Artemisium on the island of Euboea and the land pass of Thermopylae offered narrow spaces, which made it difficult or impossible for the Persians to use their numerical superiority in troops and ships effectively. It is unclear whether, or to what degree, their forces on land and sea depended on each other, and which battle was supposed to provide the decisive victory with the other aiming to hold off the enemy. It is assumed here that the Greeks pinned their hopes chiefly on Thermopylae and that the fleet in Artemisium was supposed to prevent the Persian navy from helping Xerxes on land.

See WEB **17.12.I** for Herodotus' description of the naval battle of Artemisium, and WEB **17.12.II** for Themistocles' attempt afterwards to encourage the Ionians and Carians to desert Xerxes.

At Thermopylae, the narrow passage prevented the Persians from exploiting their advantage in numbers and cavalry, and an old wall, which the Greeks intended to rebuild, was an additional obstacle. The Spartan king Leonidas took with him 7,000 troops, which were sufficient to hold the enemy off until expected Greek reinforcements arrived. This explains why only 300 Spartans came with him. Given Spartan sensitivity to their demographic inferiority at home and the need to continue the family, all 300 warriors were fathers of sons. When the Greek force came to Thermopylae, however, they were disappointed to find the Persians there sooner than expected.

17.11.A   Leonidas' Plan

Herodotus 7.207

(**7.207**) This was what they intended doing, but when the Persians approached the pass the Greeks at Thermopylae became afraid and began to discuss a retreat. All the Peloponnesians, Leonidas excepted, were for falling back on the Peloponnese and focusing their defense on the Isthmus. The Phocians and [the Eastern] Locrians, however, were very angry at the suggestion, and Leonidas voted for remaining and sending messengers to the city-states to demand assistance, seeing that they were too few to defend themselves against the army of the Medes.

See WEB **17.12.III** for Herodotus' account of a conversation between Xerxes and the exiled Spartan king Demaratus in which the latter describes the Spartan strength and ethos.

The battle began with waves of Persian infantry crashing against the Greek defense, but the Persians proved no match for the Greek hoplites, especially the Spartans. The turning point came on the third day, when Ephialtes, son of Eurydemus, a local Greek from Trachis, told the Persians about the Anopaea path, which allowed them to outflank the Greeks from the south. Ephialtes' treason immortalized him in infamy, although he did nothing substantially different from many other Greeks who advised Xerxes or fought on his side. Leonidas, who had known about this path, guarded it with 1,000 men from Phocis, but they fled upon the approach of the Persian Hydarnes and his elite unit of 10,000 "Immortals." What happened next has been a source of wonder but also some puzzlement for both ancients and moderns.

17.11.B   Leonidas Decides to Stay

Herodotus 7.219.1–220.5

(**7.219.1**) It was the prophet Megistias who, after observing the sacrificial animals, first informed the Greeks at Thermopylae of their impending death, saying that it would come with the dawn. Next came deserters, who arrived while it was still night, bearing word of the Persians taking the path around them. And then, third, news was brought by the day-scouts who came running down from the heights when day was already dawning. (**219.2**) At that point the Greeks held a meeting, at which opinions were divided. Some maintained they should not leave their position; others disagreed. After this they separated, some leaving and dispersing to their various cities, the others preparing to make their stand there with Leonidas.

(**7.220.1**) There is also a story that Leonidas himself sent them off from concern that they would die, but thought that it was improper for him and the Spartiates present there to abandon the position that they had originally come to defend. (**220.2**) The version that I am inclined to accept is the following. When Leonidas saw that the allies were discouraged and unwilling to put themselves at risk with him, he told them to leave, but said it was not right for him to go himself. In fact, though, by staying he would actually be left with great renown, and the prosperity of Sparta would not be wiped out. (**220.3**) For when the Spartiates consulted the oracle about this war, right at its start, the reply given by the Pythia was that either Lacedaemon would be laid waste by the barbarians or their king would perish. The following is the oracle she delivered to them in hexameter verse:

(**220.4**) "For you, inhabitants of wide-wayed Sparta, it is fated that either your great and glorious city will be sacked by the men of Persia or that, instead, the land of Lacedaemon will grieve over the death of a king descended from Heracles. For the strength neither of bulls nor of lions will hold the foe in conflict, since he has the might of Zeus. Nor, I tell you, will he be stopped before he has torn one of the two apart."

It was his reflection on this, as well as his wish to lay up a store of glory exclusively for the Spartans, (**220.5**) that made Leonidas dismiss the allies. This is what happened, not an unseemly departure on their part after a difference of opinion.

Even Herodotus was not entirely sure why Leonidas stayed with about 1,000 local troops in addition to his Spartans. Did he plan to escape, but failed? Did the Spartans' earlier preparations for death, as evinced by the selection of 300 Spartan fathers and the testimony of Xerxes' scout (WEB **17.12.III**), suggest that they never contemplated retreat? In the end, the Spartan ethos probably best explained their conduct.

_____   17.11.C   Commemorating the Spartans of Thermopylae

Herodotus cites two epitaphs, one about the often forgotten non-Spartan warriors who fought at Thermopylae, and the other about the Lacedaemonians who died there. Simonides is the author of the first (fr. 22 Page), and probably of the second one too (fr. 22b Page).

Herodotus 7.228.1–2

(**7.228.1**) The Lacedaemonians were buried where they fell, along with those who had lost their lives earlier, before the men dismissed by Leonidas had left. An inscription was set over them, which reads as follows:

"Four thousand from the Peloponnese once fought here against three million."

(**228.2**) This is the inscription for the whole force, but the Spartans also have one of their own:

"Stranger, report to the Lacedaemonians that here we lie, obedient to their orders."

See WEB **17.22** for a link to Simonides' epitaph.

For the Spartans' last stand at Thermopylae, the fall of Leonidas, and Xerxes' desecration of his body, see WEB **17.12.IV**.

Although the battle of Thermopylae ended in defeat, it was seen, especially in Sparta, as a moral victory. It represented a heroic struggle for freedom by the few against the many, and a model of self-sacrifice and of fighting to the bitter end regardless of the odds. This legacy led some of Sparta's foes to deduce that the Spartans entertained no other option but victory or death. In fact, the Spartans seldom if ever duplicated their last stand in Thermopylae.

Questions

1. What was the Greeks' war plan in Artemisium (WEB **17.12.I**) and Thermopylae (**17.11**)?
2. What Spartan values are highlighted in the description of the battle of Thermopylae and the events attending it (see also WEB **17.12.III–IV**)?
3. What role did non-Spartan troops play at Thermopylae? What accounted for their marginalization?
4. Was the Spartan stand at Thermopylae suicidal?
5. What were the outcomes of the battles of Thermopylae and Artemisium (see also WEB **17.12.I–II**)? What did Xerxes likely conclude from these battles?

17.13   The Evacuation of Athens

The Greek defeat at Thermopylae allowed Xerxes to enter central Greece. The Persian army raided enemy territory but spared Medized states, chief among them Thebes. Athens in the meantime evacuated most of its people.

The decision to evacuate was not easy, and our sources are unclear on how and when it was reached. The reconstruction adopted here assumes that the Athenians were well aware of their fate should Xerxes capture their city and so decided that they would leave Attica already in late 481. As can be gathered from their later actions, they planned to transfer women and children to Troezen on the Peloponnesian coast of the Saronic Gulf and to the island of Aegina. Men and the elderly were to move to the nearby Athenian island of Salamis. Salamis also served as a base for able Athenians who would meet the enemy on the sea. Themistocles most likely advocated this plan. As was common under such circumstances, before taking such a decisive step the Athenians sought the gods' approval or opinion and sent a delegation to Delphi. They received an awful response in return promising doom to the city and advising them to flee it: see WEB **17.14.I** for the first Athenian consultation of Delphi about continuing the war against Persia.

In an unusual case of bargaining or a request for reconsideration, the Athenian delegation appealed to the oracle as suppliants for another response.

17.13.A   The Athenians Ask for a Second Oracle

> Herodotus 7.141.2–142.3
>
> **(7.141.2)** … When they said this, the priestess delivered a second oracle, which ran as follows:
>
> **(141.3)** "Pallas cannot propitiate Olympian Zeus by making longwinded entreaties and using cunning sophistry. I shall make a prophecy for you again, giving it the strength of adamant. When all else within the border of Cecrops and the hollow of sacred Cithaeron is being captured, far-seeing Zeus grants to the Triton-born goddess a wooden wall, which alone will remain intact and will benefit you and your children. **(141.4)** Do not idly await the cavalry and great force of infantry that comes from the mainland, but turn your back and give way to them. You will face them in battle later. Holy Salamis, you will destroy the sons of mothers when Demeter's seed is scattered or her harvest brought in."
>
> **(142.1)** This was, both in fact and as it appeared at the time, a much milder prophecy than the earlier one, and the messengers wrote it down and went back to Athens. After they had left Delphi and made their report to the Athenians, many opinions were voiced as people tried to interpret the oracle, but two in particular stood out, and they were in conflict with each other. Some of the older people said that, in their view, the god was prophesying that the acropolis would remain safe. In fact, the acropolis of Athens had, in days of old, been surrounded by a palisade of plaited twigs, **(142.2)** and these men conjectured that this was the wooden wall that was indicated. Others, however, claimed that the god meant their ships, and they were for ignoring everything else and fitting these out. Now, those

who claimed that the wooden wall was the ships were baffled by the last two lines of the prophecy given by the Pythia:

"Holy Salamis, you will destroy the sons of mothers when Demeter's seed is scattered or her harvest brought in."

(**142.3**) The opinion of those who said the ships were the wooden wall foundered on these words, for the seers took this as meaning that, if the Athenians prepared to do battle at sea off Salamis, they would be beaten.

The opinion in favor of evacuating Athens prevailed, and the residents of Attica left for Troezen, Aegina, and Salamis (Herodotus 8.40–42). Herodotus' account, which leaves the impression that the decision to fight in Salamis and evacuate the land was taken after Artemisium, does not tally well with an inscription from Troezen that is generally known as the "Themistocles Decree." It was inscribed ca. 300 and records a popular decision, moved by Themistocles, which clearly suggested that the plan to fight the Persians in a naval battle near Salamis and to leave Attica was conceived before the battle of Artemisium. A number of scholars doubt the authenticity of the decree. They refer to other much later decrees that were falsely attributed to the time of the Persian wars in order to glorify Athens or for other reasons. Some phrases in the inscription betray a later composition or edition. It is assumed here, however, that the decree is largely authentic and that it was moved by Themistocles prior to Artemisium. The evacuation itself, which was not orderly, went into high gear after the last battle. Leaving Attica meant that the Athenians would lose their sources of income. The council of the Areopagus came to the rescue with money taken probably from the state treasury: see WEB **17.14.II** on how the Areopagus helped in the evacuation of Athens.

17.13.B Themistocles' Decree

ML no. 23 = Fornara no. 55

Translation: Fornara, pp. 54–55

[Gods.] Resolved by the Boulê [Council] and the People, Themis[tocl]es son of Neocles of Phrearrhii made the motion. The city shall be entrusted to Athena, Athens' (**5**) [Protectress, and to the] other gods, all of them, for protections and [defense against the] Barbarian on behalf of the country. The Athenians [in their entirety and the aliens] who live in Athens shall place [their children and their women] in Troezen ... the Founder of the land. (**10**) [The elderly and (movable)] property shall (for safety) be deposited at Salamis. [The Treasurers and] the Priestesses are [to remain] on the Acropolis [and guard the possessions of the] gods. The rest of the Athe[nians in their entirety and those] aliens who have reached young manhood shall embark [on the readied] two hundred ships and they shall repulse (**15**) the [Barbarian for the sake of] liberty, both their own [and that of the other Hellenes,] in common with the Lacedaemonians, Corin[thians, Aeginetans] and the others who wish to have a share [in the danger.] Appointment will also be made of trierarchs [two hundred in number, one for] each ship, by the generals, (**20**), [beginning] tomorrow, from among those who are owners [of both land and home] in Athens and who have children who are legitimate. [They shall not be more] than fifty years old and the lot shall determine each man's ship. (The generals) shall also enlist marines, ten [for each] ship, from men over twenty years old of (**25**) age [up to] thirty, and archers, four (in number). [They shall also by lot appoint] the specialist officers for each ship when they appoint [the] trierarchs by lot. A list shall be made also [of the rest, ship by] ship, by the generals, on notice boards, [with the] Athenians (to be selected) from the lexiarchic registers[1] (**30**) [the] aliens from the list of names (registered) with the Polemarch. They shall write them up, assigning them by divisions, up to two hundred (divisions, each) [of up to] one hundred (men), and they shall append to each division the name of the trireme and the trierarch and the specialist officers, so that they may know on (**35**) what trireme each division shall embark. When assignment of all the divisions has been made and they have been allotted to the triremes, all the two hundred shall be manned by (order of) the Boulê and the generals, after they have sacrificed to appease Zeus the All-powerful and Athena and Nike and Poseidon (**40**) the Securer. When they have completed the manning of the ships, with one hundred of them they shall bring assistance to Artemisium in Euboea, while with the other hundred they shall, all round Salamis and the rest of Attica, lie at anchor and guard the country. To ensure that in a spirit of concord all Athenians (**45**) will ward off the Barbarian, those banished for the [ten-]year span shall leave for Salamis and they are to remain [there until the People] decide about them.[2] Those...

Notes

1. *The lexiarchic registers listed citizens by their demes.*
2. *The banished were ostracized Athenians who were not allowed to return to Attica.*

When Xerxes captured Athens he accomplished his official goal of taking revenge. The Persians looted the empty city, and after a prolonged struggle against priests, poor men, and others who stayed to protect the acropolis, seized the citadel and set it on fire. The current ruins on the acropolis belong to later temples built on top of the destruction left by Xerxes.

The Athenians displayed communal resolve and courage when they threw everything into a single maritime battle, especially as they must have felt betrayed by their Peloponnesian allies. The latter had promised the Athenians that they would defend them in Boeotia if they retreated from Thermopylae. They did not. Instead, the Peloponnesians, including the Spartans, were busy fortifying the Corinthian Isthmus (Herodotus 8.40, 74). Defending the Peloponnese made sense because the majority of those who fought Xerxes came from there. Yet Herodotus' view of the futility of this strategy makes better sense, even if he may reflect an Athenian claim to the lion's share in the victory over Persia.

17.13.C   A Faulty Peloponnesian Strategy

Herodotus 7.139.1–5; cf. Thucydides 1.73.2–74.3

(**7.139.1**) At this point I have to express an opinion that will be found abhorrent by the majority of people, and I shall not hold back from saying what seems to me to be the truth. (**139.2**) If the Athenians had left their land from fear of the advancing peril or if, instead of leaving, they had remained in place and surrendered to Xerxes, nobody would have tried to oppose the king at sea. Now if no one had opposed Xerxes at sea, the following is what would have happened on land. (**139.3**) Even if numerous defensive walls had been drawn across the Isthmus by the Peloponnesians, the Lacedaemonians would have been deserted by their allies and left isolated – not that the allies would have done this willingly, but they would have been forced to when the cities fell one by one before the fleet of the barbarian. And, isolated, they would have died noble deaths after performing great feats of heroism. (**139.4**) Such would have been their fate; either that or, when they saw the other Greeks Medizing, they would have come to terms with Xerxes. And so, either way, Greece would have fallen to the Persians. For I cannot understand of what use walls drawn across the Isthmus could have been when the king ruled the sea.

(**139.5**) As it is, anyone claiming that the Athenians turned out to be the saviors of Greece would not be wide of the truth. Whichever side they turned to, that was the way the balance was going to tilt, and their choice was that Greece should remain free. Thus it was they who roused the rest of Greece that had not Medized and who were, after the gods, responsible for driving back the king...

Questions

1. Describe the Athenians' exchanges with Delphi about the evacuation of their city (**17.13.A**, WEB **17.14.I**). What does this suggest about Delphi's position in the conflict and about the politics of oracles?
2. How does the epigraphic evidence challenge Herodotus' description of Athens' evacuation (**17.13.A–B,** and WEB **17.14.I**)?
3. Who was involved in the city's evacuation and how (see also WEB **17.14. II**)?
4. What was the Athenian criticism of the Peloponnesian strategy and how would the Spartans have responded to it (**17.13.C**)?

17.15   The Battle of Salamis (480)

When the joint Greek navy assembled in Salamis, many Greek commanders wanted to take their ships to the Isthmus to help in its defense. Themistocles, however, first scared the Spartan chief admiral Eurybiades with the prospect of the Athenians' dispersing to their different home bases. (He would later threaten to sail to Siris in Italy.) Then he addressed the common Greek council. There is no certainty about the authenticity of the arguments Herodotus attributes to him, but they are all, as the historian puts it, "reasonable." They surely explain Themistocles' strategy.

17.15.A   Themistocles' Plan of Battle

Herodotus 8.60.a–c

(**8.60.a**) ...If you [Eurybiades] take them on in the Isthmus, you will be fighting a naval battle on the open sea, and this is not at all favorable to us, our ships being heavier and fewer in number. Furthermore, you are going to lose Salamis, Megara, and Aegina, even if we are generally successful. Also, their infantry will follow the fleet, and so you will be drawing them to the Peloponnese and putting all Greece at risk.

(**60.b**) If you do as I suggest, however, you will find the following to be to our advantage. First, by taking them on in a confined space, with our few ships facing their superior numbers, we shall, if the battle goes as one may expect, win a great victory – fighting in a confined space is to our advantage just as fighting in an open space is to theirs. In addition, there is the preservation of Salamis, where our children and women have been taken for safekeeping. And there is this further advantage in the strategy, one which you hold to be the most important. Staying here you will be fighting a battle at sea in defense of the Peloponnese just as much as you would at the Isthmus, and you will not, if you are wise, draw the enemy to the Peloponnese.

(**60.c**) If the result is what I expect and we defeat them with our navy, the barbarians will not reach the Isthmus – in fact, they will not get beyond Attica but will retreat in total disarray. We shall gain, too, by saving Megara, Aegina, and Salamis, the latter being where, it is prophesied, we shall prevail over the enemy. When men base their plans on reason, the result is usually success; if their plans are *not* based on reason, even god will not go along with men's designs...

Because Themistocles' persuasion won him only momentary success, he resorted to subterfuge. He sent a message to Xerxes informing him that the Greeks were fearful and divided and that they were planning to flee. He advised the king to seize the opportunity and win a victory. Xerxes indeed was keen on fighting the Greek navy so he could destroy it then and there. In spite of scholarly doubts about the story and Xerxes' gullibility, the precedent of the Samian fleet's defection to the Persian side in the battle of Lade (494; **15.10**: "The Fall of Miletus"; **15.11**: "The Change of Persian Policy in Ionia") made a similar action by the Athenians conceivable. Themistocles deserves credit for inducing the Persians and the Greeks to fight in the narrow straits of Salamis. He also caused the Persians to split their force into two squadrons, one on each side of the island of Psyttaleia, instead of keeping them united.

17.15.B   The Persian Movements

Herodotus 8.76.1–3

(**8.76.1**) As for the Persians, they accepted the veracity of the message [of Themistocles], and their first move was to put ashore a large number of men on the little island of Psyttaleia that lies between Salamis and the mainland. Next, in the middle of the night, they launched their western wing toward Salamis to encircle the island, while the men deployed off Ceos and Cynosura also put to sea; and they also blockaded the entire passage as far as Munychia with their ships.[1] (**76.2**) Their reason for putting to sea was to remove from the Greeks any possibility of flight, to keep them bottled up on Salamis, and have them pay for the battles off Artemisium. And the reason for putting ashore Persians on the little island called Psyttaleia was that, since the island lay in the channel where the naval battle would take place, this was where men and wreckage would be carried ashore. The Persians could now rescue or kill the survivors according to whether they were friend or foe. (**76.3**) These moves they made silently so their enemy should not become aware of them, and they did the job at night, without taking any sleep.

Note

1. *Cynosura is a peninsula on Salamis; the location of Ceos is unknown. Diodorus of Sicily (11.17.2) reports that 200 Egyptian ships sailed to prevent the Greeks from fleeing through the straits between Salamis and Megara, but his report is unsupported by other sources.*

17.15.C   The Battle Plan of Salamis

Herodotus (7.89.1) estimates that the Persians altogether had 1,207 ships, which modern historians cut to between 400 and 700 ships. The Greeks had 378 battleships (Herodotus 8.43–48 miscalculates the total of his own figures; Diodorus 11.18.1–2 has a different Greek battle order than that given by Herodotus). Even though the Persians succeeded in encircling the Greek position, it meant that their force was divided in two. Their oarsmen suffered from fatigue after rowing at night, and the narrow straits prevented them from taking advantage of their numerical superiority and their ships' greater maneuverability and speed. According to Plutarch (*Themistocles* 14.2–3), Themistocles also timed the Greek charge to coincide with a breeze that rocked the taller Persian ships but not the heavier Greek ships.

The battle of Salamis was fought on September 25, 480 (see Figure 17.3). In 472 Aeschylus won first prize in the festival of the Dionysia with a trilogy that included the *Persians*. The play portrayed the Greek victory in Salamis as

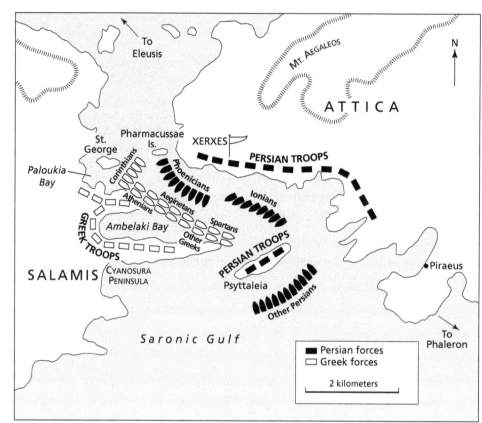

Figure 17.3
The battle plan of Salamis. Reprinted with the permission of Simon & Schuster Inc., and The Random House Group UK from *The Battle of Salamis* by Barry Strauss. © 2004 by Barry Strauss. All rights reserved.

a Persian tragedy (and according to one interpretation, as a warning of the consequences of Athenian imperialism). The poet, like many of his audience, probably took part in the battle. In the following passage, a messenger from Xerxes describes the battle to Xerxes' mother, Atossa, and other members of the Persian court in Susa.

17.15.D   Aeschylus' Description of the Battle of Salamis

Aeschylus *Persians* 395–429

(395) The trumpet with its call to battle fired their entire force. Straightway, with splashing oars dipping together, they, at the order given, hit the deep brine, and swiftly all of them came into view. The right wing, well deployed, took the lead in good order, **(400)** and then their entire force advanced; and at the same time one could hear the loud cry: "Go and free your fatherland, Sons of Greece. Free your children, your wives, the abodes of your ancestral gods and your forefathers' graves. The struggle now is for everything."

And to meet them there came from us the babble of the Persian language, and there was no longer time to hesitate. One ship rammed its brass-tipped beak on another. (**410**) The charge was started by a Greek vessel, which broke off entirely the high stern of a Phoenician craft, and then all the Greek ships bore down on various ships of ours. At first the advancing Persian navy held its own, but when the mass of our ships became crowded together in the narrow channel, no help could be brought from one to another, and they were struck by the brass-tipped rams of ships of their own side. In this situation, they sheared off all their oars, and the Greek navy, not unaware of their opportunity, encircled our ships and kept ramming them. There were upturned hulls, and the sea could not be seen – (**420**) it was covered with wreckage and slaughtered men. Headlands and reefs were full of corpses, and all the ships that were part of the barbarian force were rowing in confused flight. But the Greeks were striking and clubbing our men, as if they were tuna or some catch of fish, with broken oars and pieces of wreckage. And there was wailing and shrieking all over the sea, until the eye of murky night took away the sight. But as for the large number of our woes, I could not fully recount them to you even if I had ten days to tell the tale in order.

The battle ended in a Greek victory. The historian Diodorus of Sicily (11.19.3) mentions the loss of forty Athenian ships as opposed to more than 200 Persian ships. For Herodotus' description of the battle of Salamis, see WEB **17.16.I**.

The battle of Salamis did not decide the war; the land battle of Plataea did (**17.17**). However, this was not the way the Athenians remembered the event. For them, Salamis and their self-sacrifice saved Greece and put other Greeks in their debt. It also justified their hegemonic claim to lead the Greeks. The Athenians harped on these themes on various occasions at home and abroad.

See WEB **17.16.II** for competing claims for the honor of fighting at Salamis.

Questions

1. What were the competing Greek strategies on the eve of Salamis (**17.15.A**)?
2. What was Themistocles' contribution to the Greek victory? Who else should be given credit and why (**17.15.B–D**, WEB **17.16.I**)?
3. What tactics did the Greeks use in battle according to Aeschylus (**17.15.D**) and Herodotus (WEB **17.16.I**)?
4. Describe the Athenian–Corinthian conflict over the memory of Salamis (**17.15** and WEB **17.16.II**).

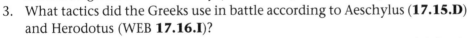
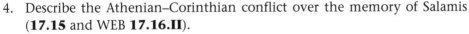

17.17 The Battle of Plataea (479)

The Greek victory at Salamis forced the Persians to rethink their strategy. Xerxes, who was concerned at being trapped in Europe and had doubts about the loyalty of Ionia, decided to leave Greece for Sardis, where he stayed until the autumn of 479. He beat a hasty retreat, the difficulties of which our sources describe in loving detail. Yet he also left in Greece part of his army under Mardonius in the hope of winning the war on land.

Mardonius, who needed a fleet to support his war efforts, tried to draw Athens to his side. The Spartans sent an embassy to Athens, not completely trusting her response. The Athenians, however, rejected Mardonius' offer. Herodotus' account of the Athenian speech to the Spartan envoys places Athens on the high moral ground and reads like a manifesto of Athenian foreign policy then and in years to come. But it also includes an early attempt to define a common Greek identity.

17.17.A   Athens Declares Loyalty to the Greek Cause

Herodotus 8.144.1–2

(**8.144.1**) ... but the Athenians' reply to the messengers from Sparta was as follows: "It may have been a normal human reaction for the Lacedaemonians to fear that we might come to some agreement with the barbarian, but it still seems to us that, knowing as you did the temperament of the Athenians, your apprehension was scandalous. You knew that nowhere in the world is there enough gold, and nowhere land sufficiently outstanding in its beauty and quality, for which we would be prepared to Medize and enslave Greece. (**144.2**) In fact, there are numerous considerations, and important ones, that would prevent us from doing that, even if we wanted to. First and foremost there is the burning and devastation of the statues and shrines of the gods; we are obliged to punish this to the fullest extent rather than come to terms with the party responsible for it. Then there is the Greek unity in blood and language, the communality of our religious buildings and rites, and our shared way of life; the betrayal of these would not reflect well on the Athenians..."

Because the Peloponnesians did not send an army to protect Athens from Mardonius, its residents evacuated the city once again to Salamis. Mardonius reoccupied Athens but his renewed peace offer to the Athenians was rebuffed. Athens used this opportunity to warn the Spartans of the consequences of dragging their feet. After some hesitation the Spartans decided to venture beyond the Isthmian wall. The Spartan force was joined shortly afterwards by 5,000 perioecic hoplites. Together with the helots, it was the largest army Sparta had ever sent to battle.

17.17.B   The Spartan Expedition to Plataea

Herodotus 9.10.1–2

(**9.10.1**) ...Saying nothing to the [Athenian] envoys who had come to them from the cities, the ephors immediately sent out five thousand Spartiates, while it was still dark, assigning seven helots to each of them[1] and giving the command to Pausanias son of Cleombrotus. (**10.2**) Overall command really belonged to Pleistarchus son of Leonidas, but he was still a boy, and Pausanias was both his guardian and his cousin (Cleombrotus, Pausanias' father and Anaxandrides' son, being no longer alive)...[2]

Notes

1. *The number of 35,000 helots seems too high, though it made sense to take many helots out of Sparta when most of its hoplites were gone. They served as light-armed troops.*
2. *The other Spartan king of the Eurypontid house, Leotychidas (II), replaced Eurybiades as commander of the Greek navy.*

The Greek army that assembled in the Isthmus and went to Boeotia numbered 38,700 hoplites with about 70,000 light troops. The largest hoplite contingents came from Sparta, Athens, and Corinth (Herodotus 9.28–29). The Persian army was slightly larger – scholars estimate it as between 30,000 and 60,000 men, though Herodotus gives the unlikely number of 300,000 troops (9.32, 66.2).

The late historian Diodorus of Sicily (11.29.2–3) reports that the Greek army took a binding oath. Two similar versions of the oath survived, one in a 330 speech by the Athenian politician Lycurgus (*Against Leocrates* 81), and the other, which most resembles an ancient oath, engraved in an Attic inscription of the last third of the fourth century. Scholars are divided about the authenticity of the so-called Plataea Oath. Because no source mentions the oath before the fourth century, some regard it as a fourth-century Athenian fabrication designed to promote a Panhellenic policy or to boost patriotism and morale. Scholars also note that the oath suspiciously forbids the destruction of Plataea, which was destroyed by Sparta at the instigation of Thebes in 427, and that it instructs the Athenians to make their ruined temples memorials of the war even though they rebuilt their temples on the acropolis. (It is possible, however, that they left one destroyed temple as a memorial.) Finally, the fourth-century historian Theopompus of Chios claimed that the Athenians fabricated this oath (*FGrHist* 115 F 153). Yet Theopompus might have been too eager a detective of forgeries. In addition, the text in the inscription uses both Athenian and Spartan terms of command: *taxiarchos* and *strategos* for Athenian military commanders, and the uniquely Spartan *enomotarches* (officer) and *hegemones* (leaders, a Spartan reference to their kings). Since there was no reason for a fourth-century Athenian forger to use Spartan terminology, the oath might be viewed as an Athenian rendition of the Spartan-inspired original.

17.17.C   The Plataea Oath

> Tod 2.204 = Fornara no. 57, lines 21–51
>
> Translation: Fornara, pp. 56–57
>
> ... (**21**) The oath which the Athenians took when they were about to fight against the barbarians: "I shall fight as long as I live, and I shall not consider it more important to be alive than to be free, (**25**) and I shall not fail the Taxiarch or the Enomotarch, be he alive or dead, and I shall not retreat unless the Hegemones lead (the army) away and I shall do whatever the generals command. Those who die (**30**), of the allied fighting-men, I shall bury on the spot and I shall leave no one unburied.
>
> After beating the barbarians in battle I shall tithe the city of the Thebans; and I shall not destroy Athens or Sparta or Plataea (**35**) or any other city of those which shared in the fighting. Nor shall I allow (them) to be coerced by famine, nor shall flowing streams be kept from them by me, be they friends or enemies. If I remain faithful to the oath's (**40**) terms, may my city be free from sickness; if not, may it become sick. And may my city go unsacked; if not, may it be sacked. And may my (land) bear (its fruits); if not, may it be barren. And may women bear children like to their parents; if not, (may they bear) monsters. (**45**) And may cattle bear issue like to cattle; if not, monsters." After swearing this, covering over the sacrifices with their shields, at the trumpet-blast, they called a curse down upon themselves if any of the terms of the oath should be violated by them and if they should not maintain (**50**) the stipulations of the oath: (namely) that pollution of guilt be upon them who swore it.

   See WEB **17.18** for Herodotus' description of the battle of Plataea.

Questions

1. How did the Athenians convince the Spartans of their loyalty to the Greek cause (**17.17.A**)?
2. What values does the Plataea Oath (**17.17.C**) promote? What rewards and penalties does it offer? What Greek anxieties does it imply?
 3. Who made the greatest contribution to the Greek victory in the battle of Plataea and why (WEB **17.18**)?

17.19   Commemorating the Battle of Plataea

As with other victories in the Persian War, the participants strove to shape the memory of battle. The poet Simonides rented his muse to different cities and individuals who wished to commemorate their particular role in the war. Other memorializations had more of an all-Greek character. The city of Plataea honored the Greeks who died in battle. Shortly after the battle, Simonides composed an elegy for the Spartans for what looked like a Panhellenic event. Fragments of the poem have been restored from badly preserved papyri. The largest fragment begins with Achilles' death and Homer's glorification of the Greek heroes, which sets the stage for the heroization of the dead of Plataea. The poet then describes the Spartans' departure for battle. The Spartans apparently saw themselves as fighting a new Trojan War in which they were the leaders of Greece. Other fragments of the poem deal with Spartans facing the Persians, a prophecy on the battle, Corinthian warriors, and Demeter. It is likely that Simonides skipped over the Spartans' hesitation before they left their homeland for the battle.

17.19.A   Simonides on the Spartans' Departure for Plataea

Simonides fr. 11, lines 20–44 (West)

But I call upon you for help, ... Muse, if you care about men who pray. And prepare, too, this delicious arrangement of our song, so that someone may remember ... men who for Sparta ... day of servitude ... Nor did they forget their valor that is high as the heavens, and the glory of men shall be deathless.

Leaving the Eurotas and the city of Sparta ... with the horse-tamer sons of Zeus, the Tyndarid heroes[1] and stalwart Menelaus ... the lords of their native city, whom the excellent son of wondrous Cleombrotus led out ... Pausanias ... and the renowned deeds of Corinth ... of Tantalus' son Pelops ... the city of Nisus,[2] where the others ... tribes of those living around them ... putting trust in ... who with ... lovely plain ... having driven ... of Pandion ... of godlike Cecrops[3] ... having subdued...

Notes

1. *That is, Castor and Pollux. Herodotus (5.57) says that only one of their images accompanied the Spartan army, but perhaps the poet refers here to the heroes themselves.*
2. *Nisus was the mythic king of Megara or of Nisaea, both possibly stations on the Spartans' march.*
3. *"Cecrops" is apparently a reference to the Spartans' arrival at Eleusis and their saving of Attica, Cecrops' land.*

For a link to images of the fragments of Simonides' poems, see WEB **17.22**.

Herodotus reports that the Greeks used the booty of the battle of Plataea to commemorate the war in three Panhellenic sanctuaries.

17.19.B   Dedications to the Gods

Herodotus 9.81.1

After gathering together all the items, they removed a tenth of them for the god at Delphi, and it was from this portion that the gold tripod was dedicated that stands nearest to the altar on the bronze, three-headed snake.[1] They also removed a tenth for the god in Olympia, from which they dedicated a ten-cubit-high bronze statue of Zeus,[2] and a tenth for the god of the Isthmus, from which was made the seven-cubit-high bronze figure of Poseidon. After setting these tenths aside, they divided the remainder. All received their just deserts with respect to the concubines of the Persians, their gold, silver, and other objects, and their pack animals.

Notes

1. *The serpent column was not made of a three-headed snake but of three intertwined serpents.*
2. *See Pausanias (Description of Greece 5.23.1–3) for Zeus' statue.*

The golden tripod of the Delphic monument was melted down by the Greek polis of Phocis ca. 354 during the Third Sacred War (see **38.6**: "Philip and the Third Sacred War"), but the bronze serpent column has survived as well as one of the snakes' heads (now in the Istanbul Archaeological Museum). The column stands in the Hippodrome in Istanbul, where it was moved by the emperor Constantine in the fourth century CE. Inscribed on the bodies of the snakes is a list of Greek poleis who fought the Persians. The inscription has a telling history of memorialization (see WEB **17.22** for images of the serpent column). The names of the Tenians and the Siphnians were added to it at a later time. Missing are the names of Croton in Italy, Pale on the island of Cephallenia, the Aegean island of Seriphus, Arcadian Mantinea, and the Opuntian Locrians, even though they are all mentioned by Herodotus as fighting on the Greek side.

17.19.C   Those Who Fought in the War

ML no. 27

The war was fought by tho[se]: Laced[aemonians], Athenians, Corinthians, Tegeans, Sicyonians, Aeginetans, Megarians, Epidaurians, Erchomenians **(5)** Phleiasians, Troezenians, Hermionians, Tirynthians, Plataeans, Thespians, Mycenians, Ceians, Melians, Tenians, Naxians, Eretrians, Chalcidians, Styrians, Halieians, Potidaeans, **(10)** Leucadians, Anactorians, Cythnians, Siphnians, Ambraciots, Lepreans.

See WEB **17.20** for Pausanias' alleged attempt to appropriate the glory of Plataea to himself.

Questions

1. How did the Greeks commemorate the victory of Plataea (**17.19**, WEB **17.20**, WEB **17.22**)? What motivated the commemorations?
2. How do you account for the deletions and omissions of names from the serpent column inscription in Delphi (**17.19.C**; cf. **17.13.C**)?

17.21   The Battle of Mycale (479)

Some of the Greek poleis mentioned in the Delphic inscription took part in the battle of Mycale in Ionia, which allegedly took place on the same day as the battle of Plataea (Herodotus 9.90.1, 100). The synchronization is perhaps too neat, but the dates of these battles must have been close.

Prior to the battle, a Greek navy assembled in the spring of 479 in Aegina under the command of the Spartan king Leotychidas II. Following the urgings of Chian and then Samian representatives, it sailed toward Samos. After Salamis, the Persians preferred not to meet the Greeks on the sea, and beached their ships on the Asian shore opposite Samos at Mycale, where they were joined by local forces. A hard battle ensued around a wall built by the Persians, which the Greeks won. The Persians retreated to Sardis, and the Greeks were left with the question of what to do with the Ionians. Many of Herodotus' contemporary readers could identify in the debate over the fate of the Ionians the future policies of Athens and Sparta and the consequent conflict between them.

The outcome of the deliberations was that the Greeks in Asia Minor, as opposed to the islanders, would remain for the time being under Persian control. The Greek fleet then sailed to the Hellespont to destroy Xerxes' bridges, but found them already broken. The Peloponnesians went home, but the Athenians, led by Xanthippus (Pericles' father), continued to the Chersonese where they laid seige to Persian-occupied Sestos. After a long siege, the city surrendered and the Athenians returned home. It was the last military operation recorded by Herodotus. The following is his description of the discussion about the Ionians' fate.

Herodotus 9.106.2–4

(**9.106.2**) On reaching Samos, the Greeks held discussions about evacuating Ionia and about where in Greece, in the area under their control, they should settle the Ionians (leaving Ionia to the barbarians). They thought it impossible for them to protect and safeguard the Ionians indefinitely, but they had no hope of the Ionians getting off scot-free with regard to the Persians without their protection. (**106.3**) The solution advocated by the Peloponnesians then in power was that they should depopulate the trading centers [*emporia*] of the Medizing Greek peoples and give that land to the Ionians as their home. However, the Athenians were, first of all, against the idea of depopulating Ionia, and they were also averse to having the Peloponnesians making decisions about Athenian colonists. Faced with their strong objections, the Peloponnesians gave way.[1] (**106.4**) Thus it was that the Athenians brought into their alliance the peoples of Samos, Chios, and Lesbos, and the other island-dwellers who had fought alongside the Greeks, and they bound them with a solemn pledge and with oaths to remain loyal to the alliance and not secede. After binding them with the oaths, the Athenians set sail to destroy the bridges, which they expected to find still in place, and headed for the Hellespont.

Note

1. *For the Spartan–Athenian debate, see also Diodorus of Sicily (11.37).*

Question

1. Explain the positions taken by the Peloponnesians and the Athenians on the future of the Ionians.

Review Questions

1. What was the Greek strategy on the eve of the Persian War (**17.3**, **17.7**, **17.9**)? How did it change and why (**17.10–11**, **17.13**, **17.15**, **17.17**)?
2. What was Themistocles' naval plan and what did it require of the Athenians (**17.3**, **17.5**, WEB **17.4**, WEB **17.6**)?
3. How did the Greeks try to foster unity (**17.7**, **17.9**, **17.17**)?
4. To what extent did internal divisions among the Greeks influence the course of the war (**17.3**, **17.7**, **17.9**, **17.13**, **17.15**, **17.17**, **17.21**, WEB **17.8**)?
5. What did Athens' evacuation entail, and what complicates its historical reconstruc- tion (**17.13**, WEB **17.14.I–II**)?
6. Why has the battle of Thermopylae been more memorable than the other battles in the Persian War in both ancient and modern times (**17.11**, WEB **17.12.III–IV**)?
7. How did the Greeks commemorate the war (**17.11**, **17.15**, **17.17**, **17.19**, WEB **17.12.I**, WEB **17.16.II**, WEB **17.18**, WEB **17.20**, WEB **17.22**)?
8. Give examples of Greek perceptions of the barbarians that influenced the sources (e.g., **17.1**, WEB **17.2.I–II**, WEB **17.12.II**).

Suggested Readings

The Persian War: Hignett 1963; Burn 1984 [1962]; Green 1996a; Briant 2002a, 525–549; Cawkwell 2005. *Perceptions of the wars*: Castriota 1992; Hall and Rhodes 2007. *The military aspects*: Lazenby 1993; Wallinga 2005. *Aeschylus' Persians*: Broadshead 1960; E. Hall 1996; Rosenbloom 2006. *Herodotus on the Persians, Xerxes, and their images*: Immerwahr 1966, 167–187; E. Hall 1993; Harrison 2002b, 560–571. *Themistocles*: Podlecki 1975; Frost 1998; Blösel 2001 (in Herodotus and in fifth-century traditions). *Themistocles' shipbuilding program*: Holladay 1987; Lazenby 1993, 83–85; Green 1996a, 53–56. *The trireme (including its reconstruction)*: Casson 1991, 81–96; Wallinga 1993; Morrison et al. 2000, but also J. Hall 1996 (criticism of its modern reconstruction). *Recalling Athenian exiles prior to the war*: Figueira 1993. *The Hellenic League*: Brunt 1953–1954; Hignett 1963, 97–102, but also Tronson 1991. *Delphi during the Persian War*: Georges 1986; Evans 1988. *Thessaly and Tempe*: N. Robertson 1976; Lazenby 1993, 109–117; Green 1996a, 85–87. *The battle of Artemisium*: Sidebotham 1982; Strauss 2004, 11–30. *Thermopylae*: Lazenby 1993, 130–148; Green 1996a, 134–144; Hammond 1996; Szemler et al. 1996; Cartledge 2006. *The evacuation of Athens and the "Themistocles Decree"*: Jameson 1960; Lazenby 1993, 102–104; Morrison et al. 2000, 108–118 (authentic); Johansson 2001 (*contra*). *The Persian sack of Athens*: Shear 1993. *The battle of Salamis*: Lazenby 1993, 151–197; Balcer 1995, 257–272; Strauss 2004, esp. 73–226; Wallinga 2005, 55–159. *Queen Artemisia*: Munson 1988. *The Plataea Oath*: Hignett 1963, 460–461;

Flower and Marincola 2002, 323–335 (a forgery); van Wees 2004, 243–244 (authentic). *The battle of Plataea*: Nyland 1992; Lazenby 1993, 198–147; Green 1996a, 201–287; Flower and Marincola 2002, 2–31, 137–231. *Simonides' Plataea elegy*: Boedeker 1998; Boedeker and Sider 2001. *The Serpent Column*: ML no. 27, 57–60. *The battle of Mycale*: Balcer 1995, 273–279; Green 1996a, 280–283; Flower and Marincola 2002, 27–28, 262, 272–282.

18

The Athenian Empire

CHAPTER CONTENTS

Ancient Greece from Homer to Alexander: The Evidence, First Edition. Joseph Roisman.
© 2011 Blackwell Publishing Ltd. Translations © 2011 John Yardley. Published 2011 by Blackwell Publishing Ltd.

Athens and Sparta were the two states that contributed the lion's share to the Greek victory in the Persian War and, hence, they were in the best position to exploit it. The period that followed the war witnessed the growth of Athenian power and Sparta's eventual realization that this power was a threat. This is the view taken by Thucydides, the historian of the Peloponnesian War, who gives the best extant account of the years between the Persian and the Peloponnesian wars (478–431; Thucydides 1.89–118; see **Introduction III.3** for his history). Ancient commentators and modern historians have called Thucydides' survey of this period the *Pentekontaiteia*, or the story of the fifty years.

Yet Thucydides' description of this period can be general and eclectic, while other sources supplement his report only partially. Hence, the chronology of many events in this period, and especially of the years between the 470s and the 450s, is uncertain. The dates used in this chapter appear to be less controversial than others.

The chapter discusses events leading to the formation of the Delian League, and especially the rebuilding of Athens' walls and Sparta's conceding to Athens the leadership of the Ionian allies. It describes the formation of the Delian League alliance, and the transformation of the league into an Athenian empire. The chapter then documents military operations in the Aegean, Asia Minor, and northern Greece under the leadership of the Athenian general Cimon that were conducive to this transformation. Sparta was occupied at this time with wars in the Peloponnese and a great helot revolt. The chapter discusses these events and their impact on the relationship between Sparta and Athens.

18.1   Rebuilding Athens' Walls (479/8)

The Greek victory over Xerxes did not eliminate the fear of a Persian retaliation. This apprehension, and Sparta's wish to keep Athens dependent on its army and good will, partly explains the affair of the rebuilding of Athens' walls in the winter of 479/8 (and see also Thucydides 1.90.1–2 below). It involved Sparta's request to Athens not to rebuild her walls and Themistocles' deception and stalling of the Spartans, which allowed the Athenians to do so. Some historians have questioned the story and the Spartan request to Athens to avoid building the walls given that practically every other polis, except for Sparta, was walled. Others suspect that the tale is inspired by the trickster image of Themistocles. Yet the Greeks' concern that Persian forces might reoccupy Athens made sense given that it had already occurred twice during the war. In addition, parts of the excavated wall at the Kerameikos are solidly built, but they also include broken columns, funerary monuments, and reliefs from statue bases, implying urgency on the part of the builders.

Thucydides 1.89.3–93.2

(**1.89.3**) When the barbarians left their land, the Athenian authorities immediately began to bring back their children, their wives, and the remains of their property from where they had placed them for safekeeping, and they set about rebuilding their city and their fortifications. For only small sections of the circuit wall remained standing, and of the houses most were in ruins, the few remaining being those in which high-ranking Persians had been quartered.[1]

(**90.1**) The Lacedaemonians, seeing what was likely to happen, sent a delegation to Athens, in part because they were not happy with the prospect of Athens, or any other city for that matter, having a defensive wall. Mostly, however, it was because of the insistence of their allies who feared the size of the Athenian fleet (which had formerly not been so large) as well as the spirit the city had shown in the war with Persia. (**90.2**) The Spartans proposed that the Athenians not build a wall, but instead join them in demolishing the defensive walls that any cities outside the Peloponnese still had standing. The Lacedaemonians did not reveal their true motives and their suspicion *vis-à-vis* the Athenians, suggesting rather that if the barbarian attacked again, he would not have a stronghold from which to operate, as he had recently had in Thebes. The Peloponnese, they said, sufficed for everyone, both as a place to retreat to and to operate from.

(**90.3**) When the Lacedaemonians made these suggestions, the Athenians, on Themistocles' advice, replied that they would send ambassadors to Sparta to deal with the matters under discussion and promptly dismissed them. Themistocles then told them to send him to Lacedaemon as quickly as possible.[2] They should also select other representatives along with him, he said, but not send them immediately. Instead, they should hold them back until such time as they had raised the wall up sufficiently for it to have the lowest height necessary for defense. Everyone in the city should take part in the building, he said, and they should spare no edifice, whether privately or publicly owned, that would be of service for the construction – they should tear them all down.

(**90.4**) After issuing these instructions, and suggesting that he would personally take care of everything else in Sparta, Themistocles left. When he reached Lacedaemon, instead of going to the magistrates he frittered away the time and fabricated excuses. Whenever anyone in authority asked him why he did not go to the assembly of the people, he said that he was waiting for his fellow-ambassadors. These had been left behind in Athens because of some business that had arisen, he said, but he was expecting them to arrive soon and was surprised that they were not there already.

(**91.1**) Because of their friendship with him the Spartans believed what he said, but when other people came from Athens and categorically stated that the wall was being built and was already reaching some height, they could no longer have any doubts. (**91.2**) Aware of this, Themistocles told them not to be misled by hearsay but to send some of their own men who could be trusted and who would bring back a reliable report after seeing for themselves. (**91.3**) The Spartans did send men, and Themistocles secretly relayed a message to the Athenians telling them to detain them, as unobtrusively as they could, and not let them go until he and the others returned. This was because his fellow-ambassadors, Habronichus son of Lysicles and Aristides son of Lysimachus, had by now arrived in Sparta with the information that the wall was high enough, and he was afraid that when the Lacedaemonians received an accurate account they would not let them go.

(**91.4**) The Athenians detained the ambassadors as directed. Themistocles then came before the Lacedaemonians and told them openly that the city of the Athenians was walled to the point where it was capable of protecting its inhabitants. If the Lacedaemonians or their allies wished to send delegations to them on any matter, he said, they would in future be going to men who understood what was in their own interests and in the interests of Greece as a whole. (**91.5**) When they had concluded that the better course was to leave their city and take to their ships, said he and his colleagues, they had decided to take this risk without consulting the Lacedaemonians, and in all their deliberations with them they had clearly been second to none in their judgment. (**91.6**) Similarly, on this occasion, it seemed better to them that their city should have a defensive wall, and that this would be more advantageous for their own citizens and for all the allies, too. (**91.7**) For, they explained, it was not possible for common consultation to take place on fair or equal terms without a balance of military strength. So either everybody in the alliance should be without defensive walls, or the Athenians' action must be considered correct.

(**92**) When they heard this, the Lacedaemonians did not openly show their anger with the Athenians. They had sent their delegation to Athens not to impede the work but (they claimed) to put forward a proposal that was to their common advantage, and they also, at that time in particular, felt well disposed toward the Athenians because of their stouthearted resistance to the Persian. But they had in fact failed to achieve their purpose and were secretly annoyed. The ambassadors of both sides then left for home without lodging any protest.

(**93.1**) Thus it was that the Athenians walled their city in a short space of time, (**93.2**) and even today it is evident that the construction was hastily effected. For the foundations are made from all sorts of stones which, in places, are not even cut to fit together but are in the same condition as when the workers brought each of them, and there are numerous stelai taken from graves and bits of dressed stone thrown in. In fact, the circumference of the wall was extended at all points, and for this reason they hurried the work along with the indiscriminate use of all sorts of materials.

Notes

1. *For what follows, see also Plutarch* Themistocles *19 and Diodorus 11.39–40.*
2. *Sending Themistocles to Sparta made sense in view of the unique honors he had received from Sparta at the end of the war (see Herodotus 8.124).*

See WEB **18.2.I** for Themistocles and the fortification of the harbor of the Piraeus, and a link to an image of "Themistocles' Wall" in Athens. For Themistocles' opposition to Sparta's plan to punish Medized states, see WEB **18.2.II**.

Questions

1. Why did the Spartans oppose the fortification of Athens, and why did the Athenians insist on it (**18.1**, WEB **18.2.I**)?
2. Describe Themistocles' vision of Athens' status and policy in light of his speech in Sparta (**18.1**), his fortification of the Piraeus (WEB **18.2.I**),

and his opposition to Sparta's demand to punish Medized states (WEB **18.2.II**).

18.3 Pausanias of Sparta, Athens, and the Allies

If the Athenians are to be believed, Sparta and its regent Pausanias, the victor of Plataea, were instrumental in Athens' becoming a hegemonic power. In 478 Pausanias sailed to Cyprus at the head of the Hellenic fleet on a mission to liberate the Cyprian Greeks. An additional, if not the primary, goal was to acquire booty for the maintenance of the fleet. From there the Greeks sailed to drive the Persians out of Byzantium. It was in liberated Byzantium that, according to Thucydides, Pausanias started behaving badly.

18.3.A Pausanias' Recall

> ## Thucydides 1.95.1–5
>
> (**1.95.1**) Pausanias was already out of control and the rest of the Greeks were exasperated with him, not least the Ionians and those recently liberated from the king's rule. They approached the Athenians and asked them, in view of their kinship, to become their leaders and not side with Pausanias if he became violent toward them. (**95.2**) The Athenians accepted their overtures, and set about considering the matter, determined not to overlook Pausanias' behavior; they would manage things as seemed best for them. (**95.3**) Meanwhile the Lacedaemonians recalled Pausanias to interrogate him on the matters about which they had been hearing, for he was being charged with gross misconduct by Greeks arriving in Sparta, and his comportment seemed to be that of a tyrant rather than a commander. (**95.4**) As it happened, he was called to the interrogation just when all the allies apart from the troops from the Peloponnese had transferred their support to the Athenians because of their exasperation with him. (**95.5**) When Pausanias reached Lacedaemon, he was called to account for injuries he had privately inflicted on individuals, but he was found not guilty on the most serious charges – he stood accused principally of Medizing, and it seemed an open-and-shut case ...

 See WEB **18.4** for additional allegations against Pausanias, especially his offer to Xerxes to put Greece under Persian rule and his behaving like a Persian lord. For Pausanias' later recall and death, see WEB **18.13.II**.

There is little doubt that Pausanias' treatment of the Greek allies caused great resentment. The result, according to Thucydides, was that Athens took up their cause.

18.3.B   The Spartans Relinquish Their Command

Thucydides 1.95.6–7

(**1.95.6**) The Lacedaemonians did not send Pausanias out as commander again; instead, they sent Dorcis and a few others with a force that was not very large, but the allies would not put overall command in their hands. (**95.7**) Realizing this, the men returned home, and the Lacedaemonians did not send out other commanders after that because they were afraid that they might become corrupt when they went abroad, as they saw had happened in Pausanias' case. They also wanted to be quit of the war against the Mede; they thought the Athenians capable of taking command, and they were on good terms with them at that point.

Thucydides' analysis of the Spartans' motives for foregoing the leadership of the Hellenic campaign is sensible but also speculative. He also ascribes to the Athenians a passive role in the affair and lets the allies take the initiative, which puts the former in a positive light. Herodotus (8.3.2), however, portrays the Athenians as more active in producing results. He says that the Athenians relinquished command of the Greek navy to Sparta during the Persian War in the common interest of Greece, but then wrested it back using Pausanias' misconduct as an excuse (see **17.9.B**: "The Greek Command"). *Ath. Pol.* supports this account.

18.3.C   Aristides and the Ionians

Ath. Pol. 23.4

And so the two men [Aristides and Themistocles] took charge of the rebuilding of the walls together, although there was animosity between them. But it was Aristides who motivated the defection of the Ionians from the alliance of the Lacedaemonians by capitalizing on the latter's disgrace because of Pausanias…

According to Plutarch (*Aristides* 23; *Cimon* 6.1–3), Cimon, the son of Miltiades, was Aristides' partner in this endeavor, although this is uncertain. Equally uncertain is Diodorus' report (11.50) of a debate among the Spartans in 475 on how to react to their loss of command, in which the option of going to war with Athens was raised. Whatever Sparta felt about her loss of leadership, she did not deem it worthy of a feud with Athens. Later, as we shall see, the Spartans were preoccupied with other problems closer to home.

Questions

1. How do the sources differ about the allies' refusal to accept Spartan command and what might explain these differences?

2. What looks suspicious and what likely in the story involving Pausanias' conduct (**18.3.A**, WEB **18.4**; cf. **17.9.B**: "The Greek Command")?

18.5   The Formation of the Delian League (478)

Once the Athenians became leaders of the war against Persia they were quick to form a new league. Modern historians call it the Delian League because until around 454/3 the league's treasury was placed in Apollo's sanctuary on Delos. The island had an important Aegean and Ionic cultic center, and it was sufficiently distant from the Persians. Central to the maintenance of the league was the tribute, *phoros* (lit. "contribution"), or less euphemistically, tax.

18.5.A   The Goals of the Delian League

Thucydides 1.96.1

This was how the Athenians gained their leadership, supported by the allies because of their hatred of Pausanias. They then made an assessment for those cities that were to make financial contributions [sg. *phoros*] for fighting the barbarian, and for those who were to supply ships. The alleged reason for this was to exact revenge for their losses by raiding the territory of the king.[1]

Note

1. *Revenge against Persia as an alleged reason or pretext* (prophasis) *is Thucydides' own* (retrospective) *interpretation of the league's goal.*

18.5.B   Liberating the Greeks

In a speech that Thucydides attributes to envoys from Mytilene to Sparta in 428, the allies' perspective of the league's goal is outlined.

Thucydides 3.10.2–3

(**3.10.2**) "The alliance between us and the Athenians dates from the time when you first abandoned the war with the Mede, and they stayed on to finish the job. (**10.3**) However, we became their allies not to make the Greeks slaves to the Athenians, but to make the Greeks free from the Mede."[1]

Note

1. *The Mytileneans may have tried to portray their revolt as in harmony with Sparta's official goal of liberating the Greeks from Athens' rule (cf. Thucydides 6.76.2–3).*

Ath. Pol. (23.5) adds that the Ionians swore eternal oaths to have the same friends and enemies (cf. Plutarch *Aristides* 25.1). The goals of exacting revenge on Persia and liberating the Greeks had Panhellenic appeal. They were also sufficiently inclusive to allow flexibility about how and when they should be accomplished. The administration of the league was more specifically defined. Thucydides says that the Athenians established which allies would provide ships for the fleet and which money, and describes how the league was managed.

--- 18.5.C   Managing the League

Thucydides 1.96.2–97.1

(**1.96.2**) It was at that time [478] that the office of "Treasurers of the Greeks" [*Hellenotamiai*] was first established by the Athenians, and these accepted the "tribute" [*phoros*], which was the name given to a contribution made in cash. The first tribute assessment was 460 talents, and the treasury was on Delos, where league meetings were held in the temple.

(**97.1**) The Athenians were, initially, leaders of autonomous allies who conferred together in meetings in which all participated, but they took the actions I shall describe, both in war and in their management of public affairs, in the interval between this [i.e., Peloponnesian] war and the Persian War. These were actions taken by them both against the barbarian and against their own allies when they defected, and also against a number of the Peloponnesian states that they came up against in the course of these various events.

Plutarch reports how the Athenian Aristides, known for his integrity, fixed the tribute.

--- 18.5.D   Establishing the Tribute

Plutarch *Aristides* 24.1–3

(**24.1**) Even under Spartan leadership of the league the Greeks used to pay some dues for fighting the war, but then they wanted a fair assessment to be made state by state. They therefore asked the Athenians for Aristides, whom they put in charge of examining the land and fixing the assessment and ability to pay in each case. (**24.2**) Aristides thus became the holder of enormous power as Greece was, in a way, putting all her affairs in his hands alone but, poor as he was when he left on his commission, he returned poorer. Moreover, his tax assessments were not merely honest and fair but also welcome and agreeable to everybody. For as the ancients sung the praises of the Age of Cronus [the golden age], so did the allies of Athens sing the praises of Aristides' tribute assessment, calling it a piece of good fortune for Greece, especially since the tribute doubled after a short period, and then tripled after that. **(24.3)** For the tribute rate of Aristides was 460 talents. To this Pericles added what almost amounted to a third as much again, for Thucydides [2.13.2] says that the revenue coming to the Athenians from the allies at the start of the war was 600 talents. After Pericles died, the demagogues [popular leaders] raised it in small increments until they brought it up to 1,300 talents. This was not because the war became inordinately expensive as a result of its length and shifting fortunes as much as because the demagogues induced the popular assembly to institute distributions of cash, public entertainments [*theorika*], and the construction of statues and temples.

 See WEB **18.6** for explanatory comments on the league's structure and on the problematic figure of 460 talents as the original annual contribution.

See also Chapter 21 on the administration of the empire and the collection of tribute.

Questions

1. What were the goals of the Delian League and the means used for attaining them?
 2. How was the league members' contribution fixed (**18.5.D**, WEB **18.6**)?
3. What in the league's structure and agenda might predict Athens' future domination of the league?

18.7   Cimon and the Athenian Empire: The Conquest of Eion, Scyros, Carystus, and Naxos (477/6–465)

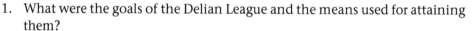

Athens' position at this stage was more of a senior partner than an imperial ruler. The latter position would be attained thanks to the efforts of Cimon, son of Miltiades of Marathon fame. An ally of Aristides and married to an Alcmeonid, Cimon became very popular as a result of his victorious campaigns and war profits. He was also the major beneficiary of Themistocles' decline, to which he contributed directly or indirectly: see WEB **18.8.I** for Themistocles' ostracism and exile (ca. 471/0).

The first recorded operation of the league under the leadership of Cimon was in 477/6 against Persian-occupied Eion in northern Greece. The campaign was in line with the league's official goal of fighting the Persians. The subsequent colonization of the site, however, benefited only the Athenians. Indeed, the region was rich in timber so important to Athenian shipbuilding. Judging from later and similar Athenian settlements, Eion became a cleruchy (*klerouchia*, from *kleros*, plot of land), a colony whose Athenian residents retained their citizen rights in their homeland, in contrast to the traditional *apoikia*, which was an independent polis (see Chapter 4: "Settlements Across the Sea"). Cleruchies enabled the Athenian poor to join the hoplite class and helped Athens protect its interests overseas (cf. Plutarch *Pericles* 11.5–6).

18.7.A   The Capture of Eion

Plutarch *Cimon* 7.1–3 (cf. Thucydides 1.98.1; Herodotus 7.107)

(**7.1**) Now that the allies had joined him, Cimon sailed to Thrace as commander-in-chief. He had heard that Persians of note and some relatives of the king were occupying the city of Eion on the banks of the Strymon River and were causing trouble for the Greeks in that area. (**7.2**) He first defeated the Persians in a pitched battle and bottled them up in the city. He then expelled the Thracians living above the Strymon, who were the source of the Persians' food supply; and, securing the entire country, he brought the Persians under siege to such dire straits that the king's general, Butes, despairing of the situation, put the torch to the city and destroyed himself along with his loved ones and possessions. (**7.3**) So although he took the city, Cimon derived no appreciable advantage from it apart from the land, since most of its possessions had gone up in flames along with the barbarians. The land, however, was very fertile and very attractive, and this he passed over to the Athenians for settlement ...[1]

Note

1. *Plutarch goes on to report how Cimon's victory was commemorated in Athens without mentioning Cimon's name, i.e., in true egalitarian fashion; cf. Aeschines 2 On the Embassy 31–33.*

Probably in 476/5, Cimon led a campaign against pirates on the island of Scyros. It is hard to see what this operation had to do with liberating Greeks or punishing the Persians. But the material gains from the campaign and a reduction in piracy benefited all the league's members. Athens, in particular, gained another settlement, and, according to Plutarch, a national hero as well. Cimon found a grave on the island and identified its occupant as the Athenian hero Theseus. See WEB **18.8.II** for Cimon's discovery and its significance.

18.7.B   The Capture of Scyros

Plutarch *Cimon* 8.3–5 (cf. Thucydides 1.98.2)

(**8.3**) They also colonized Scyros, which Cimon captured for the following reason. Dolopians inhabited the island but they were poor cultivators of the land. So, from ancient times, they practiced piracy, and eventually they did not keep their hands off even those who put in at their ports and foreigners doing business with them. They actually robbed some Thessalian traders who were anchored off Ctesium and put them in prison. (**8.4**) When these men escaped from their confinement they successfully prosecuted the city-state in the Amphictyonic court. The majority of the Scyrians were unwilling to pay the fine; instead they ordered those who were guilty of the robbery and who still had pirated goods to return them. These people were afraid, and sent a letter to Cimon, urging him to come with his fleet and take their city, which they said they would deliver to him. (**8.5**) After capturing the island in this way Cimon expelled the Dolopians and cleared the Aegean Sea [of pirates]...[1]

Note

1. *In spite of Plutarch's claim, enslaving the original inhabitants of Scyros did not clear the Aegean Sea of all pirates.*

Possibly in 472, the league went to war against the city of Carystus on the southern tip of Euboea. Following its defeat, Carystus was made into a tribute-paying member and received a cleruchy, perhaps during the 450s. The fact that it took a war to persuade a Greek city to join the league showed that participation in it was no longer voluntary. Carystus' proximity to Athens may explain why it became a target.

The war against Naxos, perhaps in 469/8, but no later than 465, showed the allies that there was no way out of the league. Naxos received an Athenian cleruchy in the late 450s. Thucydides used the episode to generalize about Athens' overbearing policy but he also blames the allies for it.

18.7.C   The Subjugation of Carystus and Naxos

Thucydides 1.98.3–99.3

(**1.98.3**) The Athenians were also involved in a war against the people of Carystus, in which the other Euboeans took no part, and in time the Carystians conditionally surrendered. (**98.4**) Subsequently, the Naxians seceded, and the Athenians fought them and brought them to heel with a blockade. This was the first allied city that was reduced to slavery in contravention of the league's constitution, but later it also happened to the others, under various circumstances.

(**99.1**) There were different reasons for seceding, the most important being an ally's arrears in tribute or failure to provide ships or, occasionally, refusal to provide any military support at all. The Athenians were exacting with regard to contributions, and were aggressive in bringing force to bear on those unused to such burdens or unwilling to shoulder them. (**99.2**) There were other reasons, too, for the Athenians' leadership being no longer as popular as it had been: they did not participate in the campaigns on equal terms with the others, and it was easy for them to force back into line those who seceded. (**99.3**) It was the allies who brought this on themselves. Because of their aversion to military service, the majority, in order to avoid leaving home, had their contributions assessed as a cash equivalent instead of contributing ships. Thus the Athenians saw their fleet augmented by the moneys that these allies contributed, while the allies themselves, whenever they seceded, found themselves lacking preparation and experience in warfare.

Questions

1. Describe Athens' path to domination over the allies and the role Cimon played in it (**18.7.A–C**, WEB **18.8.II**).
2. What fault does Thucydides find with the allies' conduct (**18.7.C**)? Is he right, or fair?

18.9 Operations in Asia Minor and the Battle of Eurymedon (469–466)

The Athenians and their allies also campaigned in and around Asia Minor, although our sources are unclear about the chronology of their operations. It appears, however, that Cimon led the Greeks against the Persians sometime between 470/69 and 467/6. Diodorus of Sicily (11.60.3–4) reports that Cimon succeeded in persuading Greek settlements on the Carian and Lycian coasts to rebel against Persia: see WEB **18.10.I**. Plutarch supplements Diodorus' account.

18.9.A   Cimon's Successes in Asia Minor

Plutarch *Cimon* 12.1–4

(**12.1**) And it is clear that nobody did more than Cimon to humble the Great King himself and deflate his arrogance. He did not simply allow him to quit Greece, but followed hard on his heels. Before the barbarians could take a breath and make a stand, he was sacking and destroying some areas, and in others he was promoting revolts and bringing them over to the Greeks. The result was that he eventually left Asia clear of Persian arms from Ionia to Pamphylia.

(**12.2**) When Cimon heard that the king's generals were lying in wait in Pamphylia with a large army and a powerful fleet, he wanted to make the Persians afraid to sail or enter the seas west of the Chelidonian Islands. He therefore set sail from Cnidus and Triopium with two hundred triremes. These vessels had initially been very well constructed for speed and maneuverability by Themistocles, and Cimon at this time broadened them and added a passageway along the decks so that they would be more effective in engaging the enemy through having a large number of hoplites on board.

(**12.3**) Sailing to the city of Phaselis, which had a Greek population but which would not admit his fleet and refused to revolt from the king, Cimon proceeded to pillage its lands and assault its walls. The Chians in his fleet, who had long been friendly with the Phaselites, tried to mollify Cimon and at the same time they shot arrows over the walls with notes for the Phaselites attached to them. (**12.4**) Cimon finally became reconciled with the townspeople, on condition that they pay him ten talents and follow him against the barbarians...

The case of Phaselis confirms that the Greeks had no alternative but to become an Athenian ally. For the first time since the Persian War, the league's actions triggered a military reaction from the Great King. He mobilized an army and fleet, which Cimon defeated in the battle of Eurymedon in Pamphylia, Asia Minor, sometime between 469 and 466. The campaign's profits helped to finance the building of the southern wall of the acropolis.

18.9.B   The Battle of Eurymedon

Plutarch *Cimon* 12.4–13.4

(**12.4**) Ephorus claims that Tithraustes was in command of the king's fleet and Pherendates in command of the infantry, but Callisthenes claims that Ariomandes son of Gobrias had supreme command of all the forces at the Eurymedon.[1] He lay at anchor there with his fleet, says Callisthenes, being reluctant to engage the Greeks, as he was awaiting the arrival of eighty ships that were sailing from Cyprus. (**12.5**) Cimon wished to strike before the ships arrived, and was prepared to force the issue should the Persians refuse a naval engagement. The Persians, in order not to be forced into a fight, withdrew upriver, but when the Athenians bore down on them they sailed out to take them on with (according to Phanodemus' record) 600 ships or (according to Ephorus) 350.[2] However, no exploit worthy of such a force was accomplished by them, at least on the water; (**12.6**) they immediately fled to land, the first of them getting ashore and fleeing to the land force deployed close by, and the rest being captured and destroyed with the ships. It is clear from this, too, that the ships manned by the barbarians were very numerous: many of them probably made good their escape, and many were shattered, but the Athenians still captured two hundred.

(**13.1**) As the Persian infantry advanced to the shoreline, Cimon thought it a massive undertaking to force a landing and then lead the exhausted Greeks against an enemy who was fresh and had vastly superior numbers. At the same time he saw that the men were full of vigor and high spirits from their victory and eager to get to grips with the enemy. He therefore put his hoplites ashore when they were still heated from the struggle at sea, and they charged ahead, shouting and at a run. (**13.2**) The Persians stood their ground and took the attack courageously, and a fierce fight followed. Of the Athenians many brave men lost their lives, men who were foremost in rank and distinction. After a great fight they drove back the barbarians with heavy losses, and then captured them and took possession of their tents, which were full of treasure of all kinds.

(**13.3**) Like a formidable athlete, Cimon had brought off two feats in the one day. Moreover, although he had eclipsed the victory at Salamis with a land battle, and that at Plataea with a naval battle, he kept on competing for victories. Learning that the eighty Phoenician triremes that had missed the battle had put in at Hydrus,[3] he sailed there swiftly while their commanders as yet had no reliable intelligence about the larger force, but were still in a state of distrust and suspense. (**13.4**) As a result they were all the more surprised. They lost all their ships, most of their crews being destroyed along with them ...[4]

Notes

1. *Ephorus was a fourth-century Greek historian whose history spanned from mythical times to his own age. Callisthenes was a fourth-century Greek historian who joined Alexander the Great's campaign to Asia. For the battle see also Thucydides 1.110.1; Diodorus 11.60.5–62.3 (based on Ephorus).*
2. *Phanodemus was an Attidograph.*
3. *The location of Hydrus is unknown, perhaps on the coast of Cilicia.*
4. *Plutarch adds that the battle moved the Persian king to agree to keep his army at a distance of a day's ride from the coast of Asia and to avoid sailing into the Aegean with warships (Cimon 13.4–5). The historicity of this agreement has been questioned since ancient times (see **20.11** on the so-called peace of Callias of 450/49).*

The Athenians commemorated the battle of Eurymedon in a variety of ways. They buried the dead of the campaign next to the main road in the Kerameikos at Athens (Pausanias *Description of Greece* 1.29.14), and heroized the Eurymedon River at Piraeus. They also advertised their victory by dedicating a bronze palm tree and a golden statue of Athena in Apollo's sanctuary at Delphi (Pausanias 10.15.3). According to some scholars, the victory at Eurymedon even inspired a vase showing a Greek man intent on buggering a barbarian (see **12.6**: "Sex, Power, and the Eurymedon Vase" and Figure 12.4). An epigram, wrongly attributed to Simonides, stressed the singularity of this victory.

————————————————————————— 18.9.C Eulogizing the Dead of Eurymedon

Simonides fr. 46 (Campbell)

These men once lost their noble young lives on Eurymedon's banks, battling the foremost of the Persian archers – some as spearmen on foot, others on swift ships. In death they left a glorious memorial to their valor.

See WEB **18.10.II** on the Athenian Painted Stoa (*stoa poikilê*), a gallery with possible associations with Cimon, and a link to its site and potential reconstruction.

Questions

1. Describe the gains from Cimon's operations in Asia Minor (**18.9.A**, WEB **18.10.I**).
2. What were the consequences of the battle of Eurymedon? How well did the battle fit within the league's agenda as described above (**18.5**)?

3. How were Cimon's victories and name advertised (**18.9**, WEB **18.10.II**)?

18.11   Operations in Northern Greece (465/4–463/2)

Most scholars date the next events between 465/4 and 463/2. After securing and cleruchizing the Chersonese, the Athenians laid seige to the island of Thasos which lasted for three years. According to Thucydides (1.101.1–2), the siege almost led the Spartans to help the island by invading Attica, but they were stopped by a helots' uprising. The sources describe Thasos' resistance as a revolt, which suggests that the status of Athens as master and the allies as subjects was already well established.

The Athenians also tried unsuccessfully to colonize a strategic site in southern Thrace called Nine Ways (later Amphipolis: see **20.20**: "The Foundation of Amphipolis"). It is possible that the Athenians' defeat there moved them to institute state funerals, where an elected speaker eulogized the dead and praised Athens and its democracy (cf. Pausanias *Description of Greece* 1.29.4–5). The territorial extent of the league at this time is unknown, but it is likely to have included cities on the Thracian coast, Chalcidice, the western and southern coast of Asia Minor, and Aegean and Cycladic islands.

Thucydides 1.100.2–3

(**1.100.2**) Some time after this [465/4] the Thasians revolted from the Athenians, with whom they had quarreled over the trading posts and a mine – all owned by the Thasians – on the coast of Thrace opposite them.[1] The Athenians sailed on Thasos with their fleet and after a victory at sea landed on the island. (**100.3**) At about this same time they also sent to the Strymon ten thousand settlers, made up of Athenians and allies, to colonize what was then called Nine Ways [*Enneai Hodoi*], but nowadays Amphipolis. The settlers did actually take possession of Nine Ways, then inhabited by the Edoni, but they went ahead into the interior of Thrace and were annihilated at Drabescus in Edonia by a combined force of Thracians, who considered the occupation of the area a hostile act.

Note

1. *Herodotus reports that the Thasians' revenues from the gold mines of Scaptesyle amounted to 80 talents (6.46.3). The dating of the first year of the siege of Thasos to 465/4 is based on an emended text of the scholiast to Aeschines 2.31, and Thucydides 4.12.2–3.*

18.12   Sparta's Wars in the Peloponnese, the Great Helots' Revolt, and the Mt. Ithome Affair (473–460)

One wonders why the Spartans allowed Athens to become so powerful with little or no interference. Thucydides thought that "they were not swift to undertake wars, unless forced into them, and they were also to some extent hampered by wars at home" (1.118.2). There must have been additional reasons. The Spartans had no ambitions to become a maritime power. They also felt that they had little reason to be concerned about Athens' plans as long as pro-Spartan Cimon was at the helm. Cimon was a *proxenos* (guest-friend) of Sparta and called one of his sons Lacedaemonius. (His other sons, Oulius and Thessalus, suggest the father's international connections.) Primarily, however, Sparta had to deal with a number of crises at home and in the Peloponnese during this period.

One crisis involved Spartan heads of state. See WEB **18.13.I** for the bribery charges against king Leotychidas and his exile (ca. 476), and WEB **18.13.II** for Pausanias' recall and punishment by starvation (ca. 470).

Pausanias' death and Leotychidas' exile deprived Sparta of commanders who might have offered the Greeks an alternative leadership to that of Athens. Sparta also had to deal with problems in the Peloponnese. The scanty evidence for these events includes Thucydides' general comment that the Spartans were "to some extent hampered by wars at home" (1.118.2), and Herodotus' listing of five conflicts ("contests") that the naturalized Spartan citizen and seer Tisamenus prophesied the Spartans would win.

18.12.A   Sparta's Peloponnesian Conflicts

Herodotus 9.35.2

The five conflicts were the following. The first was this one at Plataea; next was the one that took place in Tegea against the Tegeans and Argives; then that at Dipaea where they faced all of Arcadia apart from Mantinea; then that against the Messenians at Ithome; and the last was that at Tanagra against the Athenians and the Argives ...

The battles of Tegea (ca. 473–470) and Dipaea, or Dipaeis (ca. 470–464), suggest that Sparta was threatened by her close neighbor, Arcadia, and her traditional enemy, Argos. It is possible that Themistocles, who spent his exile in Argos and was busy working against Sparta, had a hand in events. It has also been suggested that the Spartan defeat in the battle of Oenoe against an Athenian–Argive coalition, which was depicted on the "Painted Stoa" (WEB **18.10.II**), belonged to the 460s. The battles of Mt. Ithome (ca. 460) and Tanagra (458/7) are discussed in **18.12.D** and **20.9** ("The Battle of Tanagra").

A potentially more serious threat than these conflicts was a Messenian revolt following a devastating earthquake, probably in 464.

18.12.B   The Great Earthquake and the Messenian Revolt

Plutarch *Cimon* 16.4–7; cf. Diodorus 11.63.1–64.1; Thucydides 1.101.2

(**16.4**) ... In the fourth year of the reign of Archidamus son of Zeuxidamus at Sparta, there was an earthquake that was the greatest in human memory. The territory of the Lacedaemonians subsided into numerous yawning chasms, and when Mt. Taygetus was shaken some of its peaks were shorn off. The city itself was totally destroyed, apart from five houses; all the others the earthquake demolished.

(**16.5**) The ephebes[1] and young men, it is said, were taking exercise together in the middle of a portico shortly before the earthquake when a hare appeared. The young men, for fun, ran out, all oiled as they were, and chased after it, but the ephebes remained behind. On these the gymnasium collapsed and they all died together. Their grave even today they call Seismatias.[2]

(**16.6**) Archidamus quickly surmised the danger that would follow from the present disaster and he could see that the citizens were attempting to rescue their most precious possessions from their houses. He ordered a signal of an enemy attack given on a bugle so that people would come flocking to him under arms as quickly as possible, and this was the one thing that saved Sparta at that critical juncture. For the helots came running together from all over the surrounding countryside in order to seize any Spartiate survivors. (**16.7**) When they found them drawn up under arms, however, they went back to their towns and made war on them openly, after persuading no small number of the perioeci to help them. The Messenians, too, joined the attack on the Spartiates ...

Notes

1. *The ephebes were young men aged between eighteen and twenty who performed national service before becoming adults.*
2. *Diodorus (11.63.1) mentions more than 20,000 dead in the quake, but the figure is too high.*

The duration of the helots' revolt is uncertain due to conflicting evidence, although many scholars, following an emendation of the text of Thucydides 1.103.1, put it at four years (ca. 464–460). The Laconian helots, who were joined by the Messenians and even two perioecic settlements, were eventually pushed back to Mt. Ithome. The site was well fortified and resonated with memories of the Messenians' last stand in the first and second Messenian Wars (**7.2**: "The Messenian Wars"). A Peloponnesian siege proved ineffective, and Sparta asked Athens for help based on their Greek alliance since the Persian War. Athens also had a record of successful operations against fortified places, many of which were Greek cities. The request, however, led to a crisis in the relationship between

Athens and Sparta and greatly contributed to Cimon's downfall. Plutarch reports that when the Spartans appealed for help, Cimon's advocacy of their cause met with resistance from the democratic leader Ephialtes.

18.12.C   The Debate in Athens over Helping Sparta

Plutarch *Cimon* 16.7–8

(**16.7**) ... The Lacedaemonians therefore sent Pericleidas[1] to Athens to ask for assistance. He is the man of whom Aristophanes says in a comedy that he "sits, pale, at the altars in a purple cloak, asking for an army" [*Lysistrata* 1137–1144]. (**16.8**) Ephialtes opposed this. They should not, he argued, help or set back on its feet a city that was Athens' rival; they should let overbearing Sparta lie prostrate and be trodden under. Cimon, as Critias says,[2] then set his own country's advancement behind the interests of the Lacedaemonians and persuaded the people to go out to her aid with a large force of hoplites. Ion[3] makes mention of the expression by which he most moved the Athenians – he called on them not to stand by while Greece "went lame and the city lost its partner in the yoke."

Notes

1. *Significantly, Pericleidas's son was named Athenaeus (Thucydides 4.119.2).*
2. *Critias was an extreme oligarch who led the so-called Thirty Tyrants in Athens in 404. He wrote poems and political works, which Plutarch probably used here.*
3. *Ion of Chios was a contemporary poet and an admirer of Cimon.*

The Athenians voted to aid the Spartans with a sizable force of 4,000 hoplites (Aristophanes *Lysistrata* 1142). Yet sometime after their arrival, the Spartans sent them home. Added to Thucydides' explanation of the Spartans' reasons was probably their disappointment at the Athenians' inability to decide the conflict. One of the casualties of the Spartan dismissal of the Athenian force was Cimon, who was ostracized in 461/0 for his advocacy of the Spartans and his opposition to Ephialtes' democratic reforms.

18.12.D   The Spartans Send the Athenians Back Home

Thucydides 1.102.1–4

(**1.102.1**) When their war against the helots on Mt. Ithome kept dragging on, the Spartans called upon all of their allies,[1] and especially the Athenians, for assistance, and the Athenians came with no small force, under the command of Cimon. (**102.2**) They called upon the Athenians most of all because they felt that they were strong in siege-warfare, whereas it was apparent to the Spartans, given the protracted length of the blockade, that they themselves were weak in this area – they would otherwise have already stormed the place.

(**102.3**) It was as a result of this campaign that the differences existing between the Spartans and the Athenians first became clear. When the Spartans failed to take the place with an assault, they felt apprehensive about the daring and revolutionary character of the Athenians, and they also reflected that they were of another race.[2] So, fearing that, if the Athenians remained there, they might be persuaded by the helots on Ithome to take some subversive action, the Spartans dismissed them, but not the other allies. They did not reveal what they suspected, but merely declared that they were no longer in need of their help. (**102.4**) The Athenians were aware that their dismissal was not for this quite acceptable reason. They were sure that some suspicion of them had arisen, and they were indignant, thinking that such treatment by the Lacedaemonians was undeserved. Accordingly, immediately on their return, they abandoned the alliance they had made with Sparta to combat the Persians, and instead became allies of the Argives, who were enemies of the Spartans.[3] At the same time both peoples took the same oaths to establish an alliance with the Thessalians.

Notes

1. *Among the allies who joined Sparta in the siege were Aegina (Thucydides 2.27.2), Plataea (Thucydides 3.54.5), and Mantinea (Xenophon Hellenica 5.2.3).*
2. *The Spartans were Dorians, and the Athenians, Ionians.*
3. *The Athenian–Argive alliance was celebrated about two years later in Aeschylus' Eumenides 289–291, 669–673, 762–774.*

Questions

1. What crises did Sparta face during the 470s–460s (**18.12.A**, WEB **18.13.I–II**)?

2. What can we learn about Spartan realities from Plutarch's description of the earthquake (**18.12.B**) and the Pausanias affair (WEB **18.13.II**)?
3. Why did the Spartans ask the Athenians to return home? Were they aware that this dismissal might harm their friend Cimon (**18.12.C–D**)?

18.14 The Messenians Settle Naupactus

Unable to defeat the besieged at Ithome, the Spartans agreed to let them go, and Athens helped the refugees settle in Naupactus on the northwestern coast of the Corinthian Gulf. This action gained her important allies as well as a naval base in the region. It probably also made Corinth concerned about its western trade routes and contributed to the animosity between the two states.

Thucydides 1.103.1–3

(**1.103.1**) When, in the tenth year,[1] the helots on Ithome were no longer able to hold out, they surrendered to the Spartans on condition that they leave the Peloponnese under treaty and never set foot there again, anyone caught there becoming the slave of the man who captured him. (**103.2**) In addition, the Spartans had earlier been given an oracle from Pytho to the effect that they should "release the suppliant of Zeus at Ithome." (**103.3**) So the helots left along with their children and wives. The Athenians welcomed them because of the resentment they now felt toward the Spartans, and they settled them at Naupactus, which, it happened, they had recently taken out of the possession of the Ozolian Locrians.

Note

1. *A common emendation of the text replaces the "tenth" with "fourth" year. Otherwise, the helot revolt would have been concluded in 456/5.*

Question

1. How did the Mt. Ithome affair affect the relationship between Athens and Sparta (**18.12.B**, **18.14**)?

Review Questions

1. What led to the establishment of the Delian League (**18.3**, **18.5**, WEB **18.4**, WEB **18.6**)?
2. How did the league turn into an Athenian empire (**18.7**, **18.9**, **18.11**, WEB **18.10.I**)?
3. How persistent were the Athenians in pursuing the league's declared goals (**18.5**, **18.7**, **18.9**, **18.11**, WEB **18.8.II**, WEB **18.10.I**)?
4. How do you explain Sparta's inaction in the face of Athens' growing power (**18.3**, **18.5**, **18.12**, WEB **18.13.I–II**)?
5. Whose policy toward Sparta made more sense, that of Themistocles and Ephialtes (**18.1**, **18.12.C**, WEB **18.2.I–II**), or Cimon's (**18.12.C**)?

Suggested Readings

Rebuilding of walls: Podlecki 1975, 30–31, 182–183; Wycherley 1978, 10–13; Fornara and Samons 1991, 118–121. *Themistocles and the Piraeus*: Chambers 1984; Garland 1987, 14–21. *The Pausanias affair*: Fornara 1966; Westlake 1977. *The Delian League and the Athenian empire*: Meiggs 1972; Mattingly 1996; Osborne 2000; Constantakopoulou 2007, 61–136; Low 2008; Ma et al. 2009. *The league's foundation*: Meiggs 1972, 23–49; French 1979; N. Robertson 1980; Kallet-Marx 1993, 37–69. *Aristides' assessment of tribute*: Meritt et al. 1950, vol. 3, 234–243; Kallet-Marx 1993; Osborne 2000, 86–91. *The tribute lists*: see Suggested Readings to Chapter 21. *Themistocles' exile and death*: Forrest 1960; Lenardon 1978, 108–153; Marr 1995; Frost 1998, 179–211. *Cimon's personality and career*: Blamire 1989; Schreiner 1997. *Theseus, Athens, and Athenian religious activity abroad*: Walker 1995, 55–82; R. Parker 1996, 122–151; H. Shapiro 1996; Lewis 1997 [1960]; Mills 1997, 1–86. *The Painted Stoa*: L. Meritt 1970; Sommerstein 2004; Boardman 2005; Castriota 2005; Stansbury-O'Donnell 2005. *Athenian settlements*: Zelnick-Abramovitz, 2004. *The Delian League's early years*: Meiggs 1972, 68–91; N. Robertson 1980, 64–96; Badian 1993. *Eurymedon*: Keen 1997. *The siege of Thasos and related events*: Pleket 1963; Carawan 1987, 202–205; Pritchett 1995, 94–121. *State funerals*: Jacoby 1944; Loraux 1986, esp. 15–76. *Sparta's trouble in the Peloponnese in 470s–460s*: Forrest 1960; Cartledge 1979, 214–216. *The battle of Oenoe*: Schreiner 1997, 21–37; Sommerstein 2004; and the bibliography on the Painted Stoa above. *Spartan earthquake*: Cartledge 1979, 307–317; Hodkinson 2000, 417–421. *Mt. Ithome*: Ste Croix 1972, 178–180; Luraghi 2002b, 2008.

19

Empowering Athenian Democracy (462/1–445/4)

Ancient Greece from Homer to Alexander: The Evidence, First Edition. Joseph Roisman.
© 2011 Blackwell Publishing Ltd. Translations © 2011 John Yardley. Published 2011 by Blackwell Publishing Ltd.

Popular leaders in Athens were at work strengthening its democracy even before Cimon's exile. Chief among them were Cimon's rivals Ephialtes and his younger partner Pericles. This chapter discusses the measures that these and other leaders initiated and their contribution to the development of Athenian democracy. It documents Ephialtes' reforms, which strengthened popular institutions at the expense of the Areopagus. It reports on the means that democracy used to judge the legality of motions and the qualifications of office-holders, and how officials were held accountable. The chapter examines the increased accessibility to public office and other democratic measures, including public pay, that enabled the people to participate in government. It also cites opposition to state salaries and payments by critics of democracy. The chapter then concludes with a discussion of Pericles' democratic reforms, his law restricting citizenship to sons of two Athenian parents, and his rivalry with other politicians.

19.1   Ephialtes' Reforms (462/1)

Ephialtes' most renowned measure deprived the Areopagus of its political powers. The council supervised officials and legislative procedures and had extensive judicial powers. It was composed of former archons, who were thus not elected to it directly. Areopagites also came from the two wealthiest classes and sat on the council for life. It was therefore a conservatively oriented body.

Taking advantage of the absence of Cimon and the 4,000 middle- to high-income hoplites who accompanied him to Mt. Ithome, Ephialtes relied on the people for support. He attacked the Areopagus on two fronts, charging it with arrogating powers that originally had not belonged to it and prosecuting individual Areopagites. Using a Solonian measure that allowed every citizen to initiate a public action (*graphê*), Ephialtes forced members of the Areopagus to give an account of their term (*euthynai*) as former archons.

19.1.A   Ephialtes and the Areopagus

Ath. Pol. 25.1–2

(**25.1**) ... The constitutional supremacy of the Areopagus lasted some seventeen years after the Persian Wars, though it was gradually eroding. But then the power of the people grew and, in addition, Ephialtes son of Sophonides became their leader. A man with a reputation for incorruptibility and integrity in the public sphere, Ephialtes launched an attack on this council. (**25.2**) He first removed a large number of the Areopagites by impeaching them for mismanagement of affairs. Then, in the archonship of Conon [462/1], he divested the council of all the added powers on which its guardianship of the constitution rested, assigning some of these to the Five Hundred and others to the assembly [demos] and the law courts [dikasteria].

The Areopagus was not abolished but served as a court for homicide and some religious offenses.

19.1.B   The Areopagus after Ephialtes' Reforms

Ath. Pol. 57.3

Private prosecutions of homicide and wounding are heard in the Areopagus, if the killing and wounding are premeditated, as are those of poisoning and arson. The council [of the Areopagus] hears only these cases. Prosecutions of unpremeditated homicide and intent to kill, and of killing a slave, metic [resident alien], or foreigner are heard in the court of the Palladium ...

Echoes of Ephialtes' campaign against the Areopagus for arrogating powers may be found in the assertion that its powers of watching over the government and the laws were "added" to its original jurisdiction (*Ath. Pol.* 25.2, above). Ephialtes' opponents probably defended the council's authority by emphasizing its antiquity and that it was part of the city's "ancestral constitution."

See WEB **19.2.I** for Aeschylus' description of the Areopagus and the scholarly claim that his contemporary plays are relevant to the controversy over Ephialtes' reform. WEB **19.2.I** also includes links to Aeschylus' *Oresteia*.

Ephialtes' political activity likely led to his violent death in 462/1. Even the ancients were unsure about the identity of his murderer, with some even implicating Pericles. See WEB **19.2.II** on Ephialtes' assassination.

Question

1. What powers did Ephialtes remove from the Areopagus and how?

19.3   Blocking Illegal Decrees (*Graphê Paranomon*)

The beneficiaries of Ephialtes' reforms were institutions that embodied the power and sovereignty of the people. From now on the Council (*Boulê*) was empowered to supervise legislative procedures and deal with crimes against the state (e.g., treason). When the matter or the penalty exceeded the Council's jurisdiction, it transferred it to the assembly, which dealt with the case or instructed the popular courts to take it up.

An example of the new order is the *graphê paranomon*, or public action against decrees that contradicted the existing laws. Prior to Ephialtes' reforms, the power to block legislative proposals deemed illegal or unconstitutional belonged to the Areopagus. Later in the century, any citizen could question the legality of a decree, and the matter was decided in court. Because the earliest attested use of the *graphê paranomon* is from 415 (Andocides 1.17, 22), it is questionable whether this procedure was introduced shortly after Ephialtes' measures. But even if it was established later, it was surely in the spirit of his reforms.

The best evidence for this procedure comes from the fourth century. The legislative process began when the Council discussed a proposal and formulated it as a decree (*psephisma*) to the assembly. In the assembly, any citizen could argue, before or after the vote was taken, that it was unconstitutional. Up to 403/2, the Athenians did not distinguish between permanent laws (*nomoi*) and temporary decrees (*psephismata*), hence any decision made by the assembly could be subjected to this challenge and a trial. After 403/2 the *graphê paranomon* was used against decrees while laws were subject to public actions against their suitability.

Once the decree was challenged, it was suspended and the challenger prosecuted its proponent in a court consisting of at least 501 jurors. The charge could be that the decree was illegal from a procedural or substantive point of view, or that it was damaging to the people. In the case of decrees honoring a person, the charge was often that the honor was unwarranted. For example, in 330 the politician Aeschines prosecuted the Athenian Ctesiphon for illegally moving to honor the orator Demosthenes in 336 with a crown for his public service. Demosthenes was Aeschines' bitter enemy. Aeschines alleged that Ctesiphon's motion violated a law prohibiting honors being given to a person before his conduct in office had been reviewed (*euthynai*; see **19.5** below), and especially that Demosthenes did not deserve the honor.

Significantly, the legal charge of prematurely awarding honors occupied only a small part of Aeschines' speech. The bulk of it comprised vicious attacks on Demosthenes and a defense of Aeschines' career. Prosecutions against unconstitutional proposals, then, served not just to protect existing regulations but often as a means to harm a foe and justify one's own policy or career. A person convicted of proposing an illegal decree might be subjected to a fine, at times heavy, and if convicted three times of the same offense, he was partially disenfranchised. His liability, however, was restricted to one year after proposing the motion; after that period, the proposal could be annulled without consequences for the proposer. To deter vexatious litigation, the prosecutor was liable to a fine of 1,000 drachmas if he dropped the charge before trial, and was partially disenfranchised if he failed to win at least a fifth of the jury's votes.

Aeschines 3 *Against Ctesiphon* 11–12

(**11**) Seeing this to be the case, some lawgiver established a law, and a very fine law, too, explicitly forbidding the awarding of a crown to men who have yet to render their accounts. But despite this sensible precaution on the part of the lawgiver, wording has been found to frustrate the law and, unless someone explains this to you, you will be bamboozled and caught off guard. Of those men who illegally award the crown to those who are still to render the accounts some are reasonable people, if anyone proposing illegal measures is, in fact, "reasonable." But at least they try to screen their shameful conduct; for they do add to the measures they pass that the man yet to render his accounts is to be crowned "when he provides a reckoning and accounting of his office."

(**12**) In fact, the state is harmed just as much by this, since the accounting process is swayed by praise and crowns offered in advance, but a man drafting the decree does make it clear to his hearers that he has indeed made an illegal proposal, but that he is ashamed of the infraction of which he is guilty. But Ctesiphon, Citizens of Athens, has completely transgressed the law laid down for those yet to give an accounting. Rejecting the use of that escape clause that I just mentioned, he has proposed that Demosthenes be offered the crown before an audit and before an accounting – while he is still halfway through his term of office!

Questions

1. What was democratic about Ephialtes' reforms?
2. What violations were actionable under the *graphê paranomon*? What was the procedure for making a charge? What was the penalty if the proposer was convicted?

19.4 Examination of State Officials (*Dokimasia*)

Another consequence of Ephialtes' reforms was the tightening of control over office-holders, including Council members. Almost all state officials had to undergo an "examination" (*dokimasia*) in court or in the Council, which was a sort of confirmation hearing before they could enter office. In later times public speakers called *rhetores* were also subjected to this procedure. Given the large number of offices in the state, which in the fourth century approached 700, and the fact that the Council took in 500 new members every year, it is likely that this was often a mere formality. The control mechanisms of the *dokimasia* and *euthynai* (rendering an account of office; see **19.5**) were created, and surely shaped, later than Ephialtes' reforms. But even if he only transferred powers from the Areopagus to the less exclusive and more representative Council, assembly, and courts, he nevertheless set Athens on the road to popular sovereignty.

The best evidence for the procedure of *dokimasia* is the late fourth-century *Ath. Pol.*

Ath. Pol. 55.1–5

(**55.1**) …These days the Athenians choose the six Nomothetae[1] and their secretary by lot, as they do also the archon, the king archon, and the polemarch, one from each tribe. (**55.2**) These undergo an initial candidacy examination in the Council of 500, except for the secretary, who is examined only in the court, like the other officers (for they are all examined for candidacy before entering office, whether they are chosen by lot or by show of hands). The nine archons are examined in the Council and again in the court. In earlier times anyone whose candidacy the Council rejected did not hold office, but now there is an appeal to the law court, and this is the final authority with regard to candidacy qualification.

(**55.3**) Whenever they conduct an examination, the examiners' first question is: "Who is your father and from which of the demes does he come? And who is your father's father, who is your mother, who is your mother's father and from which of the demes is he?" After this, the question is whether the man has a Family Apollo and a Household Zeus, and where the sanctuaries of these gods are located; and then whether there are family tombs and where they are located. Next he is asked if he treats his parents well, if he pays his taxes, and if he has served in the military. When the examiner has asked these questions he says, "Call witnesses to these answers." (**55.4**) When the man provides witnesses the examiner goes on to ask, "Does anyone want to prosecute this man?" If there is someone wishing to prosecute, the examiner permits the charge to be made and a defense presented, and then goes on to take a show of hands in the Council and a vote in the law court. If nobody wishes to prosecute, he takes the matter straight to the vote. In the past only one juror cast the vote, but nowadays all of them are obliged to reach a decision with their votes, the rationale being that if some reprobate has got rid of his accusers the jurors may still disqualify him.[2]

(**55.5**) When the examination has been completed along these lines, they proceed to the stone on which are to be found cut-up sacrificial victims (the same stone on which arbiters swear in rendering their decisions, and on which witnesses swear to having no evidence to give). They climb upon the stone and swear to fulfill their offices with integrity and in accordance with the laws. They swear that they will not accept gifts in connection with the office, and that they will erect a statue of gold if they do accept anything. Having taken the oath, they proceed from there to the acropolis, where they repeat the oaths, and after this they enter office.

Notes

1. *The Nomothetae, or "Lawgivers," comprised a group of judges who, in the fourth century, decided the legality of legislative change. See also **35.1.A** ("The Greater Authority of Laws").*
2. *The suspicion was that the dishonest man got rid of his accusers by bribing them.*

Questions

1. What was the purpose of the *dokimasia*?
2. What did the examiners' questions try to establish about the candidate for office?

19.5 Rendering Accounts (*Euthynai*)

In many cases the state used volunteer prosecutors to supervise the performance of magistrates during their tenure, and the assembly could suspend a
magistrate from his duty. Public officials gave an account of their term in
office and were audited at the end of their term if they had access to public
funds. The procedure of giving accounts of one's public conduct was called
euthynai (lit. "setting aright").

Ath. Pol. 54.2; 48.3–5

(**54.2**) There are also ten auditors [*logistai*], and along with them ten assistants, to whom all who have
held office are obliged to render their accounts. Only these officers can audit the accounts of those
who must undergo audit [*euthynai*] and bring the accounts to the law court. If they find anyone guilty
of embezzlement, the jurors convict him of fraud and the fine is ten times the amount involved. If
they prove someone took bribes and the jurors convict the man, they assess the amount of the bribes
and again the fine is ten times that amount. If they convict a man of maladministration of public
funds, they assess the violation and the fine is the amount of the assessment, if the man pays it before
the ninth prytany; if not, it is doubled. A penalty in ten times the amount is not doubled.

(**48.3**) The Council members choose by lot ten auditors[1] from their own number who are to verify
the accounts of officials for each prytany. (**48.4**) They also choose by lot public examiners [*euthynoi*],
one from each tribe, and two assessors [*parhedroi*] for each of the examiners, who are to sit during the
hours of the market next to [the statues of] the eponymous heroes of their tribes. If anyone wishes to
press charges, whether private or public, against any of the office-holders who have rendered accounts
in the law court, he does so within three days of the individual rendering his accounts. He writes on
a whitened tablet his own name and that of the accused, the charge on which he is prosecuting him,
and he also adds the fine he thinks appropriate. This he then gives to the public examiner, (**48.5**)
who takes the tablet and checks it. If the examiner recognizes culpability, he passes the case on.
Private cases he sends to the judges in the demes who introduce [to the court] cases for this particular
tribe, and public cases he assigns to the Thesmothetae.[2] If the Thesmothetae accept a case, they once
more bring the accounts before the law court, and whatever the jurors decide is final.

Notes

1. *These auditors are different from the auditors mentioned in 54.2.*
2. *The Thesmothetae were archons who administered the judicial system.*

Question

1. How might the *euthynai* procedure be used to attack an official's public
   service?

19.6   Expanding Eligibility to the Archonship

In Athens, only members of the two highest classes could serve as archons. In 457/6 the office was opened to people of low to middle income (*Zeugitai*). The *Thetes*, who comprised the poorest class, were excluded from the archonship and other high offices, although sometime before the late fourth century the archonship was opened to them too. The author of *Ath. Pol.*, who is critical of Athenian democracy in its radical form, links the opening of the archonship to lower classes with the rise of popular leaders and the toll taken by wars on the ranks of moderates of all classes.

Ath. Pol. 26.2–3

(26.2) The result was that, in their administration, the Athenians were in all matters not as attentive to the laws as they had been earlier, apart from in the case of the election of the nine archons. Here they introduced no innovation except that, in the sixth year after Ephialtes' death, they decided that preliminary selection of the candidates from whom the nine archons would be chosen by lot should also be open to the *Zeugitai*. The first of the *Zeugitai* to hold the office was Mneistheides. Until this time all candidates had come from the *Hippeis* and *Pentakosiomedimnoi*, while the *Zeugitai* held only the ordinary offices, unless there was some disregard of the legal provisions.[1] **(26.3)** Four years later, in the archonship of Lysicrates [453/2], came the reestablishment of the so-called deme judges.[2]

Notes

1. See **9.8** (*"Solon's Political Measures"*) for the Zeugitai, Hippeis, *and* Pentakosiomedimnoi.
2. See Ath. Pol. 16.5 (**10.7**: *"Peisistratus' Tyranny"*) for these circuit judges. Their number was increased to forty after 403/2.

19.7   Pericles' Democratic Measures

Pericles was the most famous of the democratic leaders who followed Ephialtes. He was born in the 490s to the important politician Xanthippus and the Alcmeonid Agariste (II). In 473/2 he produced Aeschylus' *Persians*, and in 463/2 he joined the unsuccessful prosecution of Cimon for bribe taking. Pericles seemed to have broken away from the traditional ways of attaining political power in Athens. Normally members of the elite relied on their *hetaireia* (lit. "companionship"), a group of relatives and friends who helped them attain and maintain political leadership. Members of the elite would also display their worth through athletic victories and public largess, and even their aristocratic lifestyle. Yet with the growth of democratic awareness and power in Athens, such conduct could provoke resentment too. Pericles did not neglect the cultivation of connections with the elite, but he conscientiously tried to disassociate himself from the elitist image of leadership, presenting himself as a politician who was above class considerations and as a man of the people. A superb orator, Pericles and other leaders who followed his policy appealed to, and relied directly on, the people and increased their power at the expense of the traditional elite. Scholars have labeled them new(-style) politicians (Connor 1971). Pericles was an important democratic leader in the 450s, yet he should not be credited with every significant democratic step taken in this period. The following passage illustrates one of the means by which he distinguished himself from the elite. WEB Chapter 22 ("The City of Athens") and Chapter 24 ("The Causes of the Peloponnesian War") discuss Pericles' leadership further.

Plutarch *Pericles* 7.3–4

(**7.3**) But, it seems, he was afraid of falling under suspicion of aiming at tyranny, and he also saw that Cimon had aristocratic sympathies and was particularly loved by the "noble and good." He therefore made overtures to the common people, thus providing for his personal safety and gaining power to counteract Cimon.

(**7.4**) In addition, he immediately gave his everyday life a different pattern. He was seen walking in the city on only one street, that which led to the agora and the council hall, and he refused dinner invitations and avoided any friendly and social interaction of that sort. The result was that during the long period that he was in office he never went to dinner at a friend's house, the sole exception being the house of his cousin Euryptolemus when the latter got married. Even then he stayed only until the libations, after which he immediately arose and left.

Question

1. How did Pericles dissociate himself from the elite and from an elitist image?

19.8 Democratic Mechanisms and State Salary (*Misthos*)

During the 450s Pericles initiated a state salary (*misthos*) of two obols per day for jurors (which was increased to three in 425/4). Business in the courts grew significantly following Ephialtes' reforms, the expansion of the Athenian empire, and the increased use of judicial procedures by the elite in their internecine rivalry for power and recognition. All of this empowered the citizen-jurors. The jurors were over thirty adult males who were assigned to courts by lot. Later evidence mentions jury bodies of 201–401 men for private actions involving more than ten drachmas, and 501 jurors or more for public actions in a judicial year of up to 200 days. The state pay was barely sufficient for sustenance but it compensated citizens for their civic service and allowed the poor to have a say in the city's judicial and political institutions. In later years Council members and many of the state office-holders were paid too, and from the early fourth century those attending the assembly received a small salary as well. Generally, state salaries for public services differentiated democracies from oligarchies. In his survey of the guiding mechanisms of democracy, Aristotle emphasizes the role of public salaries.

19.8.A   Public Pay and Offices

Aristotle *Politics* 6.1.8–9 1317b18–18a3

(**6.1.8**) Such then are the underlying principles and the nature of democracy, and the following are its characteristics:

The officers are elected by all citizens out of all the citizens. All rule over each citizen, and each citizen rules over all in turn. Offices are filled by lot, either in their totality or in such cases as do not require experience and expertise. There is no property qualification for office-holding, or only a very low one. A man should not hold an office twice, or should do so only rarely, and only in the case of a few offices outside the sphere of war. Offices should be for a short term, all of them or as many as possible. All citizens should participate in the judicial process, in all spheres or else in most of them, and in those that are the most important and critical, such as the auditing of accounts [*euthynai*], constitutional matters [*politeia*], and contracts. The assembly [*ekklesia*] has authority over all areas of government, and no official should have authority over any area or only over very few. (**1.9**) A council [*boulê*] is the most democratic of all institutions when there is not enough state pay [*misthos*] for everybody. If there is enough, then the people appropriate the power even of this office, drawing to themselves, when they are well paid, all the trials, as was noted in the previous tract.

Then there is payment for services. This should, preferably, be universal, that is for the assembly, the law courts, and the magistracies; failing that, it should at least go to the magistracies, the law courts, the council, and the principal assembly meetings [*ekklesiai kyriai*],[1] or to those magistrates who must take their meals together. And while oligarchy is characterized by birth, wealth, and education, the democratic qualities appear to be the opposite of these – mean birth, poverty, and vulgarity. With regard to the offices, none is without term; and if any has survived some ancient revolutionary change, a democracy must strip it of its power and choose by lot instead of election.

Note

1.   *There were ten principal meetings of the assembly, which were divided over the year (prytany) and had a fixed agenda.*

The author of *Ath. Pol.* makes a direct link between public expenses on political and military activity and personnel and revenues from the empire. It should be noted, however, that the Athenians continued to pay state salaries even after they had lost the empire. The text of the following passage requires emendation, especially concerning the unlikely number of 700 officials abroad and the (too small) number of Athenian forces during the "war," which probably refers to the Peloponnesian War.

19.8.B   Public Wages

Ath. Pol. 24.3

Moreover, in accordance with Aristides' proposal, the Athenians furnished an abundant food supply for the masses: from the income accruing from tribute, taxes, and the allies more than 20,000 were kept provisioned. For there were 6,000 jurors, 1,600 archers, 1,200 cavalrymen, 500 Council members, 500 guards of the dockyards, and 50 guards in the city. In terms of magistrates, there were about 700 at home, and about 700 abroad. Added to these, when the Athenians went to war later on, were 2,500 hoplites, 20 patrol vessels, and other ships conveying the tribute, with 2,000 crewmembers elected by lot. Over and above this there were the Prytaneum [town hall], the orphans, and prison guards, for all these were supported by state funds.

Questions

1. What are the principles of democratic office, according to Aristotle?
2. What does Aristotle find wrong about public wages? Why were they so important to democracy (**19.8.A**, and see **19.9**)?

19.9   Criticism of State Salaries

The increasing sovereignty of the demos during the 450s provoked sharp elitist criticism. There were Athenians who regarded the masses, and especially the poor, as their moral inferiors, as ignorant, and as incapable of governing the state. They resented the fact that payment for public service allowed the masses to participate in public life and made them the judges of those involved in running and governing the city. The state pay also undermined the link between leisure, which was the hallmark of the elite, and participation in public life. This criticism informs *Ath. Pol.*'s description of the introduction of pay for jurors. The story that Pericles tried to fight Cimon's personal patronage with public patronage is likely to be a slander. It reflected the anti-popular portrayal of poorer citizens as parasites living of the patriotic rich. It also implied that poor jurors were susceptible to bribes, even though their large number was not conducive to mass bribery. Later evidence shows that charges of bribery were flung much more frequently at members of the elite.

Ath. Pol. 27.3–5

(**27.3**) Pericles was also the first to introduce payment for service in the jury courts, and this was an attempt to gain popular leadership by countering Cimon's wealth. For Cimon possessed an estate like that of a tyrant, and not only did he at first do a brilliant job of performing his liturgies[1] but he also provided food for a large number of his fellow demesmen. Any member of the Laciadae who so wished could come to his house each day and receive a reasonable amount of provisions, and in addition his estates were all unfenced so that anyone who wished could enjoy the fruits of them.

(**27.4**) Pericles lacked the means for such extravagant gestures, and Damonides of Oea gave him some advice (Damonides was thought to be responsible for most of Pericles' measures, which was why the people later ostracized him).[2] He told Pericles that, since he was bested in terms of private resources, he should give the masses what was really their own property. Pericles therefore established payment for jury service. Some claim that there was a deterioration because of this, with random individuals rather than suitable candidates taking care to participate in the allotment of jurors. (**27.5**) It was also after this that judicial corruption started, the man first availing himself of it being Anytus, after his command on Pylos [409]. Prosecuted by some people for having lost Pylos, he escaped justice by bribing the court.

Notes

1. *Liturgies were a means of taxing the wealthy who were obliged to finance public services such as the upkeep of a trireme or performances in the festivals: see* **35.9**: *"Liturgies."*
2. *The name of Pericles' confidant was more likely Damon son of Damonides, a musician and Pericles' teacher.*

 See WEB **19.10** for an elitist perspective of Pericles' relationship with the demos.

Questions

1. What were the results of instituting public payments, according to critics of democracy (**19.9**, WEB **19.10**)?
2. What might be the democratic response to the charge that Pericles instituted jurors' fees to compete with the private largess of individuals like Cimon?

19.11   Pericles' Citizenship Law (451/0)

In 451/0 Pericles moved to change the criteria for citizenship in Athens, which hitherto required citizens to be sons of Athenian fathers and registered in their deme and phratry. Pericles added the qualification that both parents should be Athenians. Although women were not full citizens in Athens, they now became more important than before because their Athenian identity affected the status of their children. The definition of illegitimate children (*nothoi*) was thus expanded from those born to women who were not wives or concubines to those whose mothers were foreigners, albeit lawfully wedded. Scholars fail to agree on the reasons for the restriction of citizenship. See WEB **19.12** for *Ath. Pol.*'s view of Pericles' citizenship law, which the author links to a growth in the Athenian citizen body.

While the motives of Pericles and the Athenians can only be speculated, the results of the law are less in doubt. Athenian citizens could now see themselves as an elite group both at home and abroad. The law also reduced the number of beneficiaries of public rewards. Finally, it provided citizens with a new legal weapon against fellow Athenians in the form of prosecution for false claims of citizenship under the penalty of enslavement. An example of the last two outcomes occurred in 445/4 on the occasion of a gift of grain to Athens from the Egyptian king Psammetichus. The source is an ancient commentator on Aristophanes' *Wasps* who cites the highly prolific scholar and historian Philochorus (ca. 340–260). Philochorus' history of Athens (*Atthis*) in seventeen books ranged from early Athens to his own times. Yet the figures given by Philochorus and Plutarch (in the subsequent passage) for those who fell victim to the legislation have been questioned as too high, and their reported numbers of citizens were subject to widely different interpretations.

19.11.A   Philochorus on the Background of Pericles' Law

Philochorus *FGrHist* 328 F 119 = Scholion Aristophanes *Wasps* 718

Aristophanes *Wasps* 715–718: "But whenever they are frightened themselves, they offer you Euboea and promise to provide you with grain in fifty-measure portions. But they've never given it to you, except on that very recent occasion when they gave you five measures, and you got that with difficulty, facing prosecution as you did for alien status, and in measures of barley."

Scholion: That is to say that in the distributions of wheat, citizens and non-citizens were examined rigorously, to the point where it seemed that those submitting to scrutiny risked prosecution for being an alien. Philochorus says again that there were once 4,760 people found to be illegal immigrants, as was shown in the preceding text. The remarks on Euboea also accord with the didascalia [catalogues of plays], for in the previous year, the archonship of Isarchus [424/3], they launched a campaign against it, as Philochorus says. But he does not ever talk about the gift from Egypt that

Philochorus says Psammetichus sent to the demos in the archonship of Lysimachidus [445/4] – 30,000 measures (though there is never agreement on the specific figure), five for each of the Athenians. For there were 14,240 recipients.

19.11.B   Plutarch on the Background of Pericles' Law

Plutarch *Pericles* 37.3–4

(**37.3**) Years before this, when Pericles was at the height of his power within the state and had (as has been observed) legitimate children, he proposed a statute that only those born of two Athenians be Athenian citizens. Following this, the king of Egypt sent the people, as a gift, 40,000 measures of grain, and this had to be distributed amongst the citizens. The result was a large number of cases springing up against people who were, according to the statute of Pericles, illegitimate, but who until then had escaped notice and been overlooked, and many also fell prey to informers. (**37.4**) As a result, slightly fewer than 5,000 were found guilty and sold into slavery. Those who retained their citizenship and were judged to be true Athenians were enumerated as being 14,040 all told.

Pericles almost became a victim of his own law. When his last surviving legitimate son died in 429, and he refused to adopt another, his household was threatened with extinction. Pericles pleaded with the Athenians to enfranchise his son from his common law companion, Aspasia of Miletus. Pericles the Younger got his citizenship through a special procedure, but twenty years later he was executed following an impeachment trial (cf. **28.10**: "The Arginusae Affair"). During the Peloponnesian War the Athenians relaxed their qualifications for citizenship but then renewed Pericles' law in 403/2.

Question

1. What might Pericles' motives have been for the citizenship law? What were the consequences of the law (**19.11**, WEB **19.12**)?

19.13   **Pericles and Thucydides Son of Melesias**

One of Pericles' chief political opponents was Thucydides son of Melesias (not the historian). Plutarch is the best source for their rivalry, but his account is problematic. The biographer, or more likely his (unknown) sources, depicts their struggle as between the people and the oligarchs, the rich versus the poor, while in fact the conflict was within the elite, with each leader trying to enlist the people to his side. Equally dubious is Plutarch's claim that Pericles' military campaigns and festivals were designed to flatter or subsidize the demos. Lastly, there were no political parties in the modern sense in fifth-century Athens. Nevertheless, Plutarch shows how Thucydides tried to unite the divided elite behind him. (For Plutarch see **Introduction III.6.**) Thucydides also hoped to control the assembly by having his supporters sitting together, heckling and exerting group pressure on the voters. He was ostracized, however, probably in 444/3: see WEB **19.14.I.**

Plutarch *Pericles* 11.1–4

(**11.1**) The aristocrats could see even before this that Pericles had already become the greatest of the citizens, but they still wanted to have someone in the city opposing him and tempering his power so that the state would not become a complete autocracy. They therefore put up against him Thucydides of Alopece, who was a man of moderation who was related to Cimon by marriage.[1]

(**11.2**) Thucydides was less of a soldier than Cimon, but more gifted in forensic oratory and political acumen. He kept a close watch on affairs in the city, and engaged Pericles at the speaker's rostrum, quickly reestablishing parity between the parties. He would not permit the so-called "fine and good" [*kaloi k'agathoi*] men to act in isolation and be mixed in with the demos as was the case before, with their nobility of character swamped by numbers. He kept them apart from the crowd and united them in a single body, thus strengthening their collective power, and balancing the scale, as it were. (**11.3**) In fact, there had from the beginning existed in Athens a kind of hidden flaw, as found in iron, revealing the difference between the political outlook of the common people and that of the aristocracy, but it was the clash and ambition of those two men that inflicted a deep gash on the city-state, producing two parties called "the people" [*demos*] and "the few" [*oligoi*]. (**11.4**) At that time more than any other, therefore, Pericles released the reins that restrained the people and made it his policy to please them – he was ever finding some public spectacle, entertainment, or procession to put on in town, and amusing the city with pleasures that were not lacking in taste. He also sent out sixty triremes each year with large numbers of citizens on board.[2] These would sail for periods of eight months, receiving pay and also training and gaining experience as sailors.

Notes

1. *Thucydides was Cimon's son-in-law, but Pericles too was related to Cimon by marriage.*
2. *Dispatching an annual fleet of sixty triremes was too expensive and, hence, this is probably an inaccurate figure.*

See WEB **19.14.II** for Pericles' leadership following Thucydides' exile, and WEB **19.14.I** for his public building program (cf. WEB **22.1:** "Pericles' Public Building").

Questions

1. What were Thucydides' and Pericles' respective methods of garnering support?

2. What issues informed the controversy between Pericles and Thucydides (**19.13**, WEB **19.14.I**)?

3. Describe the relationship between the demos and its leader in light of Pericles' rivalry with Thucydides son of Melesias (**19.13**), and the historian Thucydides' description of Pericles' management of the state (WEB **19.14.II**).

Links to DEMOS, a collection of articles on Athenian democracy, and to a bust of Pericles can be found in WEB **19.15**.

Review Questions

1. What was democratic in Ephialtes' reforms and his methods (**19.1**, WEB **19.2.I**)?
2. To what extent were democratic reforms and laws the products of political rivalry within the elite (**19.1**, **19.7**, **19.13**, WEB **19.14.I–II**)?
3. Which democratic procedures established the accountability of public officials and how (**19.3–5**)?
4. Rank the following reforms and procedures on a scale of how they strengthened Athenian democracy and explain your ranking: Ephialtes' reforms (**19.1**), *graphê paranomon* (**19.3**), *euthynai* (**19.5**), expanding eligibility to the archonship (**19.6**), state salary (**19.8**), and Pericles' citizenship law (**19.11**).

Suggested Readings

Ephialtes' reforms: Hignett 1952, 193–213; Ostwald 1986, 34–83; Wallace 1989a, 81–87; Rihll 1995. *Aeschylus and Ephialtes*: Podlecki 1966, 80–85; Wallace 1989a. *Ephialtes' image*: L. Hall 1990; Marr 1993. *Graphê paranomon*: Hansen 1974; MacDowell 1978, 50–52; Rhodes 1993, 315–316, 544–545. *Dokimasia*: Rhodes 1985, 176–178, 1993, 542–543, 615–617; Hansen 1991, 218–220; Todd 1993, 115–116, 285–289. *Control over office-holders*: MacDowell 1978, 169–172; Hansen 1991, 220–224. *Pericles, the new politicians, and Athenian politics*: Connor 1971, 87–198; Davies 1981, esp. 114–115; Rhodes 2000, 2004a, 195–198. *State pay*: Hansen 1979; Markle 1985; Sinclair 1988, 20–21, 66–67, 108, 117, 133–134, 200–202. *Pericles' citizenship law*: Humphreys 1974; Patterson 1981; Walters 1983; Boegehold 1994; cf. Patterson 1990.

20

War and Peace in Greece (461/0–437/6)

CHAPTER CONTENTS

Ancient Greece from Homer to Alexander: The Evidence, First Edition. Joseph Roisman.
© 2011 Blackwell Publishing Ltd. Translations © 2011 John Yardley. Published 2011 by Blackwell Publishing Ltd.

The growth of Athenian democracy at home was accompanied by an aggressive foreign policy abroad. Following the Mt. Ithome incident and the breach in Athens' relationship with Sparta, Athens concluded an alliance with Thessaly and Sparta's enemy, Argos. In 461/0 the Athenians added a former Spartan ally, Megara, to their mainland allies. Their action triggered what modern historians call the "First Peloponnesian War," which lasted from 460/1 to 446/5. Unlike *the* Peloponnesian War of later years (431–404), this conflict was waged chiefly between Athens and Sparta's allies rather than the Spartans themselves, who joined hostilities only selectively. The reasons for this Spartan ambivalence are unclear and may imply a general unwillingness to escalate the conflict with Athens unless there was a promising opportunity for victory. Thus, in the initial stages of the war, most fighting involved Athens and Corinth. Corinth's expansionist policy at this time might not have been to Sparta's liking.

This chapter deals with the histories of Athens and Sparta and their conflicts between 461/0 and 437/6. It describes Athens' wars with Corinth in Egypt and on other fronts in Greece. It deals with the building of the "Long Walls" in Athens, her defeat at the battle of Tanagra against Sparta, and the signing of the so-called Peace of Callias with Persia. The chapter documents the Peloponnesian invasion of Attica in 446 and the consequent Thirty-Year Peace between Athens and Sparta. Athenian colonization around this time is illustrated by the settling of Brea in northern Greece, the foundation of Amphipolis, and a city plan of Miletus that probably resembled the plan of the Athenian colony of Thurii in southern Italy.

20.1   Athens' Clash with Corinth Over Megara (461/0)

Thucydides 1.103.4

The Megarians, too, entered into an alliance with Athens, abandoning the Lacedaemonians, and this was because the Corinthians were piling the pressure on them in a boundary war. The Athenians thus took possession of Megara and Pegae, and for the Megarians they built the long walls that run from the city to Nisaea,[1] which they then garrisoned with their own men. And that was, for the Corinthians, not the least of the reasons for their intense hatred of the Athenians, which began at this time.

Note

1. *Pegae and Nisaea were Megara's harbors in the Corinthian Gulf and the Saronic Gulf, respectively.*

    In 461/0 the Athenians won a victory over Corinth with their least able soldiers, a feat of which they were very proud. See WEB **20.2** for the commemoration of their accomplishment in this battle.

20.3   The Athenian Expedition to Egypt (460)

The Athenians' ambitions went even further. In 460 they took a large force to support an Egyptian rebellion against Persia.

20.3.A   The Egyptian Expedition

Thucydides 1.104.1–2

(**1.104.1**) Inarus, son of Psammetichus, who was a Libyan and king of those Libyans living on the borders of Egypt, set off from Mareia, a city further inland than Pharos, and succeeded in engineering the secession of most of Egypt from King Artaxerxes.[1] Then, assuming command of the area himself, he invited the Athenians in. (**104.2**) The Athenians happened to be on a campaign against Cyprus with two hundred of their own and their allies' ships, and they now left Cyprus and came to Inarus. Sailing up the Nile from the sea, and taking control of the river and two thirds of Memphis, they launched an offensive against the other third, which is called The White Fortress. Here were to be found the Persian and Medic fugitives and those Egyptians who had not supported the secession.

Note

1. *King Artaxerxes I (465–424) ascended the throne following the murder of his father Xerxes.*

See WEB **20.4** for Diodorus of Sicily's report on the Egyptian campaign, which supplements Thucydides' account.

The rebellion lasted until 454 and was restricted chiefly to the Delta region. It ended in disaster. Thucydides does not make clear the Athenian losses altogether, although around 100 ships seems to be a reasonable estimate.

20.3.B   Defeat in Egypt

Thucydides 1.109.1–110.5

(**1.109.1**) The Athenians and their allies in the meantime remained in Egypt, where they experienced war in all manner of forms. (**109.2**) First of all they gained possession of Egypt, and the king then sent the Persian Megabazus to Lacedaemon with money to induce the Peloponnesians to invade Attica, which would draw the Athenians away from Egypt.[1] (**109.3**) Since this did not go well, however, and proved a waste of money, Megabazus returned to Asia with what remained of the cash, and the king then sent out to Egypt Megabyzus son of Zopyrus, another Persian, with a large force. (**109.4**) Reaching Egypt by land, Megabyzus defeated the Egyptians and their allies in battle and expelled the Greeks from Memphis, finally keeping them pinned down on the island of Prosopitis. He blockaded them there for eighteen months. Eventually, he drained the canal by diverting the water with another canal, leaving the ships on dry land and joining most of the island to the main- land. He then crossed over by foot and captured the island.

(**110.1**) So it was that the efforts of the Greeks came to nothing after six years of fighting. Of their considerable force only a few managed to reach safety by traversing Libya to Cyrene, but most lost their lives. (**110.2**) Egypt reverted to the rule of the king, apart from the marshlands where Amyrtaeus was king – the Persians could not capture him because of the size of the marsh, and also because the marsh people are the strongest fighters in Egypt. (**110.3**) Inarus, the king of Libya and the man responsible for the entire Egyptian fiasco, was captured by treachery and crucified. (**110.4**) Fifty triremes from Athens and the allies that sailed to Egypt as a relief force put in at the Mendesian mouth of the Nile, totally ignorant of what had transpired. Some Persian infantry attacked them from the land, and a Phoenician fleet attacked them at sea, destroying most of the ships, only a few of which managed to escape. (**110.5**) So ended the great expedition to Egypt mounted by the Athenians and their allies.[2]

Notes

1. *Diodorus (11.74.6) says that Sparta declined the offer.*
2. *Two inscriptions report on Samian participation and losses in the campaign: Fornara no. 77; ML no. 34, p. 310.*

Questions

1. What might have motivated the Athenians to support the Egyptian revolt (**20.3.A**, WEB **20.4**)?

2. How did the Persians deal with the Athenian intervention in Egypt, diplo- matically and militarily (**20.3.B**, WEB **20.4**)?

20.5   Athens Campaigns on Several Fronts (460–459)

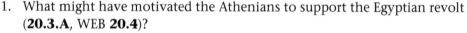

It was a testimony to the Athenians' bountiful resources in money and man- power that they could sustain their losses in Egypt. These resources also ena- bled them to fight simultaneously on several fronts. A marble stele records 177 casualties of the Athenian tribe Erechtheis in 460 or 459. The inscription mentions a campaign in Phoenicia (on the way to or from Egypt?), which is unattested elsewhere, as well as fighting in Egypt, Cyprus, and other places closer to home. Although the Athenian citizen body was divided into ten tribes, it would be wrong to deduce from the list that the Athenians lost that year ten times as many men. A casualty list of a different tribe, which seems to belong to the same year, has only forty-nine names (*SEG* 34.45). Apparently the Erechtheid losses were unusual.

*IGI*³ 1147 = ML no. 33

OF ERECHTEIS
These died in the war: in Cyprus, in
Eg(y)pt, in Phoenicia, at Halieis, on Aegina, at Megara

IN THE SAME YEAR

The three-column list includes two generals, one seer, four archers, and 170 others. See WEB **20.6** for Thucydides' report of Athenian campaigns in 460–458 that led to these losses.

Question

1. Describe how the Egyptian campaign (**20.3**) and the operations mentioned on the stele (**20.5**) and in WEB **20.2** and WEB **20.6** contributed to Athenian security and self-esteem.

20.7   The Long Walls (458)

Around 458 the Athenians built the Long Walls, which consisted of two walls going from the city to the sea, one to Phaleron and the other to Piraeus (Map 20.1, p. 288). Some years later a third, "middle," wall was added that paralleled the northern Athens–Piraeus wall at a distance of about 180 meters from it. Like the northern wall, it was built of well-cut squared blocks. When the walls were completed, Athens could expect to hold out a siege of the city and its harbors thanks to the strong fortifications and her superior navy, which protected her lines of supply. The resultant confidence likely contributed to the Athenians' already aggressive foreign policy. See WEB **20.8** for ancient accounts about the Long Walls.

20.9   The Battle of Tanagra (458)

At last the Spartans made a move. Around 458 they invaded central Greece to help Doris, the traditional motherland of the Dorians, against its neighbor Phocis. Their reasons for intervening in this local, and not terribly significant, conflict are unclear. Perhaps they were motivated by ethnic solidarity, as indicated by Thucydides (below), or they may have wanted to rival Athens for

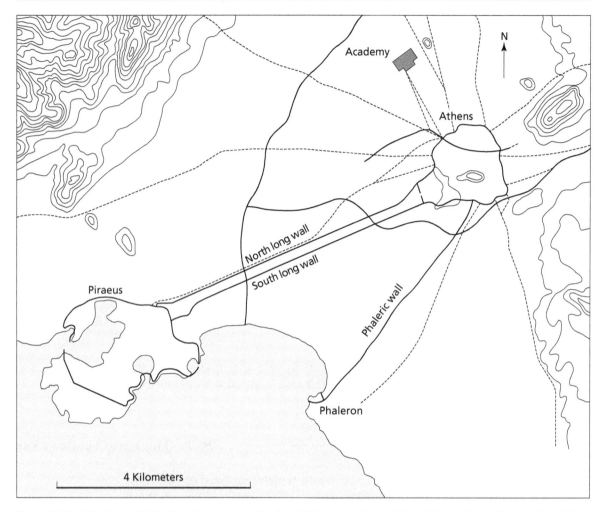

Map 20.1 The Long Walls. Drawing by John Travlos, 1968. From the archive of J. Travlos in the archive of the Archaeological Society at Athens. Reprinted with permission of the Archaeological Society at Athens.

influence in the region, especially at Delphi and in Boeotia. Diodorus suggests that they wished to strengthen Thebes as a counterweight to Athens (11.81. 2–3; cf. Justin 3.6.10). Thucydides implies that the Athenians were looking for a fight once they learned of the Spartan plans. The result was a Spartan victory at Tanagra, which earned them, however, only short-term gains.

Thucydides 1.107.2–108.3

(**1.107.2**) The Phocians had launched a campaign against Doris, original home of the Dorians, targeting Boeon, Citinium, and Erineus, and they took one of the three towns. Then, under the command of Nicomedes son of Cleombrotus (acting on behalf of the king, Pleistoanax son of Pausanias, who was still a young boy), the Lacedaemonians came to the aid of the Dorians with 1,500 of their own hoplites and 10,000 of their allies. They forced the Phocians into an agreement to surrender the town and embarked on their homeward journey. (**107.3**) If they wished to go by sea and cross the Gulf of Crisa, the Athenians, who had brought round their fleet, were likely to stop them; and with the Athenians occupying Megara and Pegae the passage through Geraneia also seemed to them to be unsafe. Geraneia was a difficult route anyway, and it was constantly guarded by the Athenians; and they realized that their enemy would block their passage there as well. (**107.4**) They therefore decided to remain in Boeotia and consider the question of the safest way through. A further reason for the decision was that they were secretly being egged on by some Athenians who were hoping to put an end to their democracy and to the construction of the Long Walls.[1]

(**107.5**) The Athenians, however, marched out against the Lacedaemonians in full force, accompanied by a thousand Argives[2] and various contingents of other allies, a force of fourteen thousand all told. (**107.6**) They took the offensive against them believing that the Spartans were at a loss as to how to get back home, and also from suspicion of some plotting against the democracy. (**107.7**) A number of Thessalian cavalry also joined the Athenians under the terms of their alliance, but they deserted to the Lacedaemonians during the operation.

(**108.1**) The battle was fought at Tanagra in Boeotia. The Lacedaemonians and their allies prevailed, but there was great slaughter on both sides.[3] (**108.2**) The Lacedaemonians then entered the Megarid and after cutting down the trees there went back home through Geraneia and the Isthmus.[4] Sixty-one days after the battle, the Athenians marched on the Boeotians under the general Myronides and (**108.3**), after defeating them in battle at Oenophyta, they seized control of Boeotia and Phocis. In addition, they demolished the walls of Tanagra and took as hostages Opuntian Locris's hundred richest men. They also completed construction of their own Long Walls.

Notes

1. *Why would the Athenian oligarchs oppose the Long Walls? Perhaps democratic allegations of a conspiracy with Sparta aimed to motivate the citizens to do battle.*
2. *An inscribed marble stele marked the burial ground in the Kerameikos of perhaps up to 400 Argives who died in this battle: ML no. 35; Pausanias Description of Greece 1.29.8.*
3. *Diodorus (11.80.6) states that the battle ended in a draw.*
4. *Cutting down trees, especially olives, was a form of agricultural destruction. Two dedications, one by the Spartans and another by the Corinthians, may have commemorated the battle in the temple of Zeus at Olympia next to a statue of Nike: Pausanias 5.10.4; ML no. 36 = Fornara no. 80.*

See WEB **20.10** for Plutarch's story about the return of the exiled Cimon, whose request to fight the Spartans at Tanagra was declined.

Questions

1. Who were the warring parties at Tanagra and what does this suggest about the expanding Athenian influence in Greece?
2. Describe the links between domestic and foreign policy in Athens in relation to the battle of Tanagra (see also WEB **20.10**).
3. What was the impact of the battle of Tanagra?

20.11   The Peace of Callias (450?)

During the 450s the Athenians incorporated Aegina into their empire (457), and established footholds in central and western Greece. See WEB **20.12.I** for Athens' campaigns in western Greece.

In 451 Cimon returned from his mandatory exile, arranged for a truce with Sparta, and then led a campaign to Cyprus where he met his death. See WEB **20.12.II** for Cimon's last campaign.

The historian Diodorus of Sicily reports around this time on an agreement between Athens and Persia, commonly known as the Peace of Callias. The peace has been a subject of vigorous scholarly debate over its historicity and date. Against its authenticity stand the explicit denials of the peace's existence by the fourth-century historians Theopompus (*FGrHist* FF 153, 154) and Callisthenes (*FGrHist* 124 F 16). There are also discrepancies among the various accounts of the peace, and Thucydides' silence on such an important agreement is significant. In favor of the peace's authenticity stands an array of (admittedly late) ancient testimonies, including the mention of an inscription that recorded it (Craterus *FGrHist* 342 F 13; Theopompus, however, argued that the inscription was forged). Scholars who regard the peace as authentic have dated it from 464 to 449. I concur with this view, with a date of 450/49. Indeed, the sources suggest a general cessation of hostilities between Athens and Persia until ca. 424/3. The peace undermined the Delian League's legitimacy as an organization whose goal was revenge against the Persians. The Athenian tribute quota lists missed a year, and if as many believe this was 449/8, it is possible that the allies refused to pay the tribute following the peace.

Diodorus of Sicily 12.4.4–6

(**12.4.4**) When he heard of the losses incurred on Cyprus, King Artaxerxes held a war council with his friends and decided that it was in his interests to make peace with the Greeks. He then wrote to his commanders on Cyprus and to his satraps, giving them notice of the terms on which they could reach a settlement with the Greeks, (**4.5**) and Artabazus and Megabazus accordingly sent ambassadors to Athens to discuss the settlement. The Athenians listened favorably and sent ambassadors with plenipotentiary powers, under Callias son of Hipponicus.

Thus a peace treaty with the Persians was concluded by the Athenians and their allies, the main points of which were the following: "All Greek cities in Asia are to be autonomous. The Persian satraps are not to approach the sea beyond a point three days' journey from it. No Persian warship is to enter the waters between Phaselis and Cyaneae.[1] The king and his commanders abiding by these terms, the Athenians will not send their forces into lands ruled by the king." (**4.6**) When the treaty was concluded, the Athenians removed their forces from Cyprus – they had won a splendid victory and achieved stunning peace terms. It also happened that Cimon died of a disease while he was on Cyprus.[2]

Notes

1. *Phaselis is on the coast of Lycia. Cyaneae is either a group of islands at the entrance to the Black Sea or a town in southern Asia Minor. Other sources define the distance from the sea as a day's ride by horse.*
2. *For more testimonies on the peace, see Fornara no. 95.*

Question

1. What led the Persians to seek peace with Athens, and what were the terms of the peace?

20.13 The Peloponnesian Invasion of Attica (446)

Between 449 and 447 Athens renewed its involvement in mainland Greece. It struggled with Sparta over influence in Delphi, and following a defeat to Boeotian forces at Coronea in 447 had to evacuate Boeotia, which regained its independence. In 446 Euboea rebelled, perhaps due to the foundation of an Athenian settlement on the island in the 450s (Pausanias *Description of Greece* 1.27.5). Megara rebelled too, and then a Peloponnesian army invaded Athenian territory.

20.13.A The Euboean Campaign and the Peloponnesian Invasion

Thucydides 1.114.1–2

(**1.114.1**) Not long after this Euboea seceded from the Athenians. Pericles had already crossed to the island with an Athenian army when he was brought the news that Megara had seceded, that the Peloponnesians were about to invade Attica, and that the Athenian garrison had been annihilated by the Megarians, apart from a number of men who escaped to Nisaea. The Megarians had actually revolted after enlisting the support of Corinth, Sicyon, and Epidaurus. Pericles then swiftly took his army back from Euboea. (**114.2**) And following that the Peloponnesians did invade, under the command of the Spartan king Pleistoanax son of Pausanias, and they plundered Attica as far as Eleusis and Thria. Advancing no further, they then returned home.

Plutarch supplements Thucydides' account and suggests that the Peloponnesians withdrew because of bribery of the king's advisor. Scholars unhappy with the allegation think that the invaders left after the Athenians promised to make concessions, pointing to the fact that Athens made peace with Sparta shortly after. Yet corruption should not be completely excluded from consideration. The Spartans would employ the invasion strategy again in the first years of the Peloponnesian War.

20.13.B   Pericles Bribes the Spartans to Retreat

Plutarch *Pericles* 22.2–23.1

(**22.2**) Pericles therefore swiftly brought his troops back from Euboea to fight the war in Attica. He dared not risk close engagement with the large numbers of powerful Spartan hoplites who confronted him, but he observed that Pleistoanax was a very young man and that he relied mostly on one of his advisors, Cleandridas (whom the ephors had, because of Pleistoanax's youth, sent along with him as his guardian and assistant). Pericles therefore made secret overtures to Cleandridas, quickly corrupted him with bribes, and persuaded him to have the Peloponnesians withdraw from Attica.

(**22.3**) When the army had left and dispersed to the various cities, the Lacedaemonians were very angry, and they fined the king so heavily that he was unable to pay most of the amount involved.[1] He accordingly moved away from Lacedaemon, and the Spartans passed the death penalty on Cleandridas, who had gone into exile.

Note

1. *Ephorus (FGrHist 70F 193 = Fornara no. 104) says that the fine amounted to 15 talents. Thucydides (2.21.1) indicates that the king was also charged with taking bribes.*

Plutarch notes that Cleandridas was the father of Gylippus, who would help Syracuse defeat Athens in 414, and later be caught out in embezzlement.

(**23.1**) In his statement of accounts for the campaign, Pericles entered an expenditure of ten talents "for necessary expenses," and the demos accepted it without any fuss or examination of the unexplained item. Some authors – the philosopher Theophrastus[1] amongst them – have recorded that ten talents would go from Pericles to Sparta every year, and that with these he "took care" of all in authority and thus averted war. He was not buying peace, these authors say, but time – time when he could, at his own convenience, prepare for the conflict, which he would then conduct with greater success.

Note

1. *Theophrastus of Lesbos (ca. 370–288) was a philosopher and scientist who studied with Aristotle and succeeded him as the head of his school.*

After this incident Pericles returned to Euboea and severely punished the elite of the city of Chalcis. He also expelled the citizens of Hestaea to Macedonia and gave their lands to Athenian settlers (see WEB **20.14**). A well-preserved inscription (ML no. 52 = Fornara no. 103) records popular decisions that regulate Athens' relationship with Chalcis. The most likely date for the decree is 446/5 (with 424/3 as an alternative date).

Questions

1. Would it be correct to say that the Spartans squandered their opportunities to make gains after both the battle of Tanagra (**20.9**) and the invasion of Attica (**20.13**)? Explain.
2. How might Pericles render an account of his term in office in light of the rules and principles of *euthynai* described in **19.5**?
3. Make arguments for and against the credibility of the story of Pericles' bribing the Spartans to leave Attica and keep the peace.

20.15 The Thirty-Year Peace Between Athens and Sparta (446/5)

In spite of the Athenian recovery of influence in neighboring Euboea, the Peloponnesian invasion of Attica and the loss of Boeotia and Megara probably convinced Pericles and the Athenians to reach an agreement with Sparta. Athens gave up places she held in the Peloponnese in return for a Thirty-Year Peace that lasted, in fact, only fifteen (446/5–432/1). For the time being, the plan to expand the Athenian empire into the Spartan sphere of influence was set aside.

20.15.A Athenian Concessions in the Thirty-Year Peace

Thucydides 1.115.1

Not long after their return from Euboea the Athenians concluded a thirty-year truce with the Lacedaemonians and their allies, returning to them Nisaea, Pegae, Troezen, and Achaea, these being lands of the Peloponnesians that the Athenians were occupying.

A speech Thucydides attributes to Pericles in 432/1 mentions that the peace required Athens and Sparta to resort to arbitration in the case of disagreements.

20.15.B   The Arbitration Clause in the Thirty-Year Peace

Thucydides 1.140.2

"That the Spartans were plotting against us was clear before, and now it is clearer than ever. It was expressly stated that any differences we had should be settled by arbitration and that meanwhile we would each keep what we have. But the Spartans have never sought arbitration, nor have they accepted it when we offered it. They want to settle grievances by war rather than dialogue, and now they come here issuing orders and no longer making requests."

 The peace induced the important state of Argos to sign a separate peace with both Athens and Sparta, which effectively made her neutral; see WEB **20.16** on the Thirty-Year Peace and Argos' neutrality.

20.17   Athenian Colonization and the Colony of Brea (447–445)

The Thirty-Year Peace between Athens and Sparta was followed by energetic bursts of Athenian activity both at home and abroad. The city continued to found cleruchies and independent colonies (*apoikiai*), which extended its influence in the Mediterranean. Plutarch lists some of these settlements, although there is no need to accept his crediting Pericles alone with Athens' colonial activity. In many cases the establishment of colonies resulted in reduced tribute for the region.

20.17.A   Athenian Foundations of Colonies

Plutarch *Pericles* 11.5

In addition, Pericles sent out citizens as settlers: a thousand to the Chersonese, five hundred to Naxos, half that number to Andros, and a thousand to Thrace for a joint settlement with the Bisaltae. He also sent others to Italy, at the time when Sybaris was being resettled as the colony they renamed Thurii. These measures he took as a means of relieving the city of its crowd of shiftless and meddlesome idlers, and of remedying the poverty of the demos, and he was also establishing settlers next to the allies as a deterrent and defense against insurgency.[1]

Note

1. Cf. *Diodorus 11.88.3. The foundation of the cleruchy in the Thracian Chersonese has been dated to 447, and those on Naxos and Andros to 450 (Meiggs 1972, 160, 123, 530). See below on the colonies in Thrace and Thurii.*

A fragmentary inscription, which many scholars date to 447–445, records the foundation of a colony in Brea in the Thraceward region. The exact site of this settlement is unknown. However, if Plutarch's mention of 1,000 settlers who were sent to live among the Thracian Bisaltae refers to this colony (and not to Amphipolis), it was west of the Strymon River and close to Argilus. The inscription endows Democleides, who is the likely founder (*oikistês*) of the colony, with somewhat extraordinary powers. An amendment to the proposal appears to exclude Athenians of the two upper classes from this enterprise. It is likely, indeed, that poor or relatively poor Athenians were among the chief beneficiaries of Athenian colonization. There is no further record of the history of the Brea settlement, perhaps because it was abandoned when neighboring Amphipolis was founded in 437/6.

20.17.B   The Foundation Decree of Brea

ML no. 49 = Fornara no. 100

Translation: Osborne 2000, no. 232, pp. 119–120

... to which a denunciation or prosecution is made, let it be introduced. But if the denunciator or prosecutor introduces [the case —][1]

The [founders of the settlement abroad] are to provide (**5**) [means for sacrificing] to obtain good omens on behalf of the settlement.

They are to choose [ten men], one from each tribe, to divide up the land and they are to divide up the land.

Democleides is to be given power to establish the [settlement] in the [best] way he can.

The (**10**) lands of the gods are to be exempted as they are now, and no other land is to be consecrated.

They are to bring a cow and a [full set of armor] to the Great Panathenaea and a phallus [to the Dionysia].

If anyone launches an expedition against [the territory] of the settlement, the [cities][2] are to help (**15**) as quickly as possible in accordance with the agreements made when [—] was Secretary [concerning the cities] in the Thraceward region.

[This] is to be written [on a stele] and placed on the Acropolis. The settlers [are to provide] the stele at their [own expense].

(**20**) If anyone puts anything to the vote contrary to the [stele or] any orator makes a proposal or [tries] to use the courts to modify in some way or rescind what has been decreed, he is to [lose his civic rights] and so are [his] children, and their property is to be confiscated and a [tenth] part given to the [goddess], (**25**) unless the settlers themselves [—] make this request.

All soldiers enlisted [to go as settlers, are to go as settlers] to Brea within thirty days of their return to Athens. The settlement is to be put into operation within thirty [days]. (**30**) Aeschines is to accompany it and give the money.

Phantocles proposed: as to the settlement at Brea, Democleides' proposal should stand, (**35**) but the Erechtheid prytany is to summon Phantocles before the Council at its first sitting. (**40**) And the settlers to be drawn from the Thetes and Zeugitai.

Notes

1.   *The purpose of this legal procedure is unclear.*
2.   *The cities were apparently in the Thraceward region and were supposed to help Brea when attacked.*

Questions

1.   Who were the beneficiaries of the Athenian settlements? Who was harmed by them and how?
2.   What were the mutual obligations of the Brea settlers and their mother-city?

20.18   A Hippodamian City Plan

More ambitious than Brea was the foundation of Thurii in southeastern Italy around 444/3. See WEB **20.19** for Thurii's foundation.

Thurii's city plan (WEB **20.19**) has all the earmarks of the architect and city planner Hippodamus of Miletus, who is linked to Thurii by a late source (Hesychius s.v. *Hippodamus' indignation*). Hippodamus had designed the master plan for the Piraeus, which included three harbors, business and residence districts, and a wall. As in Thurii, straight streets crossed one another at right angles in a linear plan that rationally divided the space to satisfy communal needs. In the Piraeus this meant a functional division of space into areas for residence, commerce, workshops, storage of goods, and so on. Alongside rectangular or square blocks, Hippodamus also recommended for cities a square or rectangular agora. According to Aristotle, who criticizes Hippodamus' ideas, his division of space was complemented by a rigid division into categories of laws, governmental structure, and residents (*Politics* 2.5.1–4 1267b23–1268a16).

Fifth-century Miletus provides a good example of a Hippodamian grid plan, although there is no evidence that Hippodamus was personally involved in Miletus' town planning (Figure 20.1). The city was built on a peninsula with two harbors. The public and commercial center was located next to the north harbor, called the Lion harbor after the discovery of lion

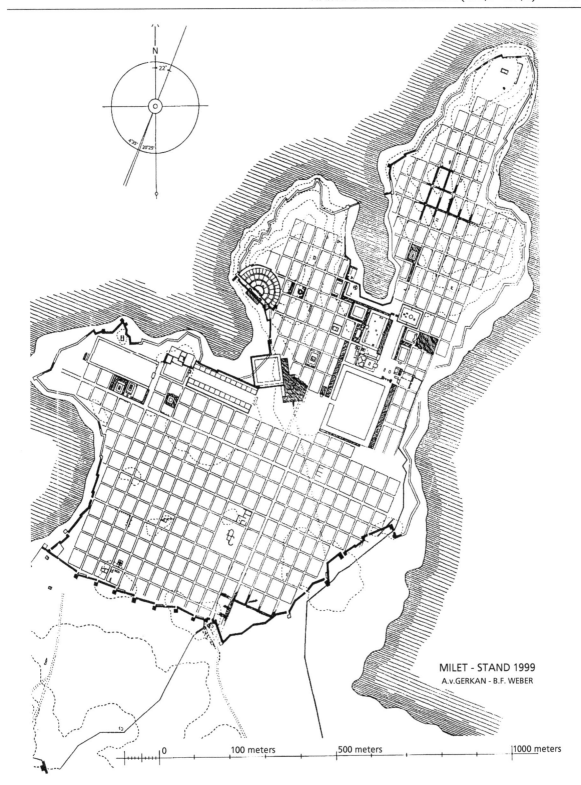

MILET - STAND 1999
A.v.GERKAN - B.F. WEBER

0   100 meters   500 meters   1000 meters

Figure 20.1   Miletus city plan. © Miletgrabung.

statues there. The older northern part of the city was divided into rectangular blocks, 20 × 25 meters, while these in the south were 30 × 40 meters big. The mostly unpaved streets were 4–5 meters wide. The two major arterial streets in the southern part were 8 meters wide. The one that ran from north to south led to the southern gate, from which a sacred way led to Apollo's shrine in Didyma. Walls, partially dated to the second century, surrounded the city, and the entrance to the north harbor could be blocked by chains. It should be said that the division of the city into northern, central, and southern districts did not create an integrated whole but three different, loosely connected areas. Generally, the Hippodamian city plan best fitted foundations of new cities. Old, established cities were normally built in an irregular, untidy fashion.

20.20   The Foundation of Amphipolis (437/6)

In 437/6 the Athenians founded the city of Amphipolis on the Strymon River in southern Thrace. The city controlled important trade routes and was close to Thracian timber and mineral resources. The settlers came from Athens and nearby garrisons (Diodorus 12.32.3). Athens became an important player in the politics of neighboring Macedonia, whose timber was coveted by Athenian shipbuilders. Corinth, however, might have been less than thrilled by the presence of an Athenian colony in the vicinity of its colony of Potidaea. Athens tried to settle the site in 466/5, but was unsuccessful (see **18.11**: "Operations in Northern Greece").

Thucydides 4.102.3

The Athenians returned 29 years later when Hagnon son of Nicias was sent out as the colony-leader, and after driving out the Edonians they settled in this place, which was earlier called Nine Ways. Their starting point was Eion, a coastal market [*emporion*] that they possessed at the mouth of the river, 25 stades distant from the present city. Hagnon named the settlement "Amphipolis" because, with the Strymon flowing on both sides, he cut off the city with a long wall running from the one point of the river to another, thus giving the foundation a remarkable view both seawards and landwards.

Review Questions

1. What were the key events of the First Peloponnesian War (**20.1**, **20.5**, **20.9**, **20.13**, **20.15**)? Did Athens win it?
2. What were the terms and significance of the Peace of Callias (**20.11**, cf. **20.3**)?
3. What motivated the Athenian colonization effort (**20.17**, WEB **20.14**, WEB **20.19**)? How was it organized (**20.17–18**, WEB **20.19**)?

4. What prevented the clashes between Athens and Sparta from developing into a full-scale war?

5. What were the terms of the Thirty-Year Peace (**20.15.B**, cf. WEB **20.16**)?

6. If a Spartan and an Athenian were to look back on events in Greece from 461 to the Thirty-Year Peace, which one was likely to be more satisfied?

Suggested Readings

The First Peloponnesian War and its causes: Holladay 1977; Lewis 1981, 1992a. *The Egyptian campaign and losses*: Westlake 1950; Meiggs 1972, 92–108; Holladay 1989. *The Long Walls*: Boersma 1970, esp. 154–156; Constantakapoulou 2007, 137–150. *The battle of Tanagra*: Roisman 1993; Plant 1994. *The Peace of Callias*: Meiggs 1972, 129–151, 487–495 (made in 450s); Sealey 1976, 278–282 (unhistorical); Badian 1987a (two agreements in 460s and 449), but see also Bloedow 1992. *The Peloponnesian invasion of Attica*: Ste Croix 1972, 196–200; Meiggs 1972, 181–182. *The regulations for Chalcis*: Balcer 1978; Ostwald 2002; Mattingly, e.g., 1992, 135–136 (opts for 424/3 as their date). *The foundation of Brea*: Vartsos 1977; Hanson 1999. *Thurii*: Ehrenberg 1948; Rutter 1973; Fleming 2002. *Hippodamus and the city plan of Miletus*: McCredie 1971; Burns 1976; Gorman 2001, 129–163; Greaves 2002, esp. 79–86. *Pericles and Thucydides son of Melesias*: Andrewes 1978; Kallet-Marx 1989; Stadter 1989, 130–187; Borthwick 2000. *Pericles and Athenian democracy*: Connor 1971, 87–198; Rhodes 2000. *Amphipolis and its archaeological remains*: Lazarides 2003.

21

The Administration of the Empire and the Athenian Tribute Quota Lists

CHAPTER CONTENTS

Epigraphic evidence provides valuable information about Athens' administration of the empire and her relationship with the allies. Probably around 454/3 the Athenians transferred the treasury of the Delian League from Delos to Athens. The reasons are unclear and might have to do with security concerns, to which the disaster in Egypt had contributed (**20.3**: "The Athenian Expedition to Egypt"). Since the Athenians were the ones who assessed and collected contributions to the treasury, its transfer to Athens changed little in practice. Probably a more significant change was the abolition of joint councils with the allies. We also hear of the presence of Athenian garrisons, settlers, and officials on allies' lands.

Starting from 454/3, 1/60 of the tribute was dedicated as "first-fruits" (*aparchai*) to Athena, the patron goddess of Athens. These annual transactions were recorded in elegantly written inscriptions, known as the "Athenian tribute quota lists." The lists allow scholars to deduce who belonged to the league at what time, how much they paid, as well as changes in both membership and the monetary demands Athens made of them. Generally, tributes were reassessed every four years and, with few exceptions, did not significantly vary before the 420s and the Peloponnesian War, when assessments were raised considerably. During that war the Athenians would also occasionally demand additional contributions. Allies had the option of appealing their assessment in Athenian courts.

This chapter discusses the ways the Athenians administered their empire. It includes a decree regulating tribute collecting, a list of tribute-paying members, and a decree illustrating Athens' intervention in her allies' affairs. It also documents Athens' suppression of a revolt by its ally, Samos. Finally, the chapter surveys allies' attitudes toward Athens and vice versa.

21.1 The Cleinias Decree

One decree, which has been dated to 448/7 or 430–426/5, gives an idea of how the tribute was collected. Evidently Cleinias, who proposed it, and the Athenians, who approved it, were concerned about irregularities in the tributes' collection and about peculation by those who came into contact with the money. They tried to deter misconduct through the democratic insistence on transparency and accountability. The decree also deals with the procedure underlying the tribute lists. The allies brought their contributions to Athens, where they were audited by public accountants (*logistai*) and then handed over to the Treasurers of the Greeks (*Hellenotamiai*: **18.5.C**: "Managing the League"). The transactions were recorded in the lists.

ML no. 46 = Fornara no. 98

Translation: Osborne 2000, no. 190, pp. 102–103

Gods. The Council and People decided, in the prytany of the tribe Oineis, when Spoudias was Secretary and [—] on (**5**) was President on the proposal of Cleinias:[1] that the Council and the magistrates in the cities and the Inspectors [*episkopoi*] should look after the collection of tribute every year (**10**) and bring it to Athens.

They are to make identification tokens for the cities to prevent those who bring the tribute from committing offences: the city is to write on (**15**) a tablet the amount of the tribute which it is sending and then seal it with the identification token before it sends it to Athens. Those who bring the tribute are to give the tablet to the Council to read whenever they hand over the tribute.

The prytaneis[2] are to hold a meeting of the Assembly after the Dionysia, at which the (**20**) Hellenotamiai[3] are to list for the Athenians separately the cities which have paid all their tribute and the cities that have defaulted.

The Athenians are to elect four men and [send] them to the cities with a record of the [tribute that has been paid] to ask for (**25**) the remaining tribute from defaulters. Two are to sail on a swift trireme [to the Island region and to Ionia and two to the Hellespont and] the Thraceward region. [The prytaneis are to introduce this matter to the] Council and the [People immediately after the Dionysia and (**30**) are to keep them up to date on this matter until it is completed.]

If any Athenian [or ally commits an offence over] the tribute which [the cities have written on the tablet and] must [send to Athens] with their tribute-carriers, any [Athenian] (**35**) or ally [shall be free to indict him before the prytaneis, and the prytaneis] are to bring [any indictment that anyone] makes to the Council [or else suffer a fine of 1,000 drachmas] each at their scrutiny. [Whatever penalty the Council] condemns [an offender to] shall only become valid when [immediately] confirmed [by the Heliaea].[4] When a [guilty verdict] is declared, (**40**) the prytaneis [are to make] a decision as to what the offender should [pay or] suffer.

If anyone commits an offence over the bringing of the cow or [the full set of armor],[5] indictment and [punishment] are to follow the same procedure.

The [Hellenotamiai are to write up and (**45**) display] on a whitened board the tribute [assessment] and [the cities that have paid all of it and] to list [—]

[10 lines missing]

... the incoming Council [is to discuss those who bring in the tribute.] All of those bringing tribute [to Athens who] are written up [on the notice-board] as owing money (**60**) [—] it is to display to the People [— if] any city [argues about the handing over of the tribute], asserting that it did [hand it over —] the common meeting of the [city —] and the cities and the (**65**) [—], it shall not be possible to indict [— or] the man who brings the indictment is to owe a fine [—] the indictment [is to be brought to the Polemarch in the month of Game]lion [December/January]. But if anyone argues [—] prosecutions, let the Council (**70**) consider the matter and [—] those [responsible for introducing cases] are to bring [to the Heliaea those who owe] tribute to the Athenians [in order, according to the record] of the denunciation. [—] the new tribute and last year's tribute [—] the Council is to consider the matter first and bring [—] at the meeting on the next day [—] arrangements for the choice [—]

Notes

1. *The dating of the decree to 448/7 is largely based on an uncertain identification of its proposer Cleinias with his namesake, who was father of the famous politician Alcibiades and died in 447/6. Those who favor a later date associate the decree with a similar decree proposed by Cleonymus in 426 (ML no. 68).*
2. *The prytaneis were fifty Council members who presided over the Council for one tenth of the year.*
3. *For the Hellenotamiai, or Treasurers of the Greeks, see Thucydides 1.96.2 = **18.5.C** ("Managing the League").*
4. *The Heliaea, or "People's Court," was the largest court in Athens, presided over by judicial officials called the Thesmothetae.*
5. *One of the allies' obligations was to bring a cow and a full suit of armor to the Panathenaea festival at Athens.*

Questions

1. Which office-holders and institutions were involved in the collection of the tribute and what function did each of them fulfill?
2. What does the inscription suggest about the hierarchy of power in Athens and its democracy?

21.2 The Tribute Quota List of 453/2

The annual tribute quota lists were inscribed on stone pillars. The first fifteen lists were inscribed on all four sides of a pillar over 3.5 meters high and 1.1 meters wide, and the next eight lists on a smaller pillar. Only few fragments survive of the annual lists past 428. The monumentality of the stones was designed to impress both Athenians and their visitors with the might of the city. It was also a pious tribute to Athena. See WEB **21.4** for a link to an image of a stele inscribed with the tribute lists of 439–431.

Starting from 446/5 the lists were organized by region, which included Ionia, Hellespont, the Thraceward, Caria (to be included in Ionia from 438/7), and the Islands. The number of the allies ranged from about 250 before the Peloponnesian War to 420 in the (optimistic?) tribute assessment of 425/4. Many allies paid only small sums. Around the 440s, only a few allies, including Samos, Chios, and Lesbos, contributed ships and did not pay tribute at all. It has been calculated that 29 percent of the tributary allies paid 86 percent of the total revenues (Osborne 2000, 89). Assessments were made on the basis of the resources, population size, and territory of the contributing state. The following is a part of the tribute quota list of 454/3–453/2, which includes a total of 208 names. The allies named below were from Caria.

The Tribute Quota List of 453/2 (*IG* I³ 260)

Column II	
Bol[bae]ans	17 drachmas and 1 obol
Lephsimani[ans]	17 drachmas and 1 obol
Erinians	68 drachmas and 5 obols
Amynand[es]	50 drachmas and 5 obols
Pactues Idum[eus]	113 drachmas and 5 obols
Oraniet[ans]	17 drachmas and 1 obol
Ola[e]ans	17 drachmas and 1 obol
T[a]rbanians	17 drachmas and 1 obol
Codapes	[amount missing]

21.3   The Erythraean Decree (453/2)

The anonymous author commonly known as the "Old Oligarch," whose work has been erroneously attributed to Xenophon, was a critic of Athenian democracy. He noted a consistent Athenian policy of putting down the elite and sponsoring democracy among the allies: see WEB **21.4.I**. The Athenians, however, had no qualms in supporting oligarchies friendly to them.

There is little doubt that Athens used the contributions to put a check on discontented members of the league. An Athenian decree, copied two centuries ago but now lost, and which is commonly dated to 453/2, provides information about Athenian instructions to the city of Erythrae in Ionia to model its government after that of Athens. The inscription implies that some Erythraeans had collaborated with the Persians, probably in a revolt against Athens. Another Athenian decree concerning the Ionian city of Colophon, tentatively dated to 450–447/6 (although some prefer to date it to 427), shows another attempt to tighten control over the city (ML no. 47). Colophon probably rebelled, and it appears that between 454 and 450 Athens had to deal with restive allies, especially in Ionia and possibly in the islands.

The Erythraean decree below shows how Athens intervened in the allies' internal affairs. The Athenians sought to establish a friendly democratic regime there under the watchful eye of a garrison commander. In later years Athens continued to infringe the allies' sovereignty when it brought allied citizens to trial in Athenian courts or prohibited allies from imposing the death penalty (probably to protect Athenian friends among them). Yet there is also evidence of agreements (*symbolai*) with individual allied states which narrowly defined the categories of judicial procedure to which allies were subjected (e.g., ML no. 31). See WEB **21.4.II** for Athens' jurisdiction over the allies.

The two fragments of the Erythraean decree were likely inscribed on the same stele.

IG I³ 14, 15 = ML no. 40 = Fornara no. 71

Translation: Osborne 2000, nos. 216A, 216B, pp. 113–114

[The Council and People decided —] when [—] was President [— that the people of Erythrae] should bring corn to the Great Panathenaea worth [not less than] three minas and distribute it to those Erythraeans present. [—] **(5)** the sacred officials [—] if [they] bring [—] worth less than three minas according to what has been laid down, [—] buy corn [—] the people [—] anyone who wants to of the Erythraeans.

There is to be a council of 120 men selected by lot [—] **(10)** on the council and [not of foreign birth] to serve on the council aged not less than thirty. [Those rejected] to be prosecuted. No one to serve twice within four years. The [Inspectors (*episkopoi*)] and Garrison Commander are to draw lots and set up the current council; in the future the council and the Garrison Commander **(15)** to do this not less than 30 days before the term of office expires. Councilors are to take an oath by Zeus and Apollo and Demeter, calling down destruction on themselves if they break their oaths. [—] and destruction on their children [—] over sacred victims [—] And the Council shall burn not less than [—] or else be fined 1,000 drachmas **(20)** [—] The People is to burn not less [—].

The council is to swear as follows: I will give the best and the most just counsel I can for the People of Erythrae and of Athens and of the allies, and I will not revolt from the People of Athens nor from the allies of the Athenians, neither myself nor will I be persuaded by another to do so **(25)** [—] I will not receive any of the exiles, nor [—] I will be persuaded by [another] of those who flee to the Persians without the agreement of the Council of the Athenians and the People, and I will not drive out any of those who have stayed without the agreement of the Council of the Athenians and the People. If any Erythraean murders **(30)** another Erythraean, let him die if condemned [—] if condemned let him be exiled from the whole Athenian alliance and let his money be confiscated and belong to the Erythraeans.

If anyone [—] the tyrants [—] the Erythraeans and [—] let him die [—] his children **(35)** [—] his children [—] the Erythraeans and [—] the Athenians —] after depositing the money [—] children [—] be [–]ed in this way [—] the Athenian People [—] **(40)** [—] of the allies [—] ten archers from the garrison [—] **(45)** Council [—] from each tribe [—] Garrison Commander [—] Athenian [—] the members of the garrison [—]

[they are to swear an oath] in front of [the council at Erythrae and the Garrison Commander, calling down] destruction [on themselves and their children if they swear falsely. The people are to swear] the following: I will not revolt [from the Athenian people nor from the allies] of the Athenians, neither myself [nor will I persuade another, and I] will obey the Athenians' [decision. This oath and the oath of the council are to be written up] on a stone stele [on the Acropolis], and on the acropolis at Erythrae [the Garrison Commander is to write up] the same.

Questions

1. How was the Erythraean Council constituted, and how did it resemble the Athenian Council?
2. How did Athens seek to guarantee Erythraea's loyalty?
3. How did the Athenians control and profit from the allies (WEB **21.4.I–II**)?

21.5 The Samian Revolt (441/0–440/39)

A major threat to Athens' control of the empire was the revolt of the island of Samos in 441/0–440/39. The island was not a tributary member of the league, and, in spite of its oligarchic regime, it maintained good relations with Athens up to the revolt.

The siege of Samos led to direct Persian intervention against Athens, thus showing their opportunistic attitude toward the Peace of Callias. In addition, it appears that the Peloponnesians contemplated aiding the Samians, although they did not take action (Thucydides 1.40.5). Lastly, a fragmentary inscription records the expenses of the Athenian campaign in Samos, which may have ranged between 1,200 and 1,400 talents. The money that was paid by the Treasury of Athena was the first attested military use of this religious fund (ML no. 55 = Fornara no. 113). Plutarch preserves a story by Duris, the third-century historian and tyrant of Samos, which records Pericles' punishment of the Samians. Duris is often criticized for his dramatic style, but the form of crucifixion (*apotympanismos*) he describes was one of the modes of execution in Athens.

Plutarch *Pericles* 28.1–3

(**28.1**) After eight months the Samians capitulated, and Pericles demolished their walls, confiscated their fleet, and fined them heavily. The Samians paid part of the fine immediately, and gave hostages after agreeing to pay the rest within a specified period. To this Duris of Samos adds aspects of tragic drama, accusing the Athenians and Pericles of considerable brutality, which Thucydides does not record, nor Ephorus, nor Aristotle. (**28.2**) Indeed, Duris seems guilty even of mendacity in saying that Pericles brought the trierarchs and marines of the Samians into the agora of Miletus and tied them to planks, that after they had suffered for ten days he gave orders that they be executed by being clubbed on the head and that their bodies were thrown aside without burial. (**28.3**) Now Duris does not usually keep his narrative within the bounds of the truth even when he has no axe to grind; all the more likely that in this case he has exaggerated the misfortunes of his country to disparage the Athenians ...

Questions

1. Who was involved in the conflict in Samos, and what was at stake for Athens?
2. How did Athens punish the Samians, and what might have moved Plutarch to harshly criticize his source?

21.6 Allies' Attitudes Toward the Empire

It is not easy to ascertain the allies' attitudes toward the Athenian empire, because our sources are overwhelmingly Athenian. In addition, the allies' attitudes were not universal or fixed. Nevertheless, two major sentiments may be discerned. One was an Athenocentric view of the empire as a blessing for the Greeks. In a funeral speech attributed to Lysias and written perhaps during the Corinthian War (395–387), the speaker describes the good services that Athens rendered the allies.

21.6.A   Athens' Services to the Allies

Lysias 2 *Funeral Oration* 56–57

(**56**) They did not think that the many should be enslaved to the few,[1] but instead they forced everybody to have egalitarian ideals; and rather than weakening the allies, they made them strong, too. They themselves demonstrated such great strength that the Great King no longer hankered after the possessions of others but surrendered some of his own and had fears for what remained. (**57**) And in that period no triremes sailed from Asia to Greece, nor were there any tyrants set up amongst the Greeks, nor did the barbarians enslave any Greek city. Such was the moderation and fear that the courage of these men instilled in all men. It is because of this that they alone should be the champions of Greece and the leaders of its cities.

Note

1. *According to Thucydides (3.10.4), envoys from Mytilene to Sparta in 428 charged the Athenians with enslaving their allies.*

Conversely, there was a hostile view of the empire that regarded the Athenians as unjust masters or tyrants. The historian Thucydides attributes to the Athenian leaders Pericles and Cleon the claim that the empire was a tyranny that should be protected if the Athenians knew what was good for them. Cleon stated this view when the Athenians debated how to punish the people of Mytilene on Lesbos, who rebelled and surrendered to them in 427 (see WEB **25.6.III**: "The Mytilenean Affair"). Cleon was in favor of killing all adult males and enslaving the women and the children.

21.6.B   Allies' Enmity Toward Athens

Thucydides 3.37.2; cf. 2.63.2

(**3.37.2**) Because there is no fear and chicanery in your daily relations with one another, you maintain the same attitude toward your allies, and you do not realize that any mistake you make through listening to their arguments, or any concession you grant from pity, shows a weakness that is not without danger for yourselves, and which does not earn you gratitude from the allies. You do not see that the empire you have is a tyranny, and that you are wielding it over unwilling subjects who are plotting against you. These people obey you not because of any favors you do them (to your own harm!) but because of whatever superiority you have imposed on them by your strength rather than established through their good will.

The "Old Oligarch" argued that the Athenian elite supported the allied elites, and the Athenian demos the allied masses, each in pursuit of its own interest (WEB **21.4.I**). In the debate over the fate of the rebel Mytileneans (428), the speaker Diodotus expressed a similar view. He opposed Cleon's motion to punish the rebels severely and recommended a more lenient punishment based on the distinction between the allies' elites and their masses.

21.6.C   A Pragmatic Attitude Toward the Allies' Conduct

Thucydides 3.47.2–3

(**3.47.2**) For at the moment the common people [*demos*] in all the city-states are well disposed toward you, and either do not join the others in seceding or, if compelled to do so, remain from the start hostile to the rebels. This means that you go to war having the masses of the opposing city as your allies. (**47.3**) But suppose you destroy the common people of Mytilene, who took no part in the secession and who readily surrendered the city to you when they acquired weapons. First of all, you will be doing wrong by killing your benefactors, and secondly you will be creating for those in power the situation they want most. For when they foment revolts in the cities, they will straightway have the common people on their side, since you will have demonstrated that the same punishment awaits the innocent as the guilty…

Questions

1. What were the blessings and the misfortunes of the Athenian empire according to its advocates and critics?

2. How was Athens supposed to treat the allies according to speakers in Thucydides (**21.6.C**) and the "Old Oligarch" (WEB **21.4.I–II**)?

Review Questions

1. How did the Athenians regulate and supervise the collection of the tribute (**21.1–2**)?

2. How did the Athenians keep the allies under control (**21.1**, **21.3**, **21.5–6**, WEB **21.4.I–II**)?

3. What was the preferable way to deal with the allies, according to the sources
    (**21.6.B–C**, WEB **21.4.I–II**)?
4. Was Athenian rule of the empire tyrannical?

Suggested Readings

The Athenian tribute quota lists: B. Meritt et al. 1939–1953; Nixon and Price 1990;
Mattingly 1996; Osborne 2000, 86–97, 101–107. *Collecting tribute and the Cleinias decree*:
Meiggs 1972 *passim*, esp. 212–213, 519–561; Lewis 1994; Osborne 2000, 86–101; and
see also Chapter 26 ("Finances and Allies During the Archidamian War"). *The Colophon
decree*: ML no. 47, pp. 123–225 (older date); Mattingly, e.g., 1966, 21–12 (427 BCE). *The
Samian revolt*: Fornara 1979; Quinn 1981, 10–17; Shipley 1987, 103–112. *Allies' attitudes toward the Athenian empire*: Ste Croix 1954–1955 (popular among the lower
classes); *contra*: Bradeen 1960.

22

The City of Athens

CHAPTER CONTENTS

Ancient Greece from Homer to Alexander: The Evidence, First Edition. Joseph Roisman.
© 2011 Blackwell Publishing Ltd. Translations © 2011 John Yardley. Published 2011 by Blackwell Publishing Ltd.

23

The Sophists, Athenian Democracy, and Democracy's Critics

Ancient Greece from Homer to Alexander: The Evidence, First Edition. Joseph Roisman.
© 2011 Blackwell Publishing Ltd. Translations © 2011 John Yardley. Published 2011 by Blackwell Publishing Ltd.

In Athens, Pericles surrounded himself with some of the best artists and philosophers of the age (Plutarch *Pericles* 4–6, 13, 31–32, 37–38). Many of these philosophers were popularly known as sophists (*sophistai*), teachers of wisdom or experts who, during Pericles' time and the Peloponnesian War, exerted significant influence, especially over members of the Athenian elite.

The sophists were the intellectual heirs of earlier Ionian philosophers, whose interest centered on the world of nature. The sophists, in contrast, focused their teaching on the polis and how to attain success and *aretê* in it. They discussed government, society, sciences, religion, language, and rhetoric. They came from many corners of the Greek world, but tended to gravitate toward Athens where their services were in demand. There they taught how to succeed in politics and litigation, primarily through the use of rhetoric. Because the sophists charged money, and at times lots of it, their students came from the ranks of those who could afford their tuition, which made them teachers of the elite. They often contested one another's philosophy or technique. The popular image of sophists, however, lumped them together as useless intellectuals. They were primarily seen as men who taught their students the art of persuasion, an art that would give its practitioners an unfair advantage regardless of the merits of their case. They were thus perceived as subverting conventional values, helping their students to outsmart individuals, the people, and the institutions of the polis (see especially Aristophanes' *Clouds*).

The teachings of the sophists have survived chiefly in fragments and in Plato's dialogues. Since Plato and his admired teacher Socrates often criticized the sophists, there is no certainty about how accurately their arguments have been preserved. Nevertheless, the extracts in this chapter show different sophists questioning the validity of popular ideas about justice, laws, and conventions. There are also passages from two plays by Sophocles and Euripides where laws and higher laws as well as tyranny and democracy are pitted against one another in a way that contributes to the debate with the sophists. To conclude, the chapter includes criticisms of Athenian democracy that echo sophistic arguments.

23.1 The Sophists' View of Justice

Generally, the sophists pitted what they called the laws of nature (*physis*) against the written and unwritten laws of human society (*nomoi*). They defined the laws of nature as the laws of life and death that were based on the principles of avoiding pain and seeking pleasure, of pursuing self-interest, and of the right of the strong to rule over the weak. Because such laws have always dominated the world of nature, including human society, they were real and permanent. In contrast, social conventions and laws were changeable and contradictory, and, unlike the laws of nature, they could be broken with impunity. The sophists' views must have sounded heretical to many contemporaries because they argued against the justice and merit of democratic measures, majority rule, and obedience to them. Yet the sophists could be very persuasive, both because of the attractive logic of their arguments and because of their rhetorical skill.

In Plato's *Republic*, Glaucon, Plato's young and ambitious brother, reported to Socrates what he had heard from the sophists. Glaucon expected Socrates to counter their arguments.

Plato *Republic* 2.358e–359c

(**2.358e**) …For they say that, if one follows nature [*physis*], to commit injustice is a good thing and to suffer it a bad thing, but that there is more bad in suffering injustice than there is good in committing it. Thus when people inflict injustice on each other and receive it in turn, and have a taste of both, those not having the ability to avoid it on the one hand, and inflict it on the other, (**359a**) decide that it is to their advantage to come to an agreement with each other not to inflict injustice and not suffer it, either. And that is the origin, they say, of legislation and covenants, and they describe what is prescribed by law [*nomos*] as being "lawful" and "just." Such is the origin and essence of "justice," they say, namely an intermediate position between the greatest good, that is to do injustice and not be punished, and the greatest bad, which is to suffer injustice and not be able to take revenge. (**359b**) Justice, lying between the two, is not liked as a "good," but is respected through its inability to do injustice, since anyone with the ability to do injustice, and who was really a man, would not make an agreement with anybody not to do or to suffer injustice – that would be madness on his part. So, Socrates, the nature of justice is this or such like, and these are the premises on which it is based, so they say.

Then there is the point that those who practice justice do so unwillingly, because they are unable to do wrong. We could understand that best if we could imagine the following scenario. (**359c**) Suppose we grant to every man, both the just and the unjust, the freedom to do whatever he likes, and suppose we follow these men and see where their desire takes them. We would then catch the just man red-handed, heading in the same direction as the unjust man because of self-interest, something that every creature naturally pursues as a good. It is only by the law that he is forced to respect the notion of reciprocity. The freedom of which I am talking would be of the order of that power that they say Gyges held, the ancestor of Gyges the Lydian.[1]

Note

1. *Gyges was a Lydian king said to possess a ring that made him invisible; it allowed him to kill his predecessor and succeed him.*

Questions

1. How did laws and justice come into being according to the sophists?
2. Why are existing laws and justice not necessarily good?
3. Why would people prefer to do injustice than justice? Do you agree with this assumption?

23.2 Right and Might

In his dialogue *Gorgias*, named after one of the most celebrated teachers of rhetoric of the age, Plato describes a conversation between Socrates and the Athenian Callicles about the nature of justice. Callicles argues for redefining might as morally just and wishes for a strong man who will introduce a new moral order.

Plato *Gorgias* 483a–484a

(**483a**) ... According to nature whatever is more disgraceful is worse, such as suffering injustice, whereas according to law inflicting injustice is worse. (**483b**) For to endure injustice is not the behavior of a man, but of a slave, for whom death is better than life – it is so for anybody who, when wronged and abused, has not the ability to help himself or anyone he cares for. In my opinion, those who make the laws are the people who are weak and these are in the majority. They therefore frame the laws with reference to themselves and in their own interest, assigning praise and blame accordingly. (**483c**) They strike fear into the stronger members of society, those able to gain an advantage, and in order to have them not gain an advantage over them, they tell them that acquisition is disgraceful and unjust, and that injustice lies in seeking to have more than other people. For as inferior people they are happy, I suppose, to have equality.

This is why, in law, it is said to be unjust and disgraceful to seek to have more than the majority, and they call this "injustice." (**483d**) But in my opinion nature reveals that it is just for the better person to have more than his inferior, and for the stronger to have more than the less strong. That this is so nature reveals in many areas. In the animal world and in humans, in their cities and their races as a whole, she shows that this is how justice is decided, by the stronger dominating the weaker and gaining the advantage. (**483e**) For on what right was Xerxes relying when he launched his attack on Greece, or his father on the Scythians? Or consider the other tens of thousands of cases of this sort. They do these things according to the true nature of "right," and, for heaven's sake, in accordance with the law of nature, though perhaps not with the law that we lay down. (**484a**) We fashion the best and strongest of our people, taking them from a tender age, like lions, and we subjugate them with our magic spells, telling them that they must have their equal share of things, and that this is what is just. But I think that if a man comes along possessing a strong enough nature, he throws all this off, breaks his bonds, and makes his escape. He tramples under foot our writings, our deceptions, our charms and laws, all of them contrary to nature, and rising up, he, the slave, is revealed as our master, and the justice of nature then shines forth ...

Questions

1. Why, according to Callicles, it is unjust and disgraceful to obey laws?
2. Why do people obey unjust laws and how might the status quo be changed?

23.3 Justice and Expediency

For Callicles, being strong meant also being worthy and meritorious. However, the sophist Thrasymachus in Plato's *Republic* presents an almost nihilistic attitude. He argues that whoever is in power, regardless of the political regime of the polis, is right because justice is measured by the interest of the strong.

Plato *Republic* 1.338c, 338d, 343d–344a

(**1.338c**) "Listen then," he said, "I say that justice is nothing other than the interest of the stronger ..."

(**338d**) ..."And each government passes laws that are in its interests, a democracy passing democratic laws, a tyranny tyrannical laws, and other forms of government doing likewise. And in passing these they have made a declaration that this is what justice is for those under the rule, namely what is expedient for themselves, and they punish anyone who departs from this as being a lawbreaker and wrongdoer. So, my good fellow, this is what I say is the 'justice' that obtains in all our states alike, namely that which is expedient for the government in power. This is what holds sway, so that, if a person is thinking straight, he will admit that 'justice' is the same everywhere, being what is expedient for the stronger ..."

(**343d**) "Oh innocent Socrates, you must see things in this way, that the just man always comes off worse than the unjust man. First of all, in their contractual dealings, when the two different characters do business with each other, you would never find that the just man has more than the unjust man when the partnership is ended – he has less. Next, in their civic obligations, when taxes are involved, the just man pays more than the unjust though their assets be equal, (**343e**) and when it is a matter of acquiring anything the one gains nothing, the other a lot.

Thus, when one of them holds a magistracy, the just man finds that, even apart from any other financial loss, his personal affairs are adversely affected because of his neglect of them, while from the public purse he benefits not at all because of his justice. So, in addition, he is resented by his relatives and acquaintances when he refuses to contravene justice to help them. The unjust man gains the opposite of all this. I am speaking, naturally, of the man I was speaking of just now, the one with the great capability for acquisition. (**344a**) So look at this man if you want to form a judgment on how much more profitable it is for him personally to be unjust than to be just."

Questions

1. What makes laws and justice both different and similar in any political regime?
2. Why is doing the right thing unprofitable?
3. How would the weak and the strong profit under a democratic regime, according to Thrasymachus?

23.4 Sophocles' *Antigone* and the Debate with the Sophists

Sophistic views of justice validated for some members of the Athenian elite their anti-democratic views. Outside politics, playwrights such as Sophocles, Aristophanes, and Euripides were both inspired by the controversy surrounding these views and contributed to it. Sophocles, for example, deals with the relationship between culture and nature and human and divine laws in his play *Antigone*, which was produced ca. 441. The play focuses on the conflict between the Theban ruler Creon and Antigone. Creon has forbidden the burial of Antigone's brother as a traitor, but Antigone defies his law as inferior to divine ordinances. Creon's discovery that Antigone has disobeyed his order leads to a confrontation between them. Their debate over which law is supreme is intimately linked to Athenian perceptions of gender. The following passages commence with Antigone's justification of her violation of Creon's ordinance.

Sophocles *Antigone* 450–496

(**450**) Antigone: "As far as I am concerned, it was not Zeus who promulgated this; nor did Justice, who lives with the gods below, establish such laws amongst men. Nor did I think your decrees to have such force that you, (**455**) a mortal, could override the unwritten and immovable statutes of the gods. For these laws live not in the present or yesterday, but forever, and no one knows when they first appeared.

I was not going to incur punishment before the gods for breaking these through fear of any man's will. (**460**) I knew it meant death, of course, even without your edict. If I am to die before my appointed time, I count that gain. For how does death *not* bring gain to anyone who lives, as I do, amidst abundant ills? (**465**) For me to meet this fate is pain of no account. But had I left my mother's son's dead body, that would have meant pain. As for this, it brings me no pain. And if my actions happen to seem foolish to *you*, (**470**) it may be that my folly is being judged by a fool."

CHORUS: "Well, the girl's fierce spirit shows she's her fierce father's child. She cannot give way before misfortune."

CREON: "But you can rest assured that spirits too obstinate are the ones most frequently brought low. Very often one might see the strongest iron, (**475**) tempered by means of fire, shattered and broken. The most spirited horses, I know, are broken in by a tiny bit. For pride is not allowed to one who is the servant of her neighbors. (**480**) She had learned her insolence at the time when she trampled upon the established laws. And here is a second piece of insolence after doing that – gloating over it, and laughing at having done it! I am not a man now, and *she* is the man, (**485**) if her show of strength will go unpunished. But even if she is my sister's child, even if she is more closely related to me than any worshipper of Zeus in our home, she and her sister will not escape the foulest doom.[1] (**490**) For her sister, too, I charge equally with planning this burial.

Call her! I just saw her inside, raving and out of control of her wits. For often the heart stands convicted as the perpetrator ahead of time, when the wicked deeds are being plotted in the dark. (**495**) But this, too, I hate, when someone caught in wicked acts tries then to make them look good."

Note

1. *Antigone's sister, Ismene, did not in fact violate Creon's order.*

Questions

1. On what basis do Antigone and Creon justify their actions and claim the other to be wrong?
2. Does Antigone defy or confirm the logic of Thrasymachus' thesis (**23.3**)?

23.5   Tyranny and Democracy in Euripides' *Suppliant Women*

Our sources suggest that Athenian democracy, which grew in strength in the second half of the fifth century, was challenged on both ideological and practical grounds. The idea that democratic laws and justice discriminated against better and smarter citizens was very much in the background of the teaching of sophists such as Callicles (**23.2**). The debate over democracy focused also on its working principles, which Aristotle described in his *Politics* in a passage quoted above (6.1.8–9; see **19.8**: "Democratic Mechanisms and State Salary"). Aristotle's dim view of democratic qualifications for office echoed years of criticism of democratic rule, including that of sophists and their pupils.

See WEB **23.6.I** for Herodotus' description of a debate about the respective merits of monarchy, oligarchy, and democracy, which allegedly took place in the Persian court ca. 550. See also WEB **23.6.II** for Pericles' praise of democracy and its principles in his funeral oration, as reported by Thucydides.

Around 422, Euripides in his play *Suppliant Women* reproduced the rhetorical and ideological conflict between democracy and tyranny. Tyranny is represented by a messenger of Creon of Thebes, who demands the surrender of the royal family of Argos receiving shelter in Athens. The other speaker is Theseus, king of Athens, who nevertheless stands for democracy. Theseus' clear victory in the debate reaffirms for the Athenian audience the superiority of democratic equality and freedom.

Euripides *Suppliant Women* 399–457

(399) HERALD: "Who is the tyrant of this country? To whom must I report the words of Creon, who has been ruler of the land of Cadmus since the time that Eteocles died at the hands of his brother Polynices near the seven-mouthed gates?"

THESEUS: "First, stranger, you were in error at the start of your speech when you asked for a tyrant here. For the city is not ruled by one individual – it is free! The people [*demos*] reigns here, taking turns in yearly succession. They do not give preference to wealth, but the poor man has equality."

HERALD: "This is one strong advantage you give us, as in checkers. **(410)** The city that I am from is ruled by one man, not a mob. There is no one who puffs her up with his talk and turns her this way and that for his own gain, no one who, momentarily captivating and giving much pleasure, later does her harm, and then hides his earlier errors with fresh slander and escapes justice. And, anyway, how could the people set a city on the right path when it cannot judge his words correctly? For it is time, not haste, that provides better instruction. **(420)** The poor farmer, even if he is not stupid, would not be able, under the pressure of work, to focus on public affairs. And, in fact, it is a dreadful thing for the better class of people when a worthless man gains credit by captivating the people with his tongue, though he was nothing before."

THESEUS: "He's a clever fellow this herald, and an amateur orator. But since *you* started this debate, listen, for it was you who threw down a challenge in words. Nothing is less in a city's interests than a tyrant. (**430**) First of all, there are under him no laws in common, but he rules alone, having taken the law into his hands. And this means there is no longer equality. When laws are written down, however, the weak man and the rich man have equal justice; weaker men are able to answer the prosperous man in kind when badly spoken of, and the smaller man overcomes the great man if his cause is just. This is what freedom is: 'Who wishes to bring forward any proposal he has that is good for the city?'[1] (**440**) The man who wants to do this gains fame, and the man who does not remains silent. What provides more equality in a city than this?

Where the people rule the land, they take delight in their supply of young citizens; but the autocrat thinks this is bad for him, and, out of fear for his tyranny, kills the best people and those he thinks intelligent. So how could a city become strong when someone cuts down and plucks off its young men like ears of wheat in a spring meadow? (**450**) Why should a person accumulate wealth and a livelihood for his children, only to see his work produce a greater livelihood for the tyrant? Why should one keep one's daughters virgins at home – a sweet delight for tyrants whenever they have the inclination, but tears for those providing it. Let me no longer live if my children will be married by force. Such are the arguments I have launched against yours."

Note

1. *Theseus quotes the invitation of the assembly's president to any citizen to speak.*

Question

1. What are the faults of democracy according to the messenger? Does Theseus discuss them? What merits does he find in democracy?

23.7 Criticizing Democracy

 In his funeral oration (WEB **23.6.II**) Pericles claimed that both rich and poor, notables and inferiors, benefited from democratic equality and freedom. Critics of democracy sharply disagreed. For example, democracy sought to insure equality of opportunities and to level the political playing field by allowing lots to decide the election of public officials. Critics pointed out that the lot put unqualified people in office. See WEB **23.8** for criticism of the democratic use of the lot.

Other types of criticism are found in the *Constitution of the Athenians* (not to be confused with the similarly titled *Ath. Pol.*), a work from probably the last third of the fifth century, which has been wrongly attributed to Xenophon. Its anonymous author is commonly known as the "Old Oligarch," although he was far from being an oligarchic ideologue. Through much of his essay the author argues that democracy wrongfully privileges the baser elements of the city at the expense of the better elements. But as a good student of the sophists, he also claims that the people are acting both wisely and justly in keeping power in their hands rather than handing it over to the elite. The "Old Oligarch" is equally ironic about the democratic principles of *isegoria*, equal access to public speech, and *parrhesia*, freedom to speak one's mind, which every law-abiding citizen could enjoy. He gives voice to the elitist perception of the masses as ignorant and incapable of recognizing the common good.

[Xenophon] *Constitution of the Athenians* 1.1–2, 4–8

(**1.1**) With regard to the Athenian constitution, this is the reason for my lack of approval of this form of government: in choosing it they have also chosen to give the worthless [*poneroi*] precedence over the competent [*chrestoi*]. That is why I do not approve. But now that they have taken this decision, I shall explain how they do a good job of protecting the constitution and taking other measures (in which the other Greeks think they are mistaken).

(**1.2**) So, first of all, I will say that in Athens it does seem fair for the *poor* [*penetês*] and the people [*demos*] to take precedence over the well-born [*gennaoi*] and the rich [*plousioi*], for this reason: it is the people who are the driving force behind the navy and who give the city its power. The helmsmen, the boatswains, the petty officers, the men at the stern, and the shipbuilders – it is these who give power to the city, more so than the hoplites, the nobles, and those from good families. Since that is the case, it seems fair for all to share the public offices by means of the current system of the lottery and elections, and for any of the citizens who so wishes to have his say.

(**1.4**) Then there is something that a number of people find amazing, namely that in every area the Athenians grant precedence to the worthless, the poor, and the common people over the competent, and this is the decisive factor that clearly reveals that they are preserving their democracy. For when the poor, the commoners, and the lower sort [*cheiroôs*] prosper, and when these types become numerous, they will strengthen the democracy. But when the rich and the competent prosper, the common people are establishing a strong opposition to themselves. (**1.5**) In every land the best people [*beltistoi*] are opposed to democracy; for amongst the best there is very little indiscipline and injustice, but scrupulous care is taken over what is good, whereas in the people there is abysmal ignorance, disorder, and disreputable behavior. For poverty draws them toward disgraceful actions, and in some men there is ignorance and lack of education because of their penury.

(**1.6**) One might say that they should not permit everyone to speak on equal terms and propose resolutions, but that they should restrict that to those who are very clever and good. But here, too, in allowing even the worthless to have their say, their decision is excellent. For if the competent spoke and made proposals, this would be beneficial for people like themselves, but not for the common people. As things are, anyone who wishes can stand up and talk, disreputable though he be, and he will gain what is beneficial for himself and those like him. (**1.7**) One might ask: "What would such an individual know about what is good for himself and the people?" But they recognize that this man's ignorance, disreputability, and support of them are more profitable for them than the good man's virtue, insight, and antipathy toward them. (**1.8**) So while a city could not reach perfection based on such institutions, this is the best way to preserve democracy. The common people do not want to be a subservient entity in a well-run state, but to have freedom and supremacy, little caring whether the constitution is bad. For it is from what you consider to be not a good constitution that the common people gain their power and freedom.

Questions

1. Why is it just for commoners to hold power, according to the "Old Oligarch?"
2. Why does it make sense that ignorant men make decisions in a democracy?

Review Questions

1. Discuss the similarities and differences in the sophists' perception of laws and justice (**23.1–3**).
2. What practical conclusions would an Athenian political aspirant draw from the sophists' teachings? Why did the democrats resent their teachings?
3. What are the working principles of democracy according to Theseus (**23.5**), Otanes (WEB **23.6.I**), and Pericles (WEB **23.6.II**)?
4. How would Theseus (**23.5**) or Pericles (WEB **23.6.II**) respond to the claim that in democracy the uneducated and the weak are given an advantage over their betters?
5. Discuss the different perceptions of law and justice of democrats and their critics.

Suggested Readings

Sophists: Rankin 1983; Ostwald 1986, 237–250; de Romilly 1992. *Sophocles' Antigone and the sophists*: M. Nussbaum 2001, 51–82. *Fifth-century views of democracy (including the "Persian debate")*: Raaflaub 1990; Brock 1991. *Democracy, its ideals, and its critics*: Hansen 1996; Ober 1998b; Robinson 2004, 152–182. *Freedom of speech in Greece*: Sluiter and Rosen 2004, 1–340. *Funeral oration*: Loraux 1986. *Pseudo-Xenophon's Constitution of the Athenians*: Forrest 1970; Ober 1998a, 16–27; Hornblower 2000 (argues for a fourth-century rhetorical piece); Osborne 2004.

24

The Causes of the Peloponnesian War and the Athenian and Spartan Strategies

Ancient Greece from Homer to Alexander: The Evidence, First Edition. Joseph Roisman.
© 2011 Blackwell Publishing Ltd. Translations © 2011 John Yardley. Published 2011 by Blackwell Publishing Ltd.

The Peloponnesian War between Athens and Sparta (431–404) was considered a watershed event in Greek history already in antiquity. The man responsible for making it relevant beyond its time is the historian Thucydides (see **Introduction III.3**). Our dependence on him for the events of the war is no more evident than in dealing with its origins. Modern discussions of this topic either follow Thucydides' analysis of the causes of the war or react to it with varying degrees of disagreement.

This chapter presents Thucydides' analysis of the causes of the Peloponnesian War. It reports on an Athenian decree against Megara that contributed to the outbreak of the conflict and on the pressures that were exerted on Sparta to go to war. The chapter then considers Spartan demands for Athenian concessions, and concludes by examining the strategies of both sides at the beginning of the war.

24.1 Thucydides' View of the Causes of the Peloponnesian War

Generally, Thucydides offers two categories of causes for the Peloponnesian War. The one he favors is what he terms as the "truest cause," which is distinguished from the publicly stated "reasons" or "complaints" that the sides proffered against each other.

Thucydides 1.23.4–6

(**1.23.4**) The Athenians and Peloponnesians started the war when they broke the Thirty-Year Peace that they concluded after the capture of Euboea [445]. (**23.5**) I have first given an account of the reasons for their breaking the treaty and for the disputes between the two states, so that no one will in future need to look for the cause of such a momentous war amongst the Greeks. (**23.6**) In my opinion the truest cause [*prophasis*] was the one least admitted, namely that the growing power of the Athenians, which inspired fear in the Lacedaemonians, forced them into war. The reasons [*aitiai*] publicly expressed by each side for breaking the peace and opening hostilities were as follows.

Having stated the "truest cause" for the war, Thucydides goes on to describe what he categorizes as complaints or grievances. These involve clashes between Athens and Corinth in conflicts that originated in the city-state of Epidamnus in northwestern Greece (436–433), and in Potidaea on the Chalcidice peninsula (433–432). See WEB **24.2.I** for the Epidamnus affair, and WEB **24.2.II** for the Potidaea affair, which includes an Athenian commemoration of their dead in Potidaea.

Questions

1. What was the "truest cause" for the Peloponnesian War, according to Thucydides? Do the events leading up to it beginning from the Thirty-Year Peace (**20.15**, **20.17**, **20.20**, **21.5**) justify his opinion?
2. What were the main arguments in Athens in favor of making Corcyra an ally (WEB **24.2.I**)?
3. What were the Corinthians' main arguments against making Corcyra an ally (WEB **24.2.I**)?
4. Why did Athens make Corcyra her ally (WEB **24.2.I**)?
5. Who was involved in the conflict in Potidaea and how (WEB **24.2.II**)?

24.3 The Megarian Decree (432?), Corinthian Pressure, and Spartan Demands

In contrast to his detailed descriptions of the Corcyran and Potidaean affairs, Thucydides is less informative about two other grievances that contemporaries apparently deemed no less important in provoking the war. One involved the island of Aegina, which was a tribute-paying city in the Athenian empire. Thucydides says that Aeginetans supported Corinth's call to go to war against Athens and complained that "they did not enjoy the autonomy prescribed by the treaty" (1.67.2). The nature of the Aeginetan autonomy, or how the Athenians suppressed it, is unclear. The other grievance is better attested and concerns what is commonly known as the Megarian Decree.

24.3.A Thucydides on the Megarian Decree

> **Thucydides 1.67.1, 4**
>
> **(1.67.1)** While Potidaea was under siege, the Corinthians did not remain inactive: they had people in the town, and they were also worried about losing the place. They immediately invited their allies to Lacedaemon, and coming there themselves they strongly accused the Athenians of having broken the truce and of committing acts of aggression against the Peloponnese ... **(67.4)** Of note amongst those who came forward with various complaints were the Megarians who, after putting forward no small number of other grievances, focused specifically on their exclusion from the ports in the Athenian empire as well as from the market of Athens, in contravention of the treaty.

The Spartans would put the Megarian Decree on top of their list of complaints against Athens (Thucydides 1.140.4). It was proposed no later than 432 and possibly earlier. Its backdrop was a dispute between Athens and Megara over sacred land near Eleusis and a Megarian refusal to return runaway slaves (Thucydides

1.139.2). Plutarch shows how the dispute with Megara evolved, stressing Pericles' adamant refusal to revoke the decree and hence his responsibility for the war. The biographer seemed to rely on a collection of Athenian decrees. Plutarch also cites verses from Aristophanes' comedy *Acharnians* (produced 425), which blame Pericles for initiating the Peloponnesian War for Aspasia's sake. See WEB **24.4** for Aristophanes on Pericles and Aspasia, and for more of his verses.

24.3.B   Plutarch on the Background to the Megarian Decree

Plutarch *Pericles* 30.2–31.1

(**30.2**) Pericles, it would seem, had some personal resentment against the Megarians. The charge he openly made against them in public, however, was that of appropriating some of the sacred land,[1] and he proposed a decree that a herald be sent to them and also to the Lacedaemonians, making that charge against the Megarians. (**30.3**) Now the decree of Pericles contained a fair and humane justification of his action, but Anthemocritus, the herald sent on the mission, was killed, and it was thought that the Megarians were responsible.[2] Charinus then proposed a decree against them to the effect that there should be a state of deadly and implacable enmity maintained against them, that any Megarian setting foot in Attica should be given the death penalty, and that when the generals took the customary oath they should also swear to invade the land of Megara twice every year.[3] It was further proposed that Anthemocritus be buried at the Thrasian Gates, now called the Dipylon.[4] (**30.4**) The Megarians for their part disclaimed responsibility for Anthemocritus' murder, and shifted the blame for everything onto Aspasia and Pericles, citing the notorious and popular lines from [Aristophanes'] *Acharnians* [524–527]:

"Young men came to Megara after drinking and *kottabos*,[5] and abducted the whore Simaetha.

Then the Megarians, infuriated with garlic-fueled pain, abducted in revenge two whores of Aspasia."

(**31.1**) The original circumstances of the decree are not easy to ascertain, but everybody lays at Pericles' door responsibility for not rescinding it. Some, however, claim that Pericles' recalcitrance stemmed from a combination of high principles and a conception of the state's best interests, that he thought that the demand for its repeal was a test of the city's assertiveness, and that submission was a confession of weakness. Others claim that it was a sort of stubbornness and truculent desire to show off Athens' strength that made him thumb his nose at the Lacedaemonians.[6]

Notes

1. *Plutarch's distinction between Pericles' real personal reasons and his ostensible public ones cannot be substantiated.*
2. *Killing a herald or envoy was considered impious and could result in divine punishment for both the killer and his community.*
3. *Scholars are divided on whether the economic sanctions against Megara were included in Charinus' decree or were proposed separately.*

4. *Later testimonies mention the landmark of Anthemocritus' tomb, which continued to remind the Athenians of what they regarded as a Megarian atrocity. The Thrasian Gates formed the most important city gate, which was rebuilt in the fourth century and renamed the Dipylon (double-gate).*

5. *Kottabos was a popular game in a symposium that involved throwing dregs of wine at a target. See* WEB **24.4** *for a fuller quotation of Aristophanes' verses.*

6. *The first interpretation of Pericles' conduct reflects Thucydides (1.140), the second is unattested elsewhere.*

Among Sparta's motives for going to war was the desire to accommodate Corinth. Corinth was Sparta's most important Peloponnesian ally whose wealth and strong navy were second only to Athens'. Well aware of their status in the league, the Corinthians used it to pressure Sparta to go to war. Thus, before Sparta made up its mind about fighting Athens, Thucydides has Corinthian envoys urging the Spartans to move against Athens, failing which Corinth would seek a better ally. The most viable candidates were Athens and Argos. Corinth, of course, did not drag a reluctant Sparta into the conflict. The vote for war in both Sparta and Athens reflected the will of their respective people. But it was the allies, rather than the big powers, who provided the spark for the conflagration.

24.3.C   Corinth Urges Sparta to Go to War

Thucydides 1.71.4–7

(**1.71.4**) "Let there be a limit to your tardiness, which has persisted until now. Bring the help you promised to your other allies, too, but to Potidaea especially, with a prompt invasion of Attica. Do not put your friends and relatives at the mercy of their bitterest enemies, and do not make the rest of us turn in despair to some other alliance. (**71.5**) We would not be acting unfairly in doing that, not in respect of the gods who witnessed our oath, nor in the eyes of judicious men. For those who break treaties are not those who turn to others when they are deserted, but those who fail to give assistance to those to whom they swore they would. (**71.6**) If you show some willingness we shall remain committed to you. We would then be acting impiously in changing sides, and we would not find more like-minded allies elsewhere. (**71.7**) Consider this matter carefully, and try by your leadership to leave the Peloponnese no less great than it was when your fathers left it to you."

The Spartans voted on a war against Athens and an assembly of their Peloponnesian allies approved a similar decision. In the winter of 432/1 the two powers exchanged charges. The Athenians denied any wrongdoing and offered to go to arbitration. The Spartans demanded that the Athenians banish the "cursed," i.e., the Alcmeonids, including Pericles through his Alcmeonid mother, for their killing of the Cylonians two centuries earlier (**6.6**: "A Failed Attempt at Tyranny in Athens: Cylon"). The Athenians retaliated by demanding the elimination of the Spartan curse following the Spartan authorities' starving to death of Pausanias, their asylum-seeking regent, a generation or so earlier (WEB **18.13.II**: "Pausanias' Second Recall and Death").

24.3.D   The Spartan Demands

Thucydides 1.139.1

(**139.1**) Such were the demands that the Lacedaemonians made on the first embassy, and the counter-demands received in turn, concerning expulsion of people under a curse. On a number of later visits to Athens the Lacedaemonians ordered the Athenians to quit Potidaea and leave Aegina independent; but the point they made most emphatically and clearly was that there would be no war if the Athenians rescinded the Megarian Decree by which the Megarians were forbidden access to the ports in the Athenian empire, and to the market of Athens.

Thucydides suggests, then, that the Spartans still gave peace a chance. In response, Pericles highlighted Sparta's refusal to go to arbitration and warned that Athens could not afford to make concessions. An unsuccessful attack by Thebes, a Spartan ally, on Plataea, an Athenian ally, in the spring of 431 constituted for Athens a clear breach of the peace. By then the Spartans had already proclaimed war on Athens (Thucydides 1.68–2.7).

Questions

1. What did the Megarian Decree entail, what were the reasons for it, and what does it suggest about Athenian power and foreign policy (**24.3.A–B**, WEB **24.4**)?
2. Why, according to the Corinthians, would they not be breaking the treaty with Sparta if they sought another alliance (**24.3.C**)?
3. What were the Spartan demands of Athens on the eve of the war (**24.3.D**)? Does this suggest Spartan fear of Athens' growing power, which according to Thucydides led to the war?

24.5   **The Spartan (Archidamian) Strategy**

Both the Athenian and the Spartan strategies for the Peloponnesian War were based on the principle of pitting their strengths against the enemy's weakness. Yet the parties' respective strengths – Athens on the sea, Sparta on land – were so overwhelming that for a long time both sides chose to avoid direct confrontation rather than put themselves at risk. This policy greatly prolonged the war and only rarely allowed the full might of one state to clash with the other.

See WEB **24.6** for the advice of the Spartan king Archidamus [II] to the Spartans to wait a few years and build up power and resources before entering the conflict.

The Spartans, however, decided to go to war with what they had. They could mobilize many allied hoplites, presumably three times as many as Athens. Yet, unlike the professional Spartan army, these hoplites included many peasants who could afford to leave their farms only for a short time. Also, in comparison to the Athenian empire, the Spartan allies were more independent and less vulnerable to sanctions from Sparta. These realities and limited financial resources dictated Spartan strategy for the first years of the war. Wishing to take advantage of their superior infantry, and based on their experience in 446 of invading Attica (**20.13**: "The Peloponnesian Invasion of Attica"), the Spartans aimed to ravage Athenian fields and thus provoke the Athenians into a battle that the Spartans would likely win. Thucydides describes Spartan hopes in a speech that Archidamus delivered to the invading Peloponnesian army in the summer of 431.

24.5.A   Spartan Estimates of the Athenian Reaction

Thucydides 2.11.6–8

(**2.11.6**) "We are advancing on a city that is not incapable of defending itself – in fact, on one very well prepared in all respects. Thus we must fully expect that they will take the field, and that, even if they are not already setting out before our arrival, they will do so when they see us in their lands plundering and destroying their property. (**11.7**) For anger inevitably strikes men when they see that they are suffering some unfamiliar loss, and see it happening right before their eyes; and at that point, unable to stop and think, they are most prone to impulsive action. (**11.8**) The Athenians are more likely than others to react in this way because they think they have the right to rule others, and that it is they who should be invading and plundering their neighbors' lands rather than seeing it happen to their own."

The Spartans' plan of engaging the Athenians in a land battle was frustrated by Pericles' strategy (**24.7**). Since Sparta left the sea to Athenian control, it could not effectively aid rebellious Athenian allies. Instead, it relied on propaganda that used the old and honorable Panhellenic slogan of freedom to the Greeks – not from Persia, but from Athens. The liberation campaign, however, enjoyed only meager success.

24.5.B   Greek Enmity Toward Athens

Thucydides 2.8.4–5

(**2.8.4**) Popular support inclined very much toward the Lacedaemonians, especially since they had declared that they were liberating Greece. Every individual and every city was eager to give the Spartan cause all possible moral and practical support, and they thought the effort was held back if they were not personally involved. (**8.5**) So great was the anger that most people felt toward Athens, some wanting to be freed from its empire, and others fearful of falling under its sway.

Question

1. What advantages and constraints shaped the Spartan strategy (**24.5.A–B**, WEB **24.6**)?

24.7   The "Periclean Strategy"

Pericles' strategy relied heavily on Athens' financial strength to sustain the war effort. He advocated a policy of avoiding fighting the Spartans on land, preserving the integrity of the empire, and shunning new territorial acquisitions. It appears that Pericles aimed to win the war by bringing the Spartans to the realization that they could not defeat Athens.

Thucydides has Pericles describe his strategy and Athens' resources in a speech prior to the Peloponnesians' first invasion of Attica in the summer of 431. See also Thucydides 2.65.6: WEB **19.14.II**: "Pericles' Leadership."

24.7.A   Pericles on the Athenian Strategy

Thucydides 2.13.2–8; cf. 1.143.4–144.1

(**2.13.2**) As for the present situation [summer 431], Pericles gave them the same advice as before, telling them to prepare for war and bring their property in from the fields. They were not to go out to battle, but come into the city and protect it, and they should fit out the fleet, their area of strength, and keep a tight grip on the allies. Their might derived from the financial revenues provided by the allies, he declared, and success in war came mostly from strategic thinking and abundant finances. (**13.3**) They should have confidence since the city had an average income of 600 talents per annum in tribute from the allies, other revenue apart, and there was still a reserve of 6,000 talents of coined silver on the acropolis (the maximum had been 9,700 talents, but from that sum moneys had been spent on the Propylaea of the acropolis, on other buildings, and on Potidaea).[1] (**13.4**) There was, in addition, uncoined gold and silver in private and public votive offerings, various religious objects used for processions and competitions, Persian spoils and the like, amounting to not less than 500 talents. (**13.5**) He further added the money in the other temples (no meager sum) on which they could draw;[2] and if they were completely bankrupt, they could make use of the gold plating of the goddess [Athena] herself (he noted that, in refined gold, the statue had a weight of forty talents, and that it was all detachable).[3] This they could use for their security, he said, but they would have to replace it in its entirety.

(**13.6**) Such were Pericles' words of encouragement in the area of finance. He then added that Athens possessed 13,000 hoplites, not including those in the garrisons and those defending the wall, who totaled 16,000. (**13.7**) These were the numbers on guard duty at the start, when the enemy made their attacks, and they comprised the oldest and youngest fighting men, and metics [resident aliens] who were hoplites. For the wall of Phaleron ran for 35 stades [ca. 6.3 km] to the wall encircling the city, and of that encircling wall 43 stades [ca. 7.7 km] were manned (though a section, between the Long Wall and the wall of Phaleron, remained unmanned). The Long Walls ran for forty stades to Piraeus, and the outer one was manned. The entire length of the wall encircling Piraeus and Munychia ran to sixty stades, and half of it was garrisoned. (**13.8**) Pericles also noted that they possessed 1,200 cavalry, including the mounted archers, 1,600 regular archers, and 300 seaworthy triremes ...

Notes

1. *The tribute quota lists mention only around 400 talents income for this year, and Thucydides' figure of 600 may include potential revenues. The 6,000 talents is a probable reference to the treasury of Athens. When Potidaea surrendered in 430/29, the total cost of its siege ran to 2,000 talents (Thucydides 2.70.2).*
2. *If what is known as Callias' decree (ML no. 58) was proposed in 434/3, those treasuries were consolidated into one.*
3. *The Athenians never used the emergency "fund" of the gold on Athena's statue.*

Given the underdeveloped stage of siege warfare in 431 as well as the Peloponnesians' inability to mount a prolonged and costly siege, Athens could feel secure behind its walls and well provided for thanks to its navy. Even so, Athens' reaction to the invasion was not entirely passive, because the Athenians harassed the enemy with their cavalry. Its navy too made seaborne raids on Peloponnesian shores. Indeed, the Athenians must have felt that as a maritime power, they had a built-in strategic advantage over Spartan land power.

The author of the *Constitution of the Athenians*, wrongly attributed to Xenophon, lists Athens' maritime advantage over a land power.

24.7.B The Superiority of Naval Power

[Xenophon] *Constitution of the Athenians* 2.3–6

(**2.3**) As for the mainland cities now under the sway of the Athenians, the large ones are ruled by fear, and the small ones entirely by necessity. For there is no city that does not need to import and export goods, and a city will not be able to engage in such activities unless it obeys those who control the seaways.

(**2.4**) Next, those who rule the seas are able to do what those with control of the land can do only occasionally, that is lay waste the land of those stronger than them; for they can sail to points where there is no enemy, or where the enemy is few in number – and if he approaches they can simply board their ships and sail off. And anyone doing that is less frustrated than the man coming to help with infantry.

(**2.5**) Next, those in control at sea can sail as far from their country as they please, but land powers cannot make a journey of many days from theirs – marching is slow, and a man on foot cannot carry food sufficient for a long period. Moreover, advancing on foot one must pass through friendly territory, or else conquer the land by fighting, while the man sailing can disembark where he is stronger, and not disembark in the area where he is not. He can, instead, sail off until he reaches friendly territory or an enemy weaker than himself.

(**2.6**) Then there are the crop diseases that are sent by Zeus. Those who have power on land are badly affected by these, but the sea power bears them easily. For not all the land is struck with the blight at the one time, so that alimentation comes to those controlling the sea from where the land is in good condition.

 See WEB **24.8.I** for Thucydides on the Athenian and Spartan "national characters" that impacted their strategies, and WEB **24.8.II** for comments on problems in the strategies of both states.

Questions

1. What were the "dos" and "don'ts" of the Periclean strategy and why?
2. What made land power inferior to maritime power, according to the "Old Oligarch"? What advantages did land power have?

Review Questions

1. Discuss the causes of the Peloponnesian War according to Thucydides. Do you agree with his ranking of them in order of significance (**24.1**, WEB **24.2.I–II**)?
 2. What was Corinth's role in the Peloponnesian War (**24.1**, **24,3**, WEB **24.2.I–II**)?
3. What were the strengths and weaknesses of the Spartan war strategy (**24.5**, WEB **24.6**, WEB **24.8.I–II**)? What accounted for them?
 4. What were the strengths and weaknesses of the Athenian war strategy (**24.7**, WEB **24.6**, WEB **24.8.I–II**)?
5. What were the risks for Athens and Sparta in *not* going to war? Do they justify their decision to fight?

Suggested Readings

The causes of the Peloponnesian War: Kagan 1969; Ste Croix 1972; Cawkwell 1997, 20–39; Lazenby 2004, 16–30; Rhodes 2006, 80–89. *The Corcyran affair*: J. Wilson 1987, 2–64; Crane 1998, 93–124. *The Megarian Decree*: Fornara 1975. *Aspasia*: M. Henry 1995, *passim*, esp. 10–28; Podlecki 1998, 109–117. *Athenian resources*: Kallet-Marx 1993; Samons 2000; Kallet 2001. *Spartan resources*: Loomis 1992. *The Athenian and Spartan strategies*: Westlake 1945 (Athens); Brunt 1965 (Sparta); Kagan 1974, esp. 17–42 (both); Cawkwell 1975 (Athens); Kelly 1982 (Sparta); Strauss and Ober 1990 (Athens); Lazenby 2004, 31–38 (both). *The short-term effect of the Peloponnesian invasions*: Hanson 1998, but see also Throne 2001. *Athenian cavalry and the Peloponnesian invasion*: Spence 1990. *Acharnia*: Whitehead 1986, esp. 397–400.

25

The Peloponnesian War

The Archidamian War (431–421)

Ancient Greece from Homer to Alexander: The Evidence, First Edition. Joseph Roisman.
© 2011 Blackwell Publishing Ltd. Translations © 2011 John Yardley. Published 2011 by Blackwell Publishing Ltd.

The Peloponnesian War is divided into three major periods. The first one, named after the Spartan king Archidamus, is known as the Archidamian War and lasted from the first Peloponnesian invasion of Attica in 431 to the Peace of Nicias in 421 which put a temporary end to the hostilities. The second period, 421–413, was marked by tense relations between Athens and Sparta and some major campaigns, including an Athenian invasion of Sicily. The last period is known as the Decelean War and lasted from 413 to Athens' defeat and surrender in 404. This chapter deals with the first period. The broad extent and sporadic character of military activities between 431 and 421 allow us to focus only on major events and developments. The chapter includes a description of a plague that hit Athens early in the war, and an archaeological find of a mass grave containing its likely victims. Pericles died in the plague, and the chapter describes his political successors, including Nicias and Cleon. It then examines a campaign in Pylos in the Peloponnese that changed the direction of the war and ended with the surprising surrender of Spartan troops to Athens. The chapter also discusses the general Brasidas, who moved Spartan operations to northern Greece, and the Peace of Nicias that concluded the Archidamian War.

25.1 Athens and the Plague

Until the Pylos campaign of 425 (**25.7**), the Spartan military efforts generally centered on annual invasions of Attica, which had only limited impact. The second Peloponnesian invasion of Attica in 430, however, came close to producing significant results. It lasted forty days, and the harm inflicted on the Athenians both by the invasion and by a plague led to the impeachment and fining of Pericles and to peace negotiations with Sparta (Thucydides 2.59.1–2). The attempt at peace failed, however, and the Athenians ree-lected Pericles to office. See WEB **25.2.I** for Plutarch's account of Pericles' conviction.

Between 430 and 426 Athens suffered from a devastating plague, which according to some estimates killed about a third of its population. Overcrowd-ing behind Athens' walls during the Spartan invasions enhanced the spread of the disease. See WEB **25.2.II** for Thucydides' famous description of the plague.

Modern attempts to identify the disease have run into difficulties. Known epidemics fail to exhibit all the symptoms described by Thucydides, who might have omitted what are thought of today as important clues. Possible mutations over time might also have obliterated the disease. The most popular identifications were smallpox and typhus. A potential hope emerged for a positive identification following excavation work for a subway station near the ancient Kerameikos cemetery in Athens in 1994. Archaeologists found a burial place of some ninety skeletons, including ten children. The burial site might have contained up to 150 dead. There was no soil separating the skeletons, and the relatively few simple burial vessels accompanying them have

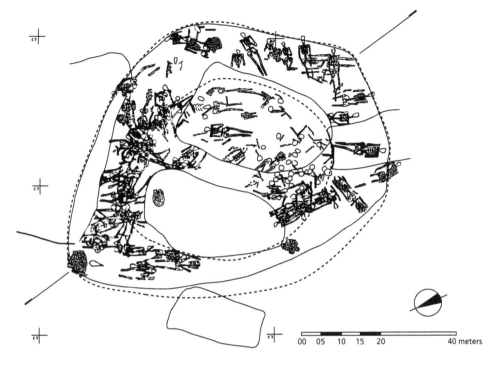

Figure 25.1
Plan of a mass burial in the Kerameikos. From E. Baziotopoulou-Valavani, "A Mass Burial from the Cemetery of Kerameikos." © Effie Baziotopoulou-Valavani. Reprinted with kind permission of the author.

00 05 10 15 20   40 meters

been dated to the second half of the fifth century. Some skeletons were piled on top of one another (cf. Thucydides 2.52.4 below and Figure 25.1). The site has been identified as a mass grave for victims of the plague.

Although DNA tests performed on the pulp of randomly selected teeth found bacteria responsible for a typhoid fever, other studies have raised questions about possible contamination, the accuracy of the results, and the small sample. It is still likely that a now-extinct disease occasioned the plague.

25.1.A   A Mass Grave in Athens

Thucydides follows his report of the symptoms of disease by describing its social and psychological effects. It appears that he was especially interested in these because they confirmed for him the (sophistic) notion that true human nature (*physis*) lurks under culture (*nomos*), or civilized conduct, and that this nature best reveals itself in times of crisis. Indeed, it may be no accident that Thucydides placed the description of the physical and social impact of the plague right after Pericles' hymn to the virtues of the Athenians and their polis in his funeral oration (WEB **23.6.II**: "Pericles' Funeral Oration"). However, the impact of the plague on Athens should not be overstated because the city continued to be militarily active and even had some successes.

25.1.B   Thucydides on Human Conduct During a Plague

Thucydides 2.52.1–53.4

(**2.52.1**) The mass exodus from the countryside into the city only aggravated the already existing difficulties, especially for those who came in. (**52.2**) There were no houses available, and as they lived in stifling huts in the summer season the loss of life knew no bounds. The bodies of the dying lay heaped on top of each other and, in the streets and around all the public fountains, people half-dead stumbled about craving water. (**52.3**) Temples in which they sought shelter were filled with the cadavers of those who died there. Under the overwhelming pressure of the calamity, people had no idea what would become of them and they began to disregard sacred and profane duties alike. (**52.4**) All customs relating to funerals that they formerly observed were upset, and they buried the dead as best they could. Many, short of friends because of the numbers that had already died before them, turned to abominable funerary expedients. Some would unload a corpse of their own family on another's pyre and set it alight before those who had built it could use it, and others would throw the corpse they were carrying on another that was burning and then run off.

(**53.1**) The plague was for the city the first step toward increasing lawlessness in other respects, too, as everyone ventured the more readily to indulge in pleasures, their proclivity for which they had previously kept hidden; for they could see the abrupt changes in circumstances, with the rich suddenly dying and those who earlier had nothing now possessing their property. (**53.2**) They accordingly saw fit to enjoy their possessions swiftly and for pleasure, thinking both their persons and their belongings to be of short duration. (**53.3**) Nobody was eager to keep struggling for what appeared an honorable cause when he thought it uncertain whether he would die before achieving it. Immediate gratification, and whatever was conducive to it – this was now what was noble and useful. (**53.4**) No fear of heaven or law of mankind held them back from anything. They reckoned that being or not being pious came to the same thing because they could see everybody dying indiscriminately, and none expected to live long enough to be judged and punished for his misdeeds. They thought that a much more serious sentence had been passed and was hanging over their heads, and before it came down on them it was reasonable for them to enjoy life a little.

Questions

1. What conventions were transgressed during the plague and how (see also WEB **25.2.II**)?
2. How were ordinary Athenians likely to interpret the plague (cf. WEB **25.2.II**)?

25.3   Pericles' Political Successors

In the summer of 427 Athens dispatched a fleet to help the Sicilian city of Leontini against Syracuse. Following a Syracusan initiative, the warring parties in Sicily reconciled and the Athenian fleet was forced to leave the island three years later. See WEB **25.4** for Thucydides on the opening of a second Athenian front in Sicily.

Athens' intervention in Sicily was a deviation from Pericles' strategy of avoiding new military commitments and yielded no significant gains. It would be inaccurate, however, to claim that Pericles' death in the plague in 429 made initiatives such as this possible. Nevertheless, Thucydides regarded Pericles' death as a crucial turning point in Athenian history, because it ushered in an age of significantly less accomplished leaders. After eulogizing Pericles' leadership and characterizing him as the first citizen in the polis (WEB **19.14.II**: "Pericles' Leadership"), the historian contrasts him with his political successors.

Thucydides 2.65.10–11

(**2.65.10**) The leaders who came after Pericles were more on a par with each other and, as they all struggled to be first, they turned to gratifying the whims of the people and putting policy in their hands. (**65.11**) The result was what one might expect in the context of a great city governing an empire: there were many blunders, and in particular the [second] expedition to Sicily [415–413]. Here it was less miscalculation with regard to the enemy than a failure by those dispatching the force to provide proper support for those who were on it. Instead, through their personal squabbles over the leadership of the demos, they both weakened the expedition's military effectiveness and, for the first time, gave rise to internal discord over state policy.

Questions

1. What, according to Thucydides, were the real and pretended reasons for Athens' intervention in Sicily (see WEB **25.4**)?
2. What was wrong with the leaders who came after Pericles, according to Thucydides?

25.5 Nicias and Cleon

Nicias and Cleon were the leading political figures to succeed Pericles before they were joined by the aristocrat Alcibiades. Neither man belonged to the great families of Athens, but both came from wealthy houses. This was especially true for Nicias, who is said to have rented to the state 1,000 slaves to work the silver mines (Xenophon *Ways and Means* 4.14). It appears that Nicias followed the traditional ways of gaining influence and popularity by spending money on public services and by holding public offices. He was a successful general before he led the Sicilian expedition of 415–413 that ended in disaster and his death. As Plutarch's description suggests, the ancient sources treated him more kindly than Cleon. Plutarch describes Nicias' and Cleon's different political styles.

25.5.A   Plutarch on Nicias

Plutarch *Nicias* 3.1–3

(**3.1**) Pericles' leadership of the city rested on genuine virtue and powerful speaking ability, and he had no need of pretensions or empty rhetoric before the masses. Nicias, however, lacked these qualities, but he did have superior financial resources, and he used these to gain leadership of the people. (**3.2**) To win over the Athenians, he did not think he could compete with Cleon's recklessness and buffoonery, all tailored to give pleasure, and he tried to win popular support with dramatic performances, athletic competitions, and other such expensive spectacles, outdoing all his predecessors and contemporaries in the costliness and splendor of the displays. (**3.3**) There remained still standing in my time some of his votive offerings: the Palladium on the acropolis, which has lost its gilding, and also, in the precinct of Dionysus, the shrine that lies below the tripods that he dedicated for his choral victories. For he won many victories as a *choregos*, and was never defeated [as a *choregos*] ...

 See WEB **25.6.I** for Nicias' piety and munificence and for a link to additional information about him.

The author of *Ath. Pol.* concurs with Thucydides' assessment of the leaders who followed Pericles (**25.3**). He describes Cleon disapprovingly.

25.5.B   Cleon and the Demos

Ath. Pol. 28.3

On the death of Pericles, Nicias (who later died in Sicily) became leader of the men of note, and Cleon son of Cleaenetus became leader of the people. It was Cleon who, more than anyone, seems to have corrupted the people with his impulsive behavior. He was the first to shout and use abusive language on the speaker's platform, and to pull his cloak up about him to harangue the people, while all others were dignified in their delivery ...

Cleon's father owned a tannery, which provided material for jokes about his son. Cleon was chiefly known for his rhetorical prowess and style, which offended traditional conventions. Thucydides describes him as "the most violent of citizens" (3.36.6), and the comic playwright Aristophanes heaps on him much abuse. In his comedy *Cavalrymen* (*Hippeis*, also translated as *Knights*), which was produced in 424, Aristophanes satirizes the Athenian political scene. He portrays the household of Demos of the Pnyx (the site of the assembly) in turmoil because of a new slave from barbarian Paphlagonia – a thinly disguised Cleon. The Paphlagonian is Demos' favorite and actually controls the house by flattering his master and extorting and intimidating other slaves. One of these slaves plans to unseat the Paphlagonian/Cleon by pitting him against a sausage seller – a lowly and vulgar trade – in a competition to flatter and pamper Demos. In the following dialogue, Aristophanes pokes fun at both the people and their leaders.

Aristophanes *Cavalrymen* 177–221

(**177**) FIRST SLAVE:	"No, all these things are for sale through you! You'll become a very big man, as the oracle here says."
SAUSAGE SELLER:	"Tell me, how am I, a sausage seller, going to become a man?"
(**180**) FIRST SLAVE:	"That's just what's going to make you great! You're worthless, you hang around the market, and you're impudent."
SAUSAGE SELLER:	"I really don't think I deserve great power."
FIRST SLAVE:	"Oh dear! What's this you're saying about not deserving it? Seems to me you have some good on your conscience! (**185**) Not from a genteel family, are you?"
SAUSAGE SELLER:	"God, no! Just from a worthless bunch."
FIRST SLAVE:	"Lucky fellow. What a great background you've got for public life!"
SAUSAGE SELLER:	"But, Sir, I got no education apart from primary, and even that's pretty shaky."
(**190**) FIRST SLAVE:	"The only thing wrong there is having it even shakily. Being leader of the people [*demagogos*] is not for an educated man or one with good character – it's for a shameless ignoramus. But don't pass by what the gods are promising you in their oracles."
(**195**) SAUSAGE SELLER:	"So what does the oracle say?"
FIRST SLAVE:	"By God, it's good – cunning and cleverly cryptic; 'But when the crooked-clawed leather eagle seizes with its beak the stupid blood-drinking snake, then will the garlic pickle of the Paphlagonian be destroyed, (**200**) and then will the god grant great renown to tripe-sellers, unless they elect to sell sausages instead.'"
SAUSAGE SELLER:	"What's that got to do with me? Tell me that."
FIRST SLAVE:	"This Paphlagonian is the leather eagle."
SAUSAGE SELLER:	"But what about 'crooked-clawed'?"
(**205**) FIRST SLAVE:	"It means that he grabs and takes with crooked hands."
SAUSAGE SELLER:	"And what about the snake?"
FIRST SLAVE:	"That's self-evident. The snake is a long thing, and a sausage is a long thing, and the sausage and snake are both blood-drinking. So it's saying that the snake will conquer the leather eagle – (**210**) unless it's softened by the heat of its words."
SAUSAGE SELLER:	"The oracle pleases me, but I'm amazed that I of all people am able to govern the demos."
FIRST SLAVE:	"That's very easy. Keep on doing what you're doing. (**215**) Keep hashing and mincing everything up, and always win the demos' favor by cooking up phrases. You have everything else that makes the demagogue: a terrible voice, low birth, and a guttersnipe's character. (**220**) You have all it takes for politics. And the oracles and Pythian shrine agree …"

See WEB **25.6.II** for Aristophanes' comic depiction of Cleon as the people's watchdog and comments on Cleon's leadership and image.

In 428 the city of Mytilene on the island of Lesbos rebelled against Athens. It surrendered to Athens the year after, and its fate was debated in Athens between Cleon, who advocated execution and enslavement, and Diodotus, who successfully argued for leniency based on utilitarian grounds. Thucydides uses the debate, commonly known as the "Mytilenean Debate," to raise questions about the relationship between speaker and audience, the tension between the rule of law and the rule of the people, and the relationship between justice and expediency (3.37.1–50.3). See WEB **25.6.III** for the Mytilenean affair.

Questions

1. How did Nicias and Cleon maintain their leadership (**25.5.A–B**, WEB **25.6.I–II**)?

2. What qualifies a man for popular leadership according to Aristophanes (**25.5.C**, WEB **25.6.II**)? Stripped of their comic cloth, what was expected of an Athenian leader?

3. To what extent does Cleon in the Mytilenean Debate (WEB **25.6.III**) fit the way he is portrayed by Aristophanes (**25.5.C**, WEB **25.6.II**)?

4. Why, according to the speakers in the Mytilenean Debate, was it good for Athens to punish the rebels, but also to be lenient toward them (WEB **25.6.III**)?

25.7 The Pylos Campaign (425)

Until 425, neither Sparta nor Athens won victories that decided or even altered the course of the war. All this changed following the Pylos campaign.

In spring 425, the Athenians sent a fleet of forty ships to Sicily. On its way there it was supposed to aid the democrats in Corcyra against oligarch exiles. A Peloponnesian navy of sixty vessels had already been sent to Corcyra to help the oligarchs. The Athenian generals in charge of the fleet were Sophocles (not the playwright) and Eurymedon. They were joined by Demosthenes, who had won a victory for Athens in Acarnania in western Greece the year before. Demosthenes also established excellent relations with the Messenians who occupied Naupactus after their exile from Mt. Ithome (cf. Thucydides 1.103.1–3: **18.14**: "The Messenians Settle Naupactus").

25.7.A Demosthenes' Plan

Thucydides 4.2.4–3.3

(**4.2.4**) …Demosthenes was just a private citizen after his return from Acarnania but, in response to a request on his part, the Athenians told him he could use these ships around the Peloponnese, if he wished.

(**3.1**) When the Athenians reached the coast of Laconia, they learned that the Peloponnesian ships were already at Corcyra. Eurymedon and Sophocles were all for pressing ahead to Corcyra, but Demosthenes insisted that they continue the voyage only after putting in at Pylos and doing what needed to be done. They opposed his idea, but as it happened a storm arose that drove the ships to Pylos. (**3.2**) Demosthenes immediately suggested that they fortify the place (which was his reason for sailing with them), and he pointed to the plentiful supply of wood and stones to be found there. He further noted that it was a naturally strong position, and that, along with much of the surrounding countryside, it was uninhabited. Pylos is some 400 stades [ca. 72 km] from Sparta, and lies in what was once the land of Messenia – the Spartans call it Coryphasium.

(**3.3**) The other two replied that there were a lot of uninhabited capes in the Peloponnese if he wanted to run up expenses for the city by seizing them. Demosthenes, however, thought this place had important differences from any other. There was a harbor nearby, and the Messenians, who in early times were natives there, and who spoke the same dialect as the Spartans, would cause the Spartans very serious damage if they could use it as their base. They would also serve as a strong garrison for the place.

What Demosthenes suggested was *epiteichismos*, that is, to establish a permanent, fortified place in enemy territory from which a force would be able to harass the locals on a regular basis, and in Pylos' case, to spread the seeds of revolt among the Messenians. The Athenians left Demosthenes in Pylos with a relatively small force and sailed to Corcyra. The Spartans were alarmed, recalled their invading army from Attica, and attacked Demosthenes by land and sea. In preparation for an expected Athenian rescue operation, they occupied the island of Sphacteria, which lay across from Pylos at the entrance to the bay where their navy was anchored (Map 25.1, p. 340). There they left 420 Spartans and their helots.

The Spartan attempt to regain Pylos failed, and then the Athenian fleet returned to defeat the Peloponnesian navy and become masters of the bay. It meant that the force on Sphacteria was now separated from the Peloponnesians on the shore and surrounded by enemy ships.

25.7.B   Sparta Offers Peace

Thucydides 4.15.1–2

(**4.15.1**) When news of the events at Pylos reached Sparta, it was seen as a major disaster, and it was decided that the authorities should go down to the camp to see how things stood and consider on the spot the action to be taken. (**15.2**) These people saw that it was impossible to help their men, and they also did not want to risk their being starved to death, or being compelled to surrender by superior numbers. They therefore decided to conclude with the Athenian generals – if they would agree – a truce limited to Pylos, and to send representatives to Athens to discuss a peace treaty and try to bring back their men as quickly as possible …

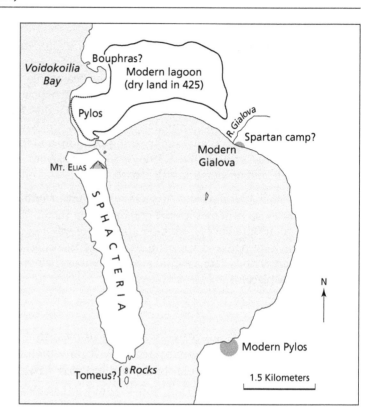

Map 25.1 Pylos and Sphacteria. After P.J. Rhodes, *Thucydides: History IV.1–V.24* (Warminster: Aris and Phillips, 1998). Reprinted with permission of Oxbow Books.

Thucydides reports the Spartan offer to Athens through a speech made by a Spartan delegation. After warning the Athenians not to be swayed by their good fortune, which might change, the Spartans made their offer.

Thucydides 4.19.1, 20.4

(4.19.1) ... The Lacedaemonians invite you to conclude a treaty and end the war, offering you peace, an alliance, and a close friendship in other respects, in return for which they ask only the men on the island. We think it better for both of us not to take the ultimate gamble ...

(20.4) ... And consider the advantages that are likely to be involved in this. If we and you agree in what we say, you can be sure that the rest of Greece, being our inferiors, will accord us the greatest respect ...

Spartan *oliganthropia*, or shortage of men, and the hope of removing the threat to Messenia from Pylos were the most likely incentives for the Spartans' peace offer. An additional incentive was the presence of important Spartans on the island. The Spartans' offer ignored their allies' interests and disavowed the official goal of liberating the Greeks, yet their hopes were disappointed.

Thucydides thought that the Athenians, led by Cleon, were too greedy in demanding in return control over places that Athens had given up in the Thirty-Year Peace (446). Both sides resumed hostilities. Thucydides proceeded to give a highly biased account that portrayed Cleon as a man entangled in the web of his own arrogant oratory. He reports that after Cleon made empty boasts about capturing Pylos, he was maneuvered by Nicias into assuming command and leaving for the island. It is more likely that Cleon had a clear plan of how to conclude the siege of the island, which was dragging on. See WEB **25.8** for the Athenians' battle with the Spartans on the island of Sphacteria.

Cleon and Demosthenes wanted the Spartans alive and offered a truce. The Spartans, whose command structure was now reduced to their third-ranking officer, agreed. They asked permission to consult with the Spartans on the mainland about what they should do.

25.7.C   The Spartans' Surrender

Thucydides 4.38.3–5

(**4.38.3**) The Athenians let none leave, but themselves called on heralds to come from the mainland. After two or three interchanges, the final herald to sail over from the Spartans on the mainland announced to them that "The Spartans bid you to decide for yourselves about your situation provided that you take no dishonorable action." After discussing the matter together, the men surrendered their weapons and themselves.

(**38.4**) Then, throughout that day and the oncoming night, the Athenians kept them under guard. The following day they set up a trophy on the island and made various preparations to sail, assigning custody of the men to the trierarchs. The Spartans sent a herald and brought back their dead. The count of the dead and prisoners that were taken alive was as follows. (**38.5**) In all, 420 hoplites had crossed to the island. Of these 292 were brought back alive, and the rest had been killed. Of those taken alive some 120 were Spartiates. Of the Athenians not many were lost, since it had not been a pitched battle.

Thucydides sums up the battle with an unkind remark about Cleon and describes the impact of the affair on Greek public opinion.

25.7.D   The Impact of Sphacteria

Thucydides 4.39.3–40.2

(**4.39.3**) The Athenians and Peloponnesians then withdrew their troops from Pylos and went home, and Cleon's promise, harebrained though it was, actually came off – within twenty days he brought back the men, as he had undertaken to do.

(**40.1**) Of all the events of the war, this one came as the greatest shock to the Greeks. They had not expected the Spartans to be starved into, or forced into, surrendering their weapons; they assumed that they would keep them and die fighting any way they could. (**40.2**) They could not believe that the men who surrendered were the equals of those who died. An Athenian ally later asked one of the prisoners-of-war from the island, in order to taunt him, whether it was the fallen who were really the Spartans tried and true [*kaloi k'agathoi*]. The man answered that a spindle [*atraktos*] – by which he meant an arrow[1] – would be very valuable if it distinguished the true men. He was thus suggesting that any man who died was simply one who chanced to be in the way of the stones and arrows.

Note

1. *The Spartan's reference to a spindle, which was associated with women, echoed the low esteem in which light-armed troops were held in comparison to the hoplites.*

25.7.E   A Spartan Shield from Pylos

A bronze cover of a shield, now on exhibit in the Museum of the Ancient Agora at Athens, is engraved with the inscription: "The Athenians from the Lacedaemonians from Pylos" (Figure 25.2).

Questions

1. What were Demosthenes' aims in fortifying Pylos (**25.7.A**)?
2. Should the Athenians have accepted the Spartan peace offer (**25.7.B**)?

Figure 25.2 A Spartan shield from Pylos. Photograph by Joseph Roisman.

3. How were the Athenians able to defeat the Spartans on Sphacteria (WEB **25.8**)?

4. When the Spartans surrounded on Sphacteria asked their authorities what they should do, the answer was: "The Spartans bid you to decide for yourselves about your situation provided that you take no dishonorable action." What does this answer mean and what does it say about the Spartan government?

5. Why did the Spartans on the island not follow the example of Thermopylae?

25.9 Brasidas

The Athenian victory at Pylos required a change in Spartan strategy. Invasions were no longer an option because the Athenians threatened to execute Spartan prisoners if their land was invaded again. There was a danger of helotic revolt, and in summer 424 Nicias added to the Spartans' worries when he captured the island of Cythera, thus making Spartan shores vulnerable to Athenian raids. The time was ripe, then, for the Spartan general Brasidas to make his mark.

Brasidas had distinguished himself in earlier operations as a daring commander. It was probably thanks to Brasidas that Sparta now redirected her efforts into hitting Athens at her most vulnerable point, namely, her allies. Brasidas chose the Chalcidian peninsula and the Thracian shore for his operations. To avoid the precedent of Pylos, he took with him only a few Spartans and an army composed chiefly of freed helots and Peloponnesian recruits and mercenaries. In the summer of 424 he showed himself in the north; after a failed attempt to cooperate with the Macedonian king Perdiccas (II), he approached the Chalcidian city of Acanthus. Thucydides says that the way he persuaded the Acanthians to desert Athens resembled his *modus operandi* elsewhere. He also assesses Brasidas' contribution to bringing the two sides to peace.

25.9.A Brasidas' Impact

Thucydides 4.81.1–3; 4.86.1–4; 4.87.2–3; 4.88.1

(**4.81.1**) The Spartans sent out Brasidas because he was very eager to have the assignment, and the Chalcidians were also very much in support of him. He was a man who was regarded in Sparta as enterprising in all situations, and who, when out of Sparta, proved to be of great value to the Spartans.

(**81.2**) In the short term he displayed a fair and even-handed attitude toward the city-states, and in many cases he engineered revolt, though some places he took through treachery. The result was that when the Lacedaemonians wanted to make terms (as they later did), it was possible for them to hand over places, and receive others in exchange, and to pull the war back from the Peloponnese. Moreover, later on in the war, following the events in Sicily, the integrity and intelligence that Brasidas revealed at this time (some experiencing it first-hand, and others knowing of it by hearsay) did much to instill positive feelings for the Spartans among the allies of the Athenians. (**81.3**) For he was the first Spartan to go out to them and, as he appeared to be an all-round good man, he left with the allied states a firm expectation that the other Spartans were just like him.

In his address to the city of Acanthus, Brasidas recalled the Spartans' promise at the beginning of the war to be the liberators of Greece and stated that he was there to implement it.

25.9.B   Brasidas' Speech to the Acanthians

(**4.86.1**) "I have come not to do harm but to liberate the Greeks, and I have made the Spartan authorities swear the greatest of oaths that any I bring on side will be autonomous allies. At the same time our purpose is not to make you our allies by attaching you to us through coercion or deception; no, rather it is to become allies to you, who have been made into slaves by the Athenians. (**86.2**) So I do not think I myself should be suspected by you, offering as I do the greatest guarantees, nor be judged incapable of helping you; you should have confidence and come over to us.

(**86.3**) And if anyone is not eager for that through personal fear of someone, feeling that I may put the city in the hands of one faction or another, he most of all should trust me. (**86.4**) For I have not come to take part in your factional quarrels, and I do not think I would be bringing you transparent freedom if, disregarding Spartan tradition, I should enslave the majority to the few or the minority to the masses…"

If, however, the Acanthians refused Brasidas' offer of freedom…

(**87.2**) "… In that case, I shall make the gods and heroes of this country witness to the fact that, though I have come well intentioned, I cannot persuade you, and that I shall try to force agreement from you by ravaging your lands. And I shall not think at that point that I am doing wrong, (**87.3**) but I shall feel justified in the face of two overwhelming considerations. These are, first, that despite your being well disposed to the Spartans, they not suffer harm from the moneys paid by you to the Athenians, if you refuse to join us [the Spartans] and in the case of the Greeks, that their release from slavery not be prevented by you…"

(**88.1**) Such were Brasidas' words. After many arguments had been put forward on both sides, the Acanthians held a secret vote. And because of Brasidas' seductive words and from fear for their grapes, the majority voted for secession from Athens; and they made Brasidas swear to keep the oaths the Spartan authorities had sworn when they sent him out, namely that any he brought on side would remain autonomous. With that they let in his army…

Brasidas succeeded in attracting other allies to his cause by similar means. The crown of his achievement was the important city of Amphipolis, which he captured under the nose of the historian Thucydides, who was the Athenian general in charge of the area. Thucydides probably went into exile because of the loss, but he reserved his resentment for those who exiled him, primarily Cleon, rather than the Spartan general whom he greatly admired.

The spread of revolt among the allies, and an Athenian defeat to a Boeotian coalition in a land battle at Delium, invigorated Athenians who were looking for a peaceful resolution of the conflict. Several Aristophanic comedies and a lost play by Euripides, *Cresphontes*, reflected the contemporary desire for peace in the city. See WEB **25.10** for how these plays reflected the yearning for peace in Athens.

Nicias was the major Athenian advocate for peace, and in early 423 Athens and Sparta agreed on a one-year truce as a preliminary to a more permanent settlement. But when the cities of Scione and Mende went over to Brasidas after the truce, he refused to give them up. Neither the Athenians nor the Spartans were able (or willing) to persuade Brasidas to change his mind, thus revealing the problems that the polis encountered and would continue to encounter in dealing with a strong man. When the term of the truce expired in 422, Cleon took an army to the Chalcidian region. He sailed to the city of Torone and captured it following a fierce battle.

25.9.C   Athens Punishes Torone

Thucydides 5.3.4

Cleon and the Athenians set up two trophies, one at the harbor and one next to the wall. Of the inhabitants of Torone they sold the women and children into slavery, and the men they sent to Athens along with the Peloponnesians and any Chalcidians in the city, a total of 700. The Peloponnesian contingent later returned home under the terms of the peace that was negotiated, and the rest were ransomed by the Olynthians on a man-for-man basis.

The harsh Athenian treatment of Torone, and in the summer of 421 that of Scione, whose adult male population was killed and the women and children enslaved (Thucydides 5.32.1), would later come back to haunt them. After the war they were afraid they would be treated similarly (Xenophon *Hellenica* 2.2.3).

Sometime after the capture of Torone in summer 422, Cleon and Brasidas met in battle near Amphipolis. The Athenians were defeated, and both bellicose generals lost their lives. Thucydides describes Cleon's conduct in the battle of Amphipolis as cowardly (5.10.9).

25.9.D   Brasidas' Last Honors

Thucydides 5.11.1

After that, with a procession under arms, all the allies gave Brasidas a state burial in the city of Amphipolis in front of what today is the agora. The people of Amphipolis fenced off his funerary monument and ever since have been making offerings to him as a hero; and they have granted him games and annual sacrifices. They have regarded him as the colony's founder, and have torn down the buildings of Hagnon and obliterated any memorial of his colonization that might survive.[1] They considered Brasidas to have been their savior, and were also cultivating their alliance with the Spartans at this time through fear of the Athenians. And because of their hostility to the Athenians, it would not be as expedient or gratifying for them for Hagnon to receive such honors.

Note

1. *Hagnon was the Athenian founder of Amphipolis in 437/6 (see **20.20**: "The Foundation of Amphipolis").*

Questions

1. What, according to Thucydides, was Brasidas' impact on the war (**25.9.A**)?
2. What, according to Brasidas, were the rewards of joining the Spartan side or the costs of refusal (**25.9.B**)?
3. Relate Brasidas' campaign and the Athenian reaction to the Mytilenean Debate on Athens' treatment of her allies (**25.6.A–C**, WEB **25.6.III**).

25.11   The Peace of Nicias (421)

Thucydides sums up the considerations of Athens and Sparta in their decision to make peace.

25.11.A   Athens' and Sparta's Motives for the Peace

Thucydides 5.14.1–15.1

(**5.14.1**) It turned out that after the battle of Amphipolis and Rhamphias' withdrawal from Thessaly[1] neither side engaged in further military operations and instead began to turn their thoughts toward peace. The Athenians had suffered a blow at Delium[2] and again at Amphipolis a little later, and they no longer had the confidence in their strength that had earlier led them to refuse the truce, when they thought that with their good fortune they would emerge on top. (**14.2**) At the same time they were afraid of disaffection spreading amongst their allies, who would be emboldened by the Athenian failures, and they were sorry they had not come to terms when they had a good opportunity to do so after the Pylos affair.

(**14.3**) The Spartans for their part found the war turning out not as they had expected. They had thought they would crush Athenian power in a few short years by ravaging their territory. But they had fallen prey to a disaster on the island the like of which Sparta had never experienced, and their land was subjected to raids from Pylos and Cythera. Furthermore, the helots were deserting, and there was always a fear that even those who remained, relying on those outside the country and considering the present circumstances, would revolt as they had before. (**14.4**) It happened, too, that their thirty-year truce with Argos was about to expire, and the Argives did not want to conclude another unless the territory of Cynuria were returned to them.[3] Taking on simultaneous wars with the Argives and the Athenians struck the Spartans as impossible. They also harbored a suspicion that some of the cities in the Peloponnese would defect to the Argives (and this actually happened).

(**15.1**) As the two sides weighed up such considerations, it seemed best to them to come to an accord, and to the Spartans especially, because of their desire to bring back the men from the island. For the Spartiates amongst them were leading citizens and also their kinsmen...

Notes

1. *Rhamphias was a Spartan commander who brought reinforcements to Brasidas. He returned home after the Thessalians refused to let him go through their land after Brasidas' death.*
2. *In 424/3 the Boeotians defeated the Athenians in the battle of Delium.*
3. *Cynuria, or Thyreatis, was a frontier zone which the Argives lost to Sparta following the "Battle of Champions" ca. 545 (see WEB **8.5**: "The Battle of Champions").*

In the spring of 421 the two states signed a peace treaty, known as the Peace of Nicias. The Spartans did not protect their northeastern allies as Brasidas had promised, but surrendered them to Athens or exposed them to future Athenian pressure. Like the Athenians, they unilaterally excluded their allies from any future negotiations on altering the peace agreement. They would pay the price for their selfish policy in later years. The following are selected clauses of the peace treaty.

25.11.B   Selected Terms of the Peace of Nicias

Thucydides 5.18.1–3, 5, 7–11

(**5.18.1**) A treaty was concluded by the Athenians and by the Lacedaemonians and their allies on the following terms, to which they swore city by city:

(**18.2**) Regarding the common sanctuaries, anyone so wishing is permitted to offer sacrifices, visit them, consult oracles, and attend festivals according to ancestral custom, by land and sea, without fear ...

(**18.3**) The treaty shall be binding on the Athenians and the Athenians' allies, and on the Spartans and the Spartans' allies, for fifty years, and is to be observed without deception or violence both by land and sea ...

(**18.5**) The Spartans and their allies are to restore Amphipolis to the Athenians. As regards such cities as the Lacedaemonians have restored to the Athenians, their inhabitants are to be allowed to go wherever they wish, taking their property with them. The cities are to pay the tribute fixed in the time of Aristides and are to be autonomous. The Athenians and their allies are not to be permitted to bear arms against them to hurt them, provided they pay the tribute, when the truce comes into force. The cities are: Argilus, Stagirus, Acanthus, Scolus, Olynthus, and Spartolus. These are to be allies of neither side, neither of the Lacedaemonians nor of Athenians, but should the Athenians succeed in persuading the cities, they may make them Athenian allies, if the cities are willing...

(**18.7**) The Spartans and their allies are to restore Panactum to the Athenians. And the Athenians are to restore to the Spartans Coryphasium [Pylos], Cythera, Methana, Ptelium, and Atalante, and all such

Spartans as are in the prison of the Athenians or in a prison elsewhere where the Athenians have power.[1] And those who are Peloponnesians amongst those under siege in Scione are to be released, along with the other Lacedaemonian allies in Scione and those whom Brasidas sent in, and any allies of the Lacedaemonians in prison in Athens or in a prison elsewhere where the Athenians have power. The Spartans and their allies are likewise to return any Athenians and Athenian allies that they are holding.

(**18.8**) With regard to Scione, Torone, Sermyle, or any other city in Athenian possession, the Athenians are to decide about these and the other cities as they see fit.

(**18.9**) The Athenians are to swear oaths to the Spartans and their allies city by city. In each case seventeen men from each city are to swear the strongest oath of the locality. The oath is to take this form: "I shall abide by the agreed terms and the treaty, justly and without deceit." The oath for the Spartans and their allies to the Athenians is to be of the same form, and both parties are to renew the oath each year. (**18.10**) They are to set up pillars at Olympia, Pytho [Delphi], the Isthmus, on the acropolis in Athens, and in the Amyclaeum in Sparta.

(**18.11**) If either party has forgotten anything with regard to any article, it shall be consistent with the oath for the two to make changes, following just discussions, at any point that the two, the Athenians and the Spartans, see fit.[2]

Notes

1. *Panactum was a site on the Attic border, which the Thebans held. The Spartans' plan to exchange it for Pylos failed. Cythera was an island south of the Peloponnese, Methana was in the Argolid, and Ptelium might have been in Thessaly on the Gulf of Pagasae. Atalante was in East Locris.*
2. *Among the Athenian signatories to the peace were Nicias and Demosthenes; among the Spartans were the two kings, Agis and Pleistoanax, and Tellis, probably Brasidas' father.*

Questions

1. Who, in your opinion, had stronger motives for signing the peace, Athens or Sparta (**25.11.A**)?
2. What was the fate of Brasidas' allies according to the terms of the Peace of Nicias (**25.11.B**)?

Review Questions

1. What does Thucydides' description of the plague in Athens share with the Mytilenean Debate (**25.1**, WEB **25.6.III**)?

2. What allegedly made Pericles' political successors inferior to him (**25.3**, **25.5**, WEB **25.4**, WEB **25.6.II**)? Does the course of the Archidamian War justify the sources' criticism of them?

3. In what ways does the Mytilenean Debate confirm or confute the sophists' views of law and justice (**23.1–3**: "The Sophists' View of Justice," "Right and Might," "Justice and Expediency," WEB **25.6.III**)?

4. Discuss the significance of the Pylos campaign (**25.7**, WEB **25.8**).

5. Make a list of gains and losses for Athens and Sparta from the beginning of the war (431) to the Peace of Nicias (421). Did any side have more reason to be glad of the conclusion of the war than the other?

Suggested Readings

Pericles' trial: Hamel 1998, 122–123, 141–142. *Mass grave in Athens*: Baziotopoulou-Valavani 2002. *Plague due to a typhoid fever*: Papagrigorakisa et al. 2006; *contra*: B. Shapiro et al. 2006; still valuable are Poole and Holladay 1979; Morens and Littman 1992, and see Littman 2006. *Pericles' successors*: Connor 1971; Rosenbloom 2004a, 2004b. *Cleon*: Woodhead 1960; Spence 1995; Bowie 1993; Wohl 2002, 73–123. *The (first) Sicilian campaign*: Lazenby 2004, 57–59, 84. *The Mytilenean Debate*: Macleod 1978; Connor 1984, 79–95; Pelling 2000, 72–81. *Pylos*: J. Wilson 1979; Rood 1998, 24–60; Lazenby 2004, 67–79. *Brasidas (and Thucydides)*: Westlake 1968, 148–168; Hornblower 1991–2008, 2: 38–61; Lazenby 2004, 91–105; Howie 2005. *The Peace of Nicias*: Kagan 1974, 305–349; Lewis 1992b, 429–432.

26

Finances and Allies During the Archidamian War

Ancient Greece from Homer to Alexander: The Evidence, First Edition. Joseph Roisman.
© 2011 Blackwell Publishing Ltd. Translations © 2011 John Yardley. Published 2011 by Blackwell Publishing Ltd.

This chapter surveys Spartan and especially Athenian means of financing the war and the impact on their relationship with their allies. It includes rare epigraphic evidence of contributions to the Spartan war fund. It also documents how the Athenians increased their revenues through a property tax and by raising the allies' tribute. Decrees involving the city of Methone demonstrate that not all allies were treated equally, and an Athenian decree enforcing the use of Athenian coins, weights, and measures in the empire implies the city's domineering attitude.

26.1   A Spartan War Fund

We know much more about Athenian finances during the war than Spartan finances, but enough to suggest that the Spartans' resources were limited. They relied on contributions from their allies in the Peloponnese and, to a lesser degree, outside it. They may have tried to borrow money from the sanctuaries in Olympia and Delphi (Thucydides 1.121.3), and were unsuccessful in obtaining financial support from Persia before 412.

An inscription found near the city of Sparta listing contributions to a Spartan war fund provides a rare glimpse into Sparta's finances. Scholars are divided about its date, with some suggesting the 420s and others 411. If it was inscribed in the 420s, it could be related to the Spartan attempt to help Mytilene during its revolt from Athens (428–427; see WEB **25.6.III**: "The Mytilenean Affair"). It is possible that the Spartan admiral Alcidas added the collection of tributes to his military mission. The list of contributions is fragmentary, but the recorded sums are relatively small and amount to about 13 talents.

IG V 1, 1 and a new fragment

Translation: Loomis 1992, p. 13

Front
The ..., who are the friends of the Lacedaemonians, gave for the war four hundred darics ...?... The Aeginetans gave to the Lacedaemonians for the war fourteen minas and ten staters.[1] The ... oi gave to the Lacedaemonians ...?... darics.

Som ... ophon of Olenus in Achaea[2] and ...?... gave to the Lacedaemonians for the war trireme ...?... and thirty-two minas of silver. The exiles of the Chians,[3] who are the friends of the Lacedaemonians, gave one thousand Aegenitan staters.

... non gave to the Lacedaemonians for the war four thousands ...?... and [four to nine] thousand other ... and of raisins ... talents. The ...?... gave ...?... many and eight hundred darics and ...?... talents. ...?... gave for the war ...?... minas and ... [two or three] thousand *medimnoi*[4] and [thir- to nine] ty ... and sixty ...?... The Ephesian gave to the Lacedaemonians for the war one thousand darics ...

Side

The Melians[5] gave to the Lacedaemonians twenty minas of silver.

Molocros[6] gave to the Lacedaemonians one talent of silver.

The Melian gave to the Lacedaemonians ...?...

Notes

1. *The daric was a Persian gold coin named after Darius, worth about 20 drachmas. 1 stater = 2 drachmas, 100 drachmas = 1 mina.*
2. *The restored name is either Olenus in Achaea or Olerus in Crete.*
3. *In 425 the Chians gave up building a wall following Athenian objections. Spartan friends in Chios probably then left the island.*
4. *The* medimnoi *were measures presumably of grain (1* medimnos *= ca. 1.5 bushels).*
5. *The island of Melos was subjugated by Athens in 416/5. Either Alcidas collected money from it or the contributions came from Melian exiles after 416.*
6. *Molocros was a Spartan and perhaps identical with Molobrus, the father of the commander of the Spartan forces in Pylos in 424 (Thucydides 4.8.9).*

26.2   Athenian Finance: Raising the Property Tax (*Eisphora*)

Thanks to literary and epigraphic evidence, we are relatively well informed about how Athens financed the war and dealt with her allies. In spite of Pericles' confidence in Athens' bountiful resources (Thucydides 2.13.2–8: **24.7**: "The 'Periclean Strategy'"), the city experienced financial strain due to running the war and responded by curbing withdrawals from the treasury, raising taxes and the tribute of the allies, and making the collection of tribute more efficient.

Thus, the tribute quota lists show that in 428 the Athenians reassessed the allies' tribute, even though reassessment was normally made every four years and the previous assessment had taken place just two years earlier. In the same year, Athens raised the *eisphora*, a property tax that was collected not regularly but on the basis of necessity from those who held a certain amount of property (see also **35.7**: "State Revenues and Taxation").

Thucydides 3.19.1–2

(**3.19.1**) The Athenians were in need of more funds to prosecute the siege [of Mytilene], even though they had for the first time levied upon themselves a tax to raise 200 talents, and had also sent twelve ships to the allies to gather money, under the command of Lysicles and four others. (**19.2**) Lysicles collected sums at various points on his journey, and after making his way inland from Myus in Caria, he was attacked by the Carians and Anaeitans – as he was going through the plain of the Maeander as far as the hill of Sandius – and was killed along with many members of his force.

Question

1. How do the Spartan inscription (**26.1**) and the Athenians' financial measures (**26.2**) illustrate Athens' financial advantage?

26.3   Raising the Tribute: The Thudippus Decree

Plutarch says that after Pericles' death, the "demagogues" increased the allies' tribute from 600 to 1,300 talents, but he does not give a precise date (*Aristides* 24.5). Among these leaders was surely Cleon, who is said by Aristophanes to have taken a particular interest in taxes and tributes, allegedly to line his own pockets: see WEB **26.4**.

In 426 the politician Cleonymus proposed a decree that facilitated tribute collection by instructing tribute-paying cities to appoint their own collectors (*eklogeis*; ML no. 68 = Fornara no. 133). As with other decrees, it tried to stem corruption by recording and displaying transactions in public and by imposing legal penalties for violations.

A year later, in 425/4, only three years after the last assessment, the Athenians reassessed the tribute of the allies once again. They justified the measure by claiming that the tribute failed to cover the expenses of the war (lines 16–17, 46 of the decree). The list of states inscribed after the decree included those that had never paid tribute or had not paid it in a long time. Altogether, the decree listed around 400 states with a total tribute of ca. 1,460 talents. Although scholars have regarded the numbers of the contributors and the total as wishful thinking, the fragmentary evidence makes it impossible to know whether Athens increased the tribute or the number of tribute-paying states. Equally uncertain is the identification of the decree's proposer, Thudippus, with Cleon's son-in-law of the same name.

The Thudippus Decree (425/4), ML no. 69 = Fornara no. 136, lines 1–7, 16–27, 44–61

Translation: Osborne 2002, no. 138, pp. 66–67

Gods. Assessment of Tribute.

The [Council and People] decided in the prytany [of the tribe —, when —] was Secretary [and —] President, [on the proposal] of Thudippus:

[to send heralds whom the Council elects by show of hands] from the – [to the] (**5**) cities: two [to Ionia and Caria], two [to Thrace, two] to the Islands, [and two to the Hellesp]ont. These [are to announce] in the assembly [of each city that ambassadors should come to Athens during] Maemacterion [November/December].[1]

Note

1. *The Julian dates in the inscription are Osborne's and are about a month later than the orthodox view.*

The inscription goes on to discuss new office-holders for assessing the tribute, procedures to allow the allies to dispute the assessment in a newly established court, and magistrates responsible for introducing the cases.

(**16**) The [Thesmo]thetae are to set up a new [court of 1,000 jurors].

[As to the tribute, since] it has become less, let [this court], together with the Council, hold an assessment during the month of Poseideion [December/January], [just as in the last] term of office, of [all the assessments] proportionately. They shall deal with the matter every day from the beginning of the month [to ensure that] the tribute [is assessed] in Poseideion. [The full Council] (**20**) is also to deal with the matter [continuously, to ensure that] the assessment happens, provided [that there is no contrary decree of the People.] They must not [assess less] tribute for any [city] than the tribute that city [has brought in before now], unless there [seems to be such shortage of resources that] that territory cannot [bring in more]. The Secretary [of the Council is to] write up this decision and this [decree and this] tribute that is assessed [for each city on two] steles and [place one in the] Council Chamber (**25**) and one (on the Acropolis). The Sellers [*Poletai*] [are to put this out to contract] and the *Colacretai* [treasurers] [are to provide the money]. [For the future, notice] about the tribute [is to be given to the] cities [before the Great [Panathenaea...]

The decree then imposes penalties on presiding Council members who fail to introduce the assessments and on citizens who propose to vote against the reassessment. It takes measures to insure speedy discussion of the decree in the assembly as well as the Council's supervision of summoners to court. It also prescribes the routes for the heralds announcing the assessments.

(**44**) [The Generals are to see to] the cities bringing in [their tribute as soon as the Council draws up the tribute] assessment, in order [that the People have sufficient money for the] war. [The Generals] must consider [about the] tribute [every year, reckoning what is needed for campaigns, both by land] and sea, [and any other expenditure.]

[At the] first [sitting] of the Council [let them always introduce cases about] this, [without the Heliaea or] the other courts, unless (**50**) the People [vote that they be introduced after the courts have] first [made a judgment.] [The *Colacretai* are to pay] the heralds who go.

[—] said: in other respects let it be as the Council propose, but [—] let the prytany that [is in office] and the Secretary [of the Council bring] the [assessments by city] to the court whenever it is assessments that are at issue in order that [the dikasts [jurors] may agree with them].

The Council and People decided (**55**) in the prytany of Aegeis, when [Phil]ip[pus] was Secretary and [—]oros President, on the proposal of Thudippus: All the cities assessed for tribute under the [Council to which Pleisti]as was first Secretary in the archonship of Stratocles [425/4] [are to bring] a cow [and a full set of armor] to the Great Panathenaea;[1] they are to take part in the procession [in the same way as Athenian settlers abroad].

The Council to which Pleistias was the first Secretary assessed the tribute for the cities [in the following way] in the archonship of Stratocles, when the (**60**) magistrates in charge of introducing cases had as secretary Ca[—].

Note

1. *For the obligation to produce a cow and set of armor, see Cleinias' decree (**21.1**).*

The decree is followed by a list of cities and their assessed tributes arranged by district.

Questions

1. List the office-holders involved with collecting the tribute and their function.
2. What is the Athenian Council instructed to do, or not do, about the tribute?

26.5 Special Treatment: The Methone Decrees

Apparently, not all allies were treated equally. A case in point is Methone in Pieria, Macedonia, which joined the Athenian empire perhaps around 432/1. The Athenians had a clear interest in keeping Methone friendly because it could serve as a launching pad for an invasion of Macedonia and because it provided access to Macedonian timber, which was important for Athenian shipbuilding. Consequently, Athens gave the city preferential treatment by raising the possibility of forgiving its debts to the Athenian (or possibly the Delian League's) treasury and by granting it access to grain from the Bosporus. In 424/3 the Athenians recorded four decrees concerning Methone in chronological order and on the same stele. Only the first three decrees from perhaps 430/29 and 426 have partially survived.

ML no. 65 = Fornara no. 128

Translation: Osborne 2000, no. 121, pp. 58–59

The people of Methone from Pieria. Phainippus son of Phrynichus was Secretary [424/3].

The Council and People decided, in the prytany of the tribe Erechtheis, when Scopas was Secretary [430/29] and Timonides President, on the proposal of [Diopei]thes (**5**) that the People should vote at

once about the people of Methone, whether they should assess tribute at once or whether it was sufficient for them to pay the share for Athena which they had been assessed to pay at the last Panathenaea
and should be free from tax as to the rest.

(**10**) As to the debts which the people of Methone are recorded as owing to the [Athenian] treasury,
if they are as friendly to the Athenians as they are now, and even more so, the Athenians [allow a
special] assessment concerning their payment, and if a [general] decree is passed about the debts
recorded on the [boards], (**15**) the people of Methone need pay nothing [unless] a separate decree is
passed about the people of Methone.

Three [ambassadors] aged over fifty are to be sent to Perdiccas [king of Macedonia] and say to
Perdiccas that [fairness] dictates that the people of Methone be allowed to use the sea and (**20**) their
movement not be limited, and allow them to import goods to the land [just as] before, and neither
doing [nor suffering injury], and that he should not [lead] an army through the territory of Methone
without permission from Methone. If [both sides] agree, the ambassadors are to broker a treaty; if not
(**25**) each side is to send an [embassy] to the Athenian Council and [People] at the Dionysia, with
power to decide disputed matters. And to say to Perdiccas that if the soldiers at Potidaea praise him,
the Athenians [will be] well intentioned towards him.[1]

The People voted that Methone (**30**) should pay the goddess' share of the tribute which they had
been assessed to pay at the last Panathenaea, and for the rest be free of taxes.

The Council and People decided, in the prytany of the tribe Hippothontis, when Megacleides was
Secretary [426] and Nicoc[–] was President, on the proposal of Cleonymus that the [people of Methone
(**35**) be allowed to import from Byzantium up to [—] thousand medimnoi of corn each year, and that
the Athenian officials at the Hellespont [*Hellespontophylakes*, lit. "the Hellespont guards"][2] should
neither themselves prevent this import nor allow any other to prevent it, on pain of a fine of 10,000
drachmas each at their scrutiny. After the *Hellespontophylakes* have been informed in writing, (**40**)
they may import the stated amount. The ships that carry the imported grain shall not be liable to any
penalty.

Any general decree that the Athenians pass concerning aid or any other demand made of the cities
either about themselves or about the cities, any that they pass mentioning by name the (**45**) [city] of
Methone, this shall apply to them, but the others not; they should guard their own land and so do
what they have been assessed to do.

As to the offences which they say Perdiccas has committed against them, the Athenians shall take
counsel as to what it is right to do when (**50**) the ambassadors returning from Perdiccas, those who
went with Pleistias and those with Leogoras,[3] report to the People. The People shall hold an Assembly
at the beginning of the second prytany immediately after the [Assembly] in the dockyard to consider
the other cities, and continue (**55**) [sitting] until these affairs are sorted out, giving nothing else priority in the discussion unless the Generals make some request.

The Council and People [decided] in the prytany of the tribe Cecropis, when [—]es was Secretary
and Hierocleides was President [?426] on the proposal of [—]

Notes

1. *The Athenians were besieging Potidaea at the time.*
2. *It is unclear when these Athenian officials, the "Hellespont guards," were introduced.*
3. *Leogoras was the father of Andocides of the notorious Mysteries affair (**27.7:** "The Herms and the Mysteries Affairs").*

Questions

1. What benefits did Athens offer Methone in the above decrees?
2. What can be learned about Athens' relations with Macedonia from the Methone decrees?

26.6 The Athenian Coinage, Weights, and Measures Decree

Around 425 the Athenians forbade the allies from minting their own silver coins, which forced the latter to use Athenian (silver) coins, weights, and measures. A likely reason was Athens' desire to facilitate her local and international trade. The fee charged for using Athenian mints constituted an added benefit. Scholars are divided between those who assume that Athens was violating the sovereignty of the allies and others who argue that local currency was never a symbol of independence, not to mention that many allies did not mint their own coins. A no longer prevalent view dates the decree to sometime before 445 based on the engraver's use of a three-bar sigma letter. This letter was allegedly replaced by a four-bar sigma around 447. Yet the possible discovery of a three-bar sigma in a 418/7 decree (ML no. 37) makes this dating criterion far less attractive. Moreover, a fragment of the coinage decree was discovered in Hamaxitus in the Troad, which joined the empire probably no earlier than the 420s. Finally, numismatic evidence shows local minting in the northeastern Aegean well into the 420s. It is now more common to date the decree to the 420s–410s, possibly around 425, perhaps even later. Indeed, the decree shares the domineering attitude toward the allies that is displayed in reassessment decrees of that period. A date of ca. 425 also makes it closer to Aristophanes' reference to a measures-and-weights decree in the *Birds*, produced in 414 (1040–1042).

The text of the decree is a composite of fragments found in different cities, hence its division into sections.

ML no. 45 = Fornara no. 97

Translation: Osborne 2000, no. 198, pp. 105–106

[— magistrates] in the cities or magistrates [—]

(2) The Hellenotamiai[1] [—] are to register. If they do not register correctly the obligation of any of the cities, [let anyone who wants immediately] bring [those who have offended] before the Heliaea[2] of the [Thesmothetae according to the law]. The Thesmothetae are to ensure [hearing for those who have brought the accusation] within five [days] in each case.

(3) If [anyone else apart from] the magistrates in the cities fails to act in accordance with the decree, either a citizen or a foreigner, he is to lose his civic rights, and his property is to be confiscated and [a tenth] given the goddess.

(4) If there are no Athenian magistrates, the magistrates [of each city are to put into effect the provisions] of the decree. If they fail to act in accordance with [the decree—]

(5) [Those who have received] the silver [in] the mint [are to strike not] less than half and [—] the cities [—three [or five]] drachmas as in the mina. They are to exchange [the other half within? months] or be liable [—]

(6) [They are to strike the] surplus of the money [exacted and hand it over] either to the Generals or [—]. Whenever it is handed over, [—] to Athena and to Hephaestus [—, and if anyone] proposes or puts to the vote a proposal on [these matters, to the effect that it should be permitted] to use or lend [this money, let him immediately be brought before] the Eleven,[3] and let the [Eleven] administer the death penalty. [But if] he appeals, [he is to be led before the court].

(7) The [People] are to choose heralds [and send them to announce what has been decreed], one to go to the Islands, [one to Ionia, one to the] Hellespont, one to the Thraceward region. [The Generals are to prescribe the route for each of these and] send them out. [If they fail to do so], they are to face a fine of ten thousand drachmas [each] at their scrutiny.

(8) The magistrates in the cities are to write up this decree on a stone stele and [place it] in the agora of [each] city, and the Overseers [*epistatai*] are to place a copy [in front of] the mint. [The Athenians are to see to] this, if the cities themselves are not willing.

(9) The herald who goes is to ask them to do all that the Athenians order.

(10) The Secretary of the [Council] is to add the following to the Council Oath [for the future]: If anyone strikes silver coinage in the cities and does not use Athenian coins or weights or measures [but foreign coins] and measures and weights, [I will administer punishments and penalties according to the former] decree that Clearchus [proposed].[4]

(11) [Anyone may hand over] the foreign silver [that he has and exchange it on the same basis] whenever he wants. The city [will give in exchange native [= Athenian] coin]. Each individual is to bring his own coins [to Athens] himself [and deposit them at the] mint.

(12) The Overseers are to write up [all that is handed over by each person] and set up [a stone stele in front of the mint] for anyone who wants to see. [They are to write up the total of] foreign coin separating [the silver and the gold, and the total of native] silver [—].

Notes

1. *See Thucydides 1.96.2 (**18.5.C:** "Managing the League") for the* Hellenotamiai.
2. *The Heliaea was the largest popular court in Athens. It was presided over by the Thesmothetae and dealt with appeals and various political cases.*
3. *For the Eleven, see Ath. Pol. 7.3–4 (**9.8.A:** "Solon's Classes and Their Respective Offices").*
4. *A Councilman by the name of Clearchus is attested for the year 408/7 (IG I³ 515.25), but it is impossible to know if he is the proposer of this decree and if the decree should be redated accordingly.*

Questions

1. What were the penalties for allies who continued to use local currency?
2. How did the Athenians try to insure transparency in the handling of currency exchange in Athens?

Review Questions

1. What contingencies did Sparta and especially Athens have to finance the war (**26.1–3**)?
2. Describe Athens' treatment of her allies in light of the above decrees (**26.2–3**, **26.5–6**, WEB **26.4**). How is this information relevant to Brasidas' campaign (**25.9**)?
3. How did the Athenians supervise the implementation of their new regulations?
4. What recourse did allies have against abuse of the demands made of them (especially **26.3**, **26.6**)?

Suggested Readings

The Spartan war fund: Loomis 1992. *Alcidas*: Roisman 1987; Kallet-Marx 1993, 139–140. *Athenian finance*: Mattingly 1968 (redating the epigraphic evidence); Kallet-Marx 1993, 71–206; Samons 2000, esp. 171–211. *Methone*: Hammond and Griffith 1979, 2: 124–128; Borza 1990, 148–150. *The coinage decree*: Mattingly 1987, 1993; Lewis 1987; Vickers 1996; Samons 2000, 330–332.

27

The Uneasy Peace and the Sicilian Expedition (421–413)

CHAPTER CONTENTS

Ancient Greece from Homer to Alexander: The Evidence, First Edition. Joseph Roisman.
© 2011 Blackwell Publishing Ltd. Translations © 2011 John Yardley. Published 2011 by Blackwell Publishing Ltd.

For Thucydides the Peloponnesian War was a continuous conflict from beginning (431) to end (404), and the Peace of Nicias of 421 was not a real peace. He saw the period that the peace ushered in as dominated by intense diplomatic and military conflicts, including between Athens and Sparta. Some of Thucydides' contemporaries might have disagreed with his view that the Decelean War (413–404) was a natural continuation of the Archidamian War (431–421).

This chapter discusses the period separating the Archidamian from the Decelean War. It focuses on the young and charismatic Athenian leader Alcibiades, who until his desertion to Sparta advocated a belligerent policy toward her. Alcibiades strongly advocated an Athenian expedition to Sicily. The chapter describes the cause that triggered the expedition, the Athenian goals in Sicily, and a scandal involving sacrilege that eventually led to Alcibiades' leaving the Athenian armada for Sparta. It then documents the Spartan reaction to the Athenian invasion of Sicily and the Athenian defeat there.

27.1 Alcibiades

The Peace of Nicias left many poleis unhappy, including the important cities of Thebes and Corinth. Argos, whose neutral status expired in 421, remained hostile toward Sparta. Even in Athens there were men who were dissatisfied with the peace, chief among them Athens' most colorful and intriguing leader Alcibiades, son of Clinias (451/0–404/3). A link to a bust of Alcibiades can be found in WEB **27.15**.

The fascination Alcibiades exerted on his contemporaries is evinced by the prominent role he plays in the histories, plays, and even speeches of the time. He came from an aristocratic family and was brought up by Pericles after his father's death. Alcibiades displayed from his youth unbounded ambition and fierce competitiveness, which together with his background, connections, and good looks placed him at the center of Athenian politics and social life. While Nicias' reputation was partly based on his public benefactions, Alcibiades' claim to fame was more individualistic. Thus, in the Olympics of probably 416, he placed seven chariots, at very great expense, in the aristocratic and highly prestigious chariot race. Olympic victory brought personal fame, but the city too partook in the honor.

27.1.A Alcibiades at the Olympic Games

Plutarch *Alcibiades* 11.1–12.1

(**11.1**) His horse-breeding was widely celebrated, as was the number of his chariots – nobody apart from him, neither private individuals nor royalty, ever entered seven at the Olympic Games. And his victory and his second and fourth places (fourth according to Thucydides [6.16.2] but Euripides says third) eclipse in distinction and glory the ambitions any might have in this area of endeavor. (**11.2**) This is what Euripides says in that ode:

> "Of you shall I sing, son of Clinias. A beautiful thing is victory, but the most beautiful thing is to do what no other of the Greeks has done, to come first, second, and third in the chariot race, to come away without fatigue, and, crowned with the olive of Zeus, to provide the herald with his loud announcement."

(**12.1**) The occasion was made even more splendid by the the various city-states competing to do him honor. The people of Ephesus set up a superbly decorated tent for him; the city of Chios provided fodder for his horses and a large number of sacrificial animals; and the people of Lesbos provided wine and other supplies for him to entertain many guests on a lavish scale ...[1]

Note

1. *Plutarch then recounts that Alcibiades was charged with registering under his own name a winning chariot team that belonged to another competitor.*

27.1.B   Alcibiades' Ambitions and the Athenians' Attitudes Toward Him

The sources often explain Alcibiades' politics as grounded in his spirited character and personal ambitions. This is how Thucydides presents him when he describes Alcibiades' role in persuading the Athenians to launch the Sicilian expedition in 415.

Thucydides 6.15.2–4

(**6.15.2**) ...The most enthusiastic proponent of the expedition was Alcibiades son of Clinias, who wanted to take a stand against Nicias because, apart from their various political differences, Nicias had made cutting remarks about him. More than anything, though, Alcibiades wanted the position of general, since he hoped to use that to take Sicily and Carthage and, if he were successful, to gain at the same time personal advancement in terms of wealth and reputation. (**15.3**) While he was held in high regard by his fellow-citizens, he indulged his passions (his horse-rearing and other expensive pastimes) to an extent that his means could not support – and this played a very important part in bringing down the Athenian state later on. (**15.4**) For the masses came to fear the extent to which his personal behavior and lifestyle transgressed the norm, and also the extent of his ambition, as revealed in every activity in which he was involved. They grew hostile to him as a man with aspirations to tyranny, and they all objected to his personal habits even though he ran military affairs in an impeccable manner on the public level. Because of this they put the city in the hands of others, and in a short time brought it to ruin...

In 420 Alcibiades was the driving force behind a defensive alliance between Athens, Argos (where he was well connected), Elis, and Mantinea. Increased tensions between Sparta and Argos led to the battle of Mantinea (I) of 418, which was the largest land battle of the entire war. The battle also pitted the Spartans against an Athenian contingent that fought on the Argive side. Sparta won the battle, which challenged the Peace of Nicias. The peace would be challenged again a few years later by Athens' invasion of Sicily (415). See WEB **27.2.I** for the first battle of Mantinea.

In 416 Athens mounted an expedition against the island of Melos. After failing to negotiate Melos' surrender, the Athenians beseiged the city and then killed all Melian men and enslaved their women and children. Thanks to Thucydides' description of the negotiations between the parties in what is known as the "Melian Dialogue," Athens' treatment of Melos has become a case study in the conflict between morality and expediency, power and justice, and humanism and realism. See WEB **27.2.II** for the Melian Dialogue.

A dubious charge against Alcibiades made him responsible for the fate of the Melians. It is found in a speech denouncing Alcibiades that has wrongly been attributed to the orator Andocides. The speech is purportedly delivered by the politician Phaeax on the occasion of an ostracism trial in 416/5 in which both Phaeax and Alcibiades were candidates. There are good reasons to regard the speech as a rhetorical exercise, although it might have been based on contemporary attacks against Alcibiades.

27.1.C   Alcibiades and Melos

[Andocides] 4 *Against Alcibiades* 22; cf. Plutarch *Alcibiades* 16.5–6

So it is that young men's occupations are confined to the law courts rather than the gymnasia, and that it is the older men who are serving in the army, while the young are making speeches in the assembly. This is the man [Alcibiades] whose example they are following. Such are the lengths to which he takes his outrageous conduct that, after expressing as his opinion that the Melians should be reduced to slavery, he purchased a woman from amongst the prisoners-of-war and had a son by her. That boy's birth was even more grotesque than that of Aegisthus[1] because he was born of parents who were each other's bitter enemies, and among his closest relatives he has one who had inflicted extreme suffering, and others who endured it.

Note

1. *Aegisthus was the son of Thyestes and Thyestes' daughter Pelopia.*

27.1.D   Alcibiades and the Ostracism of Hyperbolus

In 416 or 415 Alcibiades and Nicias participated in a political collusion. It appears that Hyperbolus, a popular politician who is much maligned by our sources, sought to get rid of either Nicias or Alcibiades through ostracism. The two combined their respective groups of supporters (*hetaireiai*) and succeeded in having Hyperbolus exiled. Their abuse of the ostracism mechanism moved the Athenians to stop using it. Potsherds (*ostraka*) have been found from this ostracism trial, which are inscribed with the names of Hyperbolus, Alcibiades, Nicias, Phaeax, and Cleophon, a politician who came to prominence later.

Plutarch *Nicias* 11.1–7

(**11.1**) Alcibiades' differences with Nicias came to a head, and there was an ostracism. This was a procedure that the people employed periodically through which they would, by voting with a potsherd, remove from the city for a period of ten years a single individual whom they either suspected because of his great reputation or else envied for his wealth. Both men were now in a nerve-racking and perilous situation, since one of them would fall victim to the ostracism, come what may. (**11.2**) In Alcibiades' case, people hated his lifestyle and feared his recklessness, as is shown more fully in my account of him. As for Nicias, his wealth exposed him to jealousy. More important than anything, however, were aspects of his comportment that were neither sociable nor egalitarian, but which were quite uncongenial and elitist, and these made him seem a strange figure; and because of the many instances of his opposing the wishes of the public, and forcing them willy-nilly to do what was truly in their interests, the common people found him a nuisance. (**11.3**) Simply put, it was a struggle between the young, who were for war, and the older generation who were for peace, the former using the potsherd against Nicias and the latter against Alcibiades.[1]

"In times of civil strife, however, the scoundrel also gains honor,"[2] and so on that occasion, too, the people became divided and provided space for the most reckless and villainous men. These included Hyperbolus of the deme Perithoedae. This man's foolhardiness came from no power that he had, but he came to power through his foolhardiness; and through the repute that he had in the city he brought disrepute upon the city. (**11.4**) At that particular time he thought himself safe from ostracism, being, as he was, more suitable for the pillory, but he hoped that with one of the two men exiled he would become a rival to the other. It was quite clear that he was delighted with their quarreling, and that he was inciting the people against both. When Nicias and Alcibiades learned of the man's unscrupulousness, they held secret discussions and, bringing together and uniting their two factions, they achieved their goal and it was Hyperbolus and not either of them who was ostracized. (**11.5**) For the moment this brought the people pleasure and amusement, but later they were annoyed at the thought that the process had been debased through being employed against an unworthy man ...

(**11.6**) ... The result was that no one at all was ostracized after Hyperbolus, who was its last victim. The first was Hipparchus of the deme Cholargus[3] who was a relative of the tyrant ...

(**11.7**) ... I am not unaware of Theophrastus' claim that Hyperbolus' ostracism occurred during the time when Phaeax, not Nicias, was at odds with Alcibiades; but most sources have reported as I do.[4]

Notes

1. *Cf. Thucydides (6.13.1) for the young–old dichotomy in Athens.*
2. *The source of this proverb, which Plutarch cites elsewhere, is unknown.*
3. *Hipparchus, who was ostracized in 488/7, actually came from the deme of Collytus.*
4. *Theophrastus of Eresus, Lesbos, ca. 370–288, was a philosopher and scientist who succeeded Aristotle as the head of his school. Thucydides dates Hyperbolus' death to 412/1. The fourth-century historian Theopompus of Chios (FGrHist 115 F 96.b) mentions Hyperbolus' burial at sea and asserts that he had been ostracized for six years, or, according to different readings of the text, after six years of popular leadership. Phaeax was sent as an envoy to Italy and Sicily in 422 (Thucydides 5.4–5). For the variant version of Phaeax's involvement in the affair, see Plutarch Alcibiades 13.*

A link to an *ostrakon* inscribed with Alcibiades' name can be found in WEB **27.15**.

Questions

1. Why was Alcibiades' lifestyle a source of consternation as well as appreciation for fellow Athenians (**27.1.A–C**)?
2. What were the grounds for ostracizing a politician, according to Plutarch's description of Hyperbolus' ostracism (**27.1.D**)?
3. Describe the organization of the Spartan army and how it was set for battle in Mantinea (WEB **27.2.I**).
4. What led to the Spartan victory at Mantinea (WEB **27.2.I**)?
5. What precepts guided the Athenians' negotiations with the Melians in the Melian Dialogue, and why did the Melians refuse to surrender (WEB **27.2.II**)?

27.3   Egesta and the Origins of the Sicilian Expedition (416)

In 415 Athens decided to intervene militarily in Sicily. Thucydides thought that the Sicilian campaign was a turning point in the Peloponnesian War and dedicated to it a large portion of his (unfinished) history. His description rises at times to literary climaxes unsurpassed elsewhere in his narrative. Undoubtedly, the Athenian defeat in Sicily was one of the greatest in their history.

The Athenians had already sent forces to Sicily in 427–424 but were forced to recall them when the Sicilians agreed to oppose foreign intervention in their island (see WEB **25.4**: "Athens Opens a Second Front in Sicily"). In 422, the Athenian Phaeax failed to establish a Sicilian coalition against Syracuse.

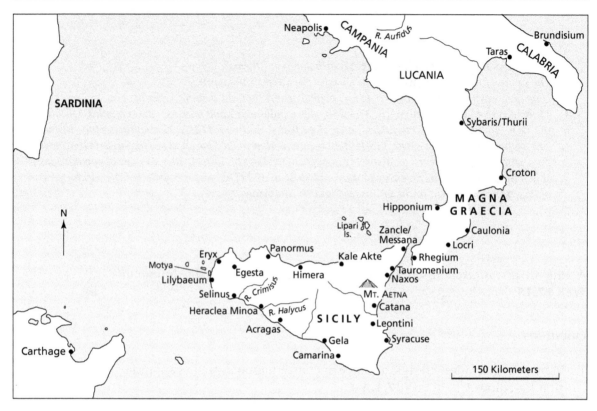

Map 27.1   Ancient Sicily.

 In the summer of 416 the Sicilian city of Egesta asked the Athenians for help against their neighbor, Selinus (see Map 27.1). Egesta may have been an Athenian ally from 418/7; this is Chambers et al.'s (1990) reading of an inscription recording the alliance (ML no. 37), but see A. Henry (1992, 1998), who argues for a date in the 450s. A link to images of the Egesta decree, and more information about it, can be found in WEB **27.15**.

Thucydides, who is critical of the Athenians' decision to invade the island, and often depicts it as less than entirely rational, thinks that the Egestan request provided Athens with a pretext to go to war. He states this view after surveying the island and its peoples.

27.3.A   Egesta Requests Help

Thucydides 6.6.1–2

(**6.6.1**) Such was the ethnic make-up of Sicily in terms of Greeks and barbarians, and such was the size of the island that the Athenians were eager to attack. The real cause was their wish to dominate the whole island, but they also wanted to seem honorable in helping their own kinsmen and the other allies they had gained.[1] (**6.2**) They were particularly aroused by ambassadors of the people of Egesta, who were present in Athens and appealing to them ever more urgently. The Egestans shared a border with the people of Selinus,[2] and had opened hostilities against them over some intermarriage arrangements and a dispute over territory. The people of Selinus had enlisted the Syracusans as allies, and were putting the Egestans under pressure in a war fought both on land and sea. Consequently, the Egestans were reminding the Athenians of the alliance they had formed with the people of Leontini in the time of Laches and the previous war,[3] and were begging them to assist them by sending ships. They produced many arguments, but the main one was as follows. Suppose, they said, that the Syracusans got away scot-free with driving the people of Leontini from their home, and then gained total domination of Sicily after destroying the remaining Athenian allies. There was danger at that point that the Syracusans, as Dorians, would provide a large force to aid their fellow Dorians, and as colonists aid the Peloponnesians who had sent them out, helping them to destroy the power of Athens. It was a sound plan, they said, to oppose the Syracusans with the remaining Athenian allies, especially since the people of Egesta would themselves supply sufficient funds for the war...

Notes

1. *See Thucydides 1.23.6 (**24.1**: "Thucydides' View of the Causes of the Peloponnesian War") for his distinction between "truest cause" and less compelling reasons.*
2. *See **4.8** for Archaic Selinus.*
3. *See Thucydides 3.86.3–4 for Athens' alliance with Leontini in 427/6.*

The Athenians decided to send envoys on a fact-finding mission to Egesta to investigate the causes of its dispute with Selinus and verify whether it had enough money to support an expedition there. See WEB **27.4** for Thucydides' description of how the Egestans successfully tricked the Athenian fact-finding mission into thinking that the city was very wealthy. In the spring of 415 the envoys returned home with Egestan ambassadors.

27.3.B   The Decision on the Sicilian Campaign

Thucydides 6.8.1–2

(**6.8.1**) At the start of the following spring the Athenian ambassadors returned from Sicily, and with them came the Egestans, who brought sixty talents of silver bullion as a month's wages for sixty ships, the number they intended asking the Athenians to send.[1] (**8.2**) The Athenians convened an assembly and listened to a number of seductive untruths from the Egestans and their own ambassadors, especially in relation to the money, which, they were told, was available in large quantities in the temples and the state treasury. They then voted to send sixty ships to Sicily, under three generals with plenipotentiary powers [*strategoi autokratores*]: Alcibiades son of Clinias, Nicias son of Niceratus, and Lamachus son of Xenophanes.[2] They were to help the Egestans against the people of Selinus, and assist them with the resettlement of Leontini, if they achieved some success in the military operations, and they were to take all other initiatives in Sicily according to what they perceived to be in Athens' best interests...

Notes

1. *A highly fragmentary inscription records a popular decree that mentions sixty ships, a "general" in one place, and "generals" in another: ML no. 78 = Fornara no. 146. Scholars are divided about its date, with some favoring 415 and others 413 in connection with the dispatch of a second armada to Sicily.*
2. *It is unclear what the plenipotentiary powers of the generals at this stage entailed. Later the people resolved to give them full powers regarding the size of the expedition and operational decisions (Thucydides 6.26.1).*

Questions

1. What were the Egestans' arguments and methods of persuading the Athenians to come to their aid (**27.3.A**, WEB **27.4**)?
2. What did the Athenian mission in Sicily entail (**27.3.B**)?

27.5   The Athenians' Goals in Sicily

The sources provide different answers to the question of what motivated the Athenians to invade Sicily. We hear of concrete goals such as helping Egesta and Leontini as well as more general ones such as promoting Athenian interests in the region (Thucydides 6.8.2: **27.3.B**). Elsewhere, Thucydides defines the goal as conquering the entire island (6.6.1: **27.3.A**). He also ascribes to Alcibiades, who was the most prominent advocate of the campaign, an even more ambitious plan. The occasion was Alcibiades' speech to the Spartans after his defection in 415/4.

27.5.A   Alcibiades Describes the Athenian Goals and Strategy

Thucydides 6.90.2–4; cf. 6.15.2

(**6.90.2**) ..."We sailed to Sicily in order to subdue the Sicilians in the first place, if we could, and then the Italian Greeks, after which we would direct our efforts against the Carthaginian empire, and the Carthaginians themselves. (**90.3**) If the enterprise succeeded, either totally or for the most part, we were then going to attack the Peloponnese, bringing with us the entire forces of the Greeks that had been added to ours in Sicily, plus large numbers of barbarians that we should have conscripted as mercenaries (Iberians and others from that region who are now acknowledged as being the best warriors of the barbarians). We were also going to build numerous triremes in addition to our own, since Italy has an unlimited supply of wood, and with these we would blockade the Peloponnese. At the same time there would be attacks made on your cities by land. Taking some of these by force, and others by siege, we expected that we would easily wear you down, and that after that we would take control of the whole of the Greek-speaking world. (**90.4**) As for finances and provisions to make each of these objectives more attainable, the lands acquired in that region were going to provide us with a sufficiency, without our touching revenues from Greece ..."

It is possible that Alcibiades was trying to scare the Spartans into taking action against the Athenian invasion by magnifying Athens' ambitions, yet there are indications elsewhere of an Athenian plan to fight Carthage (Aristophanes *Cavalrymen* 1302–1315; Thucydides 6.15.2). Ultimately, however, the difficulties of deciphering the motives or goals of the campaign go back to Thucydides. His account provides the most comprehensive treatment of events, but his view of the expedition as an avoidable mistake colored his analysis of its origins.

In truth, the Athenians were divided about the campaign. Nicias opposed it while Alcibiades supported it, but it is impossible to separate their different views of the campaign from their rivalry over power in the city: see WEB **27.6** for the debate between Nicias and Alcibiades over the campaign.

When Nicias saw that Alcibiades was gaining ground, he sought to dissuade the Athenians from sailing by depicting the campaign as requiring an immense investment in men and money. The Athenians were undeterred. Thucydides describes the reaction to Nicias' speech as dominated by passion and hopes that would prove unrealistic later.

27.5.B   Athenian Enthusiasm for the Campaign

Thucydides 6.24.1–4

(**6.24.1**) That was all that Nicias said. He thought that he would deter the Athenians by the number of problems involved, or else that, if he were obliged to undertake the expedition, he would thus set out under the safest of conditions. (**24.2**) In fact, the difficulty involved in its preparation did not make the Athenians lose their enthusiasm for the expedition; indeed, they were all the more eager for it, and the outcome of the debate was contrary to Nicias' expectations. It was thought that he had given sound advice, and that now the venture would be very secure.

(**24.3**) A passionate desire for the expedition swept over all alike. Older people thought they were going to conquer the places against which they were sailing, or at least that a great force could not come to grief; and those of fighting age had a longing to see and visit distant places, and were confident of returning safely. The masses, including the members of the expedition, were sure they would earn money in the short term, and also acquire power which would later provide them with pay without end. (**24.4**) So, faced with the overwhelming enthusiasm of the majority, anyone displeased with the idea simply kept quiet for fear of being thought unpatriotic by opposing it.

The fleet that left Athens and was reinforced on its way to Sicily was large indeed.

27.5.C   The Athenian Armada

Thucydides 6.43–44.1

(**6.43**) After this the Athenians set off from Corcyra and embarked on the crossing to Sicily with a force of the following proportions. There were all together 134 triremes and two Rhodian pentecont-ers.[1] Of these a hundred were Attic, sixty of them men-of-war, and the rest troop-carriers; and the remainder of the fleet came from Chios and the other allies. The hoplite total was 5,100. Of these, 1,500 were actually Athenians from the list, and 700 were *Thetes* who served as marines. The others taking part in the expedition were allies, some of them of subject status, but there were also 500 Argives and 250 Mantineans and mercenaries. Archers totaled 480, of whom 80 were Cretan, and there were 700 slingers from Rhodes, plus 120 light infantry who were exiles from Megara, and one cavalry-transport with thirty cavalrymen aboard.

(**44.1**) Such was the size of the first expedition that sailed over to Sicily for the war. Bringing supplies for these troops were thirty grain-bearing freighters, which also carried bakers, masons, and joiners, and all the tools for wall construction. There were also a hundred smaller vessels sailing along with the transport ships because they had been pressed into service, but there were, too, many other small vessels and freighters that voluntarily accompanied the force for trading purposes. All of them now proceeded together across the Ionic Gulf from Corcyra.

Note

1. *The penteconter was a fast warship with fifty rowers, hence the name, as opposed to the trireme, which had a complement of 170 rowers. It is possible that some ships had only a skeleton crew.*

Questions

1. What did the Athenians hope to accomplish in Sicily (**27.3**, **27.5**, WEB **27.6**)?
2. What were Nicias' arguments against going to Sicily (WEB **27.6**)? Did Alcibiades respond to them? How?

3. Why, according to Thucydides, were the Athenians so keen on going to Sicily, and how did they show it (**27.5.B–C**, WEB **27.6**)?

27.7 The Herms and Mysteries Affairs

Before the fleet sailed to Sicily, the city was gripped by one of the greatest scandals in her history involving the mutilation of the Herms (*Hermai*) and the profanation of the Mysteries. The Herms were rectangular stone pillars that stood in front of courtyards and temples and on roadsides in Athens. They were surmounted by an image of Hermes and many had a carved erect phallus. Hermes was the god of private property and travelers, and the phallus was supposed to repel evil forces. A Nolan amphora by the Micon Painter from around the mid-fifth century depicts a Herm and an altar (Figure 27.1). The

Figure 27.1   Nolan amphora by the Micon Painter showing a Herm. akg-images/Erich Lessing.

inscription on the Herm – "Glaucus is beautiful" – suggests the person to whom the vase was dedicated.

The mutilation of the Herms involved the smashing of their faces and possibly of the phalluses where these were carved. The profanation of the Mysteries, which consisted of parodying the Mysteries rites at Eleusis, was unrelated to the mutilation, but in the minds of the public the two scandals were linked. Alcibiades was arguably the most prominent figure to be suspected of participating in the Mysteries affair, although he vehemently denied it. There is no doubt that Athenian politicians tried to use the scandal to get rid of their rivals, including Alcibiades. They succeeded. A few months later, when the Athenian armada arrived at Catana, Sicily, the state-ship *Salaminia* came to summon Alcibiades back to Athens for trial (**27.9**). He was tried *in absentia* and his property was confiscated (below). See WEB **27.8** for Thucydides' succinct description of the mutilation scandal and for comments on the possible motives of those who perpetrated it.

In 400/399 the orator and politician Andocides delivered a speech in which he denied accusations that he participated in the mutilation of the Herms. (For the Attic orators, see **Introduction III.7**.) Yet he had informed on other participants, and told the following self-serving story about the plot. He named the Athenians Euphiletus and Meletus as the ringleaders.

27.7.A   Andocides on the Plot

Andocides 1 *On the Mysteries* 61–63

(**61**) Accordingly, I told the Council that I knew the culprits and I gave convincing proof of what had happened. I told them Euphiletus had brought up the idea while we were at a drinking party, but that I spoke against it and that it was thanks to me that it was not carried out at that time. Later, I said, I mounted a pony that I had, and took a fall in Cynosarges, shattering my collar-bone and fracturing my skull, and was carried home on a litter.

(**62**) Seeing the state I was in, Euphiletus told the others that I had been talked into taking part, that I had agreed with him to join the venture and mutilate the Herm beside the shrine of Phorbas. He lied to them in saying this. And that is why the Herm which you all see, the one beside our family home, the one that the Aegeis tribe dedicated, is the only one of the Herms of Athens that was not mutilated – because, as Euphiletus told them, it was I who was going to see to it. (**63**) When his accomplices learned of this they were indignant that I knew of the affair but had not done anything. Meletus and Euphiletus came to me the next day and said, "Andocides, we have succeeded in pulling this off. If you decide to take no action and to keep quiet, you will find us to be your friends just as before. Otherwise we shall be your enemies, and you will find us harder to deal with than any other friends you might make by giving us away."

One of the informers in the Herms affair, the Athenian Diocleides, gave the following testimony about what he saw the night of the mutilation. His testimony was later discredited, but even so it reflected the conspiratorial image of groups such as the *hetaireiai* (companionships) in Athens. The *hetaireia* was a group of men, usually of similar age and social background, who shared military service, spent time together, and aided one another in politics and litigation.

27.7.B   The Plotters Gather (?)

Andocides 1 *On the Mysteries* 38–39

(**38**) The man [Diocleides] said that he had a slave at Laurium, and that he needed to bring back the money the slave had earned.[1] He got up early, he claimed, mistook the hour, and set off; and there was a full moon.[2] When he was alongside the Propylaeum of Dionysus, he saw a large number of men coming down from the Odeon to the orchestra,[3] and in fear of them he went into the shadows and sat down between the grave-column and the slab on which stands the bronze figure of the general. He saw some men, about 300 in number, and they were standing in groups of five or ten, sometimes twenty. He saw their faces in the moonlight, he claims, and recognized most of them. (**39**) ... After seeing this, he said, he went on to Laurium. The following day he heard about the mutilation of the Herms and knew immediately that it was the work of these men.

Notes

1. *The Athenian silver mines were located in Laurium, where Diocleides' slave presumably worked.*
2. *Plutarch (Alcibiades 20.5) comments that the story was a lie since this was the last night of the lunar month and there was no moon.*
3. *The area described was on the southeastern slope of the acropolis. The Periclean Odeon stood next to the theater and hosted dramatic and musical performances. The orchestra was in the theater.*

Fragments of inscriptions known as the Attic Stelai record the sale at auction of the confiscated property of men involved in the Herms and Mysteries affairs. The lists provide valuable information about the minimum or approximate prices of possessions and commodities in Athens around 415/4, including of (largely non-Greek) slaves. They also name some very wealthy Athenians such as Oeonias and Aristomachus who owned property in allied states, suggesting that the empire benefited individual Athenians.

In the following partial list, the left column records the tax on the sales, the middle column the price obtained, and the right column the property sold. (The bold figures are the line numbers.) Twelve of the individuals mentioned in the list are also named by the orator Andocides among those publicly denounced for involvement in the crimes (1 *On the Mysteries* 12–18). Some of them, e.g., Cephisodorus and Adeimantus, appeared later as public figures probably following their rehabilitation. Cephisodorus' property included a diverse group of slaves.

27.7.C   The Confiscation of the Plotters' Property

IG I[3] 421, 422, 426 = ML no. 79 = Fornara no. 147 D

		[Of Alcibiades] son of Clinias (**12**) [of Scambonid]ae, the following domestic property was sold:
[–]	[–]	[–]
[–]	[–]	Bronze vessel

[–]	[–]	Bronze vessel …
[3] ob.	18 dr.	Crops (**20**) at Thria
[3] ob.	20 dr.	Crops at Athmonon
		Total with tax: 4,723 dr. 5 ob.
		Of Polystratus so Dio[dorus]
		Of Ancyle
2 dr. 1 ob.	202 dr.	Pistos (a slave)
[1] dr.	42 dr.	Crops at An-cyle
		Total with tax: 247 dr. 1 ob.
		Of Cephisodorus the metic in Piraeus
2 dr.	165 dr.	A Thracian woman
1 dr. 3 ob.	135 dr.	A Thracian woman
[2] dr.	170 dr.	A Thracian
2 dr. 3 ob.	240 dr.	A Syrian
[1] dr. 3 ob.	105 dr.	A Carian
2 dr.	161 dr.	An Illyrian slave
2 dr.	153 dr.	A Colchian
2 dr.	174 dr.	A Carian child
1 dr.	72 dr.	A small Carian child
[3] dr. 1 ob.	301 dr.	A Syrian
[2] dr.	151 dr.	A Melet[enian (male or female)
1 dr.	85 [.] dr. 1 ob.	A Lydian woman…
		[Of Adeimantus] son of Le[uc]olophides
		of Sca[m- (**53**) bonidae]
[–]	[–]	The man [Ar]istomachus
		Land [on] Thasos in I[..] and a house
[–]	[–] 250 dr.	Included are containers: 9 [amphoras]
		unbroken: 20 […] broken ones [with] lids…
		Of [P]anaetius
		Amphories of wine[1]
	[–] 20 dr.	
		unmixed: 104, 7 choes
		Beehives in the country
[3] dr.	[2] 60 dr.	
		In Is […] 15 dr. […]
[1 dr. 1 ob.]	[100] dr.	2 working oxen in Ar[…]
[1 dr.]	[7]0 dr.	[2] oxen
[–]	[–]	4 cows and calves […]
		Sheep: 84
		And their young
[7 dr. 3 ob.]	[7]10 dr.	Goats: 76 and their young…

(**110**) Payment made of the rents of the men who showed impiety toward the two goddesses.
Of Phaedrus son of Pytho[cles] of Myrrhinus:

	60 dr.	Rent paid for house
		[For land in Myrrh]inus rent
	350 dr.	[paid]

... of Oeonias of the deme Atene proceeds of unharvested land on Le[l]a[nton] plain (Euboea).[2]

Notes

1. *1 amphory = 3 choes = ca. 138 liters.*
2. *Oeonias had a vast amount of property in various places, which was sold for over 80 talents.*

Questions

1. What made Alcibiades a likely or unlikely suspect in the Herms and Mysteries affairs (**27.1**, WEB **27.8**)?
2. How did the Athenians interpret the scandal (**27.7.A–B**, WEB **27.8**)?

27.9   Alcibiades Escapes to Sparta

Alcibiades' condemnation in the affair came only later. When the Athenian navy left the Piraeus in the summer of 415, he was one of the fleet's commanders together with Nicias and Lamachus, who was known more for his military record than his political leadership. Upon reaching Corcyra, the fleet was joined by other forces that together made up a sizable armada. See Thucydides (**27.5.C**: "The Athenian Armada") for the fleet that sailed to Italy, and WEB **27.10.I** for the initial Athenian strategy in Sicily.

When the fleet arrived in Sicily, Alcibiades was recalled to stand trial in Athens for his alleged participation in the Herms and Mysteries affairs. Rather than hazard a trial, he fled first to Argos, and then to Sparta. See WEB **27.10.II** for Alcibiades' recall. Thucydides implies that recalling Alcibiades was one of the blunders that the demos and its leaders committed after the state no longer had wise Pericles to guide them: see **25.3** ("Pericles' Political Successors") and **27.1**.

Nicias now assumed primary leadership. He successfully entered the Syracusan Great Harbor by surprise and established a beachhead probably south of the Anapus River. The Syracusans in the meantime restructured their command, strengthened their armed forces and fortifications, and tried to check Athenian movements and diplomatic efforts in Sicily. They also sent envoys to the Peloponnese to request aid. Corinth, Syracuse's mother-city, gave them a warm welcome, but Sparta's reception was cooler and characterized by procrastination. According to Thucydides, it was Alcibiades's speech to the assembled Spartans that tipped the scales in favor of supporting Syracuse. He highlighted the threat to the Peloponnesians should Syracuse fall and advised them to help Syracuse as well as fight Athens on its territory. It appears, however, that Alcibiades served more as a catalyst than a policymaker or strategist.

Thucydides 6.91.3–7

(**6.91.3**) "If this city [i.e. Syracuse] is taken, then all Sicily is also in their hands, and Italy, too, right after it. And the danger from that sector that I just mentioned – that would not take long to descend on you. (**91.4**) So do not think your deliberations concern only Sicily; they concern the Peloponnese as well, unless you swiftly take the following steps. Send a sea-borne army over there, so constituted that the men can ferry themselves as oarsmen and immediately do duty as hoplites; and, what I think is even more useful than the army, send a commander who is a Spartiate to organize the troops already there and force the unwilling into service. By such means those already your friends will receive encouragement, and the waverers will be less fearful about joining you.

(**91.5**) You must at the same time give greater visibility to your prosecution of the war here in Greece so that the Syracusans will stiffen their resistance in the belief that you care about them, and so that the Athenians will be less able to send assistance to their own troops. (**91.6**) You must also fortify Decelea in Attica.[1] This is what the Athenians have always been most afraid of, and they think it the only setback they have not experienced in the war. This is the surest way of doing an enemy harm: gaining accurate intelligence and inflicting on him what you realize he fears most of all. For, naturally, everybody best knows his own perils, and fears them. (**91.7**) There are many benefits that you yourselves will gain – and will remove from the enemy – by such fortification, but I shall pass over them and highlight the most important. Whatever property is present in the surrounding countryside, most of that will come into your hands, some by capture and some through surrender. And the Athenians will be immediately robbed of the income from the silver mines of Laurium and of whatever financial benefits accrue to them from the land and the law courts[2] – and especially of the revenue from their allies. For this will come in less regularly when the allies, seeing the war is being vigorously prosecuted by you, become less responsive to them."

Notes

1. *Decelea was about 20 km north of Athens.*
2. *The law courts were viewed as a source of public revenues including in cases involving public lands and the leasing of the mines.*

Questions

1. What was Alcibiades' strategy in Sicily (WEB **27.10.I**)?
2. Why was recalling Alcibiades such a delicate mission (**27.9**, WEB **27.10. II**)?
3. Why, according to Alcibiades, should the Spartans be apprehensive of the Athenian campaign in Sicily and what should they do about it (**27.9**, **27.5.A**)?

27.11   Sparta Enters the War

In the spring of 414 the Athenians made a surprise landing north of Syracuse. See WEB **27.12** for the Athenian army's fighting there and for Nicias' later request for reinforcements to save the campaign, which the Athenians fulfilled.

In the spring of 413, Sparta reached the crucial decision to renew the war against Athens.

Thucydides 7.18.1–3

(**7.18.1**) The Lacedaemonians were meanwhile preparing to invade Attica, something that they had already decided on and which the Syracusans and Corinthians had also been pushing them to do (hoping, when they learned of the Athenian reinforcements for Sicily, that these could be stopped if the invasion went ahead). Alcibiades, too, was urgently explaining why they should fortify Decelea and not ease up on their operations.

(**18.2**) But what most invigorated the Lacedaemonians was the thought that the Athenians, having war on two fronts, against themselves and against the Sicilians, would be easier to defeat, and also their belief that it was the Athenians who had been first to break the treaty. For in the earlier war, they thought, the infringement had been more on their side: the Thebans had entered Plataea in time of truce and also, although it was stipulated in the previous treaty that recourse to arms was forbidden if there was readiness to submit to arbitration, they themselves had not accepted the Athenian invitation to arbitrate. For that reason they thought the misfortunes they had experienced were warranted, and they called to mind the disaster at Pylos and whatever others they had suffered. (**18.3**) Now, however, the Athenians had set off from Argos with thirty ships and laid waste part of Epidaurus and Prasiae, and other areas, too, while they were also conducting raids from Pylos[1] – and whenever there were disagreements over debatable items in the treaty, it was they who refused to have recourse to arbitration when the Lacedaemonians invited them to do so. The Lacedaemonians therefore thought that the same transgression of which they had formerly been guilty was now on the Athenian side, and so they were eager for war.

Note

1. *Prasiae was located on the eastern shore of the Spartan state. Pylos was not returned to Sparta and served as a basis for Athenian and Messenian raids against Laconia. In summer 414 Athenian forces, in a clear violation of the treaty with Sparta, raided Laconian land.*

Questions

1. On what grounds did the Spartans decide to renew the Peloponnesian War?
2. Compare the Spartans' considerations for making peace with Athens in 421 (**25.11.A**: "Athens' and Sparta's Motives for the Peace") with their considerations for renewing the war approximately eight years later. What has changed?

27.13   The Athenian Defeat in Sicily

The war in Sicily turned in favor of the Syracusans. They captured an Athenian base at the entrance to their Great Harbor and even succeeded in defeating the Athenian navy thanks to their modified ships, the Athenians' inability to maneuver in the confines of the harbor, and the damage inflicted on Athenian crews by Syracusan javelin throwers stationed aboard ships or small boats: see WEB **27.14** for Syracusan naval tactics prior to the arrival of Athenian reinforcements.

It was at this critical moment that the new Athenian armada led by the generals Demosthenes and Eurymedon sailed into the harbor. Shortly after, Demosthenes led a night attack on the Syracusan counter-wall that ended disastrously. The Athenians resolved on retreat, but disagreement among the generals and a lunar eclipse that was interpreted as a bad omen delayed their march (August 27, 413). An Athenian attempt to break through the Syracusan maritime blockade ended in defeat. The only option left was to retreat by land. Thucydides deploys all his literary talent, as well as emotional and hyperbolic language, to describe the misery and gloom attending the retreat.

27.13.A   The Athenian Retreat from Syracuse

Thucydides 7.75.2–7

(**7.75.2**) It was a frightful situation, and not just in one respect, namely that they were retreating after losing all their ships and with their high hopes now replaced by peril that faced both them and their city. In addition, as they were leaving the camp, each of them had the misfortune to set eyes on scenes that were painful to see and contemplate. (**75.3**) The corpses lay unburied, and whenever a man saw one of his friends lying there, he was overcome with grief and fear; and, in the eyes of the living, the men left alive, wounded and weak, were even more pitiful than the dead, more heart-rending than those who were gone. (**75.4**) These men turned to entreaty and lamentation, making them feel helpless. They begged to be taken along, and they called out for help to any individual they recognized anywhere as one of their comrades or relatives. They clung to those who had shared their tents and were now leaving, and followed them as far as they could; and, when physical strength failed them, they were left behind, not without many appeals to the gods and much lamentation. And so departure was not easy for the entire army, which was filled with tears and in such a helpless state, even though it was departure from a hostile country, and though they had endured things too great for tears and now feared what they may yet endure in future.

(**75.5**) A deep feeling of shame and self-recrimination also fell upon them. More than anything else, they looked like a people in flight from a city taken by siege, and not a small city, either. The entire crowd on the march together numbered no fewer than 40,000. They all carried whatever they could that was of use and, contrary to normal practice, the hoplites and cavalry carried their own food, some having no attendants, others mistrusting them (for desertions had long been occurring, and most them occurred right then). Nevertheless, what they carried was not enough, since there was no food left in the camp. (**75.6**) And, besides, while the humiliation and the general sharing of their miseries – the fact that they had many suffering with them – did provide comfort of a kind, even that did not seem to make things easier at the time, especially when they reflected on the splendor and pomp of the beginning and the shabbiness of the end. (**75.7**) For this was the greatest reverse ever to befall a Greek army. Men who had come to make slaves of others now, it turned out, were leaving in fear of suffering that fate themselves; and in place of the prayers and paeans with which they had sailed off from home, they were instead setting out with language of a very different kind. They were also on the march as foot soldiers, not sailors, and relying on hoplite rather than naval capability. Even so, the magnitude of the danger still hanging over them made all this seem quite bearable.

The army marched in a square, with Nicias leading the van and Demosthenes the rear (Eurymedon had fallen in an earlier naval engagement). They aimed either for Catana or for a rendezvous point with friendly Sikel forces. But supply difficulties and Syracusan harassment slowed down their pace considerably and forced them to change direction southeast toward the sea. After arriving there they followed their guides to the Erineus River. The pursuing Syracusans now surrounded Demosthenes' forces lagging behind Nicias and the vanguard and pelted them with missiles from a safe distance. Demosthenes surrendered with 6,000 of his troops. The Syracusans continued their pursuit of Nicias, who pushed toward the Assinarus River. It became the site of horrible carnage, whose vivid description by Thucydides is one of the most memorable passages in his history.

27.13.B   The Massacre at the Assinarus River

Thucydides 7.84.1–5

(**7.84.1**) With the arrival of daylight Nicias led his army on, and the Syracusans and their allies attacked them in the same manner as before, hurling projectiles and spearing them with javelins from all directions. (**84.2**) The Athenians hurried ahead to the Assinarus River. Under pressure on every side from attacks made by the large numbers of cavalry and other enemy troops, they thought things would go easier for themselves if they crossed the river; and they were also suffering from exhaustion and thirst. (**84.3**) When they reached the river they tumbled into it, no longer in any kind of formation, everybody wanting to be the first to cross, and the enemy now piling on the pressure and making the crossing difficult. They were forced to advance in a dense crowd, and they fell over each other and trampled each other down. They became victims of their own spears and equipment, some being killed immediately by the spears, and others becoming entangled in the equipment and swept downstream.

(**84.4**) The Syracusans stood on the other bank of the river – it was steep – and showered weapons down on the Athenians, most of whom were eagerly drinking in complete confusion in the deep bed of the river. (**84.5**) The Peloponnesians came down and created great slaughter, especially amongst those in the river. The water was immediately contaminated, but was drunk none the less greedily, befouled with mud and blood though it was, and was fought over by most of them.

Nicias surrendered to the Spartan general Gylippus. Some of the survivors escaped but many were enslaved. Gylippus wanted to save Demosthenes, the victor of Pylos, and Nicias, Sparta's friend, in order to bring them triumphantly to Sparta, but the Syracusans preferred to execute them. Many shared the blame for the failure in Sicily. In boxing terms, the expedition was a self-inflicted knockdown. It was not yet a knockout, but it certainly contributed to it.

This is how Thucydides describes the fate of Nicias and the Athenian prisoners-of-war and of the entire expedition.

27.13.C   The Fate of Those Captured and Thucydides' Review of the Expedition

Thucydides 7.86.5–87.6

(**7.86.5**) For this, or some very similar reason, Nicias was executed, though he was, of all the Greeks of my day, the man who least deserved to meet such a wretched end, his life having been entirely dedicated to virtuous behavior.

(**87.1**) In the early days the Syracusans were brutal in their treatment of the Athenians in the quarries. The prisoners were many, and they were in a deep, cramped hollow; and the sun and stifling heat initially brought great suffering because of the lack of cover. This was then followed by the opposite, the cold nights of autumn, which, because of the sudden variation in temperature, weakened their constitution. (**87.2**) Also, because of the lack of space, they were doing everything in the same spot, and there were, besides, the corpses piled on top of each other – corpses of the men who had died from their wounds, the variation in temperature and so on – and the stench was unbearable. At the same time they were suffering from hunger and thirst: over an eight-month period the Syracusans gave them a daily ration of a *cotylê* [cup] of water and two *cotylai* of food. Indeed, of all the tribulations men thrown into a place like that could be expected to suffer, there was not one that they did not experience. (**87.3**) They lived all together like that for some seventy days, and then the Sicilians sold them off, all but the Athenians and any Sicilian or Italian Greeks who had taken part in the expedition. (**87.4**) The total number taken prisoner is difficult to give accurately, but it was no fewer than 7,000.

(**87.5**) This turned out to be the most momentous event during this war and, in my opinion, during the whole of recorded Greek history. For the victors it was the most glorious achievement, for the defeated the most ill-starred failure. (**87.6**) The vanquished were completely defeated at every point, and their sufferings were far from small. It was what can truly be termed total destruction. Infantry, ships, and everything else were lost, and few out of many returned home. This was how things went in Sicily.

Questions

1. In what way were the Syracusan galleys and naval tactics superior to the Athenians' (see WEB **27.14**; cf. **17.5**: "The Athenian Trireme")?
2. How does Thucydides bring to life the Athenians' sufferings during their retreat and its aftermath?

Review Questions

1. Assess Alcibiades' contribution to Athenian politics (**27.1**, **27.5**, **27.7**, **27.9**, **27.11**, WEB **27.6**, WEB **27.10.I–II**).
2. Why did the Peace of Nicias collapse (**27.9**, **27.11**, WEB **27.6**)?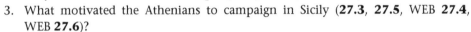
3. What motivated the Athenians to campaign in Sicily (**27.3**, **27.5**, WEB **27.4**, WEB **27.6**)?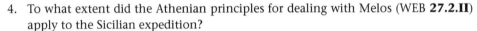
4. To what extent did the Athenian principles for dealing with Melos (WEB **27.2.II**) apply to the Sicilian expedition?
5. What do the ostracism of Hyperbolus (**27.1.D**) and the Herms and Mysteries affairs (**27.7**, WEB **27.8**) reveal about Athenian politics in this period?
6. What were the causes of the Athenian failure in Sicily (**27.5**, **27.7**, **27.9**, **27.11**, **27.13**, WEB **27.6**, WEB **27.8**, WEB **27.10.I–II**)?

Suggested Readings

Uneasy peace 421–413: Westlake 1971; Seager 1976; Rhodes 2006, 124–141. *Alcibiades*: Bloedow 1973; Ellis 1989; Forde 1989; Gribble 1999. *The Melian campaign and Dialogue*: Macleod 1974; Bosworth 1993; Seaman 1997; Kallet 2001, 9–20. *Euripides' "Trojan Women" and Melos*: Van Erp Taalman Kip 1987 (no relation); *contra*: Kuch 1998. *The battle of Mantinea*: Woodhouse 1933; Lazenby 2004, 118–126; Singor 2002. *The Egestan alliance*: Chambers et al. 1990; Chambers 1992 (dates it to 418); *contra*: A. Henry 1992, 1998 (a date in the 450s is still possible). *The motives and aims of the Sicilian expedition*: Kagan 1981, 159–191; Cawkwell 1997, 75–91; Kallet 2001, 21–84; Hornblower 1991–2008, 3: 5–22, 299–381. *The Herms and Mysteries affairs*: MacDowell 1962, esp.1–18, 167–194; Dover in Gomme et al. 1970, 4: 264–288; Osborne 1985b; Pelling 2000, 18–43. *The confiscation records or the "Attic Stelai"*: Pritchett 1956, 1961. *The Sicilian campaign*: Dover in Gomme et al. 1970, 4: 197–489; Green 1970; Roisman 1993, 52–70; Kallet 2001, 183–226; Lazenby 2004, 131–169.

28

The Peloponnesian War

The Decelean War (413–404)

CHAPTER CONTENTS

Ancient Greece from Homer to Alexander: The Evidence, First Edition. Joseph Roisman.
© 2011 Blackwell Publishing Ltd. Translations © 2011 John Yardley. Published 2011 by Blackwell Publishing Ltd.

In response to their defeat in Sicily, the Athenians selected "a board of elder statesmen [*probouloi*] to make proposals, as needed, regarding the present situation" (Thucydides 8.1.3). The board, which included the tragic poet Sophocles and the former general Hagnon, probably acted alongside the Council. The Athenians also attempted to replenish their revenues. They replaced the tribute exacted from the allies with a 5 percent custom duty (Thucydides 7.28.4), but then reverted back to collecting tribute perhaps as early as 410. The fact that they were able to carry on the war for another nine years in spite of the Persian financial backing of Sparta is a testimony to their successful recovery efforts.

This chapter discusses the last phase of the Peloponnesian War. It describes Sparta's two-pronged offensive against Athens: in Attica by the permanent occupation of Decelea, and in the Aegean with the inconsistent help of the Persians. Dissatisfaction with Athenian democracy and hopes for Persian assistance contributed to the establishment of an oligarchic regime in Athens that was toppled some months later. The chapter then examines operations involving Athens, Sparta, and Persia between 411 and 407. It documents the arrival in the region of the Persian prince Cyrus the Younger, who threw his entire support behind Sparta and her admiral Lysander. In Athens a judicial travesty involving the battle of Arginusae (406/5) resulted in the execution of a number of generals; about a year later Athens suffered a decisive defeat against Lysander's navy. The chapter concludes by documenting the extraordinary honors that Lysander was accorded by his contemporaries.

28.1   The Spartan Occupation of Decelea (413)

The Spartans decided to take advantage of the reinvigorated anti-Athenian attitude in Greece and the Aegean. They imitated the Athenian strategy of establishing a permanent base in enemy territory (at Pylos) by occupying Decelea in Attica. Their seizure of Decelea gave the name the "Decelean War" to the last stage of the Peloponnesian War in some ancient accounts.

28.1.A   Harm from Decelea

Thucydides 7.27.3–28.2

(**7.27.3**) Decelea had first been fortified that summer [413] by the whole of the army, and later it was occupied by a succession of garrisons from the allied cities, arriving at intervals to launch attacks on the countryside. This took its toll on the Athenians and, through the destruction of property and attrition of manpower, was one of the main causes of their downfall. (**27.4**) Earlier, the enemy raids had been of short duration, and did not prevent them from benefiting from the land the rest of the time, but from this point there was continuous enemy occupation. Sometimes the Spartans invaded with larger forces, and at others the garrison, which was a match for the Athenians, overran and pillaged the countryside out of need, and present with them was the Spartan king Agis, who did not accord the war secondary importance. The Athenians were thus sustaining serious damage. (27.5) They were deprived of the entire countryside; more than 20,000 slaves had run away, most of them craftsmen; and all their sheep and pack-animals had been destroyed. And since the Athenian cavalry were riding out on a daily basis, making raids on Decelea and patrolling the countryside, some of the horses were going lame on the rugged terrain and from the punishing work they faced, and others were being wounded.

(28.1) Furthermore, the transport of provisions from Euboea had previously been effected more speedily overland from Oropus via Decelea, but now it meant an expensive trip by sea around Cape Sunium. The city had to have absolutely everything imported, and became a fortress rather than a city. (28.2) For while the Athenians maintained guard on the battlements in relays during the day, everybody apart from the cavalry was on guard duty at night, some at military posts and others on the wall. Keeping this up summer and winter exhausted them.

The "Oxyrhynchus historian" is the name given by modern scholars to the anonymous fourth-century author of a fragmentary history discovered on a papyrus in Oxyrhynchus, Egypt, which continued Thucydides' unfinished history of the Peloponnesian War. The historian tells how the Thebans profited from the damage to Athens.

28.1.B   The Thebans' Gains

Hellenica Oxyrhynchia (Bartoletti) 17

… In fact, it turned out that the Thebans' lot actually improved when they joined the Lacedaemonians in fortifying Decelea against the Athenians. For they bought the slaves and everything else that had been captured in the war at a low price, and as they lived in adjacent areas they transported to their homes all kinds of materials from Attica, beginning with lumber and roof-tiles from houses.

Questions

1. How did Decelea change the Spartan strategy of the Archidamian War (cf. **24.5**)?
2. What was the impact of the occupation of Decelea on Athens? What caused the most damage and why?

28.2 Sparta's Maritime Strategy and Persia

The Spartans also directed their attention to the sea. Naval warfare had never been Sparta's field of excellence, but circumstances had changed after the Athenian fiasco in Sicily. Envoys from Athens' allies offered to secede from the Athenian empire with Spartan help, and indeed the island of Chios and the city of Miletus moved to the Spartan side. More important was the Persian initiative to aid Sparta in the war. Although Persian support proved unreliable at times, it made a crucial contribution to the final Spartan victory.

The Persians' involvement started in 413/2 when two embassies, one from the Persian satrap Tissaphernes in Sardis and the other from Pharnabazus, the satrap at Dascylium, arrived in Sparta. Thucydides says that the more senior satrap, Tissaphernes, invited the Spartans to the Aegean and promised to maintain their army.

28.2.A The Persians Offer an Alliance

Thucydides 8.5.5

...It so happened that Tissaphernes had recently been called upon by the king to produce the tribute payments from his province, and he had been in deficit since he had been unable, because of the Athenians, to gather them from the Greek cities. He thought he would be better able to bring in the tribute if he did some damage to the Athenians. He would at the same time make the Lacedaemonians the king's allies and, in accordance with the king's instructions, either take alive or kill Amorges, the illegitimate son of Pissuthnes, who had rebelled in Caria.[1] Thus it was that the Chians and Tissaphernes were acting in concert for the same goal.

Note

1. *The satrap Amorges rebelled against the Persian throne from about the 420s, very probably with Athenian support.*

Pharnabazus' invitation of the Spartans to the Hellespont was based on similar considerations. The two delegations competed with each other, and the Spartans decided to fight in the Aegean even though the Hellespontine strategy would prove to be the winning one. (Thucydides credits Alcibiades with influencing their decision: 8.6.3.)

In 412, we hear for the first time about the Spartans' willingness to forego their avowed goal of liberating the Greeks from Athens and to surrender the Ionians to Persia. Thucydides cites the first of three treaties between Sparta and Persia that was concluded after Miletus rebelled against Athens.

28.2.B   A Spartan–Persian Treaty (412)

Thucydides 8.18.1–3

(**8.18.1**) The Spartans and their allies have formed an alliance with the king and Tissaphernes on these terms:

Whatever lands and cities that the king possesses, or his forefathers possessed, are to be the king's; and with regard to all monies and anything else that accrued to the Athenians from these cities, the king, and the Spartans and their allies, are to act together to see that the Athenians do not receive the monies or anything else.

(**18.2**) The king is to conduct the war against the Athenians in partnership with the Spartans and their allies; and an end to the war against the Athenians is not to be made without the agreement of both parties, the king on the one hand, and the Spartans and their allies on the other.

(**18.3**) Any rebelling against the king are to be enemies of both the Spartans and their allies. And any rebelling against the Spartans and their allies are likewise to be enemies of the king.

Two later treaties between Sparta and the Persians included modifications of the first one but not the basic principle of Sparta's recognition of Persian rule over Asia Minor in return for help in the war. See WEB **28.7.I** for the third Spartan–Persian treaty of 411.

It is common to charge the Spartans with "selling out." The fact is that the Spartans were not of one mind on this policy, and that they rarely helped the Persians actively to resubjugate Greek cities. It can generally be said that the relationship between Sparta and Persia was based on each expecting the other to fulfill its part of the agreement but with little cost to itself. It did not help that the Persian king's subsidies were limited, probably because he expected the local satraps to pay for some of the costs. The Oxyrhynchus historian describes this royal policy in the mid-390s, which was evident already during the Decelean War.

28.2.C   The Persian King's Aegean Policy

Hellenica Oxyrhynchia 19.2

At this time it so happened that many months' pay was owing to the soldiers – they were poorly paid by their officers, which was usually the case amongst men fighting for the king. An example is the Decelean War, when the Persians were allies of the Spartans, and supplied funds in a very niggardly and tight-fisted manner; and on many occasions the allies' triremes would have been demobilized but for the commitment of Cyrus.[1] It is the king who is to blame for this. When he opens hostilities, he sends limited funds to the leaders at the start, and pays little heed to the future. If those in charge of affairs lack the means to cover costs from their own resources, they sometimes allow their forces to be demobilized.

Note

1. *Cyrus the Younger supported the Spartans generously and consistently from 407 on (see **28.8**).*

In spite of the rebellion by important Athenian allies such as Chios and Rhodes with Spartan encouragement, the satrap Tissaphernes resolved on a policy of diminishing his aid to Sparta. The ancient sources attribute this policy to Alcibiades. See WEB **28.3.I** for Alcibiades' alleged affair with the Spartan queen Timaea, which might have led to his departure from Sparta. See also WEB **28.3.II** for Alcibiades' advice to Tissaphernes to reduce subsidies to Sparta and not to fully commit to one side in the conflict. It is not unlikely that the last idea was Persian to begin with. In any case, Tissaphernes reduced his aid to the Spartans, but never helped the Athenians. The major beneficiary of the new policy was Alcibiades, who thought that he would have a better chance of returning to favor in his native land.

28.2.D   Athenian Anti-Democrats Contact Alcibiades

Thucydides 8.47.2–48.1

(8.47.2) The Athenian soldiers on Samos[1] could see that Alcibiades carried weight with Tissaphernes. This was partly because Alcibiades had sent word to the most influential men in their number to drop his name with the elite of Athens, saying that he was willing to return home provided that an oligarchy were in place and not the unconscionable democracy that had expelled him, and that he would secure for them Tissaphernes' friendship and live among them as their fellow-citizen. But more important was the fact that the Athenian trierarchs and the most influential men on the island were themselves set on bringing down the democracy. **(48.1)** The agitation began in the camp and later spread from there to the city. Some men crossed from Samos and held discussions with Alcibiades, who offered to make first Tissaphernes, and then the king, their friend, if they did not have a democracy (the king would then have greater trust in them, he said). The men of influence then, as the ones suffering most in the war, became very hopeful that they could get matters into their own hands and also prevail over the enemy.

Note

1. *The Athenians' most important base in the Aegean was democratic Samos, which remained their staunchest ally throughout the war.*

Questions

1. What motivated the Persians to offer aid to Sparta and the Spartans to accept it (**28.2.A–B**)?
2. What were the difficulties of implementing the Spartan–Persian agreement and how did the parties resolve them (**28.2.B–C**)?
3. What were Tissaphernes' considerations in changing his policy toward Sparta (WEB **28.3.II**)?
4. What impact did Alcibiades' friendship with Tissaphernes have on the Athenians (**28.2.D**, cf. WEB **28.5.1**)?

28.4 The Athenian Oligarchy of 411

 Alcibiades' negotiations with leading Athenians in Samos led to a change in the democratic government in Athens. See WEB **28.5.I** for explanatory comments on the men who led and supported the change. After the leaders of the plot failed to obtain help from Tissaphernes, they gave up on the Persian option and Alcibiades and returned to Athens. There they found that the *hetaireiai* (political companionships) had done much of the groundwork, and moved to change the government. Thucydides regarded their official motion as a means to delude the demos into agreeing to an oligarchy.

28.4.A   A Motion to Limit Political Rights to 5,000 Citizens

Thucydides 8.65.3–66.1

(**8.65.3**) A motion had earlier been produced and made public by them that declared that none should receive pay except those on military service, and participation in government should be limited to five thousand, with these being the people most capable of serving by virtue of their wealth and personal qualities. (**8.66.1**) This was just a specious façade designed for the masses, for those who were effecting the changes were going to take charge of the city. Even so the assembly and the council selected by lot were still convened, but they would deliberate on nothing not approved by the conspirators. In fact, the speakers were from amongst the plotters, and what would be said had also been vetted by these people.

The plotters' success was thus due to clever propaganda, effective leadership, and terror tactics. The proposal to limit the government to 5,000 physically and financially able men, i.e., hoplites, also created the impression that the plotters enjoyed the support of that number of men. Overall, the democratic resistance to the plotters was at best ineffective.

The next step was to propose a thirty-member committee to draft a new constitution. See WEB **28.5.II** on a proposal to set up a board for designing a new government for Athens. In an assembly meeting, the oligarch Pisander proposed another decree.

28.4.B   A Decree Concerning Public Offices and the Council

Thucydides 8.67.3

At that point it was declared, with no obfuscation, that there was to be no holding of offices under the current administration and no payment for office. They were to choose five men as presidents [*proedroi*]; these were then to choose a hundred men, and each of the hundred to choose three men. This body, now four hundred strong, should proceed to the Council chamber and, with plenipotentiary powers, govern as they thought best. They were to bring together the Council of five thousand whenever they saw fit.

Ath. Pol. provides a different version of the role of the 5,000 and the way the 400 were elected. It is likely that the 400 Council members were elected by co-option, with some power granted to the 5,000. The tribal election reported by *Ath. Pol.* was either manipulated to confirm the co-option or it may have rubber-stamped it.

28.4.C   Unpaid Offices and the Powers of the 5,000
and of the Council of 400

Ath. Pol. 29.5, 31.1–2

(**29.5**) After that they organized the constitution as follows. Revenues could be disbursed on nothing other than the war, and all magistracies were to be unpaid for as long as the war lasted, exception being made for the nine archons and whatever presidents were in office, who were each to receive three obols per day. The rest of the administration of the state they would entrust to those most able to provide service to it (personally and by virtue of their wealth) for the duration of the war, and these would number no fewer than 5,000. These men would be empowered to negotiate treaties with whomsoever they wished, and they were to select ten men from each tribe (all over forty years of age) to enroll the Council of five thousand, after swearing an oath over sacrifices performed with full rites.

(**31.1**) Such, then, was the constitution they drafted for the future, but for the current circumstances the following was to obtain. There were to be, in accordance with ancestral custom, four hundred councilors, forty selected from each tribe, these to be taken from a shortlist, drawn up by tribe members, of men over thirty years of age. These men were to appoint the magistrates and propose the oath that should be taken. They were also to take measures they thought would be beneficial for the laws, the accounts, and everything else; **(31.2)** and with regard to any laws that were passed in the area of political administration they were to uphold them and not change them or put others in place...[1]

Note

1. *The Council was supposed to choose the generals as well. Ath. Pol. 30–31 reports on two constitutions, one more democratic in appearance that was intended for the future (Ath. Pol. 30), and another that was actually adopted (Ath. Pol. 31.1–3). Perhaps the two different plans reflected a division of opinion between moderate and extreme oligarchs, or the future plan may have aimed to lull the democratic opposition.*

 Once the resolution was ratified, the Four Hundred took over the Council house by force. They dismissed the old Council, and executed, imprisoned, or exiled political opponents. See WEB **28.5.III** for the split between the oligarchic city and the democratic navy in Samos, now led by Alcibiades who had joined them there, the fall of the oligarchs, and the creation of a new government of limited democracy of which Thucydides approved.

Democracy was clearly fully restored in the summer of 410 after the Athenian navy defeated the Peloponnesians at Cyzicus. Some oligarchs deserted to Agis in Decelea, while others were put on trial and condemned to death for treason. In July, the Athenian Demophantus proposed a decree that severely punished attempts to overthrow democracy. The Council of the 500 was restored. The source is a speech by the Athenian politician Andocides, who defended himself after the war against a charge of impiety.

28.4.D   Demophantus' Decree and the Restoration of Democracy

Andocides 1 *On the Mysteries* 96–98

(96) The law:

"The decision of the Council and the assembly (in the prytany of Aeantis, with Cleigenes as secretary and Boethus as president). The following motion was drawn up by Demophantus. The decree is from the first session of the Council of Five Hundred, chosen by lot, for whom Cleigenes was the secretary.

   Anyone dissolving the democracy in Athens, or anyone serving in a public office after the dissolution of democracy, is to be an enemy of the Athenians and may be killed with impunity, his goods becoming state property and a tenth of it assigned to the goddess. **(97)** The person responsible for killing a man who does such a thing, or plots to kill him, is to be free of guilt and sin. All the Athenians are to take an oath, tribe by tribe and deme by deme, over sacrifices with full rites, to kill a man who does this. The oath is to run as follows:

'I shall, by word, by deed, by my vote and by my own hand, if I am able, kill anyone who dissolves the democracy in Athens or anyone who, if the democracy is dissolved, thereafter serves in a public office or anyone who aims at tyranny or assists putting a tyrant in power. If somebody else slays one such, I shall consider him free of sin before the gods and the powers above, in that he shall have killed an enemy of the Athenians, and I shall sell the goods of the dead man and give half to his killer and deprive him of nothing. (**98**) If a man dies in the process of killing, or trying to kill, any such person, I shall show to him and his children the kindness accorded to Harmodius and Aristogeiton and their descendants.[1] Whatsoever oaths have been sworn at Athens or in the army or anywhere else that oppose the democracy of the Athenians, these I annul and renounce.'

All Athenians are to swear to this, as the customary oath, over sacrifices with full rites before the Dionysia. And they must pray for many blessings for the person keeping the oath and, for the person who does not, destruction for him and his progeny."

Note

1. See **10.10** *("The Athenian Tyrannicides") for Harmodius and Aristogeiton.*

In an act reminiscent of the commemoration of the tyrant-slayers, the Athenians officially thanked and awarded citizenship to aliens who took part in the assassination of the oligarch Phrynichus. Some individuals are even alleged to have claimed this honor falsely (ML no. 85 = Fornara no. 155; Lysias 13 *Against Agoratus* 71). Around this time the city initiated the recodification of the "laws of Solon," i.e., the city's laws, a project that would be completed only in 400/399. Draco's homicide law (**9.1**) was thus reinscribed in 409/8. Finally, in 410/9 the popular leader Cleophon instituted a two-obol payment (*diabolia*) either as a subsidy for the needy or for jury duty. The oligarchs of 411 had abolished these payments.

Questions

1. What persuaded the Athenians to change their government (see **28.2.D** and WEB **28.5.II**)?
2. What powers were given to the 5,000 and the Council of 400 in the different plans for government in 411 (**28.4**, WEB **28.5.II–III**)?
3. What measures did Demophantus' decree establish to prevent the overthrow of democracy (**28.4.D**)?

28.6 Ransoming Captives and the Selymbrian Decree (408–407)

Thucydides' account of the war stops abruptly in the autumn of 411, probably due to his death. It is continued by the much less detailed and systematic narrative of Xenophon *Hellenica*, and complemented by the universal history of the first-century Diodorus of Sicily: see **Introduction III.4–5** for both historians.

In spring 411 the Spartans and Persians signed a third treaty in an attempt to resolve their differences: see WEB **28.7.I** for the treaty. The Spartans also began to move their operations to the northern Aegean, where Pharnabazus offered them aid. However, under the command of Alcibiades, the Athenians won several engagements against Peloponnesian fleets in the northern Aegean.

A commentator on Aristotle's *Rhetoric* preserved a report by the fourth-century historian and politician Androtion on a ransoming agreement, which was probably signed in 408 after Alcibiades took the city of Byzantium and captured Spartans there. The norm was to exchange one male prisoner for another, with ransom paid for surplus captives usually by the friends and relatives of the prisoners.

28.6.A   Ransoming Captives

Androtion *FGrHist* 324 F 44 (scholion on Aristotle
Nicomachean Ethics 5.10.1134b = Fornara no. 157, p. 187)

Aristotle *Nicomachean Ethics* 5.10.1134b: "Ransom for a mina."

Scholion: This the Athenians and the Lacedaemonians agreed in their war against each other, that is, to ransom captives for a mina each. Androtion mentions this agreement: "Euctemon of Cyathenion. In his archonship [408/7] Megillus, Endius, and Philocharidas came as envoys from Lacedaemon to Athens." And he adds: "Of the surplus (of captives), they returned them for one mina for each." For he said previously that they had agreed on this in regard to the men they captured.[1]

Note

1.   *The text is emended, because the original misidentified Euctemon as from Cyrene, and the Spartan ambassadors as Melitus, Eudicus, and Philochorus. One mina = 100 drachmas, which was a low ransom.*

Like the Spartans, the Athenians were busy collecting money and acquiring or retaining allies. Thus in 408 Alcibiades captured Chalcedon, Selymbria, and Byzantium in the Hellespont region. In Selymbria, he pursued a reconciliatory policy that encouraged the city to become Athens' ally, accept a garrison, and pay him a sum of money (Plutarch *Alcibiades* 30). An Athenian decree preserves Alcibiades' agreement with the city and his motion to ratify it a year later (407). Especially noteworthy are the respect shown for Selymbria's autonomy and the Athenian renouncement of claims to property in the city except for real estates (lines 10–12, 18–22).

28.6.B   The Selymbrian Decree

ML no. 87 = Fornara no. 162

Translation: Osborne 2000, no. 182, pp. 82–83

Selymbria decree

[–] list [–], [the Athenians are to give back] the hostages whom they hold, and in future are not to take [hostages].

(**10**) The people of Selymbria are to [set up] the constitution in whatever way they know [to be best –]
 [Whatever] the Selymbrian state [or any individual] Selymbrian owed to [–], if the property of anyone has been confiscated [or if anyone] was in debt [to the state] (**15**) or if anyone has been deprived of civic rights [–] of the Selymbrians is in exile [–] enemies and friends [–] any [Athenian] or allied [property] that was lost in the war, or if someone has a debt (**20**) or deposit which [the magistrates] exacted, there shall be no exaction except in the case of land and houses. [All] other contracts formerly concluded between private individuals or between a private individual and the state or the state and a private individual, or any other, (**25**) they are to settle mutually. In the event of dispute, the [case] is to be settled according to contractual agreements [*symbolai*].
 The agreement to be written up on a stele and placed in the temple of [–].
 The Athenian generals and [trierarchs] and hoplites and any (**30**) [other Athenian] present and all the Selymbrians took an oath.
 [Al]cib[iades] proposed: to act in accordance with the agreement that the Selymbrians made with the Athenians. And the Generals with the Secretary of the Council are to write up the agreements (**35**) [erasure here] on a stone stele at their own expense along with this decree.
 And praise [Apo]llodorus the son of Empedus and release him from being a hostage, and the Secretary of the Council to wipe out tomorrow in the presence of the prytaneis the names of the Selymbrian hostages and of their sureties (**40**) wherever they are recorded.
 And write up [–]omachus of Selymbria on the same stele as Athenian *proxenos*. And grant proxeny to Apollodorus as to his father.
 Summon the ambassadors and Apollodorus to hospitality at the Prytaneum tomorrow.

Alcibiades had not gone back to Athens since joining the Athenian fleet in Samos in 411. His victories in the north, which helped Athens regain control over the Bosporus and the Hellespont, and his election as general for 407/6, made him less apprehensive about his return, and he landed in Piraeus that year. See WEB **28.7.II** for the scene of Alcibiades' return to Athens and for Athenian opinions of him.

Questions

1. What are the differences between the first and the third Spartan–Persian treaties (**28.2.B** and WEB **28.7.I**)?

2. What were the people of Selymbria entitled to under the agreement with Athens (**28.6.B**)?

3. Compare and contrast the Selymbrian decree of 408 (**28.6.B**) with the Erythraean decree of 453/2 (**21.3**). What do the differences tell us about Athens' situation at this stage of the war?

 4. What opinions did Athenians hold of Alcibiades after his return (WEB **28.7.II**)? Which camp do you think had a better case?

28.8   Cyrus the Younger and Lysander of Sparta

In 408, Athenian and other envoys on their way to the Persian king met returning Spartan envoys who gave them bad news.

28.8.A   Cyrus' Post

Xenophon *Hellenica* 1.4.2–3

(**1.4.2**) At the start of spring they set off again on their journey to the king, and were met by the Lacedaemonian ambassadors, Boeotius and his colleagues, and the other messengers, who told them that the Lacedaemonians had gained all they wanted from the king. (**4.3**) They also met Cyrus, who was to be governor of the entire seaboard and who would be assisting the Lacedaemonians with their war effort. Cyrus was also carrying a letter bearing the royal seal and addressed to all the coastal peoples. This contained, *inter alia*, the following statement: "I am sending Cyrus down to the coast as *Karanos* over all those mustering at Castolus"[1] (*Karanos* means "lord").

Note

1.   *Castolus was a plain in Lydia and an inspection ground of the army.*

Cyrus (the Younger) was the sixteen-year-old son of Darius II. The nature of his position is unclear, but he probably ranked above the two local satraps, Tissaphernes and Pharnabazus. Cyrus' post suggested that the Persian king had resolved to throw his full – and especially financial – support behind Sparta. See WEB **28.9.I** for Cyrus' mission in Asia Minor.

The sources do not report what Sparta promised in return for Persian aid in the "Treaty of Boeotius." Apparently, she agreed that the Ionians would pay tribute to the Persians but would keep their autonomy. It was Cyrus' unequivocal support of Sparta and the generalship of the Spartan Lysander that decided the war for Sparta.

In 407/6 Lysander was appointed admiral of the Peloponnesian navy and soon established an excellent rapport with Cyrus the Younger. Cyrus raised the daily wages of the Peloponnesian oarsmen to four obols, thereby boosting the sailors' morale and encouraging desertion from the Athenian navy. Shortly after, the opposing fleets clashed in the battle of Notium, north of Lysander's base in Ephesus.

───────────────────────────────────── 28.8.B   The Battle of Notium

Diodorus of Sicily 13.71.1–4[1]

(**13.71.1**) On learning that Lysander was equipping his fleet at Ephesus, Alcibiades headed for Ephesus with all his ships. He sailed up to the harbor-mouths, but met no resistance. He accordingly anchored most of the ships off Notium, and gave command of them to his own ship's helmsman, Antiochus, ordering him not to engage at sea until he returned. He then took the troop carriers and sailed swiftly to Clazomenae. The city was an ally of Athens and was suffering badly from raids launched against it by a number of exiles.

(**71.2**) Antiochus, however, was reckless by nature and eager to bring off some brilliant feat of his own, and he ignored what Alcibiades had said. He put crews aboard the ten best ships, and issued orders to the trierarchs to keep the rest at the ready in case they had to fight a naval engagement. He then sailed toward the enemy to challenge them to fight.

(**71.3**) Now Lysander had been informed by a number of deserters that Alcibiades had left and his finest men along with him, and he decided it was the right time to bring off some coup worthy of Sparta. He therefore led out all his ships against the enemy and sank one of the ten Athenian vessels – the one on which Antiochus had taken his post for the engagement – which was sailing ahead of the rest. The others he drove back and pursued until the Athenian trierarchs manned their remaining ships and came to help them, but in total disorder. (**71.4**) A full-scale naval engagement then took place between the fleets of both sides not far from shore. Because of their disarray, the Athenians were defeated and lost 22 ships.[2] Only a few of the men on them were taken prisoner, however; the others managed to swim safely to land.

When Alcibiades learned what had happened, he swiftly returned to Notium, manned all his triremes, and bore down on the harbors sheltering the enemy. Lysander, however, dared not sail out to face him, and Alcibiades made for Samos.

Notes

1. *Diodorus apparently used for his account the Oxyrhynchus historian, whose description of the battle survived in part (4.1–4). See also Xenophon* Hellenica *1.5.11–15; Plutarch* Alcibiades *35.5–8; Lysander 5.3–5 (relying on Xenophon).*
2. *Xenophon reports the loss of only fifteen triremes.*

The defeat of Notium led to Alcibiades' second exile, for which see WEB **28.9.II**.

Alcibiades retired to Thrace, and thence to Phrygia in Asia Minor following the Athenian defeat to Sparta in the battle of Aegospotami in 405 (see WEB **28.11**). He was killed in Phrygia by the local satrap Pharnabazus at the behest of the Spartans (Plutarch *Alcibiades* 37.3–39.5).

Questions

1. What changed in the Persian policy with the mission of Cyrus the Younger, and what was his immediate impact (**28.8.A**, WEB **28.9.I**)?

2. To what extent was Alcibiades responsible for the Athenian defeat at Notium (**28.8.B**, WEB **28.9.II**)?

28.10   The Arginusae Affair (406/5)

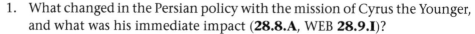

In 406/5, Lysander's successor as chief admiral was soundly defeated by the Athenian navy in a battle near the islands of Arginusae, southeast of Lesbos. The defeat moved Sparta to sue for peace, but the confident Athenians declined the offer. Ironically, they also punished their victorious generals for their conduct in the aftermath of the battle.

The Athenians had lost twenty-five ships in Arginusae, and the eight generals in command instructed several ship captains, including the politicians Theramenes and Thrasybulus, to collect the corpses and survivors. A storm prevented the rescue operation, and when six of the generals returned home, their political foes charged them with failing to recover the dead. The generals were found guilty in a clearly illegal procedure.

For ancient critics of democracy the Arginusae affair proved that the demos was controlled by emotions and demagogues. Yet Athenian democracy had, by and large, a good record of maintaining the rule of law; the Arginusae incident was an exception and had much to do with the pressures of the war.

Xenophon *Hellenica* 1.7.4–5, 8–10, 12; cf. Diodorus of Sicily 13.101–103.2

(1.7.4) After this [i.e., the pretrial imprisonment of the returning generals] an assembly was held at which some people, and Theramenes in particular, attacked the generals, saying that they should be held accountable for their failure to pick up the shipwrecked crews. As evidence that the generals blamed no one other than themselves Theramenes pointed to a letter that they had sent to the Council and the assembly, in which they attributed the disaster to the storm and nothing else. **(7.5)** The generals then each spoke in his own defense, but briefly (for according to the law they were not permitted to speak), and discussed what had happened. They themselves were going to sail against the enemy, they said, but responsibility for recovering the shipwrecked crews they assigned to competent individuals amongst the trierarchs who had already served as generals themselves, namely Theramenes, Thrasybulus, and the like.

The assembly then adjourned.

(1.7.8) This was followed by the Apaturia, at which fathers and their kinsfolk gather together.[1] Now Theramenes and his supporters procured at this festival a number of people who were dressed in black and had their heads close-shaven, and he had them come to the assembly representing themselves as kinsmen of the deceased; and they also persuaded Callixeinus to denounce the generals in the council. (**1.9**) They then convened the assembly, to which the council brought a proposal it had drafted and which Callixeinus introduced as follows:[2]

"Since they have now heard in the previous assembly both those who accuse the generals and the generals defending themselves, all the Athenians shall now proceed to the vote by tribe. For each tribe two urns shall be set out; and in the case of each tribe a herald is to announce that anyone who considers the generals guilty for not recovering the men who won the naval battle shall cast his vote in the first urn, and anyone who considers them not guilty shall cast his vote in the second. (**1.10**) If they are convicted they shall be punished by death and delivered to the Eleven[3] and their property shall be confiscated, with a tenth part to be given to the goddess."

(**1.12**) Callixeinus was summoned to court by Euryptolemus son of Peisianax and a number of others, who declared that he had made an illegal motion. Some members of the people approved of this, but the majority cried out that it was unconscionable for anyone not to allow the people to do whatever they pleased.

Notes

1. *The Apaturia was a festival of the phratries in which fathers introduced and acknowledged their male babies and when adult males joined the phratry.*
2. *The identity of Callixeinus is uncertain. He might have been a friend of Cleophon and perhaps an Alcmeonid.*
3. *The Eleven were in charge of the prison, execution, and some police duties.*

Callixeinus' proposal was illegal because it did not allow the generals to plead their case in court and because they were punished collectively. Among the generals who were condemned to death was Pericles the Younger, son of the famous politician and Aspasia.

Questions

1. What lines of defense did the generals and their supporters use in the Arginusae affair?
2. How did the people justify their rejection of the appeal of Callixeinus' decree? What does this say about the relations between democracy and the rule of law?

28.12 Athens' Defeat and the End of the Peloponnesian War (405/4)

In Sparta, pressure from the Ionians and Cyrus led to the reappointment of Lysander as commander-in-chief in 405/4. He took the Peloponnesian navy toward the Hellespont and the maritime route of the Athenian grain supply.

The Athenians followed him with 180 ships, and Lysander probably had as many vessels. The Athenian fleet anchored in Aegospotami ("Goat-Rivers"), where it suffered a crushing defeat. See WEB **28.11** for the battle of Aegospotami.

Following the victory, Lysander sent to Athens any Athenian he could find in order to swell the city with people and make it more vulnerable to siege. He also dismantled the Athenian empire by replacing the governments of the allies with friendly oligarchies, called *dekarchia* (decarchy, rule of ten), and, when necessary, a Spartan *harmostês* (governor) with a garrison.

28.12.A   Lysander Changes the Governments of the Allies

Plutarch *Lysander* 13.3–5

(**13.3**) ...He dissolved democratic governments and all other constitutions, and left one Spartan harmost [governor] in every city along with ten rulers who were chosen from the political associations that he had put together throughout the cities. (**13.4**) He did this in the cities that had been allied to him as well as in those that had been his enemies, and he sailed on at a relaxed pace, in a way acquiring for himself hegemony over Greece. For he did not appoint the rulers from considerations of nobility or wealth; instead, he based the dispensing of power on personal relationships and friendship, giving these people the right to bestow honor and punishment. He was personally involved in many massacres, and he assisted his friends in expelling their enemies, giving the Greeks no decent illustration of Spartan government. (**13.5**) In fact, the comic poet Theopompus appears to be talking nonsense in comparing the Spartans to tavern girls inasmuch as after the Greeks had tasted the sweet wine of freedom, they then gave them plonk. The taste was, in fact, *always* unpleasant and bitter, right from the beginining, since Lysander would not permit the common people in the cities to have control of their governments, and he actually put the cities in the hands of the most reckless and aggressive of the oligarchs.

Unlike many allies, the democrats of Samos refused to surrender to Sparta. The grateful Athenians gave the Samians Athenian citizenship, an extraordinary gesture that showed both their appreciation and desperate need for friends. They were careful, however, to assure the Samians that the island would remain autonomous. The resolution was passed in 405/4, but the inscription recording it was inscribed in 403/2, perhaps because the original was destroyed by the oligarchs who ruled the city after its defeat. The relief on the upper part of the decree shows Athena grasping the hand of Hera, the patron goddess of Samos.

The Samian Decree ML no. 94 = Fornara no. 166

Translation: Osborne 2000, no. 183, pp. 83–85

Cephisophon of Paeania was Secretary [403/2]. For the Samians who sided with the Athenian People.

(**5**) The Council and People decided, when the tribe Cecropis held the prytany, Polymnis of Euonymon was Secretary. Alexias was Archon [405/4], and Nicophon of Athmonon was President. A proposal of Cleisophus and his fellow prytaneis: to praise the Samian ambassadors, both those who came previously and those who have come now, and the council, generals, and other Samians because they are men good and keen to do what good they can, (**10**) and what they do they seem to do correctly for the Athenians and the Samians. And in return for their good services to the Athenians and because even now they display much concern and introduce good measures the Council and People decided that the Samians should be Athenian citizens, governing themselves as they themselves want. And in order that this may happen in whatever way is most advantageous for both parties, as they themselves propose, when peace comes, then (**15**) there will be common deliberations on other matters. They are to use their own laws and be independent, and do everything else according to the oaths and agreements that the Athenians have made with the Samians. As to any complaints that arise with each other, they are to give and receive legal cases in accordance with all the legal treaties. If some necessity happens as a result of the war which relates to the constitution before the war ends, (**20**) as the ambassadors themselves say, the People are to do whatever seems best to them in the circumstances. As to peace, if peace is made, it is to be on the same conditions for those now living on Samos as for the Athenians. And if it is necessary to fight, they will make the best preparations they can, acting together with the Generals. If the Athenians send an embassy anywhere, those from Samos who are present (**25**) are to join that embassy, if they wish, and join in counseling any good they can. To grant them the triremes which are at Samos to equip and use as they think best. [The ambassadors], with the Secretary of the Council and the Generals, are to list the names of the trierachs whose ships these are, and the dockyard superintendents are to expunge completely [any debt] recorded as incurred on the triremes anywhere against their names in the public record, (**30**) but the equipment they are to [exact as quickly as possible] and compel those who have it to give it back [in good condition] to the public store.[1]

[Cleisiphus] and his fellow prytanies [proposed]: in other respects let it be as the Council proposes, [but the gift should be made to those of the Samians who] have come, as they themselves ask, and [they] should be distributed [straightaway into demes and] ten tribes.[2] (**35**) And [the Generals should immediately provide] travelling expenses [for the ambassadors], and praise Eumachus and [all the other Samians who have come with Eumachus] as men [good to the Athenians. And summon Eum]achus to supper at the prytaneion [tomorrow].[3] The Secretary of the Council with the [Generals is to write up what has been decided on a stone stele and] set it up on the Acropolis, and the *Hellenotamiai* (**40**) [are to give the money. Also to be inscribed on Sa]mos in the same way at [their own] expense.

Notes

1. *The triremes were probably Athenian ships in Samos that did not make it to the battle of Aegospotami. Their captains were discharged from debts related to their trierarchies.*

2. *An alternative restoration is that the Samians will be distributed into (the) ten tribes.*
3. *Because the Samian Eumachus was now a citizen, he was given the honor of dining (deipnon) in the Prytaneum, which was accorded only to citizens. When non-citizens received this honor it was called "hospitality" (xenia).*

The Spartans put Athens under siege. Their king, Pausanias, came with a large Peloponnesian army to join king Agis in Attica, and Lysander arrived in Piraeus with 150 ships. Sparta demanded that Athens surrender and demolish her Long Walls. The popular leader Cleophon strongly opposed these demands, but was put to death shortly after following an allegedly rigged trial. The Athenian Theramenes, whose conduct had been questionable both in the 411 coup and the Arginusae affair, volunteered to go to Lysander to negotiate better terms. He stayed away for three months, either to soften the resolve of the starving Athenians or because Lysander detained him. When he returned to Athens, he was recommissioned with other envoys to negotiate terms at Sparta. They met the Spartan ephors in Laconia.

28.12.C   Sparta Refuses to Destroy Athens and Her Terms of Surrender

Xenophon *Hellenica* 2.2.19–20

(**2.2.19**) When Theramenes and the other representatives were at Sellasia[1] and were asked their purpose in coming, they said that they came with full powers to negotiate peace. After that the ephors gave orders that they be summoned to them. When they arrived, the ephors convened an assembly, at which the Corinthians and Thebans especially, but many other Greek communities as well, spoke against making peace with Athens, which they said they ought to destroy.

(**2.20**) The Spartans, however, said they would not reduce to slavery a Greek city that had provided such stellar service at the time when the greatest perils were facing Greece. Instead, they proceeded to make a peace treaty with her on the condition that the Athenians dismantle the Long Walls and those of Piraeus; that they surrender all but twelve of their ships; that they restore their exiles; and that they follow the Spartans wherever they should lead, on land and sea, recognizing the same enemies and friends.[2]

Notes

1. *Sellasia was in or on the border of Laconia.*
2. *According to Andocides (3 On the Peace 11–12), the terms also included giving up control over the islands of Lemnos, Imbros, and Scyros.*

Both *Ath. Pol.* (34.3) and Diodorus (14.3.2) include in the Spartan terms the instruction that Athens should be governed according to its "ancestral constitution" (*patrios politeia*). Some scholars reject the authenticity of this demand, but even if historic, it was sufficiently vague to allow different interpretations of the future government of Athens.

Xenophon *Hellenica* 2.2.21–23

(**2.2.21**) Theramenes and the other representatives with him brought these conditions back to Athens. As they entered the city a large crowd of people began to mill about them, fearing that they had returned empty-handed. For the numbers dying of starvation left no further room for delay. (**2.22**) The following day the representatives announced the terms on which the Spartans would make peace, and Theramenes delivered the report, saying that it was imperative that they accept the Spartan conditions and dismantle the walls. A number opposed him, but far more were in agreement, and their final decision was to accept the peace treaty. (**2.23**) After that Lysander sailed into Piraeus, the exiles were restored, and the Spartans, with great enthusiasm, set to tearing down the walls, accompanied by the music of flute-girls. They thought that that day spelled the start of Greece's liberation.[1]

Note

1. *It is unclear if Lysander accepted the surrender in March or April 404.*

Questions

1. What were Lysander's tactics in the battle of Aegospotami (WEB **28.11**)?
2. What did the Athenian–Samian cooperation entail, according to the Samian decree (**28.12.B**)?
3. What were the Spartan options for dealing with defeated Athens and what guided her decision (**28.12.A**, **28.12.C**)?
4. What were the Spartan terms of surrender and what do they tell us about the Spartan vision of Athens after her defeat (**28.12.C–D**)?

28.13   Honoring the Victor

Sparta won the war, and Lysander was the man who led her to victory. Tripods and victory statues commemorated his accomplishment in Sparta, and he received extraordinary honors in Greece. The Roman-era author Pausanias (10.9.7–10) describes a group of statues close to the Sacred Way in Delphi that commemorated the victory of Aegospotami. Among them were statues of the Dioscuri, Zeus, Apollo, Artemis, and Poseidon, as well as of Lysander crowned by Poseidon, in addition to his seer and pilot. Behind them stood statues of twenty-eight allied commanders. One of the statue-bases was found with an inscription whose letterforms dated it to the fourth century, although it could be a reinscription of an earlier original.

28.13.A   A Dedication in Honor of Lysander

ML no. 95 c = Harding no. 4

Translation: Harding, p. 10

He dedicated his statue [upon] this monument, when, victorious with his swift ships, he had destroyed the power of the sons of Ce[c]rops, Lysander (is his name), having crowned unsacked Lacedaemon, his fatherland with its beautiful dancing-grounds, as the acropolis of Greece. He from sea-girt Samos composed the poem. Ion (is his name).

After Lysander subjugated Samos, his local friends there honored him. According to the historian Duris of Samos (ca. 340–260; *FGrHist* 76 F 71), he was even accorded divine honors that made him the first living Greek to enjoy such status. Yet it is not impossible that Duris introduced into Samian history honors that belonged to his own times.

28.13.B   Lysander's Extraordinary Honors

Plutarch *Lysander* 18.2–4

(**18.2**) ... Now at that time Lysander held power such as no Greek before him had possessed, but he was thought to possess a pretentiousness and self-importance greater than was justified by his power. (**18.3**) He was the first of the Greeks, according to Duris' history, to whom the city-states erected altars and offered sacrifices as to a god, and the first to whom choral paeans were sung. One of these remains in the oral tradition as beginning as follows:

"We shall sing of brave Greece's commander from Sparta of the wide spaces. Oh, Io, Paean!"
(**18.4**) The Samians voted to rename the festival of Hera in their community "the Lysandrea." Lysander always kept with him Choerilus, one of the poets, to embellish his achievements with verse, while in the case of Antilochus, who composed some lines on him, Lysander was so pleased that he filled his hat with silver and gave it to him ...

The Athenian reaction to Aegospotami was predictably different. Later Athenian democrats shaped the city's collective memory of the battle in a way that denied the humiliation of defeat as well as the people's responsibility for it. In a funeral speech, whose attribution to the speechwriter Lysias is uncertain, and which might have been written in the late 390s, the speaker is careful to blame the Athenian command or evil fortune for the loss.

_____   28.13.C   An Athenian View of the Defeat

Lysias 2 *Funeral Oration* 58

Even in the midst of misfortune they displayed their usual fortitude, as when the fleet was destroyed at the Hellespont, whether through the commander's incompetence or the will of the gods. This was a crushing disaster both for us who suffered the misfortune and for the rest of the Greeks, but not long afterwards Athens showed that her power as a city provided security for Greece.

Question

1. What extraordinary honors was Lysander accorded?

Review Questions

1. Why did the Athenians lose the Peloponnesian War?
2. What major changes did Sparta make in her strategy during the Decelean War (**28.1–2**, **28.8**, WEB **28.3.II**, WEB **28.7.I**, WEB **28.9.I**)?
3. Was Alcibiades good or bad for Athens in the Decelean War (see **28.2**, **28.4**, **28.6**, **28.8.B**, WEB **28.3.II**, WEB **28.7.II**, WEB **28.9.II**)?
4. What kind of government did the opponents of Athenian democracy plan to establish in Athens in 411 and why did they fail (**28.4**, WEB **28.5.I–III**)?
5. What changed in Athens' treatment of her allies judging by the Selymbrian and Samian decrees (**28.6.B**, **28.12.B**)?
6. Discuss the Sparta–Persia relationship during the Decelean War (**28.2.B–C**, **28.8.A**, WEB **28.3.II**, WEB **28.7.I**, WEB **28.9.I**).
7. What was the impact of Athenian foreign affairs on domestic affairs and vice versa during the Decelean War (see **28.4**, **28.10**, **28.12.B**, WEB **28.5.I–III**, WEB **28.7.II**, WEB **28.9.II**)?
8. An Athenian speaker claimed that the Athenian defeat was a disaster for the other Greeks (**28.13.C**). Do you agree?

Suggested Readings

The Decelean War: Kagan 1987; Lazenby 2004, 170–250; Hanson 2005, 325–484. *Persia and the Greeks*: Wiesehöfer 2006. *Sparta and Persia up to 411*: Lewis 1977, 83–107; Hornblower 1991–2008, 3: 800–802, 924–931. *Alcibiades, Persia, and Athens*: Lateiner 1976; Aidonis 1996; Lang 1996; Hyland 2004. *The oligarchy of 411*: Ste Croix 1956;

Rhodes 1972; Andrewes in Gomme et al. 1981, 5: 107–134; Harris 1990; Munn 2000, 127–151. *The battles of Cyzicus and Notium*: Andrewes 1982b; Kagan 1987, 234–324; Lazenby 2004, 202–224. *Prisoners' exchange*: Pritchett 1991, 5: 247–249; Harding 1994, 162–164. *Selymbria*: ML, pp. 267–269. *Spartan–Persian treaties*: Lewis 1977, 83–135. *The Arginusae affair*: Andrewes 1974; Ostwald 1986, 434–442; Lang, 1992. *The battle of Aegospotami*: Strauss 1983, 1987; Wylie 1986; Lazenby 2004, 240–244. *Athens and Samos*: ML, pp. 283–287; Blanshard 2007 (questioning the identity of Hera on the relief). *Athens' surrender*: Krentz 1982, 28–56; Ostwald 1986, 445–475; Green 1991b; Wolpert 2002b, 3–15.

29

The Rule of the Thirty, the Athenian Amnesty, and Socrates' Trial

CHAPTER CONTENTS

Ancient Greece from Homer to Alexander: The Evidence, First Edition. Joseph Roisman.
© 2011 Blackwell Publishing Ltd. Translations © 2011 John Yardley. Published 2011 by Blackwell Publishing Ltd.

The Athenian defeat in the Peloponnesian War exposed the Athenian democracy to attacks from oligarchic members of the upper class as well as exiles who returned to the city. This chapter describes the oligarchic rule that these Athenians established with Spartan help. It discusses how the leading oligarchs, known as the Thirty, came to power, their oppressive rule, and their fall. Some of the Spartans who came to help the oligarchs against their democratic rivals died in battle, and the chapter produces literary and archaeological evidence of their burial in an Athenian cemetery. It also reports on the reconciliation agreement between the feuding Athenian parties and on the trial of Socrates, whose fate cannot be dissociated from the bitter memories of the Thirty's rule and Athens' defeat.

29.1   The Establishment of the Rule of the Thirty (404)

The Athenian defeat in the Peloponnesian War exposed Athenian democracy to attacks from oligarchic members of the upper class as well as exiles returning to the city. Most prominent among the latter was Critias, a pupil of Socrates, an admirer of Sparta, and an extreme oligarch. In early summer 404, a popular assembly was convened in which Lysander was present to show his support for the oligarchs. The speechwriter Lysias describes this assembly meeting in a prosecution speech, which he delivered in 403/2 against Eratosthenes. Lysias accused Eratosthenes, who belonged to the oligarchic rule of the Thirty, of responsibility for the death of Lysias' brother. (For the Attic orators, see **Introduction III.7.**)

Lysias held the Athenian political leader Theramenes chiefly responsible for the institution of the Thirty in Athens. Other sources are much more favorable toward Theramenes. Lysias' version also reflects the Athenians' wish to distance themselves from this sad chapter in their history and their acquiescing to the oligarchs.

Lysias 12 *Against Eratosthenes* 72–74, 76

(**72**) This was how matters stood, and in the presence of Lysander, Philochares, and Miltiades (Lysander's aides), they convened the assembly to discuss the constitution. At this no public speaker could oppose them or make threats against them, and you could not choose what was beneficial for the city but could merely vote for whatever they favored.

(**73**) Theramenes stood up and told you to turn the city over to thirty men, and put in service the constitution that Dracontides had publicized.[1] Despite being placed in such a position you nevertheless vociferously declared your opposition, since you well realized that on that day your debate was about slavery and freedom. (**74**) But, Gentlemen of the Jury, Theramenes declared – and to this I shall call you yourselves as witnesses – that he was not at all concerned about your uproar as he knew many Athenians who were working for the same ends as he was, and that what he was saying had the approval of Lysander and the Lacedaemonians. Following him, Lysander got up and made numerous points, in particular that he regarded you as truce-breakers, and that if you did not follow Theramenes' prescripts it was not the constitution that would be at stake but your lives ...

(**76**) They (the movers) had prior instructions to elect ten men whom Theramenes had specified, ten more who were the choice of the selected ephors,[2] and ten from the present gathering. They could see your weakness and knew their own power, to the extent that they were sure in advance of what the results of the debate in the assembly were going to be.

Notes

1. *Dracontides moved to change the government to oligarchy.*
2. *Prior to the meeting, the pro-Spartan oligarchs elected five ephors.*

Question

1. Why did the Athenians approve changing their government, according to Lysias?

29.2   The Thirty Tyrants

The Thirty appeared to have modeled themselves after the Spartan Council (*gerousia*, for which see **7.11**). From Lysander's and the Spartans' point of view they constituted an extended decarchy, a "rule of ten," which ruled other cities with Sparta's blessing (**28.12.A**: "Lysander Changes the Governments of the Allies"). Waving the banner of restoring the "ancestral constitution," the oligarchs abolished democratic legislation that empowered the popular courts and weakened the Areopagus. They also took measures against abusers of the legal system known as "sykophants." Soon, however, the Thirty become greedier for power and money and behaved tyrannically. Helped by a Spartan garrison, which they had requested, they victimized citizens and rich aliens including Lysias' family. See WEB **36.2.I** ("Good Metics") on Lysias' complaint of the Thirty's treatment of resident aliens.

Theramenes, who belonged to the Thirty but opposed their methods, demanded to increase the number of those in government. The Thirty later put him on trial and condemned him to death.

Xenophon *Hellenica* 2.3.17–18

(**2.3.17**) Large numbers were being put to death, and without justification, and it was evident that many men had formed groups and were wondering what would become of the constitution. At that point Theramenes made a further speech. It would be impossible for the oligarchy to survive unless they accepted a sufficient number of people to share power with them, he declared. (**3.18**) Critias and the other members of the Thirty were already particularly scared of Theramenes, fearing that the citizens might come flocking to his support, and this prompted them to bring together three thousand who were to share power with them...

29.3   The Fall of the Thirty (403)

The reign of terror continued, including expulsion from the city of those who did not belong to the body of 3,000 full citizens and confiscation of property. In the meantime the population of Athenian exiles grew, especially in Thebes and Argos, which gave them refuge in violation of a Spartan request to deny them support. The two cities did not care for narrow oligarchies, which could inspire imitators, and perhaps wished to display their independence from Sparta. A small number of Athenian exiles, led by the democratic leader Thrasybulus and others, seized and fortified Phyle on the border of Attica and Boeotia in 403. The Thirty's attempt to dislodge them failed, and the exiles, now more than 700 in number, took over Munychia in the Piraeus. The Thirty, helped by men from the city and Spartan troops, failed to defeat them and Critias was killed in a battle. See WEB **29.4** for Critias' alleged grave monument. The Thirty's regime now came to an end.

Xenophon *Hellenica* 2.4.23–24

(**2.4.23**) The next day the Thirty assembled for deliberation in the council chamber, thoroughly miserable and isolated, and wherever members of the Three Thousand were stationed they fell to quarreling with one another. Those who had been guilty of particularly violent conduct, and were therefore now in fear, argued strongly against giving in to the men in Piraeus; those believing they had done no wrong, however, rationalized that they need not suffer these evils and tried to convince the others. They should not listen to the Thirty, they said, or permit them to destroy the city. Finally they voted to end the administration of the Thirty and elect other leaders. They actually chose ten men, one from each tribe.

(**4.24**) The Thirty then went off to Eleusis. The Ten, in conjunction with the cavalry commanders, took charge of those in the city, who were in a chaotic state and distrustful of one another...

Question

1.   What difficulties did the Thirty encounter in maintaining their rule?

29.5 The Spartans' Grave at Athens and the Athenian Amnesty (403)

The Ten, who replaced the Thirty, resembled other decarchies and were only slightly more moderate than the Thirty. Fearful of the democrats in Piraeus, they and the Thirty in Eleusis asked the Spartans for assistance. See WEB **29.6** for the reactions of the Spartans and their allies to the Thirty's appeal for help against the exiles.

It was the Spartan king Pausanias who helped Athens to get rid of its tyrants, thereby resembling his ancestor Cleomenes I more than a century earlier (cf. **10.12**: "The Expulsion of the Tyrants"). Xenophon (*Hellenica* 2.4.29) thinks that Pausanias was moved by jealousy of Lysander. The king took a Peloponnesian army and moved against Piraeus.

29.5.A   The Battle between the Peloponnesians and Athenian Democrats

Xenophon *Hellenica* 2.4.33

As it happened, all the peltasts[1] and hoplites from the Piraeus were arming themselves in the theater. The light-armed troops accordingly made a sortie at once, and proceeded to hurl their javelins, throw stones, shoot arrows, and use their slings. Many of the Spartans were receiving wounds and, under pressure, they began to pull back, which prompted their opponents to attack with even greater determination. In that engagement Chaeron and Thibrachus, two polemarchs, lost their lives, along with the Olympic champion Lacrates and other Lacedaemonians who now lie buried before the gates in the Kerameikos.

Note

1. *For peltasts (lighter-armed troops), see* **31.10** *("Peltasts and the Battle of Lechaeum").*

29.5.B   The Spartan Grave in Athens

The Spartans practiced group burial of warriors elsewhere. Here they were buried, probably in an Athenian gesture of reconciliation, in a prominent place in the Kerameikos, next to the road leading from the Dipylon Gate to the Academy. A walled structure marked the site and thirteen skeletons were found in its chambers (Figure 29.1, p. 410). One warrior was hit by two bronze arrowheads in his right leg and another by an iron spearhead in his ribs. The heads were laid on stones. The dearth of funerary artifacts (except for one strigil) is in line with the austerity of Spartan burial practices. A fragmentary inscription

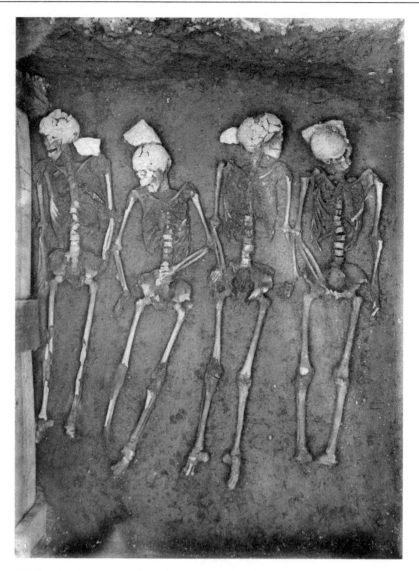

Figure 29.1   The Spartan tomb in the Kerameikos. Photo Deutsches Archaologisches Institut, Neg No D-DAI-ATH-Kerameikos 1992.

from the site has survived (*IG* II² 11678). It is written from right to left in the Laconian alphabet, and can be restored to read the words "Lacedaemonian," "Chaeron," and "Thibrachos."

The battle on the Piraeus ended in Spartan victory. This show of strength, and perhaps an appeal from the brother of Nicias, the former Athenian friend of Sparta (Lysias 18 *On the Property of Nicias' Brother* 10), moved Pausanias to reconcile the democrats of Piraeus with the oligarchs in the city. He would later be put on trial at home for his action and was narrowly acquitted. Following negotiations in Sparta with envoys from both Piraeus and the city, the two warring parties reached a reconciliation that included an amnesty.

_____   29.5.C   The Settlement Between the Democrats and the Oligarchs

Xenophon *Hellenica* 2.4.38

When the ephors and members of the Spartan assembly had heard all the representatives, they sent fifteen men off to Athens with instructions for them to act in concert with Pausanias to arrange a settlement as best they could. They succeeded in arranging the settlement, the terms of which were that peace should exist between the two sides, and that all should leave for their respective homes with the exception of the Thirty, the Eleven, and the Ten who had been in power in Piraeus. They further decided that any in the city who were in fear should take up residence in Eleusis.

Ath. Pol. adds more details on the agreement.

Ath. Pol. 39.6

Nobody was to remember in anyone's case the things he had done in the past, exception being made for members of the Thirty, the Ten, the Eleven, and those who had been in office in Piraeus, and not even in their case if they submitted an account [*euthyna*]. Those who had been in office in Piraeus should submit an account before the people of Piraeus, and those in the city before a committee of people with ratable property. Those unwilling to submit to this may, alternatively, leave their homes. Each party was to repay on its own loans taken out for the war.

The oligarchs continued to reside in Eleusis for two more years before Eleusis and Athens reunited under democratic rule. It is to the Athenians' credit that many of them abided by the terms of the reconciliation. Democrats of later generations proudly presented this fact as proof of the spirit of moderation that imbued the city.

The following example illustrates the way the city dealt with attempts to deviate from the agreement. The democratic leader Thrasybulus moved to reward everyone who fought on the side of the democrats with Athenian citizenship, including aliens and slaves. However, the politician Archinus successfully opposed the motion as illegal (*graphê paranomon*), proposing instead to establish a legal procedure called *paragraphê* (counter-suit), which was designed to prevent prosecution that violated the amnesty agreement.

29.5.D   Counter-Suit (*Paragraphê*)

Isocrates 18 *Against Callimachus* 2–3

(**2**) When you came back from Piraeus you could see a number of citizens rushing to lay false charges and trying to break the accords. You wanted to make them stop, and to demonstrate to everybody else that you drafted these accords not under duress, but in the belief that they were of benefit to the city; and so you passed a law, on a motion made by Archinus. This stated that, in the case of anyone breaking his oaths in going to law, the defendant had the right to object to the admissibility of the suit, the archons should first submit the matter to the court, and the party lodging the objection should speak first; (**3**) and, in addition, the party that loses should pay the one-sixth costs. The object of this was to insure that people having the gall to act on old grudges should not only be convicted of swearing falsely, but should also face immediate punishment and not simply await the vengeance of heaven...

Questions

1. Why did Argos and Thebes refuse the Spartan request to join the expedition against Athens, and what does their refusal suggest about Sparta's standing in Greece (WEB **29.6**)?
2. What were the terms of the reconciliation between the Athenian democrats and oligarchs (**29.5.C**)?
3. What were the challenges of implementing the amnesty and what was Archinus' solution for them (**29.5.D**, and see also **29.7**)?

29.7   Socrates' Trial (399)

The reconciliation had its limits. It was tested in court when victims of the Thirty or other Athenians prosecuted their personal and political enemies for past wrongs, even though these were supposed to be forgotten. There was also a wish to punish men viewed as responsible for the military defeat in the war and its consequences. The search for culprits also affected the philosopher Socrates. See WEB **29.8** for the background to Socrates' trial and his image.

Socrates was condemned to death, and thanks to the works of his pupils, Plato and Xenophon, his trial became a prime example of injustice in a democratic city. The fact was that he was instrumental in his own demise. He declined to go into exile, but chose to obey the city's laws, unjust as he and others deemed them to be. In the *agon timetos*, the post-trial procedure in which the disputing parties recommended penalties to the court, Socrates angered the jurors by asking not for pity but a prize, or agreed reluctantly to pay a fine (Plato *Apology* 38b; in Xenophon *Apology* 23 he refused to suggest a penalty). He had the privilege, however, of dying the quicker and more respected death of drinking poison.

Plato *Apology* 36b–d

(**36b**) ... So the man [prosecutor] is proposing the death penalty. All right; then what alternative shall I propose to you, Gentlemen of Athens? Evidently the one that I deserve! So, what is it that I deserve to suffer or pay as a fine? My crime is that, having learned lessons in life, I did not remain idle. No, I paid no attention to the things most people care about, money-making, managing one's household affairs, military commands, public speaking, and the other offices, political parties, and political associations that are part of city-life, (**36c**) for I thought myself too decent a person to be able to survive pursuing these objectives. So I did not follow a direction in which I was likely to be of no service either to you or to myself, but rather one in which – so I maintain – I was likely to benefit each of you most as individuals. I tried to persuade each one of you not to focus so much on any of his belongings as on himself, to focus rather on making oneself as good and as wise as possible; and not to focus on the affairs of the city, but on the city itself, and to do the same thing in all other areas, too.

(**36d**) So what do I deserve for being such a person? Something good, Gentlemen of Athens, if my penalty must really be what I merit. And, in addition, something good that would be appropriate for me. So what is appropriate for a poor man who is your benefactor, a man who needs the spare time to advise you? There can be nothing more appropriate for such a man, Gentlemen of Athens, than for him to receive meals in the Prytaneum[1] – something that is far more appropriate for me than for any of you who has won a victory at Olympia in a horse race, or a two- or four-horse chariot race ...

Note

1. *The Prytaneum was the seat of magistrates. Here public meals were served to officials or to honored individuals, including Olympic victors.*

Question

1. What, according to Socrates, was wrong in the public and private conduct of Athenians?

For the restored democracy following the Thirty, see **35.1** ("The Restored Athenian Democracy"), **35.2** ("The Fourth-Century Assembly and Council"), **35.4** ("Fourth-Century Democratic Leadership"), and **35.6** ("The Jury Courts").

Review Questions

1. How was the oligarchic regime of the Thirty established (**29.1**)?
2. How did the oligarchs justify their rule (**29.1–2**, WEB **29.4**)?

3. What did the amnesty agreement entail and how was it maintained (**29.3**, **29.5.C–D**, **29.7**, WEB **29.8**)?

4. What was the Spartan policy toward oligarchic Athens (see **29.1–3**, **29.5.A–B**, WEB **29.6**)?

5. How might Socrates' speech (**29.7**) have upset Athenian democrats who fought against the Thirty?

Suggested Readings

The Thirty: Krentz 1982; Ostwald 1986, 460–496; Wolpert 2002b, 3–28, 119–136. *The Lacedaemonians' tomb*: Camp 2001, 133–134. *Amnesty*: Tieman 2002; Quillin 2002; Wolpert 2002a; Ober 2002. *Paragraphê*: MacDowell 1978, 214–217; Carawan 2001. *Socrates' trial*: Stone 1988; Brickhouse and Smith 1989; Vlastos 1994, 87–109; Wallace 1994.

30

Sparta After the Peloponnesian War

Politics, Wealth, and Demography

Ancient Greece from Homer to Alexander: The Evidence, First Edition. Joseph Roisman.
© 2011 Blackwell Publishing Ltd. Translations © 2011 John Yardley. Published 2011 by Blackwell Publishing Ltd.

At the end of the Peloponnesian War, Sparta found herself *the* hegemonic power in Greece. This new reality was attended by political and social changes at home that were partly due to her new empire. Although Sparta's foreign and domestic affairs were intimately linked, we shall deal with them separately for reasons of clarity and convenience.

This chapter discusses Spartan society and politics following the Peloponnesian War. It records the accession of Agesilaus II to the throne with Lysander's help and after depriving his cousin of his inheritance. This crisis was followed by a conspiracy of Spartan residents who were less than full citizens, and its story reveals much about Spartan society and government. The chapter then examines the impact of Sparta's new wealth on her population and the related questions of land ownership and a shrinking citizen body. It concludes with a report on the Olympic victories of princess Cynisca and the reactions to her fame.

30.1 The Accession of Agesilaus II (400)

When king Agis II died in the summer of 400, the expected heir was his son, Leotychidas. However, Lysander seized the opportunity to strengthen his power by helping his friend and former beloved, Agesilaus (II), who was Agis' brother, to inherit the throne. Lysander took advantage of Leotychidas' youth (he was only in his teens) and of rumors that he was illegitimate, perhaps even a son of Alcibiades. Xenophon tells the story of Agesilaus' accession, which shows Lysander's skill in manipulating oracles.

Xenophon *Hellenica* 3.3.1–4

(**3.3.1**) After this, Agis arrived in Delphi where he offered up the usual tenth of the spoils, but on the return journey, being now an old man, he fell ill at Heraea. He was then transported back to Lacedaemon where, although he survived the journey, he soon died. His burial was on a grander scale than befits a human being.

When the hallowed days of mourning were over, and a king had to be put in place, there were two rival contenders for the throne: Leotychidas, who claimed to be a son of Agis, and Agesilaus, who was Agis' brother.

(**3.2**) "But, Agesilaus," declared Leotychidas, "the law prescribes that it is not a brother of the king who should succeed to the throne, but a son. Only in the event of there being no son could a brother succeed."

"Then I should be king."

"How is that, when I am alive?"

"Because the man you call your father denied that you were his son."

"But my mother knows the facts better than he, and she still says that I am his."

"But Poseidon showed that you were lying when he sent an earthquake to drive 'your father' from the bedroom into the open.[1] And corroborating this evidence of the god is time, which is said to give incontrovertible evidence: it was in the tenth month after he ran from the bedroom that you were born."

Such was the interchange between the two. (**3.3**) Now Diopeithes, an expert in oracles, spoke in favor of Leotychidas, declaring that there was also an oracle of Apollo to the effect that the Lacedaemonians should be on their guard against a "limping kingship." Lysander, however, rebutted him on behalf of Agesilaus by saying that he did not think the god was telling them to guard against someone limping after taking a fall, but rather to guard against someone becoming king who was not of royal birth. For, he explained, the realm would be truly limping when the stock of Heracles were not the leaders of the state.[2] (**3.4**) After hearing such arguments from both sides, the city-state chose Agesilaus as king ...

Notes

1. *Apparently, Agis took the earthquake to mean that Poseidon did not wish him to sleep with his wife.*
2. *Agesilaus had a limp. Later people would attribute to Lysander a plan to transfer kingship to selected descendants of Heracles such as himself (see WEB **31.4**: "Lysander's Alleged Plan to Reform Spartan Kingship").*

Question

1. Compare the affair of Leotychidas' succession with the dethroning of Demaratus (WEB **7.29.IV**: "Cleomenes and Demaratus"). What do both incidents tell us about how the Spartans resolved political crises?

30.2 The Cinadon Conspiracy (400/399)

One of the first challenges that Agesilaus faced was the so-called Cinadon conspiracy. Xenophon's account of it is one-sided, at best. He probably heard about the plot from government sources, perhaps even from Agesilaus whom he admired. Yet the story provides valuable information about tensions in Sparta between the *homoioi* ("similar ones"), who were full citizens, and the less privileged Spartans. It also shows the well-oiled Spartan machine for dealing with undesirables.

Xenophon *Hellenica* 3.3.4–11

(**3.3.4**) ... Agesilaus had not yet been a year on the throne when, as he offered one of the prescribed sacrifices on the state's behalf, he was told by a seer that the gods were revealing a conspiracy of dreadful proportions. Agesilaus repeated the sacrifice, and the seer told him that the auspices seemed even worse. When he sacrificed a third time, the seer said: "Agesilaus, the sign I am being given suggests that we are actually in the midst of our enemies." After this they sacrificed to the gods who ward off evil and give protection, ending only when they had, with difficulty, obtained favorable results.

Within five days of the termination of the sacrificial ceremony someone brought information to the ephors about a plot, and named Cinadon as the ringleader in the affair. (**3.5**) Cinadon was a man of youthful good looks and sturdy spirit, but not one of the *homoioi*. The ephors then asked how Cinadon said the deed would be perpetrated, and the informer replied that Cinadon had taken him to the fringe of the agora and told him to count the number of Spartiates in it.

"And I," said the man, "counted the king, the ephors, the elders, and about forty others, and I asked him: 'Why did you tell me to count, Cinadon?' His reply was: 'Regard these men as your enemies, and all the others in the agora as your allies, more than 4,000 in all.'"

The informer further claimed that Cinadon pointed to one or two people who met them here or there in the streets as being enemies, and all the others as allies. As for those people who happened to be on the farms of the Spartiates, he pointed out one, namely the owner, as the enemy, and many more on each estate as allies. (**3.6**) The ephors then asked the number Cinadon claimed as being involved in the affair, and the informer replied that, on that question, Cinadon said that they, the ringleaders, had not a large number who were actually party to it, but that these few were dependable men. The other ringleaders, however, knew about the sympathies of all the others – helots, freed helots [*neadamodeis*], the inferiors [*hypomeines*],[1] and the perioeci – since whenever talk of the Spartiates arose amongst these people there was not one able to hide the fact that he would gladly eat them raw. (**3.7**) The ephors asked the further question: "Where did they say they would acquire their weapons?" About that Cinadon, according to the informer, said: "Naturally, those of us in the armed service have acquired our own weapons, and as for the general populace …" And with that Cinadon led him to the iron market, he said, and indicated to him a large array of daggers, swords, spits, axes and hatchets, and sickles. Cinadon purportedly went on to say that these implements that men employed for work on the land, on timber, and on stone were all weapons, and that most of the other trades, too, had tools that made good enough weapons, especially against unarmed men. The ephors then questioned him further, asking at what time the action was due to take place, and the man said that his orders were to remain in town.

(**3.8**) On hearing this, the ephors thought that what he was talking about had been well planned, and they were very alarmed. Not even calling the so-called little assembly,[2] they gathered together a few members of the *gerousia* here and there and together they decided to send Cinadon to Aulon[3] along with a number of other younger men. His instructions would be to bring back some citizens of Aulon and some helots, their names having been inscribed in a *scytalê*.[4] They also ordered him to bring them the woman who was said to be the most beautiful in the town, and who was thought to be a corrupting influence on Lacedaemonians, both younger and older men, who went to Aulon. (**3.9**) Cinadon had already carried out other commissions of this sort for the ephors; and so this time it was to him that they handed the *scytalê* with the names of the individuals to be arrested inscribed in it.

Cinadon then asked which of the young men he was to take with him. "Go and tell the eldest of the commanders of the cavalry [*hippagretai*][5] to send with you six or seven men who happen to be on hand," they replied. (The ephors had, however, seen to it that the commander in question knew the ones he was to send, and that those sent knew that it was Cinadon that they were to arrest.) They also gave Cinadon a further piece of information: they would send along three wagons so that the detail would not have to bring the prisoners on foot. By doing this they were concealing as best they could the fact that the object of the mission was just one man – Cinadon.

(**3.10**) The ephors were not making the arrest in Sparta because they did not know the extent of the conspiracy; and they also wanted to hear first from Cinadon who his co-conspirators were before these men discovered that they had been given away (and thus they could prevent their escape). The arresting party would seize Cinadon, and after ascertaining from him the identity of his accomplices they were to write down the names and send them to the ephors with the utmost dispatch. So concerned were the ephors about the affair that they actually sent a cavalry squadron to assist their people in Aulon.

(**3.11**) The man was arrested, and a rider came bearing the names of the people whom Cinadon had listed, whereupon the ephors immediately proceeded to round up the seer Tisamenus[6] and the most important of the others. When Cinadon was brought back and interrogated, he made a full confession and gave the names of his co-conspirators. Finally the ephors asked him what it was he wanted to gain by taking such action, and his reply was: "To be inferior to no one in Lacedaemon." After that his hands and neck were straightaway fastened in a collar, and he and his associates were dragged through the city, all the while being whipped and poked with a cattle prod.[7]

Notes

1. Hypomeines *were probably Spartans who lost their full civic rights due to poverty or illegitimacy. Cinadon was likely one of them.*
2. *The little assembly is an unknown institution that consisted perhaps of the ephors and the elders.*
3. *Aulon was a perioecic settlement in northwest Messenia.*
4. *The* scytalê *was a dispatch written on leather wrapped around a stick. The claim that it was written in code is found only in late sources.*
5. *The* hippagretai *were commanders of the 300 "cavalrymen," an elite unit that actually fought as hoplites around the king.*
6. *Tisamenus was likely a descendant of the seer whose prophecies are interpreted by Herodotus 9.35.2 (**18.12.A**: "Sparta's Peloponnesian Conflicts").*
7. *It is likely that Cinadon was executed if he survived the ordeal.*

Questions

1. What does the Cinadon conspiracy reveal about problems in the Spartan system?
2. Who was involved in the conspiracy? Who was involved in its suppression?
3. What did the plotters want?

30.3 Empire and Wealth in Sparta

Ancient sources often tied the Spartan *oliganthropia* (shortage of men) to economic disparity. They also blamed Lysander for filling his country with riches and argued that the profits of the Peloponnesian War destroyed the moral fabric of the Spartan state and corrupted her citizens. One of the "victims" of this alleged corruption was Gylippus, the general who had helped Syracuse defeat Athens. He was caught embezzling money that Lysander shipped to the state and was forced to go into exile. Plutarch tells us about reactions in Sparta to the new wealth. The reported charges against the corrupting influence of wealth seem to be politically motivated and directed against Lysander.

Plutarch *Lysander* 17.1–2, 4

(**17.1**) After crowning a brilliant and outstanding career with such a disgraceful and sordid act, Gylippus moved away from Lacedaemon.[1] The most thoughtful of the Spartiates were now, especially because of this incident, fearful of the power of money, believing that its pernicious influence reached beyond ordinary citizens. They harshly criticized Lysander, and earnestly begged the ephors to spurn all silver and gold as being imported plagues. The ephors then turned their thoughts to the matter. (**17.2**) Theopompus claims that it was Sciraphidas (but Ephorus that it was Phlogidas)[2] who was the man who declared that they should not accept gold and silver coin in their city but avail themselves instead of their national currency. This was made of iron which was first dipped in vinegar when taken from the forge so that the piece could not be reworked, but would instead become soft and intractable; and in the second place it was very weighty and cumbersome, and even a great quantity of it, which was very heavy, was of little value ...

(**17.4**) Lysander's friends opposed this, however, and were anxious to have money remain in the city. It was thus decided that coinage of this sort be brought in for public use, but they laid down the death penalty for anyone caught acquiring it privately ...

Notes

1. *The Hellenistic author Poseidonius, however, says that Gylippus starved himself to death* (FGrHist 87 F 48c).
2. *Both Theopompus and Ephorus were fourth-century historians.*

Although Sparta did not issue coins, the Spartans could keep foreign currency before this new prohibition, which did not last long in any case.

Question

1. What measures did the Spartans take to curb corruption, according to Plutarch? Why were they ineffective?

30.4 Epitadeus' Law (?) and the Shortage of Men (*Oliganthropia*)

Plutarch tells of the Spartan ephor Epitadeus who passed a law (*rhetra*) that abolished the inalienability of plots of land (*kleroi*). Land ownership constituted one of the conditions for Spartan citizenship. Yet Plutarch's report is highly questionable and probably derived from late propaganda promulgated by the third-century reformer-kings Agis IV and Cleomenes III. These kings sought to recreate the supposed equality of Sparta of old and to explain its demise through Epitadeus' law. The biographer is correct, however, to note the decline in the number of full Spartan citizens. There were additional reasons for the shortage: war casualties, low birth rate, and natural disasters such as earthquakes. Its effect on the military was that the Spartans served primarily as the officer class, with the bulk of the army consisting of inferior citizens, freed helots, allies, and especially mercenaries.

30.4.A   Epitadeus' Law

Plutarch *Agis* 5.1–4

(**5.1**) Spartan society started to suffer the effects of corruption and decay soon after the Spartans put an end to Athenian hegemony and glutted themselves with gold and silver. Even so, through maintaining inheritance of property, the Spartiate families maintained the number defined by Lycurgus, with father leaving to son his land allotment, and as a result this egalitarian order persisted to some extent and preserved the state despite the other mistakes it made. (**5.2**) But then a powerful man called Epitadeus, who was willful and hot-tempered, became an ephor. He had some differences with his son and drafted a decree making it possible for a man to dispose of his house and land allotment, by giving it in his lifetime, or by leaving it in his will, to any one he wanted.

(**5.3**) So this man was satisfying a personal grudge in proposing the law; but greed prompted the rest of the state to accept it and ratify it, thereby destroying a fine institution. For the powerful people immediately began to accumulate property on a lavish scale, excluding family members from their rights of succession. Wealth swiftly flowed into the hands of a few, and poverty engulfed the city, bringing with it a lack of time for noble pursuits, and a servile mentality, as well as feelings of jealousy and hatred for those with means. (**5.4**) And so the total number of Spartiate families remaining was no more than 700, and perhaps there were a hundred of these who had acquired land allotments. The rest were left without means and without rights in the city, and were half-hearted and listless in fighting enemies abroad, but always on the lookout for some occasion for change and revolution at home.

Aristotle, writing in the last third of the fourth century, also discusses the Spartan demographic problem. He blames it primarily on their allowing women to own land. In Sparta, women could expect to receive a share of the family inheritance, a practice that was encouraged by male mortality in war.

30.4.B   Land Ownership and the Shortage of Male Citizens

Aristotle *Politics* 2.6.10–12 1270a15–34

(**2.6.10**) Beyond what was noted above, one might also criticize the Spartans for their uneven property distribution; for some, as it has turned out, have acquired excessive resources, and some very little indeed, which has resulted in the land falling into the hands of a few. This problem has also been poorly addressed in law, which made it dishonorable to buy or sell one's existing property – a good move – but permitted those wishing to do so to alienate it by gift or bequest. And what has happened was inevitable in either case.

(**6.11**) Moreover, the Spartan women are in possession of nearly two-fifths of the entire country because there are many women inheriting property, and also because of the practice of giving large dowries. It would have been preferable for the law to prescribe no dowry at all, or else a modest or medium-sized one. As it is, a man can give an heiress in marriage to anyone he wishes and, if he dies without making a decision about her, the person he leaves behind as his trustee gives her to anyone *he* wishes. The upshot is that while the country is capable of maintaining 1,500 cavalry and 30,000 hoplites, the total numbers were not even a thousand. (**6.12**) And it has become clear from the results that their constitutional measures in this area have been poorly framed; for the state could not withstand one blow,[1] but was destroyed because of its shortage of manpower …

Note

1. *"One blow" refers to the Spartan defeat in the battle of Leuctra, 371* (**32.13**).

Questions

1. What were the outcomes of Epitadeus' law, according to Plutarch (**30.4.A**)?
2. What effects did the Spartan system of alienating land by gift or bequest have on the state, according to Aristotle (**30.4.B**)?
3. Which social issue mentioned by Plutarch is conspicuously missing in Aristotle (**30.4.A–B**)? What might account for this?

30.5   Princess Cynisca

A fine example of the prominence of wealthy women in Sparta was Cynisca, the daughter of king Archidamus and the sister of Agis and Agesilaus. Women were barred from participating in the Olympic games, except for the chariot race in which the competitors placed chariots in the race. Cynisca won the Olympic chariot race both in 396 and in 392. That she was very wealthy is suggested by her participation in this rich people's sport, but also in the very expensive monument that she commissioned to commemorate her victories.

30.5.A   Cynisca's Olympic Victories

Pausanias *Description of Greece* 3.8.1; 6.1.6

(**3.8.1**) On his death, Archidamus left two sons. Agis was the elder, and he succeeded to the throne instead of Agesilaus. Archidamus also had a daughter called Cynisca, who was very eager to win in the Olympic games, and was the first female horse-breeder and the first to achieve an Olympic victory. After Cynisca Olympic victories fell to many other women, particularly women from Lacedaemon, though none of them is more distinguished for victories than she.

(**6.1.6**) With regard to Cynisca daughter of Archidamus, I have already discussed her pedigree and Olympic victories in my account of the kings of Lacedaemon. In Olympia, alongside the statue of Troelus, a stone base has been built, on which is a chariot with its horses and rider, and a statue of Cynisca herself, which is the work of Apelles. There are also inscriptions concerning Cynisca.

Cynisca had also arranged for another set of bronze horses to be placed in the temple of Zeus. Two bases from the sets of statues were found. As if this advertisement of distinction and fame was not enough, an epigram was added to the first set of statues that highlighted Cynisca's personal accomplishments as a woman.

30.5.B   The Cynisca Epigram

Palatine Anthology 13.16

I had Spartan kings as my forefathers and brothers. I, Cynisca, set up this statue after winning in a chariot with swift-footed horses. I claim to be the only woman from all Greece to acquire this crown.

According to Xenophon, Agesilaus undermined his sister's accomplishment. His reasons for tarnishing his sister's glory are unclear. Perhaps he was envious, or perhaps he was anxious to defend his own and Spartan masculine valor. After her death, however, Cynisca received the singular honor of a heroine shrine in Sparta (Pausanias *Description of Greece* 3.15.1).

30.5.C   Agesilaus and Cynisca

Xenophon *Agesilaus* 9.6

... He beautified his own home with artifacts and possessions befitting a man, rearing many dogs and war-horses. At the same time he persuaded his sister Cynisca to maintain chariot-horses, and by her victory he demonstrated that this animal is an indicator not of excellence [*aretê*] but of wealth.

Questions

1. How did Cynisca advertise her Olympic victories?
2. Were the Spartans proud of her?

Review Questions

1. What social problems did Sparta face and how many can be related to her newly acquired hegemonic status (**30.2–4**)?
2. What do the affair of Agesilaus' accession and the Cinadon conspiracy reveal about the operation of Spartan political institutions (**30.1–2**)?
3. How did the Spartans deal with the flow of wealth to the city (**30.3–5**)?
4. Does Cynisca confirm Aristotle's criticism of female land ownership (**30.4.B**, **30.5**)?

Suggested Readings

Spartan hegemony and king Agesilaus: Cartledge 1987; Hamilton 1991; Shipley 1997a. *Cinadon's conspiracy*: David 1979; Cartledge 1987, 162–179; Lazenby 1997. *Spartan currency and the new wealth*: Hodkinson 2000, 154–182. *Epitadeus' law*: Schütrumpf 1987; Hodkinson 2000, 43–45, 71–75, 90–94, and for Spartan women and land see also Cartledge 2001, 106–126; Pomeroy 2002, 80–86. *Cynisca*: Hodkinson 2000, 102, 321–323, 327–328; Cartledge 2003, 196–200.

31

The Spartan Hegemony, the Corinthian War, and the Peace of Antalcidas (404/3–388/7)

Ancient Greece from Homer to Alexander: The Evidence, First Edition. Joseph Roisman.
© 2011 Blackwell Publishing Ltd. Translations © 2011 John Yardley. Published 2011 by Blackwell Publishing Ltd.

A t the end of the Peloponnesian War Sparta assumed control of the Athenian empire, collected tributes, and established narrow oligarchies in the cities. But the failure of the oligarchic regime in Athens led to the abolition of Spartan-sponsored oligarchic regimes elsewhere, probably in 403. In Asia Minor, Sparta recognized the right of the Persian king to collect tribute from the Greeks, who were nevertheless supposed to remain autonomous. This chapter discusses the history of Spartan hegemony on sea and land. It records how Sparta and Persia became enemies following Spartan support of Cyrus' (failed) attempt to usurp the Persian throne and Sparta's decision to campaign in Asia Minor under Agesilaus. The chapter examines the outbreak of the Corinthian War that forced Agesilaus to return to Greece, and the loss of Spartan maritime hegemony in the Aegean following a naval defeat. The Athenians are represented in this chapter by a relief depicting a cavalryman who died in the Corinthian War, and by a description of the (unusual) defeat of a Spartan force against lighter-armed peltasts under the Athenian general Iphicrates. The chapter concludes by recording the Peace of Antalcidas (388/7), which restored Sparta's hegemonic status, and a call by the Athenian intellectual Isocrates for Greek unity by means of an all-Greek campaign against Persia.

31.1   Sparta and Persia

In 401, Cyrus tried to usurp the throne from his brother Artaxerxes II, the new Persian king, and asked Sparta to repay him for his assistance during the Peloponnesian War. The local Greeks supported his request.

31.1.A   Cyrus Requests Spartan Aid

> ## Xenophon *Hellenica* 3.1.1
>
> ... After that Cyrus sent messengers to Lacedaemon and asked the Lacedaemonians to give him the same level of support that he had given them in the war with Athens. The ephors thought that his appeal had merit. They sent word to Samius, their admiral at the time, to perform for Cyrus any service he might require, and Samius readily did what Cyrus asked of him. At the head of his own fleet, and accompanied by that of Cyrus, he skirted along the coast to Cilicia, and made it impossible for the governor of Cilicia, Syennesis, to mount any opposition on land to Cyrus during the latter's march on the king.

Xenophon's *Anabasis* ("marching upward") tells the story of Cyrus' failed attempt to take over the throne, his death, and the return of the "Ten Thousand" (actually about 8,000) Greek mercenaries in his army to Greece

(400–399). For contemporaries and especially for later generations, the failure of the Persians to stop the Greeks' return exposed the weakness of the Persian Empire. See WEB **31.2** for conclusions drawn by the Athenian intellectual Isocrates from the expedition.

Cyrus' march led the Persian king to reassess his relationship with Sparta and with the Greeks of Asia Minor who supported Cyrus.

31.1.B   Spartan Aid to Cyrus

Xenophon *Hellenica* 3.1.3–4

(**3.1.3**) Tissaphernes was reputed to have given creditable assistance to the king in the war against his brother, and he was sent to the coast as satrap both of the lands he himself had earlier governed and of those governed by Cyrus. He then immediately demanded that all the Ionian cities fall under his command. These cities, however, wished to remain free, and they also feared Tissaphernes because they had chosen Cyrus over him when Cyrus was alive. They therefore barred his entry into their cities, and sent emissaries to Lacedaemon to seek help; the Lacedaemonians were the champions of all Greece, they said, and should also look after the Asiatic Greeks, ensuring that their territory was not plundered and that their freedom was maintained. (**1.4**) The Lacedaemonians sent them Thibron as their commander [*harmostês*], and gave him troops made up of about a thousand freed helots [*neadamodeis*] and some 4,000 other Peloponnesians. Thibron also requested 300 horsemen of the Athenians, saying that he would himself furnish their pay. The Athenians sent him a number of men who had served in the cavalry under the rule of the Thirty, for they thought it would be good for the democracy if these men went abroad and were killed.

Questions

1. How did the Persian king deal with the retreating Greek mercenaries? What does this reveal about him and the Persians, according to Isocrates (WEB **31.2**)?
2. How did Cyrus' failed attempt to usurp the throne affect Persian and Spartan policies in the region (**31.1**)?

31.3   Agesilaus' Asian Campaign and Lysander's Demotion

From 400/399 the Spartans campaigned in Asia Minor against the Persian satraps Tissaphernes and Pharnabazus with meager success. In 396 king Agesilaus took charge of operations. Xenophon links his mission to intelligence about the Persians' mobilization of a large fleet, claiming that the idea to send Agesilaus there was Lysander's. Agesilaus viewed the Persian campaign or wished Greeks to see it as a Panhellenic war led by a new Agamemnon against the new Trojans. He even tried to reenact Agamemnon's sacrifices at Aulis prior to his departure to Troy. But important Spartan allies such as Athens and Corinth refused to join him, and the Boeotians added insult to injury by disrupting Agesilaus' sacrifice. Agesilaus apparently never forgot the affront, and his career showed him often initiating hostilities against the Thebans.

31.3.A   Agesilaus' Asian Campaign

Xenophon *Hellenica* 3.4.2–5

(**3.4.2**) The Spartans were agitated (about the reported build-up of a Persian fleet), and they brought together their allies and considered what to do. Lysander meanwhile calculated that the Greeks would enjoy a marked superiority with their fleet, and he also took into consideration the fact that the infantry force that had marched up-country with Cyrus had returned safely. He prevailed upon Agesilaus to undertake an expedition into Asia, if the Spartan authorities would provide him with thirty Spartiates, approximately 2,000 freed helots, and an allied contingent of about 6,000. In addition to his logistical calculations, Lysander had a personal motive for wanting to join Agesilaus' expedition. This was to reestablish, with Agesilaus' aid, the decarchies that he had established in the cities and which had been dissolved by the ephors, who had ordered a return to their traditional constitutions.

(**4.3**) When Agesilaus committed himself to the campaign, the Spartans complied with his every request and furthermore gave him provisions for six months. He then made the requisite sacrifices, and in particular those for the border-crossing, and set off. He also sent messengers to the various cities with instructions on the number of men to be sent from each and where they were to muster. He himself wished to go and offer sacrifice at Aulis, which was where Agamemnon sacrificed when he was setting sail for Troy. (**4.4**) When he reached there, however, the Boeotarchs,[1] on being apprised that he was sacrificing, sent horsemen and told him to make no further offerings; and they also hurled from the altar any already-sacrificed victims that they came across. Agesilaus, furious, called on the gods to witness this act and then boarded his trireme and sailed off. On reaching Geraestus, he gathered together as large a force as he could and embarked on a journey to Ephesus.

(**4.5**) When he arrived in Ephesus, Tissaphernes sent and asked him what his purpose was in coming. Agesilaus replied it was "to see that the cities in Asia should also be autonomous, like those with us in Greece"…

Note

1. *The Boeotarchs were the magistrates of the Boeotian confederacy.*

In a short time, Agesilaus established his own authority in camp by demoting Lysander. The two competed for power and patronage, and Agesilaus used his royal office to weaken his senior advisor and humiliate him. According to Plutarch (*Lysander* 23.7), he even gave him the servile duty of being his meat carver.

Xenophon *Hellenica* 3.4.7–8

(**3.4.7**) Agesilaus was passing his time at Ephesus in leisurely repose, and meanwhile there was constitutional upheaval in the Greek cities (there were no longer democracies as there had been during the Athenian hegemony, and no decarchies either, as during Lysander's ascendancy). Since everyone knew Lysander, they pressed him with requests to get what they wanted from Agesilaus. As a result there was always a teeming crowd fawning on him and following him around, making Agesilaus look like an ordinary citizen and Lysander like a king. (**4.8**) That this also infuriated Agesilaus was only later made clear, but the thirty Spartiates with the king could not from envy hold their tongues, and they commented to Agesilaus that Lysander was contravening the law in behaving with more-than-regal self-importance. When Lysander began to bring some people before Agesilaus, the king would invariably send off with a negative response those whom he knew Lysander was supporting. And as things were consistently turning out contrary to Lysander's wishes, he soon realized what was going on and no longer allowed the crowd to follow him about, flatly telling those asking him to work on their behalf that they would be worse off if he championed their cause.

Lysander left for the Hellespont and later went home. See WEB **31.4** for Lysander's alleged plan to reform the Spartan kingship.

Questions

1. What were Agesilaus' and Lysander's considerations in support of an Asian campaign? What was the campaign's official goal (**31.3.A**)?
2. Why was Agesilaus so furious with the Boeotians (**31.3.A**)?
3. Why did Lysander lose the conflict with Agesilaus (**31.3.B**, cf. WEB **31.4**)?

31.5   The Outbreak of the Corinthian War (395)

In 395/4 Agesilaus assumed unprecedented joint command over operations both on land and sea and would henceforth be Sparta's most powerful man until his death in 360/59. He gained a measure of success in Asia both militarily and diplomatically by exploiting the rivalry between the Persian satraps. The Persians, who failed to reach a compromise with him, supported with money anti-Spartan politicians on the Greek mainland in the hope of starting a war there and thus drawing Agesilaus away from Asia. Pro-Spartan Xenophon describes their move as nothing short of corruption and bribery. The author of the Oxyrhynchian Greek history (7), however, rightly suggests that the Greeks' enmity toward Sparta needed little encouragement. See WEB **31.6** for his criticism of the view that Persian bribes led the Greeks to fight Sparta.

31.5.A   The King Sends Money to Greece

Xenophon *Hellenica* 3.5.1–2

(**3.5.1**) [The Persian governor] Tithraustes, however, thought he had discovered that Agesilaus had scant respect for the power of the king and that he had not the slightest intention of quitting Asia but had, in fact, high hopes of getting the king in his clutches. At a loss how to exploit the situation, he sent Timocrates the Rhodian to Greece, giving him gold to the value of about fifty silver talents and instructing him to do his best to pass it on to the leading men in the various cities (taking from them the most secure guarantees) on condition that they undertake a war against Sparta.

Timocrates then went off and gave the money to Androcleidas, Ismenias, and Galaxidorus in Thebes, to Timolaus and Polyanthes in Corinth, and to Cylon and his supporters in Argos. (**5.2**) The Athenians took no part of the money but were eager for war in any case, thinking that hegemony in Greece belonged to them. Those who had accepted the money then proceeded to make anti-Spartan comments in their respective cities; and having roused them to hatred for the Spartans, they began to forge unity amongst the largest of them.

Xenophon attributes to a Theban envoy to Athens in 395 a speech that successfully appeals to the Athenians to join Thebes in a war against Sparta. The speaker lists the Greeks' grievances against Sparta and alludes to Athens' renewed imperial ambitions.

31.5.B   Greek Grievances Against Sparta

Xenophon *Hellenica* 3.5.11–15

(**3.5.11**) ... If you reflect, you will immediately see that we are telling the truth. Who is there still left sympathizing with the Spartans? Haven't the Argives always remained hostile to them? (**5.12**) Now, too, the Elians, robbed of much of their land and numerous cities, have been added to their list of enemies.[1] And what are we to say of the Corinthians, the Arcadians, and the Achaeans? In the war against you, following urgent appeals from the Spartans, these shared all the hardships and expenses, but when the Spartans had reached their goal, what share of the power, the glory, or the money did they give to them? In fact, they think it quite all right to establish helots as governors, and now that they have achieved success they have revealed themselves as tyrants over their allies, free though these are.

(**5.13**) In fact, it is clear that they have also duped those whom they detached from you. Instead of liberty, they have given them slavery twice over: these peoples endure tyranny of the governors as well as that of the decarchy whom Lysander appointed in each city. Then there is the king of Asia.

It was he who made the greatest contribution to their victory over you, but how is the treatment he now receives any different from what it would have been had he been on your side subduing *them*?

(**5.14**) So, aren't you now likely to become by far the greatest people in history if you in turn champion those who are so clearly victims of injustice? For in the time of your hegemony, your leadership was, of course, limited to maritime peoples. Now, though, you would become the leaders of all peoples – of us, of the Peloponnesians, of those whom you ruled before, and even of the king himself with his enormous power. We were very valuable allies of the Spartans, too, as you know; and it stands to reason that our support for you as allies will now be in every way stronger than it was at that time for them. For our assistance will not be given, as it was then, on behalf of islanders or Syracusans or non-Greeks, but on behalf of ourselves for injustices suffered. (**5.15**) And you should be aware of this, too, that the acquisitive power of the Spartans is much easier to overthrow than was the empire that was yours. For you had a fleet and ruled over people who did not; these people, few in number, are greedily seeking power over men many times more numerous than they and not at all their inferiors in arms. This, then, is all we have to say, but know well, men of Athens, that we think we are inviting you to enjoy advantages that will be far greater for your state than for ours.

Note

1. *In 400 Sparta defeated Elis and forced it to give autonomy to its perioeci. Sparta also disbanded Elis' navy and stripped its harbor of its defenses.*

Questions

1. What is Xenophon's view of the causes of the Corinthian War, and what does the Oxyrhynchian historian have to say about it (**31.5.A**, WEB **31.6**)?
2. What complaints did the Greeks have about the Spartan hegemony, and what were the benefits for Athens in joining the anti-Spartan coalition, according to the Theban speech (**31.5.B**)?

—————————— 31.7 The Loss of Spartan Maritime Hegemony (394)

The outbreak of the Corinthian War in Greece (395/4–387/6) and a crisis of leadership at home led to Agesilaus' recall from Asia in 394. By then the Spartan Asian campaign had already suffered a heavy blow at Cnidus. The satrap Pharnabazus recruited the former Athenian general Conon to command a fleet against the Spartans. (Conon had gone from the battle of Aegospotami in 404 to serve the Cyprian ruler Evagoras.) In 395 Conon encouraged Rhodes to defect from Sparta, and in 394 he and Pharnabazus led a Persian fleet to victory against a Spartan fleet near Cnidus. See WEB **31.8** for events leading to Agesilaus' recall and the battle of Cnidus.

The Persian naval victory put an end to Spartan supremacy in the Aegean. Conon and Pharnabazus expelled Spartan forces from Asian coastal cities and the islands and won the locals' goodwill by promising them autonomy. In 393 they arrived in Greece, raided Laconia, and garrisoned the island of Cythera south of Sparta. Conon then sailed into the Piraeus bringing money for the rebuilding of the Long Walls (a project that had already been initiated before his arrival).

Xenophon *Hellenica* 4.8.9–10

(**4.8.9**) Conon said that if Pharnabazus allowed him to take charge of the fleet, he would provide for its upkeep from the islands, and that he would also sail to his native city and help the Athenians with the reconstruction of the Long Walls and the wall around Piraeus. He knew of nothing, he declared, that would be more painful for the Spartans. "And," he added, "by this act you will have done the Athenians a service, and taken revenge on the Spartans. You will be nullifying what they worked hardest for." On hearing this, Pharnabazus happily sent Conon to Athens and supplied him with additional funds for the reconstruction of the walls.

(**8.10**) When he arrived, Conon erected a large section of the wall, providing his own manpower, paying the carpenters and masons, and covering any other necessary expenses. There were parts of the wall, however, that the Athenians themselves helped rebuild, along with volunteers from Boeotia and other cities. The Corinthians for their part used the funds left by Pharnabazus to furnish crews for ships; and, giving command to Agathinus, they attained mastery of the sea in the gulf around Achaea and Lechaeum. To counter this, the Spartans also manned a fleet, which Podanemus commanded.

Questions

1. Why would Conon's rebuilding of the Athenian Long Walls be "more painful" for the Spartans (cf. **20.7**: "The Long Walls", **28.12**: "Athens' Defeat and the End of the Peloponnesian War")?
2. What were the ramifications of the loss of their maritime hegemony for the Spartans (**31.7**)?

31.9 The Dexileus Monument

In 394 the Athenians who died in the Corinthian War received the traditional honor of a burial in the city's public burial ground (*demosion sema*), and their names were listed by tribe (*IG* II² 5221 = Harding no. 19A). Yet apparently some Athenians looked for greater distinction. A separate monument listed the names of twelve cavalrymen who died at Corinth (in the battle of Nemea of 394?) and in the battle of Coronea in Boeotia later that summer (*IG* II² 5222 = R&O no. 7). The family of young Dexileus decided to commemorate his memory by building him an individual monument in the family plot outside the Sacred Gate (Figure 31.1). By this time the legal prohibition on elaborate steles was rescinded, and important wealthy families honored their dead with

Figure 31.1 The Dexileus Monument. akg-images/Nimatallah.

expensive grave reliefs. The striking monument for Dexileus, now at the Kerameikos Museum, Athens, shows a cavalryman about to dispatch a fallen warrior in heroic fashion. He wears a short tunic (*chiton*), a cloak (*chlamys*), and boots. His bronze Thessalian hat and spear are lost. Similar scenes appear on other memorial reliefs commissioned by the state and individuals.

At the base of the monument an inscription reads (*IG* II² 6217 = Harding no. 19C, p. 33):

> Dexileus, son of Lysanius, of Thoricus, was born when Tisandros was archon [414/3], died when Eubulides was archon [394/3] at Corinth, one of the five cavalrymen.

The meaning of the "five cavalrymen" is unclear, and perhaps refers to a special unit. The dating of the young man's birth and death is exceptional in Athenian funerary inscriptions. Scholars have interpreted this as an attempt to show that Dexileus, the cavalryman, was too young to be one of the cavalry who cooperated with the tyrannical Thirty. Indeed, one vase buried in the site depicts the tyrannicides Harmodius and Aristogeiton. Yet one wonders how many readers of the inscription knew or bothered to check who were the archons during the Thirty's rule.

Question

1. What themes in the Theban speech to the Athenians about fighting Sparta (**31.5.B**) throw light on Dexileus' monument and grave?

31.10   Peltasts and the Battle of Lechaeum (390)

One event in the convoluted history of the Corinthian War had implications that ranged beyond the conflict. This was the victory of the Athenian general Iphicrates over a hoplite Spartan force near Lechaeum in the Corinthiad in 390. Iphicrates was a skilled Athenian general who was stationed in the Corinthiad at the head of a mercenary force made up largely of peltasts. Peltasts were light-armed troops whose name was derived from *peltê*, a crescent-shaped shield, which they used in battle (Figure 31.2). Originating in Archaic Thrace, peltasts became widely used in Greece during the Classical period. They went into battle with their shield, which was rimless and smaller than the hoplite shield, a spear (or in earlier times javelins), and a slashing sword, but no body armor or metal helmet. Peltasts were inexpensive to equip and especially to hire, and hence often served as mercenaries. The sources tend to ignore or marginalize their contribution on the battlefield because they were commonly used for skirmishes or similar tasks, because of their lower-class origin and status, and because their hit-and-run tactics offended hoplite ideals.

Peltasts were useful for surprise attacks, scouting, and protecting roads or fortifications. They and other light-armed troops could also be successful against hoplites and stand their ground when they had numerical superiority and fought on an uneven terrain (as in Pylos). In 390, however, Iphicrates' nimble peltasts defeated a Spartan *mora* (regiment) made up primarily of hoplites on the plain near Lechaeum. The peltasts were aided by Athenian hoplites, but the peltasts did most of the damage. The engagement started when a Spartan polemarch (officer) in charge of a garrison at Lechaeum was escorting Spartans from the village of Amyclae on part of their way home. The Amycleans were obliged to participate in the festival of Hyacinthia that was associated with a joint cult of Apollo and his beloved Hyacinthus. They were accompanied by hoplites and cavalry regiments. Xenophon describes the Spartan defeat.

Figure 31.2 A Thracian peltast. A red-figure cup from the end of the sixth century. Antikenmuseum der Universität Leipzig.

Xenophon *Hellenica* 4.5.12–17

(**4.5.12**) When they were roughly twenty or thirty stades from Sicyon, the polemarch proceeded on the return journey to Lechaeum with the hoplites, who were about 600 in number, and ordered the cavalry commander to come after him with the *mora* of cavalry once they had escorted the Amycleans as far as the Amycleans requested. The Spartans were well aware of the presence of large numbers of both peltasts and hoplites in Corinth, but because of their earlier successes they arrogantly assumed that no one would lift a hand against them. (**5.13**) In the city of Corinth, however, Callias son of Hipponicus, who commanded the Athenian hoplites, and Iphicrates, who had charge of the peltasts, could see that the Spartans were not many in number and that they also lacked the support of peltasts and cavalry, and so they thought it safe to attack them with their peltasts. If the Spartans continued along the road, they reasoned, they could be attacked with javelins on their unprotected side and wiped out; if they tried offensive action, it would be easy for peltasts, being the most lightly armed troops, to outrun hoplites. Realizing this, the two led out their men.

(**5.14**) Callias deployed the hoplites not far from the city, while Iphicrates took the peltasts and attacked the Spartan *mora*. The Spartans now came under pressure from javelins, and some were wounded and some killed, so they ordered the shield-bearers[1] to take up the casualties and carry them away to Lechaeum. And these were the only men in the *mora* who really escaped. The polemarch then ordered the ten-year men [aged 20–30] to chase off the attackers. They, however, were hoplites chasing peltasts a spear's throw away, and so they caught none of them; for Iphicrates had given the order for the peltasts to draw back before the hoplites came close. (**5.15**) And when the Spartans withdrew, they were out of order since each man had been pursuing the enemy as fast as he could. At this point Iphicrates' troops wheeled around, and some once more hurled their javelins facing the enemy, while others ran along the flank hurling them at the Spartans' unprotected side. And in the very first pursuit they brought down nine or ten of the Spartans with the javelin; and this result made them press the attack with greater bravado.

(**5.16**) The Spartans were under severe pressure, and the polemarch gave another order for pursuit, this time to the fifteen-year men [aged 20–35]. But as these withdrew, even more of them fell than on the first occasion. When their best fighters had already been killed, the cavalry joined them, and with these they once more attempted pursuit. The peltasts fell back, but at that point the cavalry botched their charge. Instead of continuing their pursuit to the point of inflicting casualties, they kept a continuous line with the hoplites both in the chase and in wheeling back. The Spartans persisted with this, and experienced the same results time and again, and their numbers were continually diminishing and their spirit ebbing, while the enemy was gaining confidence and ever greater numbers were joining the assault.

(**5.17**) At a loss what to do, the Spartans gathered in a body on a hillock, about two stades from the sea and about sixteen or seventeen stades from Lechaeum. The men in Lechaeum became aware of their plight, and they boarded some light craft and sailed along the shore until they were abreast of the hillock. But their troops on the hillock were at an impasse. They were being badly mauled and losing their lives, and there was nothing they could do about it; and when, in addition, they saw the enemy hoplites bearing down on them, they ran. Some threw themselves into the sea, and a few escaped to Lechaeum with the cavalry. In all the various engagements and in the flight roughly 250 of them died.

Note

1. *The shield-bearers were helotic attendants who, among other things, carried the hoplites' shields when on the march. A cavalry* mora *was composed of perhaps sixty horsemen.*

 See WEB **31.11** for Iphicrates' military reforms in later years.

Questions

1. Why were the peltasts so successful against the Spartan hoplites? How could they be neutralized?
 2. Compare the equipment of Iphicrates' troops (WEB **31.11**) with that of the Classical hoplite (**8.1**: "Hoplites and Their Weapons"). What were the differences and their likely impact?

31.12 The Peace of Antalcidas (388/7)

Athenian victories in Greece and in the Aegean led to a change of policy in both Persia and Sparta. Athens' support of the revolt of the Cyprian ruler Evagoras against Persia made the Persian king more attentive to Spartan claims that the greatest threat to his western front came not from Sparta but from his old Athenian enemy. Sparta also dropped its Panhellenic mission of freeing the Asian Greeks in favor of a Persian alliance that would secure Persian hegemony in Asia Minor. The man most intimately associated with these developments was the Spartan diplomat and general Antalcidas, but Agesilaus must have given Antalcidas the go-ahead.

In 388/7 Antalcidas, who held the office of admiral (*anarchies*), and Tiribazus, the satrap, obtained peace terms and promises of military aid from king Artaxerxes. The key to ending the Corinthian War was Athens. Accordingly, Antalcidas assembled a navy, took control of the Hellespont, and diverted grain ships sailing to Athens to other destinations. This, and the new Spartan–Persian alliance, convinced Athens to agree to stop the war, and her mainland allies followed suit. Xenophon sums up the motives of the warring parties for joining this common peace and reports on the royal edict their envoys heard at Sardis that defined peace terms. It became known as the Peace of Antalcidas and included the disbanding of foreign garrisons and the display of copies of the treaty in major Panhellenic sanctuaries. The two major beneficiaries of the peace were Persia, which regained control over Asia Minor, and Sparta, which was now the enforcer of peace and autonomy and the undisputed hegemonic power in Greece.

Xenophon *Hellenica* 5.1.29–31

(**5.1.29**) When they saw the large number of enemy ships, the Athenians were afraid of being totally crushed as they had been before, the king having now become an ally of the Spartans, and they were also suffering depredations at the hands of raiders based in Aegina. For these reasons they were very eager to make peace. The Spartans, too, were fed up with the war. They had a *mora* garrisoning Lechaeum, and another garrisoning Orchomenus; they were keeping an eye on their allied states, both those they trusted, so they would not be destroyed, and those they did not trust, so they would not secede; and there was all the trouble they were facing and themselves causing around Corinth. The Argives, too, were all for peace. They knew that the Spartans had called a troop-levy against them, and that the excuse of "the sacred months"[1] would no longer be of any use to them. (**1.30**) So when Tiribazus sent instructions for a meeting of all those wanting to hear the terms of the peace treaty that the king was sending them, they all quickly appeared on the scene. When they had assembled, Tiribazus showed them the king's seal and read out the message. It went as follows:

(**1.31**) "King Artaxerxes considers it just that cities in Asia should belong to him, along with Clazomenae and Cyprus of the islands.[2] The other Greek cities he thinks should be left autonomous, whether great or small, apart from Lemnos, Imbros, and Scyros, which should belong to the Athenians as they did of old. If either side refuses to accept this peace, I shall, joining the side wanting to accept it, make war on those people by land and sea, using my fleet and my resources."

Notes

1. *In 388 the Argives redated a festival and its holy truce in a failed attempt to stop a Spartan invasion.*
2. *Cyprus was in revolt at the time, and Clazomenae was independent.*

See WEB **31.13** for explanatory comments on the significance of the Peace of Antalcidas and its character as a "Common Peace."

Questions

1. Why did the main powers in Greece sign the Peace of Antalcidas?
2. What were the terms of the peace? Who were its major beneficiaries and why (**31.12**, WEB **31.13**).

31.14   The Call for a Panhellenic Campaign Against Persia

Some Greeks, full of patriotic indignation, regarded the Peace of Antalcidas as a disgraceful sellout. For them it proved the need to assert a Panhellenic identity and take common action against the barbarian Persian enemy. See WEB **36.8.I–III** ("Contrasting Greeks with Barbarians") for the Greek/barbarian dichotomy and Greek images of barbarians.

Already in the fifth century, some Greek intellectuals argued that the solution to the political, social, and economic problems that beset the Greeks at home was to unite in a war against the Persians. In the fourth century, Isocrates was among the most prominent authors to call for *homonoia* (concord) among the Greeks by conducting such a campaign. He tried in the course of his long career to persuade different states and rulers to lead it in the hope that it would solve domestic problems such as poverty and homelessness. In his literary speech *Panegyricus* (from *panegyris*, a festive assembly), written on the occasion of the 380 Olympics, he reproaches Sparta for treating Greeks like enemies and for signing the Peace of Antalcidas with Persia. He strongly promotes the claim of Athens to lead Greece, and calls upon both states to share command of a Greek campaign against Persia. Isocrates was an Athenian patriot, but he did not cynically use the idea of a Panhellenic crusade to promote Athenian interests. In the following extracts, he discusses the benefits and justice of pursuing a predatory policy against the Persians.

Isocrates 4 *Panegyricus* 133–134, 150–152, 173–174

(**133**) I think that if people coming here from elsewhere saw the current state of affairs they would charge both of us with sheer lunacy. For we expose ourselves to such risks for little gain, when it is possible for us to have considerable possessions without fear, and we are destroying our own lands while we omit to derive profit from Asia. (**134**) For the Persian king nothing is more important than looking for ways to insure that we shall never stop our internecine fighting. And we for our part are so far from throwing his affairs into confusion, or creating discord for him, that when chance produces conflicts for him we actually try to help him bring them to an end. Indeed, there are now two armies operating in Cyprus, and we allow him to make use of the one, and to put the other under siege – and both of them belong to Greece.[1]

Note

1. *Isocrates refers to Greek mercenaries who fought one another in the service of the Persians and the Cyprian king Evagoras, respectively.*

Isocrates goes on to give examples of military campaigns that showed the Persians' weakness and deficiency as warriors.

(**150**) Yet none of these events was beyond understanding; all turned out as one might expect. For it is not possible for men brought up like that, and living under such a form of government, to have courage as others do, or to set a victory trophy over their enemy in the battlefield. How could a brilliant commander or fine soldier spring up in an environment like theirs? The bulk of them constitute an unruly mob with no experience of danger, faint-hearted with regard to warfare, and better schooled in servitude than slaves are amongst us.

(**151**) Those enjoying the greatest reputation, on the other hand, have never lived on terms of equality, developing social or citizen-like sensibilities. Instead, they spend all their time humiliating some people and being subservient to others, which is the most effective way in which human nature can be corrupted. Because of their wealth they become physically soft, but because of their monarchical rule they are in spirit abject and fearful, putting in an appearance at the palace and prostrating themselves[1] and taking every opportunity to habituate themselves to self-limitation. They do obeisance before a mortal man, address him as a god, and have less regard for the deities than they do for human beings.

(**152**) As a result, those of them who come down to the coast – the so-called "satraps" – feel no shame about their upbringing there but, rather, continue with the same mores. They are treacherous to their friends and cowardly before the enemy; their lives are a combination of self-abasement and superciliousness; and they despise their allies and fawn on their enemies ...

Note

1. *Persian custom ordained inferiors to do obeisance to their superiors, which the Greeks misinterpreted as a sign of worshipping the king.*

Toward the end of the speech Isocrates sums up his plan for achieving peace and concord among the Greeks by means of a war against the barbarians.

(**173**) We must push aside these schemes and embark on such projects as will make living in our cities safer and our interrelationship more trustworthy. What is to be said about this is simple and straightforward. A lasting peace cannot be reestablished without our joining forces to combat the barbarians, nor can the Greeks be united until we derive our gains from the same peoples, and also direct our hazardous ventures against the same peoples. (**174**) Once this is achieved, and the distress engulfing our lives is removed – for distress destroys friendships, turns family ties into antipathy, and brings all men into conflict and factional strife – then it is certain that we shall be harmonious and feel sincere goodwill toward each other. Accordingly, we must consider our priority to be the removal of the theater of war from here to the continent of Asia in order that we may reap this one benefit from the dangerous situations we have put each other in, namely taking the decision to use against the barbarian the things we have experienced at his hands.

Questions

1. What are the errors of the Greeks' Persian policy and how should the policy be changed, according to Isocrates?
2. What are the Persians' deficiencies, according to Isocrates?
3. Were Isocrates' Persians a mirror image of the Greeks?

Review Questions

1. How did the Spartan–Persian relationship evolve from Agesilaus' Asian campaign to the Peace of Antalcidas (**31.3**, **31.5**, **31.7**, **31.9–10**, **31.12**, WEB **31.2**, WEB **31.6**, WEB **31.8**, WEB **31.13**)?

2. Discuss the role that Persian subsidies played in Greek affairs (see **31.1.A–B**, **31.5.A**, **31.12**, WEB **31.6**).

3. What challenges did the Spartan system face and how well did it fare in dealing with them (see **31.3**, **31.7**, **31.10**, WEB **31.4**)?
4. What was wrong with the Peace of Antalcidas, according to Isocrates? How would the Greeks who signed it disagree with him (**31.12**, **31.14**)?

5. In what way did Persia benefit from the Peace of Antalcidas (**31.12**, **31.14**, WEB **31.13**)?

Suggested Readings

The march of the Ten Thousand: G. Nussbaum 1967; Dillery 1995, 59–109. *Spartan hegemony and king Agesilaus*: see the Suggested Readings for Chapter 30. *The Corinthian War*: Hamilton 1979. *The Dexileus monument and Athenian cavalry*: Low 2002; R&O, 40–43; Fields 2003; Hurwit 2007. *Peltasts*: Best 1969; J. Anderson 1970, 111–138 (as well as other light-armed troops); Pritchett 1974, 2: 117–125; Griffith 1981; van Wees 2004, 197. *The Peace of Antalcidas and the Common Peace*: Ryder 1965; Badian 1991; Schmidt 1999. *Isocrates and Panhellenism*: Flower 2000b.

32

From the Peace of Antalcidas (388/7) to the Battle of Leuctra and Its Aftermath (371)

The Peace of Antalcidas gave Sparta the legitimacy to enforce peace and autonomy in Greece. Agesilaus soon showed how this mission could be cynically and selectively used to enhance Spartan power. This chapter focuses on the high-handed Spartan policy in Greece, the Greeks' reactions to it, and the end of Spartan hegemonic power. Agesilaus used the principle of autonomy to force the Boeotian federation to disband; the chapter describes both the structure of this confederacy and its dissolution in 386. It then discusses two cases of blatant Spartan violation of the same principle of autonomy. Athens reacted to Sparta's actions by establishing a second Athenian league, as attested in an inscription produced here. A statue of deified Peace illustrates the longing for peace in this period in Greece, and the chapter includes both an illustration of the statue and a report on the Common Peace of 371. In that same year Sparta lost the battle of Leuctra to Thebes. The chapter reports on the elite unit of the Sacred Band that contributed to the Theban victory and produces accounts of the battle itself. It then describes how the Spartans' loss was greatly augmented by the Theban foundation of an independent Messene. It concludes by documenting the dissolution of the Peloponnesian League.

32.1   The Boeotian Federation in the Fourth Century

Greek federations allegedly violated the principle of autonomy of the single polis, and Agesilaus used this principle to disband federations he regarded as a threat to Sparta. Among them were the union between Corinth and Argos and the Boeotian federation. The latter was an old institution, and a discussion about its structure is warranted at this point.

The best account of the organization and government of the Boeotian federation comes from the Oxyrhynchian historian. The author describes the federation's structure in the context of the outbreak of the Corinthian War (**31.5**). It is hard to imagine, however, that its earlier or later government were significantly different. The hegemonic status of Thebes is demonstrated by the fact that Thebes had more Boeotarchs (generals and chief magistrates) than any other state, that it provided more troops and money, and that the federal council met in its citadel of the Cadmea.

Hellenica Oxyrhynchia 16.3–4

(**16.3**) They continued to administer their own civic affairs in this manner, but the method laid down for administration of Boeotian affairs was as follows. All people living in the land were divided into eleven districts [sg. *meros*], and each of these districts would furnish one Boeotarch. The Thebans provided four, two for the city and two more for Plataea, Scolus, Erythrae, Scaphae, and for the other districts formerly part of their polity but at that time subject to Thebes. Two Boeotarchs were supplied by Orchomenus and Hysiae; two by Thespiae along with Eutresis and Thisbae; one by Tanagra; and another by Haliartus, Lebadea, and Coronea, each of the towns sending one in its turn; and one would also go from Acraephnium, Copae, and Chaeronea on the same principle.

(16.4) This, then, was the manner in which the districts produced their magistrates. They also provided sixty council members for each Boeotarch and provided them with *per diem* expenses. In the case of the army, each district was ordered to provide about a thousand hoplites and a hundred cavalrymen. Simply put, it was the number of magistrates that determined how far they profited from the common weal, to what extent they paid taxes, sent jurymen, and shared all of the disadvantages and advantages of the community. Their entire people was run in this manner, and the councils and communal assemblies of Boeotia sat on the Cadmea.

After the Boeotian federation was disbanded by Agesilaus in 386 and reconstructed in the 370s, it had an archon, an assembly, and seven Boeotarchs. The new organization was more democratic, but Thebes continued to dominate the league quite aggressively. In 373–371, Thebes destroyed the Boeotian cities of Plataea and Thespiae and turned their residents into refugees.

Figure 32.1 shows a Boeotian silver coin from 395–387. Like other federal coins it shows the Boeotian buckler or shield on the obverse. The reverse shows the infant Heracles strangling two serpents; to the right is a bow, which was one of Heracles' weapons. According to the myth, Heracles killed serpents placed in his cradle by Hera, Zeus' jealous wife. Heracles' mortal parents came from Thebes and he figured prominently on Boeotian coins. The letters Th E stand for *Thebaion*. Many federal coins were minted in Thebes.

See WEB **32.2** for more on Greek federations and the Boeotian federation before the fourth century as well as a link to Boeotian coins.

Figure 32.1 A Boeotian federal coin. © The Trustees of the British Museum.

Questions

1. Describe the structure of the Boeotian federation from the bottom up (see also WEB **32.2**).
2. How did the federation restrict the autonomy of its individual constituents?

32.3   Sparta Dissolves Greek Federations in the Name of Autonomy

One of the principles of the Peace of Antalcidas that ended the Corinthian War in 387 was the preservation of Greek autonomy. This was supposed to protect individual poleis from more powerful states. Shortly after the meeting in Sardis where the peace was announced, representatives of different states came to sign it in Sparta. Agesilaus used the occasion to dissolve the Boeotian federation; later (386), he disbanded the Argive–Corinthian union. His actions were ostensibly to promote autonomy, but in fact they were in Sparta's interests. The union between Argos and Corinth (392–386) is described by Xenophon and Diodorus in WEB **32.4**.

The disbanding of both the Argive–Corinthian union and the Boeotian federation demonstrated the failure of political units larger than the polis to face up to external threats, which had been partly the reason for their creation.

Xenophon *Hellenica* 5.1.32–34

(**5.1.32**) After listening to this, the representatives of the Greek city-states reported back to their various states. And they all swore to ratify the accords, except for the Thebans, who claimed that they should take the oath on behalf of all Boeotians. Agesilaus, however, refused to accept the oaths unless they swore, following the instructions in the king's letter, that every state would be autonomous, be it large or small. The representatives of the Thebans, however, said they had received no such instructions. "Then go now and ask your people about it," said Agesilaus. "And add this to your report, that if they do not conform, they will have no place in the treaty." With that the representatives left.

(**1.33**) Because of his animosity toward the Thebans, however, Agesilaus lost no time in winning over the ephors and immediately making the sacrificial offering. The border-crossing sacrifices were favorable, and on arrival in Tegea he sent a number of horsemen off in various directions to hurry on the mobilization of the perioeci, and he also sent mercenary commanders to the allied cities. Before he moved out of Tegea, however, the Thebans arrived declaring that they would allow the city-states to be independent. The Spartans accordingly went home, and the Thebans were obliged to comply with the treaty, leaving the cities of Boeotia independent.

(**1.34**) The Corinthians, however, would not discharge their Argive garrison.[1] Agesilaus then made a public declaration to these people threatening them with war – against the Corinthians if they failed to discharge the Argives, and against the Argives if they failed to leave Corinth. Both parties were fearful, and so the Argives left and the city of Corinth became an independent state. Those guilty of the bloodbath and their accomplices left Corinth of their own accord, and the rest of the citizens willingly took back those who had been exiled earlier.[2]

Notes

1. *Corinth and Argos formed a united polis called Argos, which Agesilaus forced them to disband: see WEB **32.4**.*
2. *Xenophon refers to a violent stasis in Corinth that preceded the union with Argos, which resulted in the temporary exile of pro-Spartan opponents of the union.*

Question

1. How did disbanding the Boeotian federation and the Argive–Corinthian union serve Spartan interests?

32.5 Spartan Occupation of the Cadmea (Citadel) of Thebes (382)

In 382, two Chalcidian cities that feared being absorbed into the Chalcidian federation led by Olynthus invoked autonomy in their appeal to Sparta for help, and the Spartans obliged. For the first time in the history of the Peloponnesian League, allies could contribute money instead of troops for the campaign, perhaps because they were unable or reluctant to send soldiers. Sparta used the money to hire mercenaries (Xenophon *Hellenica* 5.2.21–22) and sent to Chalcidice a force led by Eudamidas. Later the Spartans sent him reinforcements under the command of his brother, Phoebidas. On his way to Chalcidice, Phoebidas passed through Boeotia to collect forces drafted by his brother. There he blatantly violated the principle of autonomy espoused by the Spartans.

Xenophon *Hellenica* 5.2.25–29, 32, 35–36

(5.2.25) After bringing together what remained of Eudamidas' men, Phoebidas took command of them and set off on his march. On reaching Thebes, they encamped outside the city, in the vicinity of the gymnasium. Thebes was in the throes of factional strife, and Ismenias and Leontiades, who happened to be polemarchs,[1] were at loggerheads, and each was the leader of one of the two opposing political groups [sg. *hetaireia*]. Because of his hatred for the Spartans, Ismenias did not even approach Phoebidas. Leontiades, by contrast, made a point of cultivating him and, after establishing a close relationship, he spoke to him as follows:

(2.26) "Phoebidas, it is possible for you to render your fatherland the greatest service on this day. If you follow me with your hoplites, I shall lead you to the acropolis. Once that is done, you can count on it that Thebes will be entirely in the power of the Spartans and of us, your friends. (**2.27**) Now, as you can see, there has been a proclamation expressly forbidding any Theban from joining your campaign against Olynthus. If you join us in putting our plan into action, however, we shall immediately send many hoplites and many cavalrymen along with you. The result will be that you will assist your brother with a large force and, while he is making ready to bring Olynthus under his control, you will have already brought Thebes, a much greater city than Olynthus, under yours."

(**2.28**) Hearing this, Phoebidas was elated. To bring off some brilliant stroke was something for which he felt greater passion than he did for living; but he was an impetuous and not very prudent man. When he agreed to the plan, Leontiades told him to set off, as if he were all prepared to make his departure from the city. "When the moment arrives," said Leontiades, "I shall come to you and personally guide you."

(**2.29**) The Council was then in session in the stoa in the agora, since the women were celebrating the Thesmophoria[2] on the Cadmea; and, as it was summer and the middle of the day, the streets were pretty much deserted. This was when Leontiades rode out on his horse and made Phoebidas turn back. He led him straight to the acropolis, where he installed him and his troops, and gave him the key to the gates. Then, after instructing him not to allow anyone access to the acropolis without his authorization, he went straight to the Council.

Notes

1. *The polemarch was a Theban magistrate who replaced the former Boeotarch.*
2. *The Thesmophoria was a festival celebrated exclusively by women in honor of Demeter.*

Leontiades then told the Theban Council that the Lacedaemonians had seized the Cadmea, Thebes' citadel, and that he had arrested the democratic leader Ismenias. Three hundred of Ismenias' supporters fled to Athens.

(**5.2.32**) This done, the Thebans chose another polemarch to replace Ismenias, and Leontiades immediately proceeded to Sparta. There he found the ephors and most of the city displeased with Phoebidas for having taken such action without his city's authorization. Agesilaus' response was that if Phoebidas' initiative had been detrimental to Lacedaemon, he would deserve punishment, but if it had been beneficial then it was the custom of old to allow such improvisation. "This, then, is the one germane consideration, whether what was done was good or bad for us."

Leontiades spoke in the Spartan assembly and said that the new government would reverse Thebes' anti-Spartan policy.

(**5.2.35**) Hearing this, the Spartans decided that, since the acropolis had been seized anyway, they would keep it garrisoned and put Ismenias on trial.[1] After this they sent out as his judges three men from Sparta, and one from each allied state, great or small. It was only when the court was in session that the charges were brought against Ismenias, and they were: that he promoted the barbarian's interests; that he had done Greece no good by becoming the Persian satrap's friend; that he had taken a share of the king's money; and that he and Androcleidas were the men most responsible for all the turmoil in Greece.[2] (2.36) Ismenias mounted a defense against all the charges, but failed to convince his hearers that he was not a man of mischievous undertakings on a grand scale. He was condemned and executed. Leontiades' followers were now in possession of the city, and they provided even greater services for the Lacedaemonians than was actually required of them.

Notes

1. *According to Diodorus (15.20.2: WEB* **32.6.I**), *the Spartans fined Phoebidas.*
2. *Taking the king's money referred to Persian subsidies of Sparta's opponents prior to the Corinthian War. Androcleidas was an anti-Spartan leader at Thebes.*

Plutarch (*Agesilaus* 24.1) mentions suspicions that Phoebidas followed Agesilaus' directives, while Diodorus of Sicily reports that the Spartans planned secretly to capture the Cadmea: see WEB **32.6.I**.

Scholars are divided about Agesilaus' involvement, and it is not easy to dispel the cloud of suspicion that hangs over him. The consequences of the capture of the Cadmea are clearer, however. Sparta lost the moral high ground of enforcing autonomy on others and provided ammunition to her critics. She also made other Greek states, especially Athens, both resentful and suspicious. Even the pro-Spartan Xenophon thought that Sparta did wrong: see WEB **32.6.II**.

Questions

1. Who was chiefly responsible for Phoebidas' occupation of the Cadmea according to Xenophon (**32.5**) and Diodorus (WEB **32.6.I**)? Which version is the more likely and why (cf. WEB **32.6.II**)?
2. Why were the Spartans displeased with Phoebidas and why did they then change their minds?
3. What might have been Ismenias' defense in his trial (cf. **31.5.B**: "Greek Grievances Against Sparta")?

32.7 The Sphodrias Affair (379/8)

The pro-Spartan government in Thebes held firm for just a few years. In 379/8, Theban exiles, assisted by Athens, sneaked into the city, eliminated the oligarchy, and established democracy there. The Spartan governor of the Cadmea withdrew his force and was punished for it at home. Then came an attempted raid of Attica that exacerbated Sparta's already tense relationship with Athens. Xenophon reports that the new democratic Theban government bribed Sphodrias, the Spartan commander (harmost) in Thespiae in Boeotia, to invade Attica.

32.7.A Sphodrias Invades Attica

Xenophon *Hellenica* 5.4.20–23

(**5.4.20**) In the case of the Thebans, they too were fearful, but their fear was that nobody would take on the fight with Spartans apart from themselves, and they came up with the following ploy. They persuaded Sphodrias, the harmost in Thespiae (they gave him money, it was suspected), to invade Attica, the aim being to set the Athenians on a war footing with the Spartans. Sphodrias agreed, and claimed that he would take Piraeus because it was still without gates. He then had his men eat early, and led them from Thespiae, saying that they would complete the march to Piraeus before dawn. (**4.21**) However, they were only at Thria [in western Attica] when day was breaking, and then Sphodrias did nothing to conceal his position. In fact, when turning back, he took off cattle as plunder and put the torch to homesteads. Moreover, a number of people who had encountered him during the night fled to the city and reported to the Athenians the approach of an army of considerable size. The Athenians, cavalry as well as hoplites, immediately took up arms and stood on guard over the city.

(**4.22**) There also happened to be in Athens some ambassadors of the Spartans – Etymocles, Aristolochus, and Ocyllus – and they were at the house of their guest-friend [*proxenos*] Callias. When the incident was reported, the Athenians arrested them and kept them under guard in the belief that they, too, were involved in the plot. These men, however, were thunderstruck at what had happened, and defended themselves on the grounds that they would not have been such imbeciles as to place themselves in the hands of the Athenians within the city had they known of the attempt to capture Piraeus – and at their guest-friend's house, at that, where they would have been found in an instant! (**4.23**) They further stated that it would become clear to the Athenians, too, that the city of Sparta had no knowledge of these events – they were sure, they said, that they would hear of Sphodrias' execution by the city. The ambassadors were then judged to have no knowledge of the affair and were released.

 See WEB **32.8** for Plutarch's different version of Sphodrias' attempt to capture Piraeus and his possible motives.

What scandalized the Greeks, and especially Athens, was Sphodrias' fate. Instead of being punished, he was acquitted in a way that shows the workings of personal networks in Sparta.

32.7.B Sphodrias' Acquittal

Xenophon *Hellenica* 5.4.24–26

(**5.4.24**) The ephors recalled Sphodrias and indicted him on a capital charge. Sphodrias, in fear, did not appear to face the charge, but even so, despite his failure to appear in court, he was acquitted. To many that seemed to be the most unjust verdict ever given in Sparta. There was a reason for it, however, which is as follows.

(**4.25**) Sphodrias had a son, Cleonymus, who was at the age of having just left boyhood, and he was the finest looking and most respected of those of his generation. Archidamus [III], Agesilaus' son, happened to be in love with him. Now Cleombrotus' friends, being close comrades [*hetairoi*] of Sphodrias, were all for acquitting him, but they were afraid of Agesilaus and *his* friends and, indeed, of those who stood between the two camps – for what Sphodrias had done seemed terrible. (**4.26**) Sphodrias therefore said to Cleonymus: "Son, you can save your father if you plead with Archidamus to get Agesilaus on my side at the trial." And on hearing this, Cleonymus did venture to approach Archidamus and beg him to become, for his sake, his father's savior.

Cleonymus pleaded with Archidamus to ask his father to intervene on Sphodrias' behalf, and Archidamus reluctantly agreed. Agesilaus at first would not hear of it but later changed his mind. Xenophon lets another Spartan, Etymocles, explain his reasons.

Xenophon *Hellenica* 5.4.32

One of Sphodrias' friends, in conversation with Etymocles, remarked: "I suppose all you friends of Agesilaus want to execute Sphodrias." Etymocles replied: "By Zeus, we shan't be in accord with Agesilaus in that case. He says the same thing to everyone he talks to – that it is impossible to find Sphodrias not guilty but that, when a person as child, boy, and young man has continually acted with honor, it is difficult to execute such a man, since Sparta needs soldiers of this sort."

Questions

1. What led Sphodrias to try to attack Piraeus, according to Xenophon (**32.7.A**) and Plutarch (WEB **32.8**? What is similar and different in their accounts?
2. What made the acquittal of Sphodrias "the most unjust verdict ever given in Sparta" (**32.7.B**)?
3. Why was Agesilaus' justification of Sphodrias' acquittal acceptable in Sparta (**32.7.B**)?

32.9 The Formation of the Second Athenian League (378/7)

The Athenians formed the Second Athenian League following the Spartan blunders of capturing the Cadmea and Sphodrias' failed raid on Attica. The two incidents gave Athens the freedom and justification to build a system of alliances that promised to adhere more faithfully than Sparta to the principles of the Peace of Antalcidas.

In 378/7 Athens invited Greeks and barbarians to join it in forming a multiple defensive alliance. Xenophon fails to mention the foundation of the Second Athenian League, but Athenian inscriptions, and especially what is known as the "Decree of Aristoteles," as well as Diodorus' history provide information about it. The decree shows an effort to comply with the Peace of Antalcidas and thus not to give Sparta or the Persian king reason to oppose it. It even implies that Sparta violated the Common Peace (lines 9–12). The Athenians are careful to impress upon the allies that they do not aim to imitate their ancestors and create a second Athenian empire. The inscription is followed by a list of members that starts on the front of the stele and continues to its left side. Over a period of time names were added and erased, thus reflecting the league's history. The extant list includes approximately fifty-eight names, although Diodorus (15.30.2) mentions seventy members and the orator Aeschines seventy-five (2 *On the False Embassy* 70). Generally, new members joined the league following a show of Athenian force in their regions, either in support of or threatening them. After 375–373 the Athenians stopped adding new names for reasons that are unknown. Lines 12–15 are a modern reconstruction following their erasure, perhaps when Athens was on bad terms with Persia.

32.9.A   The Decree of Aristoteles

The Decree of Aristoteles *IG* II² 43 = R&O no. 22[1]

Translation: R&O no. 22, pp. 92–99

In the archonship of Nausinicus [378/7]; Callibius, son of Cephisophon, of Paeania, was secretary; in the seventh prytany, of Hippothontis; resolved by the council and the people; Charinus of Athmonum was chairman. Aristoteles proposed:[2]

(**7**) For the good Fortune of the Athenians and the allies of the Athenians. So that the Spartans shall allow the Greeks to be free and autonomous, and to live at peace occupying their own territory in security, [and so that the peace and friendship sworn by the Greeks and the King in accordance with the agreements may be in force and endured][3] be it decreed by the people:

(**15**) If any of the Greeks or of the barbarians living in Europe or of the islanders, who are not the King's, wishes to be an ally of the Athenians and their allies, he may be – being free and autonomous, being governed under whatever form of government he wishes, neither receiving a garrison nor submitting to a governor nor paying tribute, on the same terms as the Chians and the Thebans and the other allies.[4]

(**25**) For those who make alliance with the Athenians and the allies, the people shall renounce whatever Athenian possessions there happen to be, whether private or public, in the territory of those who make the alliance, and concerning these things the Athenians shall give a pledge.[5]

For whichever of the cities which make the alliance with the Athenians there happen to be unfavorable steles at Athens, the council currently in office shall have power to demolish them.

(**35**) From the archonship of Nausinicus it shall not be permitted either privately or publicly to any of the Athenians to acquire either a house or land in the territory of the allies, either by purchase or by taking security or in any other way. If any one does buy or acquire or take as security in any way whatever, it shall be permitted to whoever wishes of the allies to expose it to the *synedroi* [council's delegates] the allies; the *synedroi* shall sell it and give one half to the man who exposed, while the other shall be the common property of the allies.

(**46**) If any one goes for war against those who have made the alliance, either by land or by sea, the Athenians and the allies shall go to support these both by land and by sea with all their strength as far as possible.

(**51**) If any one proposes or puts to the vote, whether official or private citizen, contrary to this decree that any of the things stated in this decree ought to be undone, the result shall be that he shall be deprived of his rights, and his property shall become public and a tenth belong to the Goddess, and he shall be judged by the Athenians and the allies for breaking up the alliance.[6] He shall be punished with death or with exile from wherever the Athenians and the allies control; and, if he is assessed for death, he shall not be buried in Attica or in the territory of the allies.

(**63**) This decree shall be written up by the secretary of the council on a stone stele and set down besides Zeus Eleutherios; the money for the writing-up of the stele shall be sixty drachmas, given from the ten talents by the treasurers of the Goddess.[7] On this stele shall be inscribed the names of the cities, which are allies and any other which becomes an ally. This is to be inscribed.

(**72**) The people shall choose immediately three envoys to Thebes, who are to persuade the Thebans of whatever good thing they can.[8] The following were chosen: Aristoteles of Marathon, Pyrrhandrus of Anaphlystis, Thrasybulus of Collytus.[9]

(**79–83**) Chios; Mytilene; Methymna; Rhodes; Byzantium.

(**79**) Thebes

(**80–84**) Chalcis; Eretria; Arethusa; Carystus; Icus.

(**85–89**) Perinthus; Peparethus; Sciathus; Maronea; Dium.

(**79**) Tenedos

(**82**) Poeessa

(**i. 89**) Paros; O –; Athenae (Diades); P –

(**ii. 85–90**) Pall (?) –

(**131–134**) The People of Zacynthus in Nellus.

(**97–130**) The People of Pyrrha; Abdera; Thasos; the Chalcidians from Thrace; Aenus; Samothrace; Dicaeopolis; Acarnania; of Cephallenia: Pronni; Alcetas; Neoptolemus; [*erasure*];[10] Andros; Tenos; Hestiaea; Myconus; Antissa; Eresus; Astraeus; of Ceos: Iulis, Carthaea, Coresia; Elaeus; Amorgus; Selymbria; Siphnus; Sicinus; Dium from Thrace; Neapolis.

Notes

1. *The translation does not distinguish between the restored and legible parts of the inscription.*
2. *The third-century* CE *author Diogenes Laertius (5.1.35) identifies Aristoteles as a writer of forensic speeches.*
3. *The restoration of these lines follows S. Accame,* La lega Ateniese del sec. IV a./C. *(Rome, 1941), p. 51.*
4. *In 384/3 the Athenians made a defensive alliance with the island of Chios that might have served as a precedent or model for the present treaty: IG II² 34 = Harding no. 31, p. 45. A fragmentary inscription has also survived of an Athenian treaty with Thebes in 378/7 (IG II² 40 = Harding no. 33).*
5. *The renouncing of Athenian property abroad did not include possessions in Lemnos, Imbros, and Scyros.*
6. *It is unclear whether the violator would be judged by the* synedrion *(allies' council) and an Athenian court or, less likely, by a joint court.*
7. *The cost of sixty drachmas for the stele was at least double that of other steles. The ten talents was apparently a fund designed for such purposes.*
8. *Since Thebes was already a member, the purpose of this embassy is unclear.*
9. *The membership list follows attempts to reconstruct the order in which members were inscribed.*
10. *Following Neoptolemus, a name ending with an N was erased. Against the common restoration of it as* Iason, *that is, the Thessalian potentate Jason of Pherae, is the strong possibility that the name had six letters. For Jason see WEB Chapter 33.*

32.9.B   Diodorus on the Second Athenian League

Diodorus also reports on the foundation of the league. I follow the scholarly view that he misdates it to 377/6 instead of 379/8, and mistakenly places it prior to Sphodrias' abortive invasion of Attica. Diodorus adds elsewhere that "the Athenians also voted to restore the lands that had been made into cleruchies to those who had earlier been the owners, and passed a law that none of the Athenians should farm outside Attica" (15.29.8). The dismantling of cleruchies did not include those on Lemnos, Imbros, and Scyros. In 365 Athens colonized Samos.

Diodorus of Sicily 15.28.2–5

(**15.28.2**) The Athenians sent the most respected of their number as ambassadors to the states aligned with Sparta and appealed to them to espouse the notion of liberty that they all shared. For because of the extent of the power they wielded around them, the Spartans were disdainful and oppressive in their rule of subject states, and as a result many of those aligned with them began to fall away and turn toward Athens. (**28.3**) The first to heed the call to secession were the Chians and Byzantines, to be followed by the Rhodians, the Mytileneans, and a number of other island peoples. In the ever-increasing momentum toward this goal amongst the Greeks, a large number of city-states joined the

Athenians. The Athenian people were elated by the favor shown by the states, and established a joint council for all the allies, appointing councilors from each state. (**28.4**) By general agreement it was determined that the council should sit in Athens, but that every city, large or small, should be of equal status and have one vote, and that all should be autonomous but regard Athens as their leader.

The Spartans could see that the city-states' impetus to secede was unstoppable, but they still aspired to bring the secessionists back into line by means of deputations, kind words, and even promises of favors. (**28.5**) In addition, they applied their thoughts assiduously to war preparations, since they expected the war with Boeotia to be for them momentous and long-protracted because the Athenians, and the rest of the Greeks who were members of the council, were allies of the Thebans.

Diodorus wrongly claims that Athens appointed the allies' representatives. In fact, the allies' council (*synedrion*) did not include Athenian representatives and operated separately from the Athenian Council. The *synedrion* put proposals to the Athenian assembly, which discussed them, but it could not impose conditions that the allies opposed. It is unclear how the league's operations were financed. Apparently each member paid for its own forces on an *ad hoc* basis. Later, money was collected but, to avoid the odor of empire, the terminology was changed from *phoros* (tribute) to *syntaxis* (contribution).

32.9.C   "Contributions" to the League

Harpocration *Lexicon* s.v. Syntaxis = Harding no. 36

They used to call the payments of *phoroi* [tributes] "*syntaxeis*" [contributions] because the Greeks disliked the name "*phoroi*." Theopompus says in the tenth book of the *Philippics* that Callistratus named them thus [*FGrHist* 115 F 98].[1]

Note

1. *If Callistratus is Callistratus of Aphidna, he was a prominent Athenian politician and orator, who was put to death in 355.*

Questions

1. What were the goals of the new Athenian alliance, according to Aristotele's decree (**32.9.A**)? According to Diodorus (**32.9.B**)?
2. What were the league's institutions and how did they operate (**32.9.A–B**)?
3. What were the allies, including Athens, allowed and forbidden to do under the treaty (**32.9.A**)?
4. What might have deterred a Greek city from joining the league (**32.9.A–C**)?

Figure 32.2   Eirene with Wealth (Plutus). München, Staatliche Antikensammlungen und Glyptothek. Photo © bpk.

32.10   Desiring Peace

Following the foundation of the league, Athens and Thebes, which regained her hegemonic power in most of Boeotia, cooperated against Sparta. In 375, Sparta and Athens, as well as the Persian king who needed mercenaries, arranged for a common peace that was immediately broken. Yet Athens was unnerved by Thebes' increasing power, her destruction of Plataea, and her operations against Thespiae and Phocis. In 371 Athens called for a Greek congress in Sparta to discuss a common peace. Expectations for peace must have been high for quite some time. In 375/4, Athens instituted a cult for Eirene, Peace, and no later than 369/8 commissioned a bronze statue of this personified deity from the sculptor Cephisodotus. Eirene stood holding a scepter in one hand and carrying the child Plutus, Wealth, in the other. She wore a *peplos*, a heavy woolen garment, that underlined her maternal, nurturing figure as well as the theme of fertility. Together with the figure of Wealth, Eirene expressed the Athenian yearning for times of peace and prosperity. Figure 32.2 shows a marble Roman copy of the statue, with Eirene's right arm, Plutus' arms, and the jug restored.

32.11 The Common Peace of 371

The Greek congress in Sparta in 371 that was initiated by Athens decided on the following peace terms.

32.11.A The Terms of the Common Peace of 371

Xenophon *Hellenica* 6.3.18

... Harmosts were to be withdrawn from the cities; armed forces, both naval and land, were to be disbanded; and the city-states were to be left autonomous. In the case of contravention of these terms, anyone so wishing could help the cities suffering the injury, but anyone not so wishing was not bound by oath to fight alongside the injured parties.

The ancient accounts diverge at this point. According to Xenophon, when the Thebans asked to amend the list of signatories to the peace from "Thebans" to "Boeotians," Agesilaus refused and gave the Thebans the option of excluding themselves from the peace. Xenophon says that this made the Athenians glad and hopeful for the destruction of Thebes, while the gloomy Thebans went home (*Hellenica* 6.4.19–20). Plutarch's version of these events is different. He describes a confrontation between Agesilaus and the Theban leader Epaminondas, who spoke in the name of freedom and equality, and substituted Sparta for Persia as the Greeks' common enemy. He also extended the principle of autonomy into Laconia proper when he questioned the legitimacy of Spartan control over the perioeci. He would later give freedom and autonomy to the Messenians (but not to the cities of Boeotia: **32.15**).

32.11.B Epaminondas in Sparta

Plutarch *Agesilaus* 27.3–28.2

(**27.3**) ... A comprehensive peace seemed to all parties to be a good idea, and ambassadors from all over Greece converged on Sparta to arrange the cessation of hostilities. (**27.4**) One of these was Epaminondas, a man reputed for his learning and philosophy, but who had not yet demonstrated his capabilities in military strategy.[1] Epaminondas saw all the others deferring to Agesilaus, and he alone had the spirit to speak frankly. He embarked on a speech that was not on behalf of Thebes, but on behalf of Greece in general, pointing out that war made Sparta stronger, but only at the cost of suffering in all the other states, and he urged that peace be settled on a footing of equality and justice. Peace would endure, he said, only when all the signatories were on equal terms.

(28.1) Agesilaus saw that the Greeks were listening to Epaminondas with great admiration and rapt attention, and so he asked him if he thought justice and equality demanded that Boeotia's cities be independent. This drew a swift and bold reply from Epaminondas, who asked in turn if Agesilaus thought justice demanded that the cities of Laconia be independent. At this Agesilaus jumped to his feet and angrily told him to state clearly whether he would make the Boeotian cities independent. (28.2) Epaminondas merely restated the very same question, whether Agesilaus would make the Laconian towns independent, and Agesilaus became so truculent that he welcomed the excuse to immediately erase the name of Thebes from the treaty and declare war on her. He then told the rest of the Greeks to leave, since they were by and large reconciled and would settle what was remediable with the peace treaty, and what was not with war. For it was difficult to clear away and resolve all their disputes.

Note

1. *Epaminondas was a pupil of the Pythagorean philosopher Lysis of Taras and a man reputed to be indifferent to poverty.*

Questions

1. How was the Common Peace of 371 different from the Common Peace of Antalcidas of 388/7 (**31.12**)?
2. What was the cause of disagreement between Sparta and the Boeotians in the Greek congress of 371? Who was in the right?
3. To what extent was the dispute between Sparta and Boeotia reflected in the terms of the Common Peace of 371?

32.12   The Sacred Band

The dispute in the peace congress in Sparta led to the battle of Leuctra in 371 between the Spartans and Thebans and their respective allies. The Theban contingents included a unit called the Sacred Band (*hieros lochos*), which has attracted much attention. It was an elite force of 300 hoplites who were said to be pairs of male lovers. If true, the Thebans, like the Spartans, used homoerotic relationship to foster martial solidarity. The unit was maintained at public expense. It excelled under the Theban general Pelopidas, who was instrumental in the creation of Theban hegemony in Greece after the battle of Leuctra.

Plutarch *Pelopidas* 18.1–3, 5, 19.3

(**18.1**) It was [the Theban commander] Gorgidas, they say, who first put together the Sacred Band, which consisted of 300 hand-picked men. They had their camp on the Cadmea, and the city provided them with training and upkeep, for which reason they were also called the "City Band" (for people at that time rightly termed the acropoleis cities). Some, however, say that this corps was made up of lovers and their loved ones. (**18.2**) A playful comment is attributed to [the Theban general] Pammenes to the effect that Homer's Nestor showed no knowledge of tactics in bidding the Greeks to deploy by tribes and clans [phratries] "so that clan may help clan, and tribe help tribe" [Homer *Iliad* 2.363]. Rather, says Pammenes, he should have advocated deploying lover next to loved one. In crises, he claims, clansmen do not have much concern for clansmen, nor tribesmen for tribesmen; but a unit constituted on the basis of erotic feelings is inseparable and unbreakable. Lovers, from shame before their loved ones, and loved ones from shame before their lovers, both stand their ground in critical moments to protect each other. (**18.3**) And this is not surprising, since they have more regard for their partners, even when the partners are absent, than for all others who are present. Witness the man who, when a foe was about to finish him off as he lay on the ground, begged and pleaded with him to drive the sword through his chest, "so that my loved one may not be ashamed at seeing me with the wound in my back."...

(**18.5**) The band remained undefeated until the battle of Chaeronea, it is said.[1] After that battle, Philip purportedly looked upon the corpses, and stood at that spot on which the 300 lay dead. They had faced his pikes [*sarissas*], and all of them were lying in their armor, their bodies indiscriminately interspersed with each other. Philip was dumbfounded, and when he was told that this was the company of lovers and their beloved, he shed tears and said: "A miserable death to those who think that these men did, or had done to them, anything disgraceful!"[2]

(**19.3**) Gorgidas initially distributed members of this Sacred Band amongst the front ranks and set them in the vanguard of the entire hoplite phalanx. By doing that, however, he did not make the valor of the men conspicuous, nor did he exploit their strength by directing it against a common target. That strength was diluted and mixed in with a mass of troops of inferior quality. However, at Tegyra[3] their valor was truly conspicuous. There they fought as a unit and did so around Pelopidas, and so Pelopidas no longer kept them dispersed and scattered but employed them as a unified body, deploying them in the most dangerous positions in his greatest battles.

Notes

1. *In 338 Philip of Macedonia and a Greek coalition fought each other in the battle of Chaeronea (**38.15**).*
2. *See WEB **38.16.II** ("The Monuments of Chaeronea") for the Thebans' tomb in Chaeronea.*
3. *In 375 Pelopidas defeated two Spartan regiments at Tegyra in Boeotia.*

32.13   The Battle of Leuctra (371)

The battle of Leuctra in southwestern Boeotia in 371 was one of the most significant battles in Greek history. For reasons of age and politics, Agesilaus stayed home. King Cleombrotus, who was already in Thespiae at that time, led the Peloponnesian forces. The ancient accounts of this battle are at best incomplete, but in general Xenophon describes it from the Spartan point of view, while Plutarch (WEB **32.14**) and Diodorus (15.55.1–56.4) describe it from the Theban side. About 10,000–11,000 Peloponnesians fought 6,000–7,000 Boeotians in this battle, but the shortage of Spartan manpower allowed them to contribute only 700 Spartan citizens to the coalition army. Moreover, in the decisive clash between Cleombrotus and Epaminondas, the latter might have enjoyed a numerical superiority.

Epaminondas, the architect of the Theban victory, introduced important tactical innovations. He skillfully integrated infantry and cavalry, but more important was his deployment of the infantry. In a traditional hoplite battle, the strong right wing fought the enemy's weaker left wing, which was supposed to hold on until its right wing decided the battle. Epaminondas, however, pitted his fifty-deep left wing, that is, his main force, against the enemy's strong right wing. His advance in oblique formation encouraged Cleombrotus to try to outflank him, thus creating a gap between his troops and the rest of the line. Into this gap Pelopidas rushed with the Sacred Band.

32.13.A   Xenophon on the Battle at Leuctra

Xenophon *Hellenica* 6.4.8–15

(**6.4.8**) … Cleombrotus' last council of war was held after lunch and, as they drank a little at midday, people said the wine had stimulated them somewhat. (**4.9**) Both sides took up arms, and it was clear by now that there would be a battle. So, first of all, the people who had furnished the market, a number of camp-followers, and those who did want to fight began to withdraw from the Boeotian army; but the Spartan mercenaries under Hieron, the Phocian peltasts, and the Heraclean and Phliasian cavalry performed an encircling movement and attacked them as they retreated, turning them around and driving them back to the Boeotian camp. The result was that they greatly increased the size and compactness of the Boeotian force.

(**4.10**) Next, as the ground between the two armies was even, the Spartans deployed their cavalry before their phalanx, and the Thebans deployed theirs opposite them. The Theban cavalry force was well trained because of the wars with Orchomenus and Thespiae, whereas at that particular time the cavalry of the Spartans was in very poor condition. (**4.11**) This was because it was the richest Spartans who reared the horses, and the appointed rider came along for a horse only when the troop mobilization was called. He then simply took his mount, and whatever arms were supplied to him, and with no further ado went off to war. Moreover, the men on the horses were physically the least robust and also the least ambitious of the Spartan troops.

(**4.12**) Such, then, was the cavalry on both sides. As for the phalanx, people said that the Spartans led out each half-company [*enomotia*][1] three lines deep, and this meant that the total depth of the phalanx was no more than twelve men. The Thebans, however, were formed up no less than fifty shields deep. They reckoned that if they defeated the troops around the king everything else would be easily achieved.

(**4.13**) Cleombrotus now began to lead his men against the enemy but, right at the start, even before the troops with him were aware that he was moving them forward, the cavalry had actually engaged and that of the Spartans was quickly defeated. As they fled, the horsemen ran into their own hoplites, and in addition the Theban troops were now on the attack. Even so Cleombrotus and his men had the upper hand in the fight at the beginning, and one can confidently make this deduction from this clear piece of evidence, namely that they could not have picked him up and carried him off alive if those fighting alongside him were not then having the best of it. (**4.14**) However, when the pole-march Dinon had been killed, and Sphodrias, who was one of the king's tent-companions, and Sphodrias' son Cleonymus also fell,[2] the cavalry, the so-called polemarch's adjutants, and the others all gave ground, pushed back by the mass of Theban troops. Furthermore, when those on the left wing saw the right being pushed back, they too gave way. They had suffered many casualties and were now defeated but, even so, after crossing the ditch that was before their camp they set their weapons down on the spot from which they had started out. The camp, in fact, was not on com-pletely level terrain, but on rising ground.

After this, some of the Spartans found the disastrous result intolerable, and declared that they should block any enemy attempt to set up a trophy, and try to recover their dead by fighting, not under truce. (**4.15**) The polemarchs could see, however, that the Spartan dead totaled close to a thousand, and that of the roughly 700 Spartiates in the battle some 400 had been killed. They also observed that all their allies had lost their spirit for the fight, with some not even upset over what had happened; and so they brought together the most important members of the force and considered what to do. They all agreed to gather up the dead under a truce, and they sent a messenger to discuss its terms. After this the Thebans erected their trophy, and gave back the bodies under a truce.[3]

Notes

1. *The full complement of the "half-company" was forty men.*
2. *See **32.7** for Sphodrias' failed attempt to capture Piraeus and its consequences.*
3. *Diodorus (15.55.1–56.4) reports that Archidamus, Agesilaus' son, also fought in this battle, and that Epaminondas instructed his right wing to avoid battle and retreat if necessary. Diodorus adds that the Peloponnesians attacked both wings in a crescent formation (which is unlikely), and that the Thebans lost about 300 men.*

See WEB **32.14** for Plutarch's description of the battle of Leuctra.

The Theban messenger who came to announce the victory at Leuctra to the Athenians was given the cold shoulder. The Spartans reacted with their version of a stiff upper lip, showing, as in the battle, that they had learned nothing.

32.13.B   The Spartan Reaction to the Defeat in Leuctra

Xenophon *Hellenica* 6.4.16

Following these events, the man sent to report the calamity to Lacedaemon arrived there on the final day of the Gymnopaedia, when the men's chorus was in the theater. On hearing of the disaster, the ephors were distressed, as I suppose they were bound to be; but rather than dismiss the chorus, they allowed it to continue to the end. Furthermore, while they gave the names of the fallen to the various relatives, they ordered the women not to shriek out in lamentation but to bear their suffering in silence. The following day one saw those whose kinsmen had fallen appear in public with bright, beaming faces, but you could have seen only a few of those whose relatives had been reported alive, and these were going about sullen and dejected.

Questions

1. Try to draw the lines of the battle of Leuctra according to Xenophon's account (**32.13.A**). Who, according to this historian, was responsible for the Spartan defeat and why?

2. How does Plutarch's account of the battle of Leuctra (WEB **32.14**) modify Xenophon's (**32.13.A**)?

3. What was characteristically Spartan in the battle of Leuctra and its aftermath (**32.13.A–B**)?

32.15   The Foundation of Messene (370/69)

The battle of Leuctra effectively ended Spartan hegemony in Greece. The loss of 400 Spartans was too heavy for a state that suffered from an acute shortage of male citizens, and Epaminondas made sure he kept Sparta in a weakened position.

In 370 Arcadian Mantinea, which Sparta had disbanded in the past, reunited and Sparta was too weak to prevent it. Together with other Arcadian communities, Mantinea formed an Arcadian federation that soon allied itself with Argos, Elis, and Thebes. This meant that Sparta now had a strong new and inimical state on its border. In 370/69, for the first time in recorded Spartan history, its territory was invaded. Encouraged by information about a perioecic revolt, a coalition army led by the Theban generals Epaminondas and Pelopidas entered Laconia from different directions. In desperation the Spartans promised to free helots who would join their ranks, and 6,000 helots did so. The invaders plundered and burned Spartan property but did not converge on the unwalled city of Sparta, partially because of the Spartans' counter-measures. Instead, Epaminondas did something worse: he liberated most of Messenia. Xenophon says nothing about this event, but Diodorus fills the gap.

Diodorus of Sicily 15.66.1

Epaminondas was by nature a man of ambitious projects, one who yearned for perpetual fame. He now advised the Arcadians and the rest of the allies to resettle Messene, which had been deprived of its original inhabitants by the Spartans many years earlier, and whose territory was well situated for an attack on Sparta. All were in agreement. Epaminondas then made a search for what remained of the Messenians, and also chose volunteers for citizenship and refounded Messene, giving it a large number of inhabitants. By dividing the land amongst them, and by rebuilding, he restored a distinguished Greek city and earned a great reputation amongst all men.

Figure 32.3
Messene's walls.
© Vanni Archive/
CORBIS.

Messene's foundation was accompanied by large-scale sacrifices to the gods and traditional Messenian heroes (Pausanias *Description of Greece* 4.26–27). The site encompassed Mt. Ithome, formerly a center of resistance to Sparta, and thus contributed to the creation of an independent Messenian identity. The Messenians also built massive walls that encircled their city and the countryside. The walls were very well built, reaching in places a height of 7–9 meters (Figure 32.3).

32.16   The Dissolution of the Peloponnesian League (365)

As if losing a substantial part of its infrastructure was not enough for Sparta, in 370/69 the Arcadians founded the city of Megalopolis, perhaps on Epaminondas' initiative and certainly with his blessing. The Spartans were now surrounded by hostile neighbors to the west and north.

Sparta nevertheless managed to recover somewhat from these blows. Over the next five years Sparta, Athens, and Thebes competed for control and influence in the Peloponnese. There were also violent changes of government in various cities there. In 365, however, Sparta lost the Peloponnesian League. The initiative came from its old ally, Corinth, whose relationship with Arcadia and Athens became tense. The Corinthians sought to make peace with Thebes, with whom Sparta was at war, and the Spartans granted them their request. Sparta continued to play a role in Greek affairs afterwards, but its ability to influence them was much reduced.

Xenophon *Hellenica* 7.4.6–7, 9–10

(**7.4.6**) ... The Corinthians were now thinking that security would be difficult for them to attain. Even before this they had suffered defeats on land, and now they had to face the antipathy of Athens as well. They therefore decided to gather together mercenary troops, both infantry and cavalry. Taking charge of these, they proceeded to give the city protection, and also to inflict considerable damage on enemies living close by. In addition, they sent a deputation to Thebes to ask whether they might obtain a peace settlement if they came seeking one, and (**4.7**) the Thebans told the Corinthians to come as a settlement would be forthcoming. The Corinthians then asked the Thebans to permit them also to go to their allies so that they could include in the peace those wanting inclusion, and simply leave those who chose otherwise to continue fighting. The Thebans made this concession to them, too, and the Corinthians came to Lacedaemon and spoke as follows ...

The Corinthians pleaded with the Spartans to allow them to make peace with Boeotia and invited the Spartans to join them.

(**4.9**) On hearing this, the Spartans advised the Corinthians to make peace, and they also left it to their other allies to withdraw if they did not wish to continue the war alongside them. But they declared that they themselves would continue fighting and take whatever result heaven decided on – Messene was a land they had received from their fathers, and they would never accept being deprived of it! (**4.10**) The Corinthians accordingly made their way to Thebes to negotiate the peace. The Thebans thought they should also take an oath binding them to an alliance, but the Corinthians replied that an alliance was not a peace treaty, but only a change or wars. The point of their being there, they said, was to negotiate a fair peace, if the Thebans were in accord. The Thebans felt admiration for them because, despite their perilous situation, they were unwilling to put themselves on a war footing with their benefactors; and they granted peace to them, as well as to the Phliasians and the others who had accompanied them to Thebes, on condition that each party retain its own territory. And such were the terms on which the oaths were taken.

Questions

1. Why did the Spartans refuse to join the Corinthian peace initiative, and what did their allowing Corinth and others to pursue it mean?
2. Why did the Corinthians refuse the Theban offer to become their ally?

Review Questions

1. How did Sparta take advantage of the Common Peace (see **32.3**, WEB **32.4**)?
2. Discuss the history of the conflict between Sparta and Thebes from the Peace of Antalcidas to the Peace of 371 (**32.1**, **32.3**, **32.5**, **32.7**, **32.9**, **32.12**, WEB **32.6**, WEB **32.8**, WEB **32.14**).
3. What do the Phoebidas and Sphodrias affairs indicate about Sparta's difficulties abroad (**32.5**, **32.7**, WEB **32.6.I–II**, WEB **32.8**)?
4. What were the aims of the Second Athenian League and how did it meet the concerns of its members (**32.9–10**)?
5. How did Thebes deprive Sparta of its hegemonic status (**32.13**, **32.15–16**)?
6. It has been argued that what led to the Spartan mismanagement of their empire and defeat at Leuctra was Spartanism. Do you agree?

Suggested Readings

The Boeotian federation and its government: Demand 1982 (fifth century); Buck 1994, esp. 6–10; Beck 2000; Buckler and Beck 2008, 127–198. *The Phoebidas and Sphodrias affairs*: Cartledge 1987, 136–138, 156–159; Hodkinson 2007; V. Parker 2007; Buckler and Beck 2008, 71–84. *The Second Athenian League: date of foundation*: Rice 1975; Fauber 1999; R&O, 100; *its organization and history*: Cargill 1981; Badian 1995; Harding 1995; Baron 2006. *Eirene in Athens*: H. Shapiro 1993, 45–50; Stewart 1997, 152–153; Stafford 2001, 173–197; Smith 2003, 11. *Sacred Band*: DeVoto 1992; Ogden 1996; Leitao 2002 (questions its historical existence), but see Davidson 2007, 432–441. *Battle of Leuctra*: Cawkwell 1972; *contra*: Cartledge 1987, 236–241, and see also Tuplin 1987; V. Hanson 1988 (disputes the use of innovative tactics); Buckler and Beck 2008, 111–126. *Sparta, Thebes, and Arcadia after Leuctra*: Roy 1971; Buckler 1980; Cartledge 1987, 382–392; T. Nielsen 2002, 306–510. *Messene's foundation*: Luraghi 2002a, 2008 (argues that Messene was actually inhabited by helots and perioeci who appropriated the ancient Messenian identity to themselves).

33

Jason of Pherae (?–370)

CHAPTER CONTENTS

Ancient Greece from Homer to Alexander: The Evidence, First Edition. Joseph Roisman.
© 2011 Blackwell Publishing Ltd. Translations © 2011 John Yardley. Published 2011 by Blackwell Publishing Ltd.

34

The Second Athenian League and Theban Hegemony

CHAPTER CONTENTS

Ancient Greece from Homer to Alexander: The Evidence, First Edition. Joseph Roisman.
© 2011 Blackwell Publishing Ltd. Translations © 2011 John Yardley. Published 2011 by Blackwell Publishing Ltd.

This chapter deals with Athenian and Theban foreign policies. It shows Athens' commitment to respect the freedom of her allies as proclaimed in two separate decrees, but also reveals that Athens expelled residents from and colonized Samos (which was not an ally). Another Athenian decree reproduced here involves Arcesine on the island of Amorgus and suggests direct Athenian intervention in the polis' affairs. Thebes was the leading land power following the battle of Leuctra, and the Common Peace of 367, recorded in this chapter, reflected her new status. The chapter shows how Thebes used her power to destroy neighboring Orchomenus in 364. It concludes with accounts of the second battle of Mantinea (362), which put an end to Theban hegemony.

In addition to cities that dominated the Greek scene at this time, a new figure emerged in Thessaly, Jason of Pherae, whose death in 370 put an end to what could have been a new power in Greece. Jason of Pherae is discussed in WEB Chapter 33.

Both the Second Athenian League and Thebes' war with Sparta were responses to Spartan imperialism. Nevertheless, both Athens and Thebes ended up imitating Sparta. We shall deal with Athens first.

34.1 Athens' Treatment of Chalcis (Euboea) and the Island of Paros (378/7–372)

Athens largely stood by her commitment to respect her allies' freedom. An example of such a commitment is an alliance with Chalcis in Euboea in the year in which the Athenian League was formed (378/7). The following lines from an inscription record the popular decision concerning the alliance and detail its substance.

34.1.A Athens' Alliance with Chalcis

IG II² 44, lines 18–27 = Harding no. 38

…There shall be [allianc]e between the (**20**) [Ath]enian[s] and the Chalcidians: Alliance between the Chal[cidi]ans in Eu[b]oea [and] the [Atheni]ans. The Chalcidi[ans] shall own their own [land] in freedom [and] autonomy and … will neither have garrison placed on them (**25**) [by the Athenians], nor will they pay tribute, nor accept [a governor] contrary to the decree [of the allies. If] anyone wages war [against] the land…

The treatment of other Greeks who refused to join the league was quite different. When in 377 the city of Histiaea in Euboea refused to become a member, the league devastated its territory and forced it to take a garrison. Two years later Histiaea joined the league (Diodorus 15.30.5).

In 372 the Cycladic island of Paros joined the league following the victory of a pro-Athenian party there. Two decrees, which were inscribed on the same stele, deal with the island's membership. The earlier one, no. II, is the only extant resolution we have of the league's *synedrion* (council). It used the Athenian calendar but mentioned no prytany because it was not issued by the Athenian Council. In fact, the president was a Theban. The decree discusses the imposition of reconciliation on the island following a *stasis*. The later decree, no. I, obliged Paros as an Athenian colony to bring a cow, panoply, and phallus to the festivals of the Panathenaea and Dionysia. Significantly, similar demands were made of colonists and allies of Athens at the time of the fifth-century Athenian empire (cf. the Brea decree in **20.17**). The decree also mentions a treasurer of the people, which was a new Athenian office created ca. 376.

34.1.B   Decrees Concerning Paros

R&O, no. 29[1]

Translation: R&O, pp. 146–149

I

– in accordance with tradition, and to the Panathenaea a cow and panoply, and to send to the Dionysia a cow and phallus as a commemoration, since they happen to be colonists of the people of Athens.

(**7**) Write up the decree and the reconciliation, which the allies have decreed for the Parians, and place a stele on the Acropolis: for the writing-up of the stele the treasurer of the people shall give 20 drachmas.

(**12**) Also invite to hospitality in the *prytaneion* tomorrow the envoys of the Parians.

II

(**14**) In the archonship of Asteius [373/2]; on the last day of Scirophorion [June/July]; with [–] Thebes putting to the vote. Resolved by the allies:

(**17**) So that the Parians shall live in agreement and nothing violent shall happen there (?):

(**18**) If any one kills any one unjustly (?), he shall be put to death; and those responsible for the death shall pay the penalty (?) in accordance with the laws.

[–] or exiles any one contrary to the laws and this decree, [–]

Note

1. *The translation does not distinguish between the restored and legible parts of the inscription.*

Question

1. Did the agreements with Paros violate in letter or spirit the guidelines of the Athenian League (**32.9.A–B**)?

34.2   Athens' Colonization of Samos (365)

During the 370s–360s Athens supported rebels against the Persian throne in Egypt, Cyprus, and Asia Minor in what is known as the Satraps' Revolt. In 366, Ariobarzanes, the satrap of Dascylium, rebelled and appealed to Athens for aid. The Athenians tried to play it both ways. They sent him a fleet under Timotheus, Conon's son, but also instructed Timotheus not to violate the King's Peace. The presence of royal Persian forces on the island of Samos in violation of the peace provided Timotheus with a legitimate excuse to attack and capture it after a ten-month siege (365). Samos was not a member of the league, but this hardly justified Athens' not giving it back its freedom. Instead, Athens expelled many Samians and cleruchized the island. An aside in Aristotle's discussion of shame shows that some Athenians were distressed by this policy.

Aristotle *Rhetoric* 2.6.24 1384b32–35

People would be likely to feel shame under the following circumstances. In the first place, if there happened to be in their presence some people before whom we said they felt shame. These, remember, were persons admired by them, persons who actually admire them, or people by whom they want to be admired or from whom they stand in need of some service that they will not receive if they are without respect. They are people who see what is happening (witness Cydias' speech on the apportionment of the land of Samos, when he asked the Athenians to imagine the Greeks standing around them in a circle and seeing, not just hearing about, the decrees they were about to pass);[1] or they are people in the vicinity, or people likely to become aware of their behavior.

Note

1. *Aristotle is the only source who reports on this orator.*

34.3   Athens' Treatment of Arcesine (Amorgus; ca. 357/6)

The Athenians similarly colonized the city of Potidaea in 364/3. They were now involved in conflicts in western Greece, the Peloponnese, Thessaly, and the Aegean, and claimed to possess Amphipolis and the Thracian Chersonesus in the north. These actions, in addition to several unsuccessful and under-funded military expeditions, made the allies both fearful and resentful. In 357/6 a number of league members led by Byzantium, Cos, Chios, and Rhodes decided to secede, which led to the Social War (from *socii*, Latin for allies). The sources also blame the revolt on the Persian king, and especially Mausolus, the ruler and probably satrap of Caria, who aided the rebels, although the extent of his intervention is unclear. From around this time comes unambiguous epigraphic evidence of Athenian imperialism concerning the city of Arcesine on the Cycladic island of Amorgus. It shows the presence of an Athenian gov-ernor on allied land and the ally's obligation to maintain a garrison. Amorgus is listed as an ally in the league's foundation decree (see **32.9.A**: "The Decree of Aristoteles"). The inscription is probably from 357/6, or the beginning of the Social War, although some scholars date it a few years earlier. It honors the Athenian governor Androtion, who was a prominent politician and historian of Athens.

Arcesine Honors Androtion *IG* 12.7.5 = Tod no. 152 = Harding no. 68 = R&O no. 51

Translation: R&O, pp. 249–251

Resolved by the Council and the People of Arcesine: Since Androton had been a good man to the people of Arcesine, and when he was the governor of the city he did not harm any of the citizens (**5**) or the foreigners who came to the city, and he lent the city money in time of need, and did not wish to charge any interest; and (**10**) when the city could not pay for the garrison he advanced the pay-ment from his own pockets, and when he was repaid the money at the end of year he did not exact interest, and because of his actions the city spent twelve minas less money each year; and he ran-somed those who (**15**) became prisoners of war when he came upon them.

Androtion, son of Andron, the Athenian shall be crowned with a five-hundred drachma golden crown for his excellence and justice and good will (**20**) toward the Arcesinians, and he shall be inscribed as proxenos and benefactor of the Arcesinians, both himself and his descendants, and he shall have immunity [*ateleia*] of all things.[1]

Because it [has been also] resolved by the allies ... likewise...

Note

1. *Immunity or* ateleia *was exemption from local duties and, in particular, paying taxes.*

 The Athenians' military performance in the Social War was abysmal. See WEB **34.4** for calls for peace in Athens in response to her poor military record and financial distress, and for the conclusion of the war.

Questions

1. What impositions on Arcesine contradicted the league's foundation decree (**32.9.A**)?
2. What wrongs did the orator Cydias (**34.2**) and Isocrates (WEB **34.4**) find with Athens?

—————————   **34.5 The Theban Hegemony: A Theban Common Peace (367)**

Following Leuctra, Thebes became the strongest land power in Greece. Thebes most probably withdrew from the Athenian League and created its own league with states from central Greece, and later even with Byzantium. An Athenian–Spartan alliance and military operations against Thebes and its allies failed to change the new reality. The power of Thebes was well illustrated in 367 when representatives from different Greek states arrived at the Persian court of Artaxerxes II to ask for subsidies and support. The king readily switched his alliance from Sparta to Thebes and accepted the Theban terms for a common alliance against Sparta and Athens. Antalcidas, who had been the architect of the Spartan–Persian alliance, took his own life. The Greeks found nothing attractive in the Persian–Theban peace, and when Thebes requested that they swear to its terms, no one did.

Xenophon *Hellenica* 7.1.33–38

(**7.1.33**) The Thebans were always considering how to seize the hegemony of Greece, and thought there might be some profit derived from sending an embassy to the king of Persia. They then issued an invitation to their allies in this regard, on the grounds that the Spartan Euthycles was also at the court of the king. Those who went up-country [to the king] were: from Thebes Pelopidas, from Arcadia the athlete Antiochus, and from Elis Archidamus. An Argive also went with them. When the Athenians heard about it, they sent Timagoras and Leon.

(**1.34**) After the ambassadors arrived, it was Pelopidas who commanded the king's attention. For he was able to say that his people alone fought on the king's side at Plataea [479]; that they never after that joined an expedition against the king; and that the Spartans had opened hostilities against them simply because the Thebans were unwilling to march against him with Agesilaus, and also refused to let him sacrifice to Artemis at Aulis, where Agamemnon, sailing off to Asia, sacrificed before capturing Troy.[1] (**1.35**) Two factors, and important ones, that contributed to the respect paid to Pelopidas were that the Thebans had won the battle of Leuctra, and that they had quite clearly laid waste the territory of the Spartans. Pelopidas made the further observation that it was when the Thebans were not with them that the Argives and Arcadians were defeated in battle by the Spartans. The truth of all these declarations was corroborated by the Athenian Timagoras, who as a result came second to Pelopidas in the king's regard.[2]

(**1.36**) After this, Pelopidas was asked by the king what conditions he personally wanted included in the treaty, to which he replied that the Messenians should be independent from Sparta, and that Athens should beach her navy.[3] He added that if the two states were not persuaded, the others should open hostilities against them, and that any city refusing to go along with this should be attacked first. (**1.37**) These clauses were written into the document, and read out to the ambassadors, after which, within the king's hearing, Leon declared: "By Zeus, Athenians, it looks as if it is time for you to look to some friend other than the king." The scribe reported the Athenian's comment to the king, who then produced a revised version with a rider stating: "If the Athenians know of anything fairer than this, they should come and tell the king." (**1.38**) When the ambassadors reached home, the Athenians executed Timagoras after Leon accused him of refusing to share quarters with him and of having discussed everything with Pelopidas ...

Notes

1. *For Agesilaus at Aulis, see* **31.3.A** *("Agesilaus' Asian Campaign").*
2. *The Athenian Timagoras was rumored to have been bribed by the king (e.g., Demosthenes 19 On the False Embassy 137).*
3. *A likely reference to Iphicrates' campaign in Amphipolis at that time.*

Questions

1. What worked in the Thebans' favor in the eyes of the Persian king?
2. What were the terms of the Theban common peace and how were they different from the Common Peace of 371 (**32.11**)?

34.6 Thebes' Treatment of Orchomenus (364)

Greek hegemonic powers tended to be highly selective in implementing the principle of autonomy, and Thebes was no exception. Although at the conference in Persia she demanded that Messene's autonomy be respected (**34.5**), a year later (366) she failed to honor Achaean autonomy. See WEB **34.7.I** for Theban intervention in Achaea.

In 364 Thebes tried to rival Athens on the sea, only to abandon the plan shortly after. Thebes' maritime ambitions are examined in WEB **34.7.II**. Also in 364 Thebes displayed the ugly face of her hegemony in Boeotia. Shortly after Leuctra the Thebans had contemplated enslaving pro-Spartan Orchomenus, but Epaminondas prevailed on them to treat it more leniently. Now, however, they discovered that oligarchs in Orchomenus had cooperated with Theban oligarchs against Theban democracy and so punished the city most severely. Epaminondas, who was apparently away at the time, is said to have harshly criticized the action (Pausanias *Description of Greece* 9.15.3).

Diodorus 15.79.3–6

(**15.79.3**) It was then that the Thebans decided on a campaign against Orchomenus, and for the following reasons. A number of Theban exiles wanted to change the constitution of Thebes to give it an aristocratic character, and they persuaded the cavalry of Orchomenus, which numbered 300 men, to take part in a coup with them. (**79.4**) The cavalrymen had made a practice of meeting some Thebans on a specific day for a parade under arms, and they agreed to mount the assault on that day. Many others became involved in the cause and actively encouraged it, and they all met together at the appropriate time.

(**79.5**) The men who had organized the coup had second thoughts, however, and they revealed the plan to the Boeotarchs, betraying their co-conspirators, and by this service assured their own safety. The authorities arrested the Orchomenian cavalry and brought them before the assembly, where the demos voted to execute them, to sell the inhabitants of Orchomenus into slavery, and to raze the city to the ground. From days of old the Thebans had held a grudge against the Orchomenians, as they had been tribute-paying subjects of the Minyans in the Heroic Age, being delivered from them subsequently by Heracles.[1] (**79.6**) So the Thebans now thought the time was ripe, and seizing on these reasonable pretexts for revenge they commenced hostilities against Orchomenus. They seized the city, put the males to death, and sold children and women into slavery.

Note

1. *The mythical Minyans lived in Orchomenus and exacted a tribute from Thebes until they were defeated by the Thebans and forced by Heracles to pay a tribute to Thebes.*

Questions

1. Why and how did the Thebans intervene in Achaea (WEB **34.7.I**)?
2. How did local domestic politics influence Theban foreign policy in Achaea (WEB **34.7.I**) and Orchomenus (**34.6**)?
3. How might a Theban justify his city's treatment of Orchomenus if challenged that it violated the principle of the polis' independence?

34.8   The Battle of Mantinea (II; 362)

Thebes remained militarily active in the Peloponnese, Thessaly, and Macedonia, with mixed results. In 364 Pelopidas died in Thessaly; two years later, Thebes lost Epaminondas too. Thebes survived the death of its two greatest generals and continued to play a major role in Greece until it became entangled in the Third Sacred War with its neighbor Phocis (356). Yet the loss of these two influential men and the city's limited resources eventually undermined its ability to maintain hegemonic status.

Epaminondas died in 362 in the battle of Mantinea (II), which was the culmination of a two-year conflict between Arcadia and Elis. Other Greeks involved were members of the Arcadian federation, which was divided between pro-Spartan Mantinea and pro-Theban Tegea, in addition to almost every Greek power that counted. The battle could potentially have decided Greek affairs for years to come. Diodorus lists the warring sides.

34.8.A   The Battle Lines in Mantinea

Diodorus of Sicily 15.85.2

In order of battle, the Mantineans and the other Arcadians held the right wing, with the Spartans beside them in support, and next to these were Elians and Achaeans. Of the rest of the troops the weaker ones held the center, while the Athenians occupied the left wing. As for the Thebans, they themselves were deployed on the left wing, and had the Arcadians beside them, while they assigned the right wing to the Argives. The remainder of their huge force – Euboeans, Locrians, and Sicyonians, plus Messenians and Aenianians as well as Thessalians and the other allies – filled the middle of the line ...

According to Diodorus (15.84.4), the coalition of Mantinea, Athens, and Sparta numbered 20,000 infantry and 2,000 cavalry, while the Theban–Tegean coalition had 30,000 infantry and 3,000 cavalry. Epaminondas, who led the Theban coalition, used the same tactics in Mantinea that he had employed in Leuctra when he coordinated the movements of his cavalry and infantry (in addition to light-armed troops) and attacked the enemy with his stronger left wing. But he died of a spear wound, and although the Thebans won on their side, their adversaries claimed victory on their wing, and so the battle was undecided. A common peace was concluded but Sparta opted out when the Messenians were included in it. Xenophon concludes his *Hellenica* at this point and laments the unresolved situation.

34.8.B   Indecision in Mantinea

Xenophon *Hellenica* 7.5.26–27

(**7.5.26**) What happened as a result of these events was the opposite of what everybody expected. Practically the whole of Greece had gathered and taken sides, and there was nobody who did not believe that, should there be a battle, the winners would be rulers and the defeated would be subjects. But Heaven so arranged it that both sides erected trophies as if they were victorious, and neither side attempted to impede those erecting them. Both returned the dead under truce as if victorious, and both took back their dead under truce as though defeated. (**5.27**) Both declared they had won the victory, but it was clear that neither was better off with regard to acquisition of land, city, or power than before the battle took place. There was even greater disorder and mayhem in Greece than before.

Let my history proceed only this far. Perhaps another will take care of what followed.

Question

1. What, according to Xenophon, differentiated victory from defeat (**34.8.B**)?

Review Questions

1. What in Athens' treatment of the members of the Athenian League encouraged them to oppose her (see **34.1–3**, WEB **34.4**)?
2. What concerns and ambitions guided Theban foreign policy (**34.5**, **34.8**, WEB **34.7.I–II**)?
3. Diodorus states that the power of Thebes died with Epaminondas (WEB **34.7.II**). To what extent did Thebes' hegemony depend on him (**32.13**: "The Battle of Leuctra," **32.15**: "The Foundation of Messene," **32.16**: "The Dissolution of the Peloponnesian League," **34.5–6**, **34.8**, WEB **34.7.I–II**)?
4. Was the imperialism of Athens and Thebes similar to or different from the Spartan hegemony?
5. Which would have been judged worse in the court of Greek public opinion, Athens' treatment of Samos or Thebes' treatment of Orchomenus (**34.2**, **34.5**)?

Suggested Readings

The Second Athenian League and the Social War: in addition to the Suggested Readings in Chapter 32, see Cargill 1995; Heskel 1997. Timotheus: Sealey 1993, esp. 58–66, 80–89. *Androtion, including his governorship*: Cargill 1981, 155–159; Harding 1994; R&O, 249–252. *The Social War*: Cawkwell 1962; Buckler 2003, 377–384. *The Theban hegemony*: Cawkwell 1972; Buckler 1980; Roy 1994; Buckler and Beck 2008, 127–164. *The conference in Persia*: Ryder 1965, 137–139. *Theban maritime project*: Ruzicka 1998; Buckler 2003, 338–340, 360–366. *The Battle of Mantinea (II)*: Pritchett 1969, 2: 5–66; J. Anderson 1970, 221–224.

35

Running the Athenian Polis

*Politics, Finances, Grain, and
Trade in the Fourth Century*

CHAPTER CONTENTS

Ancient Greece from Homer to Alexander: The Evidence, First Edition. Joseph Roisman.
© 2011 Blackwell Publishing Ltd. Translations © 2011 John Yardley. Published 2011 by Blackwell Publishing Ltd.

To Athens' credit, after the fall of the Thirty the city succeeded in avoiding a renewal of civil war and enjoyed a stable democracy. This was due to the strength of the city's political institutions and democratic ideology. This chapter discusses how Athens met her political and other public needs. It shows how the Athenians ranked laws above popular will, as exemplified in popular decrees. The chapter reports on the democratic institutions of the assembly, Council, and jury courts and the nature of democratic leadership in the fourth century. It also examines state revenues and a system of taxation that relied almost exclusively on the rich to finance public functions. The chapter then discusses how state monies were allocated for civilian and military purposes. Finally, aspects of Athenian economy and society are illuminated through descriptions of grain importation, an inscription about the certification of coins, and a maritime trade contract.

35.1 The Restored Athenian Democracy: Laws and Decrees

One of the major accomplishments of the restored democracy in Athens was the completion of the codification of her laws. The project commenced in 410, but was completed only in 400/399 because of delays and interruptions. The codified laws were inscribed on the walls of the stoa of the king archon.

At the same time, the Athenians made a distinction between permanent laws (sg. *nomos*) and decrees (sg. *psephisma*) of the assembly or the Council. Decrees dealt with specific circumstances or individuals and were ranked below laws in significance and authority. In Andocides' defense speech against a charge of impiety in 399, the orator cites regulations concerning this distinction.

35.1.A The Greater Authority of Laws

Andocides 1 *On the Mysteries* 87

Laws: The authorities are not to avail themselves, in any matter, of an unwritten law. No decree, be it of the Council or the assembly, is to have greater authority than a law. A law cannot apply to an individual without the same law being applicable to all Athenians, unless a resolution is passed by the (assembly of) six thousand in a secret ballot.

So, what remained after that? The following law remained. Read it, please.

Law: All decisions reached in private suits or by arbitration as came into force when the city was a democracy are to have authority. But one may avail oneself only of laws passed since the archonship of Eucleides [403/2].

The new procedure for proposing laws assigned a major role to the annually elected board of Nomothetae, "Lawgivers." The Nomothetae also decided in cases of contradictory and unclear laws. There was no change in the procedure for passing decrees. Andocides cited a 403/2 law that established the procedure for proposing laws.

35.1.B Tisamenus' Decree

Andocides 1 *On the Mysteries* 83–84

(**1.83**) (Decree) The demos decreed, with Tisamenus proposing the motion, that the form of the Athenian government be in accord with their ancient traditions. The Athenians should follow the laws of Solon, and use his weights and measures, and the statutes of Draco, which we used in former times. If any further legislation is needed, the Nomothetae chosen by the Council are to record it on tablets, and set it out before the eponymous heroes for anyone who so wishes to inspect.[1] They are then to pass it on to the magistrates during the course of this month.

(**1.84**) When the laws have been handed over, the Council and the 500 Nomothetae[2] chosen by deme-members under oath are to give them prior examination. Any private citizen who so wishes is permitted to appear before the Council and make any suggestion that might benefit this legislation. Once the laws are ratified, the council of the Areopagus[3] is to take charge of them to insure that the magistrates put into service only those laws that have been ratified. Those of the laws that have been validated they are to inscribe on the wall on which laws were inscribed in earlier times, for anyone who wishes to see.

Notes

1. *The bases of ten statues of the eponymous heroes of the ten Athenian tribes served as an official bulletin board.*
2. *These Nomothetae are different "lawgivers" from the ones mentioned in 1.83.*
3. *It is unclear how much supervisory power the Areopagus council had.*

Questions

1. What distinguished a law from a decree (**35.1.A**)?
2. Describe the procedure for proposing a law from its initiation to publication (**35.1.B**).

35.2 The Fourth-Century Assembly and Council

The primacy of laws over decrees suggested that the postwar democracy set limits on its own powers, including that of the assembly (*ekklesia*). The assembly transferred its judicial powers to the law courts, which oversaw popular decisions and policy. At the same time, the city provided incentives for its citizens to attend the assembly. Probably starting from the late 390s, those who came on time to the assembly meetings received three obols and later six (nine for special assemblies). The place of the assembly on the Pnyx was enlarged in the second half of the century. The historian M. H. Hansen estimates a regular attendance of 6,000 men out of, in his assessment, around 30,000 citizens, which was half the number of citizens in the fifth century (Hansen 1991, 130–132; 1994). Other estimates of the Athenian citizen population on the eve of the Peloponnesian War (431), however, range between ca. 30,000 and 60,000. The restored democracy readopted Pericles' law limiting citizenship to legitimate male children of two Athenian parents. Normally, the assembly met four times every prytany (one-tenth of the year). *Ath. Pol.* reports on the agenda and procedures of the assembly and the Council.

35.2.A   The Assembly's Agenda

Ath. Pol. 43.3–6

(**43.3**) Those of their number who are *prytaneis* first of all take dinner together in the Tholos, receiving money from the city.[1] Then they schedule meetings for the Council and the assembly, every day for the Council, unless it is a holiday, and four times each prytany for the assembly. (**43.4**) The *prytaneis* also give notice in writing of the agenda of the Council, of what it is to do each day, and where it is to sit. They also give notice in writing of the meetings of the assembly. There is one principal meeting, at which they must confirm the magistrates in office if they seem to do well in their position, and discuss the grain supply and national defense. It is on that day, too, that those wishing to lay prosecutions connected with crimes against the state [*eisangeliai*] must do so; and it is the day of reading the list of confiscated properties, and of reading of applications regarding land allotments and heiresses, so that no vacancy in an estate escapes notice.

(**43.5**) In the sixth prytany they also, in addition to the above, vote by show of hands on whether an ostracism should be held, and consider litigation against vexatious litigants (sykophants), both against Athenian citizens and resident aliens (to a maximum of three cases of each), and against anyone failing to render a service to the people that he had promised. (**43.6**) Another meeting is devoted to supplications. At these anyone who wishes will, after placing an olive branch on the altar, address the popular assembly on any matter he chooses, be it of a public or private nature. The two remaining meetings are concerned with the rest of state business. At these the laws prescribe discussion of three cases concerning religious matters, three involving heralds and embassies, and three of a non-religious nature. Sometimes they even hold their meetings without an advance vote (of the Council). In addition, heralds and ambassadors come first to the *prytaneis*, and also carriers bring their letters to them.

Note

1. *The* prytaneis *were 50 Council members of the same tribe who fulfilled the functions described here for one-tenth of the year. The Tholos was a round building also called the Prytaneum.*

The assembly decided most affairs and elected magistrates who were not selected by lot. Citizens voted by show of hands except in secret ballots, when they used pebbles. See WEB **35.3** for the presidents of the assembly and their duties.

Following a ceremonial opening and oath-taking, the assembly meeting commenced when the president put up for discussion a motion (*probouleuma*) that had been previously prepared by the Council. The motion could be approved without discussion, modified, amended, or rejected. The discussion started with the proclamation "Who wishes to speak?" Many Athenians exercised this right. The equal right to speak (*isegoria*) demonstrated the citizens' liberty and equality, two principles that were identified with democracy (cf. **23.5** where these principles are articulated in Euripides' *Suppliant Women*).

Freedom and the equal opportunity to speak were intimately linked to the concept of *parrhesia*, the freedom to speak one's mind without repercussions. Speakers used this freedom to tell their audience what they did not always want to hear. The audience, for its part, regarded heckling, interrupting the speakers, mocking them, and even not allowing them to speak as their privilege and as an expression of their power and superiority.

In 392 or 391 Aristophanes produced the play *Assemblywomen*, which comically depicted some of the above practices and procedures. The play revolves around the women of Athens who decide to take control of the polis and establish a communal regime there. In the following scene, one male citizen tells another how the women, disguised as men, passed a motion in the assembly that enabled them to rule the city.

35.2.B   An Assembly Meeting

Aristophanes *Assemblywomen* 376–391, 394–426

(376) BLEPYRUS: "... But where *have* you come from?"

CHREMES: "From the *ekklesia* [assembly]."

BLEPYRUS: "It's broken up already?"

CHREMES: "Yes, and right at dawn, too. And, by Zeus, the red rope they were throwing around provided lots of fun."[1]

(380) BLEPYRUS: "Did you get the three obols, then?"

CHREMES: "Wish I had! I got there too late, so I'm ashamed to say I've nothing but my empty purse!"

BLEPYRUS: "Why's that?"

CHREMES: "There was a huge crowd of people that filled the Pnyx as never before. **(385)** Seeing them, we were all comparing them to cobblers.[2] It was really strange to see so many white faces in the *ekklesia*. So I myself and lots of others didn't get the pay."

BLEPYRUS: "So I wouldn't get it either if I go there now?"

CHREMES:	"What? You wouldn't have even if you'd gone there when the cock crowed the second time..."
(394) BLEPYRUS:	"What should draw such a crowd so early?"
CHREMES:	"What else but the *prytaneis*[3] deciding to take opinions about the safety of the city? And straightaway bleary-eyed Neocleides crept up to speak first. And then the people shouted out (you can imagine it): **(400)** 'Isn't it terrible that this man dares to address us – and on the question of safety, too? He wasn't able even to save his own sight!' He shouted out, looking around, 'What am I supposed to do?'"
BLEPYRUS:	"'Grind up some garlic with silphium, **(405)** throw in some Laconian spurge, and rub it on your eyelids in the evening.' That's what I'd have said had I happened to be there."
CHREMES:	"After him the clever dick Euaeon came forward, and he was naked, or so it seemed to most people. **(410)** He, however, claimed he was wearing a cloak; and then he gave a speech aimed at the really common people:
	'You can see that I'm needing to be saved myself – four staters is what I need! Still, I'll tell you how to save the city and its citizens. **(415)** If the clothiers provided cloaks for those who need them when the sun turns for winter, pleurisy would overtake none of us. And those who have no bed or coverlets should wash and then go to sleep in the tanners' shops. **(420)** Any tanner shutting the door on them in winter should be fined three cloaks.'"
BLEPYRUS:	"By Dionysus, that's good! No one at all would have voted against him if he'd added the further suggestion that the grain merchants must give the needy **(425)** three measures of meal for everybody's dinner, or else get a good beating."

Notes

1. *A red painted rope marked those who were late to the assembly and so lost the right to the three-obol attendance fee.*
2. *Working indoors, cobblers were pale like women.*
3. *At the time of the play's production, the assembly meetings were still run by the* prytaneis.

The speaker goes on to compare men unfavorably to women.

Questions

1. What were the fixed items on the assembly's agenda? How many of them involved the public sphere, and how many the private (**35.2.A**)?
2. What were the powers of the presidents of the assembly (WEB **35.3**)?
3. What seems to motivate those who attend the assembly and make proposals there, according to Aristophanes (**35.2.B**)?
4. What procedural and other guidelines of the assembly meeting are suggested by Aristophanes' description (**35.2.B**)?

35.4 Fourth-Century Democratic Leadership

In addition to occasional speakers and those who made proposals, there were men who were more active than others in the assembly, the Council, or the courts. The sources use different terms to describe them, but the commonest are "politicians" (*politeuomenoi*) and "speakers" (*rhetores*). They were not elected to their positions, and in the absence of political parties at Athens rhetorical skill and training were their main means of garnering support and influencing Council members, assemblymen, and jurors; this explains their limited staying power, except for a very few.

The *rhetores* often described themselves as advisors of the city as opposed to those who decided policy, i.e., the sovereign demos. This did not prevent the people from holding orators accountable for bad decisions. See, however, WEB **35.5** for Plato's criticism of the assembly's speakers and their audience.

The rise of *rhetores* marked a new development in the city's political leadership. Formerly, a leader was expected to fulfill both civic and military duties, which he did through the office of the general. In the fourth century these duties were separated. The fourth-century generals were often "professional" soldiers, while the orators focused on politics and, unlike their predecessors, came from different walks of life and seldom from the aristocracy. The trend toward expertise in leadership also encompassed financial management (see **35.11**).

Sometime after 355, the conservative Athenian intellectual Isocrates called on Athens to renounce her ambition for hegemony over other Greeks and become the champion of peace. He also made an unfavorable comparison between contemporary political leadership and that of the past, which he idealized.

Isocrates 8 *On the Peace* 54–55

(**54**) We are very different from our forefathers. They made individuals leaders of the city and chose the same people as army commanders, in the belief that if a man was able to give excellent advice on the speaker's platform, that same man would also reason very well on his own. We do the opposite. (**55**) When we have men whose advice we follow on the most important matters, we do not think we should elect these as our generals, as though they were lacking in brainpower. Instead, we send out, with plenipotentiary authority, men whose advice no one would seek either on private or on national business, as if in that capacity they will be more intelligent, and will find it easier to deliberate on matters concerning the Greeks as a whole than on those matters set before us for deliberation here.

Question

1. What faults do Isocrates (**35.4**) and Plato (WEB **35.5**) find with Athens' leaders and their followers?

35.6 The Jury Courts

The jury courts embodied the people's sovereignty perhaps even more than the assembly. We have noted that the Athenians made a distinction between private actions (*dikai*) and public legal suits (*graphai*; see **9.9**: "Solon's Judicial Regulations"). Both legal actions reflected the notion that peer citizens should decide the dispute. They also demonstrated the democratic wish to diminish individual advantage in court due to background or legal expertise. Because the state appointed public prosecutors only in special cases, any citizen who noticed a violation of public law could volunteer to prosecute the case. Needless to say, there were citizens who were more motivated and proficient than others in using the legal system.

Indeed, prosecutors or defendants who could afford it hired a speechwriter to write a speech for them in order to improve their chances. They would rarely admit it, though, and instead professed lack of skill or expertise and an inferior position to their adversary. For example, sometime after 390 Lysias wrote a defense speech for a man who had inherited from his father a charge of illegally holding state property. The speechwriter had his client plead for the court's consideration on account of his poor speaking ability and his position as a defendant.

35.6.A A Defendant's Difficulties

Lysias 19 *On the Property of Aristophanes* 1–3

(**1**) This particular trial presents me with great difficulties, Gentlemen of the Jury. I am aware that, if I do not speak persuasively now, not only shall I myself be considered guilty, but my father will, too, and that I shall be deprived of all my worldly wealth. And so, even if I am not naturally adept at this, it is incumbent on me to come to the aid both of my father and of myself, to the best of my ability. (**2**) You can see the intrigues and the fervor of my enemies, and of that I need not speak; but my own inexperience is also known to all who are acquainted with me. I shall therefore ask of you a favor that is just and easily granted, namely that you hear me, too, without anger, as you did my accusers. (**3**) For a man defending himself has to be at a disadvantage, even if you accord him an impartial hearing. You see, they have long been making their plans and have not faced personal risk as they formulated their prosecution, while we are struggling as we face fear, vilification, and the greatest danger. It is only fair, then, that your feelings for those defending themselves should be more indulgent.

35.6.B Jurors

In Athens, the category of men called *sykophantes* (sg.), or vexatious litigants, was notorious for abusing the legal system and often came to symbolize all that was wrong in an Athenian citizen. Yet the power of experts in court was limited. There were laws against sykophants, and a litigant could be helped by

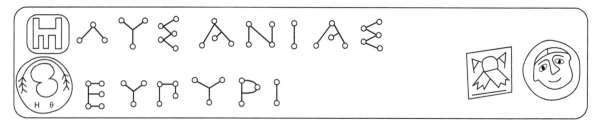

Figure 35.1   A juror's token (*pinakion*). From S.C. Todd, "A Pinakion," in *The Shape of Athenian Law* (Oxford: Oxford University Press, 1993), p. 85, fig. 6.1. Based on a photograph belonging to the Brooklyn Museum, New York 34, 678 = Kroll 1972 no. 86. Reprinted with permission of Oxford University Press and the Brooklyn Museum.

supportive speakers who served on his defense or prosecution team and thus level the playing field. Generally, the spirit of amateurism and the distaste for professionalism in court enhanced the perception of a fair legal contest.

Jurors served in large groups in an effort to curtail bribery. A water clock made sure that each litigant had the same amount of time to present his case. At the end of the pleadings, there was no deliberation by the jurors but a secret vote that was decided by majority. If a defendant was found guilty and the law did not prescribe punishment, both prosecutor and defendant recommended the desired penalty, and the jurors decided between them. The Athenian juror, then, was a composite of juror and judge.

Jurors who sat in judgment were men at least thirty years old who volunteered to serve in court. Each of the ten tribes was supposed to provide at least 600 jurors, and if the number of volunteers exceeded 6,000, those who would be called to service was decided by lot. The juror was assigned a case and a court only on the day of trial to avoid pressure and corrupting influence. He received a token (*pinakion*) that had on it his name, deme, and a letter (alpha to kappa) that was used for the selection of jurors by lottery and for assigning them to different courts. Tokens found in Athenian graves suggest that jurors were proud of their duty and social status.

The bronze token shown in Figure 35.1 belonged to Lysanias of the deme Euphyridae. The letter "eta" and the symbol of the three obols in the left corner identify him as a juror. The symbols on the right are unclear.

Question

1. What were the speaker's alleged constraints in **35.6.A** and how did they relate to democratic fairness?

35.7   State Revenues and Taxation

Athens had nothing like a national budget, not to mention a deficit. The state allocated monies on an annual basis to public institutions, say, the assembly, or to specific projects such as military campaigns. When there was surplus money it went to special funds or to temple treasuries from which the state could borrow. Conversely, when in 348 there was no money to pay for jurors, no courts were held.

State expenditures included the financing of public projects such as roads, structures, and festivals, as well as payments, albeit modest, to assemblymen, Council members, jurors, and magistrates. Athens, however, spent much of its revenue on military campaigns and the maintenance of its navy. See WEB **35.8.I** for Athens' revenues and the orator Demosthenes' description of Athens' annual income ca. 341. The bulk of public revenues came from taxing the rich, whether they were citizens or resident aliens (metics). WEB **35.8.II** describes the taxable property of Demosthenes' wealthy father.

Among the taxes that the Athenians collected was an import tax of 2 percent. Like other taxes and duties, the state auctioned tax collection to private individuals and companies. In a trial speech, the politician Andocides describes an alleged conspiracy to defraud the city of revenues by subverting the auction of this tax. The alleged chief villain was the politician Agyrrhius, otherwise best known for introducing and raising the payment for assemblymen in 403. Andocides' account should not be taken at face value because he aims to malign Agyrrhius, his legal adversary, and to praise himself while appealing to conspiratorial Athenian attitudes. Nevertheless, his report shows that the state revenues of 30–36 talents from this tax in 402–400 were relatively modest.

–– 35.7.A   Import Tax

Andocides 1 *On the Mysteries* 133–134

(**133**) I am going to tell you why these men now think like this. It is the third year since Agyrrhius here, this fine gentleman, became the chief contractor of the two percent tax, a position he bought for thirty talents. All these men who assembled with him under the poplar were involved in his business, and you are aware of their character. It seems to me that they assembled there for two purposes, which were to get money for not exceeding his bid and also to have a share in the tax, which had been sold at a bargain-basement price. (**134**) They made a three-talent profit, and discovered how the business worked and what a great amount it made. So they got together and, giving shares to the others who were bidding, they intended buying the position once more for thirty talents. Since there was nobody bidding against them, I appeared before the Council and kept on bidding above them until I bought it for 36 talents. After beating them off and providing you with guarantors, I raised the money and paid it to the city. I did not make a personal loss, either; in fact, those of us involved in the affair made a slight profit. And so I saw to it that Agyrrhius and these men did not split six talents of your money amongst themselves.

–– 35.7.B   Property Tax (*Eisphora*)

A frequently mentioned Athenian tax was the *eisphora*, or property tax, which ranged between 1 and 2 percent (see also **26.2**: "Athenian Finance"). It was imposed irregularly on people with a certain amount of property in order to finance *ad hoc* projects, mostly military ones. The second-century historian Polybius reports on the income from this tax in 378/7.

Polybius 2.62.7

They decided at that time to meet expenses for the war from taxation, and they conducted an evaluation of all of Attica, its buildings, and the rest of its property. Even so the entire evaluation fell 250 talents short of 6,000.[1]

Note

1. *Demosthenes (14 On the Symmories 19) mentions an estimated tax revenue of 6,000 talents for 354/3.*

It appears that prior to 378/7 each taxpayer paid the same amount of tax. Starting from 378/7 taxpayers of the *eisphora* were divided into one hundred companies, called symmories (*symmoriai*), which were collectively responsible for the payment. Taxpayers also paid in proportion to their assessed wealth. In this way the burden was shared more equitably. From 364/3, a procedure called *proeisphora* was introduced according to which the three richest members of each symmory advanced the state the sum due from the group, then collected it from its members. In a speech charging his enemy Midias of hubris, Demosthenes boasts of his public service and sacrifice when he advanced the *eisphora*, contrasting his conduct with that of the wealthy Midias.

35.7.C Paying the Property Tax

Demosthenes 21 *Against Midias* 157

You know, I was the head of a symmory for ten years, and I contributed the same amount as Phormio, Lysitheides, Callaeschrus, and the richest people. And I did that not from property that I actually possessed – I had been robbed of that by my guardians – but on the credit of what my father had left me, which I had the right to acquire once I came of age. So that is how I behaved toward you [the jury] – but how did Midias behave? Never yet, to this very day, has he been head of a symmory, and he was deprived by nobody of any of his inheritance – no, he received a substantial property from his father.

In 358/7, the Athenian Periander proposed that the 1,200 richest Athenians be divided into twenty symmories that were supposed to pay for trierarchies and the *eisphora*. His law divided the burden of the tax equally among these taxpayers and allowed them to pay regular small sums instead of irregular large ones. All these measures demonstrated the difficulties that the state had in securing revenues and collecting taxes fairly and effectively. Indeed, in 340, following constant criticism of the system, Demosthenes changed it by establishing that a group of 300 wealthy citizens would pay for most of the tax.

Questions

1. How did Athens manage to launch military expeditions in spite of its empty coffers, according to Demosthenes? What, does he suggest, was expected of wealthy taxpayers (WEB **35.8.I**)?
2. How did Demosthenes' father diversify his income (WEB **35.8.II**)?
3. Describe the tax collection system in Athens. How could it be abused (**35.7.A–C**, WEB **35.8.I**)?
4. Why was Demosthenes allegedly a better citizen than Midias (**35.7.C**)?

35.9 Liturgies

A common means of taxation in Athens was liturgies (sg. *leitourgia*), which were imposed on citizens whose property amounted to no fewer than 3–4 talents. One type of liturgy was the *choregia*, which assigned to a wealthy individual the duty of paying for a dramatic performance in the city's festivals (see WEB **22.6**: "Selecting and Producing Plays"). The other liturgy was the trierarchy (*trierarchia*), which required a citizen to pay for the maintenance of a trireme and often to captain it. The galley, its basic equipment, and the crew's (modest) wages were provided by the state. The trierarch, however, defrayed the considerable remaining expenses and supplemented the state payments.

There were Athenians who tried to avoid paying the liturgies by liquidating their assets and thus concealing their wealth. Of those who fulfilled their duty, some complained that they paid for the indolent poor. Yet only few wealthy Athenians appeared to have been impoverished because of taxation. Conversely, the reward for a liturgist was public recognition and honor, especially if he was victorious in dramatic competitions in the festivals, or in contests in performance of triremes. A liturgist could also expect to collect a debt of gratitude for his financial sacrifice. Speakers in Athenian courts elaborated on their public services and expenses in order to establish a record of useful citizenship and to tell jurors that it was in the city's best interests to decide in their favor. The speechwriter Lysias harped on this theme in a speech he wrote for an anonymous Athenian, who had been charged with illegally holding public property shortly after the democracy was restored in 403/2. The speaker begins his address to the court by enumerating his many public services and expenses. The list, if not inflated, is exceptional by any measure, and totals more than 63,000 drachmas. However, it tells us something about the kinds of financial obligations expected by the state.

Lysias 21 *On the Charge of Accepting Bribes* 1–5, 12

(**1**) You have been sufficiently apprised of the charges, Gentlemen of the Jury, but I think you should also hear the other pertinent information so you will know the character of the man on whose verdict you will be voting. I came of age [passed the *dokimasia*] in the archonship of Theopompus [411/0]. Then, on being made a *choregos* for tragedy, I spent thirty minas, and two months later I spent 2,000 drachmas winning with a men's chorus at the Thargelia; and in the archonship of Glaucippus [410/9] I spent 800 at the Great Panathenaea on a chorus of Pyrrhic dancers.[1] (**2**) Furthermore, in the same archonship, I won at the Dionysia as *choregos* for a men's chorus, and spent on it, with the dedication of the tripod included, 5,000 drachmas; and at the Lesser Panathenaea in the magistracy of Diocles [409/8] I spent 300 on a cyclic chorus.[2] (**3**) Meanwhile, over a period of seven years, I was trierarch and spent six talents.[3]

Despite such expenses, and despite the daily perils I faced on your behalf and despite all my journeys abroad, I still paid property tax, thirty minas in one case, and 4,000 drachmas in another. And after sailing home during the archonship of Alexias [405/4], I immediately began serving as a gymnasiarch for the Prometheia, and I won after spending twelve minas.[4] (**4**) Later on I was made *choregos* for a boys' chorus, on which I spent more than fifteen minas. In the archonship of Eucleides [403/2] I was a *choregos* for a comic production for Cephisodorus, and I won at the cost of sixteen minas (including the dedication of the equipment); and at the Lesser Panathenaea I was *choregos* for some beardless Pyrrhic dancers, spending seven minas.

(**5**) I have been victorious with a trireme in a race at Sunium, on which I spent fifteen minas, and apart from that there were the headship of sacred delegations and directorship of the procession [*errhephoria*],[5] which cost me more than 30 minas in expenses. With regard to the expenditures that I have listed, I should not have spent a quarter had I wanted my liturgies to accord with what is prescribed in law.

(**12**) If I must lose my possessions, that does not bother me so much; but I could not accept to be insulted, and to have it put into the heads of people who shirk their liturgies that what I have spent on you earns no gratitude, while *they* appear to have taken the right decision in having surrendered to you none of their own resources. So if you listen to me, you will be voting for what is right and also choosing what is expedient for yourselves.

Notes

1. *Pyrrhic dances were performed by men in arms.*
2. *The cyclic chorus was a chorus of dithyrambic hymns in honor of Dionysius.*
3. *In the fourth century a trierarchy was normally taken every three years.*
4. *The gymnasiarch was an official in charge of the upkeep and training of athletes in the gymnasion, in this case, runners in a torch-race in the Prometheia festival in the Kerameikos.*
5. *The* errhephoria *was a procession of young women carrying baskets at the Panathenaea.*

Questions

1. What public services did the speaker perform?
2. Why, according to the speaker, should the jury vote in his favor?

35.10   Lightening the Burden: The *Antidosis*

The state came up with several measures to ease the burden of liturgies. Toward the end of the Peloponnesian War, two men could share a trierarchy as syntrierarchs. Later it was customary not to impose a trierarchy more than once in three years and a choregy in two. A trierarch could additionally hire someone to replace him as the ship's captain. The Athenians also instituted in the name of fairness the procedure of *antidosis* (lit. "giving in exchange"). A man who was assigned a liturgy could challenge another, who was free of it but whom the liturgist deemed wealthier than him, either to take up the liturgy or to exchange properties. Most of those challenged opted to take up the liturgy. Those who declined went to court, which decided who should assume the liturgy. This was the case for the intellectual Isocrates, who lost a trial in which he claimed not to be sufficiently wealthy to carry a liturgy. He wrote a fictitious court speech entitled *Antidosis* in which he defended himself against the charges of being a teacher for hire (sophist), a corrupter of students, and a man who hid his own wealth to avoid public service. In the following section he makes the not-uncommon assertion that he is not as wealthy as people think him to be.

Isocrates 15 *Antidosis* 155–158

(**155**) So none of the people called sophists will be found, in general, to have amassed a lot of money; in fact, some passed their lives in straitened circumstances, and others in circumstances that were quite modest. The man who acquired most, within our memory, was Gorgias of Leontini.[1] He spent time in Thessaly in the period when its people were the wealthiest of the Greeks, and he had a long life, which he dedicated to making money. (**156**) He was also not a permanent resident of any city, and so he had no outlay for communal expenses, nor was he subject to property tax. In addition to these advantages, he did not take a wife or have children – no, he was also free of this liturgy, which is the most enduring and expensive of them! Even with this head start over all the others in terms of acquisition, Gorgias left only a thousand staters [2,000 drachmas]. (**157**) Indeed, when it comes to each other's wealth, we should not listen to those who make thoughtless claims, and we should not think of the work of sophists and actors as being equally remunerative. Rather, we should make comparative judgments about those who are in the same professions, and assume that those with similar capability in each field have like material returns.

(**158**) So if you put me on a level with the man who is the greatest achiever in our field, and compare me with him, you will not appear to be making totally wild inferences about such matters. Nor, in that case, would I be found to have been a bad manager either with regard to affairs of the city or to my own personal affairs, having in fact lived on less than I have spent on my liturgies. And it is certainly just to praise those who are more thrifty in their personal expenditures than in their spending on the state.

Note

1. *Gorgias of Leontini was a famous fifth-century sophist and teacher of rhetoric.*

Question

1. How did the management of private affairs relate to performing liturgies?

35.11   The Theoric Fund

The Theoric Fund (*Theorika*), whose origins some sources date to Periclean Athens, in the fourth century distributed money to the needy. From the mid-fourth century it assumed additional responsibilities under the guidance of the politician Eubulus. These included financing public projects, administering the navy, and, especially, organizing major festivals. The fund was mostly known for giving citizens subsidies to buy tickets to the theater during the festivals. Indeed, the late fourth-century orator Demades described the fund as "the glue of democracy" (Plutarch *Platonic Questions* 1011B). The revenues came from surplus monies, and Eubulus legislated that diverting this money to the military fund would be punishable by death. Because there was no limit on reelection to the office of the fund's manager until the 330s, Eubulus' control of it gave him political clout, which he used to oppose aggressive foreign ventures like those recommended by the famous orator Demosthenes. The second-century CE lexicographer Harpocration describes the Theoric Fund and its manager.

Harpocration *Lexicon* s.v. Theorica = Harding no. 75A

Translation: Harding no. 75A, p. 98

Demosthenes in the Philippics. Festival money was certain state money gathered from the city's revenues. This was previously kept for the needs of wartime and was called military money but later was transferred to public building-projects and disbursements, the initiator of which was Agyrrhius the demagogue.[1] Philochorus [*FGrHist* 328 F 33][2] in the third book of his *Atthis* says, "The festival fund (*theorikon*) was first considered 'the drachma for the seat in the theatre,' whence it got its name," etc. Philinus in his speech against the statues of Sophocles and Euripides, speaking of Eubulus, says, "It was called the festival fund because, when the Dionysia were imminent, Eubulus made a distribution (of funds) for the festival, so that all might take part in the festival and no one of the citizens might fail to attend through poverty."[3]

Notes

1. *For Agyrrhius, see* **35.7.A**.
2. *For Philochorus, see* **19.11**: *"Pericles' Citizenship Law."*
3. *Philinus was a late fourth-century orator. The citation is from a speech against a proposal to set up statues of the two playwrights.*

Question

1. What made the Theoric Fund democratic?

35.12 Financing Military Operations

Financial pressures and the reluctance to channel money away from civilian purposes to the military fund had an impact on Athenian military operations and foreign policy. For example, one of the reasons Athens joined a common peace in 375 was lack of money for military campaigns (Xenophon *Hellenica* 6.2.1). Underfunded military expeditions forced generals (and not just from Athens) to hire themselves and their troops as mercenaries to Persian satraps or the king. They also financed campaigns by hiring sailors as agricultural laborers, and even resorted to extortion. The Athenian general Iphicrates employed some of these means when he arrived on the island of Corcyra in 372. Sparta and Athens and their respective allies had been fighting for control of the island since 374. Iphicrates defeated a Syracusan fleet that fought for Sparta and arranged for the crews to be ransomed.

35.12.A Iphicrates' Financial Methods

Xenophon *Hellenica* 6.2.37–38

(**6.2.37**) Iphicrates supported his sailors for the most part by having them do farm work for the Corcyrans, but his peltasts and hoplites from the ships he took over with him to Acarnania. There he gave assistance to any of the cities friendly to him that needed help, and opened hostilities against the Thyrians, who were truly brave warriors and who in addition possessed a strong fortress. (**2.38**) He also attached to his navy the fleet at Corcyra, which numbered somewhere around ninety ships, and, sailing to Cephallenia first, he raised money, some giving willingly, others reluctantly. He then prepared to wreak havoc on Spartan territory and to win over those of the enemy states in the region prepared to join him, and make war on those who could not be persuaded to do so.

In his speech *On the Chersonese* (341), Demosthenes describes the general Diopeithes' fundraising methods. In 343/2, Diopeithes was sent to defend the Thracian Chersonese and Athenian settlers there who were threatened by Philip of Macedonia. His expedition was poorly funded, and he had to pay his mercenaries. So Diopeithes resorted to attacks on Greek cities in Asia and collected booty or payments from them. In addition, and not unlike modern criminals' offering "protection," he extorted money by offering his *eunoia* (favor) to Athens' allies and merchant ships, including those that sailed to Macedonia. In the following passage Demosthenes defends the general against his critics at home and abroad. His defense reveals the dilemma that many generals faced. On the one hand, they did not receive sufficient funds from the state. On the other, the Athenians expected results and were ready to punish generals for failing to achieve them or for their fundraising methods.

35.12.B   "Granting Favors"

Demosthenes 8 *On the Chersonese* 24–28

(**24**) Now some of you should learn what effect this can have. I shall speak frankly – I could not do otherwise. All commanders that have ever sailed out from you – if this is not true I condemn myself to any punishment whatsoever – gather money from the Chians, the Erythraeans, and from whatever peoples they variously can. I refer to those peoples inhabiting Asia. (**25**) Those at the head of one or two ships gather less, those with a greater force more. And those who give the money do not give it, small amount or large, in return for nothing – they are not as crazy as that! Rather, in giving it, they are also buying protection for the traders sailing from their ports, insuring that they are not robbed, and that their vessels receive safe conduct, and the like. They call such gifts "favors" [*eunoiai*], and that is the word applied to these corrupt earnings.

(**26**) And now, too, of course, since Diopeithes has an army, it is clear that all these people will give him money. For from what other source do you think he is going to finance his soldiers when he receives nothing from you, and has no personal resources from which to pay them? From heaven? No; he makes ends meet from what he gathers, begs, and borrows. (**27**) So those people amongst you who are accusing him are doing nothing other than cautioning you all not to give him anything, because he is going to pay the penalty for what he will do in future, not to mention for what he has done and achieved for himself. That is the meaning of those utterances: "He is going to conduct sieges," "He is betraying the Greeks." For is any one of these men concerned about the Greeks living in Asia? But, in that case, they would be better at looking out for others than for their own country. (**28**) This, too, is what lies behind their sending another commander to the Hellespont. For if Diopeithes is doing terrible things, and is driving merchant vessels to shore, then a short decree, Gentlemen of Athens, just a short decree could prevent all this, and the laws tell us to impeach those who commit such crimes, and not, by Zeus, to keep watch over our own men with such costs and so many triremes, since that would be extremely foolish.

Question

1. How did Iphicrates and Diopeithes finance their campaigns, and how might their methods have harmed Athens?

35.13   The Grain Import

In addition to financial concerns, Athens was much occupied with insuring a regular supply of grain to the city, preferably at affordable prices. Wheat was a fundamental staple of the Greek diet, and the demand for it by the large population of Attica could only be met by import. This affected Athenian foreign and domestic policies. For example, among the reasons for Athens' insistence on controlling the islands of Lemnos, Imbros, and Scyros in violation of Greek autonomy was that these islands were important stations on the maritime grain route from the Hellespont to Attica (as well as to central and southern

Greece). The islands also had Athenian settlers who, together with landowners in Attica, contributed to the Athenian grain supply.

A well-preserved inscription from the Athenian agora is highly informative in this regard. It records a law, which the politician and former tax collector Agyrrhius put forward in 374/3 (for Agyrrhius see **35.7.A**). The law ordained the collection of a 12 percent tax from Lemnos, Imbros, and Scyros, not in money but in kind, that is, in wheat and barley, which was cheaper and less popular. The law also insured that the grain would go nowhere but Athens. Private individuals or companies (symmories) were to bid on collecting the tax in fixed units of 500 *medimnoi* each. A *medimnos* was a measure of capacity of about 52.5 liters (1.5 bushels). In this case, however, it was a measure of weight, which was more accurate than capacity. In Agyrrhius' law, the weight of a *medimnos* of barley, 27.47 kg, and the heavier *medimnos* of wheat, 32.96 kg, are significantly lighter than the otherwise attested *medimnos*, which weighed 39.3 kg. The difference in weight may have made up the bidders' profit. Alternatively, bidders may have profited from selling grain that was left after recovering their bid and other expenses. Bidders were to ship the grain to Athens at their own risk and expense, and pay taxes on it. The city provided a free storage area in the agora, the Aeaceion, but it supervised the sale through elected officials and by letting the assembly fix the price for the grain. In keeping with democratic principles, these officials were accountable to the people. It has been estimated that Athens could expect to get from this tax about 30,000 *medimnoi* of grain, enough to sustain 70,000 people per month (R&O, 127).

Agyrrhius' Decree *SEG* 47, no. 96 = R&O no. 26

Translation: R&O, pp. 118–123

Gods. In the archonship of Socratides [374/3]. Law concerning the one twelfth of the grain of the islands.

(5) Agyrrhius proposed: in order that the people may have grain publicly available, sell the tax of one twelfth at Lemnos, Imbros, and Scyros, and the tax of one fiftieth, in grain.[1]

(8) Each share will be five hundred *medimnoi*, one hundred of wheat and four hundred of barley. The buyer will convey the grain to Piraeus at his own risk, and will transport the grain up to the city at his own expense and will heap up the grain in the Aeaceion.[2] The city will make available the Aeaceion covered and with a door, and the buyer will weigh out the grain for the city within thirty days of whatever the date when he transports it to the city, at his own expense. When he transports it to the city, the city will not exact rent from the buyers.

(21) The buyer will weigh out the wheat at a weight of a talent for five [*hekteis*] sixths [32.96 kg], and the barley at a weight of a talent for a *medimnos* [27.47 kg], dry and clean of darnel, arranging the standard weight on the balance, just as the other merchants.

(**27**) The buyer will not make a down-payment but will pay sales taxes and auctioneers' fees at the rate of 20 drachmas per share.[3] The buyer will nominate two creditworthy guarantors, whom the Council has scrutinized, for each share.

(**31**) A symmory [group] will consist of six men and the share 3,000 *medimnoi*. In the case of a symmory the city will exact the grain from each and all of those who are in the symmory, until it recovers what belongs to it.

(**36**) Let the people elect ten men from all the Athenians in the assembly, when they elect the generals [in March], to have oversight of the grain.[4] When these officials have the grain weighed according to what has been written, let them sell it in the Agora at whatever moment the people decide is right; but it is not to be possible to put to the vote the question of selling before the month of Anthesterion [February/March].

(**44**) Let the people set the price at which those elected must sell the wheat and the barley. Let the buyers of the twelfth transport the grain before the month Maemacterion [November/December]. Let the men elected by the people exercise oversight so that the grain is transported at the stated time.

(**51**) When those who have been elected sell the grain, let them render their accounts before the people and let them come before the people carrying the money and let the money raised from the grain be assigned to the military fund.

(**55**) The Receivers [*apodektai*] are to allocate the down-payment from the islands and as much of the fiftieth tax as was last year brought in from the two tenths;[5] on this occasion it is to be for the financial administration, in future the two tenths are not to be taken away from the moneys deposited.

Notes

1. *Possibly a tax on grain to be paid in Athens. A similar or identical tax was paid on exports and imports.*
2. *The Aeaceion (Aeaceum) was a sanctuary of the hero Aeacus where the city's grain was stored.*
3. *Stroud (1998, 63) estimates that the sales tax and the auctioneer's fee were around 1 percent.*
4. *Because election was normally reserved for "experts" such as generals or treasurers, it is puzzling that these officials were not chosen by lot. A cynic might say that Agyrrhius, who proposed the decree and was a former tax collector, hoped to be elected to the post.*
5. *The two-tenths were a payment advanced by the bidders.*

 See WEB **35.14.I** for Athens' cultivation of good relationships with grain producers in the Crimea, and WEB **35.14.II** for the regulations governing the grain trade and its products in Athens.

Questions

1. What roles did the state play in the grain trade, according to Agyrrhius' decree?
2. What privileges did Athens' Crimean friend grant grain importers to Attica (WEB **35.14.I**)?
3. How could the state manage the retail price of grain (**35.13**, WEB **35.14.II**)?

Figure 35.2 A counterfeit coin. From R.S. Stroud, "An Athenian Law on Silver Coinage," *Hesperia* 43 (1974), pl. 25: e. Courtesy of the Trustees of the American School of Classical Studies at Athens.

35.15   A Law of Coinage Certification

In addition to supervising trade, the state also tried to attract grain and other merchants to the city. It allowed resident aliens (metics), who were well represented among traders, the citizen's right of buying land in Attica and gave foreign merchants the right to build sanctuaries. The city also enacted laws and regulations that aimed to help traders. One such law, which was passed in 375/4, offered traders a state official and procedures to certify the value of the coins they tendered. It is unclear what exactly led to this measure. At that time Athens no longer forced its coinage on others, but the imitation of her highly valued coins, especially in the Levant and Egypt, was probably an issue. The city defaced and confiscated counterfeit or base coins, but since the value of coins was measured by their weight and metal components, it is unclear how they treated identical or close imitations of Athenian silver coins.

The chapter follows Stroud's (1974) restoration and interpretation of lines 8–9 below. Stroud thinks that it was obligatory to accept and circulate identical imitations, as opposed to others (e.g., Martin 1991, 26–27) who suggest that Athenian-like coins were returned to those who had tendered them. Of interest is the certifier or approver (*dokimastês*) of the coins. Private bankers and moneychangers employed slaves to reject or accept coins. In this case the city employed a public slave for the purpose who was probably skilled in the art, but who, unlike a citizen, could be subjected to corporal punishment if he failed to perform his duty. Figure 35.2 shows an Athenian tribolos, which the certifier has marked through with a cut as counterfeit.

Stroud (1974), pp. 158–161 = Harding no. 45 = R&O no. 25[1]

Translation: R&O no. 25, pp. 112–117

Resolved by the *nomothetai*.[2] In the archonship of Hippodamas [375/4]. Nicophon proposed:

(**3**) Attic silver shall be accepted when it is found to be silver and has the public stamp.

(**4**) The public approver [*dokimastês*] shall sit between the tables [of bankers and moneychangers] and approve on these terms every day except when there is a deposit of money, but then in the *bouleuterion* [Council house].[3] If any one brings forward foreign silver having the same stamp as the Attic [–] he shall give it back to the man who brought it forward; but if it has a bronze core or a lead core or is counterfeit, he shall cut through it immediately and it shall be scraped property of the Mother of the Gods and he shall deposit it in the council.

(**13**) If the approver does not sit, or does not approve in accordance with the law, he shall be beaten by the conveners of the people [*syllogeis tou demou*][4] with fifty lashes with the whip. If any one does not accept the silver which the approver approves, he shall be deprived of what he is selling on that day. Exposures [*phaseis*][5] shall be made for matters in the corn-market to the corn-guardians [*sitophylakes*],[6] for matters in the Agora and the rest of the city to the conveners of the people, for matters in the import-market to the overseers of the import-market [*epimeletai tou emporiou*] except for matters in the corn-market, and for matters in the corn-market to the corn-guardians. For matters exposed, those that are up to ten drachmas the officials [*archontes*] shall have power to decide, those that are beyond ten drachmas they shall introduce into the jury-court. The *thesmothetai* shall provide and allot a jury-court for them whenever they request, or they shall be fined 1,000 (?) drachmas. For the man who exposes, there shall be a share of a half if he convicts the man whom he exposes. If the seller is a slave-man or a slave-woman, he shall be beaten with fifty lashes with the whip by the officials commissioned in each matter. If any of the officials does not act in accordance with what is written, he shall be denounced [*eisangellein*] to the council by whoever wishes of the Athenians who have the right, and if he is convicted he shall be dismissed from his office and the council shall make an additional assessment up to 500 drachmas.

(**36**) So that there shall also be in the Piraeus an approver for the ship-owners and the import-traders and all others the council shall appoint from the public slaves if available or shall buy one and the *apodektai* [treasury officials] shall make an allocation of the price. The overseers of the import-market shall see that he sits in front of the stele of Poseidon,[7] and they shall use the law in the same way as has been stated concerning the approver in the city.

(**44**) Write up this law on a stone stele and put it down in the city between the tables and in Piraeus in front of the stele of Poseidon. The secretary of the council shall commission the contract from the *poletai* [auctioneers], and the *poletai* shall introduce it into the council.

(**49**) The salary payment for the approver in the import-market shall be in the archonship of Hippodamas from when he is appointed, and the *apodektai* shall allocate as much as for the approver in the city, and for the time to come the salary payment shall be from the same source as for the mint-workers.

(**55**) If there is any decree written on a stele contrary to this law, the secretary of the council shall demolish it.[8]

Notes

1. *The translation does not distinguish between the restored and legible parts of the inscription.*
2. *The Nomothetae were a board of lawgivers who decided the legality of a new law.*
3. *The approver was supposed to check in the Council house the quality of coins paid as state revenues.*
4. *The conveners of the people were a board of thirty Council members who were otherwise known to perform religious duties.*
5. *The procedure of exposing a person (phasis) was open to any citizen, who was rewarded for his initiative.*
6. *The corn-guardians regulated the grain market.*
7. *The location is unknown.*
8. *Laws (nomoi) were superior to decrees (psephismata), hence the instruction to abolish contradictory decrees.*

Questions

1. What was the penalty for circulating uncertified money?
2. What were the sanctions against those in charge of enforcing the law?

35.16 A Maritime Contract

From the mid-fourth century Athens enacted mercantile laws that were restricted to transactions performed in the Athenian market and to voyages to and from the city. The laws provided easy and speedy access to court and saved traders and ship-owners the need to wait their turn for trial. Most mercantile cases (*dikai emporikai*) revolved around written contracts, which often recorded a loan. Following the verdict, those who refused to pay the sum owed were sent to prison to reconsider. One such contract, which is preserved in a trial speech concerning an unpaid loan, shows the international character of maritime trade in Athens. The mercantile laws made no distinction between Athenian and foreign merchants, although speakers at court might appeal to the prejudices of Athenian jurors against non-Athenians. Points of interest regarding the contract are that the interest rate on the loan was about 25 percent and that it went up to 30 percent if the borrower risked sailing past the sailing season. The security for the loan was the cargo, which the borrower had yet to buy. Finally, according to the norms of maritime trade, the loss of a ship and its cargo at sea freed the borrower from his debt. Both the risks and the opportunities for dishonesty in maritime trade were considerable.

Demosthenes 35 *Against Lacritus* 10–13

(**10**) Androcles of the [Athenian] deme Sphettus and Nausicrates of Carystus [in Euboea] have made a loan of 3,000 silver drachmae to Artemon and Apollodorus of Phaselis [in Lycia] for a voyage from Athens to Mende or Scione [in Chalcidice], and from there to the Bosporus. Then, if they wish, the two can go as far as the Borysthenes [Dnieper River], following the left coast [western coast of the Black Sea], after which they will return to Athens. The rate of interest is 225 drachmae per thousand but, should they sail from the Pontus [Black Sea] to Hieron [on the Asian coast of the Bosporus] after the rising of Arcturus [September], the rate is to be 300 per thousand. Security on the loan is three thousand jars of Mendean wine, to be shipped from Mende or Scione aboard the twenty-oared ship owned by Hyblesius. (**11**) They give this security not owing anyone else any money on it, and they will not contract a further loan on it. In addition, they will bring back to Athens, in the same ship, all merchandise taken on board in exchange in the Pontus. The merchandise safely conveyed to Athens, the borrowers shall pay to the lenders the money that falls due according to the contract, and do so within twenty days of their arrival in Athens. The money shall be paid in full, exception being made for what was jettisoned [in rough water] by agreement made together by the passengers, and for any ransom paid to enemies; it shall be fully paid with respect to all else. And they shall provide the lenders with the security, untouched, to remain in their authority until the borrowers give them the money accruing under the contract.

(**12**) If the borrowers fail to pay the money within the agreed time, the lenders shall have the right to use the goods provided as security or to sell them at market price. If the money due to the lenders under the contract falls short of the loan, the lenders are to have the right of seizure from Artemon and Apollodorus of all of their property on both land and sea, wherever it happens to be, as though they had been found guilty in court and had defaulted on payment. This right shall be accorded to the lenders, both individually and jointly.

(**13**) If the borrowers do not enter the Pontus and remain in the Hellespont for ten days at the time of the dog-star [late July], setting ashore their merchandise where the Athenians have no right of reprisals[1] and then sailing from there to Athens, they are to pay the interest registered in the contract the previous year. And if the ship in which the merchandise is transported suffers irreparable damage, but the secured goods survive, whatever is left is to become the common property of the lenders. With regard to all this, nothing is to have greater validity than the contract.

Witnesses: Phormio of the deme Piraeus, Cephisodotus of Boeotia, Heliodorus of the deme Pithos [Athens].

Note

1. *The right of reprisal allowed a citizen to seize a foreigner or his property in the citizen's homeland if he had a claim against him or if the foreigner's state had harmed his state; cf. WEB **13.5**: "A Treaty Concerning Seizure of Men Abroad."*

Questions

1. What were the risks of lending money in maritime trade?
2. How did the lenders try to secure their loan?

Review Questions

1. What made the difference between laws and decrees significant (**35.1.A–B**)?
2. What hurdles did a popular decision have to pass before being voted on (see **35.1–2**, **35.4**, WEB **35.3**, WEB **35.5**)?

3. How did democracy supervise the functioning of its officials and leaders (**35.1–2**, **35.4**, WEB **35.3**, WEB **35.5**)?

4. What were Athens' major public expenses and how were they met (**35.7**, **35.9–12**, WEB **35.8.I–II**)?

5. What problems did the state face in securing its grain supply and how did it deal with them (**35.13**, WEB **35.14.I–II**)?

6. What were the constraints on trading in Athens (**35.13**, **35.15–16**, WEB **35.14.I–II**)?

7. How could a taxpayer, tax collector, and trader in Athens defraud the system and get away with it (**35.7**, **35.10–12**)?

Suggested Readings

Athenian democracy in the fourth century: Sinclair 1988; Hansen 1991; Rhodes 2004a, 1–236. *Codifying the laws and their authority*: Ostwald 1986, 412–524; Rhodes 1991. *Legislative procedure and the Athenian assembly*: Hansen 1974, 1987. *Athenian freedom*: Hansen 1996; Raaflaub 2004, esp. 166–249. *Freedom of speech*: Sluiter and Rosen 2004, 1–340. *Equality*: Roberts 1996. *Rhetores and leadership*: Hansen 1983; Ober 1989, 118–126; 1996, 86–106. *Athenian courts and legal system*: MacDowell 1978; Hansen 1990b; Todd 1993; Boegehold 1995. *Sykophants*: Osborne 1990; *contra*: Harvey 1990; Christ 1998. *Taxation and liturgies*: Davies 1981; Gabrielsen 1994 (esp. trierarchies); P. Wilson 2000, 89–95 (*choregia*). *Eisphora*: Wallace 1989b; Christ 2007. *Andocides and the 2 percent tax*: E. Burke 1985, 262–285; Roisman 2006, 102–103. *The Theoric Fund*: Hansen 1976; Harris 1996. *Antidosis*: Gabrielsen 1987; Christ 1990. *Military funds and finance*: Millett 1993. *Grain and food shortages*: Garnsy 1988, 89–164; 1998, 183–200 (downplaying Athens' dependence on foreign grain before the Peloponnesian War); *contra*: Whitby 1998. *The grain tax*: Stroud 1998; Harris 1999; Moreno 2003; R&O, 118–128. *The silver coinage law*: Stroud 1974; Giovannini 1975, 191–195; Martin 1991; R&O, 112–118. *Maritime trade and lending in Athens*: Isager and Hansen 1975; Millett 1991; E. Cohen 1992; Reed 2003.

36

Metics (Resident Aliens), Slaves, and Barbarians

CHAPTER CONTENTS

Ancient Greece from Homer to Alexander: The Evidence, First Edition. Joseph Roisman.
© 2011 Blackwell Publishing Ltd. Translations © 2011 John Yardley. Published 2011 by Blackwell Publishing Ltd.

37

Masculine and Feminine Gender in Classical Athens

Ancient Greece from Homer to Alexander: The Evidence, First Edition. Joseph Roisman.
© 2011 Blackwell Publishing Ltd. Translations © 2011 John Yardley. Published 2011 by Blackwell Publishing Ltd.

This chapter deals with portrayals of men and women chiefly in fourth-century Athens, about whom we are best informed. It describes ideals of manliness as shown in an official Athenian oath and in a statue attributed to Polyclitus. A speech in an Athenian court depicts, surely in a distorted fashion, a man who violated these and other masculine expectations. Another speech describes a violent quarrel between two men over a male lover, while a passage from Xenophon describes manual laborers' deviations from manly ideals. The chapter then discusses women in the roles of wives and mothers. A lament from Euripides' play *Medea* complains of a wife's lot, while another passage from Xenophon describes the wifely duties of running the household. Finally, a defense speech in a homicide court describes a husband's marital life and his killing of his wife's lover.

37.1   Manly Ideals: The Ephebic Oath

The ideal male Athenian citizen was a free adult man (*aner*) who was both responsible and useful in his roles of head of family, friend, and citizen. He was courageous in battle and politics, zealous of his honor, rational, and able to control his appetites and show moderation (*sophrosynê*). Some of these desirable attributes were articulated in the ephebic oath. The Athenian institution of *ephebeia* enrolled men aged nineteen to twenty (perhaps with the exception of the poor) for the purpose of training them to become good soldiers, citizens, and men. An inscription from the mid-fourth century which was put up by Dion, the priest of the Acharnian deme, records two oaths: one sworn by the ephebes and the other by the Athenians before the battle of Plataea in 479 (see **17.17.C**: "The Plataea Oath"). The antiquity of these oaths is hotly debated, with some scholars regarding them as anachronistic and others as based on historical precedents. The origins of the *ephebeia* are uncertain, although it was certainly reformed and foregrounded in the 330s. The ephebic oath is also preserved in late literary sources with some variants. The oath incorporates civic ideals that adult Athenians hoped to instill in their young. The hoplite values informing it are evident in the injunction to stand one's line and in the relief at the top of the inscription, which depicts Athena crowning the war god Ares, who is dressed like a hoplite.

Tod no. 204 = Harding no. 109A

Translation: Harding no. 109A, pp. 133–134

Gods. The priest of Ares and Athena Areia, Dion, son of Dion, of Acharnae made the dedication. (5) The ancestral oath of the ephebes, which must be sworn by the ephebes. I shall not disgrace the sacred weapons (that I bear) nor shall I desert the comrade at my side, wherever I stand the line. And I shall fight in defense of things sacred and secular and I shall not hand down (to my descendants) a lessened fatherland, (**10**) but one that is increased in size and strength both as far as in me lies and with the assistance of all, and I shall be obedient to those who on any occasion are governing prudently and to the laws that are established and any that in the future may be established prudently. If anyone tries to destroy (them), I shall resist (**15**) both as far as in me lies and with the assistance of all, and I shall honor the sacred rites that are ancestral. The witnesses (are) the Gods Aglaurus,[1] Hestia, Enyo, Enyalius,[2] Ares and Athena Areia, Zeus, Thallo, Auxo, Hegemone,[3] Heracles (and) the boundaries of my fatherland, the wheat, (**20**) the barley, the vines, the olives, the figs.

Notes

1. *Aglaurus was the daughter of king Cecrops. The oath was taken in her sanctuary on the north slope of the acropolis.*
2. *Enyo was a goddess of war. Enyalius was a god of war, but also Ares' epithet.*
3. *Thallo and Auxo were goddesses of the seasons, and Hegemone a goddess of plants.*

Question

1. What constituted an ideal male citizen, according to the oath?

37.2 The Manly Body

A man, and especially a young man, was expected to look manly. An example of the ideal body of a young man is the *Doryphoros* (spear-bearer) made by Polyclitus of Argos ca. 440 (Figure 37.1, p. 504). Although the original bronze is lost, there are several different Roman copies, with the one from Pompeii shown in the figure considered by many scholars to be modeled on the original. The title *Doryphoros* is late and might not have been the original. The warrior's spear (now lost), which probably rested on his shoulder, and his athletic body led many scholars to identify him with Achilles. To create an idealized masculine and well-proportioned body, Polyclitus used a mathematical formula that related each part to another and to the whole body. This was his famous *kanon* ("rule"), which influenced future generations of artists. The *Doryphoros* is, as the Roman antiquarian Pliny the Elder describes him, "a virile youth" (*Natural History* 34.23). He is somewhat aloof, well balanced, and "the very epitome of *sophrosynê*" (self-control; Stewart 1997, 92). It has been suggested that in addition to a spear the man also carried a shield on his left hand and held the sheath of a sword in his right.

Figure 37.1   A Roman copy of Polyclitus, *Doryphoros*. akg-images/Nimatallah.

37.3 The Unmanly Man

Needless to say, it was not easy to adhere to manly ideals. A prime example of such failure is the politician Timarchus, as depicted by the orator Aeschines. After Athens had concluded a peace with Philip II in 346, Demosthenes and Timarchus planned to prosecute their political rival Aeschines for his role in the negotiations. To forestall the attack, Aeschines brought Timarchus to trial for allegedly practicing male prostitution. This profession was not illegal, but a man who disgraced himself and his citizen status by selling his body was disqualified from holding office and public speaking. Aeschines often portrays what appeared to have been Timarchus' love affairs with different men as acts of prostitution. This was not too difficult because gifts that lovers normally bestowed on their beloved could be portrayed by biased observers as commercial transactions for sex. See **12.2** ("Homoerotic Couples") for homosexual love, and WEB **37.4** for Aristophanes on prostitution and homosexuality.

Some Athenians must have wondered why a prominent man like Timarchus would be engaged in male prostitution. Aeschines accounted for Timarchus' conduct by depicting him as a slave to his desires, a spendthrift, insolent toward others, and corrupt in private and public life. In short, Timarchus violated a cardinal expectation of manly citizens by failing to exercise self-control and moderation. Although Aeschines provided little proof for his allegations (e.g., 107 below), he won the trial. The following passage follows Aeschines' claim that young Timarchus practiced prostitution in Piraeus while living in a physician's house.

Aeschines 1 *Against Timarchus* 41–42, 105–107

(**41**) Gentlemen of Athens: One Misgolas son of Naucrates, of the deme Collytus, is in all other respects a gentleman, and one could not find fault with him in anything else, but for this sort of thing he has a phenomenal passion and always has around him musicians and lyre-players. I say this not from a vulgar superciliousness, but so that you may learn the sort of person he is. When he saw just why it was that Timarchus here was living at the doctor's house, he got him to move by paying him money in advance and he proceeded to take him into his own house – for Timarchus was well proportioned, young, degenerate, and in fact just right for what Misgolas proposed to do to him, and what Timarchus proposed to experience at his hands.

(**42**) There was no hesitation on Timarchus' part. He submitted to it although he lacked none of the things that afford a reasonable living standard; for his father had left him a very substantial estate, which he has eaten up completely, as I shall show as my exposition proceeds. But his behavior was such because he was susceptible to the most shameful passions, to extravagant living, expensive meals, flute-girls, hetaerae [courtesans],[1] dice, and all the other things to which a man noble and free should not be in thrall. And this repulsive individual felt no shame at leaving his father's house and living with Misgolas, who was not a friend of his father or a person of his age, but a stranger who was older than him – no shame in living, in the flower of his youth, with a man who was in such matters a debauchee ...

(**105**) But someone may say that, after selling the family home, he acquired another house in a different part of the city, that instead of keeping the one in the country, and the farm at Alopece, the slaves and everything else, he actually invested in the silver mines, as his father had done earlier. But no! He has nothing left, no house, no apartment, no land, no slaves, no money out on loan, nothing of what men who are not reprobates live on. Instead, all that is left to him in place of his inheritance is indecency, sykophancy [litigiousness], effrontery, licentiousness, cowardice, shamelessness, and the inability to blush at disgraceful actions, that is, the things that go toward producing the vilest and most useless citizen.

(**106**) Now it is not just his inheritance that he has swallowed up – there are also the things that belong to you all, if he ever had them in his hands. You see how young he is, and yet there is no magistracy this man has not held, gaining none of them by lot or by election, but buying them all for himself in contravention of the laws. Most I shall pass over, mentioning only two or three.

(**107**) He became a state auditor[2] and did enormous damage to the city through taking bribes from those guilty of malpractice in their magistracies, and above all through blackmailing those who were guiltless among the men undergoing audit of their accounts. He was a magistrate on Andros,[3] having paid thirty minas for the position with money that he borrowed at an interest rate of nine obols per mina, and so he made your allies rich pickings for his disgusting behavior. And the licentiousness he manifested with the wives of free men has never been matched by anybody. I summon none of these men to bear witness to his own suffering, on which he has chosen to remain silent, but I leave it to you to look into the matter.

Notes

1. *Timarchus' association with flute-girls and courtesans evinced his wasteful lifestyle more than his lust.*
2. *A board of ten auditors (logistai) went over the accounts of office-holders at the end of their terms.*
3. *The Aegean island of Andros was an ally of Athens. Timarchus might have been a governor there.*

Question

1. What moral failings did Timarchus show in his private and public life, and how were they related to each other?

37.5   Violence and Men in Love

As much as the Greeks disapproved of men who yielded to desire, they also conceded that such a failing was human and so deserving of sympathy. This attitude can be found in a defense speech by Lysias that was written sometime after 394 for an anonymous Athenian, who had been charged with "premeditated wounding" (attempted murder) before the homicide court of the Areopagus. The defendant and his prosecutor, one Simon, quarreled over a Plataean youth who was a non-citizen residing in Athens. Simon argues that he had paid the boy to stay with him but that the defendant stole him and almost killed Simon in an altercation. The speaker denies the charge. He asks for the court's understanding and sympathy for his infatuation with the boy. He also charges Simon with unreasonable belligerence and with breaking into his house where he shamed his secluded (i.e., respected) female relatives. Simon's intrusion was not an uncommon way of insulting the man of the house through his kinswomen.

Lysias 3 *Against Simon* 4–7

(**4**) Members of the Council, I think I ought to receive no leniency from you if I am guilty; but if I demonstrate that I am innocent of these charges, which Simon made under oath, and if you think moreover that my conduct *vis-à-vis* the lad is somewhat silly in view of my age, I beg you not to think any the worse of me. For you know that desire resides in all men, and the best and most judicious of them may well be the one who is able to bear its buffetings with the greatest composure. In all of which, as I shall demonstrate, Simon has stood in my way.

(**5**) I, Members of the Council, felt desire for a Plataean lad, Theodotus. I thought the best way to make him my friend was by treating him well, but this fellow thought that he would bring him to do what he wanted by treating him in an insulting and outrageous manner. To give a full account of the mistreatment the boy suffered at the man's hands would be a considerable undertaking, but I think it appropriate that you be told the wrongs he has inflicted on me personally.

(**6**) When he learned that the boy was at my place, he came to the house at night in a drunken state, broke down the doors, and went into the women's quarters. In there were my sister and my nieces, who have led such respectable lives as to feel embarrassment at being seen even by their relatives. (**7**) Now this man displayed such effrontery that he refused to leave until those who then arrived on the scene, and the men who were with him, forcefully removed him, for they thought he had behaved atrociously in appearing amongst young girls and orphans…

Question

1. What social conventions did Simon violate?

37.6 Artisans and Manual Laborers

Especially in the eyes of the elite, traders and artisans could not share in the respect accorded other men and citizens. They earned their living by providing services to others, which made them less than fully independent. They also resembled women by spending their time indoors. Manual or banausic labor and crafts in general did not bring social esteem. They deprived a man of the leisure required for politics and social activity and were associated with occupations performed by aliens, women, children, and slaves (cf. WEB **37.13** for women in the market). They also meant taking orders from others. The two exceptions were farm work and mercenary service on account of the respect accorded to agriculture and war. In Xenophon's *Oeconomicus*, Socrates and the Athenian Critobulus discuss the merits and reputations of different occupations. Socrates at first responds to Critobulus' request to point out the finest and most suitable arts for him to be engaged in.

Xenophon *Oeconomicus* 4.2–4, 6.5–8; cf. *Memorabilia* 2.8.1–5

(**4.2**) "Well said, Critobulus," replied Socrates. "For the so-called 'banausic' [manual] trades have a poor reputation, and they are, with good reason, much frowned upon by the city-states. They destroy the bodies of the workmen and those overseeing the work by forcing them into a sedentary life indoors, and some trades even make people spend the day beside a fire. And when the body grows soft, the soul becomes much more feeble still. (**4.3**) Also, the so-called 'banausic' trades leave a person no spare time to attend to his friends and civic affairs. The result is that such people are thought to have bad relationships with their friends and to be poor defenders of their native land. And in some of the city-states, particularly in those known to excel in the military sphere, none of the citizens is permitted to practice the trades."

(**4.4**) "But in my case, Socrates, what arts do you recommend that I practice?"

"Surely we would not be ashamed to follow the example of the king of Persia," replied Socrates. "For they say that he thinks agriculture and the art of war to be amongst the finest and most essential of the arts, and so he practices them conscientiously."

(**6.5**) "Now we decided that it was impossible to master all branches of learning, and we agreed with the city-states in rejecting what are called the 'banausic' trades because they seem to have a deleterious effect on the body and also because they enervate the soul. (**6.6**) We said that the clearest proof of this would be the following. Suppose an enemy invaded the country, and someone separated the farmers and the tradesmen and then asked each group whether they were in favor of defending the land or of withdrawing from the countryside and mounting guard on the city's walls. (**6.7**) In such a situation, we thought, those occupied with the land would vote for defending it, while the tradesmen would be *against* fighting and *for* doing what they had been brought up to do, namely sitting it out without exerting themselves or facing danger. (**6.8**) We decided that for a gentleman [*kalos k'agathos*] the best occupation and best specialist knowledge was farming, from which men derive the necessities of life."

Question

1. Why would people who practiced menial trades make bad ephebes (**37.1**)?

37.7 Men, Women, and the Household

We dealt with female roles and expectations associated with gender in the Archaic Age in Chapter 12 ("Archaic Society and Culture"). The following sections look at women in Classical Athens who adhered to their conventional image and others who offended it.

Once a woman changed from being a maiden to a wife, she was expected to bear her husband children, be obedient and faithful to him, and run the household (*oikos*). In his *Politics*, Aristotle observes that for the household to be functional and happy, it has to consist of a male and female, with one the ruler and the other the ruled. He regards this dichotomy as well as the differences between a female and a slave as natural.

Aristotle *Politics* 1.2.11–12 1254b3–16

(**1.2.11**) So, as we say, one may see the authority of a master and that of a statesman first of all in a living being. For the soul exercises the authority of a master over the body, and the intellect exercises the rule of a statesman and king over the appetites. In these cases it is evident that it is in accord with nature and expediency for the body to be ruled by the soul and for the emotional element to be ruled by the intellect, which is the element possessing rationality; a relationship of equality or subservience between them would be harmful for all concerned. (**2.12**) The same is true once more in the case of man and the other animals. Domesticated animals are, by nature, superior to wild animals; but it is better for them all to be ruled by men, since they gain security in this way. Likewise in the relationship between male and female: the former is ascendant and the latter inferior, the former the ruler and the latter the ruled. In the whole of humanity this pattern must be the same.[1]

Note

 1. *See WEB* **36.7** *("Aristotle on Natural Slavery") for the continuation of this passage.*

Question

1. Why is it beneficial for a woman to be ruled by a man, according to Aristotle?

37.8 Wives and Mothers

In his memoir of Socrates, Xenophon describes a conversation between the philosopher and his young son, who has been angry with his mother. Socrates' attitude toward his ill-tempered wife Xanthippe could be dismissive and patronizing (Plato *Phaedo* 60a; Xenophon *Symposion* 2.8–10). Here, however, he rebukes his son for being ungrateful to her.

Xenophon *Memorabilia* 2.2.4–6

(**2.2.4**) Naturally, you do not suppose that people have children just because of the sexual urge – the streets and brothels are full of things to satisfy that. Evidently we are on the lookout for the kind of women from whom we could have the best children, and we get together with them to procreate. (**2.5**) The male supports the woman who will have the children with him, and provides for the forthcoming progeny all things that he thinks may benefit them for living their lives, and as many of them as he can. The female conceives and carries the weight of her burden, risking her life and sharing with the foetus the food that gives her her own nourishment. With great discomfort she carries on to the end, and after giving birth she nurtures the child and looks after it, despite never having received any benefit from it, and although the baby neither recognizes the person by whom its well-being is provided nor has the ability to communicate to her its needs. Still, the mother guesses at the things that are beneficial and pleasurable for the child, and attempts to supply them, and she brings it up for a long time, laboring patiently night and day although she has no idea what benefit she will acquire from this.

Figure 37.2 A hydria by the Munich Painter with a domestic scene. © The Trustees of the British Museum.

(**2.6**) And simply providing nurture is not enough. When the children seem capable of learning, the parents also teach them whatever they are able to that will make a positive contribution to their lives; and when they think another is better able to teach them something, they send them to that person, incurring expense to do so. They do everything to see that their children become as good as they possibly can be.

The hydria or water jar shown in Figure 37.2 dates from ca. 450 and is attributed to the so-called Munich Painter. It depicts a domestic scene, with the mother sitting on a high chair and a servant or a companion handing over her baby son. The hurried movement of the woman on the left and the baby's and the mother's outstretched hands create a sense of intimacy. At the feet of the mother is a *kolathos*, wool basket, in reference to weaving, which was a common female domestic activity. The setting is probably the women's quarters. Drawing water, for which the jar was used, was the task of women and slaves.

Questions

1. Is Socrates' approach to motherhood functionalist?
2. How does the vase in Figure 37.2 conform to and contradict Socrates' description of the mother–child relationship?

37.9 A Woman's Lot

Euripides' play *Medea* (produced 431) has the heroine lament her lot as a woman and a discarded wife. Medea was told that her husband Jason, whom she had helped to obtain the Golden Fleece, wished to get rid of her in order to marry a Corinthian princess and in due course ascend the throne. It would be wrong to regard the following passage as a Greek woman's perspective on married life. Medea is not an ordinary woman but the dramatic character of a foreign princess. Her speech also aims to demonstrate to her stage audience of Corinthian women, and to the male audience in the theater, how awful her situation is. Yet Medea does inform us about Greek men's expectations of their wives. (See also Lysias *On the Killing of Eratosthenes* 6–7 in **37.12.D** for a description of the relationship between husband and wife.)

Euripides *Medea* 226–251

(**226**) I am done for and I want to die, friends, setting aside life's pleasure. For the one on whom I depended for everything, my husband, has turned out – I know it well – to be the worst of men.

Of all things that have life and reason, (**230**) we women are the most wretched creatures. First we must, with an inordinate amount of money, buy a husband and take on a master of our body – for this is an evil even more painful than the first. (**235**) And it is in this that the most important gamble lies – taking a good one or a bad one. For divorce is not respectable for women, and refusing one's husband is not possible, either.

Arriving in a situation where mores and rules are unfamiliar, a woman must have powers of divination to see what sort of man it is she must deal with in the marriage – she has not learned this at home. (**240**) And if, after we have worked hard and successfully on this, the husband lives with us in harmony and bears the yoke without constraint, our life is enviable. Otherwise, death is better. In the man's case, (**245**) whenever he is tired of living with those at home, he goes out and puts an end to the melancholy; but we have to look at the one person. They say that we live a life free of danger in the home while they fight with the spear – but they are wrong! (**250**) I would rather stand three times in the line of battle than give birth once.

Questions

1. Why is it good to be a man, according to Medea?
2. To which of Simonides' portraits of wives (**12.15**) might Medea's description serve as a counterpoint?

37.10 Running the Household

Sometime after 362 Xenophon wrote the Socratic dialogue *Oeconomicus*, which discusses farming and household management. In one part of the book he imagines a conversation between the very wealthy Ischomachus and his young and inexperienced wife, in which he teaches her the art of running the household. Ischomachus instructs his wife on how to supervise the slaves, make the household orderly, and weave, a typical female occupation that also contributed to the household economy. Ischomachus reports on his conversation with his wife to Socrates, who reports it in turn to his acquaintance, Critobolus.

Xenophon *Oeconomicus* 7.35–37; 10.10–13

(**7.35**) "Will I too have to do this?" asked my [Ischomachus'] wife.

"Yes," I said. "You will have to stay at home, sending out in a body those slaves whose work is out of doors and supervising those who must work inside. (**7.36**) You must take in the household revenues, allocating some for necessary expenditures, giving thought in advance to what must be left over after that, and seeing to it that the outlay set aside for a year is not used up in a month. And when wool is brought to you, it is your duty to have those in need of clothing supplied with it. You must also see that the dry cereal remains in good condition for eating."

(**7.37**) "One of the tasks that devolve upon you, however, you will perhaps think rather unpleasant," I said. "You must see to the nursing of any of the slaves who fall ill."

"No, by Zeus," said my wife, "that will be very pleasant – at least if those who are well nursed are going to feel grateful and be better disposed to us than before."

(**10.10**) "And my advice to her, Socrates, was not to be always sitting around like a slave, but to try, with the help of the gods, to act as a mistress. She should stand at the loom, teaching whatever she knows better than another, and learning what she knows less well than another. She should watch over the baking-woman, stand beside the housekeeper when she is distributing items, and make the rounds to see that each thing is where it ought to be. It seemed to me that this would mean that she would also have a walk around while seeing to her duties. (**10.11**) I added that mixing and kneading flour, and shaking and folding clothes and bed coverings, provided good exercise. Exercising like that, I added, she would take more pleasure in her food, enjoy better health, and develop naturally a better complexion. (**10.12**) Her looks, when set against a serving girl's, are also – because she has a purer complexion and is more gracefully dressed – very exciting, especially when one also realizes that she is giving pleasure willingly and not providing a service under duress. (**10.13**) But ladies who sit smugly around invite comparison with cheating, painted hussies. And now, Socrates, rest assured that my wife passes her days dressed as I instructed her to dress, and as I now am telling you."

Some women did not settle for the traditional roles of tending to their family and slaves. Forensic speeches in particular depict women running the household's business, which could be large and complex, and protecting its interests. Many were certainly knowledgeable about the household's assets, including commercial transactions. See WEB **37.11** for a speech by Lysias that portrays one such woman.

For a plan of a Greek house from Olynthus, see **38.9.B** ("Plan of an Olynthian House").

Questions

1. How was the mistress of the house supposed to deal with slaves? What should she be careful about?
2. Contrast Xenophon's portrait of a wife with the woman depicted in Lysias' speech *Against Diogeiton* (WEB **37.11**).
3. How did the woman in Lysias' speech (WEB **37.11**) handle the conflict between her roles as daughter and mother?

37.12 Virtuous and Unfaithful Women

Social virtues are often espoused in funerary inscriptions, and the Greeks were no exception. The following early fourth-century inscription from a tomb relief in Piraeus commemorates the qualities of Theophile. The inscription does not mention her male relatives as is common practice in other epigrams. In Athens, naming a woman in public was often a sign of disrespect, because a woman's place and reputation were indoors. A woman's death, however, legitimized the advertising of her merits.

37.12.A   A Woman of Virtue

W. Peek, *Griechische Vers-Inschriften* I: *Grab-epigramme* (Berlin, 1955), no. 1490

Translation: Fantham et al. (1994, 83), slightly modified

> The memory of your virtue, Theophile, will never die.
> [You were] self-controlled, good, and industrious, possessing every virtue.

Honor and modesty encouraged upper-class women in particular to remain indoors. A fragment of a late fourth-century speech by the orator Hyperides suggests that elderly women alone did not have to account for their presence outdoors. Some scholars have attributed the fragment to a speech against the courtesan Aristagora who, being a metic, had been charged for failing to obtain a *prostates* (citizen sponsor or patron).

37.12.B   Female Propriety

Hyperides fr. 205 (Jensen)

If a woman goes out of her house, she should have reached the age where those who meet her will ask not whose wife she is but whose mother.

Women could legitimately show themselves in public on religious occasions, at funerals, or when they went to fetch water from the public fountain or even to light a torch at a neighbor's house. Economic contingencies, however, forced poorer women to work outdoors and deal with male strangers. This could expose them to suspicion of promiscuity or adultery. An Athenian law that punished the slandering of persons who worked in the agora suggests the dis-respect that attended their way of earning a living. In addition, resident aliens and slaves, who often did business in the agora, diminished by association the reputation of free retailers. See WEB **37.13** for the case of a man whose citizenship was challenged because his mother sold ribbons in the market.

   Staying indoors, however, did not equate with virtue. Lysias' *On the Killing of Eratosthenes* (date unknown) is a speech written in defense of Euphiletus, who had killed his wife's lover Eratosthenes. Eratosthenes' relatives charged Euphiletus with premeditated murder, but Euphiletus argued in his defense that his action was a justified homicide (justified homicides were tried in the court of the Delphinium). Athenian homicide law allowed the head of the household (*kyrios*) to kill with impunity an adulterer caught in the act (see also Plutarch *Solon* 23.1: WEB **13.4**: "Solon's Laws Concerning Inheritance, Dowry, Women Outdoors, Parental Support, and Sexual Misconduct").

37.12.C   Homicide and Adultery

Demosthenes 23 *Against Aristocrates* 53

…Law: If someone unintentionally kills a man in an athletic contest, or in overpowering him in a street brawl, or not recognizing him in battle, or while he is having intercourse with his wife, mother, sister, or concubine that he is keeping for the purpose of producing free children, he shall not in these cases go into exile for the killing.

Although the law legitimized such killing, many contemporary Athenians regarded the act as too extreme. The more usual procedure was to reach a financial settlement or even to ignore the affair. In Euphiletus' case, the defense's strategy was to portray him as a somewhat naïve man, one who acted as he did in order to defend the law, family, and honor. The speech throws light on daily life and the division of space in Athenian houses.

37.12.D   The Killing of Eratosthenes

Lysias 1 *On the Killing of Eratosthenes* 4, 6–14, 16, 23–27, 32–34

(**4**) I think, Gentlemen, that what I have to prove is that Eratosthenes committed adultery with my wife, corrupted her, brought shame on my children, and greatly insulted me by coming into my house. I must prove that, this apart, there was no bad blood between him and me; that my action was not taken for money, so that I could rise from poverty to riches; and that there is no other benefit in view apart from the vengeance authorized by the laws.

(**6**) Men of Athens: When I decided to get married and I took my wife home, my feelings were that I would not be hard on her, but that I would also not allow her too much latitude to do as she liked. So I kept a watchful eye on her, as far as I could, and paid her a reasonable amount of attention. But when my child was born, I began to have trust in her and I turned over to her all my affairs, thinking this the best way to live together. (**7**) In the early days, Gentlemen of Athens, she was the best of all women, a deft and economical housekeeper who ran everything with precision. But then my mother died, and her death was what brought on all my problems. (**8**) For it was when my wife was attending the funeral that she was spotted by this fellow and, in time, seduced by him. He kept an eye out for our slave-girl who went to the market, used her to carry messages, and so precipitated my wife's ruin.

(**9**) Now first of all, Gentlemen (for I must supply you with these details), my house has two stories, the upper being equal in size to the lower, with the former constituting the women's quarters, and the latter the men's. When the child was born to us, its mother breastfed it; and, so she would not be at risk climbing down the stairs whenever the child needed to be bathed, I lived upstairs while the women lived downstairs. (**10**) This then became routine, so much so that my wife would often go downstairs to sleep by the child to give it the breast and stop it crying. This went on over a long period, and I never suspected anything; I was so naïve that I believed that, of all the women in the city, my wife was the most virtuous.

(**11**) Time passed, Gentlemen, and I came home from the country unexpectedly. After dinner, the child began to cry and become irritable – it was being deliberately aggravated by the slave-girl so it would do this. That was because the man was there – I learned the whole story later. (**12**) I told my wife to go and give the child the breast so it would stop its wailing. She refused at first – she was so delighted to see me come home after so long, she said. But when I became angry and ordered her to go, she said, "Yes, so you can then have a go at the little serving girl! You were pulling her about when you were drunk once before." (**13**) I laughed and she got up, went off and closed the door, pretending to joke with me, and then pulled the bolt across. I, thinking nothing of it, and having no suspicions, went happily to sleep after my return from the country.

(**14**) When it was close to daylight, she came back and opened the door. I asked her why the doors had made a noise during the night, and she said that the lamp beside the child had gone out, and that she had then got a light from the neighbors. I remained silent, supposing this to be the case. But it seemed to me, Gentlemen, that her face was made up, and it was not yet thirty days since the death of her brother! Nevertheless I made no comment on the matter; I simply left and went out in silence...

Some time later, an old woman, sent by one of Eratosthenes' former lovers, told Euphiletus about the affair.

(16) ..."Euphiletus," she said, "do not think I have approached you wishing to pry into your affairs. It turns out that the man bringing shame on you and your wife is an enemy of ours. If you get hold of the slave-girl who goes to the market and who waits on you, and if you interrogate her under torture, you will learn everything. 'It is Eratosthenes of the deme Oe who is the culprit,' she said. 'He has seduced not just your wife, but many others, too. This is his line of work ...'"

Euphiletus interrogated the maid and learned about the affair. He arranged with her to tell him when Eratosthenes would come to his house, and on the fateful night he caught his wife and her lover in bed, legitimizing his killing of him. We do not know the result of the trial or the fate of the wife. The law, however, ordained that the husband divorce his adulterous wife. It also forbade her from appearing in public in the city's sacred areas and during public rituals ([Demosthenes] *Against Neaera* 59.87). In the following passage, Euphiletus describes his motives for the action. He is anxious to show that he did not lure the victim to his death, as the prosecution had argued.

(23) ...Eratosthenes came in, Gentlemen, and the slave-girl immediately woke me up and informed me that he was in the house. Telling her to keep an eye on the door, I went down and silently left the house. I then went to the houses of one friend after another, finding some at home and others not in town. (24) I took with me as many as I could of those who were available and started for home. We picked up some torches in the closest tavern and entered the house, the door having been left open in readiness by the slave-girl. Pushing open the bedroom door, those of us who entered first could still see the man lying beside my wife, and those coming in later saw him standing up on the bed, naked. (25) And I, Gentlemen, hit him and knocked him down. I pulled his arms behind his back and tied them, and then asked him what prompted him to enter my house and commit such an outrage. He admitted that he was in the wrong, and begged and pleaded with me not to kill him but to demand payment from him. (26) "It is not I who will kill you," I replied, "but the law of the city. This you have broken, considering it of less importance than your pleasures, and preferring to commit such a heinous offense against my wife and my children than to obey the laws and show some decency." (27) So it was, Gentlemen, that this man received the punishment that the laws prescribe for that sort of thing...

To emphasize the evils of adultery, Euphiletus ranks it above rape in villainy. He supports his assertion by contrasting the killing of adulterers to the more lenient penalty of fining rapists. However, he neglects to mention that rape could also be punished by death according to the law of *hubris*.

(32) You hear what the law prescribes, Gentlemen. If someone forcefully violates a free person or a child, he is to pay double the amount of damages. In the case of a woman, the same penalty applies in instances where killing is allowed. And so, Gentlemen, the lawgiver considered those using violence deserving of a lesser penalty than those using persuasion, since he condemns the latter to death and the former to double the amount of damages. (33) His thinking was that those who use force in performing the act are hated by those on whom the force is used, while those using persuasion so corrupt the souls of their prey that they have other men's wives more under their influence than the husbands do. They bring the whole household under their control, and render it unclear to whom the children belong, to the husbands or to the adulterers. That is why the man framing the law instituted the death penalty for them.

(34) In my case, Gentlemen, the laws not only cleared me of wrongdoing but actually ordered me to take this satisfaction. It is for you to decide whether these laws should have authority or be worthless…

See WEB **37.14** for the courtesan Neaera and other women whose life and identity were shaped outside the traditional household.

Questions

1. Describe what might constitute an insult to an Athenian woman in light of the tomb epitaph (**37.12.A**), Hyperides' fragment (**37.12.B**), and the speech on the working mother in WEB **37.13**.
2. How does Euphiletus describe his marriage prior to his discovery of his wife's infidelity (**37.12.D**)?
3. What wrongs has Eratosthenes committed, according to his killer (**37.12.D**)?
4. If Euphiletus' wife had been given a voice in the trial, what might she have said?

Review Questions

1. What constituted a manly and unmanly man in Athens (**37.1–3**, **37.5–6**)?
2. How could men threaten masculine control of the household (**37.3**, **37.5**, **37.12**)?
3. How could women threaten men and their household (**37.12**, WEB **37.13–14**)?
4. What were women's contributions to the household (**37.7–10**, **37.12**, WEB **37.11**, WEB **37.13**)?

5. How were gender and class related in Athens (**37.3**, **37.6**, WEB **37.13**)?
6. How did the courtesan Neaera negotiate her way in a man's world (WEB **37.14**)?
7. In your view, would Neaera have been better off as a wife (WEB **37.14**)?

Suggested Readings

Greek and Athenian manhood: Rosen and Sluiter 2003, 1–234; Roisman 2005. *The ephebes and their oath*: Siewert 1977; Vidal-Naquet 1986, 106–128 (interpreting the institution as a rite of passage, but see Hesk 2000, 29–30, 86–89). *Polyclitus and the Doryphoros*: Moon 1995; Borbein 1996; (and masculinity) Stewart 1997, 86–97. *Aeschines, Timarchus, politics, and sexuality*: Harris 1995, 96, 101–106, 151; Davidson 1997, 252–274; Fisher 2001; Roisman, 2005, esp. 89–90, 164–184. *Attitudes toward labor, including handicrafts*: Ste Croix 1983, 179–192; Balme 1984; Cartledge 2002, 148–150. *Xenophon's Oikonomikos and women in the household*: S.I. Johnstone 1994; Pomeroy 1994; Cox 1998. *Naming women*: Schaps 1977. *Working women and their reputation*: D. Cohen 1991, 150–154; Brock 1994; Scheidel 1995, 1996; S. Johnstone 2002. *Rape and adultery*: D. Cohen 1991, 101–132; Carey 1995; Patterson 1998, 114–197; Omitowoju 2002; Harris 2004. *Euphiletus' case*: Carey 1989, 59–86; D. Cohen 1991, 114–132; Porter 1997 (doubting the historicity of the case); Wolpert 2001; Todd 2007, 43–148. *Courtesans and prostitutes*: Halperin 1990, 88–112; Davidson 1997, 73–108, 194–205; Kurke 1999, 175–227; Skinner 2005, 96–104, 113–114, cf. 163–169. *Neaera's trial*: Carey 1992; Kapparis 1999; Hamel 2003; Glazebrook 2005.

38

Philip II of Macedonia (359–336)

CHAPTER CONTENTS

Ancient Greece from Homer to Alexander: The Evidence, First Edition. Joseph Roisman.
© 2011 Blackwell Publishing Ltd. Translations © 2011 John Yardley. Published 2011 by Blackwell Publishing Ltd.

Philip II of Macedonia was a man who transformed the history of both his country and Greece. The accomplishments of his son Alexander the Great were to a large extent based on the groundwork that Philip had prepared. Macedonia was roughly divided into Lower and Upper Macedonia. Its ruler initially dominated only Pieris and most of Bottice. The rest of the Macedonian principalities from Pelagonia in the north to Tymphaea in the south were ruled by local dynasts who acknowledged the authority of the kings only periodically (see Map 38.1).

Before the rise of Philip, many Greeks viewed Macedonia as a peripheral state to be exploited for its timber, minerals, and other resources. The debate about whether the Macedonians were Greek has engaged many more modern people than it did the ancients. The Macedonians spoke a distinct dialect, and some sources – often hostile – called them "barbarians." Yet Greek attitudes toward the Macedonians and their ethnic identity were changeable; in any case, many accepted the Greekness of the ruling Argead dynasty. The Macedonian royal house claimed Heracles as its ancestor, and although no Macedonian ruler before Alexander the Great seemed to have taken up the title "king," they certainly acted like kings once they established their rule. Their authority was often challenged from within and without. Macedonia's neighbors, whether Thracians, Illyrians, Chalcidian towns, Athens, Thessalians, and even rulers of Upper Macedonia, continued to threaten the central government. The result was that the borders of the Macedonian kingdom were highly unstable.

 WEB **38.2** describes the military reforms of king Archelaus (413–399) and provides a link to coins from his reign.

The Macedonian army consisted in this period of infantrymen, recruited from the local peasantry, and of cavalry, dominated by the nobility. From at least Philip II's time, the nobles were called "Companions" (*hetairoi*). They advised the king and served as his pool of military commanders. Their collective name of Companions denotes their closeness to the king. To elicit similar closeness to the infantry the kings called them "foot-companions" (*petzhetairoi*). Evidence from the time of Philip and Alexander refers to popular assemblies or to the Macedonians assembled under arms. Scholars are divided about the jurisdiction of these assemblies, with some granting them the power to elect or confirm the election of kings and to serve as a court for treason, and others regarding them as largely impotent.

This chapter focuses on Philip's reign and accomplishments. It discusses the challenges the king faced upon ascending the throne and how he overcame them. The chapter then reports on Philip's military reforms, coinage, court, and many wives. Philip's intervention in Greece is shown through his involvement in the Third Sacred War, the capture of Olynthus, and the peace he signed with Athens in 346. Philip took over Greece after the renewal of the war with Athens and his victory over a Greek coalition at Chaeronea (338). The chapter concludes by documenting Philip's subsequent settlement of Greek affairs, including the establishment of a Panhellenic league of Corinth, and his assassination in 336.

A link to a small ivory head identified as Philip II can be found in WEB **38.21**.

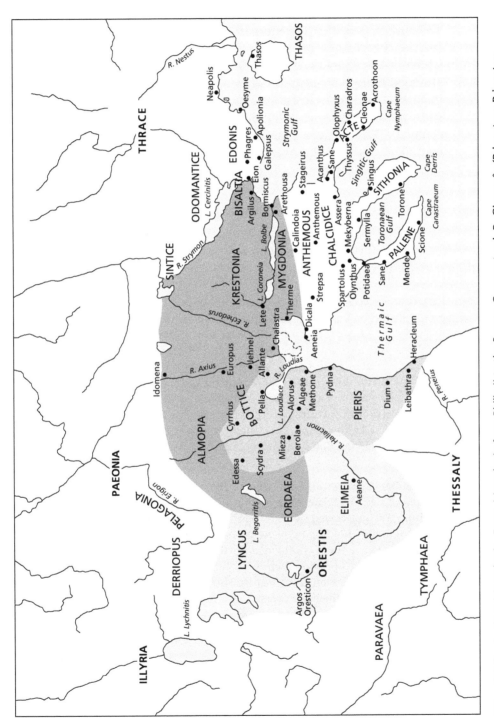

Map 38.1 Ancient Macedonia. From *Macedonia from Philip II to the Roman Conquest*, ed. R. Ginouvès (Princeton: Princeton University Press, 1994), fig. 15, p. 27.

38.1 Philip's Accession and Challenges to his Rule (359)

The authority of the Macedonian king depended on his personality no less than on his office. This is why turmoil often followed the death of a king, which in Macedonia was rarely due to natural causes. Chaos and danger also attended Philip's assumption of power. His brother, Perdiccas III, died in 359 in a battle against an invading Illyrian army, and Perdiccas' son Amyntas was still a minor. Consequently, Philip became king (and not regent as used to be claimed). Diodorus describes the challenges that Philip faced upon assuming command and how he overcame them. Philip's *modus operandi* at this time also characterized much of his later career.

Diodorus of Sicily 16.2.4–3.6; cf. Justin *Epitome of Pompeius Trogus' Philippic History* 7.6.3–10

(**16.2.4**) …Perdiccas, however, was beaten in a great battle by the Illyrians and fell in the engagement. His brother Philip, who had escaped from his situation as hostage, then took over the kingdom, which was in a sad state. (**2.5**) More than 4,000 Macedonians had been killed in the battle, and the rest, left demoralized and terrified of the forces of the Illyrians, had no will to see the war through to the end. (**2.6**) At about the same time the Paeonians, close neighbors of Macedonia, began to raid the land out of contempt for the Macedonians; the Illyrians also proceeded to muster strong forces and prepare for a campaign against Macedonia; and a certain Pausanias, who was related to the country's royal family, was attempting to take over the throne of Macedon through the agency of the king of Thrace. Like them, too, the Athenians were hostile to Philip; they were trying to restore Argaeus to the throne, and had sent off a commander, Mantias, with 3,000 hoplites and a substantial naval force.

(**3.1**) Because of the military disaster and the immensity of the dangers threatening them, the Macedonians were absolutely at a loss. However, despite all the frightening and dangerous situations facing the country, Philip was not cowed by the magnitude of the anticipated hazards. Instead, he kept the Macedonians together by holding frequent assemblies; and by his shrewd use of language he inspired them to courage and gave them confidence. Furthermore, he took measures to reorder and strengthen the armed forces, and to provide them with appropriate weapons; and he held frequent maneuvers and competitive martial exercises. (**3.2**) He also developed the tight formation and the equipment of the phalanx, copying the close ordered fighting of the heroes at Troy,[1] and was really the first to organize the Macedonian phalanx.

(**3.3**) He was affable in his interrelationships; he used gifts and promises to win over the crowd to the deepest loyalty to him; and he took shrewd countermeasures against the plethora of dangers bearing down on him. For example, he saw the Athenians focusing all their hopes on the recovery of Amphipolis,[2] and trying to restore Argaeus to the throne in pursuit of this end, and so he voluntary retreated from the city – after first making it independent! (**3.4**) He also sent a deputation to the Paeonians and, after bribing some with gifts and bringing others over by magnanimous assurances, got them to agree to peace for the time being. Similarly, he blocked Pausanias' return by bribing the [Thracian] king who was on the point of having him restored.

(**3.5**) The Athenian general Mantias had sailed to Methone and, staying there himself, he sent Argaeus ahead to Aegae with a force of mercenaries. Argaeus came up to the city and called on the people of Aegae to accept his return and become the prime sponsors of his kingship. (**3.6**) Nobody paid any heed, however, and he returned to Methone. Philip then came on the scene with some of his forces, joined battle with Argaeus, and wiped out large numbers of his mercenaries. The rest took flight to some high ground, and these he released under a truce, taking from them the exiles, whom they delivered to him …

Notes

1. *The reference is to Homer* Iliad *13.131–133, which is cited by Polybius in **38.3.A** below. Both Philip and Alexander modeled themselves on Homeric heroes.*
2. *Athens lost Amphipolis during the Peloponnesian War but did not renounce its ambition to regain it. Philip withdrew a garrison put there by his brother Perdiccas.*

Questions

1. What foreign powers threatened Philip and how did he deal with each of them?
2. What did Philip's domestic reforms consist of?
3. Which of Archelaus' projects (WEB **38.2**) might still have been serviceable in Philip's time?

38.3   Philip's Military Reforms and Coinage

It is likely that Diodorus compressed Philip's military reforms into a single period and that he credited him with some of his predecessors' work. The result, however, was the best army of the period.

The main offensive weapon of the Macedonian infantryman, that which gave the Macedonian phalanx its advantage, was the *sarissa*. This was a pike approximately 4.5–5.5 meters long, weighing about 6 kg, with a spearhead and a butt-spike. The *sarissa* both outreached the enemy's spears and provided protection from missiles when held upright. Since it took both hands to wield the pike, Macedonian warriors hung their small shields around their necks, which induced many to renounce their body armor. They also used slashing swords, and occasionally spears and greaves. Alexander's phalanx, which was likely modeled on that of Philip, consisted of six brigades (sg. *taxis*) of infantry, each comprising 1,500 men, and an elite brigade of 3,000 (and more) *hypaspistai* (shield-bearers).

Iron parts from a *sarissa* apparently belonging to a Macedonian warrior were found in a late fourth-century grave in a cemetery in Aegae (Vergina) (Figure 38.1, p. 524). They include a 0.51-meter-long spearhead, a 0.44-meter-long butt-spike (called *sauroter*, lit. "lizard-killer"), and a connecting socket that probably joined together the two parts of the shaft, which measured ca. 5 meters.

The second-century historian Polybius discusses phalanx formations and tactics, which probably resembled those of Philip's army.

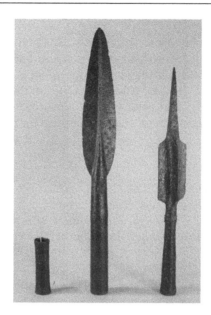

Figure 38.1 The metal parts of a *sarissa*: spearhead, butt-spike, and connecting socket. From the Museum of the Royal Tombs of Aegae, Vergina (BM 3014-16), in D. Pandermalis, *Alexander the Great: Treasures from an Epic Era of Hellenism* (New York: Alexander S. Onassis Public Benefit Foundation, 2004), p. 58, fig. 10. Photo: Archaeological Receipts Fund – TAP Service.

38.3.A   Phalanx Formations

Polybius 18.29.1–30.4

(**18.29.1**) Many considerations make it easy to see that, when the phalanx has its usual characteristics and strength, nothing could withstand its head-on charge or hold out against its attack. (**29.2**) When the ranks close up for battle, a man, with his weapons, takes up three feet of space. The length of the *sarissa* is, in its original design, sixteen cubits [ca. 7.2 m],[1] but this has been reduced to fourteen [ca. 6.3 m] for practical purposes. (**29.3**) From this fourteen one must deduct four cubits [ca. 1.8 m] for the space between the holder's hands and the weapon's counterweight projecting behind him. (**29.4**) It is therefore clear that the *sarissa* must extend ten cubits [ca. 4.5 m] in front of each hoplite's body when he advances on the enemy, holding it before him with both hands. (**29.5**) It follows from this that the *sarissas* of the fifth rank, while those of the second, third, and fourth ranks project further than these, still stretch two cubits [ca. 0.9 m] beyond the men in the front line, when the phalanx has its normal pattern and close order in the rear and on the flanks. As Homer puts it:

> "Shield pressed against shield, helmet against helmet, and man against man; and when they bent their heads the horns of their horse-hair crested helmets would touch. So close was the order in which they faced each other." [*Iliad* 13.131–133]

If my suggestions are accurate and precise, it is clear that every man in the front rank must have five *sarissas* projecting in front of him, each separated from the other by a space of two cubits.

(**30.1**) From this it is easy to get an impression of what the advance and charge of the entire phalanx is probably like, and the force that it has, when it is sixteen ranks deep. (**30.2**) Those behind the fifth rank cannot use their *sarissas* to engage in the fight. They accordingly do not hold the weapons level (**30.3**) but keep them up over the shoulders of the ranks before them in order to give protection to the whole formation from above; for the *sarissas* are massed together and so ward off any projectiles flying over the foremost ranks that can fall on men standing at the rear. (**30.4**) These men, however, put pressure on those before them in the formation and by their sheer bodily weight increase the force of the charge while at the same time making it impossible for the forward ranks to turn around.

Note

1. *The cubit is a Latin term for the Greek* pechys, *which is the distance between the elbow and the tip of the little finger, ca. 45 cm (18 inches).*

The Macedonian cavalry was recruited regionally and in Alexander's time consisted of eight squadrons (sg. *ilê*). The royal squadron (*ilê basilikê*) included mostly nobles and other men close to the king. During Alexander's campaign it was the cavalry that delivered the decisive blow to the enemy in set-piece battles. They rode without saddles or spurs, and their weapons included spears, body armor, and a helmet. In the Pompeii mosaic depicting the battle of Issus of 333 between Alexander and the Persians, Alexander is shown as a cavalryman dispatching a Persian warrior (see **39.4.B**: "The Alexander Mosaic," p. 561).

In addition to Macedonian infantry and cavalry, Philip employed allies and mercenaries, some of them as light-armed troops and engineers. He was a warrior king, and his frequent use of the Macedonian army helped him to consolidate his power in the kingdom. Conversely, military defeats could and did weaken his position at home.

—————————————————————————————— 38.3.B Philip's Coinage

In 357 Philip captured Amphipolis, which Athens regarded as her own colony. His control of this strategic city became a bone of contention between Athens and Macedonia. Philip, perhaps sincerely, perhaps not, promised to restore it to Athens, but he never did. Athens declared war on Philip but did little to pursue it. In 356 Philip captured the city of Crenides in Thrace and, after adding to it territory and settlers, renamed it Philippi. The polis' new name suggested the king's ranking above his subjects and the state, because hitherto foundations of cities were not named after their founder. The possession of Philippi and Amphipolis allowed Philip to mine silver and gold ore in the region and thus to become one of the wealthiest men in Greece. His silver and gold coins soon replaced Athenian coins as the preferred means of exchange. However, Philip was also a great spender, and when he died his son found himself in debt.

Diodorus of Sicily 16.8.6–7

(**16.8.6**) After this Philip proceeded to the city of Crenides [356]. This he enlarged by adding significant numbers to its population, and he changed its name to Philippi, calling it after himself. He then developed the gold mines in the area, which were hitherto very unproductive and of little importance, to the point where they were able to provide him with an income of more than a thousand talents.[1] (**8.7**) From these mines he swiftly built up his wealth, and he brought the kingdom of Macedon to great preeminence through his abundant riches. For he struck the gold coinage that was known as the Philipeios after him, and then established a considerable force of mercenaries and also used the money to bribe a large number of Greeks to turn traitor to their native lands ...

Note

1. *In comparison, the Athenians in 425/4 made the (probably dubious) claim that they collected 1,460 talents in contributions from about 400 cities.*

 There is a link to Philip's coinage in WEB **38.21**.

Questions

1. Compare the phalanx formation to that of the hoplites (**8.2–3**). How were they similar and how did they differ from each other?
2. What were the phalanx's vulnerable points?
3. Did the Macedonians benefit from Philip's use of gold (**38.3.B**)?

38.4 Philip's Court: Companions and Royal Boys (Pages)

Philip gained his nobles' support by giving them land, gifts, commands, and royal posts. Land grants also won him the friendship and services of Greek and Thessalian families. His court in Pella was the political, social, and cultural center of the kingdom. Greeks and barbarians came there as envoys, friends, or seekers of employment and patronage. The fourth-century historian Theopompus of Chios described Philip's court in his universal history entitled *History of Philip* (also known as *Philippica*), which centered on Philip and which survives only in fragments. Theopompus depicted the king negatively, explaining his success as due to the Greeks' moral decline. Accordingly, his description of Philip's court

appealed to the Greeks' disapproval of heavy drinking and homosexual relationships between male adults. The Macedonian elite, however, subscribed to
different protocols. Polybius, the source of the Theopompus fragment, cites the
author as an example of historians who write with bias about kings.

38.4.A   Philip's Companions

Polybius 8.9.1–13 (Theopompus *FGrHist* 115 FF 27, 225a)

(**8.9.1**) On this one might level criticism at Theopompus more than anyone. He states at the beginning of his history of Philip that what most induced him to undertake the enterprise was the fact that
Europe had never produced anyone who was at all comparable with Philip son of Amyntas.[1] (**9.2**)
And yet right after this, in his introduction, and throughout his history, he shows Philip to be completely lacking in self-control as regards women, to the point of doing his best to ruin his own household by his flamboyant passions.[2] (**9.3**) He then reveals the king as being unprincipled and mischievous
in his treatment of friends and allies; as one who had subjugated and outfoxed many cities by duplicity and force; (**9.4**) and as one so passionately fond of drink as to be often seen by his friends clearly
inebriated even in the daytime. (**9.5**) Anyone wishing to read the beginning of Theopompus' 49th
book will be thoroughly shocked by the writer's eccentricities. Amongst other things he has pre-
sumed to make the following statement (I have cited the passage verbatim):

(**9.6**) "Those amongst the Greeks and barbarians who were depraved and shameless in character would
all flock to Macedonia to Philip's court, where they were saluted as 'the king's companions.' (**9.7**) For
Philip for the most part rejected men of good character who took care of their own property, and showed
regard for, and promoted, wastrels and men who spent their lives drinking and dicing. (**9.8**) He not only
supported them in these activities but actually made them into virtuosos in all sorts of iniquitous and
repulsive behavior. (**9.9**) Of disgusting or degrading qualities they lacked none, and of good and upright
qualities they possessed none. Some of them spent their time shaving and making their bodies soft, men
though they were, and others shamelessly had sex with each other despite being bearded. (**9.10**) They
would go around with two or three of their 'boyfriends,' but would themselves also provide the others
with the same services as these provided to them. (**9.11**) So one would have been right in supposing
these to be not *hetairoi* [companions] but *hetaerai* [prostitutes], and in calling them not soldiers but rent-
boys. (**9.12**) Their nature was to be killers of men [*androphonoi*], but in practice they were whores of men
[*andropornoi*]. (**9.13**) Let me put it simply and stop going on at length (says Theopompus), especially
since I have so many matters to deal with. It is my opinion that the so-called friends and companions of
Philip were worse animals, and worse in character, than the Centaurs that inhabited Pelion, the
Lystrygonians living on the plain of Leontini, or any other beasts you care to think of."[3]

Notes

1. *Polybius' criticism of Theopompus was perhaps unwarranted, because Theopompus' statement about
   Philip's singularity is ambivalent.*
2. *The reference is probably to the circumstances attending Philip's death (**38.19**).*
3. *The Centaurs were mythological creatures who were part human, part horse, and were known for their
   uncivilized way of life and unbridled conduct. The Lystrygonians were cannibal giants who killed many
   of Odysseus' sailors.*

Young sons of important local families served as the king's Royal Boys, or Pages (*paides basilikoi*). They were educated with the royal children, attended to the king's personal needs, and may have been used as hostages to insure their families' loyalty. Quintus Curtius Rufus, a Roman historian of Alexander the Great, reports on the institution.

38.4.B   The Royal Boys or Pages

Q. Curtius Rufus 8.6.2–6

(**8.6.2**) As was observed above, it was customary for the Macedonian nobility to deliver their grown-up sons to their kings for the performance of duties that differed little from the tasks of slaves. (**6.3**) They would take turns spending the night on guard at the door of the king's bedchamber, and it was they who brought in his women by an entrance other than that watched by the armed guards. (**6.4**) They would also take his horses from the grooms and bring them for him to mount; they were his attendants both on the hunt and in battle, and were highly educated in all the liberal arts. (**6.5**) It was thought a special honor that they were allowed to sit and eat with the king. No one, apart from the king himself, had the authority to flog them. (**6.6**) This company served the Macedonians as a kind of seminary for their officers and generals, and from it subsequently came the kings whose descendants were many generations later stripped of power by the Romans.

Questions

1. How did Philip control his Companions, according to Theopompus (**38.4.A**)?
2. Describe Philip's court without Theopompus' moral judgments (**38.4.A**).
3. What duties did the nobles' sons owe the king? Do these duties explain their education in military and administrative leadership (**38.4.B**)? If so, how?

38.5   Philip's Wives

While the institution of the Royal Boys served to foster ties at home, Philip used marriages to cement alliances abroad. The third-century literary scholar Satyrus listed all of Philip's wives. In the Macedonian polygamist's court, the queen was the woman who gave birth to the crown prince. In Philip's case this was Olympias of Molossia, Epirus, the mother of Alexander (III, the Great). Satyrus' report belies his own statement that Philip's marriages were always connected to his military campaigns. The dates of Philip's marriages, some of which are insecure, are: Phila (359/8), Audata (359/8), Philinna (358), Olympias (357), Nicesipolis (353), Meda (352), and Cleopatra (337).

Athenaeus *Learned Conversationalists at Table* (*Deipnosophistae*) 13.557b–e

(**13.557b**) …Philip had a new wedding with every campaign. In his *Life of Philip* Satyrus states: "In the twenty-two years of his rule (**557c**) Philip married the Illyrian Audata, by whom he had a daughter, Cynnane (?), and he also married Phila, sister of Derdas and Machatas. Then, since he wished to extend his realm to include the Thessalian nation, he had children by two Thessalian women, Nicesipolis of Pherae, who bore him Thessalonice, and Philinna of Larissa, by whom he produced Arrhidaeus. In addition, he took possession of the Molossian kingdom by marrying Olympias, by whom he had Alexander and Cleopatra, (**557d**) and when he took Thrace the Thracian king Cothelas came to him with his daughter Meda and many gifts. After marrying Meda, Philip also took her home to join Olympias as his second wife.

In addition to all these wives he also married Cleopatra, with whom he was in love; she was the daughter of Hippostratus and niece of Attalus. By bringing her home as yet another wife alongside Olympias he made a total shambles of his life. For straightaway, right at the wedding ceremony, Attalus remarked: 'Well, now we shall certainly see royalty born who are legitimate and not bastards.' Hearing this, Alexander hurled the cup he had in his hands at Attalus, and Attalus in turn hurled his goblet at Alexander. (**557e**) After that Olympias took refuge with the Molossians and Alexander with the Illyrians, and Cleopatra presented Philip with a daughter who was called Europa."

Philip's Family

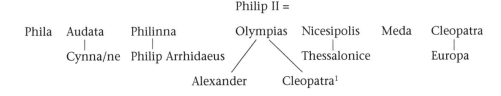

Note

1. *Scholars disagree on whether Philip fathered a son named Caranus from Cleopatra or from another woman.*

Question

1. Reconstruct the network of Philip's alliances through his marriages.

38.6   Philip and the Third Sacred War (356–346)

What brought Philip to central Greece and eventually made him ruler of Greece were the Third and Fourth Sacred Wars.

During the 360s Delphi supported Sparta in its conflict with Thebes. In the 350s Thebes encouraged the Amphictyonic league of states connected to the oracle of Apollo at Delphi to charge Phocis (where Delphi was located) with sacrilege for cultivating land sacred to Apollo and to fine it. The charge was hardly new, but the Phocian reaction was novel. In 356 the Phocian general Philomelus occupied Delphi, obtained the support of Thebes' enemies, and built up a mercenary army. The affair escalated into an all-Greek conflict. On the one side stood Thebes, Thessaly, East Locrian communities, and other Greeks representing the Amphictyonic league. On the other side were Phocis and Thebes' adversaries, namely, Athens and Sparta, which was also charged and fined by the Amphictyonians for sacrilege. In 354/3, Philomelus took the unprecedented action of using Delphi's sacred treasures to finance his war.

38.6.A   The Phocians Pillage Delphi

Diodorus of Sicily 16.30.1–2

(**16.30.1**) It became clear that the Boeotians were going to fight the Phocians with a mighty force, and Philomelus decided to muster a large number of mercenaries. But the war called for greater expenditure, and he was obliged to lay his hands on the dedicatory offerings and pillage the oracle.[1] He increased the pay for his mercenaries by half as much again, and so a large number swiftly came together, many of them responding to the call to arms simply because of the size of the pay. (**30.2**) Out of respect for the gods, no right-minded man signed up for the campaign, but the worst scoundrels and men who, because of their greed, had only contempt for the gods eagerly joined Philomelus, so that a strong force of men bent on plundering the temple was quickly assembled…

Note

1. *Elsewhere Diodorus exonerates Philomelus of the sacrilege (16.56.5), but the present version seems preferable.*

Philomelus was victorious against the Amphictyonic coalition, but in 354 he was defeated by the Thebans and took his own life. He was replaced by Onomarchus, who continued to use the sacred treasures and was as successful a general and diplomat as his predecessor. Onomarchus defeated the Boeotians, the Locrians, and then Philip, who in 353 came to help his Thessalian friends in the war. The king, however, recovered and in 352 returned to Thessaly where he was apparently elected as archon of the Thessalian League. Philip then met Onomarchus in the Battle of the Crocus Field off the Gulf of Pegasae. He won the battle, and although Athens saved Phocis from Macedonian conquest, Philip made significant gains. He now controlled Thessaly and its excellent cavalry, earning the status of a champion of a sacred cause and a legitimate player in Greek affairs.

   We have two accounts of this battle, one by Diodorus and the other by the late Roman epitomist Justin, who stresses the religious character of Philip's position and campaign. See WEB **38.7** for Justin's account of the Battle of the Crocus Field. The following is Diodorus' account.

38.6.B   Diodorus on the Battle of the Crocus Field

Diodorus of Sicily 16.35.3–6

(**16.35.3**) Later Philip retired to Macedonia, and Onomarchus launched a campaign against Boeotia, defeating the Boeotians in battle and taking the city of Coronea. In Thessaly, Philip, who had recently arrived with his army from Macedonia, opened hostilities against Lycophron, the tyrant of Pherae. (**35.4**) Being no match for Philip in the field, Lycophron sent for support from his allies the Phocians, promising in return to join the Phocians in effecting a political reorganization of all Thessaly; and Onomarchus swiftly came to his assistance with 20,000 infantry and 5,000 cavalry. Philip therefore persuaded the Thessalians to take up the war along with him, and he brought together a total of more than 20,000 infantry and 3,000 cavalry.

(**35.5**) There was a hard-fought battle, from which Philip emerged as victor thanks to Thessalian superiority in cavalry numbers and in courage. Onomarchus fled toward the sea, and it so happened that the Athenian Chares was coasting by with a large number of triremes.[1] The result was a massacre of the Phocians. This was because the fugitives stripped off their armor and tried to swim to the triremes, Onomarchus being one of them. (**35.6**) In the end more than 6,000 Phocians and mercenaries were killed, including the general himself, and no fewer than 3,000 were taken prisoner. Philip hanged Onomarchus, and hurled the others into the sea as men guilty of sacrilege.[2]

Notes

1. *It is likely that Chares came to help the Phocians rather than by accident.*
2. *The sources provide different accounts about Onomarchus' death, including that he died at the hands of his troops. If the "general" killed was Onomarchus, Philip might have punished his corpse.*

Questions

1. How did the Phocian Philomelus' use of money (**38.6.A**) resemble or differ from Philip's use of gold (**38.3.B**)?
2. What does Justin's account of the Battle of the Crocus Field (WEB **38.7**)
   add to Diodorus' description of the battle (**38.6.B**)?

38.8   Demosthenes' War Plan Against Philip (352/1)

In spite of Philip's military operations in northern and central Greece in the late 350s, neither he nor Athens were interested in fighting each other. The orator Demosthenes, however, thought that Athens should confront the king and, starting from 352/1, he tried to persuade the Athenians that Philip was a threat. His calls remained unheeded until the late 340s. The Athenians did not regard Philip as a viable danger, and Eubulus, who administered the city's affairs through his control of the Theoric Fund (cf. **35.11**), approved of military operations only when they were financially feasible or did not impact the quality of life at home.

The extant assembly and court speeches of Demosthenes provide valuable information about both Philip's actions and Athens' reactions. In his assembly speech titled the *First Philippic*, delivered in 352/1, Demosthenes encourages the Athenians to fight Philip and upbraids them for their apathy. His portrayal of the citizens as indolent and reluctant to act, however, was not always warranted. He criticized the city for making grand albeit futile plans to employ large numbers of mercenaries instead of citizens, yet the expeditionary force he envisioned consisted of only 25 percent citizens, with mercenaries making up the rest. Athenian citizens still answered the call to service, but there was a growing reliance on mercenaries, who were in abundant supply. Demosthenes offered to pay them two obols per day. Mercenaries' wages varied considerably, but this offer was clearly on the lower scale, hence, Demosthenes' suggestion that they supplement their wages with plunder. The Athenians, however, did not endorse his plan.

Demosthenes 4 *First Philippic* 8, 16–17, 19–26, 28–29

(**8**) Indeed, do not imagine that Philip's present power is immutably fixed, like divine power. No, even amongst those who seem to be on very good terms with him, men of Athens, there are some who hate him, fear him, and envy him. You must understand that all the reactions to him found in other men are also present in those who are around him. But all these emotions remain subdued at the moment: because of your apathy and idleness – which, I maintain, you should now cast off – they have no way out.

(**16**) First, Men of Athens, I say we must fit out fifty triremes. Then I say you must resolve to board them and sail them yourselves if needs be. In addition, I urge you to make ready cavalry-transports and freighters to accommodate half our cavalry. (**17**) These measures must be taken, I think, to counter the lightning attacks he makes from Macedonia against Thermopylae, the Chersonese, Olynthus, and anywhere else he wants to go …

(**19**) …But more important than this, Men of Athens, I say you should mobilize a force to maintain continuous operations that do him damage. Do not talk to me about ten or twenty thousand mercenaries, or about those huge forces that exist only on paper! I am talking about a force from our city, one that will obey and follow its leader – whether you choose a single general or more, or whether it be one particular individual or anyone else. I further urge you to provide the upkeep for this force. (**20**) What kind of force will it be, and of what size? Whence will come its upkeep, and how will it be made ready to discharge these duties? I shall explain, going into each of these questions individually. I am talking about mercenaries now, and about how you should avoid what has often done you harm in the past – thinking that everything falls short of what is needed and so opting with your decrees for the greatest projects, but then failing to take even the smallest steps to put them into effect. Instead, you must take those smallest steps and make due provision for them, adding further resources if they seem to fall short. (**21**) My suggestion is that the troops should total 2,000 men, and that of these 500 should be Athenian. They should be of any age that seems to you appropriate, and should serve for a prescribed period of time, not a long one but just for as long as you think sufficient, in successive tours of duty.

The others, I propose, should be mercenaries. Alongside these there should be 200 cavalry, at least 50 being Athenian, thus preserving on campaign the same ratio as there will be in the infantry.[1] These should also have cavalry-carrying vessels. (22) Right, then – so what else? Ten swift triremes; for since Philip has a fleet we need speedy triremes so that the force can be secure when under sail. And where is their maintenance to come from? That, too, I shall explain and illustrate after I tell you why I think a force of such a size to be sufficient, and why I recommend that citizens serve in it.

(23) This is why I specify these dimensions, Men of Athens: we do not at present have the capability to raise a force that could face him in battle. Instead, we must play the pirate and apply such tactics to the early stages of our fight with him. Accordingly the force should not be overlarge – we can afford neither the pay nor the support for that – nor yet should it be completely wretched. (24) The reasoning behind my recommendation that citizens be present to take part in the expedition is this. I am told that in earlier days the city maintained in Corinth a mercenary force that Polystratus, Iphicrates, Chabrias, and some others commanded, and that you yourselves served in it.[2] And I know from what I have been told that these mercenaries fought alongside you, and you alongside them, and defeated the Spartans. However, ever since mercenary forces on their own have been fighting for you, they have been defeating only your friends and allies, while your enemies have gained more power than they should have. They take a nonchalant look at the war assigned to them by the city and then choose rather to go sailing off to Artabazus or anywhere else, with their general understandably following – for he cannot command them unless he provides their pay.[3]

(25) What do I propose, then? That you deprive both general and soldiers of their pretexts for doing this by providing them with pay and also by setting alongside them some home-grown soldiers to keep an eye on them. For the way we run things now is ridiculous. Should someone ask, "Men of Athens, do you have peace?" the reply would be, "Of course we don't – we are fighting a war with Philip." (26) But have you not been electing from your number ten battalion commanders [*taxiarchs*], ten generals, ten squadron commanders [*phylarchs*], and two cavalry commanders? So what are these men doing? Apart from the one man that you send out to the war, the rest are organizing religious processions alongside the public sacrificers [*hieropoioi*]. Just like those who fashion clay figurines, you are electing your battalion commanders and squadron commanders for the marketplace, not the war.

(28) …Now for the finances. There is upkeep, just the provision of food, which for this force is 90 talents and a bit more. Forty talents will be needed for the swift triremes (twenty minas a month per ship); another forty for two thousand infantrymen, so that each soldier can get ten drachmas a month as a provision-allowance; and twelve talents for the two hundred cavalry, if each man is to get thirty drachmas a month. (29) If anyone thinks that providing supplies for men on active service is a trifling investment, he is mistaken. I know full well that, if this is enacted, the army will itself provide everything else from the proceeds of the war, making up the pay without causing loss to any of the Greeks or the allies. I am willing to join the expedition and am ready to suffer any penalty if this turns out not to be the case…

Notes

1. *Unlike mercenaries, citizen soldiers saved the state their wages, but they could serve only for limited periods, hence the need to rotate them.*
2. *For Iphicrates' victory near Lechaeum (390), see **31.10** ("Peltasts and the Battle of Lechaeum"). Chabrias defeated a Spartan navy in 376, and Polystratus' victory is unknown.*
3. *Artabazus, son of Pharnabazus, was a satrap in Asia Minor who rebelled against the Persian king. Demosthenes refers to the Athenian generals' need to finance their underfunded expeditions, here by hiring themselves as mercenaries for Artabazus; cf. **35.12** ("Financing Military Operations").*

Questions

1. How did Demosthenes plan to fight Philip? What constraints framed his plan?
2. How did Athens' methods of financing campaigns (**35.9**: "Liturgies," **35.12**: "Financing Military Operations") affect Demosthenes' view of the struggle with Macedonia?

38.9 Philip's Capture of Olynthus (348)

Since 432, much of Chalcidice was organized as a federal state centered on the city of Olynthus. The federation was dissolved or greatly weakened by Sparta in 379, but came back to life in the 360s. The Chalcidians' major adversaries were Macedonia and Athens, and when these states were in conflict the Chalcidians had to pick sides. In 352, fear of Philip's growing power as well as disagreements within the Chalcidian federation led to a change in its alliance from Philip to Athens and later to supporting pretenders to the Macedonian throne. In response, Philip declared war on Olynthus in 349. The city requested aid from Athens, and in spite of Demosthenes' best efforts in what are known as his Olynthiac speeches, Athens' help came too little and too late. The Athenians were more concerned at that time about the island of Euboea, which was nearer and where they fought to maintain their influence against hostile local leaders. Thus Philip was able to beseige Olynthus and capture it in the autumn of 348.

38.9.A   Philip's Capture of Olynthus

Diodorus of Sicily 16.53.2–3

(**16.53.2**) In this period [348/7] Philip was eager to conquer the cities on the Hellespont, and took Mecyberna and Torone through betrayal and without running any risk.[1] He then embarked on a campaign, with a large force, against Olynthus, the greatest of the cities in that area. He initially bested the Olynthians in two engagements and hemmed them in under siege; but while launching a series of attacks on them he lost large numbers of men in battles at the walls. In the end he bribed Euthycrates and Lasthenes, the two foremost Olynthians,[2] and took Olynthus after it was betrayed to him through their agency.

(**53.3**) Philip pillaged the city, enslaved its inhabitants, and sold them off. After doing this he found himself with a lot of money to carry on the war, and he also struck fear into the other states that were opposing him. He rewarded those soldiers who had fought bravely in battle with appropriate prizes and he also distributed largesse to the powerful men in the various cities, thereby providing himself with many men ready to betray their own. And he would himself declare that he had expanded his kingdom by means of gold far more than by arms.

Notes

1. *Mecyberna was the harbor of Olynthus. Torone was located on Sithonia in Chalcidice.*
2. *Euthycrates and Lasthenes were two cavalry commanders who defected with their cavalry to Philip. Their betrayal became notorious.*

In WEB **38.10**, Demosthenes makes use of Olynthus' destruction and a story about the abuse of a captive Olynthian woman to attack a political rival.

The tragedy of Olynthus turned out to be a blessing in disguise for excavators. Archaeologists have found in Olynthus sling bullets and arrowheads, some of which bear the name of Philip or of his generals. More importantly, because the city was resettled only in a sporadic way, it has become a primary archaeological source for Greek town planning, private houses, and public buildings in the Classical era. Of course, not all Greek houses looked alike but responded to the specific character of their environment.

38.9.B   Plan of an Olynthian House

The "House of Many Colors," which owes its name to its painted and colored stucco walls, belongs to a common Classical type called the pastas (or portico) house (Figure 38.2, p. 536). Two vertical and horizontal axes divide the house plan almost equally. The house occupies a plot 17 meters by 17 meters. At its center is the courtyard, made up partly of earth floor (l) and partly of cobblestones (i). It served as the main entrance and illuminated the adjacent rooms, although privacy was attained in general at the expense of light. A square altar is built on the court's west side. The pastas (e) was an additional open space. Rooms (c), (d), (f), and (j) had earth floors. The other rooms had cement floors with a mosaic in room (f), and a central mosaic apparently embedded in the floor of a shallow pool in room (d), which probably served as the *andron* (men's dining room). Room (a) was used for manufacturing and coloring woven fabric. Other Greek houses also included commercial production as part of the household economy. Room (h) operated as the kitchen. The use of the rooms was not fixed but changed according to the needs of the family and seasons of the year.

For more information and images of ancient Olynthus, see a link in WEB **38.21**.

Questions

1. Why did Philip treat Olynthus as he did?
2. To what extent does Demosthenes' description of the party in Macedonia (WEB **38.10**) resemble Theopompus of Chios' account of the Macedonian court (**38.4.A**)? What moral values do both descriptions appeal to?

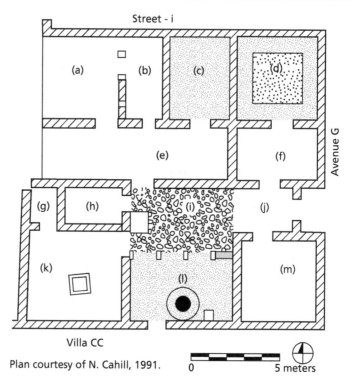

Figure 38.2 Plan of an Olynthian house. © Nick Cahill. Reprinted with kind permission of the author.

3. Try to map the domestic activities described by Lysias in his speech concerning the killing of an adulterer (**37.12.D**: "The Killing of Eratosthenes") in the space of the Olynthian house (Figure 38.2).

38.11 The Peace of Philocrates and the End of the Third Sacred War (346)

Philip's gains in the Sacred War and Olynthus and his expressed desire to repair his relationship with Athens led to a peace initiative in Athens. After two Athenian embassies, which included the rival politicians Demosthenes and Aeschines, had gone to Macedonia and come back, a third embassy, this time without Demosthenes and Aeschines, went to inform Philip, now in central Greece, about the latest Athenian resolution. (For the resolution, see Demosthenes in WEB **38.12.I**, which also describes the background to the Peace of Philocrates and the difficulties faced in reaching it.) When the embassy discovered that Phocis had surrendered to Philip, however, it returned home. The frightened Athenians thought that Philip was about to march on their city and began preparing for a siege. But Philip had no such intention. Instead, he convened the Amphictyonic council to decide how to end the war.

The Peace of Philocrates, named after one of its Athenian proponents, concluded the war and generally confirmed that Athens and Philip would keep what they already held. However, the agreement favored Philip, who gained control over the Amphictyonic council through his and the Thessalian votes, while his opponents and even allies fared much worse. Phocis was ordered to be dissolved, and Athens failed to defend its mainland allies, including Halos. Thebes got very little for its prolonged conflict with Phocis. Philip was arguably now the strongest man in Greece. The following is Diodorus' account of the Amphictyonic decision that ended the Sacred War.

Diodorus of Sicily 16.59.4–60.5

(**16.59.4**) Contrary to his expectations, the king had finished off the sacred war without a battle, and he held a council meeting with the Boeotians and Thessalians. He then decided to bring together the council of the Amphictyonies and leave to that body the decision on all matters in question.

(**60.1**) The council members accordingly decided to make Philip and his descendants members of the Amphictyonic League, holding the two votes that the Phocians held before their defeat. They further ordered that the walls of the three cities in the hands of the Phocians be removed, that the Phocians should have no association with the shrine or the Amphictyonic League, and that they should have no right to acquire either horses or weapons until they paid back the god the amount of money they had plundered.[1] Further, those Phocians who had fled, and all others who had participated in the looting of the shrine, were everywhere to be under a curse and outlawed, and (**60.2**) all the cities of the Phocians were to be razed to the ground and their populations transferred to villages. Each village was to have no more than fifty houses, and the villages were to be no less than a stade's distance from each other. The Phocians would keep their lands and every year bring to the god sixty talents in tribute, until they paid off the amount of cash officially registered in the shrine at the time of its desecration. In addition, Philip was to put on the Pythian Games, along with the Boeotians and Thessalians, because the Corinthians had joined the Phocians in their religious transgression.[2] (**60.3**) The members of the Amphictyonic League and Philip were to smash the weapons of the Phocians and their mercenaries on rocks, burning the remnants of them, and to sell off their horses. In conformity with these decisions, the members of the Amphictyonic League formulated regulations for the care of the oracle and all other matters pertaining to religious observance, the common peace, and the harmony of the Greek world.

(**60.4**) After that, when he had assisted the Amphictyonic League in carrying out its resolutions and shown kindness to all, Philip went back to Macedonia, having now not merely acquired a reputation for godliness and excellence as a commander, but also having laid down a solid groundwork for the greatness that he was to achieve. (**60.5**) For he dearly wished to be appointed the commander-in-chief [*strategos autokrator*] of Greece and to embark upon the war against Persia, something that was going to come about ...

Notes

1. *The plundered money was estimated at ca. 10,000 talents, which the Phocians repaid over the years in varied annual installments starting with sixty talents down to ten in the mid-330s.*
2. *It appears that Corinth lost its votes or privileges in the Amphictyonic League. The Spartans too were expelled from it.*

Philip's clear prominence put him in Isocrates' sights. In 346, the ninety-year-old Athenian author tailored his plan to save and unify Greece through a war on Persia to fit the Macedonian king. It is uncertain, however, that Philip seriously entertained the idea of a Persian campaign at this time. See WEB **38.12.II** for Isocrates' appeal to Philip to lead a Persian campaign by virtue of his Heraclid ancestry.

Questions

1. What were Philip's constraints in signing the peace, according to Demosthenes (WEB **38.12.I**)?
2. How was Phocis punished for its sacrilege, and what did Philip gain from the Amphictyonic settlement (**38.11**)?
3. Why, according to Isocrates, should Philip go to war against Persia (WEB **38.12.II**)?

38.13   Athens Proclaims War on Philip (340)

Dissatisfaction with the Peace of Philocrates soon emerged in Athens, which politicians tried to use to get rid of their rivals. In 343 Demosthenes prosecuted Aeschines for his conduct as an envoy to Philip, and Aeschines was acquitted by a small majority. Philocrates, the man most associated with the peace, was convicted the same year in an impeachment trial (*eisangelia*) and went into exile. Demosthenes also intensified his calls to confront Philip (see WEB **38.14.I**).

Philip was busy consolidating his power both at home and abroad. In 340 he attacked the city of Perinthus on the Propontis. Perinthus received aid from the Persians and from the city of Byzantium. The Byzantine intervention led Philip to put this city under siege too, and Athens sent a navy to help Byzantium. See WEB **38.14.II** for Philip's siege of Perinthus, which shows advancement in siege warfare, and for the Byzantine and Persian aid to the city.

The Athenian fleet to Byzantium, under the command of Chares, anchored at Hieron on the Asian coast north of Byzantium in order to protect a large number of merchant ships sailing from the Bosporus to the Aegean. Philip, however, took advantage of Chares' departure for a meeting with Persian satraps and captured the merchant ships. The blow to Athenian imports and manpower enabled Demosthenes to persuade the Athenian assembly to declare war on Philip. We learn of these events from the fourth-century historians Philochorus and Theopompus. They are cited by the first-century Alexandrian scholar Didymus in his commentary on Demosthenes' speeches, and by the literary critic and historian of Augustus' time, Dionysus of Halicarnassus. In 339, Philip pulled his forces out of both Perinthus and Byzantium.

38.13.A   Philip Seizes Ships to Athens

[Demosthenes] 11.1; Didymus *Demosthenes* 10.34–11.5 = Theopompus *FGrHist* 115 F 292; Philochorus *FGrHist* 328 F 162 = Harding no. 95B

[Demosthenes] 11.1: "It has become clear to you, Men of Athens, that Philip did not establish peace with this but merely postponed the war."

Didymus: The war the Athenians fought against the Macedonian was kindled ... all the other transgressions of Philip against the Athenians while he feigned to be observing the peace, and most of all his campaign against Byzantium and Perinthus. He was eager to have these cities on his side for two reasons: to eliminate the Athenian grain supply, and to prevent the Athenians from having cities on the coast for their fleet and from possessing in advance operational bases and places of refuge for the war against him. He then brought off his most lawless action: he seized the ships of the traders at Hieron. In Philochorus' account, these numbered 230, but in Theopompus' 180; and from the ships he raised a total of 700 talents. According to other sources, and Philochorus in particular, these events took place in the archonship of Theophrastus [340/39], whose term followed that of Nichomachus. Philochorus' account runs as follows:

"Chares went off to a meeting of the commanders of the Persian king and left ships at Hieron to gather up the freighters from the Pontus. When Philip saw that Chares was no longer there, he initially tried to send ships to seize the freighters, but, unable to take them by force, he shipped troops over to Hieron and took possession of the freighters there."

38.13.B   Philip and Athens Go to War

Dionysus of Halicarnasus *To Ammaeus* 1.741F. = Philochorus *FGrHist* 328 F 56a = Harding no. 96A

The two sides went to war with each claiming to have been wronged by the other. Philochorus, in his *Attica* Book Six, is very precise in his account of the reasons for this, as he is concerning the time at which they broke the peace, and I shall cite the most important elements from this work.

Theophrastus of Halae. It was during his archonship [340/39] that Philip first sailed up and attacked Perinthus. Failing in that venture, he next blockaded Byzantium, bringing up siege-engines.

Philochorus then goes through all the charges Philip leveled against the Athenians in the letter, and adds the following (which I quote verbatim): "After they heard the letter and Demosthenes inciting them to war and proposing decrees, the people voted to tear down the stele that had been erected commemorating the peace and alliance with Philip, to man their ships, and put all other war measures into effect."

Questions

1. Why did Philip attack Perinthus and Byzantium, according to Didymus (**38.13.A**)?
2. According to Demosthenes, what were the arguments for peace in Athens, what stood behind them, and why should they be rejected (WEB **38.14.I**)?
3. What were Philip's tactics and instruments of war in the siege of Perinthus (WEB **38.14.II**)?

38.15   The Battle of Chaeronea (338)

What led Philip back to central Greece and eventually to the decisive battlefield of Chaeronea was the Fourth Sacred War of 340/39. Following an Amphictyonic invitation to fight Locrian Amphissa, Philip came with his army and occupied Elatea in Phocis. This was perceived as a threat both in Boeotia and in Attica. See WEB **38.16.I** for Philip's capture of Elatea and the reaction to it in Athens.

Demosthenes recommended forming an alliance with Thebes against Philip. He went to Thebes with nine other envoys and had not only to compete against Philip's offer of an alliance, but also to overcome the mutual animosity that frequently characterized the relationship between the two states. Demosthenes regarded (and presented) his success in forming an alliance with Thebes as a crowning achievement, but it came at a price. Athens promised to help Thebes secure its rule over Boeotia, pay for two thirds of the expenses of the coalition army and all the expenses of the joint navy, and give seniority in command to the Thebans.

Following intensive diplomatic activity and small-scale military operations, including Philip's punishment of Amphissa for its sacrilege, the two sides faced each other on the battlefield of Chaeronea in Boeotia in early August 338. On one side were Philip and his allies, and on the other forces from Boeotia, Athens, Euboea, Megara, Corinth, Achaea, Leucas, and Corcyra. Chaeronea is considered one of the most decisive battles in Greek history. For many modern historians it marks the end of the Classical Age and the beginning of the Hellenistic Age when the Greek poleis of the mainland lost much of their independence. It is unfortunate, however, that we are not well informed about the fighting. The two chief sources for the battle are Diodorus of Sicily and the second-century CE Macedonian author Polyaenus, who wrote a didactic military work entitled *Strategmata* (stratagems). Diodorus commences his description of the battle following a report that Philip failed to convince the Boeotians to move to his side.

38.15.A   Diodorus on the Battle of Chaeronea

Diodorus of Sicily 16.85.5–86.6

(**18.85.5**) After this Philip failed to gain an alliance with the Boeotians; even so, he decided to take on the fight against both of them [i.e., the Boeotians and the Athenians]. After waiting for the latecomers of his allies to arrive, he came into Boeotia at the head of more than 30,000 infantry and no fewer than 2,000 horse.[1] (**85.6**) Both sides were ready for battle, both were psychologically prepared and full of spirit, and both were the other's equal in courage; but it was the king who had the edge in numbers and leadership qualities. (**85.7**) Having fought many different kinds of battle, emerging victorious from most encounters, he had extensive experience in the conduct of warfare. On the Athenian side the finest commanders were dead – Iphicrates and Chabrias, and Timotheus as well – and of those remaining the best was Chares, who was in no way superior to your ordinary, run-of-the-mill officers in terms of action and judgment in military leadership.

(**86.1**) The two forces were drawn up at break of day. On one of the wings the king stationed his son Alexander, in years just a boy, but distinguished for courage and speed in action, and he set beside him his most outstanding officers. Philip himself took charge of the other wing, keeping with him his elite troops, and the other squadrons he deployed in order as circumstances dictated. (**86.2**) The Athenians arranged their line-division by nationality, giving one part to the Boeotians and themselves assuming command of the rest. The battle was hard fought for a long time, with large numbers falling on both sides, and for a while the struggle still offered both sides hope of victory.

(**86.3**) Alexander, however, was eager to demonstrate his personal courage to his father, and he did not lay aside his overpowering greed for glory. With many of his brave soldiers fighting alongside him, he first of all breached the dense front of the enemy line and, felling large numbers, put heavy pressure on the troops ranged against him. (**86.4**) Since his companions did the same, the enemy front was repeatedly being broken. As the pile of bodies kept rising, Alexander, ahead of the others, forced his way through and drove back the enemy. After this, the king himself came to the forefront of the battle, refusing to concede credit for the victory even to Alexander. First of all he thrust back those deployed in front of him, and then, by also forcing them to take flight, he became the author of the victory. (**86.5**) Of the Athenians more than a thousand fell in battle, and no fewer than two thousand were taken prisoner. (**86.6**) Many of the Boeotians, too, were killed, and not a few were captured. After the battle Philip erected a trophy and gave up the bodies for burial. Then he offered victory sacrifices to the gods and made appropriate awards to those who had performed valiantly.

Note

1. *The size of the army that opposed Philip is uncertain. In addition to citizen troops, it included between 10,000 and 15,000 mercenaries and 1,000–2,000 cavalry. Scholars estimate their totals at between 30,000 and 35,000 men.*

38.15.B   Polyaenus on the Battle of Chaeronea

Polyaenus *Stratagems* 4.2.2, 4.2.7

(**4.2.2**) Drawn up against the Athenians at Chaeronea, Philip was retreating and giving ground before them when Stratocles the Athenian commander shouted out, "We must not stop piling on the pressure until we bottle up the enemy in Macedonia," and he would not halt his pursuit.

"The Athenians do not know how to win," said Philip, and he gave ground gradually, keeping the phalanx in tight formation, and sheltered by shields. In a short time he gained some higher ground and, encouraging the rank and file, he turned and vigorously attacked the Athenians. And after putting up a superb fight he won the victory.

(**4.2.7**) At Chaeronea Philip was aware that the Athenians were hotheaded and poorly trained, while the Macedonians were disciplined and well trained. He therefore drew out the battle, swiftly sapping the Athenians' strength and making them easy to defeat.

38.15.C   Plutarch on the Battle of Chaeronea

Plutarch reports on Alexander's role in the attack in his biography of the king.

Plutarch *Alexander* 9.2

Alexander was also present at Chaeronea and took part in the battle against the Greeks, and it is said that it was he who was the first to burst into the Sacred Band of the Thebans. Even down to our time they show near the Cephisus River an old oak, called "Alexander's Oak," near which he encamped on that occasion, and not far from it is the communal grave of the Macedonians.

38.15.D   Reconstructing the Battle

Scholars have offered different reconstructions of the battle and the positions of the opposing sides. One suggestion is that Philip commanded the Macedonian right wing and Alexander the left. At first Philip approached the enemy with his line at an oblique angle, but when the enemy attacked he feigned a retreat (see Polyaenus above). This provoked the Athenians into pursuit, which created a gap in the Greek front, and which Alexander exploited when he charged the Thebans at the head of the Macedonian cavalry. At about the same time, Philip reversed to attack the Athenians, and he and Alexander (now on foot fighting

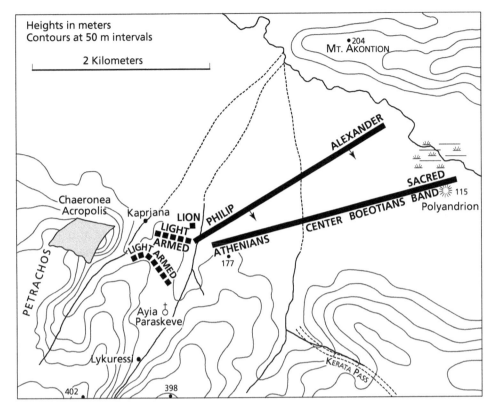

Figure 38.3
Plan of the battle of Chaeronea. From *Macedonian State* by N.G.L. Hammond (Cambridge: Cambridge University Press, 1989), fig. 5, p. 117. Reprinted with permission of Cambridge University Press.

the Sacred Band) brought the battle to a conclusion. This is N.G.L. Hammond's reconstruction of the battle (1973, 534–557). See Figure 38.3.

It should be said, however, that no source mentions Alexander leading the cavalry into battle, or, as has been suggested, that he commanded the entire left-wing phalanx against the Sacred Band (Rahe 1981). An alternative view dissociates the monument of the Macedonian dead from the battle's reconstruction and positions the Thebans on the left against Philip (Ma 2008, 74). See WEB **38.16.II** for the likely Macedonian and Theban monuments commemorating the battle of Chaeronea. WEB **38.18** includes Demosthenes' eulogy of the Athenian dead of Chaeronea and his patriotic depiction of the battle.

Questions

1. What was the reaction in Athens to the news about Philip at Elatea, and what qualified Demosthenes to save the day? What did he do (WEB **38.16.I**)?
2. What advantages did Philip have over his opponents in Chaeronea (**38.15.A–C**)?

38.17   Philip and the Greeks after Chaeronea (338–336)

Following Chaeronea Philip moved to regulate his relationship with the Greeks and settle their affairs. He must now have been planning his campaign against Persia and hoped to encourage the Greeks to support it, or to prevent them from spoiling it. In general, Philip's hegemony over the Greeks was not oppressive. He treated each city-state or group of peoples on an individual basis, favoring some, punishing others, so that they would have little in common. For example, Athens was a well-fortified city with a strong navy that could be used against the Persians, so Philip gave back the Athenians their dead and prisoners-of-war without ransom and allowed them to retain some of their holdings in the Aegean. But he also forced Athens to give up her empire and territorial claims elsewhere and to become his friend and ally. His treatment of Thebes was very different. He allowed the city's Boeotian enemies, Plataea, Thespia, and Orchomenus, to rebuild and engineered a change in Thebes' government to a pro-Macedonian regime, placing a Macedonian garrison in the city's citadel of the Cadmea. The Greeks called this and other garrisons in Corinth, Ambracia, and later in Euboean Chalcis the "fetters of Greece." Philip did not wish to fight a second Chaeronea.

Most Greeks acknowledged Philip's supremacy, except for Sparta, which was punished with loss of territory. In early 337 Philip called a meeting in Corinth at which Greek representatives endorsed a common peace under his leadership. The result was the so-called League of Corinth.

38.17.A   The Corinthian League

Diodorus of Sicily 16.89.1–3

(16.89.1) In the archonship of Phrynichus at Athens [337/6], the Romans appointed as consuls Titus Manlius Torquatus and Publius Decius. It was during these men's terms of office that king Philip, swollen-headed from his victory at Chaeronea, and having now stunned the most famous city-states, began to aspire to becoming leader of all Greece. (89.2) He put out the word that he wanted to conduct a war against the Persians on behalf of the Greeks, and make them pay for their lawless treatment of the temples [under Xerxes], and by this he won their loyalty and good will. He showed kindness to everybody on the private as well as the public level, and to the city-states he made a show of wanting to discuss their interests.

(89.3) A general assembly was therefore brought together in Corinth, and there Philip discussed the war against Persia, holding out to them great hopes and thereby pushing the delegates to support a war. Finally, the Greeks chose him as a commander-in-chief [*strategos autokrator*] of Greece, and he proceeded to make large-scale preparations for the campaign against the Persians. He fixed the number of troops for each city to contribute to the alliance and then returned to Macedonia.

Two fragmentary inscriptions found in Athens tell more about the oath taken by the Greeks. The numerals next to the names in the second fragment may represent the number of votes each state had in the council.

38.17.B   The Greeks' Oath on a Common Peace

The Greeks' Oath *IG* II² 236 = Harding no. 99 = R&O no. 76

A

[Oath. I swear by Zeus, Ge (Earth), Helios (Sun), Pos]eidon, A[thena, Ares and by all gods and goddess]es. I shall abide [by the peace and shall not break] the treaty [(**5**)...] nor shall I bear weapons [to do harm against those who keep the oaths, neither by land] nor by sea. [And] I shall not capture [any city nor a fo]rt [nor a harbor in order to make w]ar, of any of those who participate (**10**) in the [peace] by any device [or plot; nor] shall I overthrow the kingdom of Ph[ilip and his descendant]s, not the [existing constitutions] in each state when they swore [the oaths regarding] the peace; (**15**) [nor shall I myself do anything] contrary to these [agreements nor] shall I allow any one else as far as it is [in my power. And if any one does anything] to breach [the agreements, I shall give aid] as requested by [those who are wronged], and I shall make war against (**20**) the one who transgresses [the common peace] as [resolved by the common Coun]cil [*synhedrion*] and the *hegemon*; and I shall not abandon [...]

B

[..] 5 [...] [The]ssalians: 5. ...]ans: 2. ...]iots: 1. [Samothracians and] Thasians: 2.] ... ans: 2. Ambraciot[s: 1 (?)].] ... f]rom Thrace and [...]. Phocians: 3. Locrians: 3. ... Oet]aeans and Malians and [Aenianians ... Ag]raeans and Dolopians: 5. ... Pe]rrhaebians: 2. Acynthu]s and Cephallenia: 3.

An assembly speech, whose attribution to Demosthenes is uncertain, includes charges against Alexander the Great for violating his agreement with the Greeks. Some of the charges refer to obligations under the treaty. Even if the treaty was with Alexander, it is likely that it was based on a former treaty with Philip. The speech and the above inscription show that the treaty resembled other common peace treaties that ordained the cessation of war and local autonomy under a hegemonic control. But the treaty with Alexander (and the one with Philip if its reconstruction above is correct) also differed from previous peaces in their insistence on preserving the status quo within the polis. It also provided a mechanism to enforce the peace.

38.17.C   Alexander's Treaty with the Greeks

[Demosthenes] 17 *On the Treaty with Alexander* 6, 8, 10, 15, 16, 19–20

(**6**) Such a situation cannot be permitted if you want to maintain justice; for there is an additional statement in the peace accords that anyone behaving as Alexander has behaved is to be treated as an enemy – and his country along with him – by all participants in the peace, and that these should all make war on him. So if we follow the terms of the treaty, we shall treat as an enemy the man who restored the exiles.

(**8**) Moreover, the treaty explicitly states at the beginning that the Greeks must be free and autonomous. So how is it not truly absurd that the statement that they be free and autonomous should stand at the head of the accords, while the man who led them into servitude is not regarded as having contravened our common accords? So, Men of Athens, if we are to stand by the accords and our oaths, and to take the just course that they require – as I just called on you to take – then it is incumbent on you to take up arms and launch a campaign, alongside those who are willing to join us, against those who have broken the treaty.

(**10**) I come now to another point of justice relating to the accords. There is a clause in them to the effect that any who subvert the constitutions that existed in the various states at the time when they took the oaths ratifying the peace treaty – these men are to be considered enemies by all participants in the treaty. Consider this, Men of Athens. The Achaeans in the Peloponnese had democratic governments, but the Macedonian has subverted the democracy in Pellene, driving out most of its citizens; and he has turned their property over to their slaves and installed Chaeron the wrestler as tyrant.

(**15**) But there's something even more ridiculous. Amongst the accords is the stipulation that members of the Council [*synedrion*] and those responsible for public safety are to insure that in the states that are signatories to the peace treaty there be no killings or banishment in contravention of the laws established in the cities. There are to be no confiscations of property, either, no redistribution of land, no canceling of debts, and no emancipation of slaves to promote revolution ...

(**16**) I will point out another violation of the treaty. It is stated that exiles are not permitted to make cities that are participants in the peace treaty their base of operations for an armed assault on any of the cities that are signatories to the treaty ...

(**19**) None of the Greeks is ever going to reproach you with having in any way breached the common accords; in fact, they will be thankful to you for having been the only people to point the finger at those guilty of doing this. And so you may be more certain of this fact, I shall merely touch upon some minor points relevant to the issue, though there is much that can be said.

It is stated in the agreement that all signatories to the peace treaty may sail the seas, with no one obstructing them or forcing a vessel to shore. Anyone contravening this is to be considered an enemy by the signatories to the peace. (**20**) Well, Men of Athens, you have very clearly observed such actions taken by the Macedonians ...

Figure 38.4
The Philippeum.
© Netfalls/
Shutterstock.

38.17.D   The Philippeum

In addition to regulating his relationship with the Greeks, Philip sought to enhance his stature among them. This was probably the purpose of his building the Philippeum at Olympia (Figure 38.4). This monument stood on what was prime real estate near the most popular entrance to the sanctuary of Olympia next to the Temple of Hera. It was a *tholos* building made of limestone and marble and consisting of a circular colonnade of eighteen Ionic columns. The rotunda enclosed a circular interior with nine Corinthian half-columns used for decorative purposes. Inside were statues of Philip, his parents Amyntas (III) and Eurydice, his wife Olympias, and his son Alexander. The sculptor was Leochares, who used gold for the statues' attire and ivory (Pausanias *Description of Greece* 5.17.4, 20.9–10) or marble (archaeologists, including Schultz 2007) for the flesh. Philip may have wished to display thus the continuity, legitimacy, and authority of his dynastic rule. Yet the shrine-like structure also suggests his desire to accord himself and his family superhuman, if not divine, status.

Questions

1. Describe the goals, institutions, and officials of the League of Corinth (**38.17.A–C**).

2. Compare the speech on Alexander's treaty with the Greeks (**38.17.C**) with the Greeks' oath on the common peace (**38.17.B**). Which peace terms in the oath does the speech confirm? Which does it add?
3. What did the Greeks gain from Philip's common peace (**38.17.A–C**)?
4. What themes are highlighted in the commemorations of Chaeronea and its aftermath (**38.17.D**, WEB **38.16.II**, WEB **38.18**)?

38.19   The Murder of Philip II (336) and the Royal Tombs at Vergina

Philip returned to Macedonia to plan his Persian campaign and even sent an advanced force into Asia Minor. The preparations were cut short, however, by his assassination in the summer of 336. Unnatural deaths of political leaders have always encouraged allegations of conspiracy, and Philip's death is no exception.

In 337 Philip married his seventh wife, the Macedonian Cleopatra. At the wedding banquet Cleopatra's uncle, Attalus, questioned Alexander's legitimate birth. The incident led to a conflict between Alexander and Philip and the exile of the young prince and his mother Olympias (see **38.5** for Philip's wives). The sources agree that Philip married Cleopatra for love, although some scholars have detected behind the marriage Philip's desire to replace Alexander with an heir from his new wife.

The murder of Philip took place during the celebration of the marriage of his daughter and Alexander's sister, (a different) Cleopatra, to Olympias' brother, Alexander of Epirus. Philip used the occasion to officially launch the campaign against Persia. Delegations arrived from all over Greece (Athens included) to pay honor to the king. The celebration included games, banquets for the guests, and a procession in which Philip's statue was carried among statues of the Olympic gods, thus demonstrating his claim to divine status. Diodorus' description of the event includes reports (omitted here) of omens that foretold Philip's death and which the self-confident king failed to understand.

38.19.A   The Death of Philip II

Diodorus of Sicily 16.92.5–94.4

(**16.92.5**) Eventually the drinking party broke up, and the games were due to start the next day. It was still dark when the crowds moved hastily to the theater and at daybreak the procession took place in which Philip put on display, along with all the other paraphernalia, statues of the twelve gods, superbly crafted and amazingly decked out in rich splendor. But with these he also displayed a thirteenth image that was appropriate for a god, one of Philip himself – the king was actually showing himself seated among the twelve gods.

(**93.1**) The theater was full when Philip himself came in wearing a white cloak. He had given orders for his bodyguards to follow him at some remove, for he was showing the world that he had the universal goodwill of the Greeks to safeguard him and needed no protection from bodyguards. (**93.2**) While he was basking in such success and while everybody was showering praise and congratulations on the man, there suddenly appeared – unexpectedly and completely out of the blue – a plot against the king, followed by his death. (**93.3**) To make my account of these events clearer, I shall preface it with the reasons for the plot.

Pausanias was a Macedonian by birth who came from the area called Orestes. He was a bodyguard of the king, and because of his good looks he had become Philip's lover. (**93.4**) When Pausanias saw another Pausanias – the man had the same name – receiving Philip's amorous attentions he used insulting language to him, saying that he was effeminate and ready to submit to sex with anyone who wanted him. (**93.5**) The fellow could not bear such malicious abuse, but for the moment he held his tongue. Then, after informing Attalus,[1] one of his friends, about what he was going to do, he committed suicide in an extraordinary manner. (**93.6**) For, a few days later, when Philip was in combat with king Pleurias of the Illyrians, this second Pausanias stood before the king and on his own body took all the wounds aimed at the king, dying in the act.

(**93.7**) The event gained notoriety. Then Attalus, who was one of Philip's courtiers and had great influence with the king, invited Pausanias to dinner, and there poured large quantities of neat wine into him and handed him to muleteers for them to abuse his body in a drunken orgy. (**93.8**) When Pausanias sobered up after the drinking bout, he was deeply hurt by the physical outrage and charged Attalus before the king. Philip, too, was angered by the enormity of the deed, but he was unwilling to show his disapproval because of his close ties with Attalus and because he needed his services at that time. (**93.9**) Attalus, in fact, was the nephew of the Cleopatra who had become the king's new wife, and he had been chosen as commander of the force that was being sent ahead into Asia – he was a man of courage on the battlefield. Thus the king preferred to mollify Pausanias' legitimate anger over what he had endured, and he bestowed on him substantial gifts and promoted him to positions of honor in the bodyguard.[2]

(**94.1**) The resentment of Pausanias, however, remained unchanged, and he passionately longed for revenge not only on the perpetrator of the deed but also on the man who failed to exact punishment for him. The sophist Hermocrates also greatly helped him decide to take action. Pausanias had studied under Hermocrates, and during his schooling had asked him how one could gain great fame. The sophist replied that it was by killing a man who had accomplished great deeds, since the person who brought off the killing would become part of posterity's memory of the man. (**94.2**) Pausanias took the remark in the context of his personal indignation and, his anger brooking no delay in the plan, scheduled his enterprise for the upcoming games.

It went as follows. (**94.3**) Placing horses at the city gate, he came to the entrance to the theater with a Celtic dagger concealed on his person. Philip had told the friends who were with him to go ahead to the theater, and his bodyguards were some distance from him. Seeing the king completely alone, Pausanias ran up to him and, delivering a dagger thrust that went clean through his ribs, left him dead on the ground. He then ran to the gate for the horses that had been prepared for his getaway. (**94.4**) Immediately, some of the bodyguards rushed to the king's body while others – Leonnatus, Perdiccas, and Attalus amongst them – poured out in pursuit of the murderer. Pausanias had a head start on his pursuers and would have mounted his horse before they caught him had he not fallen when his sandal became entangled in a vine. As he was getting up, Perdiccas and his group caught up with him and stabbed him to death.

See WEB **38.20** for Justin on Philip's assassination and for the incrimination of Olympias and possibly Alexander in Philip's murder.

38.19.B   The Vergina Royal Tombs

The amazing discovery in 1977–1978 of royal tombs at modern Vergina, which was the ancient Macedonian capital of Aegae, renewed interest in Philip and his death. Under a great mound (tumulus), excavators found four tombs dated to the late fourth and early third centuries. Tomb I is a cist tomb that was pillaged in antiquity and contained the remains of a mature male, a younger female, and an infant. One wall had a large painting depicting the rape of Persephone by Hades with Hermes running in front of their chariot. Tomb II, which was spared looting, produced the most spectacular finds.

Tomb II is a barrel-vault tomb with a main chamber and an antechamber. Its Doric façade has at its top a large painting of a hunting scene (Figure 38.5). The main chamber included grave goods such as silver vessels, tripods, the remains of what looks like a ceremonial shield, greaves, helmet, decorated body armor, and fragments of wooden furniture that was ornamented with small ivory heads. It also contained a round object, which was probably a diadem (crown), and a marble sarcophagus. The sarcophagus contained a solid gold chest weighing approximately 11 kilos that bore the Macedonian sun- or star-burst. In it were the burned and cleaned bones of a mature male, topped by a magnificent golden wreath. A marble door led to the antechamber, which contained assorted grave goods including a golden Scythian bow and arrow case, greaves, a golden wreath, and a marble sarcophagus. The sarcophagus had a smaller golden coffin that contained the bones of a female shrouded with gold and purple brocade. Tomb III, also unlooted, was built like Tomb II but on a smaller scale. The antechamber had a frieze showing two horse chariots. The tomb included many grave goods and a silver vessel that contained the bones of a male teenager. Tomb IV was too damaged to allow meaningful reconstruction.

Figure 38.5 shows the reconstructed fresco of the hunting scene on the façade of Tomb II. While the doors and the rest of the façade were preserved, the painting needed a great amount of restoration. Some scholars have identified the rider on the right with Philip and the rider at the center with Alexander, but the identification is uncertain.

Figure 38.5   A reconstruction of the façade of Tomb II, Vergina. Photo: Archaeological Receipts Fund – TAP Service.

Manolis Andronikos, the excavator of the site, identified Tomb II as that of Philip II and his wife Cleopatra and dated it to Alexander's reign. He thought that Tomb III was the tomb of Alexander IV, the young son of Alexander the Great and Roxane, who was murdered with his mother by the Macedonian ruler Cassander in 310/9. This identification is less controversial than that of Tomb II. Scholars who dispute Andronikos' view date Tomb II to after Alexander's era. They suggest that the pottery found in this tomb belongs to the last quarter of the fourth century, and detect in the hunting frieze references to Alexander's royal hunts during his Asian campaign. Accordingly, they have identified the human remains in Tomb II with Philip III Arrhidaeus, who was Alexander's half-brother and successor, and of his wife Eurydice. Both Philip III and Eurydice were murdered by Olympias in 317 and later buried in Aegae by Olympias' rival, Cassander. It has also been suggested that Tomb I is in fact the burial place of Philip II, his wife Cleopatra, and their baby daughter. The absence of inscriptions makes any identification uncertain, although current opinion tends to favor the identification of Tomb II as that of Philip Arrhidaeus and Eurydice.

Questions

1. What Panhellenic themes did Philip display in his daughter's marriage celebration (**38.19.A**)?
2. To what extent might the Pausanias affair (**38.19.A**) have influenced Theopompus' depiction of Philip's court (**38.4.A**)?

3. Construct two different conspiracy scenarios for the death of Philip II, each with a different arch plotter (**38.19**, WEB **38.20**).

Review Questions

1. Why was Philip so successful?
2. Describe life in the Macedonian royal court (**38.4–5**, **38.19**, WEB **38.10**, WEB **38.20**).

3. What shaped Athens' reactions to Philip (**38.6**, **38.8–9**, **38.11**, **38.13**, **38.15**, WEB **38.12.I**, WEB **38.14.I–II**, WEB **38.16.I**, WEB **38.18**)?

4. Describe Philip's army and military tactics (**38.3**, **38.6**, **38.8–9**, **38.13**, **38.15**, WEB **38.7**, WEB **38.14.II**).
5. How did Philip settle Greek affairs after Chaeronea (**38.17**, WEB **38.18**)?

6. Write an outline for a speech describing Philip's death and its consequences in the way an Athenian might have reported it to the Athenian assembly (**38.4–5**, **38.19**, WEB **38.14.I**, WEB **38.18**, WEB **38.20**).

Suggested Readings

Early Macedonian history and Macedonian institutions: Hammond and Griffith 1979, 3–200, 383–404; Borza 1990, 1999. *Macedonian and Greek ethnicity*: Borza 1996; J. Hall 2001; Sourvinou-Inwood 2002; Anson 2004, 191–232; cf. Adams 1996. *Philip's reign and career*: Ellis 1976; Cawkwell 1978; Hatzopoulos and Loukopoulos 1981; Hammond 1994; Worthington 2008. *Royal Boys/Pages*: Carney 2008. *Philip and Macedonian royal women*: Ogden 1999, esp. 17–29; Carney 2000, 51–81; 2003. *Macedonian army, arms, and Philip's reforms*: Griffith in Hammond and Griffith 1979, 405–449; Markle 1982; Bosworth 1988, 259–266; Anson 1991. *Theopompus on Philip*: Flower 1997, 98–112. *Philip's coinage and economy*: Thompson 1982; Hammond 1995; Jones 1999. *Philip and the Greeks*: Ryder 1994; Harding 1995. *The Third Sacred War*: Buckler 1989; Markle 1994. *Philip, Olynthus, and its houses*: Carter 1971; McQueen 1986, esp. 6–19; Cahill 2002. *Philip, Athens, and the Peace of Philocrates*: Sealey 1993, 137–159; Harris 1995, 41–16; Buckler 2000; Ryder 2000. *Isocrates and Philip*: Perlman 1957, 1969; Markle 1976; cf. Buckler 1994. *Demosthenes, Athens, and Philip*: Sealey 1993, 160–193; Ryder 2000; Buckler 2003, 463–488. *The Fourth Sacred War*: Londey 1990; Harris 1995, 126–132; Roisman 2006, 133–145. *The battle of Chaeronea*: Cawkwell 1978, 144–149; Rahe 1981; Hammond 1994, 143–154; Ma 2008; Worthington 2008, 147–151. *The Philippeum*: Fredricksmeyer 1979; Baynham 1994; Carney 2007; Schultz 2007. *Philip and the Greeks after Chaeronea*: Roebuck 1948; Ryder 1965, 102–115, 150–162; Hammond and Griffith 1979, 604–646; Buckler 1994. *The death of Philip II*: Badian 1963; Bosworth 1971; Fears 1975; Carney 1992. *The Royal tombs of Vergina*: Andronikos 1984 (Philip's tomb); Borza 1987 and Palagia 2000 (Philip Arrhidaeus' tomb).

39

Alexander the Great (336–323)

CHAPTER CONTENTS

Ancient Greece from Homer to Alexander: The Evidence, First Edition. Joseph Roisman.
© 2011 Blackwell Publishing Ltd. Translations © 2011 John Yardley. Published 2011 by Blackwell Publishing Ltd.

Since antiquity, views of Alexander the Great have ranged from great admiration to harsh criticism and hostility. Our extant sources on the king belong to both categories. Of those used here, Arrian and Plutarch tend to favor the king while Diodorus of Sicily and especially Q. Curtius Rufus criticize him on more than one occasion. This chapter follows the career of a

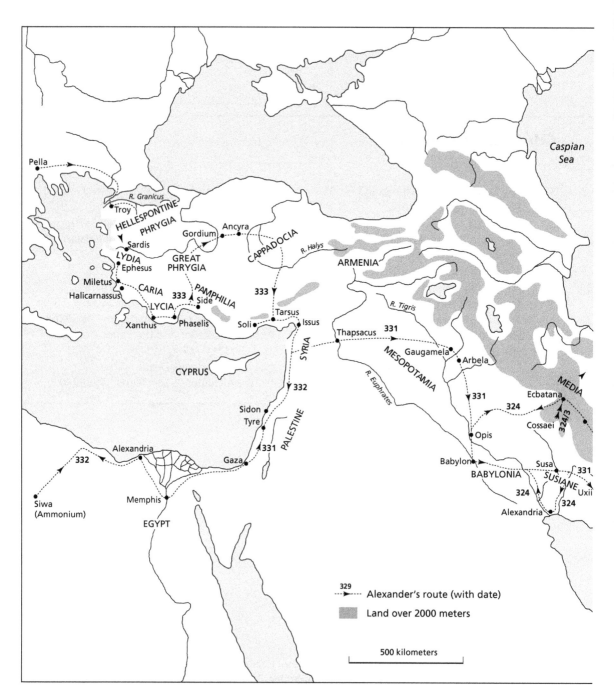

Map 39.1   Alexander's campaigns, 334–323.

king who is said to have transformed the ancient world. It describes Alexander's relations with Greeks early in his reign, which encompassed the destruction of Thebes to a more peaceful incorporation of Asian Greeks into the empire. It describes his victory over the Persian king Darius III at Issus, and his visit to an oracle in Egypt where he was told he was the son of Ammon/Zeus. The chapter

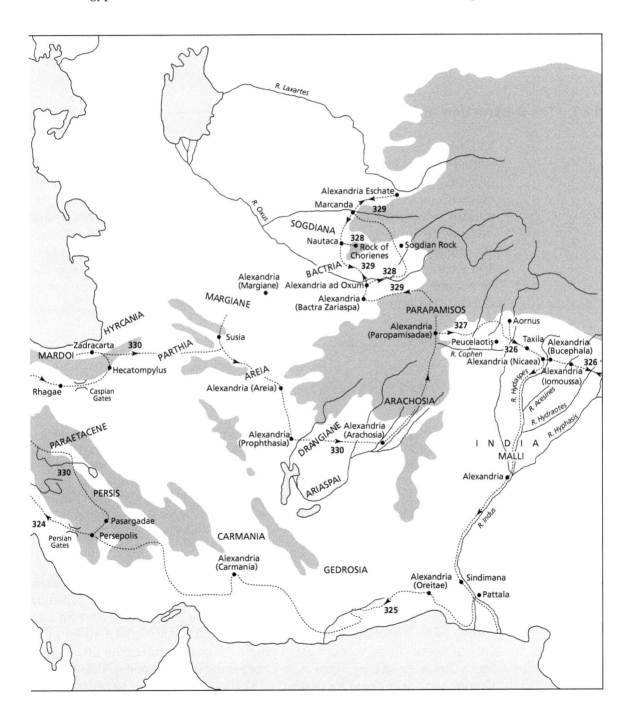

then examines Alexander's burning of buildings in the Persian city of Persepolis and the significance of this act. It also scrutinizes Alexander's relationship with his military elite and the related issues of his adoption of Iranian practices and his divine aspirations. The chapter records Alexander's victory in India and an army mutiny at Opis following his return to Mesopotamia. The mutiny casts light on Alexander's relations with both Macedonians and Iranians. The chapter concludes with Alexander's decree ordering the return home of Greek exiles and his death.

Map 39.1 shows a map of Alexander's military campaigns from 334 to 323.

39.1   The Destruction of Thebes (335)

Following his confirmation as king by the Macedonian assembly, Alexander wasted no time in eliminating potential rivals to the throne. He then made a quick march to Greece to insure that both Thessaly and other Greek states recognized him as the heir to Philip and his settlements. He spent the next few months completing the subjugation of Thracian tribes in the north, which involved crossing the Danube and fighting Illyrians in northwestern Greece. His campaign was interrupted by news that Thebes had rebelled against him. The second-century CE Greek historian Flavius Arrianus, or Arrian, who was an admirer of Alexander and wrote the best extant account of his campaign (*Anabasis*), was unsympathetic to the Thebans' cause.

39.1.A   The Theban Revolt

Arrian *Anabasis* 1.7.1–2

(**1.7.1**) In the meantime, a number of the exiles from Thebes slipped into the city at night – some people there had invited them with the intention of starting a revolution – and they seized and killed Amyntas and Timolaus, who were two of those occupying the Cadmea, suspecting no hostile movement from outside. (**7.2**) They came into the assembly and induced the Thebans to defect from Alexander, claiming "liberty" and "freedom of speech" as their goals, fine historic words, and urging them to rid themselves finally of the oppressive rule of the Macedonians. They made their appeal more persuasive with the people at large by steadfastly maintaining that Alexander had died in Illyria.

The Theban revolt of 335 posed a challenge for Alexander. Some of his contemporaries viewed him as too young or unprepared for the job of ruling Macedonia and Greece, and there was a danger that the revolt might turn into a wider Greek war of liberation. On the other hand, if Alexander destroyed this famous Greek city as an example to others, he would undermine his claim to lead a campaign against Persia in revenge for the harms it had inflicted on the Greeks. Alexander opted for destroying Thebes as a deterrent to other Greeks, although he "allowed" the Greek council of the Corinthian League to make the formal decision on Thebes' fate. The most vocal members against Thebes were her enemies, who recommended destruction. In spite of Alexander's efforts, the Greeks blamed him for the result.

39.1.B   The Punishment of Thebes

Plutarch *Alexander* 11.6–12

(**11.6**) Then when told of the defection of the Thebans and the support voiced for them by the Athenians, Alexander immediately led his forces through [the pass at] Thermopylae. Demosthenes, he said, had called him a child while he was amongst the Illyrians and Triballians, and a young whipper-snapper when he was in Thessaly; and now he wanted to look like a man before the walls of Athens.

(**11.7**) Approaching Thebes Alexander still gave its people the chance to show contrition for what had been done; he demanded only the surrender of Phoenix and Prothytes[1] and he proclaimed an amnesty for any who went over to him. (**11.8**) However, the Thebans in turn demanded that Alexander surrender to them Philotas and Antipater[2] and proclaimed that those wishing to join the Thebans in the liberation of Greece should make a stand with them. At this point the king sent his Macedonians into battle.

(**11.9**) The Theban defense was conducted with courage and spirit above and beyond their actual strength in a struggle against an enemy that outnumbered them many times over. (**11.10**) But when the Macedonian garrison, leaving the Cadmea, also fell on them from behind, most of the Thebans found themselves surrounded and went down fighting. The city was then taken, sacked, and razed to the ground. (**11.11**) For the most part this measure was prompted by Alexander's expectation that the Greeks would be shocked by a disaster of such proportions and be too frightened to take action. But the king also prided himself on responding to the complaints from his allies, for both the Phocians and the Plataeans had condemned the conduct of the Thebans. (**11.12**) Making an exception of priests, all those with ties of hospitality to the Macedonians, the descendants of [the poet] Pindar, and any who had opposed the decision to revolt, he sold them all into slavery, some 30,000 souls. The number of those who died there was in excess of 6,000.

Notes

1. *Phoenix and Prothytes were probably anti-Macedonian leaders.*
2. *Philotas and Antipater might have been local Macedonian commanders of the garrison at the Cadmea.*

Question

1. Could Alexander claim that the Thebans had violated Philip's common peace (cf. **38.17.B–C**)?

39.2   Alexander in Asia Minor (334–333)

39.2.A   Alexander's Invading Army

Alexander launched his campaign in 334/3 and justified it as a Greek war of revenge against ancient Persian wrongs. Like the Trojan War, it was a conflict between Europe and Asia, and Alexander stressed his descent from Achilles through his mother by sacrificing at this hero's tomb at Troy. According to Diodorus (below), he also claimed Asia by the right of conquest or the spear.

At the beginning of his campaign, Alexander's meager resources supported a force of about 30,000 infantry and ca. 5,000 cavalry. Among his officers, Philip's general Parmenion and his family held the most important commands. They would be replaced later in the campaign by men whose dependence on Alexander was greater.

Diodorus of Sicily 17.17.1–5

17.17.1 …After marching to the Hellespont with his army, Alexander shipped it across from Europe to Asia, (**17.2**) and he himself sailed to the Troad with sixty war ships. There, ahead of the other Macedonians, he hurled a spear from his ship, fixed it in the ground, and jumped ashore, declaring that he was receiving Asia from the gods as his possession won by the spear. (**17.3**) He paid his respects to the tombs of Achilles, Ajax, and the other heroes with funerary offerings and the other conventional marks of honor, and then personally conducted a thorough enumeration of the troops that were with him.

It was found that, in terms of infantry, there were 12,000 Macedonians, 7,000 allies, and 5,000 mercenaries. These were all under the command of Parmenion. (**17.4**) The Odrysians, Triballians, and Illyrians accompanying him numbered 7,000 and there were a thousand archers and so-called Agrianians, so that the infantry totaled 32,000. Cavalry numbers were as follows: 1,800 Macedonians, commanded by Parmenion's son Philotas; 1,800 Thessalians, commanded by Callias son of Harpalus; from the rest of Greece a total of 600 under Erigyius; and 900 Thracian guides and Paeonians, with Cassander as their commander. This made a total of 4,500 cavalry [in fact, 5,100]. Such was the strength of the army that crossed to Asia with Alexander. (**17.5**) The number of soldiers left behind in Europe, who were under Antipater's command, totaled 12,000 infantry and 15,000 cavalry.

 See WEB **39.3.I** for the battle of the Granicus between Alexander and the Persians, and WEB **39.3.II** for a Roman copy of what might be his statue commemorating the fighting there.

Following Alexander's victory in the battle of the Granicus, many Greeks in the Aegean and Asia Minor welcomed him as their liberator from Persian rule. To insure their loyalty to him, Alexander initiated or supported changes of local government from pro-Persian oligarchies to democracies. He also placed garrisons in some cities. There are several inscriptions from this region that attest to the complex nature of his dealings with the Greeks. One of them records a letter from Alexander to the island of Chios that was probably written in 334. Chios had apparently supported Philip's invasion of Asia Minor in 336, but in 335 had moved over to Memnon of Rhodes, who led the Persian counteroffensive. Chios changed sides once again in 334 when it supported Alexander. Each of these volte-face was accompanied by a change of government and the exile of the previous rule.

The following inscription is in two parts. The first includes Alexander's instructions to the Chians to take back the anti-Persian exiles and requests twenty triremes for his fleet. Alexander would disband his navy later that year because of his reliance on the land conquest of Asia Minor. Chios was asked to pay the expenses as well as the maintenance of a garrison. The reference to trials of pro-Persians by the Greek council suggests that the island was treated as a member of the Corinthian League. Not all Asian Greek cities were members, and some paid Alexander the tribute given to the Persians. The second part of the inscription (which is not reproduced here) includes a demand not to harm a friend of Alexander. Due to the fragmentary nature of the document, it is uncertain whether it was intended to protect one Alcimachus from prosecution or to prevent Alcimachus from prosecuting exiles. The inscription illustrates the political upheavals that the invasion had caused as well as Alexander's direct interference in local affairs. In 333, when Alexander was away, Chios rejoined the Persian cause only to change sides once again the following year.

39.2.B   Alexander and the Chian Decree

Tod no. 192 = R&O no. 84. A

From King Ale[xander] to the People [of] Chios, written in the Prytany of Deisitheos [334]: All those exiled from Chios are to return, and the constitution of Chios is to be democratic. Drafters of legislation are to be selected to write (**5**) and emend the laws as to insure that there are no impediments to a democratic constitution and the return of the exiles. Anything already emended or drafted is to be referred to Alexander. The people of Chios are to supply twenty triremes, with crews, at their own expense, and these are to sail as long (**10**) as the rest of the Greek naval force accompanies us at sea. With respect to those men who betrayed the city to the barbarians, all those who escaped are to be exiled from all the cities that share the peace, and to be liable to seizure under the decree of the Greeks. Those who have been caught are to be brought back and tried in the (**15**) Council of the Greeks. In the event of disagreement between those who have returned and those in the city, in that matter they are to be judged by us. Until a reconciliation is reached among the people of Chios, they are to have in their midst a garrison of appropriate strength installed by King Alexander. The people of Chios are to maintain the garrison.

It took diplomacy and hard fighting to capture the rest of western Asia Minor. The Persians continued to be active in the Aegean until Alexander's general Hegelochus established firm Macedonian control over the area in 333–332. In 330/1, the Spartan king Agis III, subsidized by Persian money, tried to challenge Macedonian rule in Greece, but his revolt was crushed by Antipater, Alexander's regent in Macedonia.

See WEB **39.3.III** for the story of Alexander and the Gordian knot and its significance.

Questions

1. What did Alexander mean to convey by hurling his spear at the Asian shore (**39.2.A**) and cutting the Gordian knot (WEB **39.3.III**)?
2. What was the Persians' plan at the Granicus (WEB **39.3.I**)?
3. How did Alexander secure his control of Chios (**39.2.B**)?

39.4 The Battle of Issus (333)

Turning south to Cilicia, Alexander marched unhindered to the northern Levant. His army met the Persian forces at Issus in northern Syria. Alexander took to the battle 40,000 infantry and 5,000 cavalry. Darius' force greatly outnumbered Alexander's, although it is difficult to assess the Persian size accurately given the sources' tendency to augment Alexander's victory by inflating the numbers of the opposition (Arrian 2.8.8 gives Darius 600,000 troops). What contributed to Alexander's victory was the poor choice by Darius of a battlefield between hills and sea that did not allow him to exploit his numerical superiority. As at the Granicus, the king waited for Alexander behind a river, the Pinarus, and his cavalry and infantry were no match for their Macedonian counterparts. When Alexander came dangerously close to the Persian center, Darius fled the battlefield. The fate of the Persian Empire depended on the king's survival. See WEB **39.5** for Arrian's description of the battle of Issus up to the following passage.

39.4.A   Alexander's Victory at Issus

Arrian *Anabasis* 2.11.4–10

(**11.4**) As soon as his left wing was repulsed by Alexander and he observed that it was severed from the rest of the army, Darius, in his chariot, lost no time and was amongst the first to flee. (**11.5**) While the ground he came upon in his flight was even he was secure in the chariot but when he encountered gullies and other difficult terrain he abandoned it, casting off his shield and his cape, and also leaving his bow in the chariot. He then mounted a horse and fled, and it was the imminent onset of darkness that saved him from capture by Alexander. (**11.6**) For while there was daylight Alexander kept up a vigorous pursuit, but when it grew dark and seeing what was before him became impossible he turned back again to the camp. He did, however, take with him Darius' chariot with his shield, cape, and bow. (**11.7**) In fact, time had been lost in his pursuit because he had turned back at the moment when the phalanx began to break formation, and did not take up the chase until he saw the foreign mercenaries and the Persian cavalry pushed back from the river.

(**11.8**) Amongst the Persian dead were Arsames, Rheomithres, and Atizyes, who had been cavalry commanders at the Granicus; and Sauaces, the satrap of Egypt, and Bubaces, both members of the Persian nobility, also lost their lives. Some 100,000 common soldiers, including more than 10,000 cavalry, were killed. Consequently, according to Ptolemy son of Lagus, who accompanied Alexander on the campaign,[1] the men who were along with them in pursuit of Darius came to a ravine during the chase and made their way over it on Persian bodies.

(**11.9**) The camp of Darius was immediately taken by storm, and with it were also taken Darius' mother, his wife (who was also his sister), and his infant son. Two daughters were also captured, and a few noble Persian ladies waiting on them. The rest of the Persians had actually sent their women and their baggage to Damascus, and (**11.10**) Darius too had sent to Damascus most of his money, plus all the other appurtenances that go along with the Great King to support his extravagant lifestyle even when he is on campaign. As a result no more than 3,000 talents were taken in the camp. In fact, the money in Damascus was also captured a little later by Parmenion, who had been sent there for this purpose. Such was the end of that battle. It took place when Nicocrates was archon in Athens, in the month of Maemacterion [November/December 333].[2]

Notes

1. *Ptolemy FGrHist 138 F 6. Ptolemy, the future king of Egypt, was Arrian's chief source for Alexander's history, including probably the battle of Issus.*
2. *Another primary source is the Alexander historian Callisthenes. His account of the battle has been preserved by the Hellenistic historian Polybius, who criticizes it (not always justifiably): Callisthenes FGrHist 124 F 35 = Polybius 12.17–22.*

39.4.B   The Alexander Mosaic

One of the most famous artistic renditions of Alexander's campaign is the so-called Alexander Mosaic from the House of Faun at Pompeii (Figure 39.1). The mosaic, measuring 5.84 by 3.17 meters, was created ca. 100 BCE. At the center of this floor decoration stands Darius a moment before fleeing the battlefield.

Figure 39.1
The Alexander Mosaic. Museo Nazionale, Naples/SCALA.

Alexander is riding a horse on the left and threatens to strike him. Many scholars have located the scene at the battle of Issus and identified the mosaic's source of inspiration as a painting by Alexander's near contemporary Philexenus of Eretria, but this is uncertain. One attractive suggestion is that the original was a didactic painting about the art of war, and that the scene is a composite of a number of battles (A. Cohen 1997). The mosaic depicts Alexander's ferocious combativeness, while Darius' portrayal is sympathetic and much closer to the ancient accounts that describe him as fleeing only when his life was in danger than to Arrian's depiction of him as a cowardly king.

Questions

1. What considerations guided Darius' and Alexander's lines of battle at Issus (WEB **39.5**)?
2. What was the turning point in the battle of Issus (**39.4**, WEB **39.5**)?
3. What were the battle's outcomes and their significance (**39.4**, and see also **39.6** below)?

4. What are the similarities between the statue of Alexander by Lysippus (?) in WEB **39.3.II** and his depiction in the mosaic (**39.4.B**)?

5. Assuming that the scene in the mosaic (Figure 39.1) is of the battle of Issus, how does it complement or contradict Arrian's description of the battle (**39.4.A,** WEB **39.5**)?

39.6   Alexander Visits the Oracle of Ammon at Siwa (332/1)

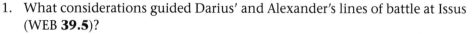
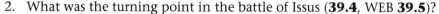

The battle of Issus had important consequences. It led to the capture of Darius' treasury and his family as well as the families of important Persian nobles. Darius offered Alexander a ransom for his family, territories, and alliance, but Alexander would not hear of it. He enjoyed clear military superiority over Darius, as well as possession of Darius' money, and he aimed to become king of Asia, with Darius at best as his vassal.

Darius' retreat to Mesopotamia exposed Phoenicia and Egypt to Alexander's offensive. Alexander went to Tyre, which refused to capitulate to him. It took Alexander seven months of hard-fought siege before he entered the city and slaughtered its inhabitants. He captured Gaza after two months' siege, and dragged its governor behind his chariot in imitation of Achilles' treatment of Hector. Alexander reached Egypt in the autumn of 332 and was welcomed as liberator from the Persians by this often-rebellious province. He paid his respects to local deities, in clear contrast to acts of sacrilege allegedly commit-ted by Persian kings. He was also given the traditional title of pharaoh. In the winter Alexander visited the Libyan shrine of Ammon (Amun) in the oasis of Siwa. The Greeks were long familiar with this god, whom they identified with Zeus, and they held the local oracle in high regard.

The first-century geographer Strabo both paraphrased and criticized the account of Alexander's companion, Callisthenes, of the journey to the oracle and what he heard there: see **Introduction III.1** ("Investigation of Sources and Fragments of Lost Historians").

Other sources, based on traditions of uncertain value, report with some variations Alexander's questions to the oracle and the answers he received. The historicity of a dialogue between Alexander and the priest has been questioned. Strabo, based on Callisthenes, does not record such an exchange and says that only Alexander was allowed to enter the temple. Archaeologists who have inspected the ruins have seriously doubted whether anyone outside could have heard or seen what transpired inside. At the least, Alexander confirmed to himself and others that he was the son of Zeus/Ammon. It was the first step on the road to deification. Discontented Macedonians regarded his claim to divine parenthood as an attempt to disown Philip and them.

Plutarch *Alexander* 27.5–9

(**27.5**) When Alexander reached the oasis, after the desert crossing, the prophet of Ammon addressed to him greetings from the god, who he implied was Alexander's father. Alexander then asked if any of his father's assassins had escaped him. (**27.6**) The prophet told him not to blaspheme, for he had no mortal father, at which point Alexander reworded the question, asking if he had succeeded in punishing all Philip's assassins. He then asked about his own empire and inquired whether the god granted him mastery over all men. (**27.7**) The god replied that he was granting him this and that the revenge of Philip was now complete. Alexander presented the god with spectacular offerings, and his human assistants with money. (**27.8**) Such is the account of the oracles that most authors give, but Alexander himself in a letter to his mother says that a number of secret responses were given to him, which he would tell her on his return, but in the strictest confidence. (**27.9**) Some say the prophet, to be friendly, wanted to address him in Greek as "O paidion" ("Oh my son"), but because of his foreign accent he lapsed into a sigma at the end of the phrase and said "*O paidios*," using the sigma instead of a nu. Alexander, they say, was pleased with this slip of the tongue and the story got around that the god had addressed him as the son of Zeus (*pai Dios*).

Alexander returned to found Alexandria at a site he had chosen before his Siwa trip. Egyptian Alexandria was the most successful of his foundations of Alexandrias, which ranged from new cities in uninhabited places to military colonies and the refoundation of existing settlements. See WEB **39.7** for a list of eighteen foundations of Alexandrias attributed to Alexander.

See also **Introduction II** ("Coins") and Figure I.3 for a silver tetradrachm from Memphis, Egypt, minted during Alexander's reign.

Questions

1. What happened to Alexander on the way to Ammon and what does this add to the story of his visit (see **Introduction III.1**)?
2. How does Plutarch suggest his reservations about the consultation in Siwa?

39.8 Fire in Persepolis (331–330)

From Egypt Alexander marched to Mesopotamia where Darius was waiting for him with a large army (331). The battle on the plain of Gaugamela ended in a Macedonian victory and Darius' second flight. He was later assassinated by his companions, and one of his killers and relatives, Bessus, would assume the title of King Artaxerxes (V) and lead the resistance against Alexander in central Asia until his capture and execution.

From Gaugamela Alexander marched unopposed to the Persian capital of Babylon. There he reappointed the Iranian Mazaeus as the local satrap and thus started a trend for integrating the local elite in his administration. From Babylon Alexander captured the Persian capital of Susa and its treasury. After overcoming local resistance he entered the Persian capital of Persepolis in the early winter of 330; in early spring he set on fire the Apadana, or Audience Hall, the Treasury, and Xerxes' palace. Archaeological evidence suggests arson and that the palace was systematically looted prior to its destruction. The ancient sources offer two different versions of the sack of the city. One portrays the destruction as premeditated revenge for Xerxes' ruinous invasion of Greece, while the other describes it as more spontaneous and carried out after a drunken orgy. The historian Arrian thinks that the fire was intentional but also unwise. The Roman historian Q. Curtius Rufus gives the more famous story, which places the courtesan Thais at its center.

Although many scholars see the destruction as calculated, they are divided about its interpretation. Some regard it as a proclamation to the Greeks that Alexander was still pursuing his Panhellenic mission of revenge, and others see it as a message to the Persians that a new ruler had arrived to replace the Achaemenid dynasty. There are also historians who see Alexander as essentially a marauding conqueror. The sources favor the first interpretation, although Alexander's regret suggests that he did not think his actions through and that Thais might have played a role in instigating them. The way this episode is described by the sources and their modern interpreters is often indicative of how they view Alexander.

Q. Curtius Rufus 5.7.1–7, 10–11

(**5.7.1**) Alexander had some great natural gifts: a noble disposition surpassing that of all other monarchs; resolution in the face of danger; speed in undertaking and completing projects; integrity in dealing with those who surrendered and mercy toward prisoners; restraint even in those pleasures which are generally acceptable and widely indulged. But all these were marred by his inexcusable fondness for drink. (**7.2**) At the very time that his enemy and rival for imperial power was preparing to resume hostilities and when the conquered nations, only recently subdued, still had scant respect for his authority, he was attending day-time drinking parties at which women were present – not, indeed, such women as it was a crime to violate, but courtesans who had been leading disreputable lives with the soldiers.

(**7.3**) One of the latter was Thais. She too had had too much to drink when she claimed that, if Alexander gave the order to burn the Persian palace, he would earn the deepest gratitude among all the Greeks. This was what the people whose cities the Persians had destroyed were expecting, she said. (**7.4**) As the drunken whore gave her opinion on a matter of extreme importance, one or two who were themselves the worse for drink agreed with her. The king, too, was enthusiastic rather than acquiescent. "Why do we not avenge Greece, then, and put the city to the torch?" he asked. (**7.5**) They were all excited by the wine, and so they got up, when drunk, to burn the city which they had spared when under arms. Alexander took the lead, setting fire to the palace, to be followed by his drinking companions, his attendants, and the courtesans. Large sections of the palace had been made of cedar so they quickly took flame and spread the conflagration over a large area. (**7.6**) The army, encamped not far from the city, caught sight of the fire and, thinking it accidental, came running in a body to help. (**7.7**) But when they reached the palace portico, they saw their king himself still piling on torchwood, so they dropped the water they had brought and began throwing dry wood into the blaze themselves…

(**7.10**) The Macedonians were ashamed that a city of such distinction had been destroyed by their king during a drunken orgy, so the whole episode was given a serious explanation and they convinced themselves that this was the most appropriate method of destruction for it. (**7.11**) As for Alexander, it is generally agreed that, when sleep had brought him back to his senses after his drunken bout, he regretted his actions and said that the Persians would have suffered a more grievous punishment at the hands of the Greeks had they been forced to see him on Xerxes' throne and in his palace.

Questions

1. How does the story of the fire show Alexander's moral decline, according to Q. Curtius Rufus?
2. What was wrong in avenging Greece in the manner described above, according to Curtius?

39.9 Conspiracy in Court: The Philotas Affair (330)

The next phase of the campaign was not easy. Alexander had to deal with bad weather and fierce local resistance in Bactria and Sogdiana (today Afghanistan and Pakistan), and his forces suffered several defeats in guerilla-like warfare. There were also problems in the court. In 330, Philotas, the commander of the cavalry and the son of Alexander's most senior general, Parmenion, was implicated in a conspiracy against the king's life. A friend of one of the plotters had told Philotas about the conspiracy, but Philotas said nothing to the king and was consequently charged with participating in it. He was executed following a trial, and his father, who stayed behind in Ecbatana, was put to the sword. Most historians agree that Philotas played no part in the plot. One influential view suggests that Alexander used the conspiracy to get rid of the old marshal through his more vulnerable son. Parmenion was the only Macedonian who could rival Alexander in authority and popularity. Another view detects in the affair a struggle between Parmenion's group and an *ad hoc* coalition of Macedonian commanders who, with Alexander's support, used it to promote themselves as the new marshals of the empire. One should not discount the possibility that Philotas kept silent about the conspiracy in the hope that it would succeed. The Roman historian Q. Curtius Rufus (6.11.21–33) even has him confess under torture that he, his father, and the veteran general Hegelochus had formed tentative plans in Egypt to take Alexander's life.

Plutarch *Alexander* 48.4–49.13

(**48.4**) As it happened, incriminating remarks about Philotas had been passed along to Alexander for quite some time. When Darius had been defeated in Cilicia [i.e., Issus] and his treasure was subsequently captured at Damascus, a large number of prisoners were taken to the Macedonian camp. Amongst these was found a woman called Antigone who came from Pydna and who was pleasing to the eye. She fell to Philotas. (**48.5**) He chattered on to her, making the usual opinionated and boastful comments a young man makes to his mistress, especially as the drink flows; and he declared that the greatest exploits belonged to himself and his father. Alexander he styled a mere youngster who enjoyed only nominal power, and that thanks to them. (**48.6**) These remarks the woman reported to one of her friends and he, as usually happens, passed them on to another, until the story came to Craterus.[1] Craterus then took hold of the woman and brought her secretly to Alexander. (**48.7**) The king heard her out and told her to continue her relationship with Philotas, and to come and report back to him whatever she learned from him.

(**49.1**) And so Philotas was unaware that a trap was being laid for him. He continued his meetings with Antigone, during which he would let drop many impulsive and boastful comments and many remarks disrespectful of the king. (**49.2**) Much incriminating evidence against Philotas was now coming to Alexander but he still suffered in silence and held back, either through confidence in Parmenion's good will toward him or because he feared the reputation and power the two men commanded.

(**49.3**) Now at that time a Macedonian called Limnus[2] from Chalaestra was hatching a plot against Alexander, and he invited Nicomachus, one of the young boys – Limnus was infatuated with him – to join him in the enterprise. (**49.4**) Nicomachus did not accept the invitation but he informed his brother Cebalinus of the proposed coup. Cebalinus then went to Philotas and told him to bring the two of them before Alexander as they had urgent and important matters to communicate to him. (**49.5**) Philotas, however, for some reason – what it was is unknown – would not show them in, claiming the king was involved in more important matters. And he refused to do so on two occasions.

(**49.6**) The brothers now began to suspect Philotas and turned to somebody else, by whom they were taken to see Alexander. They began by recounting the Limnus affair and then gradually revealed Philotas' failure to attend to them on the two occasions. (**49.7**) And this cut Alexander to the quick. A man was sent to fetch Limnus, but the man killed the conspirator when he tried to resist arrest. Alexander was even more unnerved by this because he thought the proof of the plot had slipped through his fingers. (**49.8**) He felt bitterly angry with Philotas, and he brought in those who had long held grudges against him. These now openly declared that the king had been too complacent in assuming that Limnus, a man from Chalaestra, had independently taken on such a daring act. (**49.9**) No, they said, he was just a pawn, an instrument employed by a greater authority, and the source of the plot was to be sought amongst those who had most to gain from it being concealed.[3] (**49.10**) The king was by this time giving his ear to such innuendo and insinuations, and these people then proceeded to pile accusation on accusation against Philotas. (**49.11**) He was apprehended and interrogated, the *hetairoi* [Companions] being present at the torture session and Alexander listening from behind a curtain drawn between them. (**49.12**) They say that Philotas resorted to pathetic and abject wails of entreaty to Hephaestion, and Alexander said: "Did you attempt such a major coup, weakling and coward that you are?"[4]

(**49.13**) Immediately after Philotas' execution Alexander also sent men into Media and had Parmenion killed. Parmenion was a man who had shared many of Philip's exploits and, amongst the older friends of Alexander, he was the only, or at least the most vigorous, proponent of his crossing to Asia. Of his three sons he had seen two die on the campaign before this and now he had been dispatched along with the third.[5]

Notes

1. *Craterus was a popular general and one of Alexander's most trusted men. He was also one of the major beneficiaries of the affair.*
2. *Limnus is a manuscript error for Dimnus or Dymnus.*
3. *Prominent among Philotas' foes were the commanders Hephaestion and Coenus.*
4. *According to the Roman historian Q. Curtius Rufus (6.7.33; 10.34), Philotas explained his silence by his disdain for the informant and because Alexander in the past was scornful of warnings about a plot.*
5. *Parmenion's other dead sons were Nicanor, the commander of the elite infantry unit of the hypaspists, and young Hector.*

Questions

1. What can be learned from the Philotas conspiracy about the inner workings of Alexander's court and command?
2. Who was responsible for the death of Philotas and Parmenion?

-------------------- **39.10   Alexander Kills the Veteran General Cleitus (328)**

Following the executions of Philotas and Parmenion, Alexander took the precautionary measure of dividing Philotas' single command of the cavalry between his loyal friend Hephaestion and the veteran general Cleitus. Cleitus had saved Alexander's life in the battle of the Granicus (WEB **39.3.I**) and was the brother of Alexander's nurse. In 328, at Maracanda (Samarkand), Alexander killed Cleitus in a drunken quarrel. The hard fighting, wine, and the sympotic culture of put-down contributed to the affair, but the protagonists' verbal exchange also revealed strains in the king's relationships with his commanders and troops. These revolved around the respective status of the Macedonians, Greeks, and Iranians in the camp and their competition for honor and influence. Other issues related to the changes in Alexander's status and power since he became king of Asia, his divine parenthood, and his fear of plots against his life.

39.10.A   The Killing of Cleitus

Plutarch *Alexander* 50.1–51.11

(**50.1**) The Cleitus affair followed not much later.[1] Those who are told the simple facts of it may find it more brutal than the Philotas episode, (**50.2**) but when we consider its origin and context we find that it was not a premeditated affair but arose through an unfortunate set of circumstances. It was the king's anger and drunkenness that gave Cleitus' evil genius its chance. It happened as follows.

(**50.3**) Certain people came from the coast bringing the king some Greek fruit. Alexander was full of admiration for the freshness and beauty of the fruit, and he sent for Cleitus, wishing to show it to him and share it with him. (**50.4**) Cleitus happened to be offering sacrifice at that moment, but he abandoned that and went to the king; and three sacrificial sheep that had already been consecrated came following after him. (**50.5**) When the king was told this, he passed on the information to his seers, Aristander and Cleomenes the Spartan. The seers declared that it was a sinister omen, and Alexander issued orders that expiatory sacrifices be immediately offered on Cleitus' behalf. (**50.6**) For, two days earlier, the king himself had had a strange dream: Cleitus appeared to him in black clothes sitting with the sons of Parmenion, who were all dead. (**50.7**) But before the sacrifices ordered for Cleitus were concluded, Cleitus himself came to dine with the king, who had been sacrificing to the Dioscuri.

(**50.8**) Some lively drinking got under way, and poems were sung. These were the compositions of one Pranichus (or Pierion, according to some) on the generals who had recently suffered defeat at the hands of the barbarians, subjecting these men to humiliation and ridicule.[2] (**50.9**) Older diners were offended and had harsh words for the poet and the singer, but Alexander and his group were enjoying the performance and told the singer to carry on. By this time Cleitus was drunk and, a man of truculent and willful temperament, he flew into a rage. It was not right, he said, in the presence of barbarians and enemies, to insult Macedonians who were far better than the men mocking them, even if they had fallen on bad luck. (**50.10**) Alexander then remarked that in representing cowardice as bad luck Cleitus was pleading for himself, (**50.11**) at which Cleitus sprang to his feet and declared: "Yes, it was this cowardice of mine that saved the offspring of the gods when he was turning his back to Spithridates' sword! And it is by the blood of Macedonians and by these wounds that you have become so high and mighty as to disown Philip and claim to be the son of Ammon."

(**51.1**) Alexander was stung by the remark. "You bastard," he said, "do you think you are going to get away with saying such things about me all the time and causing friction amongst the Macedonians?"

(**51.2**) "We are not getting away with anything even now," replied Cleitus, "considering the rewards we receive for our efforts. We think those already dead are the lucky ones for not living to see Macedonians flogged with Median rods and pleading with Persians for a chance to see our king."

(**51.3**) Cleitus had spoken too freely. Alexander's companions stood up to face him and proceeded to shower him with abuse, while the older men attempted to calm the disturbance. (**51.4**) Turning then to Xenodochus of Cardia and Artemius of Colophon Alexander said: "Don't you think Greeks walking amongst Macedonians are like demi-gods walking amongst wild animals?" (**51.5**) Cleitus would not give up. He told Alexander to let him say what he wanted or else not invite to dinner men who were free and spoke their minds – he should live with barbarians and slaves who would prostrate themselves before his Persian girdle and snow-white tunic.

No longer able to control his temper, Alexander threw one of the apples within his reach at Cleitus and hit him, after which he looked round for his sword. (**51.6**) But Aristophanes [Aristonus?], one of his bodyguards, got to it first and removed it. The others surrounded the king and begged him to stop, but he jumped to his feet and summoned his guards, loudly shouting in the Macedonian tongue, which indicated that there was a serious crisis. He also ordered the bugler to sound the alarm and hit him with his fist when the man hesitated and was unwilling to obey. (**51.7**) This man was subsequently held in high regard as he was thought to be the one mostly responsible for the camp not having been thrown into turmoil.

(**51.8**) Cleitus still would not give up, however, and his friends with difficulty jostled him out of the dining room. But he reentered by another door, reciting this iambic verse from Euripides with derisive bravado: "Alas! What a sad state of government there is in Greece."[3] (**51.9**) At this Alexander grabbed a spear from one of the guards and, when Cleitus was drawing back the curtain before the door and came face to face with him, ran him through. (**51.10**) Cleitus fell with a groan that grew to a howl of pain, and Alexander's anger straightway left him. (**51.11**) Coming to his senses, and seeing his friends standing there speechless, he drew the spear from the body and made to stab himself in the throat. He was prevented from doing so, however, when his guards grabbed his hands and carried him under duress into his room.

Notes

1. *The affair actually occurred two years after the Philotas affair, but the sources linked them together.*
2. *Perhaps in reference to a recent Macedonian defeat against the local rebel leader Spitamenes.*
3. *The verse is from Euripides'* Andromache *(683), a play which Alexander probably knew well, and where the following lines bitterly complain against generals who unjustly appropriate to themselves the honor of victory.*

39.10.B   Legitimizing Cleitus' Death

Q. Curtius Rufus 8.2.10–12

(**8.2.10**) …The king shut himself away for three days. (**2.11**) When his attendants and Bodyguards[1] realized that he was determined to die, they burst into his tent in a body and, though he long resisted their entreaties, finally prevailed upon him to take nourishment. (**2.12**) To ease his feeling of shame over the killing, the Macedonians formally declared that Cleitus' death was justified, and they would have refused him burial had not the king ordered it.

Note

1. *Besides the regular bodyguards, the seven Bodyguards were selected commanders and royal friends.*

Questions

1. What tensions informed the Cleitus episode?
2. What factors, besides wine, influenced Alexander's reactions in the incident?
3. Why do the sources tend to link the Philotas affair (**39.9**) to that of Cleitus?

39.11   Alexander Turns "Asian"

Alexander adopted Persian royal protocols and insignia in the hope of becoming less of a foreign conqueror and more an heir to established imperial traditions of the Persian Empire. Yet some Macedonians resented his policy for these very reasons. They were concerned that Alexander was losing his Macedonian identity and feared for their superior rank in the realm as well as Alexander's decreasing dependence on them. See WEB **39.12** for Alexander's adoption of Persian dress and customs.

Of all the Persian practices that Alexander had adopted, the *proskynesis*, or obeisance, was the most sensitive. In the Near East people acknowledged a person's superior rank, king included, by prostrating themselves and blowing a kiss up in his direction. The practice had no known religious significance and did not make the Persian king divine. The Greeks and the Macedonians, however, reserved this act for worship, and when it was done to mortals they equated it with servility and impiety. Alexander may have been concerned that Asians would think less of him if they saw the Macedonians and Greeks avoiding the *proskynesis*. He might also have wished to eliminate differences among these groups in court as far as acknowledging his supreme status was concerned. Finally, even if the act was primarily a social ritual, Alexander surely knew what it meant in Europe. Indeed, the historian Callisthenes, who articulated the opposition to *proskynesis*, highlighted the religious aspect of prostration. Alexander decided not to press the issue, but Callisthenes fell out of favor and was later arrested and perhaps executed for his alleged involvement in a conspiracy of Royal Boys (Pages) against the king in 327.

The sources have two versions of the introduction of *proskynesis*. One reports that Callisthenes frustrated the experiment by giving a speech on the danger of blurring the line between divine honors and those given to mortals. In the other version reproduced below, Plutarch summarizes Callisthenes' main arguments and reports his refusal to perform the ritual during a *symposion*. This episode may have followed or preceded his speech against the practice.

Plutarch *Alexander* 54.2–55.4

(**54.2**) So Aristotle was apparently not far off the mark in stating that while Callisthenes was a capable and powerful speaker, he had no judgment. (**54.3**) But Callisthenes' firm and philosophical rejection of *proskynesis*, when he alone listed openly the objections secretly harbored by all the best and oldest of the

Macedonians, was rather different. By restraining Alexander from establishing the practice of *proskynesis*, he saved the Greeks from great disgrace, and Alexander even more so. However, he precipitated his own destruction because he appeared to have forced the king's hand rather than to have persuaded him.

(**54.4**) Chares of Mytilene[1] claims that when Alexander was once at a symposium he took a drink and passed the cup to one of his friends. The friend took the cup and rose to face the household altar; then, after drinking, he first did *proskynesis* before Alexander, and after that kissed him and took his seat once more. (**54.5**) All present followed this procedure in turn. Callisthenes then took the cup, but at that point Alexander, who was in conversation with Hephaestion, was paying no attention. Callisthenes drank and went forward to kiss the king, (**54.6**) at which juncture Demetrius, who was surnamed Pheidon, said, "Your majesty, do not kiss him. He is the only one not to have done *proskynesis* before you." Alexander turned away from the kiss, and Callisthenes declared in a loud voice, "So I shall leave short of a kiss."

(**55.1**) The first development while this rupture between the two was growing was Hephaestion's assertion that Callisthenes had promised to do *proskynesis* before the king but had then broken his word, and this was readily believed. (**55.2**) Next came the insistent claims of such people as Lysimachus and Hagnon that the sophist was going around very haughtily expressing ideas about overthrowing tyranny, and that the young were running to him and following him around – the only man amongst all those thousands who was truly free! (**55.3**) So it was that when Hermolaus and his friends conspired against Alexander and their plot was uncovered, the smears of Callisthenes' detractors seemed to have the ring of truth. They had said that when Hermolaus asked how he could become a very famous man Callisthenes answered, "By killing a very famous man." (**55.4**) And they added that in spurring on Hermolaus to do the deed, he told him not to fear the golden couch but to remember that he would be dealing with a human being who fell sick and got wounded like any other.

Note

1. *Chares was Alexander's chief chamberlain and historian, and likely well informed about events in the court.*

Questions

1. What was so wrong about Alexander's adoption of Persian dress and protocols, according to the sources (**39.11**, WEB **39.12**)?
2. What was wrong with Callisthenes' conduct?
3. How does the *proskynesis* episode relate to the Cleitus affair (**39.10**)?

39.13   Victory in India (326)

In 328/7 Alexander married Roxane, and her father, the noble Bactrian Oxyarthes, helped the king to quell local revolts. Alexander marched into India in 326, reportedly in emulation of Dionysus. It is possible, however, that the stories about Dionysus in India were invented by men in Alexander's camp with the cooperation of eager-to-please locals. It was in India that Alexander fought the last of his pitched battles against the local king Porus

Figure 39.2
The Porus medallion.
© The Trustees of the British Museum.

at the Hydaspes River. The battle was preceded by a march in a torrential thunderstorm. Alexander had to cross the river at night to effect a surprise, and before clashing with Porus he fought Porus' son and a large number of elephants. As in other set-piece battles, Alexander's cavalry inflicted a major blow on the enemy. Following his victory, Alexander gave Porus back his kingdom in the interests of regional politics but also out of appreciation for his valor. It is highly likely that he issued the so-called Porus medallions in commemoration of this battle. The large medallion (*decadrachm*) shown in Figure 39.2 depicts on the observe a horseman attacking two men riding an elephant, and on the reverse a warrior holding a *sarissa* in one hand and a thunderbolt in the other, with the goddess Nike crowning him from above. Although Alexander did not fight Porus in person, it is likely that he is represented as charging the Indian ruler and his mahout on the observe. On the reverse, a heavily armed warrior, most probably Alexander, holds Zeus' thunderbolt, which suggests appropriation of divine properties as well as a reference to the thunder that preceded the battle.

39.14   Alexander, the Macedonians, Iranians, and the Opis Mutiny

 See WEB **39.15** for a survey of Alexander's campaign until his return to Iran, and the weddings at Susa between Macedonians, himself included, and Asians.

Alexander integrated Asian cavalry and infantry into his army. Already in central Asia he had initiated a military training program for 30,000 young Asians whom he called *Epigoni*, or Successors. He was not intending to give up on the Macedonians, who were too good as warriors, but the number of Macedonians available for service was limited, and the dependence of the *Epigoni* on him was greater.

The increasing reliance on Asian troops alarmed and angered Macedonian veterans. In 324 when Alexander decided in Opis on the Tigris River to send home old and disabled soldiers, many Macedonians, including those he intended to keep, saw it as an attempt to replace them with oriental troops.

39.14.A   Resentment in the Army

Arrian *Anabasis* 7.8.1–3

(**7.8.1**) When he reached Opis, Alexander brought the Macedonians together and proclaimed that he was releasing from active service and sending home the men whom old age or physical impairment rendered unfit for fighting. On those who remained, he said, he would confer so much that it would make them the envy of people at home, and fire the rest of the Macedonians with a wish to share with them those very hardships and dangers that they were experiencing. (**8.2**) It was certainly with the intention of humoring the Macedonians that Alexander said this, but they felt they were already despised by him and were in his eyes totally unfit for fighting, and so they were indignant at the speech he made – and not without reason. It came on top of the numerous other things that had hurt them throughout the entire length of the campaign. Many were the occasions on which they had already been stung by his Persian dress (a deliberate insult), by the barbarian *Epigoni* being equipped in Macedonian manner, and the inclusion of foreign cavalry in the ranks of the Companions. (**8.3**) As a result, they did not suffer this indignity in silence. They told him to release them all from service – he should continue the campaign with his father (a snide reference to Ammon). Alexander was, in the circumstances, more sensitive than usual, anyway, and after receiving all the attentions from the barbarians he was no longer as understanding with the Macedonians as he had been in the past. On hearing these comments, he leaped down from the dais with the officers who were around him and ordered the arrest of the most prominent of the rabble-rousers, personally indicating to the hypaspists with his finger the men who should be arrested. They numbered about thirteen. These he ordered to be hauled away for execution, and when the others fell into a stunned silence he mounted the dais once more and spoke as follows...

The authenticity of Alexander's speech as reproduced by Arrian is questionable. According to Arrian, Alexander stressed the debt the Macedonian people owed Philip and the even greater debt to him after he had given them power, wealth, and honor.

39.14.B   The Opis Mutiny and Its Aftermath

Arrian *Anabasis* 7.11.1–9

(**7.11.1**) With these words he leaped swiftly from the dais and proceeded to the palace where he remained, oblivious to his personal needs, and was not seen by any of the Companions. In fact, he was not seen the next day, either. On the third day he called in his select group of Persians and allocated amongst them command of the army battalions. He designated some as his kinsmen, and to these he restricted the right to kiss him.

(**11.2**) In the immediate aftermath of the speech the Macedonians simply stood there by the dais stunned to silence by his words and none followed the king as he took his leave, save for the Companions who were in attendance on him and the Bodyguards. The mass of the soldiers had nothing to do or say as they loitered there, but they did not want to leave, either. (**11.3**) Then the facts about the Persians and Medes were reported to them, the granting of commands to Persians and barbarian troops being enlisted in the Macedonian companies. They heard about the Macedonian names being used. They heard about a Persian agema, so-called, and Persian *pezhetairoi* [foot-companions]; they heard of others called *astheteroi*, of a Persian contingent of argyraspids [silver shields] and of a Persian Companions' cavalry, which now had another royal agema.[1] At this point they were no longer in control of themselves. (**11.4**) They ran in a body to the palace and there threw down their weapons before the doors as a gesture of supplication to the king, and standing before the doors themselves they called out to him begging for admission. They said they were willing to surrender those responsible for the disorder, and that they would certainly not leave the doors day or night, unless Alexander showed some compassion for them.

(**11.5**) When this was reported to the king, he quickly came forth. He saw their dejection and heard most of them weeping and wailing, at which he also shed tears. He went forward as if to say something, and they remained where they were, pleading with him. (**11.6**) Then one of their number, a man called Callines, who enjoyed some distinction because of his age and his position as officer in the Companion cavalry, said something like: "Your Majesty, what hurts the Macedonians is the fact that you have now made some of the Persians our kinsmen, that Persians are called 'Alexander's kinsmen' and that they kiss you while no Macedonian has yet enjoyed that honor." (**11.7**) But I regard all of you as my kinsmen," said Alexander in reply, "and from now on I shall call you that." When he said that, Callines went up to him and kissed him, and was followed by all the others who wished to kiss him. And with that they shouldered their weapons and went off to the camp shouting and singing a song of victory.

(**11.8**) Alexander celebrated the occasion with a sacrifice made to his usual gods, and hosted a public feast. Here he was seated in the midst of all the guests, the Macedonians beside him, the Persians next to them, and after these members of the other races, ranked according to their station or some other distinction. Alexander and those next to him drew from the same mixing-bowl and made the same libations, with the Greek soothsayers and the Magi initiating the proceedings. (**11.9**) Foremost among the blessings for which Alexander prayed was that the empire of Macedonians and Persians enjoy harmony and accord.[2] It is said that participants in the feast numbered 9,000, and that they all poured one and the same libation, singing a victory song immediately afterwards.

Notes

1. *The Persian agema served as a bodyguard. The* astheteroi *were a heavy infantry unit whose exact function is unclear.*
2. *The thesis of scholars such as Tarn (1948) that Alexander's prayer for accord (*homonoia) *reflected his dream of the brotherhood of mankind is no longer generally accepted.*

Questions

1. What aggrieved the Macedonians at Opis?
2. How did Alexander put down the revolt?
3. Can the Susa marriages (WEB **39.15**) be linked to the Opis mutiny?

39.16 Alexander and the Exiles Decree (324)

In addition to a mutinous army, Alexander had to deal with a restive empire. His settlements in Bactria, Sogdiania, and India largely collapsed and many mercenaries left their posts and made their way home. Greece too had a large homeless population. Alexander's solution was to repatriate exiles, many of whom served as mercenaries. It was a blatant violation of the treaty with members of the Corinthian League, which was supposed to preserve the autonomy of the cities (**38.17**: "Philip and the Greeks after Chaeronea"). The decree brought joy to the exiles, but also created a host of problems and especially the prospect of *stasis* between the returnees and residents who held their properties. Athens, for example, which had banished the locals in Samos in 365 and taken over their possessions, was concerned about the fate of her colonists there (see **34.2**: "Athens' Colonozation of Samos"). A number of inscriptions from other Greek cities show similar concerns elsewhere.

Diodorus reports on the king's exile decree, which was proclaimed at the 324 Olympics.

Diodorus of Sicily 18.8.1–5

(**18.8.1**) In Europe, the Rhodians freed their city after driving out the Macedonian garrison, and the Athenians commenced the so-called Lamian War against Antipater [323].[1] I must first set out the causes of this war in order to clarify the events that took place within it.

(**8.2**) Shortly before his death, Alexander decided to recall all exiles in the Greek cities. This was, in part, to enhance his reputation, but partly, too, because he wanted to have in each city large numbers of men personally attached to him to face rebellions and secessions amongst the Greeks. (**8.3**) Accordingly, since the Olympic Games were approaching, he gave Nicanor of Stageira a letter concerning the return of the exiles and sent him to Greece with orders to have the letter read out to the crowds during the festival by the winning herald.[2]

(**8.4**) Nicanor did as he was instructed, and the herald took from him and read out the letter, which ran as follows:

"A message from King Alexander to the exiles from the Greek Cities. Though we were not responsible for your exile, we shall be responsible for your return – apart from those under a curse – to your various cities. We have informed Antipater of this in writing so that he may bring force to bear on those of the cities refusing to recall you."

(**8.5**) When this was announced the crowd loudly applauded, those attending the festival showing their joyful appreciation of the king's gift and responding to his benefaction with shouts of praise. All the exiles had assembled for the festival and there were more than 20,000 of them.

Notes

1. *Antipater was Alexander's deputy in Macedonia.*
2. *A contest of heralds opened the Olympic Games.*

Question

1. To what extent was the exiles decree different from Alexander's letter to Chios (**39.2.B**)? What were the Greek reactions in each case?

39.17   Alexander's Death

Around October 324 Alexander lost his best friend and confidant, Hephaestion, to an alcohol-induced death. Hephaestion was given a hero cult, and it was perhaps then that Alexander received divine honors in Greece. Late and unreliable sources report that he demanded divine status, but the more contemporary sources imply that the initiative came from Greece.

A more pressing issue on the royal agenda was the preparations for an expedition against Arabia, but Alexander's death in 323 cut them short. According to Diodorus of Sicily (18.4.1–6), there were other plans, no less ambitious and costly, that Alexander had formulated, but that Alexander's generals and army decided to cancel following his death. See WEB **39.18** for Alexander's last plans.

Alexander died on June 10, 323 at the age of thirty-two, without designating an heir. As might be expected, his death was preceded by bad omens and followed by different allegations about its cause. One account is based on the *Ephemerides*, or Diaries, which were written by the unknown Diodotus of Erythrae and the much better known Eumenes of Cardia, who was Alexander's chief secretary and a major player in the wars of the Successors. The (court) diaries give a detailed description of Alexander's last days and ascribe his death to illness. Some historians accept the authenticity of the Diaries and even see them as the ultimate source for a number of primary histories on Alexander. A more recent and prevalent view, however, regards them as a later document designed to refute suspicions that Alexander had been poisoned. There was no shortage of fearful, resentful, or ambitious Macedonians in 323 who might have resorted to such means. The symptoms of Alexander's illness have led to diagnoses of different local diseases as well as poisoning.

Plutarch *Alexander* 76.1–77.5

(**76.1**) The following account of the illness is given in the *Ephemerides*. On the 18th of Daesius Alexander slept in the bathhouse because of his fever. (**76.2**) The next day he took a bath and went back to his bedroom, where he spent the day playing dice with Medius.[1] Then, late in the day, he bathed again and sacrificed to the gods, after which he took a bite and spent the night in a fever. (**76.3**) On the 20th he bathed once more, and made his usual sacrifice. He then made his bed in the bathhouse and spent his time with Nearchus and his officers listening to an account of their sea voyage and the ocean. (**76.4**) The 21st he passed in the same manner, but his temperature was higher. He had a bad night and the following day his fever was extremely high. (**76.5**) Removed from the bathhouse he then lay by the large swimming pool, conversing here with his generals on the subject of assessing personnel with a view to fulfilling the vacant posts in the army command. (**76.6**) On the 24th his fever was again extremely high, and he was carried outside to perform the sacrifice. He gave orders for his highest-ranking officers to remain in the court, and for the taxiarchs [battalion commanders] and pentakosiarchs [commanders of 500 men] to spend the night outside. (**76.7**) He was then transported on the 25th to the palace on the other river bank and here he slept a little, but the fever did not subside.

When his generals came to his side he was unable to speak, and that remained the case on the 26th. As a result the Macedonian rank and file thought he was dead. (**76.8**) They came to the doors shouting and uttering threats to the Companions until they had to give way. The doors were flung open for them, and they filed past his bed, one by one, wearing only their tunics. (**76.9**) That day, Python and Seleucus were sent to the temple of Sarapis to ask if they should bring Alexander there, but the god's reply was that they should leave him where he was. On the 28th, toward evening, he died.

(**77.1**) Most of the above account follows the *Ephemerides* word for word. (**77.2**) There was no suspicion of poisoning in the immediate aftermath, but they say that five years later Olympias was given information which led to her putting many to death and scattering the remains of Iolas,[2] now dead, alleging that he had poured the poison for Alexander. (**77.3**) Those who maintain that Aristotle advised Antipater on the deed, and that it was he who was entirely responsible for providing the poison, say that their account comes from one Hagnothemis who purportedly heard it from King Antigonus. (**77.4**) According to them the poison was a chilly water, cold as ice, that came from a certain cliff situated in Nonacris. This they gathered as a fine dew and set in an ass's hoof since no other receptacle could hold it (any other it would shatter with its coldness and pungent strength). (**77.5**) Most authors, however, believe the story to be a complete fiction and there is a piece of evidence favoring them, which is not insignificant. During the quarrels between Alexander's generals, which lasted several days, the corpse lay unattended in hot and stifling conditions and yet showed no sign of the deterioration a death of that kind would cause, but remained clean and fresh.

Notes

1. *Medius is otherwise known as Alexander's flatterer. Sources of dubious credibility involve him in Alexander's poisoning.*
2. *Iolas was Antipater's son who served in Alexander's court.*

Questions

1. Where did Alexander plan to march according to the *Ephemerides* (WEB **39.18**)?
2. Which of Alexander's future projects (WEB **39.18**) can be related to the celebrations after the Opis mutiny (**39.14.A–B**)?

Review Questions

1. To what extent was Alexander the champion of the Greeks (see **39.1–2**, **39.8**, **39.11**, **39.14**, **39.16**, WEB **39.3.I–II**, WEB **39.12**, WEB **39.15**)?

2. How did Alexander and his army excel on the battlefield (**39.2**, **39.4**, WEB **39.3.I**, WEB **39.5**)?

3. How did Alexander treat the conquered population (**39.2**, **39.4**, **39.6**, **39.8**, **39.11**, **39.14**, WEB **39.7**, WEB **39.12**, WEB **39.15**)?

4. How did Alexander control the Macedonian elite and his troops (**39.2**, **39.9–11**, **39.14**, **39.17**, WEB **39.15**)?

5. Describe the evolution of Alexander's ambitions and self-perception (**39.2**, **39.6**, **39.9–11**, WEB **39.3.II**, WEB **39.15**, WEB **39.18**).

6. What characterized Alexander's commemoration of his victories (**39.4**, **39.13**, WEB **39.3.II**)?
7. What cultural challenges did Alexander and his Macedonians encounter? How did they react to them?

Suggested Readings

Alexander the Great: Bosworth 1988; Green 1991a; Roisman 2003; Cartledge 2004. *Sources on Alexander in translation*: Worthington 2003a; Heckel and Yardley 2004. *Alexander and the Greeks (including Thebes' destruction)*: Heisserer 1980; Rubinsohn 1997; Faraguna 2003; Worthington 2003b. *Alexander's military campaign, army, and generals*: Fuller 1958; Heckel 1992, 2002, 2007; Strauss 2003; Lonsdale 2006. *Alexander's aims*: Flower 2000a; Fredricksmeyer 2000; Bloedow 2003. *Alexander in art*: Bieber 1964; Killerich 1993; Stewart 1993, 2003. *Alexander and the Asian Greeks*: see Alexander and the Greeks above, and Nawotka 2003b; for Chios: Heisserer 1980, 79–95; Piejko 1985; R&O, no. 84, pp. 418–424. *Gordian knot*: Fredricksmeyer 1961; Bosworth 1980–1995, 1: 184–188; cf. B. Burke 2001; Munn 2008. *Battle of Issus*: Devine 1985a, 1985b; Bosworth 1988, 55–64; Hammond 1992. *The Alexander Mosaic*: Stewart 1993, 130–135; A. Cohen 1997; Badian 1999; Stewart 2003, 42–44. *Alexander's divine aspirations*: Balsdon 1950; Edmunds 1971; Badian 1981; Cawkwell 1994; Fredricksmeyer 2003. *Foundation of cities*: Tarn 1948, 2: 232–259; Fraser 1996; Hammond 1998. *Persepolis*: Borza 1972 and Nawotka 2003a (message to the east); Sancisi-Weerdenburg 1993 (a conqueror in action); Badian 1994 and Flower 2000a, 113–115 (message to Greece); cf. Morrison 2001 (an emotional outlet). *The Philotas affair*: Badian 1960, 2000, 64–74 (Alexander's plot against Parmenion); Heckel 1977, 2003, 202–220, and Rubinsohn 1977 (a power struggle within the elite); cf. Adams 2004. *The Cleitus affair*: Carney 1981; Bosworth

1996; Tritle 2004. *The proskynesis affair*: see Alexander's divine aspirations above, and Brown 1949; Bosworth 1980–1995, 2: 68–101. *The battle at the Hydaspes and the "Porus medallions"*: Bosworth 1996, 5–21; Lane Fox 1996; *contra*: Holt 2003. *Alexander in India*: Bosworth 1996, 1–165; cf. Badian 1998. *Susa marriages and the policy of integration*: Bosworth 1980; O'Neil 2002; Brosius 2003. *Opis mutiny*: Carney 1996, esp. 31–44; cf. Nagle 1996 (Alexander's speech). *The exiles decree*: Bosworth 1988, 220–228; Green 1991a, 249–251; Faraguna 2003, 124–127; Dmitriev 2004. *Alexander's future plans*: Tarn 1921 (forgery); Badian 1967 and Flower 2000a, 132–135 (authentic). *Alexander's death and the Diaries*: Badian 1987b; Heckel 1988; Anson 1996 (an authentic document); O'Brien 1992, 217–228 (death by alcoholism); Borza and Reames-Zimmerman 2000 (from typhoid).

References

Adams, W.L. 1996. "Historical Perceptions of Greco-Macedonian Ethnicity in the Hellenistic Age." *Balkan Studies* 36, 205–222.

Adams, W.L. 2004. "The Episode of Philotas: An Insight." In W. Heckel and L.A. Tritle, eds., *Crossroads of History: The Age of Alexander*. Claremont, CA, 113–126.

Adkins, A.W.H. 1960. *Merit and Responsibility: A Study in Greek Values*. Oxford.

Aidonis, T. 1996. "Tissaphernes' Dealings with the Greeks." *Classica & Mediaevalia* 47, 89–108.

Akbar Khan, H., ed. 1994. *The Birth of the European Identity: The Europe–Asia Contrast in Greek Thought, 490–322 BC*. Nottingham.

Almeida, J.A. 2003. *Justice as an Aspect of the Polis Idea in Solon's Political Poems: A Reading of the Fragments in Light of the Researches of New Classical Archaeology*. Leiden.

Anderson, G. 2003. *The Athenian Experiment: Building an Imagined Political Community in Ancient Attica, 508–490 BC*. Ann Arbor.

Anderson, G. 2005. "Before *Turannoi* were Tyrants: Rethinking a Chapter of Early Greek History." *ClAnt* 24, 173–222.

Anderson, J. 1970. *Military Theory and Practice in the Age of Xenophon*. Berkeley.

Andrewes, A. 1956. *The Greek Tyrants*. London.

Andrewes, A. 1974. "The Arginusai Trial." *Phoenix* 1974, 112–122.

Andrewes, A. 1978. "The Opposition to Pericles. *JHS* 98, 1–8.

Andrewes, A. 1982a. "The Growth of the Athenian State." *CAH* 3.3, 360–391.

Andrewes, A. 1982b. "Notion and Kyzikos: The Sources Compared." *JHS* 102, 15–25.

Andronikos, M. 1984. *Vergina: The Royal Tombs and the City*. Athens.

Anson, E.M. 1991. "The Evolution of the Macedonian Army Assembly (330–315 B.C.)." *Historia* 40, 230–247.

Anson, E.M. 1996. "The Ephemerides of Alexander the Great." *Historia* 45.4, 501–504.

Anson, E.M. 2004. *Eumenes of Cardia: A Greek Among Macedonians*. Leiden.

Archibald, Z.H. 2000. "Space, Hierarchy, and Community in Archaic and Classical Macedonia, Thessaly and Thrace." In R. Brock and S. Hodkinson, eds., *Alternatives to Athens: Varieties of Political Organization and Community in Ancient Greece*. Oxford, 212–233.

Arthur, M.B. 1973. "Early Greece: The Origins of Western Attitude Toward Women." *Arethusa* 6, 7–58. Reprinted in J. Peradotto and J.P. Sullivan, eds., 1984, *Women in the Ancient World: The Arethusa Papers*. Albany.

Ault, A. and L.C. Nevett, eds. 2005. *Ancient Greek Houses and Households: Chronological, Regional, and Social Diversity*. Philadelphia.

Bäbler, B. 2005. "Bobbies or Boobies? The Scythian Police Force in Classical Athens." In D. Braund, ed., *Scythians and Greeks: Cultural Interactions in Scythia, Athens and the Early Roman Empire (Sixth Century BC–First Century AD)*. Exeter, UK, 114–122.

Badian, E. 1960. "The Death of Parmenio." *TAPhA* 91, 324–338.

Badian, E. 1963. "The Death of Philip II." *Phoenix* 17, 244–250.

Badian, E. 1967. "A King's Notebooks." *HSCP* 72, 183–204.

Badian, E. 1971. "Archons and *Strategoi*." *Antichton* 5, 1–34.

Badian, E. 1977. "The Battle of Granicus: A New Look." *Ancient Macedonia* 2, 271–293.

Badian, E. 1981. "The Deification of Alexander the Great." In H.J. Dell, ed., *Ancient Macedonian Studies in Honor of Charles F. Edson*. Thessaloniki, 27–71.

Badian, E. 1987a. "The Peace of Callias." *JHS* 107, 1–39.

Badian, E. 1987b. "The Ring and the Book." In E. Will and J. Heinrichs, eds., *Zu Alexander dem Grossen: Festschrift Gerhard Wirth zum 60. Geburtstag am 9.12.86*. Amsterdam, Vol. 1, 605–625.

Badian, E. 1991. "The King's Peace." In M.A. Flower and M. Toher, eds., *Georgica: Greek Studies in Honour of George Cawkwell*. London, 25–48.

Badian, E. 1993. *From Plataea to Potidaea: Studies in the History and Historiography of the Pentekontaetia*. Baltimore.

Badian, E. 1994. "Agis III: Revisions and Reflections." In I. Worthington, ed., *Ventures into Greek History*. Oxford, 258–292.

Badian, E. 1995. "The Ghost of Empire: Reflections on Athenian Foreign Policy in the Fourth Century." In W. Eder, ed., *Die athenische Demokratie im 4. Jahrhundert v. Chr.* Stuttgart, 79–106.

Badian, E. 1996. "Alexander the Great between Two Thrones and Heaven: Variations on an Old Theme." In A.M. Small, ed., *Subject and Ruler: The Cult of the Ruling Power in Classical Antiquity*. Ann Arbor, 11–26.

Badian, E. 1998. "The King's Indians." In W. Will, ed., *Alexander der Grosse: Eine Welteroberung und ihr Hintergrund*. Bonn, 205–224.

Badian, E. 1999. "A Note on Alexander Mosaic." In F.B. Titchener and R.F. Moorton, eds., *The Eye Expanded: Life and the Arts in Greco-Roman Antiquity*. Berkeley, 73–92.

Badian, E. 2000. "Conspiracies." In A.B. Bosworth and E.J. Baynham, eds. *Alexander the Great in Fact and Fiction*. Oxford, 50–95.

Bakker, E.J., I.J.F. de Jong, and H. van Wees, eds. 2002. *Brill's Companion to Herodotus*. Leiden.

Balcer, J.M. 1978. *The Athenian Regulations for Chalkis: Studies in the Athenian Imperial Law*. Wiesbaden.

Balcer, J.M. 1995. *The Persian Conquest of the Greeks, 545–450 B.C.* Konstanz.

Balme, M. 1984. "Attitudes to Work and Leisure in Ancient Greece." *G&R* 31.2, 140–152.

Balsdon, J.P.V.D. 1950. "The 'Divinity' of Alexander." *Historia* 1, 363–388.

Barber, G.L. 1993. *The Historian Ephorus*, 2nd ed. Chicago.

Baron, C.A. 2006. "The Aristoteles' Decree and the Expansion of the Second Athenian League." *Hesperia* 75.3, 379–395.

Barrett, A.A. and M. Vickers, 1978. "The Oxford Brygos Cup Reconsidered." *JHS* 98, 17–24.

Barringer, J.M. and J.M. Hurwit, eds. 2005. *Periklean Athens and Its Legacy: Problems and Perspectives.* Austin.

Bauslaugh, R.A. 1990. "Messenian Dialect and Dedications of the 'Methanioi.'" *Hesperia* 59, 661–668.

Baynham, E. 1994. "The Question of Macedonian Divine Honours for Philip II." *Mediterranean Archaeology* 7, 35–43.

Baynham, E. 2003. "Antipater and Athens." In O. Palagia and S.V. Tracy, eds., *The Macedonians in Athens 322–229 BC.* Proceedings of an International Conference held at the University of Athens, May 24–26, 2001. Oxford, 23–29.

Baziotopoulou-Valavani, E. 2002. "A Mass Burial from the Cemetery of Kerameikos." In M. Stamatopoulou and M. Yeroulanou, eds., *Excavating Classical Culture: Recent Archaeological Discoveries in Greece.* Studies in Classical Archaeology. Oxford, 187–201.

Beck, H. 2000. "Thebes, the Boiotian League, and the 'Rise of Federalism,' in Fourth Century Greece." In P.A. Bernardini, ed., *Presenza e Funzione della Città di Tebe nella Cultura Greca. Atti del Convegno Internazionale (Urbino 7–9 iuglio 1997).* Pisa, 331–344.

Beck, H. 2001. "'The Laws of the Fathers' versus 'The Laws of the League': Xenophon on Federalism." *CPh* 96.4, 355–375.

Bellinger, A.R. 1963. *Essays on the Coinage of Alexander the Great.* New York.

Best, J. 1969. *Thracian Peltasts and Their Influence on Greek Warfare.* Groningen.

Bieber, M. 1964. *Alexander the Great in Greek and Roman Art.* Chicago.

Blamire, A. 1989. *Plutarch: Life of Kimon.* London.

Blanshard, A.J.L. 2007. "The Problems with Honouring Samos: An Athenian Document Relief and its Interpretation." In Z. Newby and R. Leader-Newby, eds., *Art and Inscriptions in the Ancient World.* Cambridge, 19–37.

Block, J.H. and A.P.M.H. Lardinois, eds. 2006. *Solon of Athens: New Historical and Philological Approaches.* Leiden.

Bloedow, E.F. 1973. *Alcibiades Reexamined.* Wiesbaden.

Bloedow, E.F. 1992. "The Peaces of Callias." *Symbolae Osloenses* 67, 41–68.

Bloedow, E.F. 2003. "Why Did Philip and Alexander Launch a War Against the Persian Empire?" *Acta Classica* 72, 261–274.

Blösel, W. 2001. "The Herodotean Picture of Themistocles: A Mirror of Fifth-Century Athens." In N. Luraghi, ed., *The Historian's Craft in the Age of Herodotus.* Oxford, 179–197.

Boardman, J. 1966. "Evidence for Dating the Greek Settlements in Cyrene." *Annual of the British School at Athens* 61, 149–156.

Boardman, J. 1974. *Athenian Black-Figure Vases.* London.

Boardman, J. 1975. *Athenian Red-Figure Vases: The Archaic Period: A Handbook.* London.

Boardman, J. 1978. "Exekias." *AJA* 82, 11–25.

Boardman, J. 1989. *Athenian Red-Figure Vases: The Classical Period.* London.

Boardman, J. 1991a. *Greek Sculpture: The Archaic Period.* London.

Boardman, J. 1991b. *Greek Sculpture: The Classical Period.* London.

Boardman, J. 1996. *Greek Art,* 4th rev. ed. London.

Boardman, J. 1999. *The Greeks Overseas: Their Early Colonies and Trade,* 4th ed. London.

Boardman, J. 2005. "Composition and Content on Classical Mural and Vases." In J.M. Barringer and J.M. Hurwit, eds., *Periklean Athens and Its Legacy: Problems and Perspectives.* Austin, 63–72.

Boardman, J. 2006. *The History of Greek Vases: Potters, Painters and Pictures*. London.

Bodel, J., ed. 2001. *Epigraphic Evidence: Ancient History from Inscriptions*. London.

Boedeker, D. 1993. "Hero Cult and Politics in Herodotus: The Bones of Orestes." In C. Dougherty and L. Kurke, eds., *Cultural Poetics in Archaic Greece: Cult, Performance, Politics*. Cambridge, 164–177.

Boedeker, D. 1998. "The New Simonides and Heroization at Plataia." In N. Fisher and H. van Wees, eds., *Archaic Greece: New Approaches and New Evidence*. London, 231–249.

Boedeker, D. and D. Sider, eds. 2001. *The New Simonides: Contexts of Praise and Desire*. New York.

Boegehold, A.L. 1994. "Perikles' Citizenship Law of 451/0 BC." In A.L. Boegehold and A. Scaffuro, eds., *Athenian Identity and Civic Ideology*. Baltimore, 57–66.

Boegehold, A.L. 1995. *The Lawcourts at Athens: Sites, Buildings, Equipment, Procedure, and Testimonia*. Princeton.

Boersma, J.S. 1970. *Athenian Building Policy from 561/0–405/4 BC*. Groningen.

Borbein, A.H. 1996. "Polykleitos: Personal Styles in Greek Sculpture." In O. Palagia and J.J. Pollitt, eds., *Personal Styles in Greek Sculpture*. Cambridge, 66–90.

Borthwick, E.K. 2000. "Aristophanes and the Trial of Thucydides, Son of Melesias." *Phoenix* 54.3–4, 203–211.

Borza, E.N. 1972. "Fire from Heaven: Alexander at Persepolis." *CPh* 66, 233–245.

Borza, E.N. 1987. "Royal Macedonian Tombs and the Paraphernalia of Alexander the Great." *Phoenix* 41, 105–121.

Borza, E.N. 1990. *In the Shadow of Olympus: The Emergence of Macedon*. Princeton.

Borza, E.N. 1996. "Greeks and Macedonians in the Age of Alexander: The Source Traditions." In R.W. Wallace and E.M. Harris, eds., *Transitions to Empire: Essays in Greco-Roman History, 360–146 BC, in Honor of E. Badian*. Norman, 122–139.

Borza, E.N. 1999. *Before Alexander: Constructing Early Macedonia*. Claremont, CA.

Borza, E. and J. Reames-Zimmerman, 2000. "Some New Thoughts on the Death of Alexander the Great." *Ancient World* 31.1, 22–30.

Bosworth, A.B. 1971. "Philip II and Upper Macedonia." *CQ* 21, 93–105.

Bosworth, A.B. 1980. "Alexander and the Iranians." *JHS* 100, 1–21.

Bosworth, A.B. 1980–1995. *A Historical Commentary on Arrian's History of Alexander the Great*, 2 vols. Oxford.

Bosworth, A.B. 1986. "Alexander the Great and the Decline of Macedon." *JHS* 106, 1–12.

Bosworth, A.B. 1988. *Conquest and Empire: The Reign of Alexander the Great*. Cambridge.

Bosworth, A.B. 1993. "The Humanitarian Aspect of the Melian Dialogue." *JHS* 113, 30–44.

Bosworth, A.B. 1996. "The Tumult and the Shouting: Two Interpretations of the Cleitus Episode." *Ancient History Bulletin* 10.1, 19–30.

Bosworth, A.B. 2002. *The Legacy of Alexander: Politics, Warfare and Propaganda Under the Successors*. Oxford.

Bosworth, A.B. and E.J. Baynham, eds. 2000. *Alexander the Great in Fact and Fiction*. Oxford.

Bowden, H. 2005. *Classical Athens and the Delphic Oracle: Divination and Democracy*. Cambridge.

Bowersock, G.W. 1967. "Pseudo-Xenophon." *HSCP* 71, 33–55.

Bowie, C.M. 1993. *Aristophanes; Myth, Ritual and Comedy*. Cambridge.

Bowra, M. 1961. *Greek Lyric Poetry: From Alcman to Simonides*, 2nd ed. Oxford.

Bradeen, D.W. 1960. "The Popularity of the Athenian Empire." *Historia* 9, 257–269.

Bremmer, J.N. 1980. "An Enigmatic Indo-European Rite: Paederasty." *Arethusa* 13, 279–298.

Bremmer, J.N. 1990. "Adolescents, *Symposion*, and Pederasty." In O. Murray, ed., *Sympotica: A Symposium on the "Symposion."* Oxford, 135–148.

Bremmer, J.N. 1994. *Greek Religion*. Oxford.

Briant, P. 2002a. *From Cyrus to Alexander: A History of the Persian Empire*. Trans. P.T. Daniels. Winona Lake, IN.

Briant, P. 2002b [1989]. "History and Ideology: The Greeks and the 'Persian Decadence.'" In T. Harrison, ed., *Greeks and Barbarians*. New York, 193–210.

Brickhouse, T.C. and N.D. Smith, 1989. *Socrates on Trial*. Princeton.

Broadhead, H.D. 1960. *The Persae of Aeschylus*. Cambridge.

Brock, R. 1991. "The Emergence of Democratic Ideology." *Historia* 40, 160–169.

Brock, R. 1994. "The Labour of Women in Classical Athens." *CQ* 44: 336–346.

Brosius, M. 2003. "Alexander and the Persians." In J. Roisman, ed., *Brill's Companion to Alexander the Great*. Leiden, 169–193.

Brosius, M. 2006. *The Persians: An Introduction*. London.

Brown, T.S. 1949. "Callisthenes and Alexander." *AJP* 70, 225–248.

Brunt, P.A. 1953–1954. "The Hellenic League Against Persia." *Historia* 2, 135–163. Reprinted in P.A. Brunt, 1993. *Studies in Greek History and Thought*. Oxford, 47–83.

Brunt, P.A. 1965. "Spartan Policy and Strategy in the Archidamian War." *Phoenix* 19, 255–280. Reprinted in P.A. Brunt, 1993. *Studies in Greek History and Thought*. Oxford, 84–111.

Buck, C.D. 1965. *The Greek Dialects*, 2nd ed. Chicago.

Buck, R.J. 1994. *Boiotia and the Boiotian League, 423–371 BC*. Edmonton.

Buckler, J. 1980. *The Theban Hegemony 371–362 BC*. Cambridge, MA.

Buckler, J. 1989. *Philip II and the Sacred War*. Leiden.

Buckler, J. 1994. "Philip II, The Greeks, and the King, 346–36 BC." *Illinois Classical Studies* 19, 99–122.

Buckler, J. 2000. "Demosthenes and Aeschines." In I. Worthington, ed., *Demosthenes: Statesman and Orator*. London, 114–158.

Buckler, J. 2003. *Aegean Greece in the Fourth Century*. Leiden.

Buckler, J. and H. Beck, 2008. *Central Greece and the Politics of Power in the Fourth Century*. Cambridge.

Burke, B. 2001. "Anatolian Origins of the Gordian Knot Legend." *GRBS* 42, 255–261.

Burke, E.M. 1984. "Eubulus, Olynthus, and Euboea." *TAPhA* 114, 111–120.

Burke, E. M. 1985. "Lycurgan Finances." *GRBS* 26.3, 251–264.

Burkert, W. 1985. *Greek Religion: Archaic and Classical*. Trans. J. Raffan. Oxford.

Burkert, W. 1987. *Ancient Mystery Cults*. Cambridge, MA.

Burkert, W. 1992. *The Orientalizing Revolution: Near Eastern Influence on Greek Culture in the Early Archaic Age*. Trans. M.E. Pinder and W. Burkert, Cambridge, MA.

Burkert, W. 2004. *Babylon, Memphis, Persepolis: Eastern Contexts of Greek Culture*. Cambridge, MA.

Burn, A.R. 1984 [1962]. *Persia and the Greeks: The Defense of the West, 546–478 BC*, 2nd ed. Stanford.

Burns, A. 1976. "Hippodamus and the Planned City." *Historia* 25, 414–428.

Cahill, N. 2002. *Household and City Organization at Olynthus*. New Haven.

Cairns, D.L. 1993. *Aidôs: The Psychology and Ethics of Honour and Shame in Ancient Greek Literature*. Oxford.

Calame, C. 1997. *Choruses of Young Women in Ancient Greece: Their Morphology, Religious Role, and Social Function*. Trans. J. Orion and D. Collins, Lanham.

Calame, C. 2003. *Myth and History in Ancient Greece: The Symbolic Creation of a Colony*. Trans. D. Berman. Princeton.

Camp, J.M. 2001. *The Archaeology of Athens*. New Haven.

Carawan, E.M. 1987. "*'Eisangelia' and 'Euthuna'*: The Trials of Miltiades, Themistocles, and Cimon." *GRBS* 28, 167–208.

Carawan, E.M. 1998. *Rhetoric and the Law of Draco*. Oxford.

Carawan, E.M. 2001. "What the Laws Have Prejudged: Παραγραφή and Early Issue-Theory." In C.W. Wooten, ed., *The Orator in Action and Theory in Greece and Rome*. Leiden, 17–51.

Carey, C. 1989. *Lysias: Selected Speeches*. Cambridge.

Carey, C., ed. 1992. *Apollodorus Against Neaira (Demosthenes 59)*. Greek Orators, Vol. 6. Warminster, UK.

Carey, C. 1995. "Rape and Adultery in Athenian Law." *CQ* 45, 407–417.

Cargill, J. 1981. *The Second Athenian League: Empire or Free Alliance?* Berkeley.

Cargill, J. 1995. *Athenian Settlements of the Fourth Century*. Leiden.

Carney, E.D. 1981. "The Death of Clitus." *GRBS* 22, 149–160.

Carney, E.D. 1992. "The Politics of Polygamy: Olympias, Alexander and the Murder of Philip." *Historia* 41, 169–189.

Carney, E.D. 1996. "Macedonians and Mutiny: Discipline and Indiscipline in the Army of Philip and Alexander." *CPh* 91.1, 19–44.

Carney, E.D. 2000. *Women and Monarchy in Macedonia*. Norman, OK.

Carney, E.D. 2003. "Women in Alexander's Court." In J. Roisman, ed., *Brill's Companion to Alexander the Great*. Leiden, 227–252.

Carney, E.D. 2007. "The Philippeum, Women, and the Formation of Dynastic Image." In W. Heckel, L.A. Tritle, and P. Wheatley, eds., *Alexander's Empire: Formulation to Decay*. Claremont, CA, 27–60.

Carney, E.D. 2008. "The Role of the *Basilikoi Paides* at the Argead Court." In T. Howe and J. Reames, eds., *Macedonian Legacies: Studies in Ancient Macedonian History and Culture in Honor of Eugene N. Borza*. Claremont, CA, 145–164.

Carradice, I. 1995. *Greek Coins*. Austin.

Carter, J.M. 1971. "Athens, Euboea and Olynthus." *Historia* 20, 418–429.

Cartledge, P.A. 1979. *Sparta and Lakonia: A Regional History, 1300–362 BC*. London.

Cartledge, P.A. 1987. *Agesilaos and the Crisis of Sparta*. London.

Cartledge, P.A. 1992. "Early Lakedaimon: The Making of a Conquest State." In J.M. Sanders, ed., *ΦΙΛΟΛΑΚΩΝ: Lakonian Studies in Honour of Hector Catling*. London, 49–55.

Cartledge, P.A. 2001. *Spartan Reflections*. Berkeley.

Cartledge, P.A. 2002. *The Greeks: A Portrait of Self and Others,* 2nd ed. Oxford.

Cartledge, P.A. 2003. *The Spartans*. New York.

Cartledge, P.A. 2004. *Alexander the Great: The Hunt for a New Past*. New York.

Cartledge, P.A. 2006. *Thermopylae: The Battle that Changed the World*. New York.

Casson, L. 1991. *The Ancient Mariners: Seafarers and Sea Fighters of the Mediterranean in Ancient Times,* 2nd ed. Princeton.

Castriota, D. 1992. *Myth, Ethos and Actuality: Official Art in Fifth Century BC Athens*. Madison, WI.

Castriota, D. 2005. "Feminizing the Barbarian and Barbarizing the Feminine: Amazons, Trojans, and Persians in the Stoa Poikile." In J.M. Barringer and J.M. Hurwit, eds., *Periklean Athens and Its Legacy: Problems and Perspectives*. Austin, 89–102.

Cavanaugh, M.B. 1996. *Eleusis and Athens: Documents in Finance, Religion and Politics in the Fifth Century BC*. Atlanta.

Cawkwell, G.L. 1962. "Notes on the Social War." *Classica & Mediaevalia* 23, 34–49.

Cawkwell, G.L. 1971. "The Fall of Themistocles." In B.F. Harris, ed., *Auckland Classical Essays Presented to E.M. Blaiklock*. London, 39–58.

Cawkwell, G.L. 1972. "Epaminondas and Thebes." *CQ* 22, 254–278.

Cawkwell, G.L. 1975. "Thucydides' Judgment of Periclean Strategy." *YCS* 24, 53–70.

Cawkwell, G.L. 1978. *Philip of Macedon*. London.

Cawkwell, G.L. 1993. "Cleomenes." *Mnemosyne* 46, 506–527.

Cawkwell, G.L. 1994. "The Deification of Alexander the Great: A Note." In I. Worthington, ed., *Ventures into Greek History*. Oxford, 293–306.

Cawkwell, G.L. 1995. "Early Greek Tyranny and the People." *CQ* 45, 73–86.

Cawkwell, G.L. 1997. *Thucydides and the Peloponnesian War*. London.

Cawkwell, G.L. 2005. *The Greek Wars: The Failure of Persia*. Oxford.

Chambers, M. 1984. "Themistocles and the Piraeus." In A.L. Boegehold et al., eds., *Studies Presented to Sterling Dow on his Eightieth Birthday*. Durham, 43–50.

Chambers, M. 1992. "Photographic Enhancement of a Greek Inscription." *CJ* 88, 25–31.

Chambers, M., R. Galluci, and P. Spanos, 1990. "Athens' Alliance with Egesta in the Year of Antiphon." *ZPE* 83, 38–63.

Christ, M. 1990. "Liturgy Avoidance and Antidosis in Classical Athens." *TAPhA* 120, 147–169.

Christ, M. 1998. *The Litigious Athenians*. Baltimore.

Christ, M. 2007. "The Evolution of the *Eisphora* in Classical Athens." *CQ* 57.1, 53–67.

Christien, J. 2002. "Iron Money in Sparta: Myth and History." In A. Powell and S. Hodkinson, eds., *Sparta: Beyond the Mirage*. London, 171–189.

Clay, J. S. 2003. *Hesiod's Cosmos*. Cambridge.

Clinton, K. 1974. *The Sacred Officials of the Eleusinian Mysteries*. Philadelphia.

Clinton, K. 1993. "The Sanctuary of Demeter and Kore at Eleusis." In N. Marinatos and R. Hägg, eds., *Greek Sanctuaries: New Approaches*. London, 11–24.

Clinton, K. 2009. "The Eleusinian Sanctuary During the Peloponnesian War." In O. Palagia, ed., *Art in Athens During the Peloponnesian War*. Cambridge, 52–65.

Cohen, A. 1997. *The Alexander Mosaic: Stories of Victory and Defeat*. Cambridge.

Cohen, D. 1991. *Law, Sexuality, and Society: The Enforcement of Morals in Ancient Athens*. Cambridge.

Cohen, E.E. 1992. *Athenian Economy and Society: A Banking Perspective*. Princeton.

Coldstream, J.M. 2003. *Geometric Greece: 900–700 BC*, 2nd ed. London.

Cole, S.G. 1993. "Procession and Celebration at the Dionysia." In R. Scodel, ed., *Theater and Society in the Classical World*. Ann Arbor, 25–38.

Connor, W.R. 1971. *The New Politicians of Fifth-Century Athens*. Princeton.

Connor, W.R. 1984. *Thucydides*. Princeton.

Connor, W.R. 1987. "Tribes, Festivals, and Processions: Civic Ceremonial and Political Manipulation in Archaic Greece," *JHS* 107, 40–50.

Connor, W.R. 1989. "City Dionysia and Athenian Democracy." *Classica & Mediaevalia* 40, 7–32.

Constantakapoulou, C. 2007. *The Dance of the Islands: Insularity, Networks, the Athenian Empire, and the Aegean World*. Oxford.

Cooper, C. 1995. "Hyperides and the Trial of Phryne." *Phoenix* 49.4, 303–318.

Corso, A. 1997–1998. "Love as Suffering: The Eros of Thespiae of Praxiteles." *British Institute of Classical Studies* 42, 63–91.

Cox, C.A. 1998. *Household Interests: Property, Marriage Strategies, and Family Dynamics in Ancient Athens*. Princeton.

Crane, G. 1992. "Fear and Pursuit of Risk: Corinth on Athens, Sparta, and the Peloponnesians (Thucydides 1.68–71, 120–21)." *TAPhA* 122, 227–256.

Crane, G. 1998. *Thucydides and the Ancient Simplicity: The Limits of Political Realism*. Berkeley.

Csapo, E. and W. Slater, 1995. *The Context of Ancient Drama*. Ann Arbor.

Dahmen, K. 2007. *The Legend of Alexander the Great on Greek and Roman Coins*. London.

David, E. 1979. "The Conspiracy of Cinadon." *Athenaeum* 57, 239–259.

Davidson, J. 1997. *Courtesans and Fishcakes: The Consuming Passions of Classical Athens*. New York.

Davidson, J. 2005. "Theatrical Production." In J. Gregory, ed., *A Companion to Greek Tragedy*. Oxford, 194–211.

Davidson, J. 2007. *The Greeks and Greek Love: A Radical Reappraisal of Homosexuality in Ancient Greece*. London.

Davies, J.K. 1981. *Wealth and the Power of Wealth in Classical Athens*. New York.

Davies, J.K. 1997. "The 'Origins of the Greek *Polis*': Where Should We Be Looking?" In L. Mitchell and P.J. Rhodes, eds., *The Development of the Polis in Archaic Greece*. London, 24–38.

Davies, J.K. 2005. "The Gortyn Laws." In M. Gagarin and D. Cohen, eds., *The Cambridge Companion to Ancient Greek Law*. Cambridge, 305–328.

De Angelis, F. 2003. *Megara Hyblaia and Selinous: The Development of Two Greek City-States in Archaic Sicily*. Oxford.

de Romilly, J. 1992. *The Great Sophists in Periclean Athens*. Trans. J. Lloyd. Oxford.

Demand, N. 1982. *Thebes in the Fifth Century*. London.

Demand, N. 1990. *Urban Relocation in Archaic and Classical Greece: Flight and Consolidation*. Norman.

Descoeudres, J.-P., ed. 1990. *Greek Colonists and Native Populations*. Oxford.

Develin, R. 1977. "Miltiades and the Parian Expedition." *L'Antiquité classique* 46, 571–577.

Develin, R. and M. Kilmer, 1997. "What Kleisthenes Did?" *Historia* 64, 3–18.

Devine, A.M. 1975. "Grand Tactics at Gaugamela." *Phoenix* 29, 374–385.

Devine, A.M. 1985a. "Grand Tactics at the Battle of Issus." *Ancient World* 12, 39–59.

Devine, A.M. 1985b. "The Strategies of Alexander the Great and Darios III in the Issus Campaign (333 BC)." *Ancient World* 12, 25–38.

Devine, A.M. 1986. "The Battle of Gaugamela: A Tactical and Source-Critical Study." *Ancient World* 13, 87–116.

Devine, A.M. 1988. "A Pawn-Sacrifice at the Battle of the Granicus: The Origins of a Favorite Stratagem of Alexander the Great." *Ancient World* 18, 3–20.

De Voto, J.G. 1992. "The Theban Sacred Band." *Ancient World* 23.2: 3–19.

Dewald, C. 1981. "Women and Culture in Herodotus' *Histories*." In H.P. Foley, ed., *Reflections of Women in Antiquity*. New York, 91–125.

Dewald, C. 2003. "Form and Content: The Question of Tyranny in Herodotus." In K. Morgan, ed., *Popular Tyranny: Sovereignty and Its Discontents in Ancient Greece*. Austin, 25–58.

Dewald, C. and J. Marincola, eds. 2006. *The Cambridge Companion to Herodotus*. Cambridge.

Dillery, J. 1995. *Xenophon and the History of His Times*. London.

Dillon, M. 1997. *Pilgrims and Pilgrimage in Ancient Greece*. London.

Dillon, M. and L. Garland, 2000. *Ancient Greece: Social and Historical Documents from Archaic Times to the Death of Socrates (c. 800–399 BC)*, 2nd ed. London.

Dmitriev, S. 2004. "Alexander's Exiles Decree." *Klio* 86, 348–381.

Donlan, W. 1980. *The Aristocratic Ideal in Ancient Greece*. Lawrence.

Donlan, W. 1989. "The Unequal Exchange between Glaucus and Diomedes in Light of the Homeric Gift-Economy." *Phoenix* 43, 1–15.

Donlan, W. 1993. "Duelling with Gifts in the *Iliad*: As the Audience Saw It." *Colby Quarterly* 29, 155–172.

Donlan, W. 1997. "The Relations of Power in the Pre-State and Early State Polities." In L. Mitchell and P.J. Rhodes, eds., *The Development of the Polis in Archaic Greece*. London, 39–48.

Dover, K.J. 1988. *The Greeks and Their Legacy: Collected Papers, Vol. 2: Prose, Literature, History, Society, Transmission, Influence*. Oxford.

Dover, K.J. 1989. *Greek Homosexuality*, 2nd ed. Cambridge, MA.

Dubois, P. 2003. *Slaves and Other Objects*. Chicago.

Ducat, J. 2006. *Spartan Education: Youth and Society in the Classical Period*. Trans. E. Stafford et al. Swansea.

Dunkley, B. 1935–1936. "List of Fountain Scenes in Attic Vase Paintings." *Papers of the British School at Athens* 36, 198–207.

Edmunds, L. 1971. "The Religiosity of Alexander." *GRBS* 12, 363–391.

Edwards, A.T. 2004. *Hesiod's Ascra*. Berkeley.

Edwards, C. 1996. "Lysippos." In O. Palagia and J.J. Pollitt, eds., *Personal Styles in Greek Sculpture*. Cambridge, 130–153.

Edwards, M. J., ed. 1995. *Andocides*. Greek Orators, Vol. 4. Warminster, UK.

Edwards, M. J. and S. Usher, trans. and eds. 1985. *Antiphon and Lysias*. Greek Orators, Vol. 1. Warminster, UK.

Ehrenberg, V. 1948. "The Foundation of Thurii." *AJP* 69, 149–170.

Ellis, J. R. 1976. *Philip II and Macedonian Imperialism*. London.

Ellis, W.M. 1989. *Alcibiades*. London.

Engels, D.W. 1978. *Alexander the Great and the Logistics of the Macedonian Army*. Berkeley.

Eremin, A. 2002. "Settlements of Spartan περίοικοι: πόλεις or κῶμαι?" In A. Powell and S. Hodkinson, eds., *Sparta Beyond the Mirage*. London, 267–284.

Evans, J.A.S. 1988. "The 'Wooden Wall' Again." *Ancient History Bulletin* 2, 25–30.

Fantham, E. et al. 1994. *Women in the Classical World: Image and Text*. New York.

Faraguna, M. 2003. "Alexander and the Greeks." In J. Roisman, ed., *Brill's Companion to Alexander the Great*. Leiden, 99–130.

Faraone, C.A. 1996. "Taking the 'Nestor Cup Inscription' Seriously: Erotic Magic and Conditional Curses in the Earliest Inscribed Hexameters." *ClAnt* 15, 77–112.

Fauber, C.M. 1999. "Deconstructing 375–371 BC: Towards a Unified Chronology." *Athenaeum* 87, 481–506.

Fears, J.R. 1975. "Pausanias, the Assassin of Philip II." *Athenaeum* 53, 111–135.

Ferrari, G. 2008. *Alcman and the Cosmos of Sparta*. Chicago.

Fields, N. 2003. "Dexileos of Thorikos: A Brief Life." *Ancient History Bulletin* 17.1–2, 108–127.

Figueira, T.J. 1993. *Excursions in Epichoric History: Aigenetan Essays*. Lanham, 173–196.

Figueira, T.J. 1999. "The Evolution of the Messenian Identity." In S. Hodkinson and A. Powell, eds., *Sparta: New Perspectives*. Swansea, 211–244.

Figueira, T.J. 2002. "Iron Money and the Ideology of Consumption in Laconia." In A. Powell and S. Hodkinson, eds., *Sparta: Beyond the Mirage*. London, 137–170.

Figueira, T.J. 2004. "The Nature of the Spartan *Kleros*." In T.J. Figueira, ed., *Spartan Society*. Swansea, 47–76.

Figueira. T.J., ed. 2004. *Spartan Society*. Swansea.

Figueira, T.J. and G. Nagy, eds. 1985. *Theognis of Megara: Poetry and the Polis*. Baltimore.

Finkelberg, M. 2006. "The City Dionysia and the Social Space of Attic Tragedy." In J. Davidson, F. Muecke, and P. Wilson, eds., *Greek Drama III: Essays in Honour of Kevin Lee*. London, 17–26.

Finley, M.I. 1978. *The World of Odysseus*, rev. ed. New York.

Finley, M.I. 1986. "Sparta." In *The Use and Abuse of History*, 2nd ed. London, 161–178.

Fisher, N., ed. 2001. *Aeschines Against Timarchos*. Oxford.

Fleming, D. 2002. "The Streets of Thurii: Discourse, Democracy, and Design in the Classical Polis." *Rhetoric Society Quarterly* 32.3, 5–32.

Flower, M.A. 1997. *Theopompus of Chios: History and Rhetoric in the Fourth Century BC*. Oxford.

Flower, M.A. 2000a. "Alexander the Great and Panhellenism." In A.B. Bosworth and E.J. Baynham, eds., *Alexander the Great in Fact and Fiction*. Oxford, 96–135.

Flower, M.A. 2000b. "From Simonides to Isocrates: The Fifth-Century Origins of Fourth-Century Panhellenism." *ClAnt* 19.1, 65–101.

Flower, M.A. 2002. "The Invention of Tradition in Classical and Hellenistic Sparta." In A. Powell and S. Hodkinson, eds., *Sparta: Beyond the Mirage*. London, 191–217.

Flower, M.A. and J. Marincola, eds. 2002. *Herodotus. Histories, Book IX*. Cambridge.

Foley. H.P., ed. 1994. *The Homeric Hymn to Demeter: Translation, Commentary, and Interpretative Essays*. Princeton.

Fontenrose, J. 1978. *The Delphic Oracle, its Responses and Operations, with a Catalogue of Responses*. Berkeley.

Forde, S. 1989. *The Ambition to Rule: Alcibiades and the Politics of Imperialism in Thucydides*. Ithaca.

Fornara, C.W. 1966. "Some Aspects of the Career of Pausanias of Sparta." *Historia* 15, 257–271.

Fornara, C.W. 1970. "The Cult of Harmodios and Aristogeiton." *Philologus* 114, 155–180.

Fornara, C.W. 1971. *The Athenian Board of Generals from 501–404*. Wiesbaden.

Fornara, C.W. 1975. "Plutarch and the Megarian Decree." *YCS* 24, 213–228.

Fornara, C.W. 1979. "On the Chronology of the Samian War." *JHS* 99, 7–19.

Fornara, C.W. and L.J. Samons II, 1991. *Athens from Cleisthenes to Pericles*. Berkeley.

Forrest, W.G. 1960. "Themistokles and Argos." *CQ* 10, 221–241.

Forrest, W.G. 1970. "The Date of Pseudo-Xenophontic Athenaion Politeia." *Klio* 52, 107–116.

Forsdyke, S. 2005. *Exile, Ostracism, and Democracy: The Politics of Expulsion in Ancient Greece*. Princeton.

Foss, C. 1977. "The Battle of the Granicus: A New Look." *Ancient Macedonia* 2, 495–502.

Foucault, M. 1986. *The History of Sexuality, Vol. 2: The Use of Pleasure*. Trans. R. Hurley. New York.

Foxhall, L. 1996. "The Law and the Lady: Women and Legal Proceedings in Classical Athens." In L. Foxhall and A.D.E. Lewis, eds., *Greek Law in Its Political Setting: Justifications Not Justice*. Oxford, 133–152.

Foxhall, L. 1997. "A View from the Top: Evaluating the Solonian Property-Classes." In L. Mitchell and P.J. Rhodes, eds., *The Development of the Polis in Archaic Greece*. London, 113–136.

Foxhall, L. 2005. "Cultures, Landscapes, and Identities in the Mediterranean World." In I. Malkin, ed., *Mediterranean Paradigms and Classical Antiquity*. London, 75–92.

Frangeskou, V. 1999. "Tradition and Originality in Some Attic Funeral Orations." *Classical World* 92.4, 315–336.

Fraser, P.M. 1996. *Cities of Alexander the Great*. Oxford.

Fredricksmeyer, E.A. 1961. "Alexander, Midas, and the Oracle of Gordium." *CPh* 56, 160–168.

Fredricksmeyer, E.A. 1979. "Divine Honors for Philip II." *TAPhA* 109, 39–61.

Fredricksmeyer, E.A. 2000. "Alexander the Great and the Kingship of Asia." In A.B. Bosworth and E.J. Baynham, eds., *Alexander the Great in Fact and Fiction*. Oxford, 136–166.

Fredricksmeyer, E.A. 2003. "Alexander's Religion and Divinity." In J. Roisman, ed., *Brill's Companion to Alexander the Great*. Leiden, 253–278.

French, A. 1979. "Athenian Ambitions and the Delian Alliance." *Phoenix* 33, 134–141.

Frost, F.J. 1998. *Plutarch's Themistocles: A Historical Commentary*, rev. ed. Chicago.

Fuller, J.F.C. 1958. *The Generalship of Alexander the Great*. London.

Gabrielsen, V. 1987. "The *Antidosis* Procedure in Classical Athens." *Classica & Mediaevalia* 38, 7–38.

Gabrielsen, V. 1994. *Financing the Athenian Fleet: Public Taxation and Social Relations*. Baltimore.

Gagarin, M. 1974. "Hesiod's Dispute with Perses." *TAPhA* 104, 103–111.

Gagarin, M. 1986. *Early Greek Law*. Berkeley.

Gagarin, M. 2001. "The Gortyn Code and Greek Legal Procedure." In G. Thür, ed., *Symposion 1997: Vorträge zur griechischen and hellenistischen Rechtsgeschichte*. Cologne, 41–52.

Gagarin, M. 2005. "Early Greek Law." In M. Gagarin and D. Cohen, eds., *The Cambridge Companion to Ancient Greek Law*. Cambridge, 82–96.

Gagarin, M. and D. Cohen, eds. 2005. *The Cambridge Companion to Ancient Greek Law*. Cambridge.

Garlan, Y. 1988. *Slavery in Ancient Greece*. Trans. J. Lloyd. Ithaca.

Garland, R.S.J. 1987. *The Piraeus: From the Fifth to the First Century BC*. London.

Garnsey, P.D.A. 1988. *Famine and Food Supply in the Graeco-Roman World*. Cambridge.

Garnsey, P.D.A. 1998. *Cities, Peasants and Food in Classical Antiquity*. Cambridge.

Gentili, B. 1988. *Poetry and Its Public in Ancient Greece: From Homer to the Fifth Century*. Baltimore.

Georges, P.B. 1986. "Saving Herodotus' Phenomena: The Oracles and Events of 480 BC." *ClAnt* 5, 14–59.

Gershevitch, I., ed. 1985. *The Cambridge History of Iran, Vol. 2: The Median and Achaemenian Periods*. Cambridge.

Gill, C., N. Postlethwaite, and R. Seaford, eds. 1998. *Reciprocity in Ancient Greece*. Oxford.

Gill, D.W.J. 2001. "The Decision to Build the Temple of Athena Nike (IG I3 35)." *Historia* 50.3, 257–278.

Giovannini, A. 1975. "Athenian Currency in the Late Fifth and Early Fourth Century BC." *GRBS* 16, 185–195.

Glass, S.L. 1988. "The Greek Gymnasium: Some Problems." In W.J. Raschke, ed., *The Archaeology of the Olympics: The Olympics and Other Festivals in Antiquity*. Madison, WI, 155–173.

Glazebrook, A. 2005. "The Making of a Prostitute: Apollodoros's Portrait of Neaira." *Arethusa* 38.2, 161–187.

Golden, M. 1998. *Sport and Society in Ancient Greece*. Cambridge.

Goldhill, S. 1987. "The Great Dionysia and Civic Ideology." *JHS* 107, 58–76.

Gomme, A.W., A. Andrewes, and K.J. Dover, eds. 1945–1981. *A Historical Commentary on Thucydides*, 5 vols. Oxford.

Gorman, V. B. 2001. *Miletos, the Ornament of Ionia: A History of the City to 400 BCE*. Ann Arbor.

Gouschin, V. 1999. "Athenian Synoikism of the Fifth Century BC, or Two Stories of Theseus." *G&R* 46.2, 168–187.

Graham, A.J. 1983. *Colony and Mother City in Ancient Greece*. Chicago.

Gray, V. 1989. *The Character of Xenophon's Hellenica*. Baltimore.

Gray, V. J. 1996. "Herodotus and the Images of Tyranny: The Tyrants of Corinth." *AJP* 117, 361–389.

Greaves, A.M. 2002. *Miletos: A History*. London.

Green, P. 1970. *Armada from Athens: The Failure of the Sicilian Expedition, 415–413 BC*. London: Hodder and Stoughton.

Green, P. 1991a. *Alexander of Macedon, 356–323 BC: A Historical Biography*. Berkeley.

Green, P. 1991b. "Rebooking the Flute-Girls: A Fresh Look at the Chronological Evidence for the Fall of Athens and the ὀκτάμηνος ἀρχή of the Thirty." *Ancient History Bulletin* 5, 1–16.

Green, P. 1996a. *The Greco-Persian Wars*. Berkeley.

Green, P. 1996b. "The Metamorphosis of the Barbarian: Athenian Panhellenism in a Changing World." In R.W. Wallace and E.M. Harris, eds., *Transitions to Empire: Essays in Greco-Roman History 360–146 BC in Honor of E. Badian*. Norman, OK, 5–36.

Green, P. 2003. "Occupation and Coexistence: The Impact of Macedon on Athens, 323–307." In O. Palagia and S.V. Tracy, eds., *The Macedonians in Athens 322–229 BC*. Proceedings of an International Conference held at the University of Athens, May 24–26, 2001. Oxford, 1–7.

Green, P. 2006. *Diodorus Siculus, Books 11–12.37.1: Greek History 480–431 BC – The Alternative Version*. Austin.

Gribble, D. 1999. *Alcibiades and Athens: A Study in Literary Presentation*. Oxford.

Griffith, G.T. 1950. "The Union of Corinth and Argos (392–386 BC)." *Historia* 1, 236–256.

Griffith, G.T. 1981. "Peltasts and the Origins of the Macedonian Phalanx." In H. Dell, ed., *Ancient Macedonian Studies in Honor of Charles F. Edson*. Thessaloniki, 161–167.

Habicht, C. 1977. *Athens from Alexander to Antony*. Trans. D. Lucas. Cambridge, MA.

Hall, E. 1989. *Inventing the Barbarian: Greek Self-Definition Through Tragedy*. Oxford.

Hall, E. 1993. "Asia Unmanned: Images of Victory in Classical Athens." In J. Rich and G. Shipley, eds., *War and Society in the Greek World*. London, 108–133.

Hall, E., ed. 1996. *Persians: Aeschylus*. Warminster, UK.

Hall, E. and P.J. Rhodes, eds. 2007. *Cultural Responses to the Persian Wars: Antiquity to the Third Millennium*. Oxford.

Hall, J. 1996. "The Lost Technology of Ancient Greek Rowing." *Scientific American* May, 66–71.

Hall, J.M. 1997. *Ethnic Identity in Greek Antiquity*. Cambridge.

Hall, J.M. 2001. "Contested Ethnicities: Perceptions of Macedonia within Evolving Definitions of Greek Identity." In I. Malkin, ed., *Ancient Perceptions of Greek Ethnicity*. Cambridge, 159–186.

Hall, J.M. 2002. *Hellenicity: Between Ethnicity and Culture*. Chicago.

Hall, J.M. 2007. *A History of the Archaic Greek World ca. 1200–479 BCE*. Oxford.

Hall, L.G.H. 1990. "Ephialtes, the Areopagus and the Thirty." *CQ* 40, 319–328.

Halperin, D.M. 1990. *One Hundred Years of Homosexuality and Other Essays on Greek Love*. New York.

Hamel, D. 1998. *Athenian Generals: Military Authority in the Classical Period*. Leiden.

Hamel, D. 2003. *Trying Neaira: The True Story of a Courtesan's Scandalous Life in Ancient Greece*. New Haven.

Hamilton, C.D. 1979. *Sparta's Bitter Victories: Politics and Diplomacy in the Corinthian War*. Ithaca.

Hamilton, C.D. 1991. *Agesilaus and the Failure of Spartan Hegemony*. Ithaca.

Hammer, D. 2002. *The Iliad as Politics: The Performance of Political Thought*. Norman.

Hammond, N.G.L. 1973. *Studies in Greek History*. Oxford.

Hammond, N.G.L. 1989a. "Casualties and Reinforcements of Citizen Soldiers in Greece and Macedonia." *JHS* 109, 56–68.

Hammond, N.G.L. 1989b. *The Macedonian State: The Origins, Institution, and History*. Cambridge.

Hammond, N.G.L. 1992. "Alexander's Charge at the Battle of Issus in 333 BC." *Historia* 41, 395–406.

Hammond, N.G.L. 1994. *Philip of Macedon*. Baltimore.

Hammond, N.G.L. 1995. "Philip's Innovations in Macedonian Economy." *Symbolae Osloenses* 70, 22–29.

Hammond, N.G.L. 1996. "Sparta at Thermopylae." *Historia* 45, 1–20.

Hammond, N.G.L. 1998. "Alexander's Newly-Founded Cities." *GRBS* 39.3, 243–270.

Hammond, N.G.L. and G.T. Griffith, 1979. *A History of Macedonia, 550–336 BC, Vol. 2*. Oxford.

Hansen, M.H. 1974. *The Sovereignty of the People's Court in Athens in the Fourth Century BC and the Public Action Against Unconstitutional Proposals*. Odense.

Hansen, M.H. 1976. "The Theoric Fund and the Graphe Paranomon against Apollodorus." *GRBS* 17, 235–246.

Hansen, M.H. 1979. "Misthos for Magistrates in Classical Athens." *Symbolae Osloensis* 54, 5–22.

Hansen, M.H. 1983. "*Rhetores* and *Strategoi* in Fourth-Century Athens." *GRBS* 24, 151–180.

Hansen, M.H. 1987. *The Athenian Assembly in the Age of Demosthenes*. Oxford.

Hansen, M.H. 1990a. "Solonian Democracy in Fourth-Century Athens." In W.R. Connor et al., eds., *Aspects of Athenian Democracy*. Copenhagen, 71–99.

Hansen, M.H. 1990b. "The Political Power of the People's Court in Fourth Century Athens." In O. Murray and S. Price, eds., *The Greek City from Homer to Alexander*. Oxford, 215–243.

Hansen, M.H. 1991. *The Athenian Democracy in the Age of Demosthenes*. Oxford.

Hansen, M.H., ed. 1993. *The Ancient Greek City-State: Symposium on the Occasion of the 250th Anniversary of the Danish Academy of Science and Letters July 1–4, 1992*. Copenhagen.

Hansen, M.H. 1994. "The Number of Athenian Citizens Secundum Sekunda." *Échos du monde classique* 38, 299–310.

Hansen, M.H. 1996. "The Ancient Athenians and the Modern Liberal View of Liberty as a Democratic Ideal." In J. Ober and C. Hedrick, eds., *Demokratia*. Princeton, 91–104.

Hansen, M.H., ed. 2000. *A Comparative Study of Thirty City-State Cultures: An Investigation*. Copenhagen.

Hansen, M.H. 2006a. *Polis: An Introduction to the Ancient Greek City-State*. Oxford.

Hansen, M.H. 2006b. *Studies in the Population of Aigina, Athens and Eretria*. Copenhagen.

Hansen, O. 1999. "The Athenian Colony of Brea = Amphipolis?" *Hermes* 127, 121–122.

Hanson, V. 1988. "Epameinondas, the Battle of Leuktra (371 BC), and the 'Revolution' in Greek Battle Tactics." *ClAnt* 7, 190–207.

Hanson, V.D. 1989. *The Western Way of War: Infantry Battle in Classical Greece*. London.

Hanson, V.D., ed. 1991. *Hoplites: The Classical Greek Battle Experience*. London.

Hanson, V.D. 1998. *Warfare and Agriculture in Classical Greece*, 2nd ed. Berkeley.

Hanson, V.D. 1999. *The Other Greeks: The Family Farm and the Agrarian Roots of Western Civilization*, 2nd ed. Berkeley.

Hanson, V.D. 2005. *A War Like No Other: How the Athenians and Spartans Fought the Peloponnesian War*. New York.

Harding, P. 1994. *Androtion and the Atthis*. Oxford.

Harding, P. 1995. "Athenian Foreign Policy in the Fourth Century." *Klio* 77, 105–125.

Harl, K. 1997. "Alexander's Cavalry Battle at the Granicus." In C. Hamilton and P. Krentz, eds., *Polis and Polemos: Essays on Politics, War, and History in Ancient Greece in Honor of Donald Kagan*. Claremont, CA, 303–326.

Harris, E.M. 1990. "The Constitution of the Five Thousand." *HSCP* 93, 243–280.

Harris, E.M. 1995. *Aeschines and Athenian Politics*. New York.

Harris, E.M. 1996. "Demosthenes and the Theoric Fund." In R.W. Wallace and E.M. Harris, eds., *Transitions to Empire: Essays in Greco-Roman History 360–146 BC in Honor of E. Badian*. Norman, OK, 57–76.

Harris, E.M. 1999. "Notes on the New Grain-Tax Law." *ZPE* 128, 269–272.

Harris, E.M. 2004. "Did Rape Exist in Classical Athens? Further Reflections on the Laws about Sexual Violence." *Dike* 7, 41–83.

Harrison, E.B. 1972. "The South Frieze of the Nike Temple and the Marathon Painting in the Painted Stoa." *AJA* 76, 353–378.

Harrison, T., ed. 2002a. *Greeks and Barbarians*. New York.

Harrison, T. 2002b. "The Persian Invasions." In E.J. Bakker, I.J.F. de Jong, and H. van Wees, eds., *Brill's Companion to Herodotus*. Leiden, 551–578.

Harvey, F.D. 1990. "The Sykophant and Sykophancy: Vexatious Redefinition?" In P. Cartledge et al., eds., *Nomos: Essays in Athenian Law*. Cambridge, 103–121.

Harvey, F.D. 2004. "The Clandestine Massacre of the Helots (Thucydides 4.80)." In T.J. Figueira, ed., *Spartan Society*. London, 199–217.

Hatzopoulos, M.B and L.D. Loukopoulos, eds. 1980. *Philip of Macedon*. Athens.

Havelock, C.M. 1995. *The Aphrodite of Knidos and Her Successors: A Historical Review of the Female Nude in Greek Art*. Ann Arbor.

Head, B.V. 1881. *On the Chronological Sequence of the Coins of Boeotia*. London.

Heckel, W. 1977. "The Conspiracy against Philotas." *Phoenix* 31, 9–21.

Heckel, W. 1988. *The Last Days and Testament of Alexander the Great: A Prosopographic Study*. Stuttgart.

Heckel, W. 1992. *The Marshals of Alexander's Empire*. London.

Heckel, W. 2002. *The Wars of Alexander the Great: 336–332 BC*. Oxford.

Heckel, W. 2003. "King and Companions: Observations on the Nature of Power in the Reign of Alexander." In J. Roisman, ed., *Brill's Companion to Alexander the Great*. Leiden, 197–225.

Heckel, W. 2007. *The Conquests of Alexander the Great*. Cambridge.

Heckel, W. and J. Yardley, 2004. *Alexander the Great: Historical Texts in Translation*. Oxford.

Hedreen, G. 2001. *Capturing Troy: The Narrative Functions of Landscape in Archaic and Early Classical Greek Art*. Ann Arbor.

Hedrick, C. 2006. *Ancient History: Monuments and Documents*. Oxford.

Heisserer, A.J. 1980. *Alexander the Great and the Greeks: The Epigraphic Evidence*. Norman, OK.

Henry, A.S. 1992. "Through a Laser Beam Darkly: Space-Age Technology and the Egesta Decree (I.G. i³ 11)." *ZPE* 91, 137–146.

Henry, A.S. 1998. "The Sigma Enigma." *ZPE* 120, 45–48.

Henry, M.M. 1995. *Prisoner of History: Aspasia of Miletus and Her Biographical Tradition*. Oxford.

Herman, G. 1987. *Ritualized Friendship and the Greek City*. Cambridge.

Hesk, J. 2000. *Deception and Democracy in Classical Athens*. Cambridge.

Heskel, J. 1997. *The North Aegean Wars, 371–360 B.C.* Stuttgart.

Hignett, C. 1952. *The History of the Athenian Constitution to the End of the Fifth Century B.C.* Oxford.

Hignett, C. 1963. *Xerxes' Invasion of Greece*. Oxford.

Hodkinson, S. 1997. "The Development of Spartan Society and Institutions in the Archaic Period." In L.G. Mitchell and P.J. Rhodes, eds., *The Development of the Polis in Archaic Greece*. London, 83–102.

Hodkinson, S. 2000. *Property and Wealth in Classical Sparta*. London.

Hodkinson, S. 2007. "The Episode of Sphodrias as a Source for Spartan Social History." In N. Sekunda, ed., *Corolla Cosmo Rodewald*. Monograph Series Akanthina 2. Gdansk, 43–65.

Hölkeskamp, K.-J. 1992. "Written Law in Archaic Greece." *Proceedings of the Cambridge Philological Society* 38, 87–117.

Holladay, A.J. 1977. "Sparta's Role in the First Peloponnesian War." *JHS* 97, 54–63.

Holladay, A.J. 1987. "The Forethought of Themistocles." *JHS* 107, 182–187.

Holladay, A.J. 1989. "The Hellenic Disaster in Egypt." *JHS* 109, 176–182.

Holst-Warhaft, G.L. 1992. *Dangerous Voices: Women's Laments and Greek Literature*. London.

Holt, F.L. 2003. *Alexander the Great and the Mystery of the Elephant Medallions*. Berkeley.

Hopper, R.J. 1968. "Observations on the *Wappenmünzen*." In C.M. Kraay and G.K. Jenkins, eds., *Essays in Greek Coinage Presented to S. Robinson*. Oxford, 16–39.

Hornblower, S. 1991–2008. *A Commentary on Thucydides*. 3 vols. Oxford.

Hornblower, S. 2000. "The Old Oligarch (Pseudo-Xenophon's *Athenaion Politeia*) and Thucydides: A Fourth-Century Date for the Old Oligarch?" In P. Flensted-Jensen et al., eds., *Polis and Politics: Studies in Ancient Greek History Presented to Mogens Herman Hansen on His Sixtieth Birthday, August 20, 2000*. Copenhagen, 263–284.

Howie, J.G. 2005. "The Aristeia of Brasidas: Thucydides' Presentation of Events at Pylos and Amphipolis." In F. Cairns, ed., *Papers of the Langford Latin Seminar, Vol. 12: Greek and Roman Poetry, Greek and Roman Historiography*. Cambridge, 207–284.

Howland, J. 2004. "Plato's Reply to Lysias: Republic 1 and 2 and Against Eratosthenes." *AJP* 125.2, 179–208.

Hubbard, T.K. 1988. "Popular Perceptions of Elite Homosexuality in Classical Athens." *Arion* 6, 48–78.

Hubbard, T.K., ed. 2003. *Homosexuality in Greece and Rome: A Sourcebook of Basic Documents.* Berkeley.

Humphreys, S.C. 1974. "The Nothoi of Kynosarges." *JHS* 94, 88–95.

Humphreys, S.C. 1985. "Lycurgus of Butadae: An Athenian Aristocrat." In J.W. Eadie and J. Ober, eds., *The Craft of the Ancient Historian: Essays in Honor of Chester G. Starr.* Lanham, 199–252.

Hunt, P. 1998. *Slaves, Warfare, and Ideology in the Greek Historians.* Cambridge.

Hurwit, J.M. 1985. *The Art and Culture of Early Greece, 1100–480 BC.* Ithaca.

Hurwit, J.M. 2007. "The Problem with Dexileos: Heroic and Other Nudities in Greek Art." *American Journal of Archaeology* 111, 35–60.

Hyland, J.O. 2004. "Waiting for Tissaphernes: Athens and Persia in Thucydides VIII." *Syllecta Classica* 15, 71–101.

Immerwahr, H.R. 1966. *Form and Thought in Herodotus.* Cleveland.

Isager, S. and M.H. Hansen, 1975. *Aspects of Athenian Society in the Fourth Century BC: A Historical Introduction to and Commentary on the Paragraphe-Speeches and the Speech Against Dionysodorus in the Corpus Demosthenicum (XXXII–XXXVIII and LVI).* Trans. J.H. Rosenmeier. Odense.

Jablonka, P. and C.B. Rose, 2004. "Late Bronze Age Troy: A Response to Frank Kolb." *AJA* 108, 615–630.

Jacoby, F. 1944. "*Patrios Nomos*: State Burial in Athens and the Public Cemetery in the Kerameikos." *JHS* 64, 37–66.

Jameson, M.H. 1960. "A Decree of Themistokles from Troizen." *Hesperia* 29, 198–233.

Jeffrey, L.H. 1976. *Archaic Greece: The City-States c. 700–500 BC.* London.

Jeffrey, L.H. 1990. *The Local Scripts of Archaic Greece: A Study of the Origin of the Greek Alphabet and Its Development from the Eighth to the Fifth Centuries BC,* rev. ed. Oxford.

Johansson, M. 2001. "The Inscription from Troizen: A Decree of Themistocles?" *ZPE* 137, 69–92.

Johnstone, S. 2002. "Apology for the Manuscript of Demosthenes 59.67." *AJP* 123, 229–256.

Johnstone, S. 2003. "Women, Property, and Surveillance in Classical Athens." *ClAnt* 22, 247–274.

Johnstone, S. 1994. "Virtuous Toil, Vicious Work: Xenophon on Aristocratic Style." *CPh* 89, 219–240.

Jones, J.R.M. 1999. "Ancient Greek Gold Coinage Up to the Time of Philip of Macedon." In M. Amandry and S. Hurter, eds., *Travaux de numismatique grecque offerts à Georges Le Rider.* London, 257–275.

Joshel, S.R. and S. Murnaghan, eds. 1998. *Women and Slaves in Greco-Roman Culture: Differential Equations.* London.

Kagan, D. 1969. *The Outbreak of the Peloponnesian War.* Ithaca.

Kagan, D. 1974. *The Archidamian War.* Ithaca.

Kagan, D. 1981. *The Peace of Nicias and the Sicilian Expedition.* Ithaca.

Kagan, D. 1987. *The Fall of the Athenian Empire.* Ithaca.

Kallet, L. 2001. *Money and the Corrosion of Power in Thucydides: The Sicilian Expedition and Its Aftermath.* Berkeley.

Kallet-Marx, L. 1989. "Did Tribute Fund the Parthenon?" *Classical Antiquity* 8, 252–266.

Kallet-Marx, L. 1993. *Money, Expense and Naval Power in Thucydides' History 1–5.24.* Berkeley.

Kapparis, K.A., ed. 1999. *Apollodoros "Against Neaira" [D. 59].* Berlin.

Keen, A.G. 1997. "Eurymedon, Naxos, and the Purpose of the Delian League." *Journal of Ancient Civilizations* 12, 57–79.

Kelly, T., 1982. "Thucydides and Spartan Strategy in the Archidamian War," *American Historical Review* 87: 25–54.

Kennedy, G.A. 1963. *The Art of Persuasion in Greece: Political Propaganda from Aeneas to Brutus*. Princeton.

Kennell, N.M. 1995. *The Gymnasium of Virtue: Education and Culture in Ancient Sparta*. Chapel Hill.

Kern, P.B. 1999. *Ancient Siege Warfare*. Bloomington.

Keuls, E.C. 1993. *The Reign of the Phallus: Sexual Politics in Ancient Athens*, 2nd ed. Berkeley.

Khurt, A. 2001. "The Achaemenid Persian Empire (*c*.550–*c*.330 BCE): Continuities, Adaptations, Transformations." In S.E. Alcock et al., eds., *Empires: Perspectives from Archaeology and History*. Cambridge, 93–123.

Killerich, B. 1993. "The Public Image of Alexander the Great," In J. Carlsen et al., eds., *Alexander the Great: Reality and Myth*. Rome, 85–92.

Kinns, P. 1986. "The Coinage of Miletus." *Numismatic Chronicle* 146, 234–260.

Kolb, F. 2004. "Troy VI: A Trading Center and Commercial City?" *AJA* 108, 577–613

Konstan, D. 1997. *Friendship in the Classical World*. Cambridge.

Kraay, C.M. 1976. *Archaic and Classical Greek Coins*. London.

Krasilnikoff, J.A. 1993. "The Regular Payment of Aegean Mercenaries in the Classical Period." *Classica & Mediaevalia* 44, 77–95.

Krentz, P. 1982. *The Thirty at Athens*. Ithaca.

Krentz, P. 1985. "Casualties in Hoplite Battles." *GRBS* 26, 13–20.

Krentz, P., ed. 1989–1995. *Xenophon Hellenika*, 2 vols. Warminster, UK.

Kroll, J.H. and N.M. Waggoner. 1984. "Dating the Earliest Coins of Athens, Corinth and Aegina." *AJA* 88, 325–340.

Kuch, H. 1998. "Euripides und Melos" *Mnemosyne* 51, 147–153.

Kurke, L. 1999. *Coins, Bodies, Games and Gold: The Politics of Meaning in Archaic Greece*. Princeton.

Lacy, W.K. 1968. *The Family in Classical Greece*. Ithaca.

Lambert, S.D. 1986. "Herodotus, the Cylonian Conspiracy and the πρυτάνιες τῶν ναυκράρων." *Historia* 35, 105–112.

Lane, E.A. 1933–1934. "Lakonian Vase-Painting." *Annual of the British School at Athens* 34, 99–189.

Lane Fox, R. 1996. "Text and Image: Alexander the Great, Coins and Elephants." *Bulletin of the Institute of Classical Studies* 41, 87–108.

Lane Fox, R. 2000. "Theognis: An Alternative to Democracy." In R. Brock and S. Hodkinson, eds., *Alternatives to Athens: Varieties of Political Organization and Community in Ancient Greece*. Oxford: 35–51.

Lang, M.L. 1967. "The Kylonian Conspiracy." *CPh* 62, 243–249.

Lang, M.L. 1990. *The Athenian Agora XXV: Ostraka*. Princeton.

Lang, M.L. 1992. "Theramenes and Arginousai." *Hermes* 120, 267–279.

Lang, M.L. 1996. "Alcibiades vs. Phrynichus." *CQ* 46, 289–295.

Lapatin, K. 2007. "Art and Architecture." In L.J. Samons II, ed., *The Cambridge Companion to the Age of Pericles*. Cambridge, 125–152.

Larsen, J.A.O. 1968. *Greek Federal States: Their Institutions and History*. Oxford.

Lateiner, D. 1976. "Tissaphernes and the Phoenician Fleet (Thucydides 8.87)." *TAPhA* 106, 267–290.

Lateiner, D. 1982. "The Failure of the Ionian Revolt." *Historia* 31, 129–160.

Lateiner, D. 1989. *The Historical Method of Herodotus*. Toronto.

Lavelle, B.M. 1992. "Herodotos, Skythian Archers, and the *Doryphoroi* of the Peisistratids." *Klio* 74, 78–97.

Lavelle, B.M. 1993. *The Sorrow and the Pity: A Prolegomenon to a History of Athens under the Peisistratids*. Stuttgart.

Lavelle, B.M. 2005. *Fame, Money, Power: The Rise of Peisistratus and "Democratic" Tyranny at Athens*. Ann Arbor.

Lawton, C.L. 2009. "Attic Votive Reliefs and the Peloponnesian War." In O. Palagia, ed., *Art in Athens During the Peloponnesian War*. Cambridge, 66–93.

Lazarides, D. 2003. *Amphipolis*, 2nd ed. Trans. D. Hardy. Athens.

Lazenby, J.F. 1985. *The Spartan Army*. Warminster, UK.

Lazenby, J.F. 1993. *The Defence of Greece 490–79 BC*. Warminster, UK.

Lazenby, J.F. 1997. "The Conspiracy of Kinadon Reconsidered." *Athenaeum* 85, 437–447.

Lazenby, J.F. 2004. *The Peloponnesian War: A Military Study*. London.

Leahy, D.M. 1955. "The Bones of Tisamenus." *Historia* 4, 26–38.

Lee, J.W.I. 2001. "Urban Combat at Olynthos, 348 BC." In P. Freedman and A. Pollard, eds., *Fields of Conflict: Progress and Prospect in Battlefield Archaeology. British Archaeological Reports*. BAR International Series 958, 11–22.

Lefkowitz, M.R. 1976. "Fictions in Literary Biography: The New Poem and the Archilochus Legend." *Arethusa* 9, 181–189.

Legon, R.P. 1981. *Megara: The Political History of a Greek City-State to 336 BC*. Ithaca.

Leitao, D.D. 2002. "The Legend of the Theban Sacred Band." In M.C. Nussbaum and J. Sihvola, eds., *The Sleep of Reason: Erotic Experience and Sexual Ethics in Ancient Greece and Rome*. Chicago, 143–169.

Lenardon, R.J. 1978. *The Saga of Themistocles*. London.

Lethaby, W.R. 1918. "Greek Lion Monuments." *JHS* 38, 37–44.

Lewis, D.M. 1977. *Sparta and Persia: Lectures Delivered at the University of Cincinnati, autumn 1976 in Memory of Donald W. Bradeen*. Leiden.

Lewis, D.M. 1981. "The Origins of the First Peloponnesian War." In G.S. Shrimpton and D.J. McCargar, eds., *Classical Contributions: Studies in Honor of Malcolm Francis McGregor*. Locust Valley, NY, 71–78.

Lewis, D.M. 1985. "Persians in Herodotus." In M. H. Jameson, ed., *The Greek Historians: Literature and History: Papers Presented to A.E. Raubitchek*. Stanford, 101–117.

Lewis, D.M. 1987. "The Athenian Coinage Decree." In I. Carradice, ed., *Coinage and Administration in the Athenian and Persian Empires*. Oxford, 53–63. Reprinted in P.J. Rhodes, ed., 1997, *Selected Papers on Greek and Near Eastern History*. Cambridge, 116–130.

Lewis, D.M. 1990. "Public Property in the City." In O. Murray and S. Price, eds., *The Greek City from Homer to Alexander*. Oxford, 245–263.

Lewis, D.M. 1992a. "Mainland Greece, 479–451 BC"; "The Thirty Years' Peace." In D.M. Lewis et al., eds., *The Cambridge Ancient History, Vol. 5: The Fifth Century BC*, 2nd ed. Cambridge, 96–146.

Lewis, D.M. 1992b. "The Archidamian War." In D.M. Lewis et al., eds., *The Cambridge Ancient History, Vol. 5: The Fifth Century BC*, 2nd ed. Cambridge, 370–432.

Lewis, D.M. 1994. "The Athenian Tribute-Quota Lists, 453–450 BC." *Annual of the British School at Athens* 89, 285–301.

Lewis, D.M. 1997 [1960]. "Apollo Delios." In P.J. Rhodes, ed., *Selected Papers on Greek and Near Eastern History*. Cambridge, 150–157.

Lissarague, F. 1990. "The Sexual Life of Satyrs." In D.M. Halperin, J.J. Winkler, and F.I. Zeitlin, eds., *Before Sexuality: The Construction of Erotic Experience in the Ancient Greek World*. Princeton, 53–82.

Lissarague, F. 2002 [1997]. "The Athenian Image of the Foreigner." In T. Harrison, ed., *Greeks and Barbarians*. New York, 101–124.

Littman, R.J. 2006. "The Plague of Athens: Current Analytic Techniques." *Amphora* 5, 10–12.

Lloyd-Jones, H. 1975. *Females of the Species: Semonides on Women*. London.

Londey, P. 1990. "The Outbreak of the Fourth Sacred War." *Chiron* 20, 239–260.

Lonsdale, D.J. 2006. *Alexander the Great: Lessons in Strategy*. New York.

Loomis, W.T. 1992. *The Spartan War Fund: IG V 1, 1 and a New Fragment*. Stuttgart.

Loraux, N. 1986. *The Invention of Athens: The Funeral Oration in the Classical City*. Trans. A. Sheridan. Cambridge, MA.

Low, P. 2002. "Cavalry Identity and Democratic Ideology in Early Fourth-Century Athens." *Proceedings of the Cambridge Philological Society* 48, 102–119.

Low, P., ed. 2008. *The Athenian Empire*. Edinburgh.

Luraghi, N. 2002a. "Becoming Messenian." *JHS* 122, 45–69.

Luraghi, N. 2002b. "Helotic Slavery Reconsidered." In A. Powell and S. Hodkinson, eds., *Sparta: Beyond the Mirage*. London, 227–248.

Luraghi, N. 2008. *The Ancient Messenians: Constructions of Ethnicity and Memory*. Cambridge.

Luraghi, N. and S. Alcock, eds. 2003. *Helots and Their Masters in Laconia and Messenia: Histories, Ideologies, Structures*. Cambridge, MA.

Ma, J. 2008. "Chaironeia 338: Topographies of Commemoration." *JHS* 128, 72–91.

Ma, J., N. Papazarkadas, and R. Parker, eds. 2009. *Interpreting the Athenian Empire*. London.

McCoy, W.J. 1989. "Memnon of Rhodes at the Granicus." *AJP* 110, 413–433.

McCredie, J.R. 1971. "Hippodamos of Miletos." In D.G. Mitten et al., eds., *Studies Presented to G.M.A. Hanfmann*. Mainz, 95–100.

MacDowell, D.M., ed. 1962. *Andokides: On the Mysteries*. Oxford.

MacDowell, D.M. 1978. *The Law in Classical Athens*. Ithaca.

McGlew, J.F. 1993. *Tyranny and Political Culture in Ancient Greece*. Ithaca.

McKechnie, P. 1994. "Greek Mercenary Troops and Their Equipment." *Historia* 43, 297–305.

Macleod, C.W. 1974. "Form and Meaning in the Melian Dialogue." *Historia* 23, 385–400.

Macleod, C.W. 1978. "Reason and Necessity: Thucydides III.9–14, 37–48." *JHS* 98, 64–78.

McQueen, E.I., ed. 1986. *Demosthenes: Olynthiacs*. Bristol.

Malkin, I. 1987. *Religion and Colonization in Ancient Greece*. Leiden.

Malkin, I. 1994. *Myth and Territory in the Spartan Mediterranean*. Cambridge.

Mansfeld, J. 1980. "The Chronology of Anaxagoras' Athenian Period and the Date of His Trial: Part II, The Plot against Pericles and His Associates." *Mnemosyne* 4.33, 17–95.

Manville, P.B. 1990. *The Origins of Citizenship in Ancient Athens*. Princeton.

Marconi, C. 2007. *Temple Decoration and Cultural Identity in the Archaic Greek World: The Metopes of Selinus*. Cambridge.

Mark, I.S. 1993. *The Sanctuary of Athena Nike in Athens: Architectural Stages and Chronology*. Princeton.

Markle, M.M., III. 1976. "Support of Greek Intellectuals for Philip: A Study of Isocrates' *Philippus* and Speusippus' *Letter to Philip*." *JHS* 96, 80–99.

Markle, M.M., III. 1982. "Macedonian Arms and Tactics under Alexander the Great." In B. Barr-Sharrar and E.N. Borza, eds., *Macedonia and Greece in Late Classical and Early Hellenistic Times*. Studies in the History of Art No. 10. Washington, DC, 87–111.

Markle, M.M., III. 1985. "Jury Pay and Assembly Pay at Athens." In P.A. Cartledge and F.D. Harvey, eds., *Crux: Essays in Greek History Presented to G.E.M. de Ste Croix on His 75th Birthday*. London, 265–297.

Markle, M.M., III. 1994. "Diodorus' Sources for the Sacred War in Book 16." In I. Worthington, ed., *Ventures into Greek History*. Oxford, 43–69.

Marr, J.L. 1993. "Ephialtes the Moderate?" *G&R* 40, 11–19.

Marr, J.L. 1995. "The Death of Themistocles." *G&R* 42, 159–167.

Marsden, E.W. 1964. *The Campaign of Gaugamela*. Liverpool.

Marsden, E.W. 1969. *Greek and Roman Artillery: Historical Development*. Oxford.

Marshall C.W. and S. van Willigenburg, 2004. "Judging Athenian Dramatic Competitions." *JHS* 124, 90–107.

Martin, T.R. 1991. "Silver Coins and Public Slaves in the Athenian Law of 375/4 BC." In W.E. Metcalf, ed., *Mnemata: Papers in Memory of Nancy M. Waggoner*. New York, 21–47.

Mattingly, H.B. 1966. "Periclean Imperialism." In E. Badian, ed., *Ancient Society and Institutions: Studies Presented to Victor Eherenberg*. Oxford, 193–223. Reprinted in H.B. Mattingly, 1996, *The Athenian Empire Restored: Epigraphic and Historical Studies*. Ann Arbor, 147–179.

Mattingly, H.B. 1968. "Athenian Finance in the Peloponnesian War." *Bulletin de correspondance hellénique* 92, 450–485. Reprinted in H.B. Mattingly, 1996, *The Athenian Empire Restored: Epigraphic and Historical Studies*. Ann Arbor, 215–257.

Mattingly, H.B. 1987. "The Athenian Coinage Decree and the Assertion of Empire." In I. Carradice, ed., *Coinage and Administration in the Athenian and Persian Empires*. Oxford, 65–71. Reprinted in H.B. Mattingly, 1996, *The Athenian Empire Restored: Epigraphic and Historical Studies*. Ann Arbor, 477–486.

Mattingly, H.B. 1992. "Epigraphy and the Athenian Empire." *Historia* 41, 129–138.

Mattingly, H.B. 1993. "New Light on the Athenian Standards Decree (*ATL* II, D 14)." *Klio* 75, 99–102.

Mattingly, H.B. 1996. *The Athenian Empire Restored: Epigraphic and Historical Studies*. Ann Arbor.

Meadows, A. and K. Shipton, eds. 2001. *Money and Its Uses in the Ancient Greek World*. Oxford.

Meiggs, R. 1972. *The Athenian Empire*. Oxford.

Meritt, B.D., H.T. Wade-Gery, and M.F. McGregor, 1939–1953. *The Athenian Tribute Lists*. 4 vols. Cambridge, MA.

Meritt, L.S. 1970. "The Stoa Poikile." *Hesperia* 39, 233–264.

Mertens, N. 2002. "Οὐκ οἴμαι, ἀγαθοὶ δέ: The Peroikoi in the Classical Lakedaimonian Polis." In A. Powell and S. Hodkinson, eds., *Sparta: Beyond the Mirage*. London, 285–303.

Mikalson, J. D. 2005. *Ancient Greek Religion*. Oxford.

Miller M.C. 1997. *Athens and Persia in the Fifth Century BC: A Study in Cultural Receptivity*. Cambridge.

Miller, S.G. 2004. *Ancient Greek Athletics*. New Haven.

Millett, P.C. 1984. "Hesiod and His World." *Proceedings of the Cambridge Philological Society* 30, 84–115.

Millett, P.C. 1991. *Lending and Borrowing in Ancient Athens*. Cambridge.

Millett, P.C. 1993. "Warfare, Economy and Democracy in Classical Athens." In J. Rich and G. Shipley, eds., *War and Society in the Greek World*. London, 177–196.

Mills, S. 1997. *Theseus, Tragedy, and the Athenian Empire*. Oxford.

Mirhady, D.C. 1996. "Torture and Rhetoric in Athens." *JHS* 116, 119–131.

Mitchell, L.G. 2000. "A New Look at the Election of Generals at Athens." *Klio* 82, 344–360.

Mitchell, L.G. and P.J. Rhodes, eds. 1997. *The Development of the Polis in Archaic Greece*. London.

Moon, W.G., ed. 1995. *Polykleitos, the Doryphoros, and Tradition*. Madison, WI.

Morel, J.P. 1983. "Greek Colonization in Italy and the West." In T. Hackens, N.D. Holloway, and R.R. Holloway, eds., *The Crossroads of the Mediterranean*. Leuven, 123–162.

Moreno, A. 2003. "Athenian Bread-Baskets: The Grain-Tax Law of 374/3 BC Reinterpreted." *ZPE* 145, 97–106.

Morens, D.M. and R.J. Littman, 1992. "Epidemiology of the Plague of Athens." *TAPhA* 122, 271–304.

Moretti, J.-C. 1999–2000. "The Theater of the Sanctuary of Dionysus Eleuthereus in Late Fifth-Century Athens." *Illinois Classical Studies* 24–25, 377–398.

Morgan, C. 2003. *Early Greek States Beyond the Polis*. London.

Morgan, K., ed. 2003. *Popular Tyranny: Sovereignty and Its Discontents in Ancient Greece*. Austin.

Morris, I. 1987. *Burial and Ancient Society: The Rise of the Greek City-State*. Cambridge.

Morris, I. 1990. "The Gortyn Code and Greek Kinship." *GRBS* 31, 233–254.

Morris, I. 1991. "The Early Polis as City and State." In J. Rich and A. Wallace-Hadrill, eds., *City and Country in the Ancient World*. London, 25–58.

Morris, I. 1992. *Death-Ritual and Social Structure in Classical Antiquity*. Cambridge.

Morris, I., ed. 1994. *Classical Greece: Ancient Histories and Modern Archaeologies*. Cambridge.

Morris, I. and B. Powell, eds. 1997. *A New Companion to Homer*. Leiden.

Morrison, G. 2001. "Alexander, Combat Psychology, and Persepolis." *Antichthon* 35: 30–44.

Morrison, J.S, J.F. Coates, and N.B. Rankov, 2000. *The Athenian Trireme: The History and Reconstruction of an Ancient Greek Warship*, 2nd ed. Cambridge.

Mossé, C. 2004. "How a Political Myth Takes Shape: Solon, 'Founding Father' of the Athenian Democracy." In P.J. Rhodes, ed., *Athenian Democracy*. Oxford, 242–259.

Mossman, J., ed. 1997. *Plutarch and His Intellectual World: Essays on Plutarch*. London.

Munn, M. 2000. *The School of History: Athens in the Age of Socrates*. Berkeley.

Munn, M. (2008) "Alexander and the Gordian Knot, and the Kingship of Midas." In T. Howe and J. Reames, eds., *Macedonian Legacies: Studies in Ancient Macedonian History and Culture in Honor of Eugene N. Borza*. Claremont, CA, 107–144.

Munson, R.V. 1988. "Artemisia in Herodotus." *ClAnt* 7, 91–106.

Murphy, T. M. 1989. "The Vilification of Eratosthenes and Theramenes in Lysias 12." *AJP* 110, 40–49.

Murray, O. 1988. "The Ionian Revolt." In J. Boardman et al., eds., *The Cambridge Ancient History*, Vol. 4, 2nd ed. Cambridge, 461–490.

Murray, O. ed. 1990. *Sympotica: A Symposion on the "Symposion."* Oxford.

Murray, O. 1993. *Early Greece*, 2nd ed. Cambridge, MA.

Mylonas, G.E. 1962. *Eleusis and the Eleusinian Mysteries*. Princeton.

Nagle, D.B. 1996. "The Cultural Context of Alexander's Speech at Opis." *TAPhA* 126, 151–172.

Nawotka, K. 2003a. "Alexander the Great in Persepolis." *Acta Antiqua Academiae Scientiarum Hungaricae* 43, 67–76.

Nawotka, K. 2003b. "Freedom of the Greek Cities in Asia Minor in the Age of Alexander the Great." *Klio* 85, 15–41.

Nevett, L.C. 1999. *House and Society in the Ancient Greek World.* Cambridge.

Nielsen, A.M. 1987. "'… fecit et Alexandrum Magnum multis operibus': Alexander the Great and Lysippos." *Acta Archaeologica* 58, 151–170.

Nielsen, T.H. 2002. *Arkadia and Its Poleis in the Archaic and Classical Periods.* Göttingen.

Nixon, L. and S. Price, 1990. "The Size and Resources of Greek Cities." In O. Murray and S. Price, eds., *The Greek City from Homer to Alexander.* Oxford, 137–170.

Nussbaum, G. 1960. "Labour and Status in the *Works and Days.*" *CQ* 10.3–4, 213–220.

Nussbaum, G. 1967. *The Ten Thousand: A Study in Social Organization and Action in Xenophon's Anabasis.* Leiden.

Nussbaum, M. 2001. *The Fragility of Goodness: Luck and Ethics in Greek Tragedy and Philosophy.* Cambridge.

Nyland, R. 1992. "Herodotos' Sources for the Plataiai Campaign." *L'Antiquité classique* 61, 80–97.

Ober, J. 1989. *Mass and Elite in Democratic Athens: Rhetoric, Ideology, and the Power of the People.* Princeton.

Ober, J. 1996. *The Athenian Revolution: Essays on Ancient Greek Democracy and Political Theory.* Princeton.

Ober, J. 1998a. *Political Dissent in Democratic Athens: Intellectual Critics of Popular Rule.* Princeton.

Ober, J. 1998b, "Revolution Matters: Democracy as Demotic Action (A Response to Kurt A. Raaflaub)." In I. Morris and K.A. Raaflaub, eds., *Democracy 2500? Questions and Challenges.* Dubuque, IA, 67–85.

Ober, J. 2002. "Social Science History, Cultural History, and the Amnesty of 403." *TAPhA* 132, 127–137.

Ober, J. 2005. *Athenian Legacies: Essays on the Politics of Going on Together.* Princeton.

O'Brien, J.M. 1992. *Alexander the Great: The Invisible Enemy, A Biography.* London.

Ogden, D. 1996. "Homosexuality and Warfare in Ancient Greece." In A. Lloyd, ed., *Battle in Antiquity.* London, 107–168.

Ogden, D. 1998. "What Was in Pandora's Box?" In N. Fisher and H. Van Wees, eds., *Archaic Greece: New Approaches and New Evidence.* London, 213–230.

Ogden, D. 1999. *Polygamy, Prostitutes and Death: The Hellenistic Dynasties.* London.

O'Hara, R.J. *Ancient Greek Coins of Miletus.* http://www.rjohara.net/coins/.

Omitowoju, R. 2002. *Rape and the Politics of Consent in Classical Athens.* Cambridge.

O'Neil, J.L. 2002. "Iranian Wives and Their Roles in Macedonian Royal Courts." *Prudentia* 34.2, 159–177.

Osborne, M.J. 1981–1983. *Naturalization in Athens.* 4 vols. Brussels.

Osborne, R. 1985a. *Demos: The Discovery of Classical Attika.* Cambridge.

Osborne, R. 1985b. "The Erection and Mutilation of the Hermai." *Proceedings of the Cambridge Philological Society* 31, 47–73.

Osborne, R. 1990. "Vexatious Litigation in Classical Athens: Sykophancy and the Sykophant." In P. Cartledge et al., eds., *Nomos: Essays in Athenian Law, Politics and Society.* Cambridge, 83–102.

Osborne, R. 1994. Looking On – Greek Style. Does the Sculpted Girl Speak to Women Too?" In I. Morris, ed., *Classical Greece: Ancient Histories and Modern Archaeologies.* Cambridge, 81–96.

Osborne, R. 1996. *Greece in the Making, 1200–479 BC.* London.

Osborne, R. 1998. *Archaic and Classical Greek Art*. Oxford.

Osborne, R. 2000. *The Athenian Empire*, 4th ed. London.

Osborne, R. 2002. "Archaic Greek History." In E.J. Bakker, I.J.F. de Jong, and H. van Wees, eds., *Brill's Companion to Herodotus*. Leiden, 497–522.

Osborne, R., trans. 2004. *The Old Oligarch: Pseudo-Xenophon's Constitution of the Athenians*, 2nd ed. London.

Ostwald, M. 1969. *Nomos and the Beginnings of Athenian Democracy*. Oxford.

Ostwald, M. 1986. *From Popular Sovereignty to the Sovereignty of the Law: Law, Society, and Politics in Fifth-Century Athens*. Berkeley.

Ostwald, M. 2002. "Athens and Chalkis: A Study in Athenian Control." *JHS* 122, 134–143.

Palagia, O. 2000. "Hephaestion's Pyre and the Royal Hunt of Alexander." In A.B. Bosworth and E.J. Baynham, eds., *Alexander the Great in Fact and Fiction*. Oxford, 167–206.

Papagrigorakisa, M. J., et al. 2006. "DNA Examination of Ancient Dental Pulp Incriminates Typhoid Fever as a Probable Cause of the Plague of Athens." *International Journal of Infectious Diseases* 10, 206–214.

Paradiso, A. 2004. "The Logic of Terror: Thucydides, Spartan Duplicity and an Improbable Massacre." In T.J. Figueira, ed., *Spartan Society*. Swansea, 179–198.

Parke, H.W. 1933. *Greek Mercenary Soldiers from the Earliest Times to the Battle of Ipsus*. Oxford.

Parke, H.W. and D.E.W. Wormell, 1956. *The Delphic Oracle*. 2 vols. Oxford.

Parker, H.N. 1993. "Sappho Schoolmistress." *TAPhA* 123, 309–351.

Parker, R.C.T. 1983. *Miasma: Pollution and Purification in Early Greek Religion*. Oxford.

Parker, R.C.T. 1994. "Athenian Religion Abroad." In R. Osborne and S. Hornblower, eds., *Ritual, Finance, Politics: Athenian Democratic Accounts Presented to David Lewis*. Oxford, 339–346.

Parker, R.C.T. 1996. *Athenian Religion: A History*. Oxford.

Parker, V. 1993. "Some Dates in Early Spartan History." *Klio* 75, 45–60.

Parker, V. 2007. "Sphodrias' Raid and the Liberation of Thebes: A Study of Ephorus and Xenophon." *Hermes* 135, 13–33.

Patterson, C. 1981. *Pericles' Citizenship Law of 451–450 BC*. New York.

Patterson, C. 1990. "Those Athenian Bastards." *ClAnt* 9, 40–73.

Patterson, C. 1998. *The Family in Greek History*. Cambridge, MA.

Pearson, L. 1962. *Popular Ethics in Ancient Greece*. Stanford.

Pearson, L. 1984. "Ephorus and Timaeus in Diodorus: Laqueur's Thesis Rejected." *Historia* 33, 1–20.

Pelling, C. 2000. *Literary Texts and the Greek Historian*. London.

Percy, W.A. 1996. *Pederasty and Pedagogy in Archaic Greece*. Urbana.

Perlman, S. 1957. Isocrates' *Philippus*: A Reinterpretation." *Historia* 6, 306–317.

Perlman, S. 1969. "Isocrates' *Philippus* and Panhellenism." *Historia* 18, 370–374.

Perlman, S. 1976. "Panhellenism, the Polis and Imperialism." *Historia* 25, 1–30.

Phillips, D.J. 2003. "Athenian Political History: A Panathenaic Perspective." In D.J. Phillip and D. Pritchard, eds., *Sport and Festival in the Ancient Greek World*. Swansea, 197–232.

Phillips, D.J. and D. Pritchard, eds. 2003. *Sport and Festival in the Ancient Greek World*. Swansea.

Pickard-Cambridge, A.W. 1946. *The Theatre of Dionysus in Athens*. Oxford.

Pickard-Cambridge, A.W. 1968. *The Dramatic Festivals of Athens*, 2nd ed. Oxford.

Piejko, F. 1985. "The Second Letter of Alexander the Great to Chios." *Phoenix* 39, 238–249.

Pipili, M. 1987. *Laconian Iconography of the Sixth Century BC*. Oxford.

Plant, I.M. 1994. "The Battle of Tanagra: A Spartan Initiative?" *Historia* 43, 259–274.

Pleket, H.W. 1963. "Thasos and the Popularity of the Athenian Empire." *Historia* 12, 70–77.

Podlecki, A.J. 1966. *The Political Background of Aeschylean Tragedy*. Ann Arbor.

Podlecki, A.J. 1975. *The Life of Themistocles: A Critical Survey of the Literary and Archaeological Evidence*. Montreal.

Podlecki, A.J. 1998. *Perikles and His Circle*. London.

Polignac, F. de. 1995. *Cults, Territory, and the Origins of the Greek City-State*. Chicago.

Pomeroy, S.B. 1975. *Goddesses, Whores, Wives, and Slaves: Women in Classical Antiquity*. New York.

Pomeroy, S.B. 1994. *Xenophon's Oeconomicus: A Social and Historical Commentary*. Oxford.

Pomeroy, S.B. 1997. *Families in Classical and Hellenistic Greece: Representations and Realities*. Oxford.

Pomeroy, S.B. 2002. *Spartan Women*. Oxford.

Poole, J.C.F. and A.J. Holladay, 1979. "Thucydides and the Plague of Athens." *CQ* 29, 282–300.

Porter, J.R. 1997. "Adultery by the Book: Lysias I (On the Murder of Eratosthenes) and Comic Diegesis." *Échos du monde classique* 16, 421–453.

Powell, A. 1998. "Sixth-Century Lakonian Vase-Painting: Continuities and Discontinuities with the 'Lykourgan Ethos.'" In N. Fisher and H. van Wees, eds., *Archaic Greece: New Approaches and New Evidence*. London, 119–146.

Powell, B.B. 1989. "Why Was the Greek Alphabet Invented? The Epigraphical Evidence." *ClAnt* 8, 320–350.

Pownall, F.S. 2004. *Lessons from the Past: The Moral Use of History in Fourth-Century Prose*. Ann Arbor.

Pownall, F.S. 2007. "The Panhellenism of Isocrates." In W. Heckel, L.A. Tritle, and P. Wheatley, eds., *Alexander's Empire: Formulation to Decay*. Claremont, CA, 13–26.

Price, M.J. 1991. *The Coinage in the Name of Alexander the Great and Philip Arrhidaeus*. 2 vols. Zurich.

Price, S. 1999. *Religions of the Ancient Greeks*. Cambridge.

Pritchett W.K. 1956. "The Attic Stelai, II." *Hesperia* 25, 178–317.

Pritchett W.K. 1961. "Five New Fragments of the Attic Stelai." *Hesperia* 30, 23–29.

Pritchett W.K. 1965–1991. *The Greek State at War*. 5 vols. Berkeley.

Pritchett, W.K. 1969. *Studies in Ancient Greek Topography*, Vol. 2. Berkeley.

Pritchett, W.K. 1995. *Thucydides' Pentekontaetia and Other Essays*. Amsterdam.

Project Troia. http://www.uni-tuebingen.de/troia/eng/index.html.

Purcell, N. 1990. "Mobility and the *Polis*." In O. Murray and S. Price, eds., *The Greek City: From Homer to Alexander*. Oxford, 29–58.

Quillin, J.M. 2002. "Achieving Amnesty: The Role of Events, Institutions, and Ideas." *TAPhA* 132, 71–108.

Quinn, T.J. 1981. *Athens and Samos, Lesbos and Chios, 478–404 BC*. Manchester.

Raaflaub, K.A. 1990. "Contemporary Perceptions of Democracy in Fifth-Century Athens." In J.R. Fears, ed., *Aspects of Athenian Democracy*. Copenhagen, 33–70.

Raaflaub, K.A. 1997. "Homeric Society." In I. Morris and B. Powell, eds., *A New Companion to Homer*. Leiden, 624–648.

Raaflaub, K.A. 1998a. "Historian's Headache: How to Read 'Homeric Society'?" In N. Fisher and H. van Wees, eds., *Archaic Greece: New Approaches and New Evidence*. London, 169–193.

Raaflaub, K.A. 1998b. "Power in the Hands of the People: Foundations of Athenian Democracy." In I. Morris and K.A. Raaflaub, eds., *Democracy 2500? Questions and Challenges*. Dubuque, IA, 31–66.

Raaflaub, K.A. 1998c. "The Thetes and Democracy (A Response to Josiah Ober)." In I. Morris and K.A. Raaflaub, eds., *Democracy 2500? Questions and Challenges*. Dubuque, IA, 87–103.

Raaflaub, K.A. 1999. "Archaic and Classical Greece." In K.A. Raaflaub and N. Rosenstein, eds., *War and Society in the Ancient and Medieval Worlds: Asia, the Mediterranean, Europe, and Mesoamerica*. Cambridge, MA, 129–161.

Raaflaub, K.A. 2004. *The Discovery of Freedom in Ancient Greece*. Chicago.

Rahe P. 1981. "The Annihilation of the Sacred Band at Chaeronea." *AJA* 85, 84–87.

Rankin, H.D. 1983. *Sophists, Socrates and Cynics*. London.

Reed, C.M. 2003. *Maritime Traders in the Ancient Greek World*. Cambridge.

Renfrew, C. and P. Bahn, 1996. *Archaeology: Theories, Methods, and Practice*. London.

Rengakos, A. and A. Tsakmakis, eds. 2006. *Brill's Companion to Thucydides*. Leiden.

Rhodes, P.J. 1972. "The Five Thousand in the Athenian Revolution of 411 BC." *JHS* 92, 115–127.

Rhodes, P.J. 1985. *The Five Thousand and the Athenian Revolution of 411*. Oxford.

Rhodes, P.J. 1991. "The Athenian Code of Laws, 410–399 BC." *JHS* 111, 87–100.

Rhodes, P.J. 1993. *A Commentary on the Aristotelian Athenaion Politeia*, 2nd ed. Oxford.

Rhodes, P.J. 2000, "Who Ran Democratic Athens?" In P. Flensted-Jensen et al., eds., *Polis and Politics: Studies in Ancient Greek History presented to Mogens Herman Hansen on his Sixtieth Birthday, August 20, 2000*. Copenhagen, 465–477.

Rhodes, P.J., ed. 2004a. *Athenian Democracy*. Oxford.

Rhodes, P.J. 2004b. "Political Activity in Classical Athens." In P.J. Rhodes, ed., *Athenian Democracy*. Oxford, 185–206 = *JHS* 1986. 106, 132–144.

Rhodes, P.J. 2006. *A History of the Classical Greek World: 478–323 BC*. Oxford.

Rice, D.G. 1975. "Xenophon, Diodorus and the Year 379–378 BC: Reconstruction and Reappraisal." *YCS* 24, 95–130.

Rice, D.G. 1997. "Litigation as a Political Weapon: The Case of Timotheos of Athens." In C.D. Hamilton and P. Krentz, eds., *Polis and Polemos: Essays on Politics, War, and History in Ancient Greece, in Honor of Donald Kagan*. Claremont, CA, 229–240.

Richardson, N.J., ed. 1974. *The Homeric Hymn to Demeter*. Oxford.

Richter, G.M.A. 1970. *Kouroi: Archaic Greek Youths: A Study of the Development of the Kouros Type in Greek Sculpture*. London.

Ridgeway, D. 1992. *The First Western Greeks*. Cambridge.

Rihll, T.E. 1995. "Democracy Denied: Why Ephialtes Attacked the Areiopagus." *JHS* 115, 87–98.

Robb, K. 1994. *Literacy and Paideia in Ancient Greece*. New York.

Robbins, E. 1994. "Alcman's *Partheneion*: Legend and Choral Ceremony." *CQ* 44, 7–16.

Roberts, J.T. 1996. "Athenian Equality: A Constant Surrounded by Flux." In J. Ober and C. Hendrick, eds., *Dêmokratia: A Conversation on Democracies, Ancient and Modern*. Princeton, 187–202.

Robertson, M. 1992. *The Art of Vase-Painting in Classical Athens*. Cambridge.

Robertson, N. 1976. "The Thessalian Expedition of 480 BC." *JHS* 96, 100–120.

Robertson, N. 1980. "The True Nature of the Delian League, 478–461 BC." *American Journal of Ancient History* 5, 64–96, 110–133.

Robinson, E.W., ed. 2004. *Ancient Greek Democracy: Readings and Sources*. Oxford.

Roebuck, C. 1948. "The Settlements of Philip II with the Greek States in 338 BC." *CPh* 43, 73–92.

Roisman, J. 1987. "Alkidas in Thucydides." *Historia* 36, 385–421.

Roisman, J. 1988. "On Phrynichos' 'Sack of Miletos' and 'Phoinissai.'" *Eranos* 86, 15–23.

Roisman, J. 1993. "The Background of the Battle of Tanagra and Some Related Issues." *L'Antiquité classique* 62, 69–85.

Roisman, J., ed. 2003. *Brill's Companion to Alexander the Great*. Leiden.

Roisman, J. 2005. *The Rhetoric of Manhood: Masculinity in the Attic Orators*. Berkeley.

Roisman, J. 2006. *The Rhetoric of Conspiracy in Ancient Athens*. Berkeley.

Rood, T. 1998. *Thucydides: Narrative and Explanation*. Oxford.

Rosen, R.M. and I. Sluiter, eds. 2003. *Andreia: Studies in Manliness and Courage in Classical Antiquity*. Leiden.

Rosenbloom, D. 1993. "Shouting 'Fire' in a Crowded Theater: Phrynichos's *Capture of Miletos* and the Politics of Fear in Early Attic Tragedy." *Philologos* 137, 159–196.

Rosenbloom, D. 2004a. "*Ponêroi* vs. *Chrêstoi*: The Ostracism of Hyperbolos and the Struggle for Hegemony in Athens after the Death of Perikles, Part I." *TAPhA* 134, 55–105.

Rosenbloom, D. 2004b. "*Ponêroi* vs. *Chrêstoi*: The Ostracism of Hyperbolos and the Struggle for Hegemony in Athens after the Death of Perikles, Part II." *TAPhA* 134, 323–358.

Rosenbloom, D. 2006. *Aeschylus: Persians*. London.

Roy. J.G. 1971. "Arcadia and Boeotia in Peloponnesian Affairs, 370–362 BC." *Historia* 20: 569–599.

Roy, J.G. 1994. "Thebes in the 360s BC." *CAH²* 6: 187–208.

Rubicam, C.I.R. 1987. "The Organization and Composition of Diodorus *Biblioteke*." *Échos du monde classique* 31, 313–328.

Rubinsohn, W.Z. 1977. "The Philotas Affair – A Reconsideration." *Ancient Macedonia* 2, 409–420.

Rubinsohn, W.Z. 1997. "Macedon and Greece: The Case of Thebes." *Journal of Ancient Civilization* 12, 99–123.

Runnels, C., D.J. Pullen, and S. Langdon, eds. 1995. *Artifact and Assemblage: The Finds from a Regional Survey of the Southern Argolid, Greece*. Stanford.

Russell, D.A. 2001. *Plutarch*. Bristol.

Rutter, N.K. 1973. "Diodorus and the Foundation of Thurii." *Historia* 22, 155–176.

Ruzicka, S. 1998. "Epaminondas and the Genesis of the Social War." *CPh* 93.1, 60–69.

Ryder, T.T.B. 1965. *Koine Eirene: General Peace and Local Independence in Ancient Greece*. Oxford.

Ryder, T.T.B. 1994. "The Diplomatic Skills of Philip II." In I. Worthington, ed., *Ventures into Greek History*. Oxford, 228–257.

Ryder, T.T.B. 2000. "Demosthenes and Philip II." In I. Worthington, ed., *Demosthenes: Statesman and Orator*. London, 45–89.

Sacks, K.S. 1990. *Diodorus Siculus and the First Century*. Princeton.

Saïd, S. 2002 [1984]. "Greeks and Barbarians in Euripides' Tragedies: The End of Differences." In T. Harrison, ed., *Greeks and Barbarians*. New York, 62–100.

Sakellariou, M.B. 1990. *Between Memory and Oblivion: The Transmission of Early Greek Historical Traditions*. Athens.

Salmon, J.B. 1977. "Political Hoplites?" *JHS* 97, 84–101

Salmon, J.B. 1984. *Wealthy Corinth: A History of the City to 338 BC*. Oxford.

Samons, L.J., II. 1998. "Mass, Elite, and Hoplite-Farmer in Greek History." *Arion* 5, 99–123.

Samons, L.J., II. 2000. *Empire of the Owl: Athenian Imperial Finance*. Stuttgart.

Sancisi-Weerdenburg, H. 1993. "Alexander and Persepolis." In J. Carlsen et al., eds., *Alexander the Great: Reality and Myth*. Rome, 177–188.

Sancisi-Weerdenburg, H. 2000. "Cultural Politics and Chronology." In H. Sancisi-Weerdenburg, ed., *Peisistratus and the Tyranny: A Reappraisal of the Evidence*. Amsterdam, 79–106.

Scanlon, T.F. 1998. "*Virgineum Gymnasium*: Spartan Females and Early Greek Athletics." In W.J. Raschke, ed., *The Archaeology of the Olympics: The Olympics and Other Festivals in Antiquity*. Madison, WI, 185–216.

Schaps, D.M. 1977. "The Woman Least Mentioned: Etiquette and Women's Names." *CQ* 27, 323–331.

Schaps, D.M. 1979. *Economic Rights of Women in Ancient Greece*. Edinburgh.

Schaps, D.M. 2004. *The Invention of Coinage and the Monetization of Ancient Greece*. Ann Arbor.

Scheidel, W. 1995. "The Most Silent Women of Greece and Rome: Rural Labour and Women's Life in the Ancient World, I." *G&R* 42: 202–217.

Scheidel, W. 1996. "The Most Silent Women of Greece and Rome: Rural Labour and Women's Life in the Ancient World, II." *G&R* 43: 1–10.

Schmidt, K. 1999. "The Peace of Antalcidas and the Idea of the *koine eirene*: A Panhellenic Peace Movement." *Revue internationale des droits de l'Antiquité* 46, 81–96.

Schreiner, J.H. 1997. *Hellanikos, Thukydides and the Era of Kimon*. Aarhus.

Schultz, P. 2007. "Leochares' Argead Portraits in the Philippeion." In R. von den Hoff, ed., *Early Hellenistic Portraiture: Image, Style, Context*. Cambridge, 205–233.

Schütrumpf, E. 1987. "The Rhetra of Epitadeus: A Platonist's Fiction." *GRBS* 28, 441–457.

Schwartz, A. 2009. *Reinstating the Hoplite: Arms, Armour and Phalanx Fighting in Archaic and Classical Greece*. Stuttgart.

Scully, S. 1981. "The Polis in Homer: A Definition and Interpretation." *Ramus* 10, 1–34.

Scully, S.P. 1999. "Orchestra and Stage in Sophocles: 'Oedipus Tyrannus' and the Theater of Dionysus." *Syllecta Classica* 10, 65–86.

Seager, R. 1976. "After the Peace of Nicias: Diplomacy and Policy, 421–416 B.C." *CQ* 26, 249–269.

Sealey, R. 1976. *A History of the Greek City States ca. 700—338 BC*. Berkeley.

Sealey, R. 1981. "Ephialtes, *Eisangelia*, and the Council." In G.S. Shrimpton and D.J. McCargar, eds., *Classical Contributions: Studies in Honour of Malcolm Francis McGregor*. Locust Valley, NY, 125–34. Reprinted in P.J. Rhodes, ed., 2004, *Athenian Democracy*. Oxford, 310–324.

Sealey, R. 1993. *Demosthenes and His Time: A Study in Defeat*. New York.

Seaman, M.G. 1997. "The Athenian Expedition to Melos in 416." *Historia* 46, 385–418.

Sekunda, N. 2002. *Marathon 490 BC: The First Persian Invasion of Greece*. Oxford.

Sergent, B. 1986. *Homosexuality in Greek Myth*. Trans. A. Goldhammer. Boston.

Shapiro, B., et al. 2006. "No Proof That Typhoid Caused the Plague of Athens (a Reply to Papagrigorakis et al.)." *International Journal of Infectious Diseases* 10, 334–335.

Shapiro, H.A. 1989. *Art and Cult Under the Tyrants in Athens*. Mainz.

Shapiro, H.A. 1993. *Personifications in Greek Art: The Representations of Abstract Concepts, 600–400 BC*. Zurich.

Shapiro, H.A. 1996. "Athena, Apollo, and the Religious Propaganda of the Athenian Empire." In P. Hellstrom and B. Alroth, eds., *Religion and Power in the Ancient Greek World: Proceedings of the Uppsala Symposium, Boreas* 24, Uppsala, 101–113.

Shapiro, S.O. 1996. "Herodotus and Solon." *ClAnt* 15, 348–364.

Shear, T.L. 1978. "Tyrants and Buildings in Archaic Athens." In W.A.P. Childs, ed., *Athens Comes of Age: From Solon to Salamis*. Princeton, 1–19.

Shear, T.L. 1993. "The Persian Destruction of Athens: Evidence from Agora Deposits." *Hesperia* 62, 383–482.

Shipley, G. 1987. *A History of Samos 800–188 BC*. Oxford.

Shipley, G. 1997a. *A Commentary on Plutarch's Life of Agesilaos: Response to Sources in the Presentation of Character*. Oxford.

Shipley, G. 1997b. "The Other Lakedaimonians: The Dependent Perioikic *Poleis* of Laconia and Messenia." In M.H. Hansen, ed., *The Polis as an Urban Center and as a Political Community*. Copenhagen, 189–281.

Sidebotham, L.S. 1982. "Herodotus on Artemisium." *Classical World* 75, 177–186.

Siewert, P. 1977. "The Ephebic Oath in Fifth-Century Athens." *JHS* 97, 102–111.

Sinclair, R.K. 1988. *Democracy and Participation in Athens*. Cambridge.

Singor, H.W. 1999. "Admission to the *Syssitia* in Fifth-Century Sparta." In S. Hodkinson and A. Powell, eds., *Sparta: New Perspectives*. London, 67–89.

Singor, H.W. 2000. "The Military Side of the Peisistratid Tyranny." In H. Sancisi-Weerdenburg, ed., *Peisistratus and the Tyranny: A Reappraisal of the Evidence*. Amsterdam, 107–126.

Singor, H.W. 2002. "The Spartan Army at Mantinea and Its Organization in the Fifth Century BC." In W. Jongman and M. Kleijwegt, eds., *After the Past: Essays in Ancient History in Honour of H. W. Pleket*. Leiden, 235–284.

Skinner, M.B. 2005. *Sexuality in Greek and Roman Culture*. Oxford.

Slings, S.R. 2000. "Literature at Athens, 566–510 BC." In H. Sancisi-Weerdenburg, ed., *Peisistratus and the Tyranny: A Reappraisal of the Evidence*. Amsterdam, 57–77.

Sluiter, I. and R. Rosen, eds. 2004. *Free Speech in Classical Antiquity*. Leiden.

Smith, A.C. 1999. "Eurymedon and the Evolution of Political Personifications in the Early Classical Period." *JHS* 119, 128–141.

Smith, A.C. 2003. "Athenian Political Art from the Fifth and Fourth Centuries BCE: Images of Political Personifications." http://www.stoa.org/projects/demos/article_pe rsonifications?page=11&greekEncoding=UnicodeC, 1–26.

Snodgrass, A. 1964. *Early Greek Armour and Weapons*. Edinburgh.

Snodgrass, A. 1967. *Arms and Armour of the Greeks*. Ithaca.

Snodgrass, A. 1980. *Archaic Greece: The Age of Experiment*. Berkeley.

Snodgrass, A.M. 1987. *Archaeologies of Greece*. Berkeley.

Snodgrass, A.M. 1997. "Homer and Greek Art." In I. Morris and B. Powell, eds., *A New Companion to Homer*. Leiden, 560–598.

Sommerstein, A.M. 2004. "Argive Oenoe, Athenian Epikouroi and the Stoa Poikile." In S. Keay and S. Moser, eds., *Greek Art in View: Essays in Honour of Brian Sparkes*. Oxford, 138–147.

Sorkin Rabinowitz, N. 2002. "Excavating Women's Homoeroticism in Ancient Greece: The Evidence from Attic Vase Painting." In N. Sorkin Rabinowitz and L. Auanger, eds., *Among Women: From the Homosocial to the Homoerotic in the Ancient World*. Austin, 106–166.

Sourvinou-Inwood, C. 1994. "Something to Do with Athens: Tragedy and Ritual." In R. Osborne and S. Hornblower, eds., *Ritual, Finance and Politics: Athenian Democratic Accounts Presented to David Lewis*. Oxford, 269–290.

Sourvinou-Inwood, C. 2002. "Greek Perceptions of Ethnicity and the Ethnicity of the Macedonians." In L. Moscati Castelnuovo, ed., *Identità e prassi storica nel Mediterraneo greco*. Milan, 173–204.

Spence, I.G. 1990. "Perikles and the Defense of Attika During the Peloponnesian War." *JHS* 110, 91–109.

Spence, I.G. 1993. *The Cavalry of Classical Greece: A Social and Military History with Particular Reference to Athens*. Oxford.

Spence, I.G. 1995. "Thucydides, Woodhead, and Cleon." *Mnemosyne* 48, 411–437.

Sprawski, S. 1999. *Jason of Pherae: A Study on History of Thessaly in Years 431–370 BC*. Krakow.

Sprawski, S. 2004. "Were Lycophron and Jason Tyrants of Pherae? Xenophon on the History of Thessaly." In C. Tuplin, ed., *Xenophon and His World*. Stuttgart, 437–452.

Stadter, P.A. 1989. *A Commentary on Plutarch's Pericles*. Chapel Hill.

Stadter, P.A., ed. 1992. *Plutarch and the Historical Tradition*. London

Stafford, E. 2001. *Worshipping Virtues: Personification and the Divine in Ancient Greece*. Swansea.

Stahl, H.-P. 2003. *Thucydides: Man's Place in History*. Swansea.

Stansbury-O'Donnell, M.D. 2005. "The Painting Program in the Stoa Poikile." In J.M. Barringer and J.M. Hurwit, eds., *Periklean Athens and Its Legacy: Problems and Perspectives*. Austin, 73–87.

Stanton, G.R. 1990. *Athenian Politics c. 800–500 BC*. London.

Starr, C.G. 1986. *Individual and Community: The Rise of the Polis 800–500 BC*. New York.

Ste Croix, G.E.M. de. 1954–1955. "The Character of the Athenian Empire." *Historia* 3, 1–41.

Ste Croix, G.E.M. de. 1956. "The Constitution of the Five Thousand." *Historia* 5, 1–33.

Ste Croix, G.E.M. de. 1972. *The Origins of the Peloponnesian War*. London.

Ste Croix, G.E.M. de. 1983. *The Class Struggle in the Ancient Greek World: From the Archaic Age to the Arab Conquest*. Ithaca.

Ste Croix, G.E.M. de. 2004. *Athenian Democratic Origins and Other Essays*. Ed. D. Harvey and R. Parker. Oxford.

Stewart, A. 1993. *Faces of Power: Alexander's Image and Hellenistic Politics*. Berkeley.

Stewart, A. 1997. *Art, Desire and the Body in Ancient Greece*. Cambridge.

Stewart, A. 2003. "Alexander in Greek and Roman Art." In J. Roisman, ed., *Brill's Companion to Alexander the Great*. Leiden, 31–66.

Stone, I.F. 1988. *The Trial of Socrates*. Boston.

Strauss, B. 1983. "Aegospotami Reexamined." *AJP* 104, 24–35.

Strauss, B. 1987. "A Note on the Topography and Tactics of the Battle of Aegospotami." *AJP* 108, 741–745.

Strauss, B. 2003. "Alexander: The Military Campaign." In J. Roisman, ed., *Brill's Companion to Alexander the Great*. Leiden, 133–158.

Strauss, B. 2004. *The Battle of Salamis: The Naval Encounter That Saved Greece – and Western Civilization*. New York.

Strauss, B. 2006. *The Trojan War: A New History*. New York.

Strauss, B. and J. Ober, 1990. *The Anatomy of Error: Ancient Military Disasters and Their Lessons for Modern Strategists*. New York.

Stroud, R. 1968. *Drakon's Law on Homicide*. Berkeley.

Stroud, R. 1974. "An Athenian Law on Silver Coinage." *Hesperia* 43, 157–188.

Stroud, R. 1998. *The Athenian Grain-Tax Law of 374/3 BC*. Princeton.

Suter, A. 2002. *The Narcissus and the Pomegranate: An Archaeology of the Homeric Hymn to Demeter*. Ann Arbor.

Svenbro, J. 1993. *Phrasikleia: An Anthropology of Reading in Ancient Greece*. Trans. J. Lloyd. Ithaca.

Szemler, G.J., W.J. Cherf, and J.C. Kraft, 1996. *Thermopylai: Myth and Reality in 480 BC*. Chicago.

Tandy, D.W. 1997. *Warriors into Traders: The Power of the Market in Early Greece*. Berkeley.

Tarn, W.W. 1921. "Alexander's Hypomnemata and the World Kingdom." *JHS* 41, 3–17.

Tarn, W.W. 1948. *Alexander the Great*. 2 vols. Cambridge.

Taylor, M.W. 1991. *The Tyrant Slayers: The Heroic Image in Fifth-Century BC Athenian Art and Politics*, 2nd ed. Salem, MA.

Thomas, C.G. and C. Conant, 1999. *Citadel to City-State: The Transformation of Greece 1200–700 B.C.E.* Bloomington.

Thomas, R. 1989. *Oral Tradition and Written Record in Classical Athens*. Cambridge.

Thomas, R. 1996. "Written in Stone? Liberty, Equality, Orality and the Codification of Law." In L. Foxhall and A.D.E. Lewis, eds., *Greek Law in Its Political Setting: Justifications not Justice*. Oxford, 9–32.

Thompson, M. 1982. "The Coinage of Philip II and Alexander III." In B. Bar Sharrar and E.N. Borza, eds., *Macedonia and Greece in Late Classical and Early Hellenistic Times*. Washington, DC, 113–121.

Throne, J.A. 2001. "Warfare and Agriculture: The Economic Impact of Devastation in Classical Greece." *GRBS* 43, 225–253.

Thür, G. 1996. "Reply to D.C. Mirhady: 'Torture and Rhetoric in Athens.'" *JHS* 116, 132–134.

Tieman, W. 2002. "'Cause' in History and the Amnesty at Athens: An Introduction." *TAPhA* 132, 63–70.

Tigerstedt, E.N. 1965–1978. *The Legend of Sparta in Classical Antiquity*. 3 vols. Stockholm.

Tod, M.N., ed. 1985. *Greek Historical Inscriptions: From the Sixth Century BC to the Death of Alexander the Great in 323 BC*. 2 vols. Chicago.

Todd, S.C. 1993. *The Shape of Athenian Law*. Oxford.

Todd, S.C. 2007. *A Commentary on Lysias, Speeches 1–11*. Oxford.

Tomlinson, R.A.T. 1972. *Argos and the Argolid: From the End of the Bronze Age to the Roman Occupation*. Ithaca.

Tracy, S.V. 1995. *Athenian Democracy in Transition: Attic Letter-Cutters of 340–290 BC*. Berkeley.

Traill, J.S. 1975. *The Political Organization of Attica: A Study of Demes, Trittys, and Phylai and their Representation in the Athenian Council*. Princeton.

Traill, J.S. 1986. *Demos and Trittys: Epigraphical and Topographical Studies in the Organization of Attica*. Toronto.

Trevett, J. 1992. *Apollodoros, the Son of Pasion*. Oxford.

Trevett, J. 1996. "Did Demosthenes Publish His Deliberative Speeches?" *Hermes* 124, 425–441.

Tritle, L.A. 2004. "Alexander and the Killing of Cleitus the Black.' In W. Heckel and L.A. Tritle, eds., *Crossroads of History: The Age of Alexander*. Claremont, CA, 127–146.

Tronson, A. 1991. "The Hellenic League of 480 BC: Fact or Ideological Fiction?" *Acta Classica* 34, 93–110.

Troxell, H.A. 1997. *Studies in the Macedonian Coinage of Alexander the Great*. New York.

Trundle, M. 2004. *Greek Mercenaries: From the Late Archaic Period to Alexander*. London.

Tuplin, C.J. 1982. "The Date of the Union of Corinth and Argos." *CQ* 32, 75–83.

Tuplin, C.J. 1987. "The Leuctra Campaign: Some Outstanding Problems." *Klio* 69, 72–107.

Tuplin, C.J. 1993. *Failings of Empire: A Reading of Xenophon Hellenica 2.3.11–7.5.27*. Stuttgart.

Tuplin, C.J., ed. 2004. *Xenophon and His World: Papers from a Conference held in Liverpool in July 1999*. Stuttgart.

Ure, P.N. 1922. *The Origin of Tyranny*. Cambridge.

Usher, S. 1999. *Greek Oratory: Tradition and Originality*. Oxford.

van der Vin, J.P.A. 2000. "Coins in Athens at the Time of Peisistratos." In H. Sancisi-Weerdenburg, ed., *Peisistratos and the Tyranny: A Reappraisal of the Evidence*. Amsterdam, 147–153.

van Erp Taalman Kip, A. 1987. "Euripides and Melos." *Mnemosyne* 40, 414–419.

van Wees, H. 1992. *Status Warriors: War, Violence and Society in Homer and History*. Amsterdam.

van Wees, H. 1995. "Politics and the Battlefield: Ideology in Greek Warfare." In A. Powell, ed., *The Greek World*. London, 153–178.

van Wees, H. 1999. "Tyrtaeus' *Eunomia*: Nothing to do with the Great Rhetra." In S. Hodkinson and A. Powell, eds., *Sparta: New Perspectives*. London, 1–42.

van Wees, H. 2000a. "The Development of the Hoplitic Phalanx: Iconography and Reality in the Seventh Century." In H. van Wees, ed., *War and Violence in Ancient Greece*. London, 125–166.

van Wees, H. 2000b. "Megara's Mafiosi: Timocracy and Violence in Theognis." In R. Brock and S. Hodkinson, eds., *Alternatives to Athens: Varieties of Political Organization and Community in Ancient Greece*. Oxford, 52–67.

van Wees, H. 2004. *Greek Warfare: Myths and Realities*. London.

Vartsos, J. 1977. "The Foundation of Brea." *Ancient Macedonia* 2, 13–16.

Vernant, J.-P. 1982. "From Oedipus to Periander: Lameness, Tyranny, Incest in Legend and History." *Arethusa* 15, 19–38.

Vickers, M. 1996. "Fifth Century Chronology and the Coinage Decree." *JHS* 116, 171–174.

Vickers, M. 1999. "Alcibiades and Melos: Thucydides 5.84–116." *Historia* 48, 265–281.

Vidal-Naquet, P. 1986. *The Black Hunter: Forms of Thought and Forms of Society in the Greek World*. Trans. A. Szegedy-Maszak. Baltimore.

Vinogradov, Y. 1998. "The Greek Colonisation of the Black Sea Region in the Light of Private Lead Letters." In G.R. Tsetskhladze, ed., *The Greek Colonisation of the Black Sea Area: Historical Interpretation of Archaeology*. Stuttgart, 153–178.

Vlastos, G. 1994. *Socratic Studies*. Ed. M. Burnyeat. Cambridge.

Vogt, J. 1975. *Ancient Slavery and the Ideal of Man*. Trans. T. Wiedemann. Cambridge, MA.

Walbank, F.W. 1976–1977. "Were There Greek Federal States?" *Scripta Classica Israelica* 3, 27–51.

Walbank, F.W. 2002 [1951]. "The Problem of Greek Nationality." In T. Harrison, ed., *Greeks and Barbarians*. New York, 234–256.

Walker, H.J. 1995. *Theseus and Athens*. Oxford.

Wallace, R.W. 1983. "The Date of Solon's Reforms." *American Journal of Ancient History* 8, 81–95.

Wallace, R.W. 1989a. *The Areopagos Council, to 307 BC*. Baltimore.

Wallace, R.W. 1989b. "The Athenian *Proeisphorontes*." *Hesperia* 58, 473–490.

Wallace, R.W. 1994. "Private Lives and Public Enemies: Freedom of Thought in Classical Athens." In A. Boegehold and A. Scafuro, eds., *Athenian Identity and Civic Ideology*. Baltimore, 127–155.

Wallace, R.W. 1998. "Solonian Democracy." In I. Morris and K.A. Raaflaub, eds., *Democracy 2500? Questions and Challenges*. Dubuque, IA, 11–29.

Wallinga, H.T. 1993. *Ships and Sea-Power Before the Great Persian War: The Ancestry of the Ancient Trireme*. Leiden.

Wallinga, H.T. 2000. "The Athenian Naukraroi." In H. Sancisi-Weerdenburg, ed., *Peisistratus and the Tyranny: A Reappraisal of the Evidence*. Amsterdam, 131–146.

Wallinga, H.T. 2005. *Xerxes' Greek Adventure: The Naval Perspective*. Leiden.

Walters, K.R. 1983. "Perikles' Citizenship Law." *ClAnt* 2, 314–336.

Welwei, K.-W. 2004. "Orestes at Sparta: The Political Significance of the Grave of the Hero." In T.J. Figueira, ed., *Spartan Society*. Swansea, 219–230.

Westlake, H.D. 1935. *Thessaly in the Fourth Century B.C.* London.

Westlake, H.D. 1945. "Seaborne Raids in Periclean Strategy." *CQ* 39, 75–84. Reprinted in H.D. Westlake, 1969, *Essays on the Greek Historians and Greek History*. Manchester, 84–100.

Westlake, H.D. 1950. "Thucydides and the Athenian Disaster in Egypt." *CPh* 45, 209–216. Reprinted in H.D. Westlake, 1969, *Essays on the Greek Historians and Greek History*. Manchester, 61–73.

Westlake, H.D. 1968. *Individuals in Thucydides*. Cambridge.

Westlake, H.D. 1971. "Thucydides and the Uneasy Peace – A Study in Political Incompetence." *CQ* 21, 315–321. Reprinted in H.D. Westlake, 1989, *Studies in Thucydides and Greek History*. Bristol, ch. 7.

Westlake, H.D. 1977. "Thucydides on Pausanias and Themistocles: A Written Source." *CQ* 27, 95–110. Reprinted in H.D. Westlake, 1989, *Studies in Thucydides and Greek History*. Bristol, ch. 1.

Whatley, N. 1964. "On the Possibility of Reconstructing Marathon and Other Ancient Battles." *JHS* 84, 119–139.

Whitby, M. 1984. "The Union of Corinth and Argos: A Reconsideration." *Historia* 33, 295–308.

Whitby, M. 1998. "The Grain Trade of Athens in the Fourth Century BC." In H. Parkins and C. Smith, eds., *Trade, Traders, and the Ancient City*. London, 102–128.

Whitehead, D. 1977. *The Ideology of the Athenian Metic*. Cambridge.

Whitehead, D. 1986. *The Demes of Attica 508/7–ca. 250 BC: A Political and Social Study*. Princeton.

Wiesehöfer, J. 2006. " 'Keeping the Two Sides Equal': Thucydides, the Persians and the Peloponnesian War." In A. Rengakos and A. Tsakmakis, eds., *Brill's Companion to Thucydides*. Leiden, 657–667.

Wiles, D. 1997. *Tragedy in Athens: Performance Space and Theatrical Meaning*. Cambridge.

Willetts, R.F. 1967. *The Law Code of Gortyn*. Berlin.

Willetts, R.F. 1991. *The Civilization of Ancient Crete*. Amsterdam.

Wilson, J. 1979. *Pylos 425 BC: A Historical and Topographical Study of Thucydides' Account of the Campaign*. Warminster, UK.

Wilson, J. 1987. *Thucydides: Athens and Corcyra: Strategy and Tactics in the Peloponnesian War*. Bristol.

Wilson, J.-P. 1997. "The Nature of Greek Overseas Settlements in the Archaic Period: *Emporion* or *Apoikia*?" In L.G. Mitchell and P.J. Rhodes, eds., *The Development of the Polis in Archaic Greece*. London, 199–207.

Wilson, L.H. 1996. *Sappho's Sweetbitter Songs: Configuration of Female and Male in Ancient Greek Lyric*. London.

Wilson, P. 2000. *The Athenian Institution of the Khoregia: The Chorus, the City and the Stage*. Cambridge.

Wilson, P., ed. 2007. *The Greek Theatre and Festivals: Documentary Studies*. Oxford.

Winkler, J.J. 1990. *The Constraints of Desire: The Anthropology of Sex and Gender in Ancient Greece*. New York.

Wohl, V. 2002. *Love Among the Ruins: The Erotics of Democracy in Classical Athens*. Princeton.

Wolpert, A. 2001. "Lysias 1 and the Politics of the Oikos." *CJ* 96, 415–424.

Wolpert, A. 2002a. "Lysias 18 and the Athenian Memory of the Civil War." *TAPhA* 132, 109–126.

Wolpert, A. 2002b. *Remembering Defeat: Civil War and Civil Memory in Ancient Athens*. Baltimore.

Woodford, S. 2003. *Images of Myths in Classical Antiquity*. Cambridge.

Woodhead, A.G. 1960. "Thucydides' Portrait of Cleon." *Mnemosyne* 13: 289–317.

Woodhouse, W.J. 1933. *King Agis of Sparta and His Campaign in Arcadia: A Chapter in the History of the Art of War Among the Greeks*. Oxford.

Worthington, I., ed. 2000a. *Demosthenes: Statesman and Orator*. London.

Worthington, I. 2000b. "Demosthenes' (In)activity During the Reign of Alexander." In I. Worthington, ed., *Demosthenes: Statesman and Orator*. London, 90–113.

Worthington, I. 2003a. *Alexander the Great: A Reader*. London.

Worthington, I., 2003b. "Alexander's Destruction of Thebes." In W. Heckel and L.A. Tritle, eds., *Crossroads of History: The Age of Alexander the Great*. Claremont CA, 65–86.

Worthington, I., ed. 2007. *A Companion to Greek Rhetoric*. Oxford.

Worthington, I. 2008. *Philip II of Macedonia*. New Haven.

Worthington, I. 2009. "*IG* II² and Philip's Common Peace of 337." In L. Mitchell and L. Rubinstein, eds., *Greek History and Epigraphy: Essays in Honour of P.J. Rhodes*. Dublin, 213–223.

Wycherley, R.E. 1978. *The Stones of Athens*. Princeton.

Wylie, G. 1986. "What Really Happened in Aegospotami." *L'Antiquité classique* 55, 125–141.

Zanker, G. 1986. "The *Works and Days*: Hesiod's *Beggar's Opera*?" *Bulletin of the Institute of Classical Studies* 33, 26–36.

Zanker, G. 1994. *The Heart of Achilles: Characterization and Personal Ethics in the Iliad*. Ann Arbor.

Zeitlin, F. 1996. *Playing the Other: Gender and Society in Classical Greek Literature*. Chicago.

Zelnick-Abramovitz, R. 2004. "Settlers and Dispossessed in the Athenian Empire." *Mnemosyne* 4, 325–345.

Zelnick-Abramovitz, R. 2005. *Not Wholly Free: The Concept of Manumission and the Status of Manumitted Slaves in the Ancient Greek World*. Leiden.

Index of Ancient Sources

Note: Numbers in roman refer to the ancient texts, numbers in **bold** refer to pages in the book. Page references to web material are prefixed by **WEB**.

General Index

Note: Page references to web material are prefixed by WEB.

Ancient Greece from Homer to Alexander: The Evidence, First Edition. Joseph Roisman.
© 2011 Blackwell Publishing Ltd. Translations © 2011 John Yardley. Published 2011 by Blackwell Publishing Ltd.

Lightning Source UK Ltd.
Milton Keynes UK
UKHW032343060919
349284UK00001B/6/P